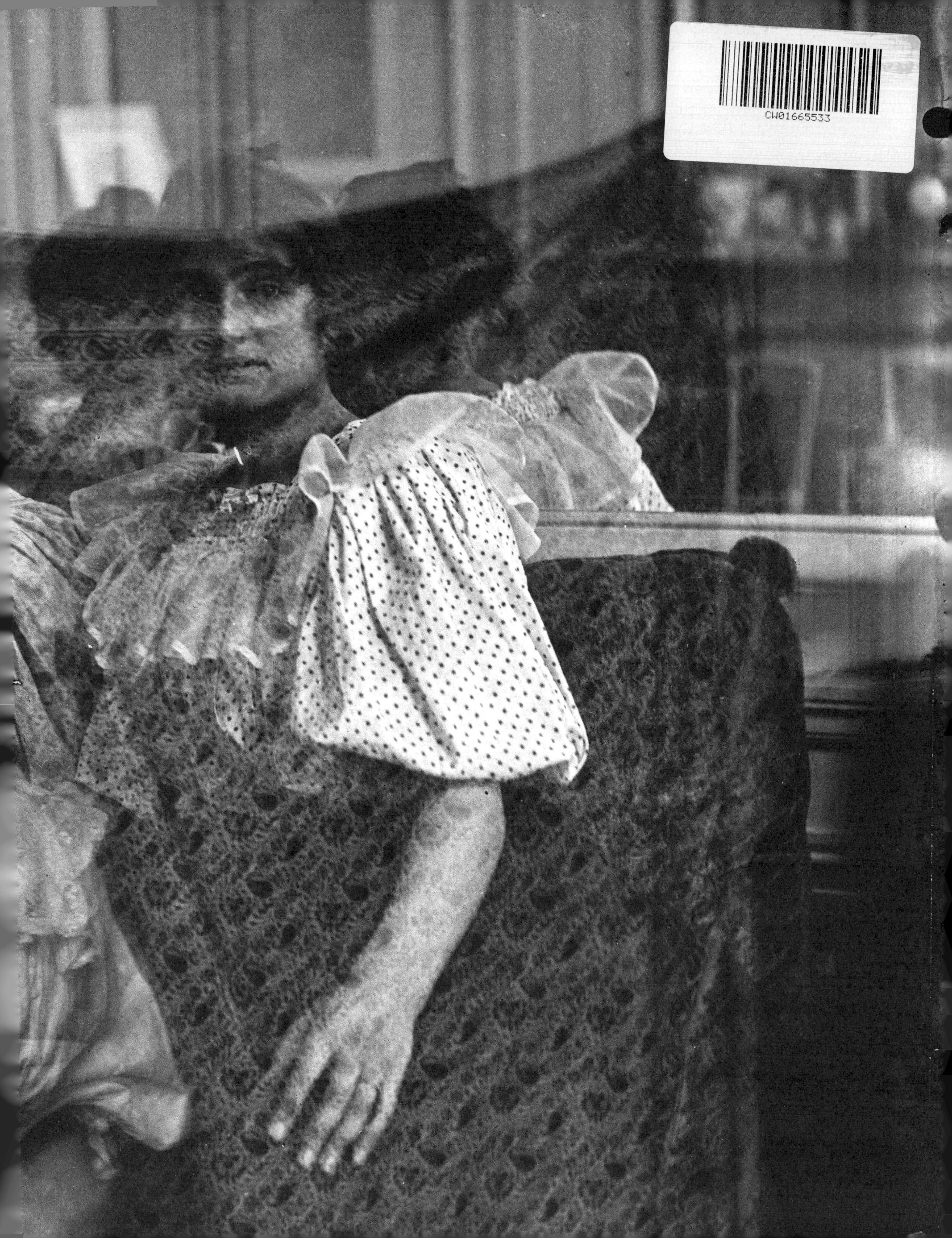

JULIE MANET

Front cover
Berthe Morisot (1841–1895)
Julie Daydreaming, 1894
Oil on canvas, 65 × 54 cm
Private collection

Back cover
Ernest Rouart (1874–1942)
Julie Manet Writing, n.d.
Oil on canvas, 116.7 × 89.2 cm
Private collection

Flyleaf
Jeannie Gobillard and Julie Manet posing in the living room in the rue de Villejust, late 1895–98
Archives BS, Paris, Musée Marmottan Monet

ISBN: 9780300264098
Printed in Italy
Library of Congress Control Number: 2021941539
A catalogue record for this book is available from The British Library
Legal deposit: October 2021

EDITED BY MARIANNE MATHIEU

JULIE MANET

AN IMPRESSIONIST HERITAGE

HAZAN

MUSÉE MARMOTTAN MONET

Distributed by Yale University Press, New Haven and London

This book is being published on the occasion of the exhibition "Julie Manet: an Impressionist Heritage," organized by the Musée Marmottan Monet, Paris, from October 19, 2021 to March 20, 2022.

With the generous support of:

LVMH
MOËT HENNESSY • LOUIS VUITTON

With the cooperation of:

ACKNOWLEDGMENTS

The Musée Marmottan Monet is deeply grateful to the private collectors, museums, and institutions who made generous loans, and in particular:

Brazil
São Paulo, Museu de Arte de São Paulo Assis Chateaubriand, Adriano Pedrosa, director

Denmark
Copenhagen, Ny Carlsberg Glyptothek, Gertrud Hvidberg-Hansen, director

England
London, Tate Modern, Frances Morris, director

France
Annecy, Musées d'Annecy,
Lionel François, director of Museums and Heritage
Lille, Palais des Beaux-Arts, Bruno Girveau, director
Lyon, Musée des Beaux-Arts,
Sylvie Ramond, director, chief heritage curator
Montpellier, Musée Fabre,
Michel Hilaire, director, general heritage curator
Paris, Musée du Louvre, Jean-Luc Martinez, president
Paris, Musée d'Orsay, Laurence des Cars, president
Paris, Petit Palais, Musée des Beaux-Arts de la Ville de Paris, Christophe Leribault, director
Pau, Musée des Beaux-Arts, Aurore Méchain, director
Saint-Germain-en-Laye, Musée Déparemental Maurice Denis, Marie-Aline Charier, director, chief heritage curator
Toulouse, Musée des Augustins,
Axel Hémery, chief heritage director, director

Germany
Bremen, Kunsthalle Bremen,
Prof. Dr. Christoph Grunenberg, director

Japan
Tokyo, Artizon Museum, Ishibashi Foundation,
Hiroshi Ishibashi, director

Monaco
David and Ezra Nahmad

Portugal
Lisbon, Museu Calouste Gulbenkian,
António Filipe Pimentel, director

Switzerland
Zürich, Emil Bührle Collection,
Christian Bührle, president, Lukas Gloor, director

United States
Notre Dame, Snite Museum of Art, University of Notre Dame,
Joseph Antenucci Becherer, director

As well as all those who preferred to remain anonymous.

Érik Desmazières, Marianne Mathieu, Dominique d'Arnoult, and Claire Gooden would like to express their gratitude to:

the grandchildren, cousins, and rights-holders of Julie and Ernest Rouart

for their trust, assistance, generosity and their unwavering support.

They would like to thank for their precious help:
Yohan Agnero, Sébastien Allard, Jean-Marie Andriveau, Jacques Bailly, Christian Baraja, Manon Baroni, Noël Barriati, Maxime Becker, Loïc Bégard, Bruno Benoiste, Véronique Berecz, Martine Boivin-Champeaux, Dominique Bona, Hélène Bonafous-Murat, Me Gilles Bonnet, Tanja Borghardt, Franck Boucourt, Clarisse Bouvet, Gérard Bruyère, Liv Bulteau, Sébastien Castel, Christian Chatellier, Marion Cinqualbre, Jean-Paul Claverie, Sylvie Colomb, Grégory Couderc, Caroline Couzineau, Penelope Curtis, Dominique David, Claire Denis, Nathalie Derra, Mathilde Despois, Flavie Durand-Ruel, Paul-Louis Durand-Ruel, Christophe Duvivier, Emilie Faneuil, Marie-Louise Favre, Amélie Ferlay, Isabelle Gaëtan, David Gallais, Agata Graczyk, abbé Gabriel Grimaud, Isabelle Groux de Mieri, Dorothee Hansen, Michaël Landat, Erik Lasalle, Antoine Lefort, Jean-Louis Leloir, Dominique Lobstein, Sophie Marin, Françoise Marnoni, Maud Marron Wojewodzki, Claire Martin, Pascal Martin-Lavigne, Paul Menoux, Christian Michel, Roberto Morane, Alexis Morat, Clémence Morat-Mathieu, Nadine Musy, Ruth Nagel, Victoria Perdomo, Pascal Perrin, Sophie Pietri, Jules Pinet, Anthony Pontabry, frère Jean-Michel Potin, Gaël Quintric, Antoine Rauffet, Marc Rauffet †, Mélanie Rivault, Françoise Rouart, Jean-Marie Rouart, Yves Rouart, Virginie Roure, Bertrand Sachs, Anne-Pascale Saliou, Crystal Salmon, Bernadette et Bruno Schmitz, Isabelle Séruzier, Florie Sitt, Cheryl Snay, Fabienne Stahl, Alain Tapié, Laure Tapié, Bernard Thomas, Annabelle Thouveny, Anna de Torrès, Giulia Trabaldo Togna, Anna Ueda, Charles-Ambroise Valéry, Monique Valéry, Élisabeth Verbecq, Marie Vercambre, Bernard Vidal, and Gabrielle Welti.

They also thank Anne Gratadour for the exhibition design and Julien Boitias for the graphics.

MUSÉE MARMOTTAN MONET

Érik Desmazières
Member of the Institut
Director

Marianne Mathieu
Deputy director
Head curator

Véronique Pelloie
Deputy director, administration, finance, operations

Aurélie Gavoille, Claire Gooden, Anne-Sophie Luyton
Assistant curators

Laurène Marin
Registrar of collections and exhibitions

Manon Paineau
Head of communications

Thibaud Oscar
Administrative and financial assistant
Group reservations and workshops

Hatem Soualhi, Hervé Facompré
Security

Aurélien Sebire
Technical service and maintenance

Céline Ducrocq
Sales assistant

Stéphanie Closier, Maurice Correa, Larissa Yimga
Sales personnel

EXHIBITION CURATORS

Marianne Mathieu
Art historian, head curator
of the Musée Marmottan Monet

Assisted by
Claire Gooden
Assistant curator, Muséc Marmottan Monet

Victoire Annezo
Researcher

With
Laurène Marin
Registrar, Musée Marmottan Monet

CATALOG EDITED BY

Marianne Mathieu
Art historian, head curator
of the Musée Marmottan Monet

With contributions from

Dominique d'Arnoult
PhD in art history

Claire Gooden
Assistant curator, Musée Marmottan Monet

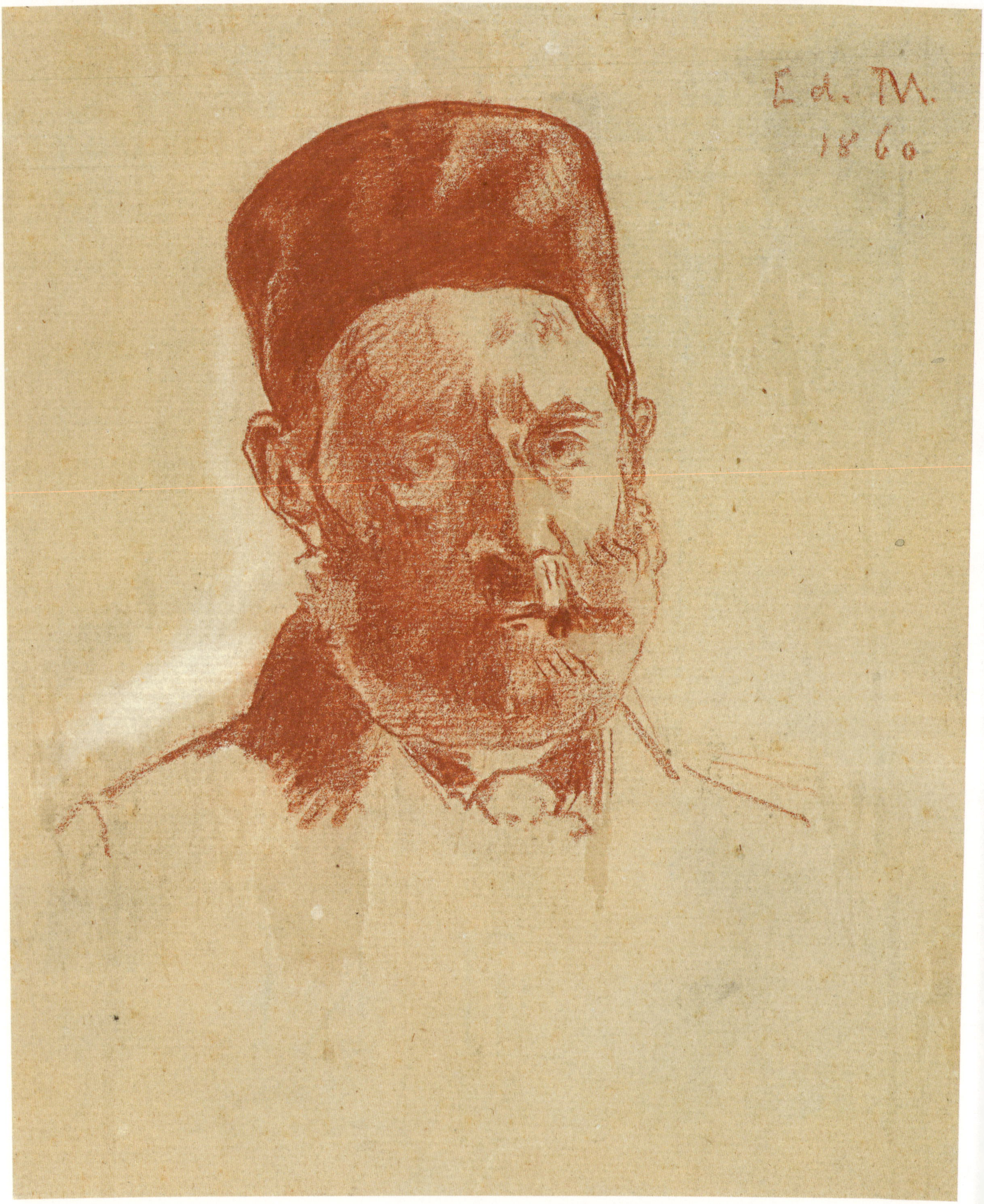
Ed. M.
1860

CONTENTS

Édouard Manet (1832–1883)
Portrait of Auguste Manet, the Artist's Father, 1860
Red chalk on paper, 17 × 13.7 cm
Private collection

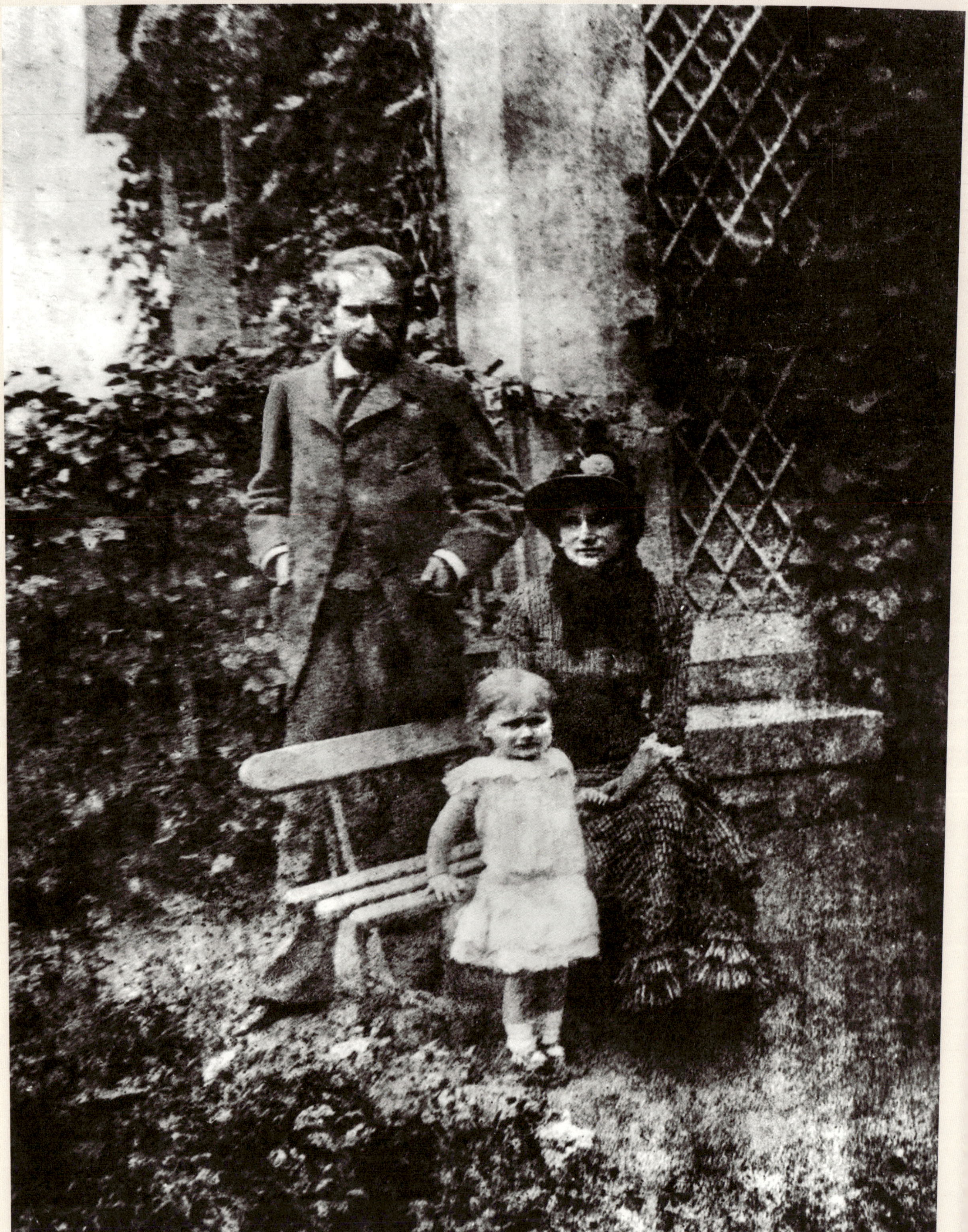

FOREWORD

Paris, November 1878. The Exposition Universelle, set up on the Champ-de-Mars, at the exact spot where the Grand Palais Ephémère now stands, had just closed. Mac Mahon still had a few months ahead as president of the Republic and France was in the throes of industrial expansion as it began to recover from the twin traumas of the defeat of 1870 and the Commune.

Julie Manet was born on the 14th of that month, in the 16th arrondissement. Daughter of Berthe Morisot and sole niece of Édouard Manet, her father's brother, she grew up in a very Parisian milieu where, as a young child, she knew Degas, Pissarro, Renoir, Mallarmé and many other figures. She had everything she needed to be happy.

But it did not last. Her father, a man of fragile health, died when she was only thirteen, and her mother followed him unexpectedly three years later. It was now that the good fairies of her childhood stepped in and became kindly guardian angels. Degas arranged her marriage to Ernest Rouart, the son of his great friend Henri Rouart and his only student as a painter. A charming child, a ravishing young girl, a much-courted young woman, she was a model for her mother, of course, but also for Manet, Renoir, and, later, her own husband.

The little girl holding a cat in her arms in the Renoir painting, who became a ravishing and generous young woman and diarist and, in her later years, an elderly figure usually dressed in black, never left the family home in the rue de Villejust that was built by her parents. She lived alongside friends and relations on all floors, surrounded by a host of memories on the walls.

All their life, Julie and Ernest worked devotedly for the recognition of Berthe Morisot. They organized exhibitions and donated generously to museums, thus perpetuating the memory of that remarkable artist. Ernest died in 1942, Julie in 1966, aged eighty-eight. Practicing painters and discriminating connoisseurs, they built up a sizeable collection.

Julie was austere and generous, with a religious personality that was very different from her mother's. Between 1893 and 1899, she briefly kept a diary that shows her to be a perspicacious observer.

Thanks to the generosity of her children and grandchildren, the Musée Marmottan Monet has long been bound up with this story as a recipient of the many generous donations made by the Rouart family over the decades—paintings, of course, but also letters and photographs. It is with deep gratitude that we would like to extend our special thanks to Françoise and Yves Rouart, Julie Manet's grandchildren, who recently added to the outstanding documentation already held by the museum. We also thank the late lamented Marc Rauffet and his son Antoine for their unfailing support.

Julie Manet is a witness to past times, to the time that was, in a sense, frozen on the walls of her home—a time that we can revisit here thanks to the paintings, drawings, prints, photographs, and letters in this exhibition. We wanted to pay homage to this woman who fervently and loyally preserved the memory of her mother and to recall her youth at the heart of the Impressionist movement. By their astute historical sleuthing, Marianne Mathieu with Dominique d'Arnoult and Claire Gooden have managed to untangle the threads and capture the truth of this long life dedicated to art. I thank all three profusely for this book that is much more than an exhibition catalogue.

Érik Desmazières
Member of the Institut
Director of the Musee Marmottan Monet

Eugène Manet, Berthe Morisot and their daughter in Bougival, c. 1882
Paris, Musée Marmottan Monet

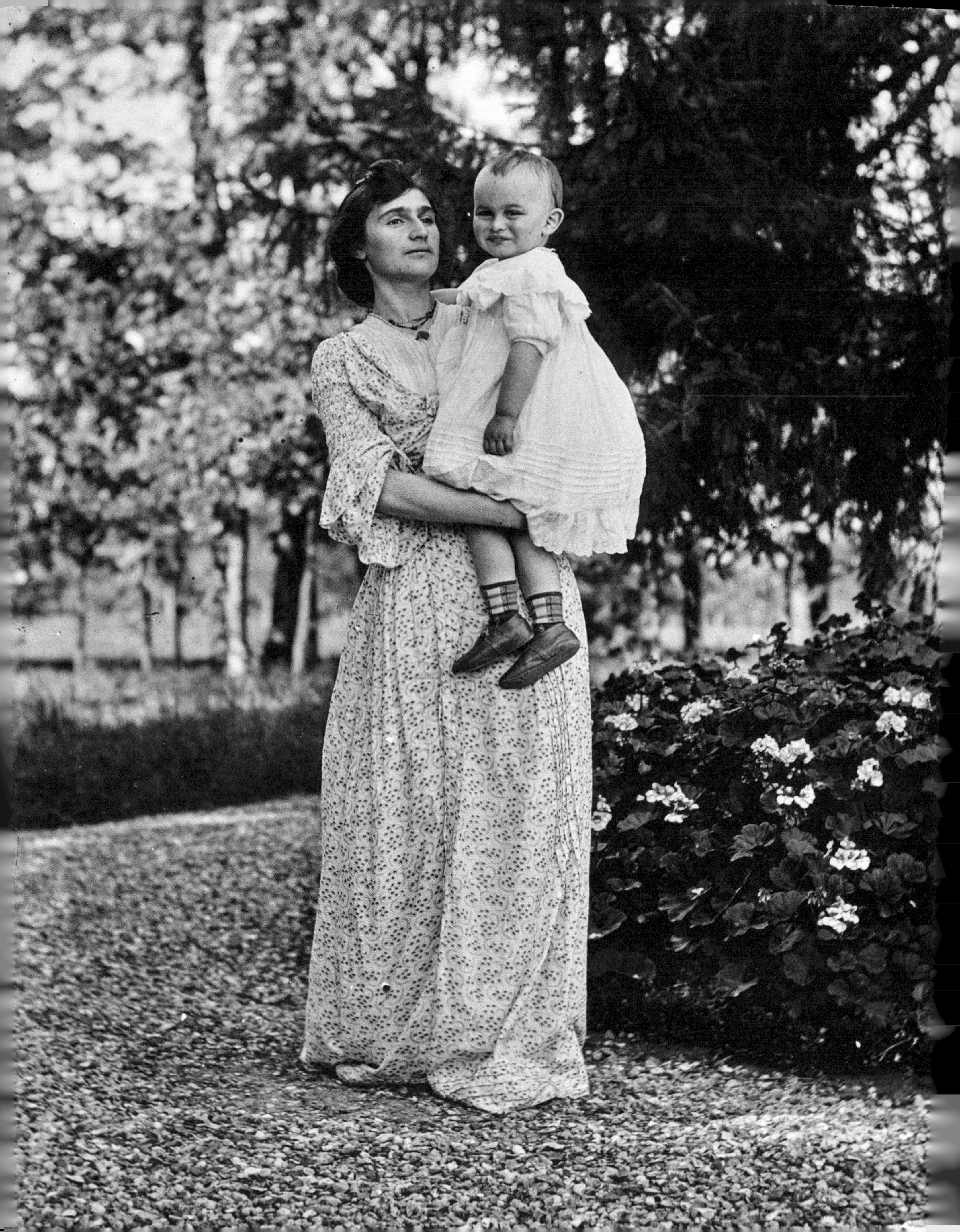

JULIE MANET

A BIOGRAPHY

MARIANNE MATHIEU

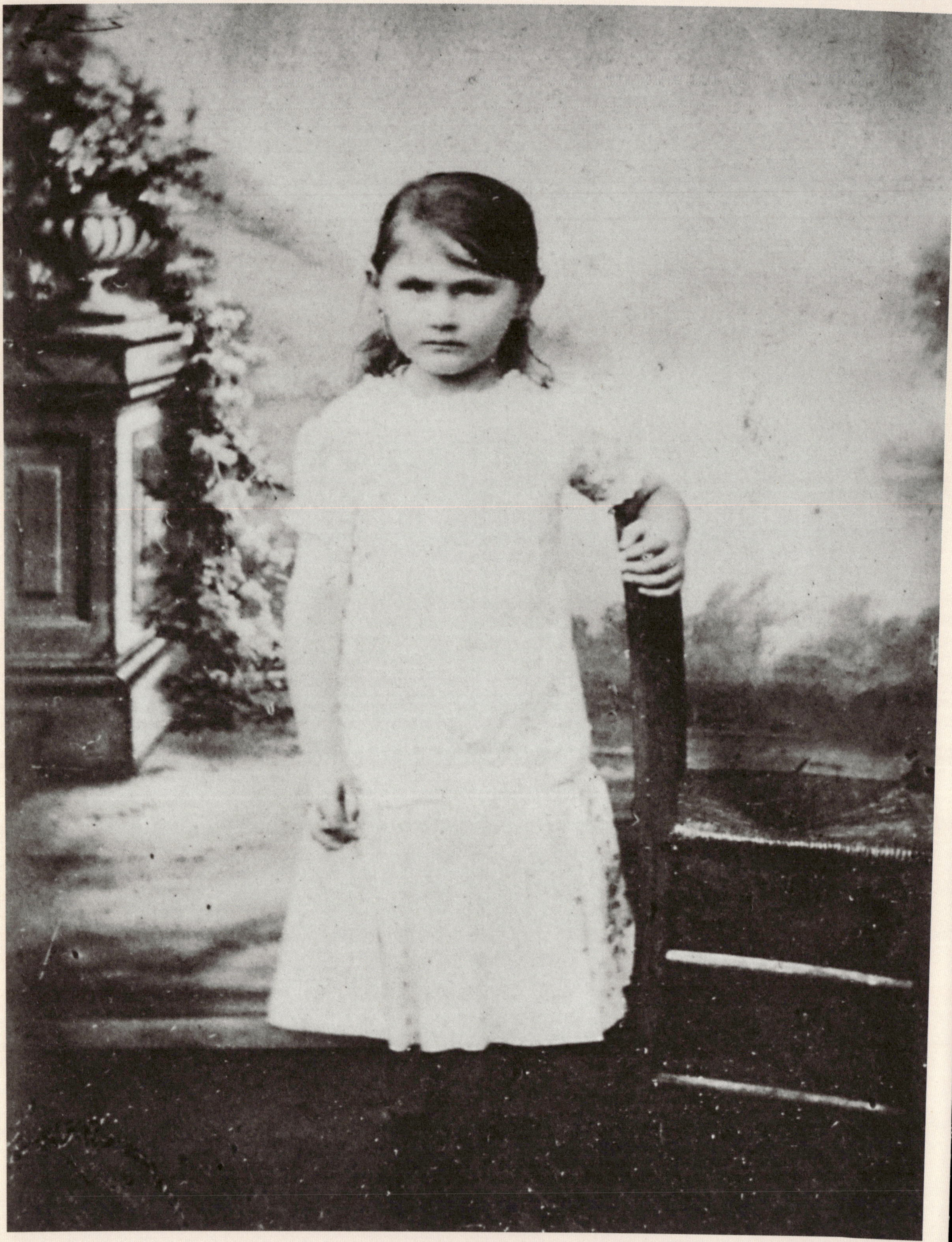

PASSY, A FAMILY PENCHANT

1878–1881

The daughter of Berthe Morisot and Eugène Manet, brother of the painter, Julie, the child who came into the world in 1878, was born into wealthy families from Paris and Gennevilliers whose history can be comprehensively established thanks to the abundance and precision of the archives.

THE MORISOTS OF PASSY

It was shortly before the birth of their tenth and last child,[1] in 1832, that Jean Simon Joseph Thomas,[2] "Bon Papa Thomas,"[3] and his wife, Marie Françoise Caroline Mayniel,[4] moved in at 15, rue Franklin in Passy. The family of this general inspector of finances and central cashier at the Trésor Public (tax office)[5] put down roots in what in those days was still a village on the edge of Paris.[6] Three of their seven surviving children also made it their home. Marie Joséphine Clémentine Thomas,[7] the wife of Alexandre Chevalier,[8] lived 900 meters from her parents at Villa Fodor, at 2, rue Jean Bologne. In 1848, after his marriage[9] to Félicie Louise Cosnard[10]—"Aunt Félicie" to her family—Marie Joseph Charles Thomas,[11] a central cashier at the Trésor Public like his father, made his home at 10, rue Franklin,[12] a short walk from "Bon Papa," then later moved to number 14. Three of their ten children were born at this address,[13] including Marie Gabriel Thomas (p. 35), who came into the world on January 15, 1854.[14] He went on to found the Musée Grévin and to serve as an administrator of the Eiffel Tower and the Théâtre des Champs-Élysées. A discerning collector, he was the most illustrious descendant.[15] Marie Joséphine Cornélie Thomas (p. 14),[16] wife of Edme Tiburce Morisot (p. 14),[17] a former prefect who would soon be made a counsellor at the Cour des Comptes, arrived in the village in 1852. The couple later moved in order to be as close as possible to their family at 12 and, later, 16, rue Franklin.[18] It was in Passy, since 1860 officially part of Paris, that their daughters Yves Élisabeth (p. 14),[19] Marie Edma Caroline (p. 14),[20] and Berthe Marie Pauline (p. 14),[21] and their son Marie Charles Tiburce (p. 14)[22] all grew up. That, too, is where Berthe became aware of her vocation as a painter. And it was at the local town hall, in 1866, that Yves married Théodore Gobillard[23] before returning to Quimperlé, where the young husband had a position as district tax collector. It was there, too, that in 1869 Edma married the ship's lieutenant Adolphe Pontillon.[24] And although she lived in Lorient after her wedding, it was again at 16, rue Franklin that the young Mme Pontillon gave birth to her two daughters: Jeanne[25] in 1870 and Blanche[26] in 1871. It was also in the protected setting of this quarter and, especially, of this home, that Berthe Morisot produced her first important canvases: in 1872, Edma posed watching over a sleeping Blanche for *The Cradle* (p. 125), then with her four-year-old niece Paule Gobillard[27] for *Woman and Child on a Balcony*.[28] Only Tiburce chose to go into debt[29] in order to explore the world and live a life of adventure—a choice that was sometimes problematic for his family and friends. As for Berthe, she remained attached to the neighborhood. In 1873, still unmarried at the age of thirty-four, she moved with her parents into what was no doubt a more modest apartment at 7, rue Guichard. However, the death of her father on January 24, 1874 forced her to make new choices.

From the age of seventeen, Berthe had been devoted, body and soul, to painting. Trained by Guichard and then

Previous double page
Attributed to Ernest Rouart (1874–1942)
Julie Manet-Rouart and her son Julien, c. 1902–03
Archives BS, Paris, Musée Marmottan Monet

Facing page
Julie Manet as a child, c. 1883
Private collection

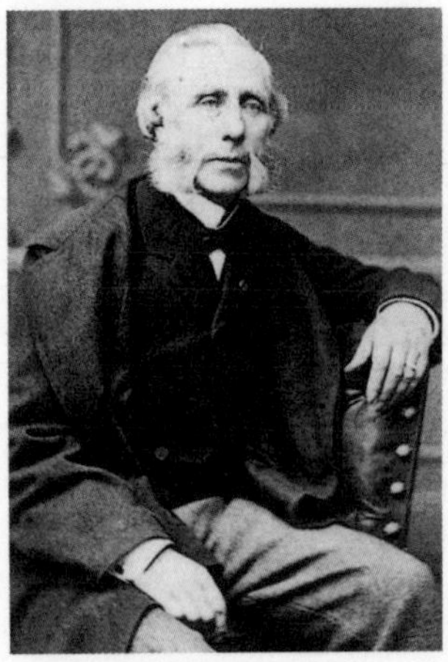

Edme Tiburce Morisot

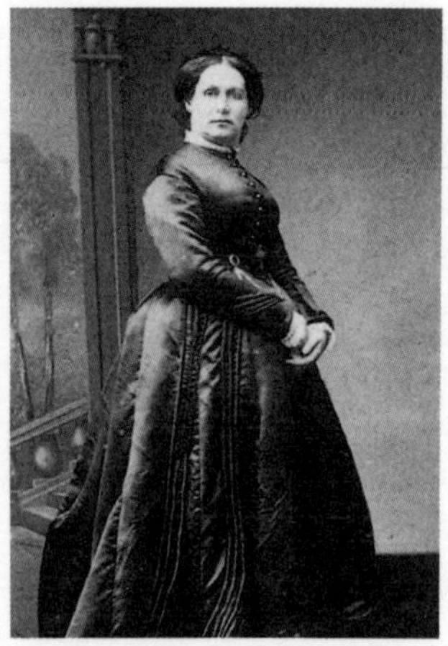

Marie Joséphine Cornélie Thomas, married name Morisot

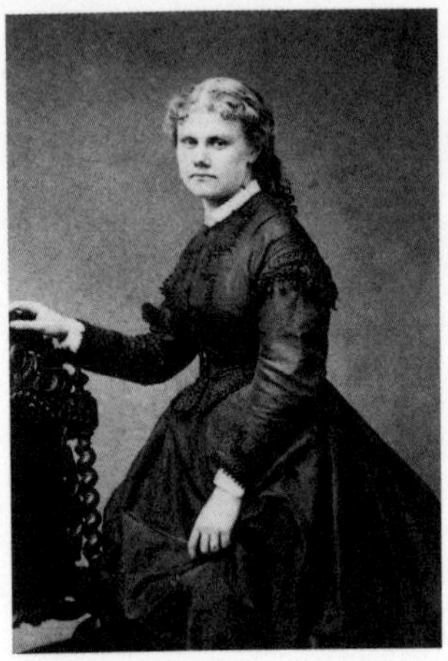

Yves Élisabeth Morisot, married name Gobillard

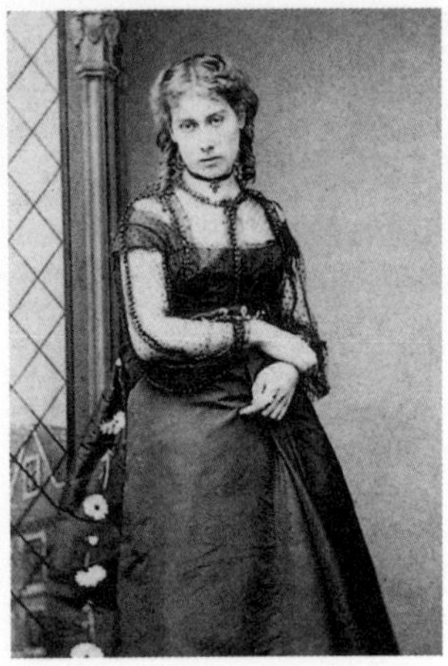

Edma Morisot, married name Pontillon

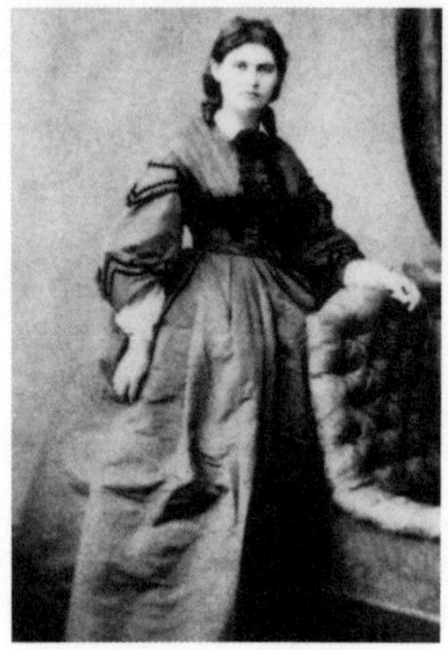

Berthe Morisot, married name Manet

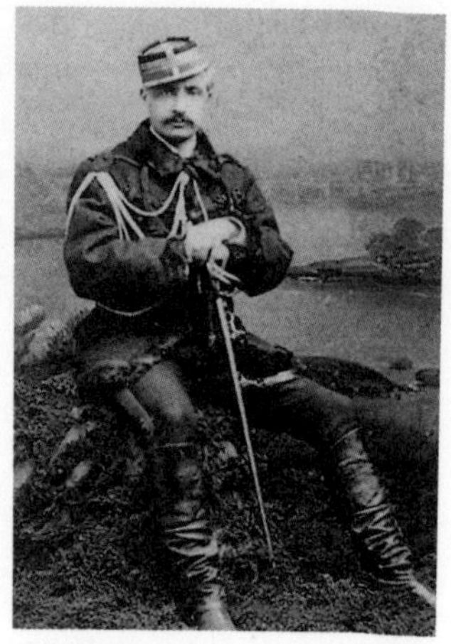

Tiburce Morisot

by Corot,[30] she began exhibiting regularly at the official Salon in 1864.[31] Her interest in outdoor work was something she shared with the experiments of Frédéric Bazille, who died in 1870, and of his contemporaries Claude Monet, Pierre-Auguste Renoir, Camille Pissarro, and Alfred Sisley. Encouraged by two painters who, like her, came from the upper reaches of society—the illustrious Édouard Manet, who first had her pose in 1869, and the intransigent Edgar Degas, who painted the portrait of Yves in the rue Franklin[32]—Berthe dreamed of a career and was determined, at the very least, to produce a body of work. But in the aftermath of the 1870 war the situation grew tense. The Salon once again closed its doors to the proponents of a new way of painting and prospects shrank.[33] Berthe boldly chose to forgo exhibiting there and to pursue her artistic development outside official circles. In April 1874, she took part in the first exhibition of the Association Anonyme des Peintres, Sculpteurs, Graveurs, etc. organized in Nadar's old studio, on which occasion the term "Impressionist" was coined. This presence earned her the posthumous and prestigious title of "first woman Impressionist." At the time, her choice was all the more daring in that the Morisots' financial situation was deteriorating. Comprised mainly of shares and bonds from the Compagnie du Gaz, the capital that Mme Morisot inherited from her spouse represented 83,988.84 francs, while her son Tiburce was already indebted to the tune of 17,791.55 francs.[34] In other words, the Morisots did not have the wealth of the highest bourgeoisie. This made the question of maintaining their lifestyle cruelly acute.[35] This was one of the circumstances that made Berthe opt for early marriage. Only eleven months after her father's death, she married the younger brother of Édouard Manet, Eugène.

The question of Berthe's suitors and her relations with Édouard Manet has been amply discussed and will not be rehashed here. In marrying Eugène, she was joining a family that was both open to the arts and bourgeois, combining two essential dimensions around which she structured her life.

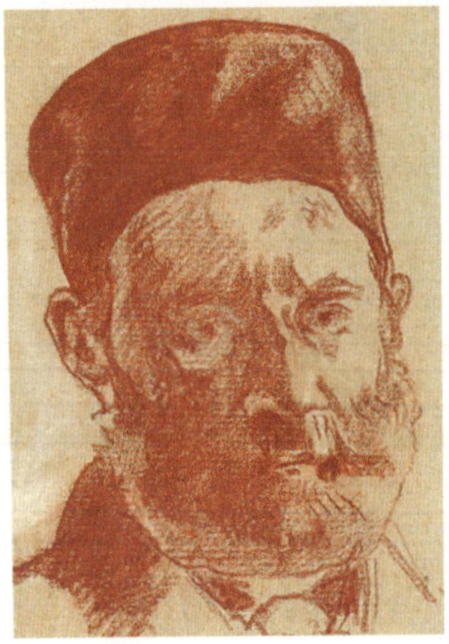

Auguste Manet

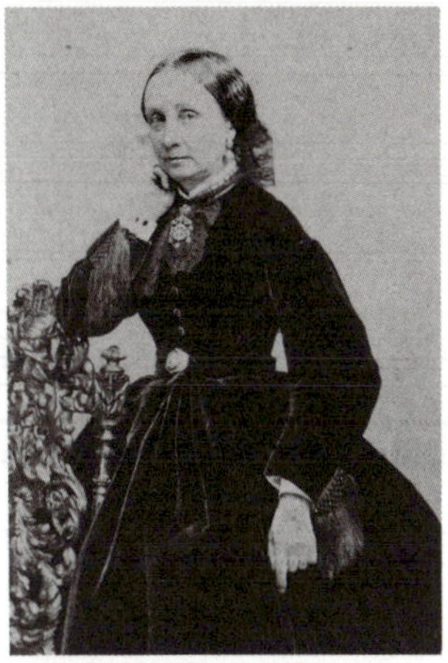

Eugénie Désirée Fournier, married name Manet

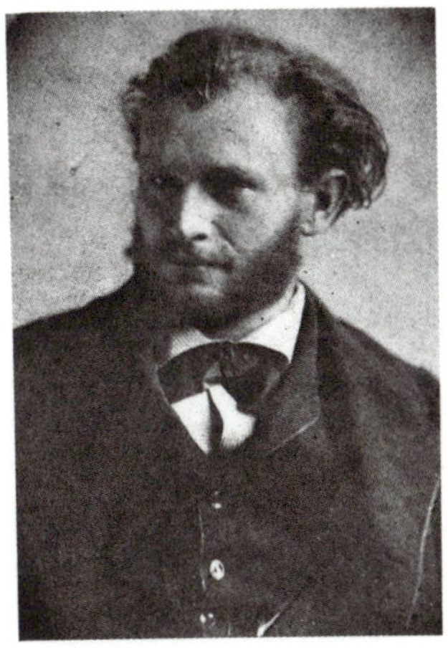

Édouard Manet

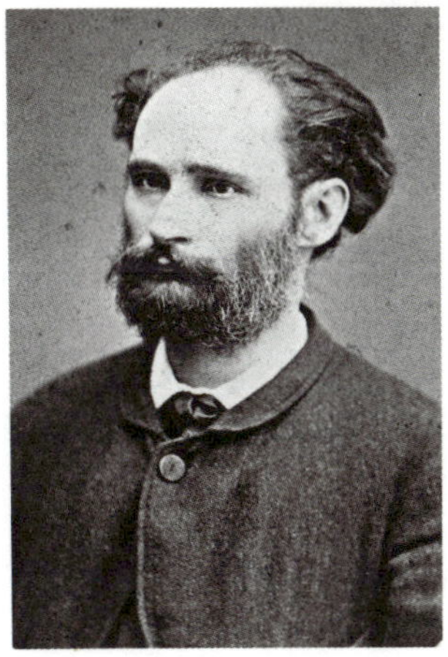

Gustave Manet

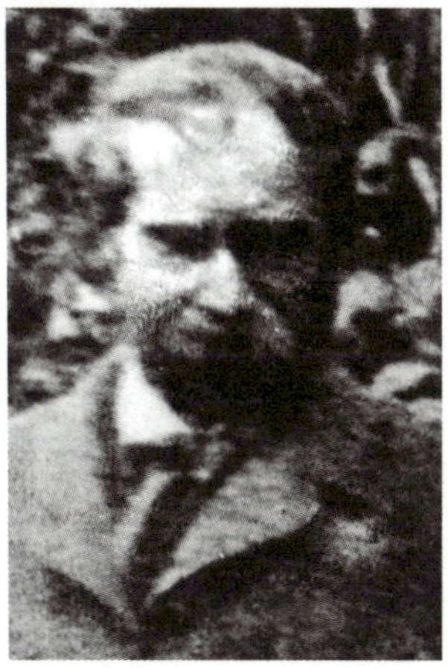

Eugène Manet

THE MANETS OF GENNEVILLIERS

The Manet family fortune had been amassed by Eugène's grandfather, Clément Manet, treasurer and property manager of the parish before the Revolution, then mayor of Gennevilliers.[36] In the space of a generation he acquired so much land in Gennevilliers that people used to say he owned the town. The three surviving children[37] born to him and his wife Marguerite (née Quesnel)[38] shared this considerable heritage. While not much is known about Félicité Clémence Manet, married to a Monsieur Marchais,[39] except that she had no children, we have a little more information about the two others. Émilie Manet[40] married Denis François Claude de Jouy.[41] Their son, Anatole Jules,[42] a barrister at the appeal court of Paris, who married Marie Geneviève Quatremère[43] on April 27, 1847, in what was a childless marriage (she died on November 23 that year),[44] was a key figure in the clan. Auguste Manet (above),[45] Julie's grandfather, was division head at the Ministry of Justice, private secretary of the Garde des Sceaux (justice minister), and judge. He married Eugénie Désirée Fournier (above),[46] daughter of the French Consul in Sweden and goddaughter of Bernadotte, with whom he had three children. In 1863, after his father's death, and much to his mother's displeasure, the oldest child, the painter Édouard (above), married Suzanne Leenhoff (p. 16), the mother of an eleven-year-old son, Léon Édouard Koëlla (p. 16);[47] the painter had no direct heirs. His brother, Gustave (above),[48] a municipal councilor in Paris, prison inspector,[49] and inspector of public finances,[50] remained a bachelor, and childless. Finally, Berthe's future husband, Eugène (above),[51] who was briefly mentioned as a copywriter (*rédacteur*) in a ministry,[52] is often described as a landowner.[53] It is true that the Manets lived on the income from their land in Gennevilliers, a large part of which was held in common ownership, forcing them to co-manage, under the auspices of their first cousin Jules de Jouy. While Gustave's position ensured a comfortable income and guaranteed his independence, Édouard and Eugène benefited from

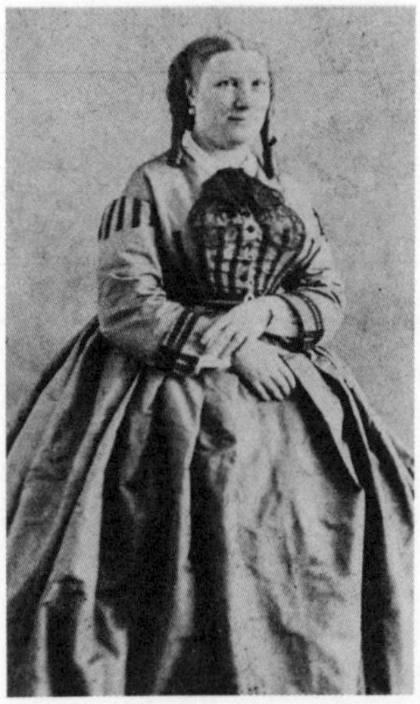

Suzanne Leenhoff, married name Manet

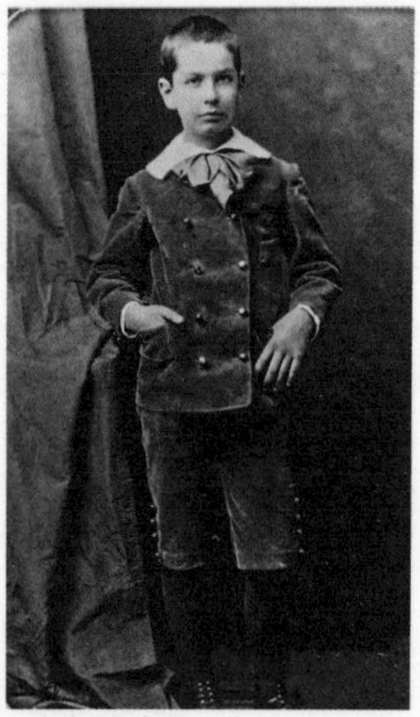

Léon Koëlla known as Leenhoff

the constant support of their mother, who would remind them of the fact at the opportune moment.

This is evident in the contract drawn up by the Morisots' notary and neighbor, Maître Amy,[54] for the wedding of Berthe and Eugène. The couple was given 202,000 francs to start out in life together. Eugène's wealth was estimated at 166,000 francs; 150,000 francs were property, half of it held in indivision with his brothers, although the ensemble was burdened with 75,500 francs of mortgages. Berthe had 36,000 francs to her name, including 16,000 francs in shares and bonds.[55] A dowry of 10,000 francs set aside for each person was also taken into account. This sum, well below the 40,000 francs that was the norm in wealthy Parisian circles,[56] which had been promised to Yves and Edma,[57] would be paid when their mothers were still alive only by Mme Auguste Manet. The day after the signing of the marriage certificate, the civil wedding was celebrated "in the customary way" at the town hall of the 16th arrondissement, in the presence of their close circle. Jules de Jouy and Édouard Manet were the groom's witnesses, while Jean Joseph Simon Thomas (Bon Papa) and Adolphe Pontillon were Berthe's.

CHOOSING THE 16TH ARRONDISSEMENT

Not for a minute did the "Eugène Manets," as they were now called, consider moving to Gennevilliers, or even to the rue Saint-Pétersbourg, close to Mme Manet *mère*, as Édouard and Suzanne Manet had done. Instead, the young couple chose the 16th arrondissement and stayed very close to Berthe's family. They settled into the apartment at 7, rue Guichard that Marie Joséphine Cornélie had made available to them. The latter moved to 2, rue Jean Bologne, home not only to her sister Marie Joséphine Clémentine, aunt Chevalier, but also, more recently to her daughter, Edma Pontillon, who felt more comfortable in Passy than she did in Lorient during the long absences of her ship's lieutenant husband.[58] When Marie Joséphine Cornélie died (December 15, 1876),[59] Berthe and Eugène started looking for a new lease. They found one at 9, avenue d'Eylau. Her elder sister soon joined her in this apartment that Berthe immortalized in several of her paintings.

Suffering from mental illness, Théodore Gobillard was interned in 1876.[60] The greatest discretion was required, as this letter attests: "The best house would be Blanche's[61] but how could they keep that secret? Best look elsewhere."[62] Placed in a nursing home in Ville Evrard on 24 June,[63] Théodore was transferred to the national establishment in Charenton on 24 October.[64] He stayed there until his death on January 6, 1883.[65] Yves, Paule, aged nine, and Marcel, five,[66] were soon welcomed to avenue d'Eylau.[67] That was where Yves gave birth to her last daughter, Jeannie Claudine,[68] on January 16, 1877. This Gobillard would never know her father: her parents were legally separated in the year of her birth,[69] which was declared by the family doctor, Martin, in the presence of a neighbor and of Eugène Manet. A few years after Jeannie's arrival, Yves wrote to request a place for Paule in the Maison d'Éducation, a young girls' establishment in Saint-Denis:

> Monsieur the Grand Chancelier,
>
> I write to ask that my daughter be admitted to the school in Saint Denis. The child is nine years old. Her father, M. Gobillard, was awarded the Légion d'Honneur and made a captain in the 51st infantry regiment after undergoing the amputation of a limb in Puebla, and on his return from Mexico entered the financial administration. He lost his position as a tax collector a few months ago because of insanity. His military pension, which constitutes his only personal wealth, pays for his keep at the establishment in Charenton. The misfortune that has befallen him has left me to bring up a family of three children on my own, with an income that is completely insufficient for that onerous task. I dare hope that her father's service and misfortune may give my daughter the credentials that would recommend her to your benevolence and without delay, open to her the refuge reserved for the children of officers without means.
>
> I am,
>
> Monsieur the Grand Chancelier,
>
> With respect, your humble and obedient servant,
>
> Y. Gobillard, Paris,

January 25, 1877
9, avenue d'Eylau.[70]

On April 27, 1877, Paule entered the École de la Légion d'Honneur, where she would spend seven years.[71] The purpose of this institution was to provide free instruction for the legitimate daughters of needy *légionnaires*.[72] Yves herself was philosophical about her loss of social status: "Society. I do not regret that I am no longer part of it."[73]

It was in the refuge on the avenue d'Eylau that Jeannie took her first steps under the loving gaze of her aunt, who herself would soon be with child. Although she painted little during her pregnancy, Berthe could not resist limning little Nini,[74] the child whose awakening she was witnessing, in three quick pastel portraits.

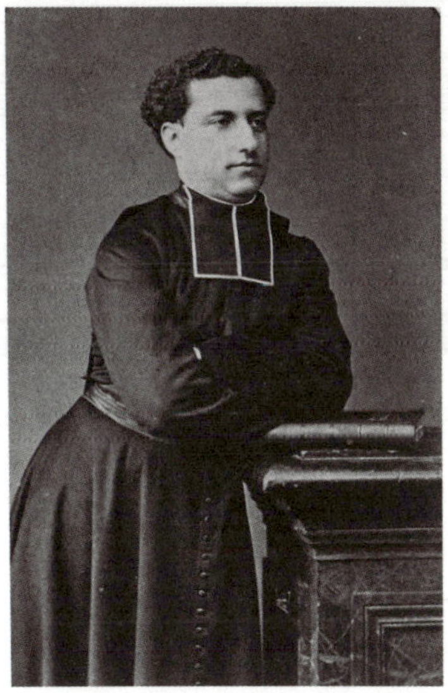
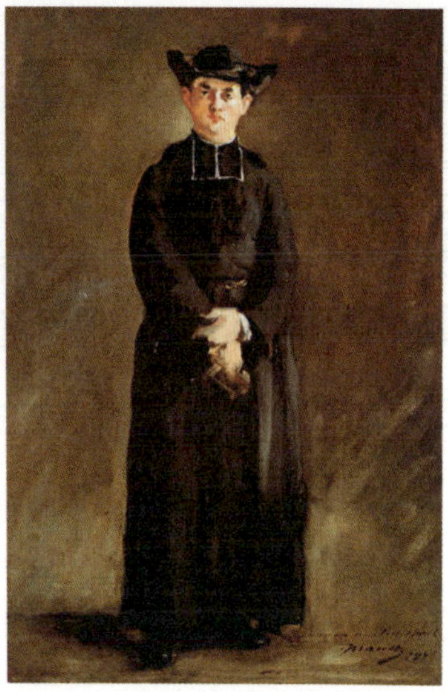

The Abbé Hurel, photographed (left) and painted by Édouard Manet (right)

EUGÉNIE JULIE MANET

The daughter of Berthe Morisot and Eugène Manet was born on the avenue d'Eylau on November 14, 1878.[75] Yves reported on the event for Edma:

> Berthe was doing very well last night, my dear Edma: her skin was good and she had slept perfectly the night before, but Mr. Martin had to catheterize her as was done for you at your first childbirth. For her the operation is without importance. I saw her twice in the day, making only short visits for fear of tiring her out. I felt the child was prettier when I looked at her again; there is still Eugène but while I saw the Manet mouth on her at the moment of her birth, I could not see it again yesterday. Berthe is a little concerned about something to which, she tells me, Mr. Martin attaches no importance. The child has not performed all the natural functions since birth. She came into the world almost strangled by the cord, wrapped three times round her neck, but went only a few seconds without breathing. Paule was the same, I am told.[76]

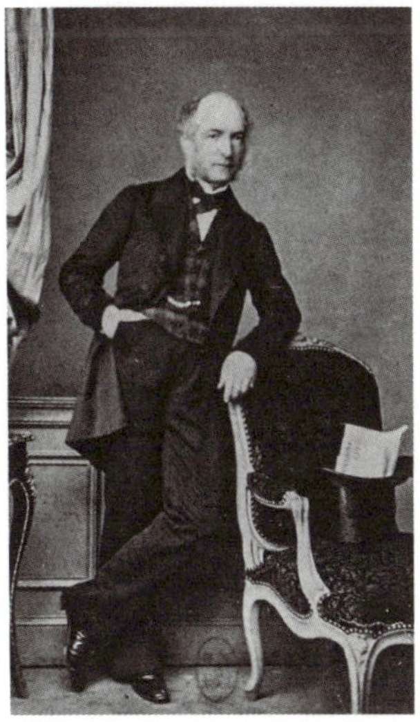
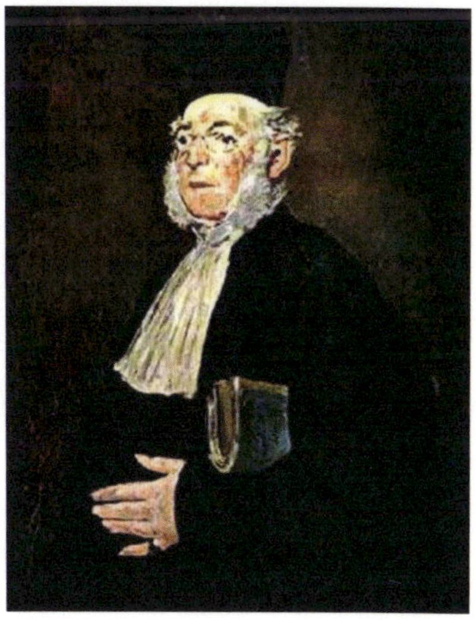

Jules de Jouy, photographed (left) and painted in his lawyer's gown by Édouard Manet (right)

Congratulations came thick and fast, with Edma the first to respond:

> My dear Eugène,
> I opened the telegram bringing me the good news with real emotion. I had been waiting impatiently for it for some days; how happy I am today to be able to congratulate you and to know that Berthe is free of her burden. Now I cannot wait to hear how she is. My daughters wanted to write to their aunt at once. You can give her their letters when you deem it appropriate. They seem happier at the arrival of this little cousin than at their father's. Auntie's child must be a true beauty.
>
> If you have a moment, send me news and please do give our love to Berthe. Adolphe sends his most affectionate congratulations.[77]

She enclosed a few lines to Berthe from the young Blanche:

> My dear Auntie, I am very happy that you have a little girl. What will you call her? Do you find her pretty? Does she cry a lot? She must tire you a great deal. I would like to see her. I kiss you with all my heart, Little Blanche.[78]

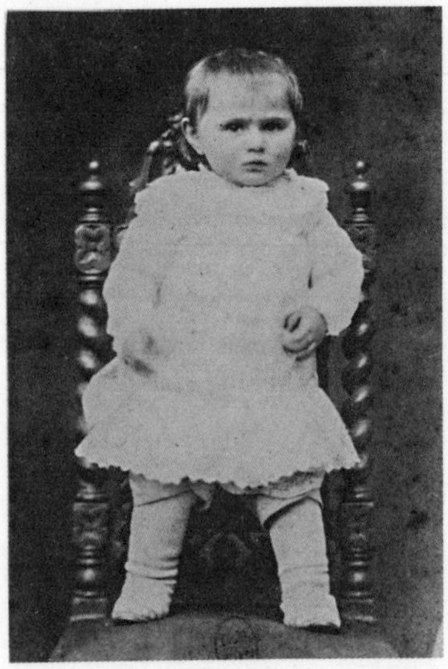

Julie Manet as a baby, c. 1880
Paris, Bibliothèque Nationale de France

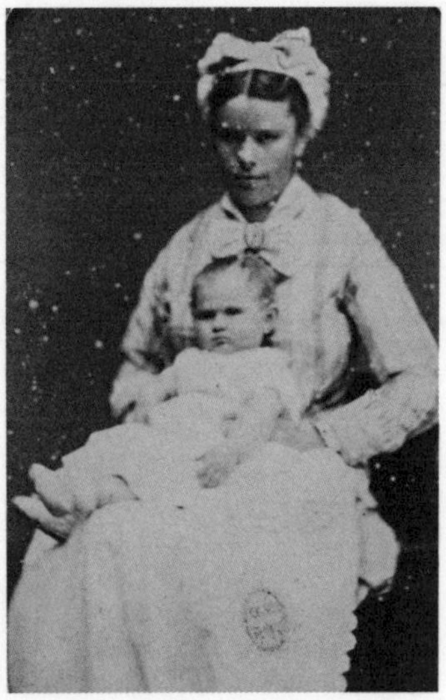

Julie Manet and her nanny Angèle, c. 1880
Paris, Bibliothèque Nationale de France

The birth was declared on November 17, 1878 by her father, in the presence of her two Manet uncles, Édouard and Gustave.[79] The child was to be called Eugénie Julie in homage to the two people named as godparents at the baptism: her maternal grandmother, Eugénie Désirée Manet, on one side, and her first cousin, Jules de Jouy, on the other. This baptism was celebrated at the Madeleine church[80] because of the friendship between Mme Manet *mère* and the vicar of the parish, Abbé Hurel (p. 17).[81] Julie's affection for Bonne Maman[82] and for the uncle-godfather, whom Édouard portrayed that year in his barrister's gown (p. 17),[83] would never fail.

Julie would be the Eugène Manets' only child, even if Yves, who shared her daily life, confided to Edma a few days later:

> Did not Berthe tell me the other day that she would gladly do it again if she could be sure of bringing into the world a boy, for, deep down, that is what she desired before the birth of her daughter. She told me quite the opposite a few months ago.[84]

The parents, of course, were over the moon with their offspring, as Yves recalls:

> She [Julie] has not had the slightest upset since her birth and she is all plump. Her mother is very proud of her. The first smile went straight to her heart. She laughs at Eugène who thinks his daughter already looks intelligent, but she herself tells me very seriously that this little one seems already to see and know certain things. I was careful not to answer that Paule showed the same surprising signs of intelligence at the same age.[85]

Berthe did not fail to inform her niece Jeanne Pontillon:

> I would love to see you again, my dear little one, you whom I think of rather as my older daughter. And of course, I really wouldn't mind showing you my little Bibi![86]

FIRST STEPS (1879–1883)

The family got organized. Apart from domestics, the subject of much complaining in avenue d'Eylau, a nanny, Angèle, looked after "Julie Bibi" from 1879 to 1880. Though rarely mentioned in the correspondence, she appears in the first photographic portrait of Julie (left) and strikes a similar pose for Berthe, who was gradually getting back to her painting (p. 19). Soon, Mademoiselle Bibi was posing on her own in front of the lens, sitting or, later, standing (p. 12).

The family gathered around Julie. They went to visit Bon Papa Morisot[87] in the rue Franklin, and soon, too, his brother, Uncle Octave,[88] who had just moved in there. They loved to meet in avenue d'Eylau. Edma even made impromptu visits.[89] Jules de Jouy, the uncle and godfather, developed a relationship not only with his goddaughter but also with his aunt Yves, with Jeannie and with Marcel, who was now old enough to pose nicely for his aunt.[90] The name of Mallarmé, not yet a close acquaintance, crops up like a promise in Yves' account of these happy moments:

> We went for a walk with M. de Jouy. It was a superb night yesterday evening, Eugène was eloquent and Berthe in a semi-somnolent state in which scraps of "poets' words" came back to her along with religious impressions. Mass, says Mallarmé, is never ridiculous; nothing is more beautiful, grander, than the actions of the priest, the moment when he holds up his arms, the right hand a little higher than the other. And what a noble poetic meaning in this book that is moved on the altar![91]

Not surprisingly, Bibi's health was a priority. In keeping with the contemporary concern with hygiene, the overriding preoccupation was to ensure she got fresh air. Hence the family's choice of the little village of Bougival. As Yves confided to her older daughter, Paule:

> Your aunt Berthe has decided all of a sudden to go and live in Bougival which was not rented out, where she hopes that Bibi will start to look healthier. It has been agreed that we will go to be with her during the holidays and she has had me remove a few pieces of furniture for their future installation.[92]

When they were not on holiday in Beuzeval and Houlgate, the "Eugène Manets" moved back and forth

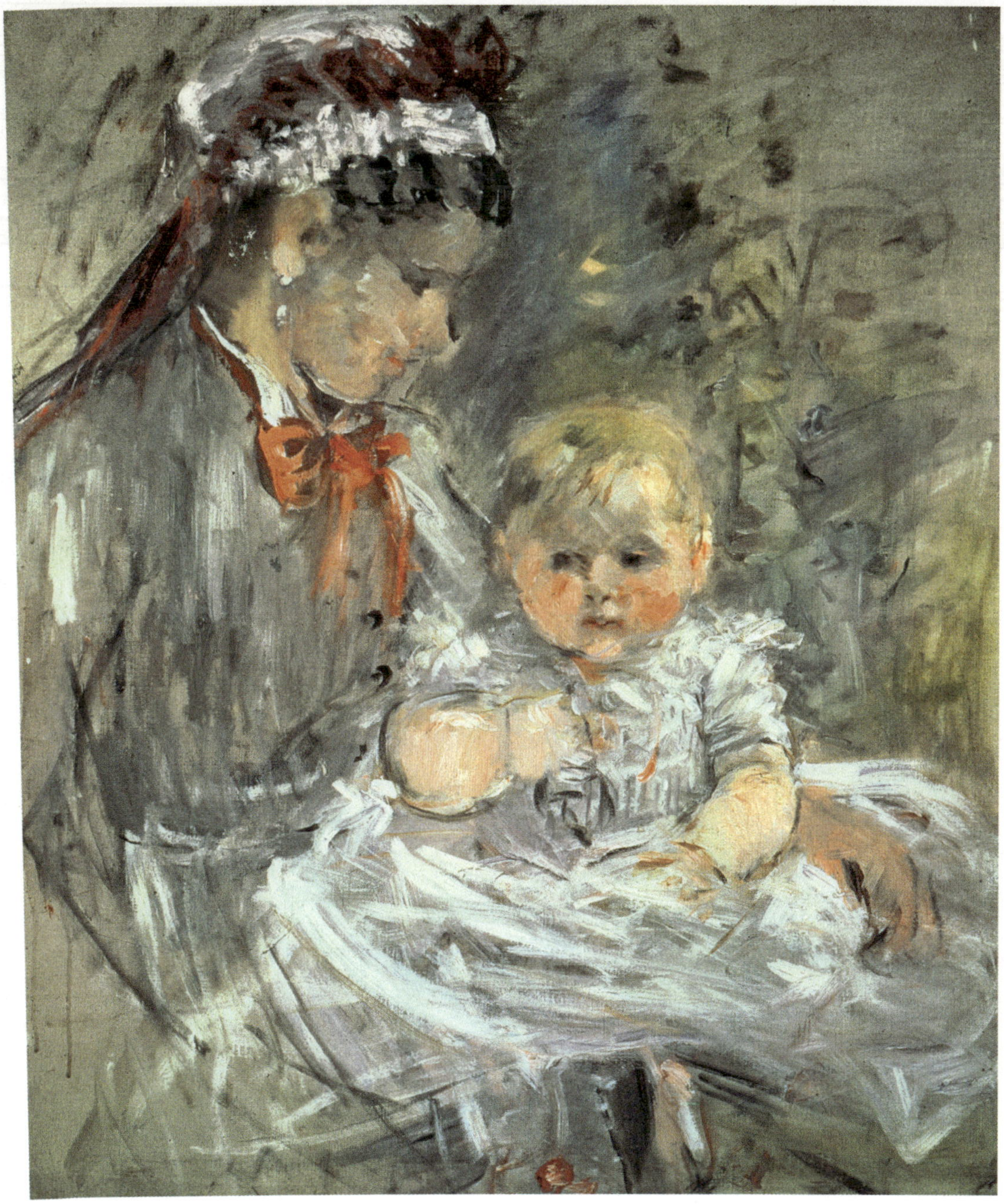

Berthe Morisot (1841–1895)
The Wet Nurse, 1880
Oil on canvas, 73 × 60 cm
Copenhagen, Ny Carlsberg Glyptotek

between Bougival and Paris,[93] where Bon Papa Morisot passed away at the age of ninety-two on November 11, 1880.[94] The following year, the family rented the house at 4, rue de la Princesse in Bougival, where they posed for the only family photograph that has come down to us (p. 8). In 1881, the nanny Angèle gave way to the young and elegant Pasie, who was now tasked with watching over Julie. Both posed for Berthe in the verdant garden at Bougival (above). And as the place was perfectly to their taste, the "Eugène Manets" left their rented accommodation on the avenue d'Eylau.

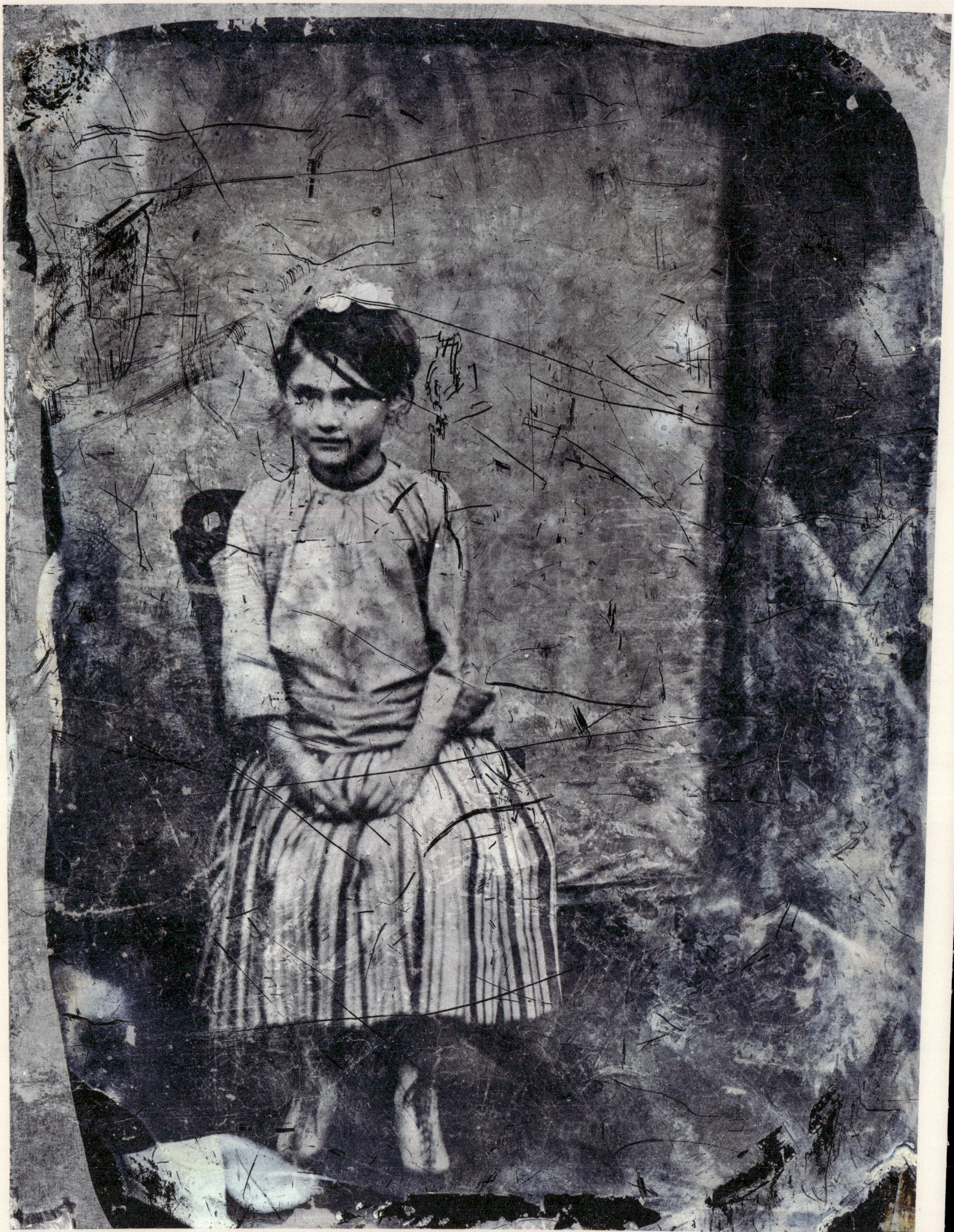

A PLACE OF ONE'S OWN

1881–1892

RUE DE VILLEJUST

In 1881, Berthe and Eugène made the kind of investment that comes only once in a lifetime. They acquired a plot of land for the construction of a rental property, thereby acquiring their own home but also a possible source of revenue. The "Eugène Manets" decided that they would stay in the 16th arrondissement and purchased from one M. Henri Jennings a plot of 522.34 square meters at 40, rue de Villejust for the sum of 173,127 francs.[95] The exact financial arrangements are not known. Berthe probably contributed 43,500 francs[96] from the estate of her mother, Marie Joséphine Cornélie, who died in 1876, and of Bon Papa, who died in 1880. For his part, Eugène sold a plot of land in Gennevilliers[97] for an unknown sum and, with his brothers, took out a loan of 55,000 francs from the Crédit Foncier, to be reimbursed over sixty years. It was no doubt thanks to the support of Julie's paternal grandmother that the sum could be paid in cash in April 1881.

This was also the month when Julie entered the art world: the young girl appeared in two of the works submitted by her mother to the sixth Impressionist Exhibition:[98] a profile in pastel, not unrelated to the portrait painted by Uncle Édouard at the age of fifteen months, heralded her future as a model (right).[99]

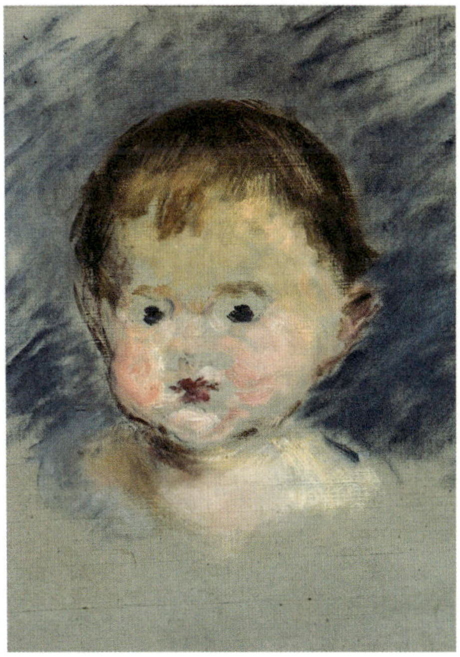

Édouard Manet (1832–1883)
Julie Manet at Fifteen Months, 1880
Oil on canvas, 36 × 33 cm
Private collection

It was at this time that "the Eugène Manets" terminated their lease in the avenue d'Eylau. Yves, Paule, Marcel, and Jeannie Gobillard moved in near to Edma, at 2, rue Jean Bologne,[100] then left the capital. They were next in Versailles, Neuilly, Compiègne, and then Marly-le-Roi:[101] while waiting for the construction of the building in the rue de Villejust, designed by the architect Morize, Berthe, Eugène, and Julie thus went from place to place. In spring 1881 they were in Bougival, while the winter was spent in Nice. Bibi's health having worsened, Berthe extended their stay, and delighted in seeing Julie become "all pink in the sun."[102] Eugène returned to Paris, where he had various matters of business to attend to. He stayed with his brother Gustave in avenue Trudaine.[103] While there, he also selected the canvases by Berthe that would feature in the 1882 Impressionist Exhibition.

Facing page
Julie Manet as a child, c. 1885
Archives BS, Paris, Musée Marmottan Monet

Once again, Julie featured prominently: Berthe's child was the subject of four[104] of the ten works exhibited,[105] in Bougival or on the beach at Nice, playing alone, with Pasie, or with her father.

"If you decide to rent an apartment, I think it would be better to look in our neighborhood, so that Bibi's daily life won't change and she can get plenty of air every day," Berthe suggested to her husband.[106] "I await your guidance to choose an apartment," was Eugène's conciliatory answer, although he did argue in favor of the streets close to the Champs-Élysées, pointing out that "there Julie will be at the center of children's pleasures. Wooden horses, artistic guignol, goats."[107]

In the end, in early 1882 "the Eugène Manets" rented a pied-à-terre in the 1st arrondissement at 3, rue du Mont Thabor,[108] then decamped to à Bougival for the summer. Uncle Édouard, who was in a very bad way, was vacationing nearby, in Rueil. Julie, who benefited from the outdoor life all summer long, also gave her mother and uncle one of their choice subjects. Both immortalized her making sandcastles (p. 188). The countless paintings of Julie and her toys reflect the new perception of childhood that had begun to pervade privileged milieus during the late nineteenth century.

In order to finance work in the rue de Villejust, Eugène Manet took out a new loan from the Crédit Foncier, a substantial 160,000 francs.[109] The couple's debt now represented 72% of their capital. Although the lack of a tax declaration[110] means that we cannot determine their annual income (bank interest, various property revenues), it is clear that Berthe and Eugène were committing all their capital to this ambitious project. The building was completed by late 1882. Four apartments and their service rooms extended over as many floors. The first tenants, Monsieur and Madame Koechlin, moved in to the fifth floor in October 1882 where their annual rent was 4,500 francs.[111] The apartment occupying the first floor and entresol was designed for an artist[112] and more particularly for Berthe, which would explain why Eugène declined the offer from a prospective tenant, the sculptor Bartholomé,[113] conveyed to him by his friend Degas. In 1883 the owners finally moved in. A garden ensured that Bibi and her mother could enjoy the good fresh air that they both needed. On the street side, an adaptable room was designed both for painting and receiving guests. The architect had done his best to allow this twin function. The drawing room/studio, which was to be directly accessible to visitors, was close to the entrance. It was a handsomely sized room notable for its high ceiling, which was unusual for a first-floor room on the street side, and for its three double windows, forming a kind of glass wall. However, it faced south/southwest and not north, as artists usually prefer. According to Jacques-Émile Blanche, Berthe had rejected this, saying that she preferred strong light.[114] This, then, was very much her apartment.

1883: THE TURNING POINT

The beginning of 1883 was a sad time. Théodore Gobillard passed away on January 6,[115] Édouard Manet on April 30. Eugène organized his brother's funeral and acquired a plot in Passy cemetery on behalf of his widow, who, with her daughter, left the rue Saint-Pétersbourg for the 16th arrondissement. On May 7, 1883, Eugénie wrote to her daughter-in-law:

> I am very well looked after by Eugène and Berthe who are full of attention, consideration, and affection for me. I am trying to overcome the despondency and disorder that such sorrow has brought to my mind. You have found a letter of mine bringing good financial news. Answer it at once or have Léon answer, he has become the consummate businessman. This good news has brought forth in my mind a thought that would make me very happy if you would agree to join with me to rent an apartment from Eugène. Berthe has spoken of all the happiness you would give me.
>
> Eugène wants to rent me his third 3,500 = 2,400 of my rent in the rue Saint-Pétersbourg and 1,100 that you would put in would make up the total. You know the apartment: 3 bedrooms with a WC and bathroom, scullery, very fine kitchen, 2 cellars, 2 servants' rooms.[116]

A few days later, Léon wrote to Eugène:

> My dear Eugène,
>
> My Sister [in fact, his mother, Suzanne Leenhoff] has told me that Madame Manet plans to go and live in your house and that she would be glad to have me in her home, for which I am most grateful to her.
>
> Your brother raised me like his own son; I have always lived in your family, and it would be a great wrench to leave you.[117]

The new arrivals were settled before June, with countless paintings decorating their apartment. Mme Manet *mère* moved in with some thirty works. These included two portraits of her deceased son, one by Fantin-Latour,[118] the other by Monet,[119] several other canvases by Monet,[120] a Sisley,[121] a Pissarro,[122] and even two Morisots.[123] As for her son's work, she clearly brought only the double portrait for which she had posed with her husband[124] (p. 235) and a landscape (p. 221).[125] The artist's widow, Suzanne Leenhoff, brought only mementoes: five portraits of her and Léon by her husband.[126] There was no lack of canvases on the first floor, either. In addition to Manet's portrait of Berthe[127] (p. 239) and the one of Eugène given by Degas[128] (p. 223) for their wedding, there was a copy of a Boucher painted by Berthe,[129] two Pissarros,[130] a seascape by Monet (p. 252) [131] plus one of his views of Bordighera (p. 253) and Japanese prints.[132] The Manets were the most numerous. The twelve items acquired for 20,000 francs in the posthumous sale constituted a "gallery," noted Berthe. "Mme Manet's heritage is shrinking,"[133] she observed. *Woman with Fans* (p. 280–281), *Laundry* (p. 226),[134] *Girl in the Garden,*[135] *Singer at a Café-Concert,*[136] *Nude Arranging Her Hair* (p. 245),[137] and *Oysters and Champagne*[138] were the main works on show.[139] *Boy with Cherries* (p. 243), which Berthe would soon let go, was part of Eugène's heritage. Such was the setting in which the young girl developed—a private, Impressionist world, an environment in which memories, art, and family history merged into one.

LÉON VERSUS JULIE

Julie, painted by her mother playing in her mourning clothes,[140] spent her first years with Manet's wife and daughter. Now aged four, the young girl brought them all joy. As Berthe told a friend:

> My husband was deeply affected and so was my poor mother-in-law . . . it is all so sad! And nothing less than the sight of Bibi's gaiety and robust health of can restore a little charm to our interior.[141]

Despite the apparent harmony, the situation was tense. Eugénie warned:

> I have ruined myself enough as it is for my 2 sons [Édouard and Eugène] without yet bringing myself down to nothing.[142]

The "Leenhoff world"[143] drew some particularly harsh words:

> They are adversaries, not to use another word.[144] . . . There are some things about which I shall speak no more. It is the crime she was made to commit by her affection for this poor boy who is merely the victim of his sad birth. She [Suzanne] wants more than she should have, that is the punishment for her crime, and she must suffer it.[145]

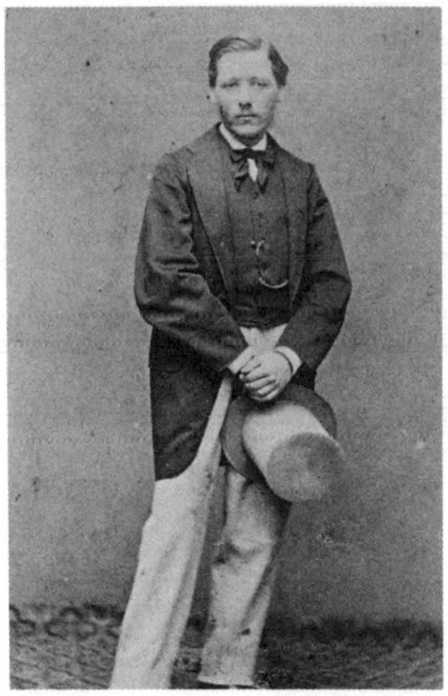

Léon Koëlla known as Leenhoff, c. 1872
Paris, Bibliothèque Nationale de France

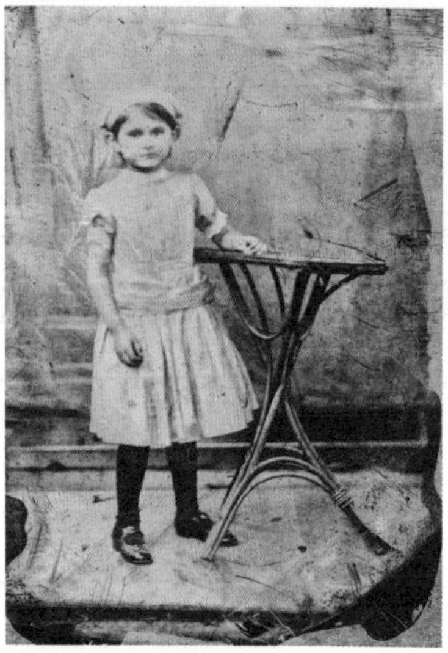

Julie Manet as a child, c. 1884
Archives BS, Paris,
Musée Marmottan Monet

Mme Manet did not hear the wish half-expressed in Édouard's will, which was that Léon should be given a place with the Manets, by making him, after his mother Suzanne, his sole legatee. Mme Manet would never accept him as a grandson. She took no measures in his favor, making Julie her one and only heir. As of June 7, 1883, when an estimate was being made of the furniture in her son's estate, Eugénie Désirée Fournier added a codicil in favor of Julie:

> I give and bequeath to My Dear granddaughter Julie Manet daughter of my son Eugène Manet for whom I feel the greatest affection: all my jewelry . . . ownership of capital yielding six hundred francs of income . . . as a result of the decease of my poor dear Édouard, I find myself his heir for a quarter in bare ownership, the usufruct belonging to his widow Suzanne Manet in accordance with his marriage contract, I give my granddaughter Julie Manet the share that will come to me . . . The bequest that I have made above to My Dear granddaughter Julie Manet, to serve as her dowry, I desire and wish that the goods and capital or values that will come to her as a result of this bequest should be used as goods or bonds in Julie's name, so that she remembers her grandmother kindly.[146]

As for Léon, he was given no more consideration than would be extended to servants: "I give Léon my wardrobe with a mirror and the vases on it and I thank him again for the very tender, devoted care that he gave my poor Édouard during the two cruel months of suffering."[147] This was much less than the works that she set aside for the Abbé Hurel![148]

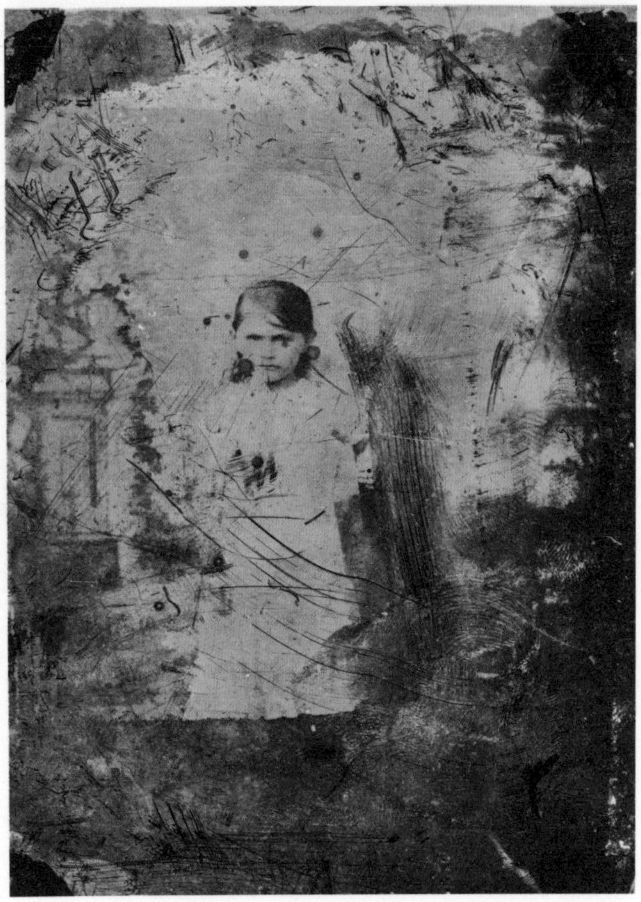

Julie Manet as a child, c. 1883
Archives BS, Paris, Musée Marmottan Monet

As usufructuary of the property and sole legatee with full ownership, what Suzanne actually inherited was above all debts. Édouard's estate presented liabilities of 49,907 francs toward Eugénie. The failure of the posthumous sale meant the widow was unable to settle her accounts as she was hoping to do.[149] The only reimbursement that she was able to make, for the sum of 21,888.20 francs, was from the sale of land held in common that she had inherited.[150] Suzanne still owed nearly 30,000 francs. At the age of six, then, Julie was a child with a rich endowment and, without knowing it, the instrument of undeclared family score-settling.

HOME TEACHING

Julie was now old enough to receive her first tuition. Despite the abundant correspondence and numerous references to the young girl, little is said about the arrangements for her instruction. One thing is certain: Julie was given the kind of education expected of the upper bourgeoisie of her time.[151] The idea, certainly, was not to lead her to a diploma or a profession—her parents both declared that they had none—but to inculcate the manners and way of living appropriate to their milieu. Seemingly unconcerned by Camille Sée's law which, in 1880, opened secondary education to young girls, Eugène and Berthe gave Julie a home education provided by tutors, punctuated by short spells of private lessons. Berthe was particularly aware of developments in teaching practice, which aimed to "replace constraint and monotony with affection and variety."[152] To make the education process even more lively for Bibi, in 1883 the artist illustrated her reading book. Her father was unstinting in his efforts and encouraged her learning from the age of three: "I am counting that when I see you again you will be perfectly able to read French," he wrote her in 1884.[153] In addition to French, Julie was immediately introduced to English, learning which had been a central part of the education of young bourgeois girls since the July Monarchy. Eager to keep their distance from the teaching dispensed in schools, which they imagined to be almost exclusively written and dominated by grammar and technique, good families employed English nannies whose job it was to give future mothers a classical, literary education that was as much oral as written. Berthe Morisot had herself been looked after by a memorable English nanny, Louisa.[154] Apart from the language, Louisa relentlessly inculcated an impassivity that was close to the feigned indifference of the bourgeoisie, which always muffled its feelings, whatever the circumstance. Berthe confided:

> **When I was in England, I made no effort to see Louisa again, I was too frightened to see a narrow-minded old English woman. I loved her as only children can love. I thought she was perfect, understand me, perfect with a flaw. I saw her as pretty, and it seems that she was very ugly. She instilled in me, first of all, an absolute faith, even in miracles, a faith that I lost shortly afterwards. And also a certain moral strength, the courage to suffer in silence. As a little girl I used to cry in bed because of my sorrows, and she pretended not to hear me and did not console me.[155]**

"The Eugène Manets" would inculcate in Julie the same sense of restraint and, as was the custom, resorted as of 1881[156] to the services of one Miss Reynolds. In 1884 the tutor posed with her student for a canvas and a watercolor eloquently titled *The English Lesson*.[157]

VISITORS TO THE RUE DE VILLEJUST

Coming in close succession, the deaths of Gustave Manet, on December 18, 1884, and Eugénie Désirée Manet, on January 8, 1885, marked another turning point. Apart from the canvases that he inherited (portraits of Auguste and Eugénie Manet; p. 235, and Isabelle Lemonnier; p. 224), Eugène now became sole owner of the property portfolio left by Auguste Manet, which had been largely reconstituted as a result of his mother and brother's successions. The apartment on the fourth floor was let to Mme Tenré when Suzanne left to live in Gennevilliers, moving into a house that Jules de Jouy made freely available to her in the rue Croix-des-Vignes.[158]

Berthe Morisot decided that she would receive guests on Thursdays, in memory of Eugénie Désirée's receptions on the same day. As of 1885 her salon-cum-studio become one of the places where Manet's friends and young colleagues would meet. The artist's circle is one of the most extensively studied aspects of her life,[159] and my purpose here is not to trace its development but to place it in the context of Julie's childhood. While following the codes of bourgeois sociability, Berthe gave her daughter a unique opportunity to grow up surrounded by the artists of her day. The children of her male counterparts were less fortunate: their fathers met in town rather than at home. Neither Monet and Renoir's sons, nor the children of Pissarro and Sisley benefited from a similar experience.

The young Julie had her place in a landscape of great men—Degas, Monet, Renoir, and Mallarmé, to name but a few.

More than ever, painting was part of her everyday life. Bibi witnessed the lessons her mother gave to her cousin Paule, who, since leaving the Légion d'Honneur school on July 13, 1884, had decided that she would be a painter. As a cousin wrote to Berthe: "Your sister Yves, is very happy about your lessons for her daughter and seems, alas, to be full of hope. Everything is so difficult that hope is nearly always our only pleasure."[160] Paule herself assured her: "I work every morning when I have time, scraping, erasing, frowning, never achieving anything very good. How difficult it is. There are days when I wonder how the thought of painting ever came to me and where it will lead me."[161] To which Berthe replied: "You have not reached the end of your ordeals with painting. They are infinitely varied, but they will keep you busy for life."[162]

Julie also took to the brush and worked with her mother. An habitué of museums, Bibi no doubt frequented the Louvre with Paule, whom Berthe had just registered as a copyist. Following their friend Degas's dictum, that "You don't talk about painting, you observe it,"[163] the artist honed her daughter's gaze and taught her to see like a painter. "I tell her to observe," she wrote. "With her, I look for the relation between shadow and light. She sees pink in the light, purple in shadows."[164] Painting was not a formula. Phrasemakers led it astray.

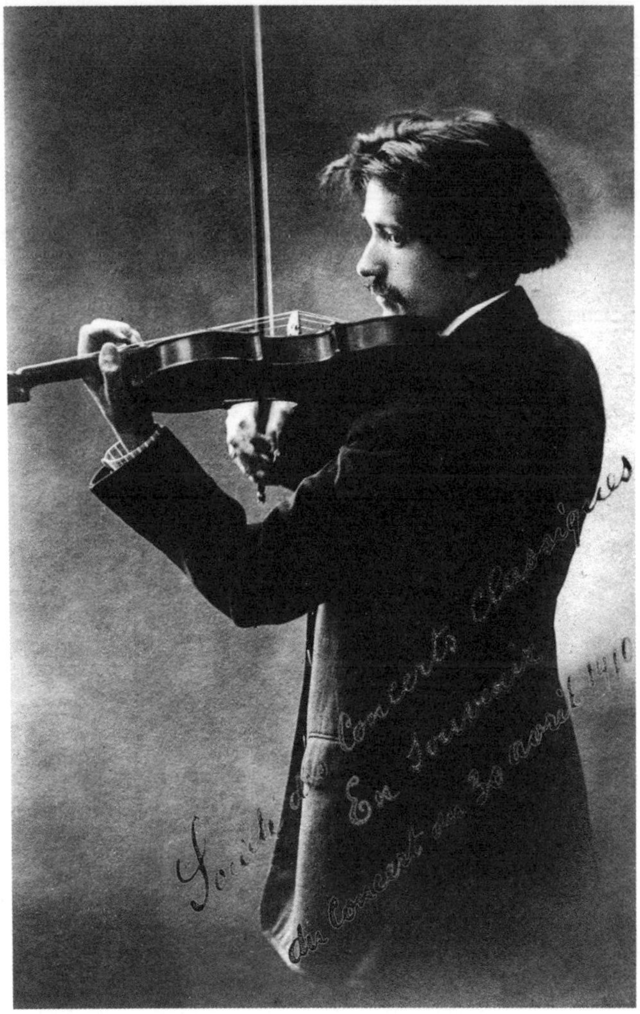

Jules Boucherit with violin, 1905

> **Explaining how painting is done may interest onlookers because they will never understand a thing. Values, chiaroscuro, muted colors—these are hieroglyphs on which, in fact, painters should sit an exam before printing them. True artists understand brush in hand. . . . Is this vulgarization of matters artistic really necessary? What can you do with rules? Nothing of interest. What is needed are new, personal sensations. Where can you learn those?[165]**

Her mother warned: "Ah, when the whole of France is quibbling over painting, it will crush it like a big printing roller."[166] Renoir summed up this idea that was so important to the Impressionists: "Music and painting should never be literary."[167] And he added: "When I try to capture an individual's physiognomy, then I become literary."[168]

And so when, in 1887, Eugène and Berthe asked Renoir to make a portrait of their daughter, the two painters no doubt discussed the most appropriate way of representing Bibi whom, at her birth, her mother had described as "Like a little cat, always in a good mood . . . as round as a ball and with sparkling eyes and a big mouth that she puckers."[169]

The highly composed, meticulously executed portrait of Julie Manet, known also as *Child with Cat* (p. 209), no doubt required numerous sittings, and it is likely that these encounters would have helped forge a genuine friendship between Julie and Renoir, who was quick to encourage his young protégé in her painterly ambitions.[170] The apple never falls far from the tree.

As firm friends of her parents, the Mallarmés, also took a keen interest in Julie. The poet was mindful of Bibi's efforts and asked Berthe to "not forget to kiss the forehead of the painter in the avenue du Bois: for we also keep one of her paintings in our sight."[171] His daughter Geneviève (right) was soon a member of the closest circle. As was Paule, "Vève" was like a much-loved older sister. Berthe charged her with assembling groups of young readers. As she wrote:

> **I am sending you this invitation on behalf of my daughter, just on the off chance, thinking that you may have a few young friends, girls or boys, who might be glad to receive it, and that if so you would be so kind as to escort them to me. The innocence of our readers is an attraction, for they are between 8 and 13 years old.**[172]

During the summer of 1887 "the Eugène Manets" made their first trip to the vicinity of Valvins, where the Mallarmés were renting a small house, Les Plâtreries. The forest of Fontainebleau and the banks of the Seine now became a familiar part of Julie's world. Mallarmé had wasted no time informing Eugène of the improvements made to the site that might please the child. "I was thinking of you in this heat wave, and do tell Mlle Julie that we quickly cleared the river and erected a footbridge just for her."[173]

They saw one another all the time, forming such a bond that in 1888 Berthe wrote a first will making Mallarmé Julie's deputy guardian.[174] This meant that, were her parents to die before Julie reached her majority, he would take responsibility for overseeing the management of her guardian. The Mallarmés were now part of the family. The poet belonged to that inner circle invited to celebrate, for example, the induction of Jules de Jouy into the order

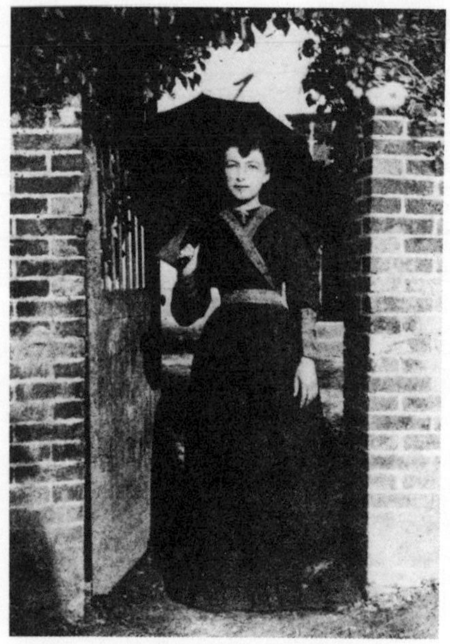

Geneviève Mallarmé, c. 1885

of barristers.[175] Unable to attend the dinner, Mallarmé recommended to "Mademoiselle Bibi my toast for the uncle-godfather."[176]

PAINTING WITH WORDS

The pleasure of having their own home sweet home did not keep "the Eugène Manets" from travelling. They never spent the full year in the 16th arrondissement, cultivating the bourgeois art of vacation residences. After their summers in Bougival and their jaunt to stay with Yves in Compiègne, they would go away for weeks, sometimes even months. One year it might be Belgium and Holland, another, the island of Jersey, or again the châteaux of the Loire and Tours, ending at the Château de Vassé, owned by their cousins the Mayniels. Their stay in Nice, where they rented the Villa Ratti from November 1888 to April 1889, is the most significant and best known. In her letters Berthe stresses Julie's painting and lessons, which kept her very busy.[177] English, so important on the Riviera, was even more to the fore, and, as she wrote Mallarmé, Berthe also took the opportunity to brush up her own skills: "I have found a 'little philology of English words' owned by Julie's English teacher and I am studying it assiduously in order to get my English beyond what is required for domestics."[178]

Mallarmé maintained a keen interest in his ward's reading.[179] For the New Year he sent her *L'Homme à la flûte*

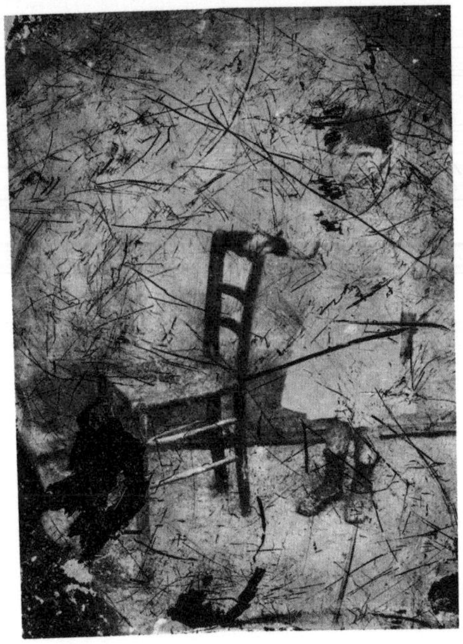

Julie Manet, c. 1883
Archives BS, Paris, Musée Marmottan Monet

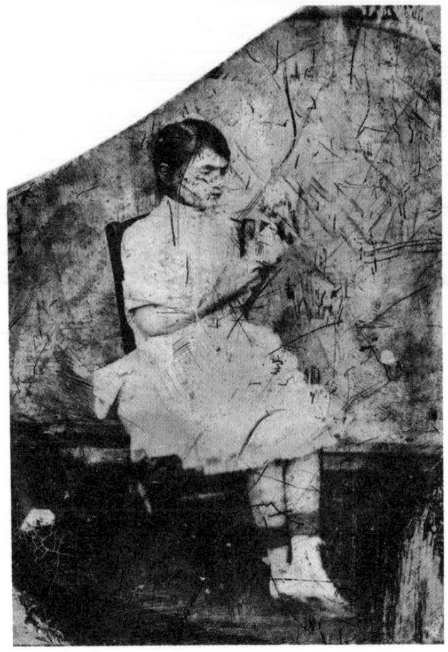

Julie Manet, c. 1885
Archives BS, Paris, Musée Marmottan Monet

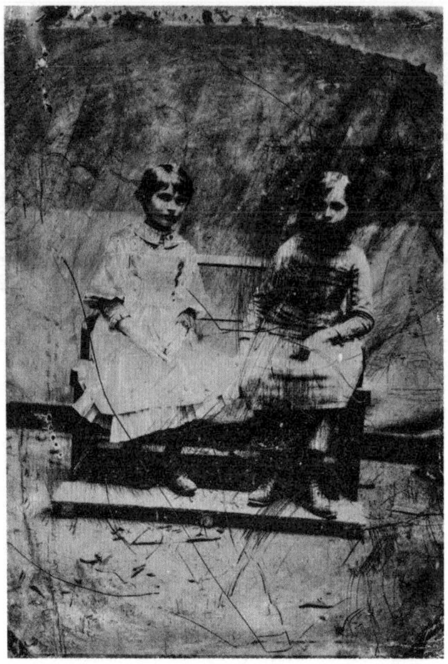

Julie Manet and her cousin Jeannie Gobillard, c. 1887
Archives BS, Paris, Musée Marmottan Monet

(*The Pied Piper of Hamelin*) by the English poet Robert Browning, then, the following year, *François le Champi* by George Sand. He also made a point of writing from time to time, including a quatrain for New Year's Eve. She received these every year[180] and treasured each one:[181]

Ce poème devenu prose,
Comme tout se passe à l'envers !
Moi qui devrais pour chaque rose
Ne vous envoyer que des vers[182]

Sent to Nice in January 1889, this quatrain announced the next:

Sur Pégase si bien en selle
Où que vous jette son élan
Restez Bibi, Mademoiselle
Julie, avec le nouvel an[183]

Despite all the moving, Bibi's days were highly organized, as can be seen from the "Timetable" on the first page of the exercise book in which the young girl copied out her geography lessons, consisting of droll poems in English and French (p. 28).[184] When she was eleven, this world of words, which was so important to her parents, was manifested to Julie in a new light. A teacher, Edgar Bèhne,[185] came to Nice, then directed her studies by mail when the family returned to Paris in the spring. The letter he wrote to Eugène Manet on May 7 goes into some detail about Julie's education:

Allow me to begin by telling you how delighted I am to be giving lessons to your charming young lady, and particularly in such an interesting way, by correspondence, but repeating the express condition that the moment you find this somewhat unusual system complicated you should feel free to stop these lessons forthwith.

Here are what I suggest as the general principles of this program:

1. Avoid all tiredness, imperatively. On this condition we can be sure of obtaining the most brilliant results, and of seeing Mlle Julie Manet become a very remarkable and accomplished person. These precautionary measures concern you, Madame Manet and yourself, exclusively, and you cannot be too vigilant on this score.

2. Take as the basis of the lessons what the pupil has [around her]; that is to say, she should send me an account of what she observes; I shall send it back as we go along with corrections and annotations. These essays can be about her reading or her excursions, or descriptions of the house, the garden, an enumeration of its flowers, about which I shall give her botanical explanations, etc. Let her send me the copies she makes and tell me what pieces she is learning. For the time being, the exhibition offers an endless reserve. But beware tiredness! Short, short days only.[186]

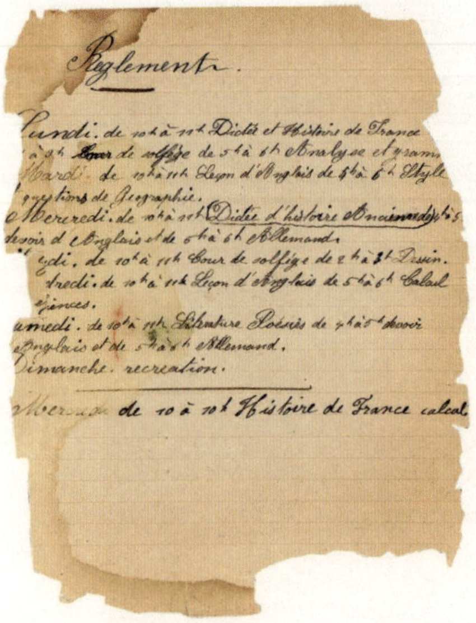

Reglement.

Lundi. de 10h à 11h Dictée et Histoire de France à 3h ~~Cour~~ de solfège de 5h à 6h Analyse et gram...
Mardi. de 10h à 11h Leçon d'Anglais de 5h à 6h Style questions de Geographie.
Mercredi. de 10h à 11h Dictée d'histoire Ancienne ... devoir d'Anglais et de 6h à 6h Allemand.
...udi. de 10h à 11h Cour de solfège de 2h à 3h Dessin.
...dredi. de 10h à 11h Leçon d'Anglais de 5h à 6h Calcul ...ences.
...amedi. de 10h à 11h Litterature Poésies de 4h à 5h devoir d'Anglais et de 5h à 6h Allemand.
Dimanche. recreation.

Mercredi de 10 à 10h Histoire de France calcul

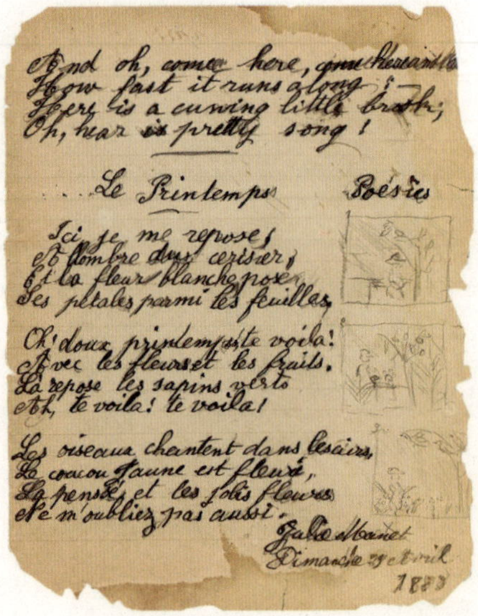

And oh, come here, ...
How fast it runs along;—
Here is a cunning little brook;
Oh, hear its pretty song!

Le Printemps   Poésies

Ici je me repose,
A l'ombre d'un cerisier,
Et la fleur blanche pose
Ses petales parmi les feuilles.

Oh! doux printemps te voila!
Avec les fleurs et les fruits.
La repose les sapins verts
Ah, te voila! te voila!

Les oiseaux chantent dans les airs,
Le coucou jaune est fleuré,
La pensée et les jolis fleurs
Ne m'oubliez pas aussi.

Julie Manet
Dimanche 29 avril
1888

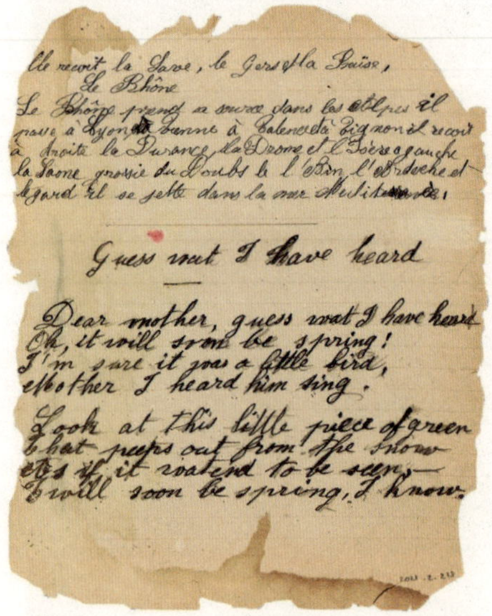

...lle recoit la Save, le Gers & la Baïse,
Le Rhône
Le Rhône prend sa source dans les Alpes il passe à Lyon ... à Valence à Avignon il recoit à droite la Durance la Drome et l'Isère a gauche la Saone grossie du Doubs le l'Ain l'Ardeche et le gard il se jette dans la mer Méditerranée.

Guess wat I have heard

Dear mother, guess wat I have heard
Oh, it will soon be spring!
I'm sure it was a little bird,
Mother I heard him sing.

Look at this little piece of green
that peeps out from the snow
As if it watend to be seen,—
It will soon be spring, I know.

Julie Manet's learning book: timetable and poetry, c. 1889
Archives BS, Paris, Musée Marmottan Monet

While Berthe trained her daughter to see the world as a painter, her teacher trained her to find the right words to depict it. One of her first pieces of homework was to describe the event of the year: the Exposition Universelle of 1889. What a pity that Julie's essays about the Eiffel Tower, of which her cousin Gabriel Thomas was delegated administrator,[187] and her first essays composed under her mother's loving gaze[188] have not come down to us!

Other private teachers would also be hired to instruct Julie. The "French teacher as learned as she is ugly who oversaw her work"[189] shortly after this was no doubt the severe Mlle Bordier, mentioned by Berthe in her letters.[190] On occasions, too, Julie frequented private institutions: "Julie goes very regularly to the courses and enjoys herself greatly there. This young girl has a real love of work, and this time her teachers do not tire her brain with their lessons."[191]

Berthe Morisot's position was clear: a good education was not force feeding: "Nowadays, little girls take 5 or 6 courses a week . . . We fuss and fidget and have lost sight of the fact that nothing beats 2 hours lying on a chaise longue. Dreaming is life – and dreams are truer than reality, that is where we are really ourselves – if we have a soul, that is where it is."[192] To compromise Julie's awakening was out of the question!

Her education would not have been complete without music. Berthe Morisot knew where music theory was taught in the capital[193] and made sure that her daughter was taught perfectly. Julie tried the mandolin and, above all, the violin, providing the subject of countless pictures by her mother. At this moment, too, Jeannie Gobillard acquired a passion—and a virtuosic talent—for the piano. The cousins very likely attended the musical mornings given by the Société des Concerts Bleus which, from 1890,[194] brought together the most brilliant students from the Conservatoire aged between seven and fourteen. One of these young musicians, Lucie Léon, posed at rue de Villejust for a series of canvases.[195] Julie and Jeannie saw mainly the troupe's violinist, Jules Boucherit, whose parents were great music lovers. Julie also went regularly to the Concerts Lamoureux, accompanied by her mother or tutor on Sunday mornings.[196] More, even, than her musical talents, it was her ability to listen that was called upon. For while "paintingology" was mistrusted in the rue de Villejust, musicology was seen as an art. Properly appreciating a performance and assessing the quality of an interpretation was an integral part of Julie's bourgeois education. To converse knowledgeably about music was as important as being able to play it.

"MADEMOISELLE FORMERLY BIBI" OR "THE CATECHUMEN"

Julie was growing up. Her guardian, still prone to slips of the tongue, observed this and wrote of "Mademoiselle formerly Bibi."[197] The quatrain he wrote for her on New Year's Eve in 1890 was intended for a young woman:

> **Ici l'humble greffier**
> **Atteste la mélancolie**
> **Qui le prend d'orthographier**
> **Julie autrement que Jolie**[198]

Renoir praised "the young girl with handsome hair like Pan."[199] Her mother's many canvases of her record the transformation.[200] The passing time also widened Julie's social circle. She cultivated a close friendship with Germaine Hoschedé, Monet's daughter-in-law, visiting her several times in Giverny. And as Berthe was close to Henriette Caroline Renault,[201] Julie frequented her daughter, also called Berthe,[202] who was soon one of her best friends, and who gave her and her cousin Jeanne roles in a four-act comedy she had written, *Le Service intéressé*, which they performed on Monday May 11, 1891 (right).[203]

With her cousins, Paule and Jeannie, Julie began to enter society. The talk about Villiers de L'Isle-Adam, given by Mallarmé in the rue de Villejust on February 27, 1890, was an event. Some fifty friends were invited: the cream of Paris society and the Mallarmé-Monet-Morisot clan. "This effort is great fun for our young entourage and it will be an opportunity to bring new dresses out of the wardrobes," wrote Eugène of an event that sounds very much like a rite of passage.[204]

Julie was also concerned not to have had her first communion, which was usually celebrated at the age of seven or thereabouts. Her insistence finally paid off: Louise Riesener wrote Berthe, "I heard that Julie was very concerned about her first communion. I can assure you that she is right to want to go ahead. These things cause only fleeting trouble but are a burden if one does not do them in time."[205]

Berthe, for whom "this grand name God . . . means nothing" and was "empty of meaning,"[206] approached the event as a chore.[207] The preparation, which she hoped to entrust to their friend the Abbé Hurel,[208] was not enough. The family's move to Mézy-sur-Seine in 1890 meant that she had to deal with the priests of Les Yvelines.

Mallarmé, who attended the farewell dinner with Degas, Renoir, the Olliviers, and the Abbé Hurel,[209] closely followed his ward's progress, with questions in every letter: "Bibi; how many theological virtues are there?"[210] "Bibi, how many deadly sins?"[211] After the event, Berthe related her communion mishaps to Monet: "First communion is done and we have acquitted our debt to society. But it was not easy. I was lucky to meet a perfect priest here, who was totally on my side, but then he went and took ill and they replaced him with two phrasemongers who gave me a really hard time."[212] Indeed, as she confessed to Mallarmé, who was unfortunately unable to attend,[213] the priests terrified her, leading the poet to conclude: "So, the dark nightmare was tripled, and you had to possess learning to satisfy three *abbés*. Julie sailed through all that, unscathed, holding the candle like a flower, and so much the better. . . . Warm greetings to you, Manet and the catechumen.[214]

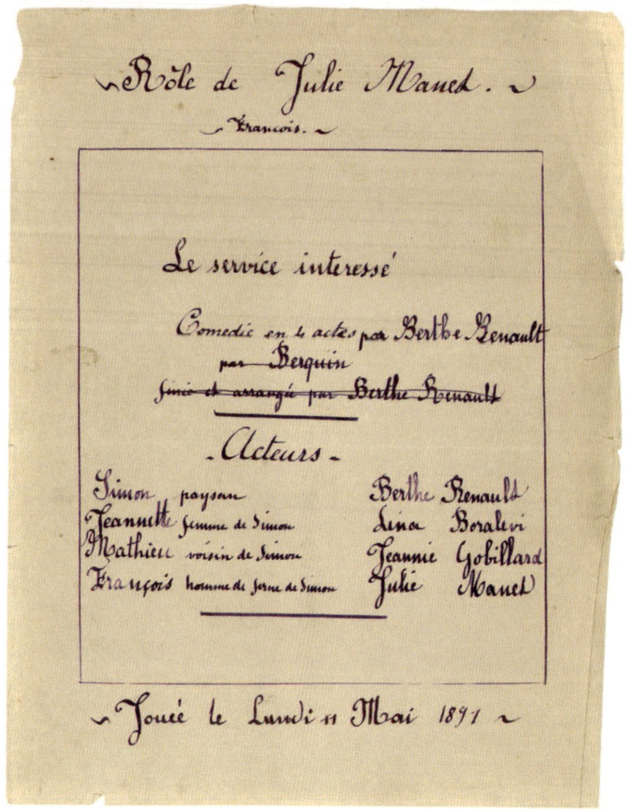
Rôle de Julie Manet.
François.

Le service intéressé

Comédie en 4 actes par Berthe Renault
par Berquin
finie et arrangée par Berthe Renault

Acteurs

Simon	paysan	Berthe Renault
Jeannette	femme de Simon	Lina Boralevi
Mathieu	voisin de Simon	Jeannie Gobillard
François	homme de ferme de Simon	Julie Manet

Joué le Lundi 11 Mai 1891

First page of *Le Service intéressé*, a four-act comedy by Berthe Renault, in which a role was assigned to Julie Manet, May 11, 1891
Archives BS, Paris, Musée Marmottan Monet

"EDMA, WOULD YOU LOOK AFTER THE LITTLE ONE?"

Although Berthe Morisot laid out the house in Mézy so that she could receive guests—Mallarmé, who did not come, Renoir, who set up his easel next to hers, and Paule

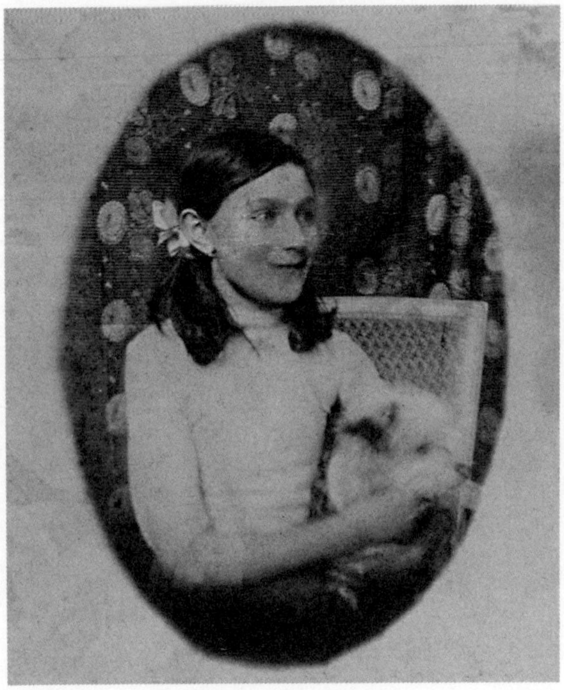

Julie Manet, c. 1889
Paris, Musée Marmottan Monet

and Jeanne, who posed with their cousin—the real reason for their move outside Paris was Eugène's declining health.[215] When she too fell ill, Berthe imagined the worst. The letter she sent to her sister Edma in late 1890 is perfectly clear on this point:

> I am well now, but not yet recovered from the blow to morale. I saw myself struggling with death and remain terrified at the idea of what might happen when I am gone, especially to Julie. Did I tell you that my will makes Mallarmé her deputy guardian? But—so many buts. If Eugène were no longer there, or became just too ill, would you look after the little one?[216]

Edma replied at once. To which Berthe responded as follows:

> Thank you for your affectionate letter. In a word, this is what I had: rheumatism of the heart. It is perhaps not as dangerous as it feels for the patient: the sensation is exactly that of life ebbing away from you, and since that eventuality will certainly come about some day or other, best make arrangements for one's loved ones.
>
> I have always thought of life as a great gift and will do everything in my power to hang on to it as long as possible. Thank you for so kindly answering with a "yes," and assuring me of your affection for Julie.[217]

It was certainly to find better air for Eugène that the couple acquired a small château not far from Meulan. On November 29, 1891, Mme Étienne, a widow, sold to them for 30,000 francs a property of two hectares at Le Mesnil, in the commune of Juziers, in the canton of Limay.[218] At around the same time, the apartments in the rue de Villejust, which had manifestly remained empty, were put up for rent. The second floor was given to the Comte de Riancey and the third to M. and Mme Dieudonnée Bertin, for annual rents of 3,750 and 3,600 francs respectively. A loan of 40,000 francs taken out in March 1892 from M. Jolivard ensured sufficient liquidity to buy the château.[219] Eugène took advice on this acquisition from the uncle-godfather, also asking him about Julie's interests in the estate of his brother Édouard: ten years after the painter's death, the affair remained unsettled.

> My dear Jules,
>
> Would you be so kind as to find out about the liquidation of Édouard's estate?
>
> There is one important chapter, which is Julie's debt claim toward her aunt. The sums accruing from the sale of paintings and reused as annuities (like my mother's guaranteed share) were sold and used to reimburse Suzanne's property loan.
>
> Consequently, Julie is the creditor on what remains.[220]

Julie was indeed her aunt's creditor by virtue of the liquidation pronounced on March 25, 1892. A few days later, on April 13, her father passed away. Julie was now the last of the Manets.

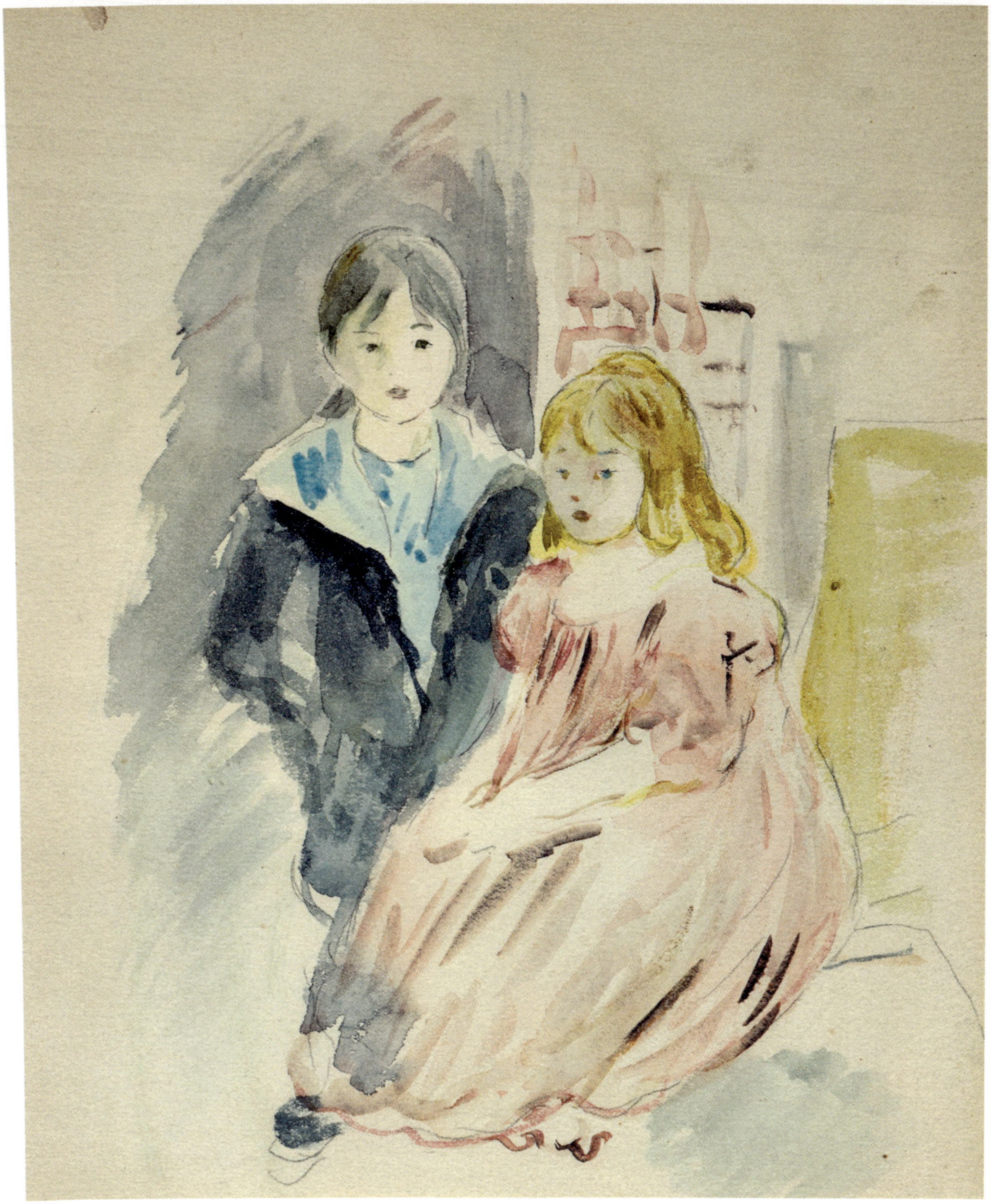

Berthe Morisot (1841–1895)
The Children of Gabriel Thomas, c. 1893–94
Watercolor on paper, 24 × 20 cm
Private collection

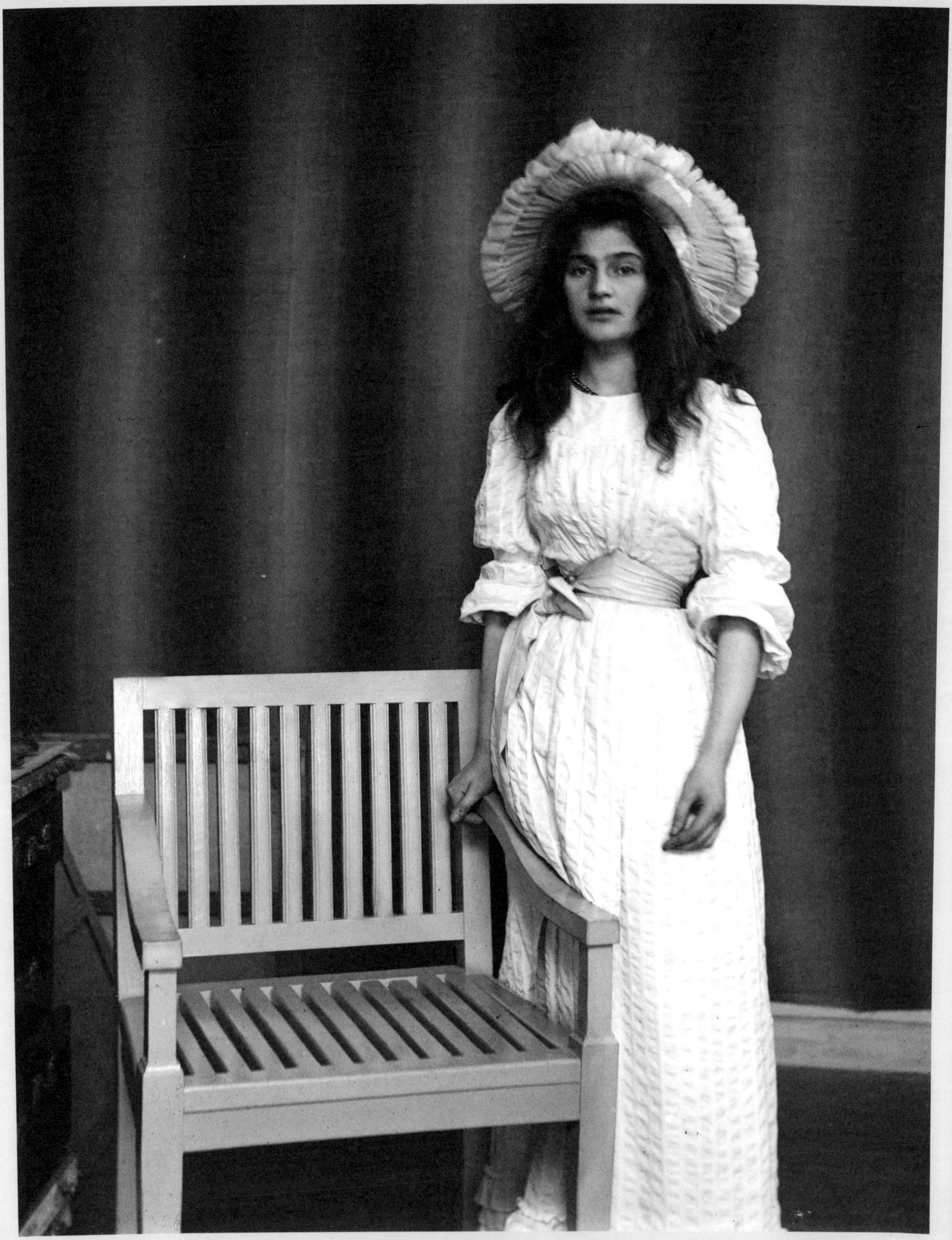

JULIE IN THE LIBERTY HAT

1892–1894

"WITH TEARS WELLING UP, I SEND YOU MY LOVE"[221]

The family was extremely discreet about Eugène's demise. Little is known about his last moments, or about those that followed. A few letters written shortly before March 25 hold out little hope for Julie's father:

> My dear friend, I would like to talk to you as Julie's guardian. Tell this man to let me know if you are free today, Thursday. At around 10 am I am usually alone in the living room; be sure to have a pretext ready to explain your unlikely presence at such an early hour. Or would you rather I came to you? But it is difficult to commit myself to a time an hour ahead. Eugène is so agitated that. . . .
>
> This all sounds very mysterious, but it is just sad.[222]

Paule, who was with the Gobillards in Clermont-Ferrand, sent a few pages describing her impressions. In her PS, she concludes:

> Oh my dear Aunt Berthe, I do believe there is nothing gay in what I have written, despite my best intentions. But there is something so sad in my heart knowing that you are so worried about Uncle Eugène, my Bon Oncle, my thoughts are with him as ever, with his suffering, and with you, Aunt Berthe, alone at his side.[223]

On April 13, 1892 Degas came in haste to be with his dying friend.[224] The same day, Berthe wrote six words to Mallarmé, announcing the worst:

> Dear friend, it is all over
> B. Manet[225]

In the press we found neither obituaries nor death notices. As for Eugène's funeral, there is not much to say except that he was buried alongside Édouard in Passy cemetery, attended by only the closest family and friends. Regarding the inhabitants of the rue de Villejust, only Berthe followed the bier. Julie was considered too young to attend her father's funeral. Silence became and would remain the best way of facing the future. The placid expression in the photograph of Berthe in full mourning speaks volumes (p. 34). Reflecting her upbringing rather than any belief, her demeanor shows that she respected the codes of the Catholic bourgeoisie. "God gave, God has taken back" (Job 1:21), and so to complain would be like judging God. Berthe's behavior toward Julie followed the same logic: "Rather than outpourings, I must contain myself and spare her childhood the spectacle of my grief."[226]

Julie followed her mother's example; interiorizing the conventions, she remained silent:

> When I think that I have never dared to speak to Maman about Papa since his death! Not once have I pronounced his name, it is extraordinary; we were both grieving for him yet I join my tears with Maman's . . . Why did I never talk about Papa, what did Maman think of me? Perhaps she understood me if she was so shy and withdrawn; she knew well that I adored Papa.[227]

Facing page
Julie Manet in a hat, rue Weber, c. 1894
Paris, Musée Marmottan Monet

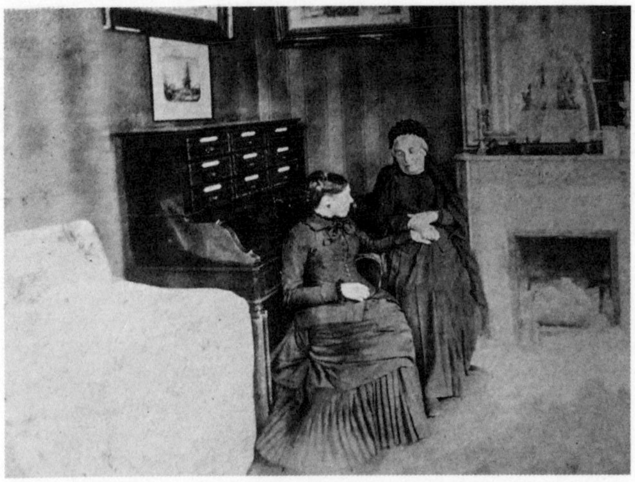

Paule and her mother Yves Gobillard at Marly-le-Roi, c. 1890–93
Private collection

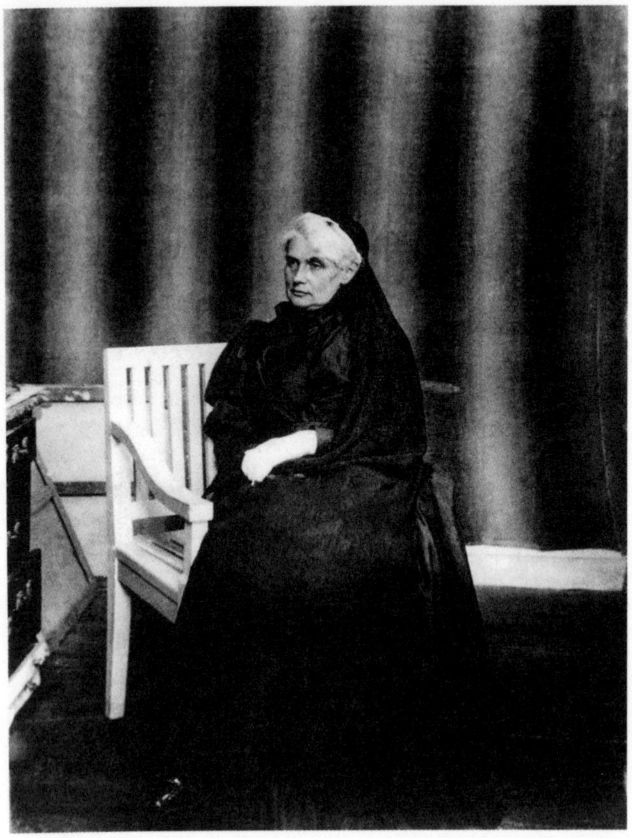

Berthe Morisot in mourning, rue Weber, 1892

THE FAMILY COUNCIL

To protect the interests of orphans or adults without legal agency, the French Code Civil makes provision for a family council (art. 390). Comprising a minimum of four members, it is assembled by a justice of the peace in order to choose a guardian and deputy guardian,[228] to oversee their actions, and even to arbitrate the most important decisions. The usual practice is for the surviving parent to be designated as guardian. In the eyes of the law, therefore, Berthe Morisot was the "natural and legal guardian of Mlle Julie Manet, her daughter,"[229] and this is the title used in official documents, rather than "mother." As women could not otherwise sit on the family council (this changed in 1917), Berthe was the only female presence to watch over Julie's interests. For want of access to the official proceedings,[230] the correspondence tells us about the make-up of this family council.[231] Jules de Jouy, the godfather-uncle, although very much involved in managing the family's affairs, was not a member, no doubt because of his age, seventy-seven, and his lack of mobility. In fact, Julie's family on her father's side was not at all represented, an incongruity which reminds us that the Manet family and name was dying out. On the Morisot side, Berthe appealed to her brother-in-law, Adolphe Pontillon, who replied at once: "My dear Berthe, I am utterly at your disposal to be part of the family council . . . for Julie."[232] Two cousins, it appears, were also members. Émile Marie Mayniel (p. 35),[233] state councillor, was an eminent descendant of Berthe's grandmother. Gabriel Thomas (p. 35),[234] who, as we know, was a highly successful entrepreneur, came from the family of the artist's grandfather. The other members of the council were from the close circle. Their friend Mallarmé (p. 35), as we have seen, was deputy tutor. Also to be mentioned is the architect of the rue de Villejust, Julien Morize,[235] who was in attendance when the first meeting of the family council was held at Passy town hall on May 6. Degas, who was regularly informed of the course of events, was also informed of this first meeting.[236] Held in the presence of the notary Maître Fermé, from Suresnes, with whom Eugène had deposited the handwritten will he wrote in 1886, the assembly set out to determine the calendar for the post-mortem inventory. Another meeting was held on June 10, 1892, in the presence of Berthe Morisot and Stéphane Mallarmé. They quickly agreed to continue their deliberations at a later date. For the time being, there were other ways of honoring Eugène's memory.

THE BOUSSOD & VALADON EXHIBITION VERSUS JUZIERS

It was Eugène who had the idea of the *Berthe Morisot* exhibition at the Boussod & Valadon gallery, and so to proceed with it, from May 25 to June 18, 1892, was a way of respecting his will. Featuring forty-three works and a catalogue prefaced by Gustave Geffroy, this was the one and only solo exhibition of the artist's work during her lifetime. But, given her mourning, Berthe could follow it only at a distance, as she told her faithful friend Louise Riesener:

> **I left Paris the day after the opening, which of course I did not attend.**[237]

As for Julie, she was deprived not only of that final farewell to her father, but also of the pleasure of celebrating her mother. Julie, whose portrait by Berthe was on the cover of *La Revue des deux mondes* in 1891, was also kept away from the gallery. But while unable to experience the success of the exhibition, she did get an echo of the admiration inspired by her mother's portraits of her.[238]

Berthe Morisot had made up her mind. A change of scene was in order. The house at Le Mesnil on which Eugène had set his heart was put up for rent. The sole purpose of the months she spent there with Bibi was to freshen up the residence. But despite the offers that were soon being made, Berthe had no plans to sell: she wanted to preserve Julie's inheritance:[239]

> **Having spent three weeks supervising the workers, putting up hangings, repainting, and all those ruinous things, I am coming to find this house increasingly pretty. It was certainly a real find, and it is a great satisfaction to me to think that Julie will enjoy it and fill it with children. For myself, though, I feel mortally sad here and cannot wait to leave.**[240]

Let on January 1, 1893, to a distant relation of Émile Henry Mayniel,[241] the widowed Mme Jagerschmidt,[242] Le Mesnil was hardly mentioned again, except when Mallarmé thought he had glimpsed the place from the train, near Gargenville. To which Berthe replied: "It may well be Le Mesnil that you saw: something long, sad, a big mansard roof, a bunch of pines breaking up the façade."[243] Julie, growing up in the most refined circles, and with a growing sense of ownership, remarked: "I think it is quite charming to have a château that one does not live in, and that now and again one sees from a railway, looming up like a shadow in the night, and to say, 'That is mine.'"[244]

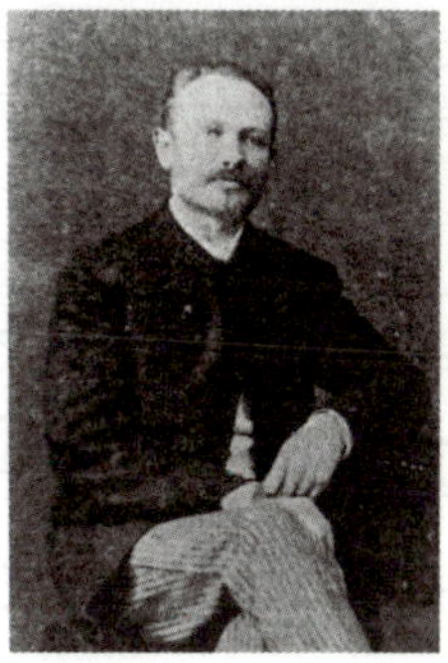

Gabriel Thomas

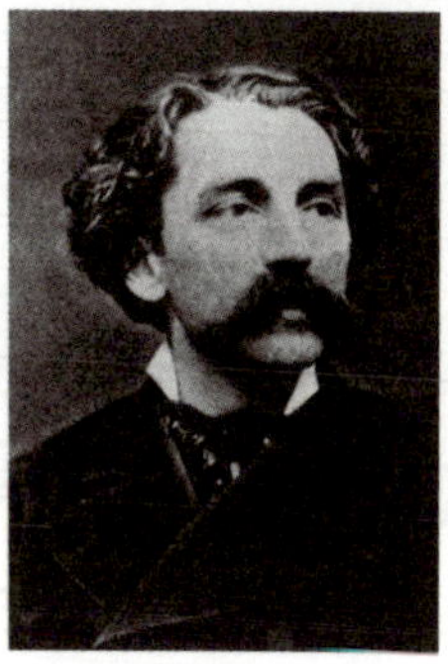

Stéphane Mallarmé

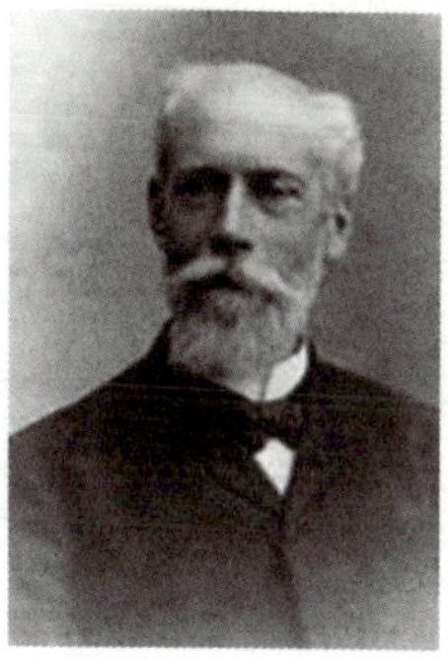

Émile Mayniel

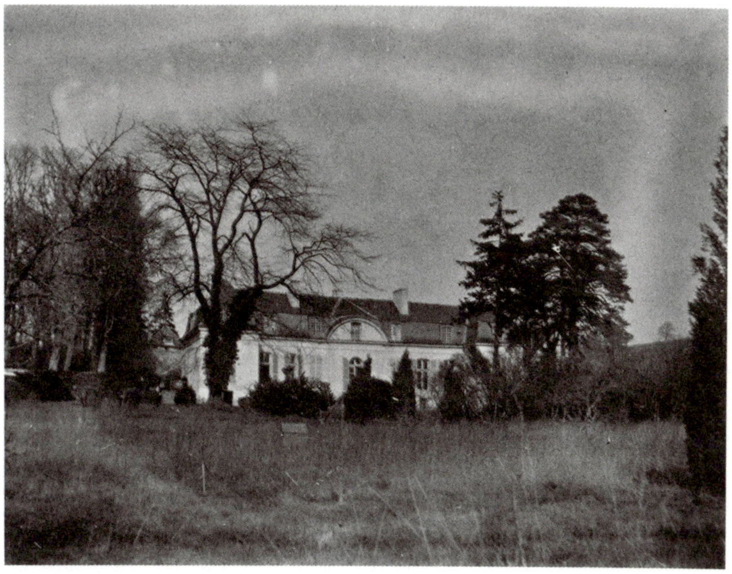

Julie Manet (1878–1966) or Ernest Rouart (1874–1942)
Le Mesnil, exterior view
Archives BS, Paris, Musée Marmottan Monet

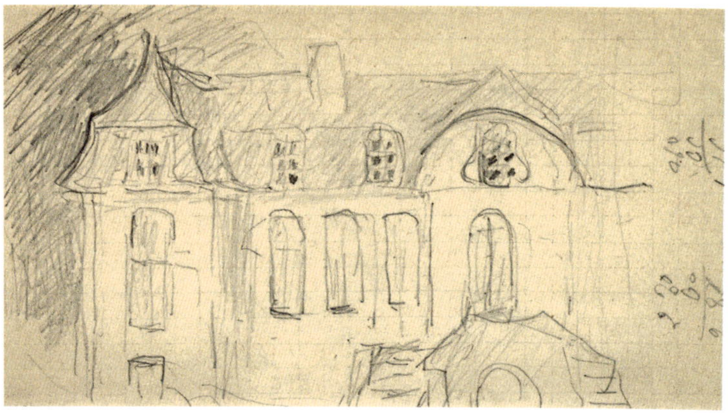

Berthe Morisot (1841–1895)
The Façade of Le Mesnil, page from the Mézy notebook, also known as the "black notebook," 1891
Pencil on paper, 8.5 × 15 cm
Paris, Musée Marmottan Monet

As of spring 1892, Julie made only occasional stays in the rue de Villejust. When she was not in Le Mesnil with her mother, she was visiting her cousins and her aunt Yves Gobillard,[245] whose health was also declining, in the rue Saint-Cyr in Marly-le-Roi.[246] At the age of thirty-one, Berthe's niece Paule Gobillard was perfectly able to look after the younger ones. She had Julie stay with her in Marly, thereby sparing her the uncomfortable sight of her father's post-mortem inventory, which took nine days and was carried out in the presence of her mother and deputy tutor. This was still unfinished when a tenant was found for the apartment.[247] On June 29, the Comte de Suarez d'Aulan asked that it be cleaned and its painting refreshed for October, in exchange for an annual rent of 3,800 francs.

> I have grown accustomed to the idea of leaving this interior where Julie grew up and where I faded. My memories are within me, impenetrable, and my death will interest no one. I have always found it very hard to part with places and persons, and even animals, and the worst thing is that they think I am utterly insensitive.[248]

On October 1, 1892, Berthe and Julie moved to within a ten-minute walk of the rue de Villejust, on the fourth floor of a building at 10, rue Weber—it was, naturally, in the 16th arrondissement. For a rent of 3,200 francs, the mother and daughter had the run of an apartment comprising a kitchen, antechamber, library, living room, two bedrooms, a bathroom and a maid's room. A room on the fifth floor could be used as a studio. There was the same Empire style furniture, the Chinese basin, the mahogany Pleyel piano, and a guitar. The one or two paintings depicting this interior are not sufficient to determine what artworks hung there and how. However, we do catch a glimpse of some family portraits: *Berthe Morisot Reclining* by Manet (p. 239),[249] and Eugène painted by Degas (p. 223)[250] were hung as pendants in the living room, where the *Portrait of Isabelle Lemonnier* (p. 224),[251] inherited from uncle Gustave, was also visible. Art as memento.

In the attic, Berthe's *The Black Bodice*[252] hung on the studio wall with a few Japanese screens (could they be the ones that Édouard Manet placed around Nina de Callias in the portrait now at the Musée d'Orsay?),[253] while the other paintings lay in a pile.[254]

Eugène's succession was settled shortly after Berthe and Julie's move on October 12, 1892. Berthe inherited shares of the jointly held family properties, which made her a creditor of Suzanne Leenhoff, who inherited a modest usufruct from Édouard. She also received a quarter of all the property and a quarter of the usufruct of the moveable and immoveable goods that belonged to her husband. The rest went to Julie. The family fortune was estimated at about 250,000 francs, 184,591.06 francs of which came to Julie in unrestricted ownership.[255] Managing these assets, collecting rents, selling land, and repaying loans became part of Berthe's daily routine. Now, as well as a painter and mother, she was an asset manager. Suzanne, who was used to chasing after unpaid rents, encouraged her: "I do not doubt for a moment that you will be able to manage; you are so intelligent that these matters of interest which you have not yet dealt with will come naturally to you, like a habit."[256]

AN IMPRESSIONIST FAMILY

It was at this moment that Julie's Impressionist family really took shape. By deciding to involve her artist friends Mallarmé and Degas in the family council, as champions of Bibi's interests, and giving them real responsibility for her future, Berthe was extending the family circle. This important moment in Berthe and Julie's life was shared by her friends. Their tragedy was their friends' tragedy. For months, they had the same concerns, and even the same everyday life, as they all attended the same "solemn" and "grave meetings."[257] Mallarmé, who had been watching over Julie since she was eight years old,[258] gave her a greyhound which he called Laërtes, in homage to the character in Shakespeare's *Hamlet*. The poet thus gave Julie's new companion the name of a hero who, like her, had lost his father.[259] He was offering his ward a friend, who, by the symbolic power of words, shared something of her history. In his *Notes sur le théâtre*, he also recognized that Shakespeare's young man had "the finest qualities":[260] "'Good Laërtes' says Hamlet,"[261] he wrote to Berthe. The man of letters saw the shakesperean Laërtes as the perfect image of family devotion. The mallarmean Laërtes was Julie's guardian.

But the poet's role did not end there. As he was informed from the outset, Berthe wished to make way for him in dealing with the succession:

> You will shortly be hearing from Gustave Hubbard, deputy for S. et O.,[262] and a lawyer who is my counsel in this entangled liquidation. It is your role, as deputy guardian, to direct things. . . . This solution rather reassures me. I was the victim of that horrid notary, I had the impression that at the helm I was sinking the ship, failing in my duties to my daughter and also to Eugène's memory.[263]

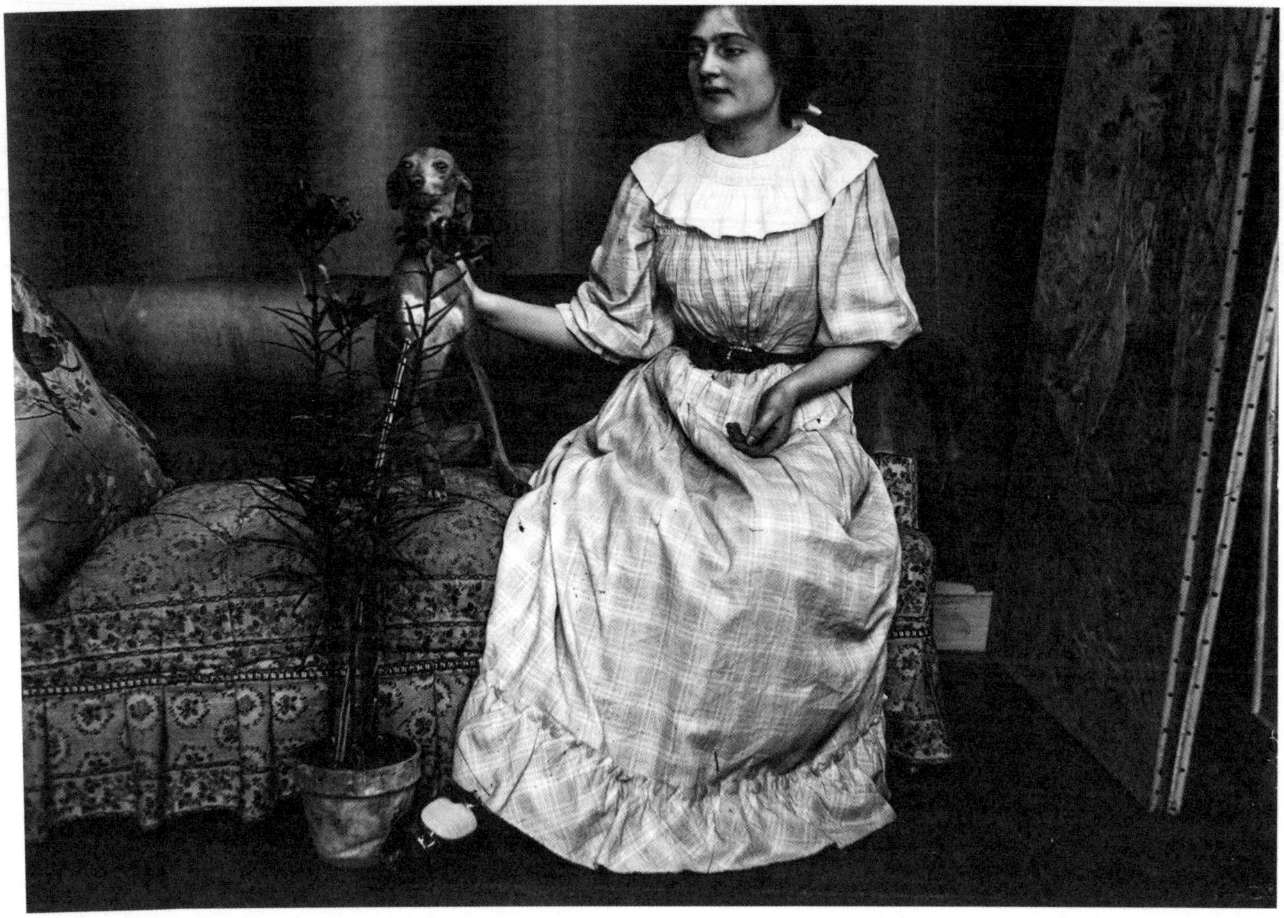

Julie Manet and her greyhound Laërtes in the rue Weber, c. 1892–95
Paris, Musée Marmottan Monet

The trust between them was total. Mallarmé, who lived very modestly on his pension as an English teacher, and whose estate was less than 1,000 francs,[264] watched scrupulously over the heiress's interests. And if the Mallarmés' modest dwelling in Valvins was not big enough to accommodate their friends, then they would stay at the inn. The initial invitations to come on Thursdays were soon informally extended; they were welcome to come and dine *en famille* on any day of the week.[265] Mallarmé, Degas, at whose home they would soon be dining, and Renoir were the three musketeers of the rue Weber. And while Renoir had no legal responsibility for Julie, his presence—he had her pose for him in that sad year of 1892—and his unfailing friendship made him a full-fledged member of this Impressionist family.

Julie and her mother were always together. The demoiselles Gobillard, who were already very close, became even more so by the force of circumstance. When Doctor Martin diagnosed Yves with cancer of the mouth, Berthe responded to Paule's distress:

> Nothing is being hidden from you, my dear child. Your mother's situation can be become serious only in the future, and that future, believe me, is something the doctors have no more idea of than you or I. . . . I say to you in all sincerity, she neither looks nor moves like an afflicted person. Which is not to say that I do not understand your distress and alarm, but please, do not let them get the better of you: stay where you are because she is happy to know that you are getting fresh air and are surrounded with affection. If your presence here were to become useful, rest assured, I will let you know, you can count on that. Your mother first told me about that lump one evening in the wood; the very next day she went to see Martin, so there has been no time lost on her part. The doctor believes this goes back a long way.[266]

While Paule was watching over her mother in Marly-le-Roi, Berthe looked after Jeannie. In her description of Easter Sunday, on April 2, 1893, Nini evokes the pomp of the solemn Mass at the church of the Trinité, and the wonderful experience of hearing Beethoven's Mass in C Minor. Overlooking the assembly from a gallery, Julie and Jeannie had front-seat views:

> Never had a hallelujah seemed more beautiful. Then the music continued, now soft and tender, now majestic, and then it all stopped and the organ alone continued its song with clarinet sounds: the moment for communion had come: all the worshippers came and kneeled at the holy table in the deepest silence and reverence: even a pagan would have been converted. I wish Berthe had been able to witness it all, but she was hidden away in her dark corner where all you could see was her white hair, the white rim of her hat and dark eyes in the shadow—the effect was fantastical.[267]

They spent the rest of the day at the Meissonier exhibition at the Galerie Georges Petit.[268] Jeannie continues:

> In the last room was exhibited a famous work, the grandest of them all, representing some charge under Napoleon. . . . We stayed in that spot for nearly a quarter of an hour and for 10 minutes we were seated on an excellent red sofa. There, Aunt Berthe told us that music was prettier than painting.[269]

Such a pronouncement was bound to make an impression on the young pianist.

YOUNG GIRLS IN BLOOM—YOUNG GIRLS IN MOURNING

Two months later, on June 8, Yves passed away in Marly.[270] The very private funeral was held on the 10th at Père-Lachaise cemetery, where her mother, Marie Cornélie, was buried.[271] Jules de Jouy wrote:

> When I think of the great void that this death will leave you, you were so close to your sister, whose warmth and intelligence I had ample occasion to appreciate. I am also concerned for your dear daughter. Here is another sorrow in her young life, and at her age it is very sad to be afflicted as she has been this past year. My thoughts are also with those who are orphaned.[272] How horrible this life can be . . . All I can say is this: my heart is torn at the idea of what she suffered and the thought of those three orphans grieves me.[273]

Berthe and the uncle-godfather immediately came to Paule's aid in settling the succession. The urgent priority was to terminate the lease on the apartment at 89, avenue de Neuilly in Neuilly-sur-Seine, where the Gobillard ladies, Marcel and their maid, Charlotte Philippeaux, had been living those last few years.[274] The whole of the family pitched in, and soon the young Gobillards were living a short walk away from the rue Weber, at 8, rue Marbeau[275] in the 16th arrondissement. Shortly after their arrival, Suzanne Leenhoff wrote her sister-in-law: "How are you faring? And my dear little Julie, how is she? I am so happy for you both that you have your nieces so close by. It occurs to me that on occasion Paule might replace you with Julie, when you are not well."[276]

Aunt Berthe did not always lean on Paule, however, and took charge of Jeannie's education. She wrote to Jeannie's former piano teacher, now living in Geneva for health reasons, who was delighted to hear from "Jeany [*sic*]."[277] Julie was worried: "Have you given up with the conservatoire?" she asked, signing off as "your cousin who loves you so much."[278] A few days later, she returned to her theme: "You have not told me, either, if you still plan to enter the Conservatoire. It would surprise me if you had given up that idea, and I understand why it should be so important to you."[279]

Given Jeannie's desire to enter the Conservatoire, Berthe enrolled her for piano lessons at the Institut Rudy[280] in the rue Royale, where, for convenience, she also planned to enroll Julie for French lessons.[281] We have no idea whether Jeannie also took the general courses given by Mme Jammès at 54, faubourg Saint-Honoré, where Julie was enrolled at the end of the year.[282] It was no doubt at 77, avenue de Wagram, through the Société Civile Anglaise Protestante, according to the directory an office for placing young English women "only,"[283] that Berthe recruited a new English teacher. In a touchingly fulsome letter, Minnie Vos wrote: "I believe I have the honor of being your daughter's professor of English."[284] Judging by the bond she forged with the family, to which she remained close for several decades, there can be no doubt that she taught more than one young lady in the family circle.

Julie, Jeannie, and Paule were soon joined by their Pontillon cousins who, when their father Adolphe retired in October 1893, took up residence nearby at 12, rue Mignard.[285] The diary that Julie began keeping in August 1893[286] records their everyday existence. Between 1893 and 1895 the old village of Passy became, once again, pivotal to family life.[287] Like their mothers before them, the cousins would go walking around the "village," doing the rounds of their relations. They visited Aunt Edma, Aunt Félicie, Aunt Chevalier, and their friend Sophie Canat.[288] They turned up impromptu and

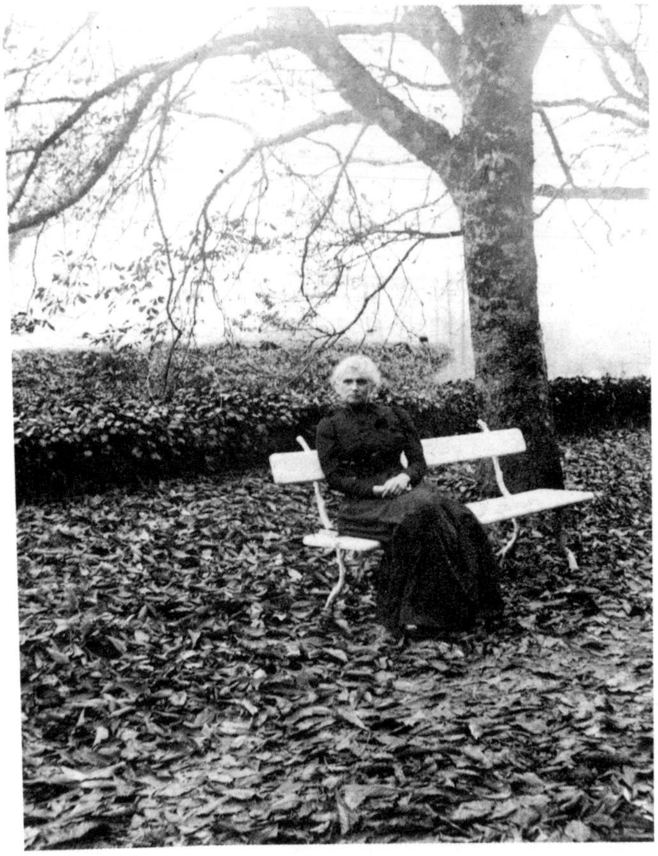

Julie Manet (1878–1966)?
Berthe Morisot in the garden at the Château de Vassé, c. 1892
Paris, Musée Marmottan Monet

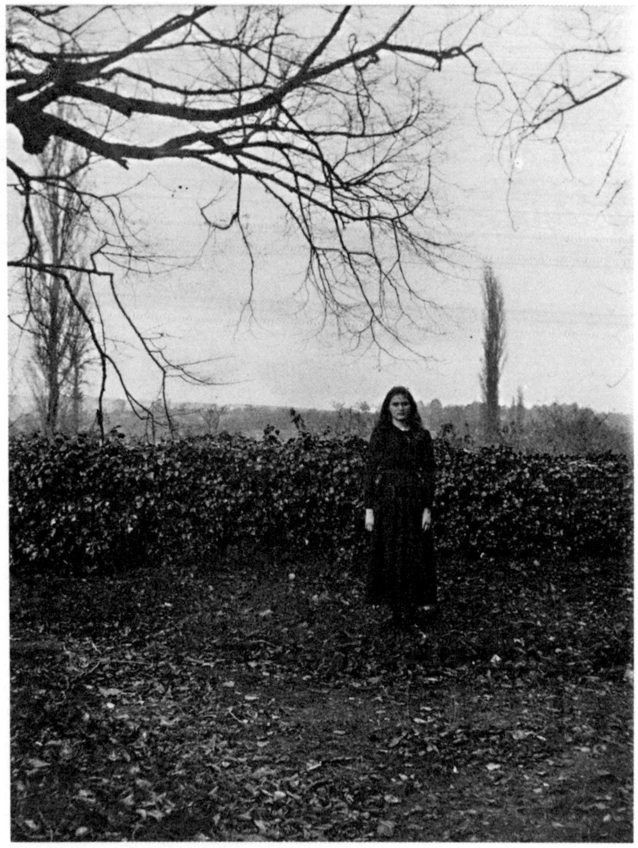

Berthe Morisot (1841–1895)?
Julie Manet in the garden at the Château de Vassé, c. 1892
Paris, Musée Marmottan Monet

stayed to dine with this or that relative. The maids were careful to see these young people safely home, leaving them free to enjoy the pleasure of being together. Berthe was now surrounded by young girls in bloom, five young ladies aged between fifteen and twenty-six, each a companion and a model. These were the years when their particular genius, with its mix of bourgeois mores and artistic spirit, produced its most felicitous moments. Whereas the bourgeoisie perceived art as a pleasure, a simple pastime, at the rue Weber it was seen as a way of life. At the age of fifteen, Julie was perfectly free to follow her mother and share her daily life as a painter. Wherever Berthe set up her easel, the young woman did likewise and painted the same subjects. *On the Chaise Longue* (p. 161),[289] *The Two Sisters*,[290] and *Woman and Young Girl beside a Lake* (p. 163)[291] are some of the themes of which mother and daughter each produced a version.[292] Julie's visual judgment was gaining in confidence, as can be seen from her description of Monet's *Rouen Cathedral* series, which she saw, still fresh, at Monet's home in October 1893.[293] More than ever, too, music had its place—indeed, one could say it was everywhere. First of all, because they painted it. Berthe immortalized Julie and Blanche playing the violin and Jeannie at the piano playing a Mozart sonata. All these canvases would seem to indicate that music was one of their main occupations. In 1892 their former comrade from Les Concerts Bleus, Jules Boucherit, won first prize at the Conservatoire. At the age of sixteen, this rising star in the musical world was Julie's violin teacher. They went to hear him at the Conservatoire, and to attend the annual competitions in which his sister Magdeleine also took part. That same year, Jeanne followed the harmony lessons given by the great violinist Raoul Pugno.[294] They continued, as ever, to frequent the Colonne and Lamoureux concerts, they heard Ysaïe play in Brussels and the solemn masses, which Julie and Jeannie so loved, must for Berthe have been more a musical intermezzo than a moment of prayer. Then there was literature, which was always Mallarmé's gift. Having asked

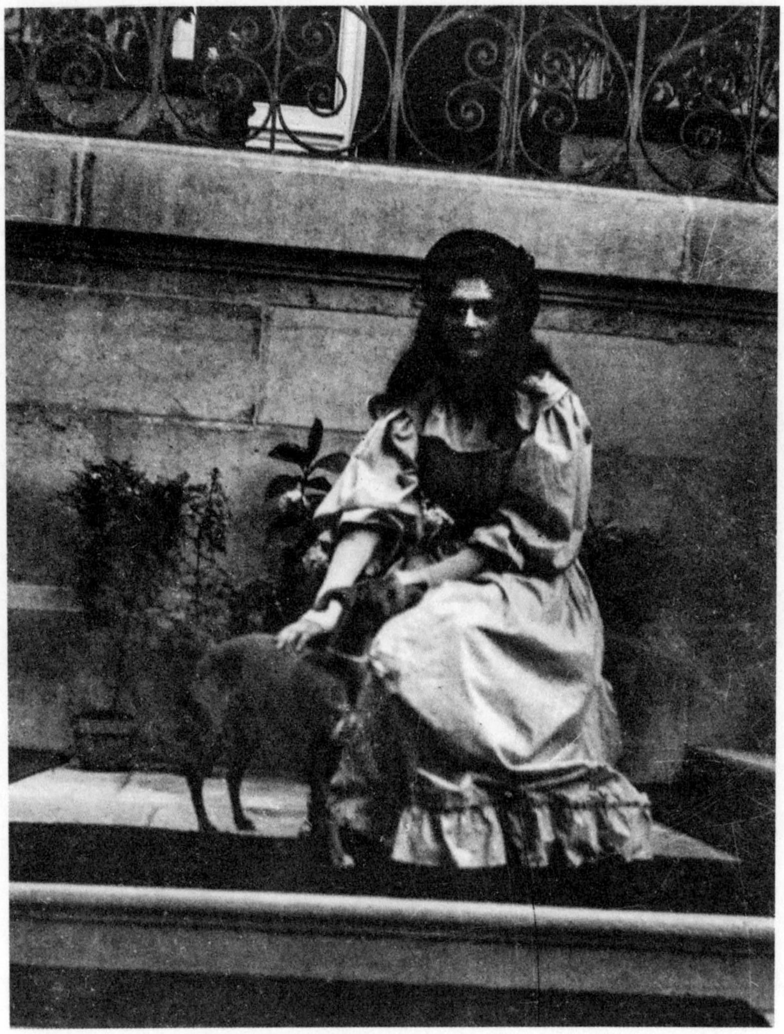

Attributed to Berthe Morisot (1841–1895)
Julie Manet and her greyhound Laërtes, c. 1892–94
Archives BS, Paris, Musée Marmottan Monet

Camille Mauclair to initiate "Mlles Julie and Jenny" into mythology and religion, the poet wrote:[295]

> Julie avant que ne se fixe
> Sur chaque page votre œil clair
> Suivi de vos cheveux de nixe
> Interrogez Monsieur Mauclair[296]

"HOW WRETCHED TO WITNESS THE DEATH OF YOUR FAMILY"[297]

To start the year 1894, Julie told Jules de Jouy of a cherished wish, as he informed Berthe:

> My dear cousin,
> I was hoping to see you yesterday with Julie. Another day, then.
>
> Your dear daughter writes to tell me that for her present she would like a camera. It is rather vague because they come in all kinds of sizes and systems. Is it to take snapshots or bigger photographs? I would like to be clear about this. I have written to one of my friends, Mr Lagrénée, who takes photographs, to find out where I could obtain what your daughter has asked for and what accessories are necessary, etc. Do you have any guidance to give me in this respect?

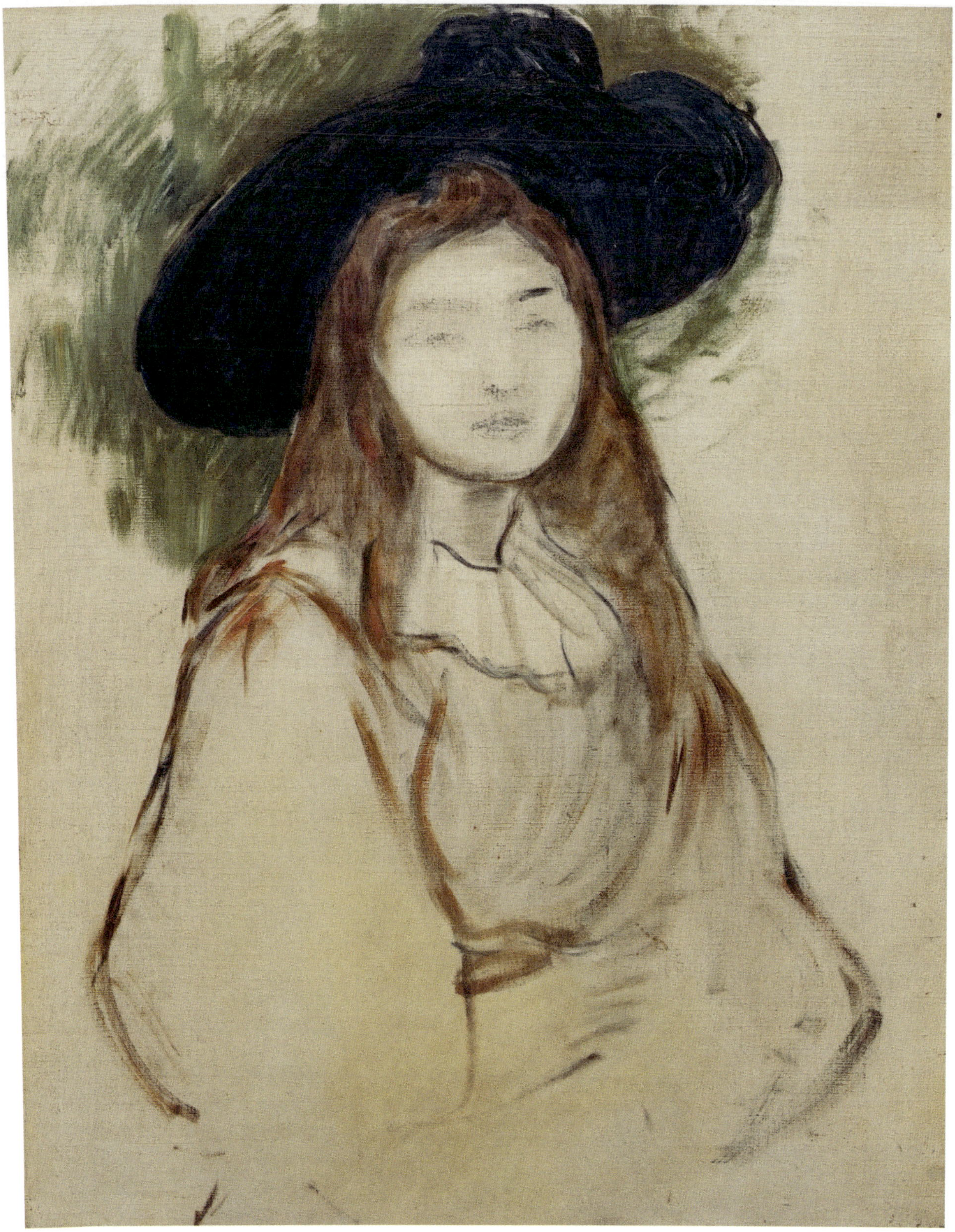

Berthe Morisot (1841–1895)
Julie Manet in the Liberty Hat, 1895
Oil on canvas, 73 × 55 cm
Private collection

Give Julie all my love, with all my heart, and my most affectionate greetings to you. Dejouy[298]

This gift was doubly important for Julie. First of all, it added another string to her bow. Forthwith, she offered to make photographic portraits of Jules Boucherit and Gabrielle Hubbard.[299] Painter, musician, author—she was now a photographer as well. This practice stayed with her for many years, as can be seen from her diary and her unpublished correspondence. Is the previously photograph of her mother in mourning (p. 39 left) by her? No doubt. Did Berthe borrow the camera and have her daughter pose in return (p. 39 right)? Probably. Occasionally reproduced, diversely captioned, never listed or indexed, these images have yet to be studied. We may note simply that the oldest provide precious documentation of that family of Impressionists, and that many of them are contemporaneous of Degas's efforts in the medium, about which more later.

The camera had another, symbolic import: it was Jules de Jouy's last gift to his goddaughter. The lawyer died at the age of sixty-nine on March 9, 1894.[300] His was the first funeral Julie attended. The Mass was held at the Madeleine, in keeping with the Manet way of doing things. The succession throws up this disenchanted observation by Julie: "My good godfather, the last descendant of the Manets. Now I am the only descendant of the three Manet brothers. All that remains is one wretched girl and two widows grieve for them."[301]

Having acquired the sad status of unique descendant of Édouard, Gustave, and Eugène Manet in 1892, it seems that Julie inherited a new title when her uncle-godfather died, that of "last of the Manets." In other words, she was the last not only in the line that descended from Auguste, this Bon Papa Manet whom she knew only as the subject of paintings, but also that of her great aunts, Clémence Manet (Mme Marchais) and Émilie Manet (Mme de Jouy). This is why Julie is the only Manet heir to appear among Jules's assignees, when there were four beneficiaries, the nephews from the line of his widow, née Quatremère. For her part, Julie inherited half of the uncle-godfather's fortune. Having deducted particular bequests, one of which guaranteed Suzanne Leenhoff use of the house in the rue de la Croix-des-Vignes for five years from the date of his death, the fortune due to her was valued at 401,255 francs.[302] "I am happy to think that Julie will have a fine fortune," wrote Suzanne to her sister-in-law. "I do wish her well, I love her so much, her too. She is so good."[303] Her mother and Stéphane Mallarmé, represented by Me Fermé[304] in the post-mortem inventory, acted in her name.

After the sharing out of personal property, and particularly family portraits,[305] the apportionment of the land in Gennevilliers did bring its problems. Lots of equal value were constituted and selected in random order by Me Pinguet. As the house occupied by Suzanne was not part of the lot that fell to Julie, the situation grew tense. Suzanne confided to her sister-in-law:

Above all, do nothing for me that could be costly for Julie. I am old, I could perhaps obtain (after the distribution) a rent that would be provided to me for 5 years, all that indirectly For I may be dead in 5 years.[306]

She continued a few days later: "I make no secret of my feelings but I wish I could have stayed there all my life. I fear the move, I fear everything that is fatigue. I am used to this place, and where I go I shall take my grief with me."[307] Berthe suggested an exchange in order to integrate the house into Julie's share.[308] Without success. To help her sister-in-law, she paid the new owner, M. Collomp, annual compensation of 300 francs to cover the resulting costs.[309]

The year 1894 was richly eventful. The journey to Brussels to the Libre Esthétique exhibition, the Duret sale at which the French state bought its first painting by Berthe[310] and Berthe, the model, bought *Berthe Morisot with a Bouquet of Violets* (p. 218),[311] the sittings for Renoir for his double portrait of Berthe and Julie (p. 43 and 217), the summer in Brittany with Paule and Jeannie, the improvised concerts in Morlaix at the Boucherit home and at Suzanne Leenhoff's home in Gennevilliers formed a veil of happiness that covered but did not hide Berthe's sorrow. One of her main concerns was to put her papers in order. "I used up all my writing paper in Fermé,"[312] she sighed. She went about settling her outstanding loans. Against the advice of the uncle-godfather, who encouraged her to delay,[313] on April 10, 1894 she sold land in Gennevilliers for 110,000 francs. The loan of 160,000 francs taken out with the Crédit Foncier for the rue de Villejust, 60,000 francs borrowed from the Dubreuils and the 20,000 francs from debts owed by Eugène from before their marriage[314] were all paid off. The death of Adolphe Pontillon in September could only encourage Berthe's resolutions. All was gradually put in order for Julie's birthday. She wrote movingly of the event in her diary:

14 November 1894: It's my sixteenth birthday today. The sunrise was quite extraordinary—it was magical,

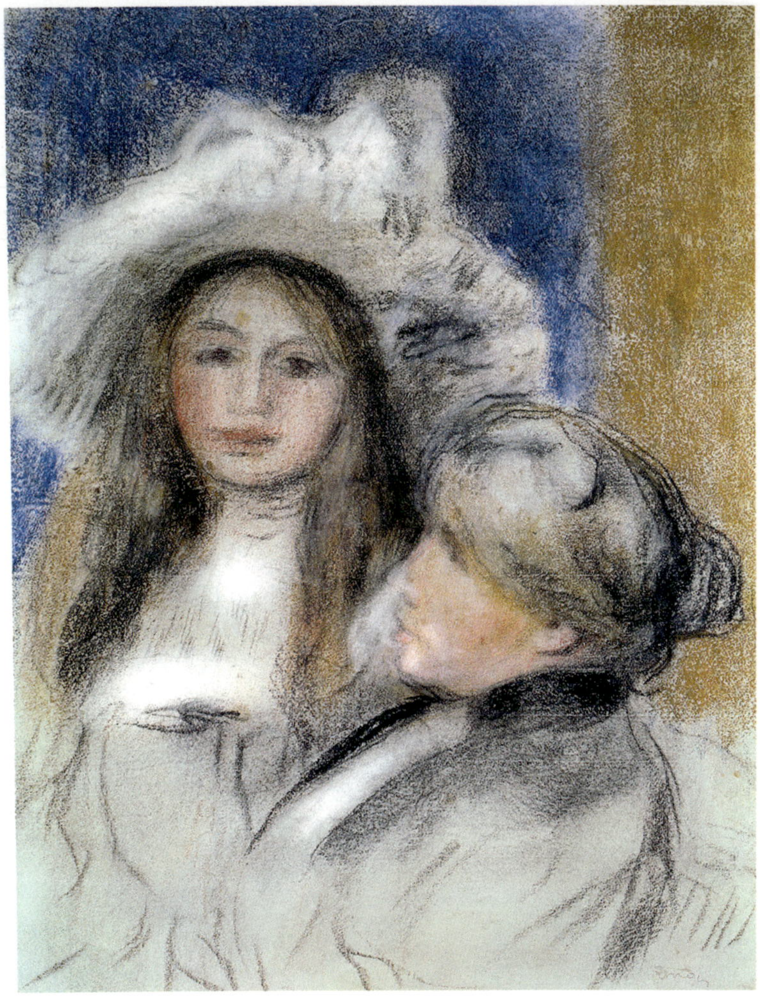

Pierre-Auguste Renoir (1841–1919)
Berthe Morisot and Her Daughter Julie, 1894
Pastel and charcoal on paper glued on cardboard, 58.5 × 46 cm
Paris, Petit Palais – Musée des Beaux-Arts de la Ville de Paris

pink, pink, pink everywhere like a firework display, everything looked as though it was enveloped in tulle—truly marvellous! Paule and Jeannie brought me flowers and Berthe [Renault] sent me some lovely plants. We had supper at Madame Renault before the "Français." First we saw Molière's *Mariage Forcé* . . . *La joie fait peur* [by Mme Émile de Girardin] . . . *Il ne faut jurer de rien* by Alfred de Musset. It was Maman's idea to go to the "Français" for my birthday.[315]

Dressed in and behatted in white, Julie posed for her most famous photograph (p. 32). She is the flower evoked by Mallarmé in another photograph (p. 40):

Celle qui sous le ciel si vite
Atteint une exacte hauteur
Fleurit svelte lys et n'évite
Qu'à son pied reste le tuteur[316]

Charmed by *Julie Manet in the Liberty Hat* (p. 41), Berthe Morisot's last portrait of her daughter, the poet wrote again:

Le rire prompt à se taire
Dont votre air grave est diverti
L'ombrage d'un autre mystère
Que le seul chapeau Liberty.[317]

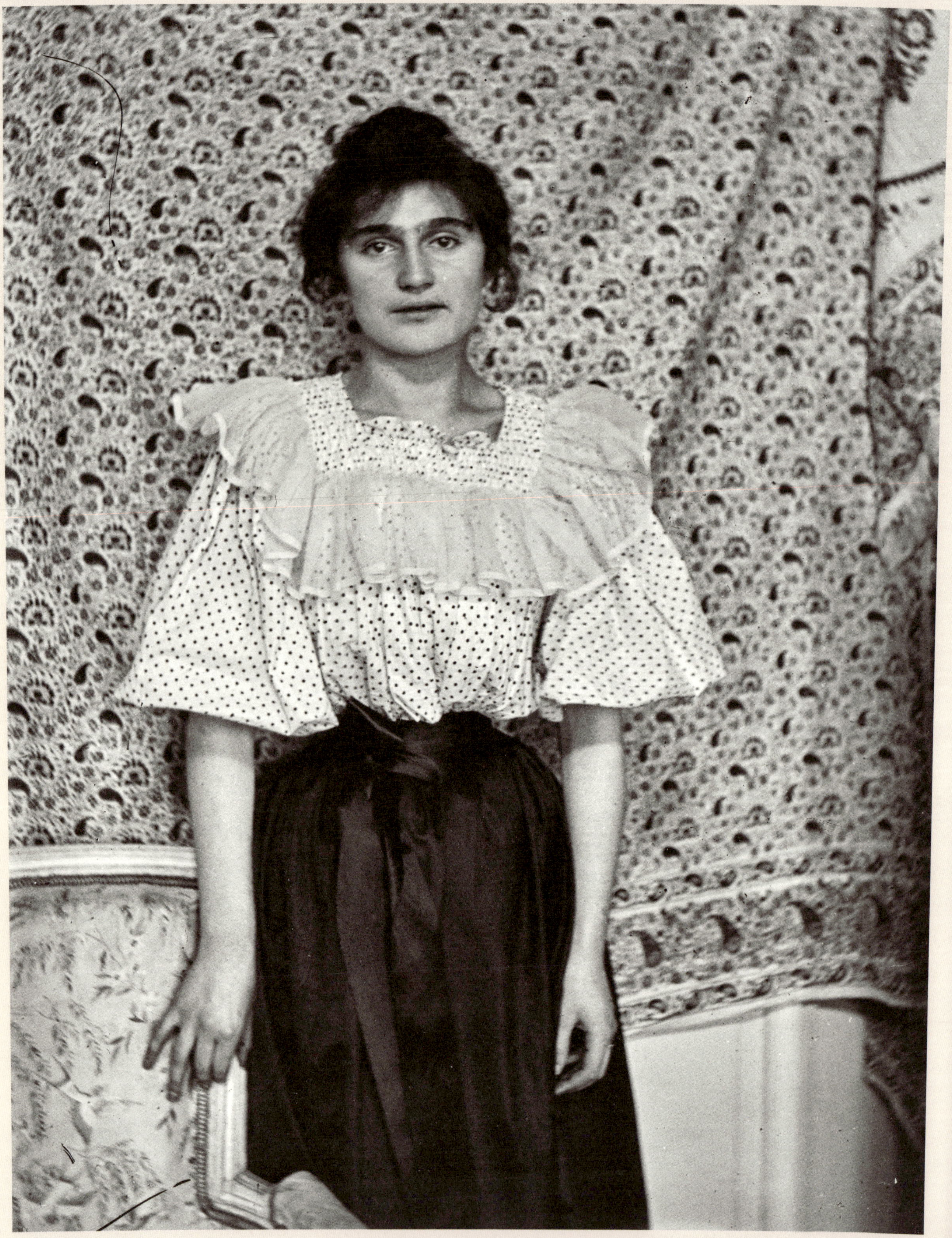

"THE FLYING SQUADRON"

1895–1899

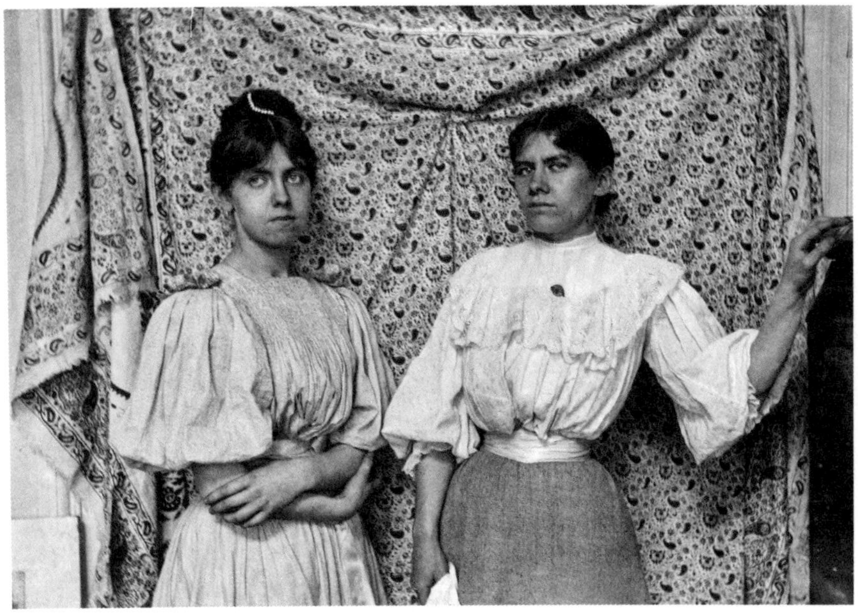

LAST WISHES

The happiness of celebrating Julie's sixteenth birthday was short-lived. Ten months later, the young girl fell ill, followed by her mother. Berthe never recovered. Julie herself does not mention these days in early 1895 in her diary, but the lapidary if instructive notes left by her cousin Jeannie Gobillard do help to establish a succinct chronology of this sad time. On January 8, 1895, Julie took ill.[318] A month later, it was her mother: "Aunt Berthe and Julie sick," notes Jeanne on February 5.[319] On February 25, Berthe expressed her dying wishes and wrote a new will at rue Weber,[320] intended not for Julie but others in her care. Berthe set aside 60,000 francs for her nieces Jeannie and Paule Gobillard, and 20,000 francs for Geneviève Mallarmé. She granted Suzanne Manet a life annuity of 600 francs, representing the heritage of Édouard that the wife of Auguste Manet had sought to keep from the Leenhoff branch of the family by bequeathing it to Julie instead.[321] In this way she was redressing the balance. On March 1, Julie made a few notes in her diary, ending with a supplication: "Dear God, please make Maman better."[322] Berthe had lost hope and on the same day wrote her last wishes:

> My dearest little Julie, I love you as I die; I shall still love you when I am dead; I beg of you, do not cry; this parting was inevitable. I hoped to be with you until you

Facing page
Attributed to Paule Gobillard (1867–1946) or Jeannie Gobillard (1877–1970)
Julie Manet in the rue de Villejust, late 1895–98
Archives BS, Paris, Musée Marmottan Monet

Above
Attributed to Julie Manet (1878–1966)
Jeannie and Paule Gobillard rue de Villejust, late 1895–98
Archives BS, Paris, Musée Marmottan Monet

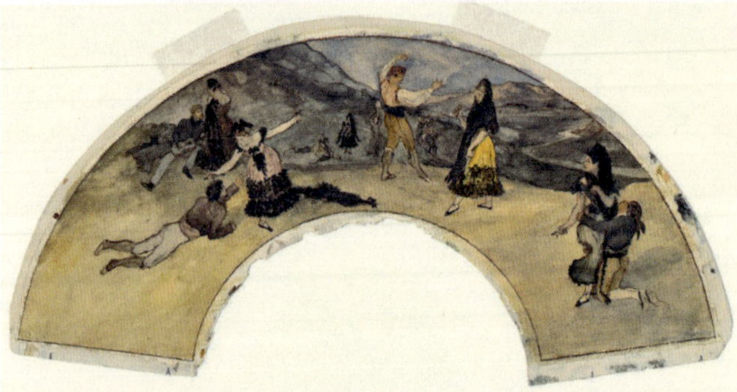

Edgar Degas (1834–1917)
Spanish Dancers and Musicians, c. 1868–69
Watercolor, pen and black ink on wove paper, 51.4 × 26 cm
Washington, D.C., National Gallery of Art, Woodner Collection

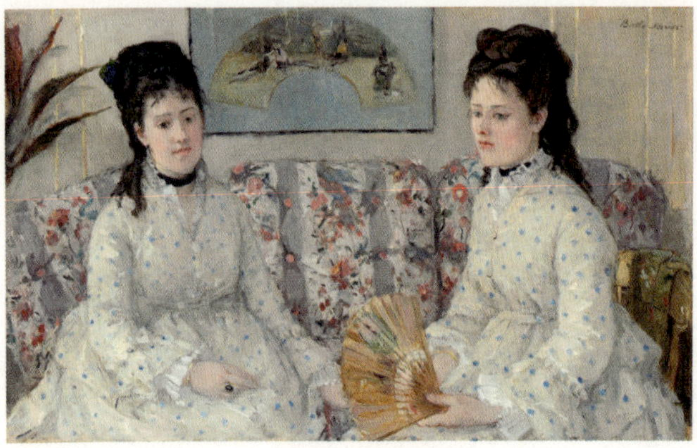

Berthe Morisot (1841–1895)
The Sisters, 1869
Oil on canvas, 52.1 × 81.3 cm
Washington, D.C., National Gallery of Art, gift of Mrs. Charles S. Carstairs

> married . . . Work hard and be good as you have always been. You have not caused me any chagrin in your young life. You have beauty, money; make good use of them. I think the best thing would be for you to live with your cousins in the rue de Villejust, but I do not wish to force you in any way. . . . Do not cry; I love you more than I can tell you. Jeannie, take care of Julie.[323]

Berthe's plans for the future life of her daughter and nieces were most unusual. Given the status assigned to women in the late nineteenth century, the idea of bringing together three orphans, two of them still minors, in the same apartment, and of offering them independence while ensuring their security, was most untypical. The close family that would now surround Julie was already at her side when Berthe breathed her last, on March 2. "Julie—terrible fright"[324] is Jeannie's entry for this date. Her cousin Gabriel Thomas and Aunt Edma were at the dying woman's bedside, where they no doubt heard her last wishes. Renoir came in haste from the South: "I have never forgotten the way he arrived in my room in the rue Weber and held me close to him," Julie recalled.[325] He was, along with Mallarmé,[326] one of those who gave notice of the funeral: Berthe did not want an official death notice, but only "to personally inform those who are not strangers to me."[327] Hence the paucity of information. There is no record describing the cortège that took Mme Eugène Manet from the church of Saint-Honoré-d'Eylau to the cemetery in Passy. Uncle Tiburce, unable to leave Cairo, and his wife and daughter-in-law Alice Gamby, then in Nice, were absent as, probably, was Berthe's nephew Edme Pontillon,[328] of whom nothing had been heard since his military service. Marcel Gobillard's discretion, too, is notable. These figures gradually disappear from the family photograph, their absence serving to further justify the construction of a purely female mythology. Given that men were expected to lead processions, we may assume that this role fell to the guardians, Gabriel Thomas and Émile Mayniel. Aunt Edma, Jeanne and Blanche Pontillon, and Paule and Jeannie Gobillard were all there. On March 5, Jeanne simply notes: "Friends of Aunt B[erthe] coming."[329] A succinct summary of the book of condolences attests the presence of Degas, Puvis de Chavanes, Mme Claude Monet (representing her husband, in Norway at the time),[330] Fantin-Latour, Mary Cassatt, and Jules Chéret.[331] Pissarro evoked this last homage in a poignant note.[332] We cannot tell whether Suzanne, seriously weakened by the influenza that had taken Berthe, was able to travel from Gennevilliers. The concern and devotion expressed in her letters suggest that she was certainly present, in thought if not in person.

> I proceed from the idea that Berthe's desire for her daughter to live with her cousins must be our law, that there is not even any need for deliberation by the family council. This combination is certainly what is most desirable for Julie from the point of view of her moral interests, but from the point of view of her material interests, which are more particularly the guardian's responsibility, it will be costly. There is no doubt that we must disregard this expense which cannot compromise the equilibrium of her budget. For it is clear that we cannot subject Julie to the privations that Paule and Jeanne have thus far had to impose on themselves, and the latter are unable to pay into the common chest a contribution representing two thirds of expenditure. They will therefore live in part at Julie's expense. I do not doubt that the family council

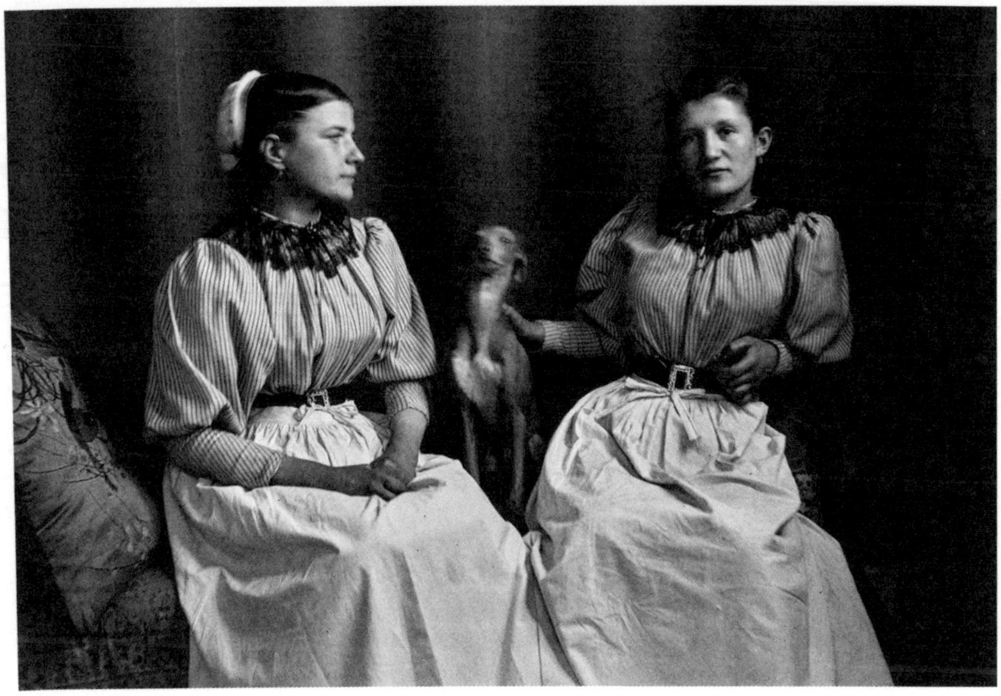

Attributed to Julie Manet (1878–1966)
Presumed portraits of Marie and Octavie holding Laërtes in the rue Weber, c. 1892–95
Archives du Mesnil, on permanent loan at the Musée Marmottan Monet

will understand and adjudicate this situation equitably. . . . this is a moral question.[333]

And that is how things went.

Appointed guardian (*tuteur datif*) for Julie's possessions by the family council on March 8, 1895, as expected, Gabriel Thomas was thus in charge of protecting the minor's inheritance, while the surrogate guardian, Mallarmé, had simply an oversight role, which oversight was consolidated by the annual presentation of the management reports. Julie's first cousin directed the post-mortem inventory[334] and winding-up of the estate. Mallarmé, indeed, was present only on March 13, the first day of the assessment. He was subsequently represented by Jules Adrien Barbier, a notarial clerk. Gabriel Thomas was thus the only person to attend the sessions of March 16, April 3, 5, and 6, and May 4, 6, 7, 8, 9, 11, 13, and 22, which were held in the rue Weber. Appointed guardian of the seals, Marie Guarrigues, who was present when the artist breathed her last,[335] acted as witness and signed off at the bottom of each set of minutes.

Julie was no doubt spared this sad process and the details of all these operations. She did not open her diary again until July, and so tells us nothing about her everyday life before the summer of 1895. Our only information comes, once again, from Jeannie's notes. In March, she writes: "Julie in black dress." In the margins of her notes for April and May she mentions current exhibitions, like reference points. No doubt the three orphans attended the homage organized at the Palais Galliera to mark the centenary of Corot's birth[336] and the exhibition of Monet's *Cathedrals* at Durand-Ruel.[337] Jeannie's description—"Julie looking unwell the paintings"[338]—may evoke the atmosphere. During this period Julie also went on a retreat at the church of Saint-Augustin and stayed at the Mas Marvent with the Havilands.[339]

Jeannie sets the scene for June thus: "Downhearted: Julie unhappy."[340] The three orphans left Paris shortly afterwards and spent the summer in Brittany with Renoir. On September 2, the deed of conveyance, setting the estate at 163,821 francs, was drawn up.[341] Julie was still far from the capital, in Douarnenez. There is a passage about her arrival in her diary, but not a word about her affairs.[342] The daily *Gil Blas* was certainly interested in these, however. In 1896, it published an insert titled "The Fortune of Mademoiselle Manet," saying that this "consists of buildings yielding a pre-tax income of 33,321 francs and securities bringing in a monthly 1100 fr. in interest."[343] Every month, this sum was paid in gold coin, either in a purse presented at the office of M. Bouts[344] or deposited by her

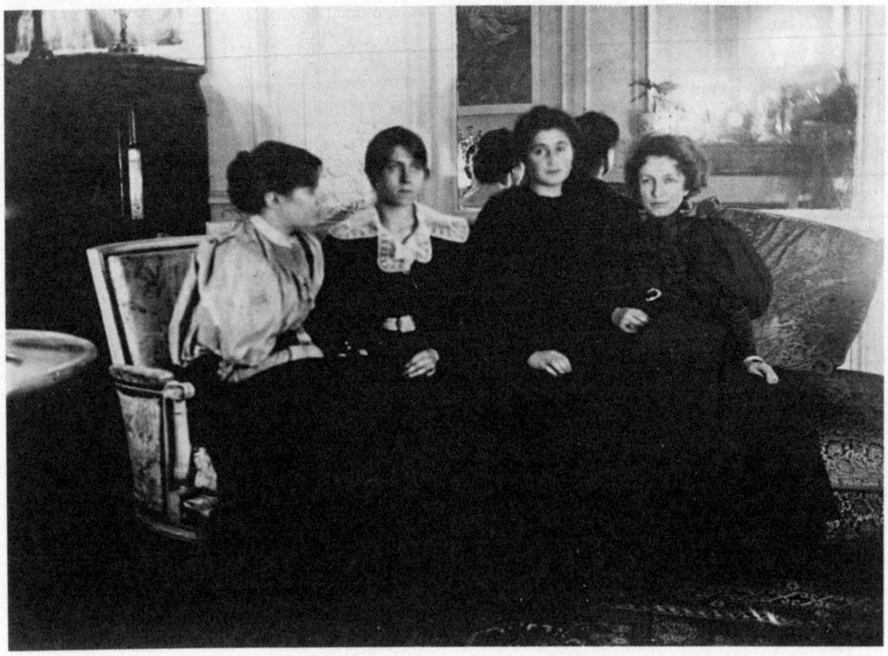

Edgar Degas (1834–1917)
Paule Gobillard, Jeannie Gobillard, Julie Manet, and Geneviève Mallarmé, December 16, 1895
New York, The Metropolitan Museum of Art, gift of Paul F. Walter, 2000

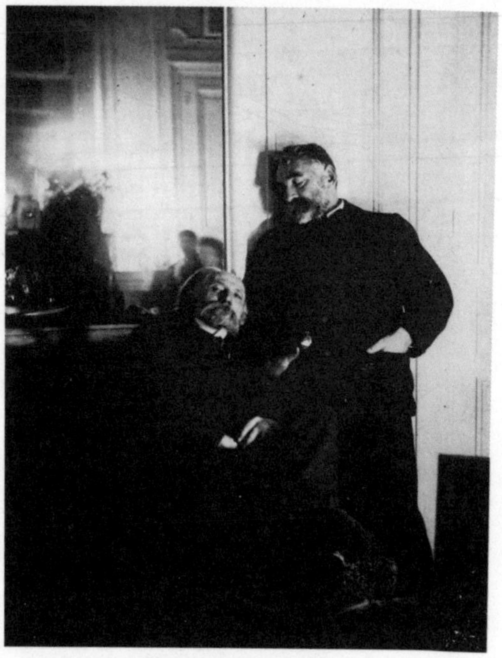

Edgar Degas (1834–1917)
Pierre-Auguste Renoir and Stéphane Mallarmé in the rue de Villejust, December 16, 1895

cousin Gabriel.[345] Gabriel Thomas completed the reorganization of the movable property—including debts—begun by Berthe Morisot. But where Morisot had wanted to pay back some of her loans by selling land at a low price,[346] the guardian in charge of Julie's possessions preferred a contractual arrangement based on novation with settlement over the medium term that brought together all movable debts under the same contract.[347] In this way he preserved his ward's real estate heritage until she became independent, on June 29, 1897.[348] Despite the importance of these transactions, Julie's diary does not contain a single line about finance, management, or administration. These considerations simply did not come to her as she was writing. Julie was spared such concerns, her family having no wish to make her bear burdens inappropriate both to her age and her status. The orphan had lost her parents but not her youth.

"TO LIVE AMONG MEMORIES IS STILL THE MOST COMFORTING THING WHEN ONE IS SAD"[349]

In keeping with Berthe's recommendations, Julie and her two cousins moved house. This change of address probably occurred in May. Jeannie mentions her departure from the rue Marbeau twice in her notes.[350] Did Julie leave the rue Weber shortly afterwards? All the evidence suggests that she did.[351] The cousins moved back to the rue de Villejust, where they lived on the fifth floor, that being the only apartment left vacant after Berthe's death. Previously occupied by the Koechlins, it comprised a hall, living room, library, dining room, and three bedrooms. More than ever, art filled the space, taking center-stage and revealed in new forms. Jeannie refers to "pictures being hung" as early as June 1895.[352] The canvases that Berthe had stacked away[353] were now part of the decoration. For the first time in the history of the Manet-Morisot family, paintings by the first woman Impressionist graced the walls of the family home. In keeping with the most progressive ideas, Julie chose plain frames, with flat, wide, white sides. *The Cherry Tree*[354] and *The Goose*[355]—part of the pile in the rue Weber (p. 37)—dominated the living room, *Young Woman and Child on an Isle*[356] hung in the dining room (p. 185). Already, in 1895, Berthe Morisot's painting was the soul of the fifth floor. As Julie notes, "I love to come back to our pretty interior, to cast my eyes over these delightful canvases through which I can live so close to my dear Maman."[357]

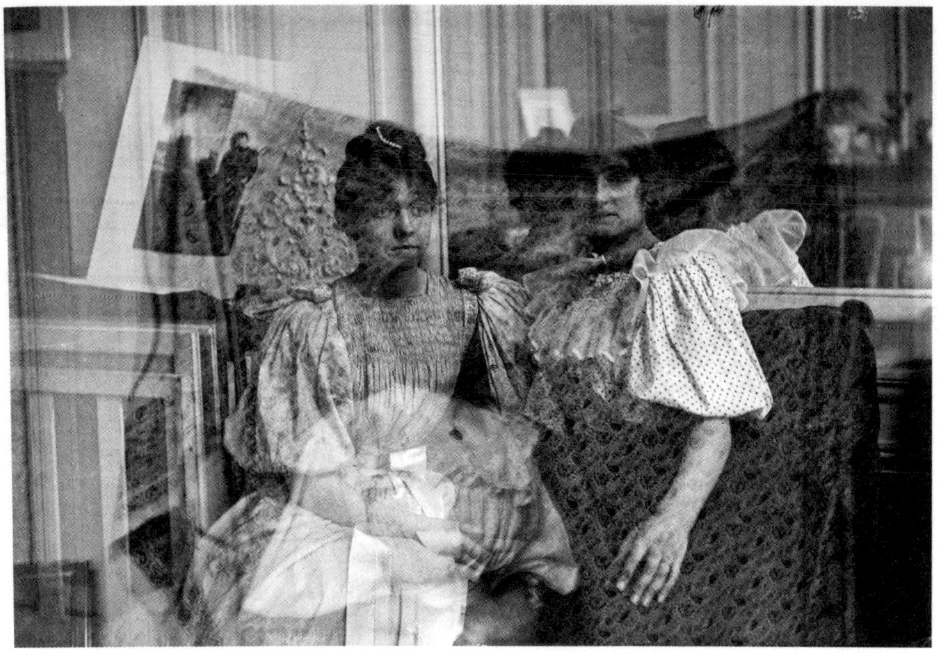

Jeannie Gobillard and Julie Manet in the living room of the rue de Villejust, late 1895–98
Archives BS, Paris, Musée Marmottan Monet

The hanging changed with the circumstances, but the number of canvases was constantly increasing. *Young Woman in Gray Reclining,*[358] *On the Lake in the Bois de Boulogne,*[359] and a red chalk *Large Nude*[360] are among the works it has been possible to identify (p. 79 and 258). There were also works from the painter's close circle. *Young Woman in the Garden* by Manet[361] and a view of Bordighera by Monet (p. 253) hung on the walls of the living room. A fan that once belonged to Degas (p. 46) was placed on a half-moon console in its little frame (p. 182).[362] In the music room, Julie and Jeannie's pianos were crowned with canvases by Uncle Édouard: *Oysters,*[363] *Madame Manet in the Garden at Bellevue* (p. 251),[364] and *Singer at a Café-Concert,*[365] flanked *Child with Cat* by Renoir (p. 209). The *Portrait of Eugène Manet* by Degas faced them (p. 223). Where was *Nina de Callias* (p. 280–281)? In the first-floor dining room, as in the old days?[366] Julie occupied a bedroom giving onto the garden.[367] There she no doubt installed her mother's bed and full-length mirror. In addition to the portrait of her grandparents on the Manet side (p. 235), she put up *Berthe Morisot with a Bouquet of Violets* (p. 218), which she loved to look at from her bed.[368] Did she also hang Manet's *Berthe Reclining* (p. 239), as her mother had done before?[369] In this spacious apartment, Paule and Jeannie seem, oddly enough, to have shared the same bedroom.[370] And there were also the service rooms. One of these was used to store paintings.

Close friends immortalized the three cousins' domestic arrangements. On December 16, 1895,[371] Degas had them pose for him in the rue de Villejust. Today, we know of four photographs taken in the living room: Geneviève and Marie Mallarmé, Stéphane Mallarmé and Paule Gobillard, Paule, Jeannie, Julie, and Geneviève Mallarmé posing in front of *The Goose* (p. 48 left) and, last but not least, Renoir seated and Mallarmé standing, the camera, and the ghostly figure of Degas and the silhouettes of Mallarmé's wife and daughter in the mirror (p. 48 right).

Notice was given to the tenant on the fourth floor, Mme Tenré, so that Aunt Edma could move in there,[372] and thus make good her promise to look after Julie. But this was no simple matter, as Julie told her guardian: "Mme Tenré is still not leaving. On Wednesday she sent word to ask if it was absolutely certain that Aunt Edma is coming to live here. She is most stubborn. It upsets me that Aunt Edma should have to continue waiting to move, for I would very much like to have her with us."[373] On October 11, Edma informed Gabriel Thomas: "I am now about to move and must make an appointment with M. Bouts in order to agree on the repairs that need to be made. I wish now to settle financial matters

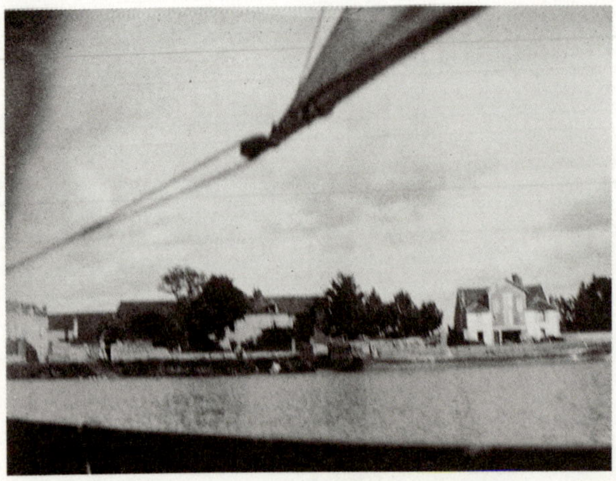

Attributed to Julie Manet (1878–1966)
Photograph taken from Mallarmé's boat on the Seine, c. 1896
Archives du Mesnil, on permanent loan at the Musée Marmottan Monet

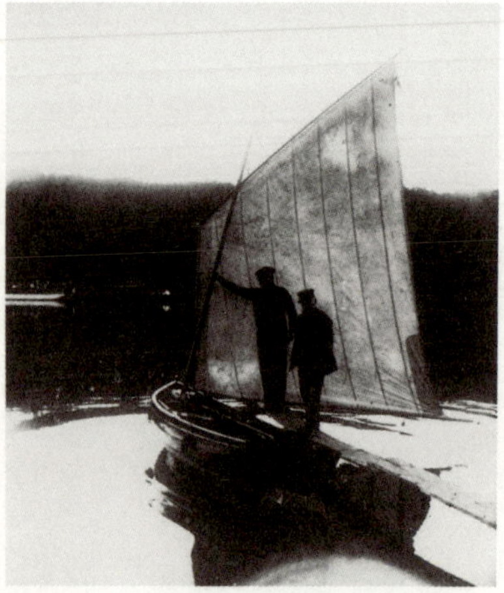

Attributed to Julie Manet (1878–1966)
Thadée Natanson and Stéphane Mallarmé on La Voile blanche, c. 1896

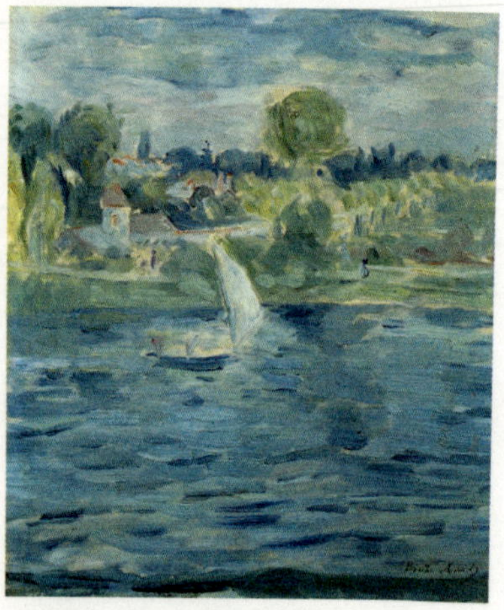

Berthe Morisot (1841–1895)
The Seine at Valvins, 1893
Oil on canvas, 35 × 28 cm
Private collection

in writing in order to have them out of the way. . . . As I have already told you, these conditions are forced upon me by the demands of my modest budget, which I must absolutely balance."[374]

Aunt Edma benefited from a modest rent of 1,700 francs up to January 1, 1897 and 1,300 francs after that date.[375] Madame Pontillon watched over the young women's daily life—the coming and going between floors, the banging of doors, everyone in their own home but everyone always together. Such was the prevailing spirit in the rue de Villejust.

Within this guardianship structure, the role of Berthe Morisot's former colleagues was significant. It was on their initiative that a posthumous exhibition was organized to mark the first anniversary of the artist's death. Gustave Geffroy wrote an article about the event: "The friends of Mme Eugène Manet, the painter Berthe Morisot, who died a year ago this same week of March, thought to put on a commemorative exhibition of her work, and have acted on their idea. Leaving their own art, their work, all that is their care and their joy, Mallarmé, Degas, Renoir, and Monet have come actively and attentively to revive through the legacy of her spirit, before our eyes, this great artist who is no longer with us."[376]

Julie, who had a great deal on her plate, was guided step by step. But it is clear that her greatest contribution to the exhibition was her detailed account of it in her diary, leaving future generations a unique insight and art historians a vital source.[377] We are not always aware of the significance of our acts.

CIRCLES

Three circles formed Julie's immediate entourage. There, was of course, the set of republican intellectuals frequented by her surrogate guardian, Mallarmé. In Valvins and at Tuesday meetings in the rue de Rome, Julie and her cousins frequented the director of *La Revue Blanche*, Thadée Natanson. Julie photographed her with the poet in front of her boat, *La Voile blanche* (above), and pictured Paule by the waterside.[378] Other pictures of the area taken during this stay and not shown before were discovered when working on this book, including a surprising image of Mallarmé looking down from the window of his house in Valvins at his wife Marie (p. 51). The concerts given by Misia, Natanson's charismatic wife, were much admired by the young women. Through the Mallarmés they also met Marguerite Normant (p. 55), who happened to be the sister of Henry Roujon, director of the Beaux-Arts and former secretary of Jules Ferry. They did not frequent Méry Laurent, who was too close to Mallarmé, but they were invited to listen to her in the poet's box, when, in April 1897, he inaugurated the Saturday evenings dedicated to old and modern poetry at the Théâtre de l'Odéon. Whistler, whose *Arrangement In Grey and Black No. 1 (Portrait of the Artist's Mother)*,[379] was acquired by the state through the intermediary of Roujon and Mallarmé's intervention, observed the little group in the rue de Villejust and dubbed Paule the "demoiselle Patronne,"[380] a nickname quickly taken up by the poet.[381] Odilon Redon, contacted by Vollard in 1896 to illustrate a text by Mallarmé for publication, became an

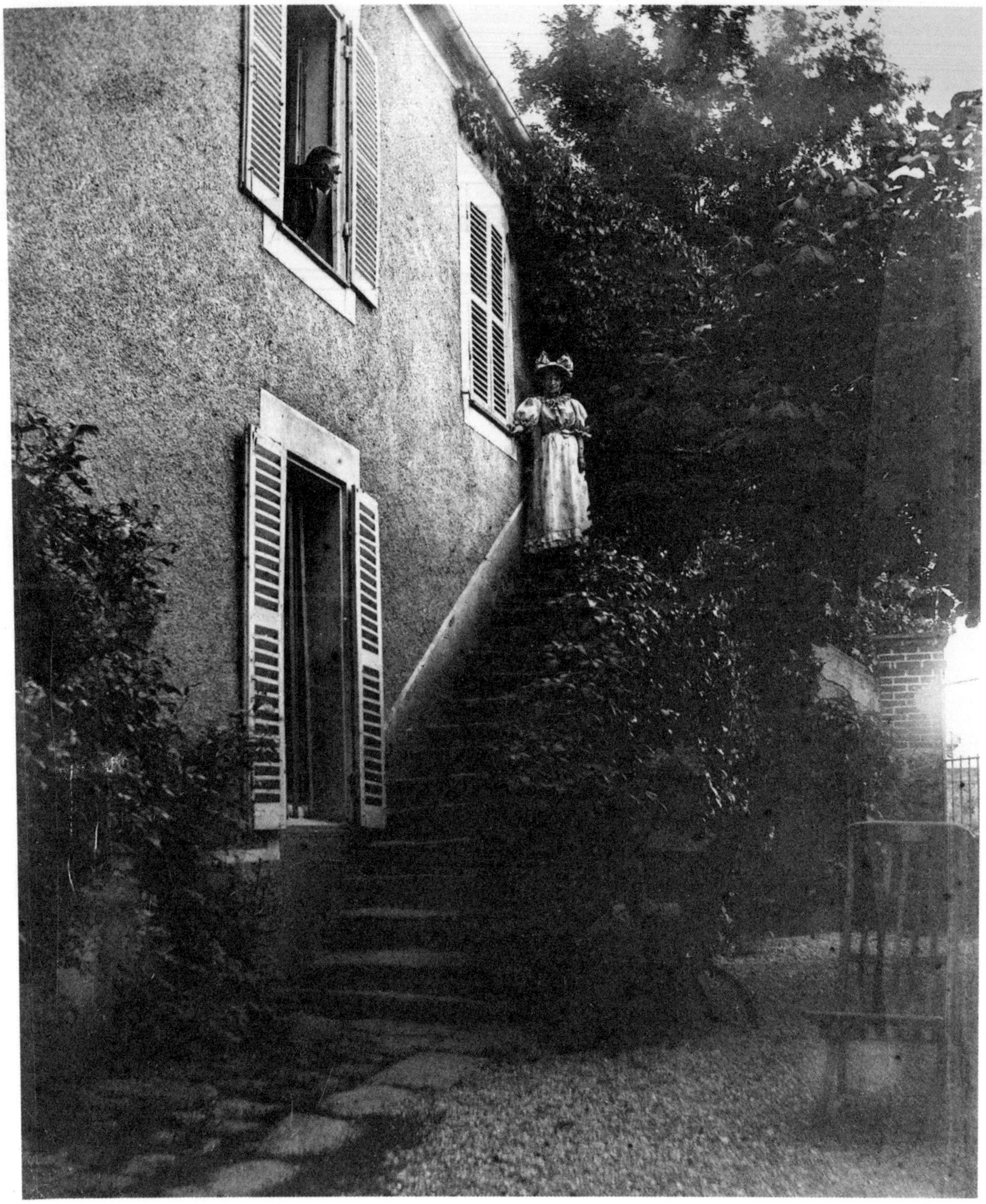

Attributed to Julie Manet (1878–1966)
Stéphane Mallarmé and his wife Marie in their house at Valvins, c. August–September 1896
Archives du Mesnil, on permanent loan at the Musée Marmottan Monet

admirer of the young woman who inspired one of his finest portraits.[382] They formed a strong friendship; the artist now belonged in the "Patronne's" close circle.[383] No doubt they also met Vuillard, who was involved as illustrator of another of Vollard's Mallarmé publications, *Hérodiade*.

Renoir, who was an anti-Dreyfusard, was the life and soul of a youthful circle full of gaiety and joie de vivre. Jeanne Baudot was its dominant figure. Born in 1877, the doctor's daughter discovered Impressionist painting at the home of collector Paul Gallimard, a friend of the family. Described by many as an assertive young woman, she

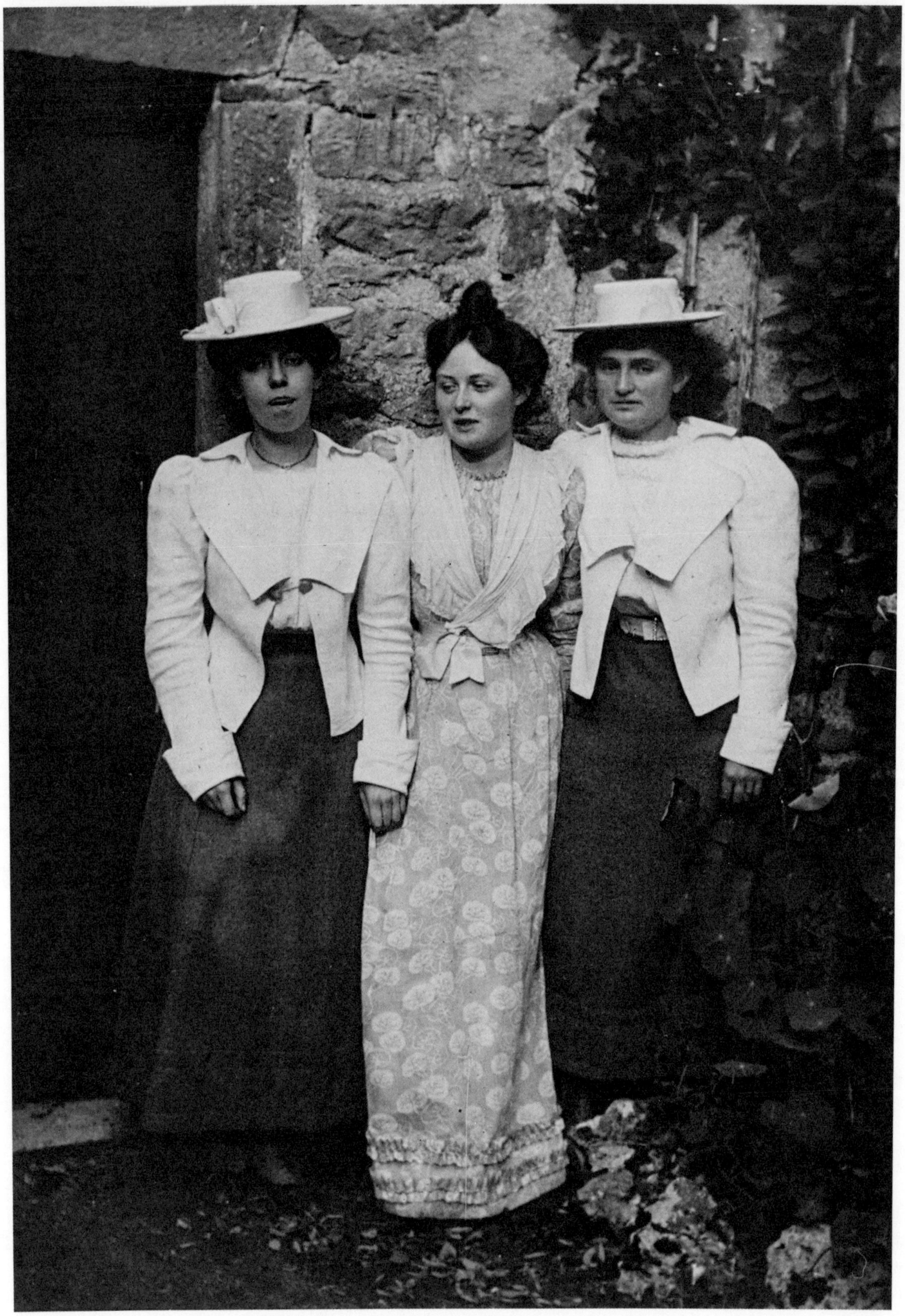

Jeannie Gobillard, Jeanne Baudot, and Julie Manet in Givry, August–September 1898
Private collection

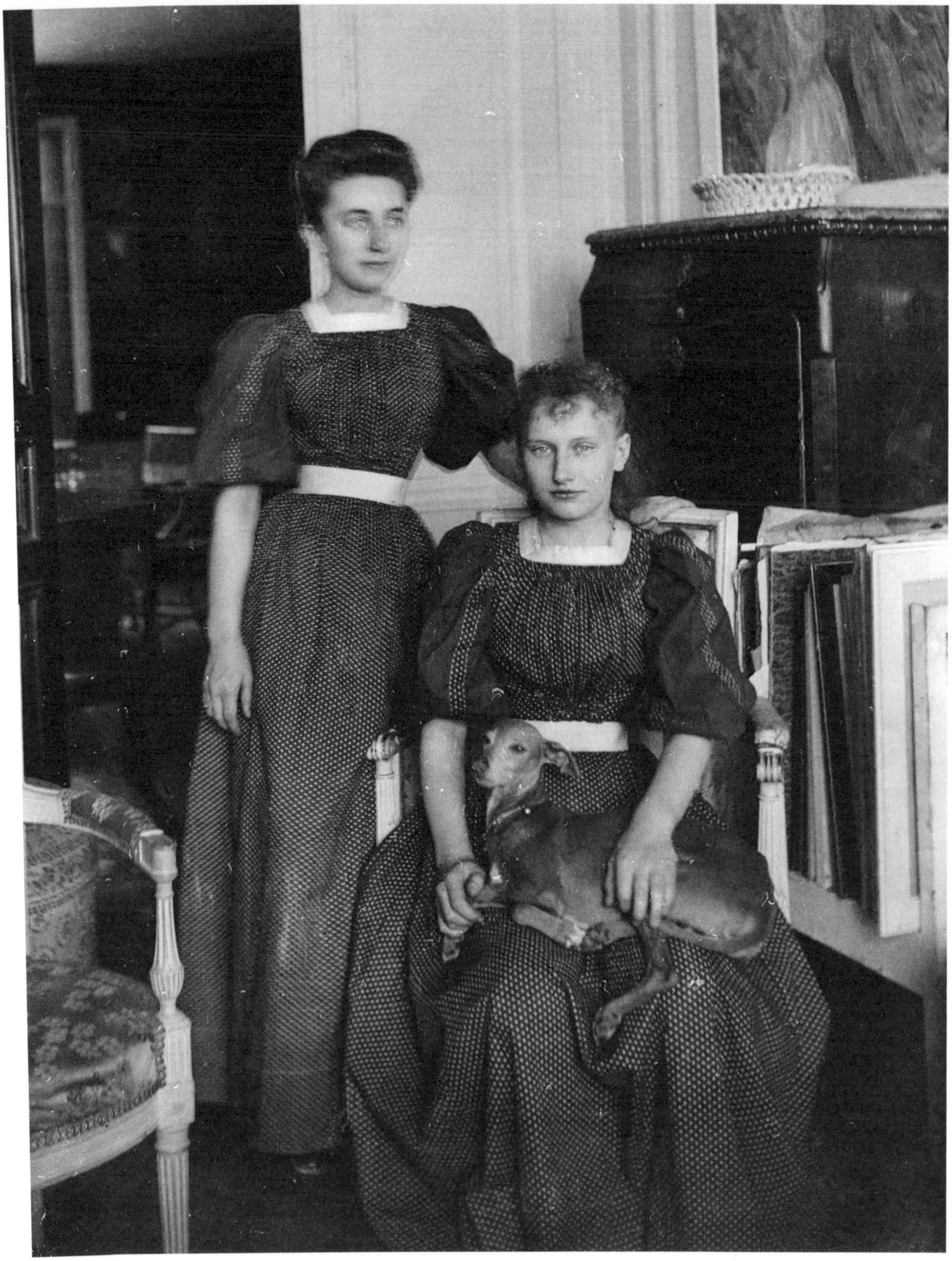

Attributed to Julie Manet (1878–1966)
Fernande Angoulvent and her sister Gabrielle Angoulvent with Laërtes on her knees, in the rue de Villejust, late 1895–98
On permanent loan at the Musée Marmottan Monet

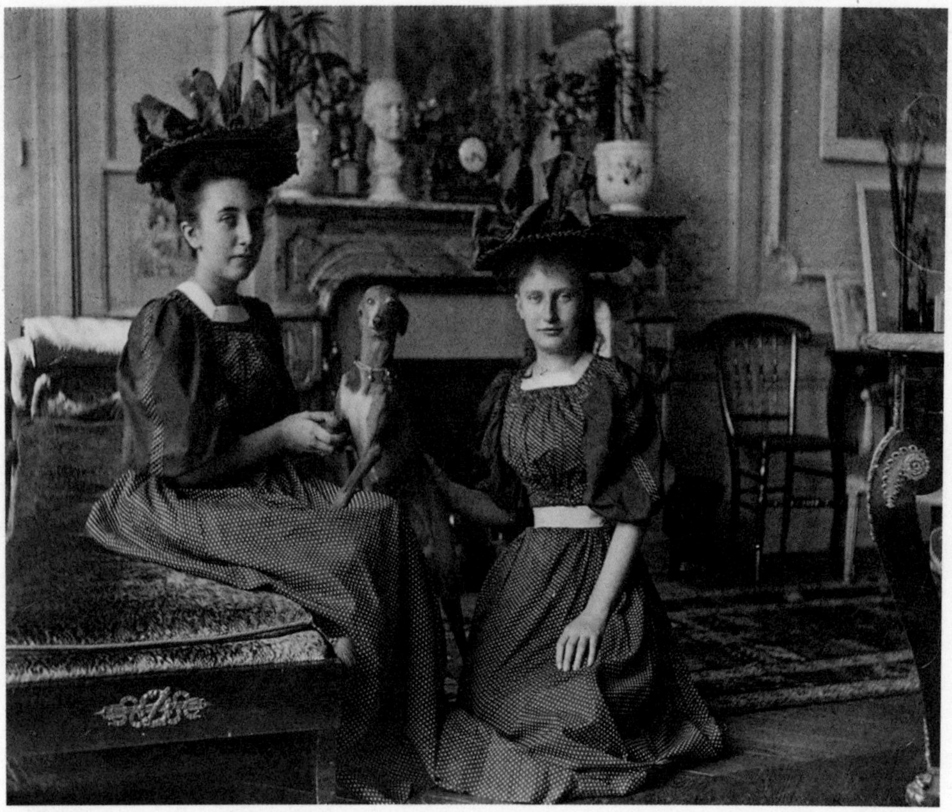

Attributed to Julie Manet (1878–1966)
Fernande Angoulvent seated and her sister Gabrielle Angoulvent kneeling, and Laërtes in the rue de Villejust, late 1895–98
Archives du Mesnil, on permanent loan at the Musée Marmottan Monet

managed to get Gallimard to introduce her to Renoir and by 1893, at the age of sixteen, she was his student[384] while the two families grew close and met up in Louveciennes. She was close enough to be the godmother of Jean Renoir, born in 1894.[385] Jeanne was a young woman of good breeding and real beauty (the ever-present Degas teasingly offered to marry her)[386] and was passionate about painting. She had a touch of artistic *bohème* while remaining, as Berthe Morisot put it, on the level with society. In other words, she had a great deal in common with the young ladies in the rue de Villejust. The circle that they formed soon widened to include the Baudots' cousins, the Cléments, enjoying the company of the general as much as that of his daughter, Jeanne. Two Lyonnais, Jacques Drogue and Abel Faivre, also joined the group. Trained at the École des Beaux-Arts de Lyon and then at the Académie Julian in Paris, both were outstanding illustrators. Drogue tried his hand at woodblock printing and collaborated with the *Mercure de France*, while Faivre specialized in satirical drawings and, later, posters. The company of these gentlemen amused, their art less so—that, in any case, is what we may gather from Julie's unsparing judgement: "[Faivre] shows us his painting and we are lost for words. They are truly gaudy. It is pitiful, and one really has to ask if Faivre is intelligent."[387]

Other circles, other mores—those of the late Mme Eugène Manet's good friends in the 16th arrondissement. The fidelity of the Renaults could be counted on. Henriette Caroline Renault and her daughter Berthe, the children of their friends the Angoulvents,[388] Léon,[389] Fernand,[390] and Gabrielle (p. 53 and above),[391] the daughter of the Roudiers, Raymonde, and her cousin Jacques Cor, author of a musical and textual study of Richard Wagner's *Mastersingers of Nuremberg*,[392] were regulars. Pierre Étienne Marie Lahalle, introduced by the Angoulvents, was aiming for a career in architecture, which he was studying at the Beaux-Arts.[393] As for the Avoines, who made a few appearances with Aunt Edma, all we know is their name. The anonymity surrounding these figures, although they were close to Julie, demonstrates, if that were necessary, that one did not need to be famous to be part of the circle in the rue de Villejust, merely to share its art of living.

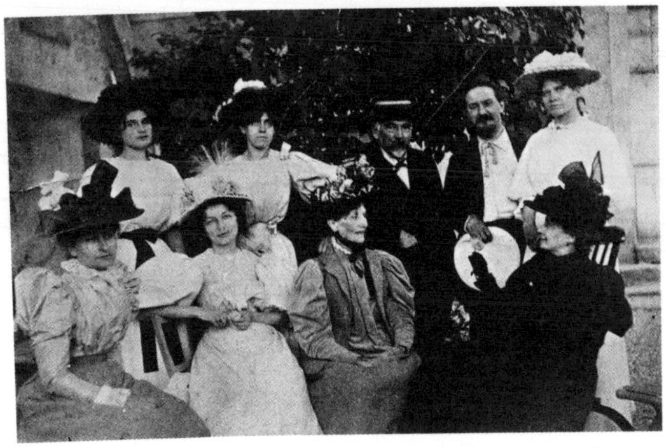

From top to bottom and left to right: *Julie Manet, Jeannie Gobillard, Stéphane Mallarmé, Gabriel Séailles, Paule Gobillard, Mme Séailles, Geneviève Mallarmé, Mme Mallarmé, Mme Normant at Valvins*, summer 1896

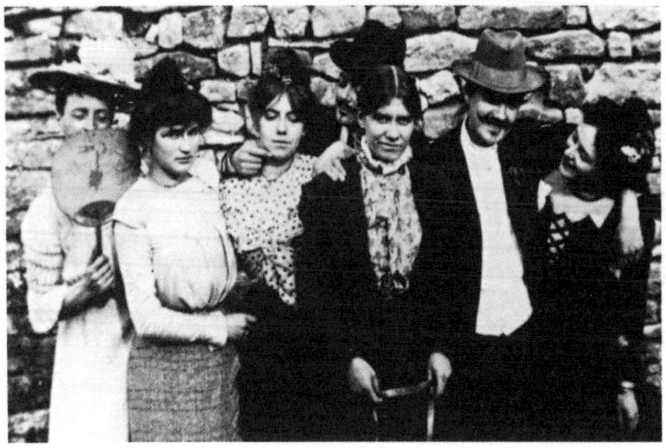

Julie Manet, Jeannie Gobillard, Paule Gobillard (center), Jeanne Baudot (on the far right), and three of their friends, summer 1898 or summer 1899

"THE FLYING SQUADRON"[394]

Mallarmé found just the right words for the comings and goings of the young ladies in the rue de Villejust. The inseparable three were not raised to the rank of musketeers, but formed, instead, a "Flying Squadron."[395] What with one holiday and the next, they were active at least two months a year. Julie confided: "We are so used to travelling that I find it strange when people go away without us."[396]

Between 1895 and 1898, they spent their summers and the early days of autumn moving from one place and circle to another. Even so, it was unusual for them to stay with friends—the spaces were rarely able to accommodate so many visitors—and found their pied-à-terre in the neighborhood, be it in an inn that someone recommended or in a rented house. Although Julie does not say much about the matter in her diary, an attentive reading reveals the presence of servants. They were regularly accompanied by a cook who oversaw the transferal of trunks and the greyhound Laërtes from one spot to another. When Berthe died, Octavie was present through the transition. Then along came Charlotte Lecoq, recommended by Mallarmé in 1896.[397] These free young women were chaperoned as was expected in their milieu.[398] In 1895, they travelled to Brittany; the "Squadron" visited the Renaults in Saint-Enogat and met the Angoulvents and Boucherits, who were from Morlaix. Next they joined the Renoirs in Pont-Aven. The following year they spent a month at Valvins in Mallarmé's social circle. The stay ended with an excursion to Rouen where, chaperoned by Mme Normant, they met Pissarro. Julie took photographs and later developed them herself in the rue de Villejust in a dark room she had set up in the loft.[399] In October they were back in Valvins and then in Essoyes, Mme Renoir's home town. The summer of 1897 again illustrates this broad-minded nomadism. The two months of holidaying began in Touraine, followed by a stay with their cousins the Vaissières, who had inherited from their forebear, Laurent Casimir Fournier, a deputy and member of the departmental council of Sarthe in 1830, the Château de Vassé, which dated from the 16th and 17th centuries. The main building, or *grand pavillon*, with its eleven windows along the façade, a chapel dedicated to Saint Pétronille, built under Louis XIV, and numerous outbuildings including a dovecote that could house up to eight thousand pigeons, the little mill along the pond, the terraced park and its fortifications—all this formed an outstanding ensemble that could not fail to please Julie. Soon, they moved on to Saint-Yrieix-sous-Aixe, and to another château, the Mas Marvent, owned by the Havilands, who were particularly close to the Gobillards.[400] Regularly extended since the eighteenth century, the building, if less imposing than Vassé (its façade numbered only eight bays), had just gained a new pavilion with bow windows. "Château life is most pleasurable," wrote Julie.[401] She would never forget this, although without forsaking her usual simplicity. Holidays also included a spell among the country folk of Essoyes, where, as always when in his company, Julie painted under the kindly gaze of Renoir. In 1898, the squadron met the master in Dieppe, the Renaults at Saint-Enogat, the Roudiers and the Angoulvents also in Ille-et-Vilaine. Renoir, looking to see them in September, wrote to them in Paris, "since I do not know in which châteaux you are holidaying."[402] In October they headed for Givry in Burgundy, to be with "Baudot's band" (Jeanne Baudot, Jeanne Clément, and Jacques Drogue). The stay was an extremely joyous one, making for an unforgettable memory. "They are so high-spirited, these young girls. They dance in their nightdresses,"[403] she told Drogue. In Givry, they "laugh like whales," noted Renoir.[404] They wrote a play, "La Princesse Jolie Mine." Julie played the title role, Jeanne Baudot that of the knight in love with Jolie Mine, and Jeannie was the *grande coquette*, Paule the duenna, Drogue a mushroom grower, Jeanne Clément the maid and "Dr Baudot, the noble father they forget to bring on stage."[405]. Before they left, Julie added: "We are writing a letter to Colonel Clément with our caricatures blowing into bagpipes and signed with our nicknames."[406]

PARISIAN LIFE

Julie lived Parisian life the way she had learned it. She received visitors, first in the day, then, starting in 1899, in the evening. She chose the same day as her mother and grandmother before her and stated this on an elegant visiting card: "Julie Manet, Thursday."[407] Cleverly shot against the light, a fine photograph of Julie at the window skillfully reveals the figure of the young woman that Julie had become, dressed and coiffed as such, her hair in a bun (p. 57). The time of studying humanities was behind her,[408] as was school with Mme Jammès. She was still taking lessons, but in piano and violin, as an accompanist. Jeannie, ever more the virtuoso, was continuing her studies at the Institut Rudy and followed the Cours Pugno. She sat on Mme Boucherit's student jury and took care to attend the "women's piano" competition at the Conservatoire, to which she dreamed of being admitted like her friends Lucie Léon and Magdeleine Boucherit, who eventually both won a first prize.

As always, they went to the Concerts Lamoureux and Concerts Colonne, where Jules was made a solo violinist in 1897.[409] A little later Mlle and M. Boucherit formed a duo that toured Europe. Both became professional musicians. Music was also played in the rue de Villejust. Small concerts were given in the music room, where stood two pianos belonging, respectively, to Julie and Jeannie (p. 172).[410] They played Carl Maria von Weber, Damien Dubois, Camille Saint-Saëns, Felix Mendelssohn, and Benjamin Godard.[411] They performed in the company of Fernand and Gabrielle Angoulvent, Blanche Pontillon, and Berthe Renault. They also played in public, as on Thursday February 25, 1897, in front of numerous guests. Christine and Yvonne Lerolle, a friend from Berthe's day, and Jeanne Baudot, were rivals in elegance, as Julie noted: "The Lerolles had ravishing low-necked dresses and Mlle Baudot wore a white dress made by Marie Callot, which was very particular."[412] They also learned to dance. The "Squadron" organized lessons in its salon on Fridays and encouraged participants to share the costs.[413] Friday became a festive day. "These lessons are great fun. Yes, we have fun dancing at home. That sounds extraordinary to me."[414]

The most faithful attendees came from the circle of Mme Renault, to whom it fell to organize the first ball attended by these young ladies. They particularly enjoyed masked balls, where they dressed as flowers: Julie was a rose and Jeannie a buttercup.[415] Disguises were also in order for the party held to inaugurate Jeanne Baudot's new studio. Jacques Drogue, Abel Faivre, Jeanne Clément, Julie, Jeannie, and Paule made up in the Italian style.[416] The day was so memorable that a "brilliant idea was born in someone's brain," recalled Jeanne Baudot:

> **The foundation of "piglet society"; members were to meet once a month at each of their homes. The proposal was unanimously popular and the society was placed under the protection of Saint-Doux[417] and founded under the capital of Saint-Émilion. Abel Faivre wrote the statutes; he illustrated a copy and my father [the doctor] was made doctor of the association.[418]**

Saint-Anthony's day was decreed a feast day, and they gathered in the rue de Villejust to celebrate the occasion.[419] They called each other by diminutives. There was a bit of mild flirting. Favier was Paule's *chevalier servant*, Cor was Jeannie's and Drogue was Julie's.

They went to all the exhibitions and auction sales. Nor did they forget to paint. They drew concert programs and decorated menus. Julie even painted wardrobes. Berthe Morisot's daughter was not without ambition. Accepted by the Salon des Indépendants in 1896,[420] rejected by the Salon National des Beaux-Arts in 1897,[421] she was back at the Indépendants in 1898,[422] as indicated by the *Revue Blanche*, a fact that did not displease her guardian.[423] Although she could not and did not wish to call herself the student of M. Renoir, she followed in his wake and relied on his advice. The physical types painted by Julie are, like those of Jeanne and Paule, the same as those of her mentor, with round faces and firm lines. The theme of her painting was laid out before her: everyday life in the rue de Villejust was an endless source of inspiration. What Julie particularly appreciated was the effect of mirrors and *mise-en-abyme*; she painted both the model and the painter at work. Sometimes it was Julie painting Jeanne Baudot, sometimes Jeanne held the brush. Here, Julie took a vantage-point that is found neither in her mother's work nor in Renoir's. Her singularity brought the risk of not getting beyond anecdote. She painted their life. Would that amount to an *œuvre*?

STORY OF A SOUL[424]

The early deaths of Eugène and Berthe Manet deprived Julie of the possibility of constructing her identity in opposition to her parents. Her mental dispositions were still those of a teenage orphan who, to prove her love to those around her, sought to be like them. Never to do anything that would displease Papa and Maman is a mantra in the pages of her diary, and it became the foundation of her existence. Reproducing a way of life, preserving a heritage, sharing a memory, painting—it all maintained the link with lost loved ones, brought the past back to life. "I am an orphan, all alone to remember the life of Papa and Maman."[425] The solitude weighed on her. Julie was always looking for advice and regretted Mallarmé's discretion (he seldom aired his ideas) while drinking in Renoir's words, including his trenchant anti-Dreyfusard opinions. "One could not find an intelligence greater and more incisive in all matters than that of M. Renoir; he sees true both in life and in his paintings."[426]

Then there were the opinions of Degas. Another context was possible, another direction of consciousness: Julie was awakening to religion. She openly embraced her faith, as she had never dared do when her mother was alive. "And to think that she could not understand whether or not I was religious; what weakness not to dare to say so when she said that she would like it better if I was, how wrong of me, dear God forgive me."[427]

She recalled her first communion, a day she now considered the most important in her life.[428] She implored God "that we will always be together, that these three young orphans always get on together and that there will never be even a tiny disagreement between them to please their mothers."[429] She looked to sermons for ideas as to how to achieve her goal, without ever thinking this might displease her mother, who had a quarrel with God. "Dear God! tell me that Papa and Maman are happy, and all those I have mourned. Keep me under the power of communion and your goodness. . . . Let me serve you as a true Christian. I have the resolution, dear God, give me your grace."[430]

She was influenced by the curate of Vulaines and stayed at the Providence convent in Blois, which she began to support in 1897.[431] In 1898, she went on a three-day retreat at Saint-Pierre-de-Chaillot, and joined Les Enfants de Marie de Saint-Honoré-d'Eylau as an aspirant, to be received into the order on December 11th:

> **Saint Mary, mother of God and still a virgin, I Julie Manet choose you on this day for my Queen, my Patroness, and my Champion. I make the firm and unwavering resolution never to abandon you, never to say or do anything against your service, never to allow those who depend on me to wound in any way the honor that is due to you, I implore you then, take me as your perpetual servant; help me in my actions and do not forsake me at the hour of my death. So be it.[432]**

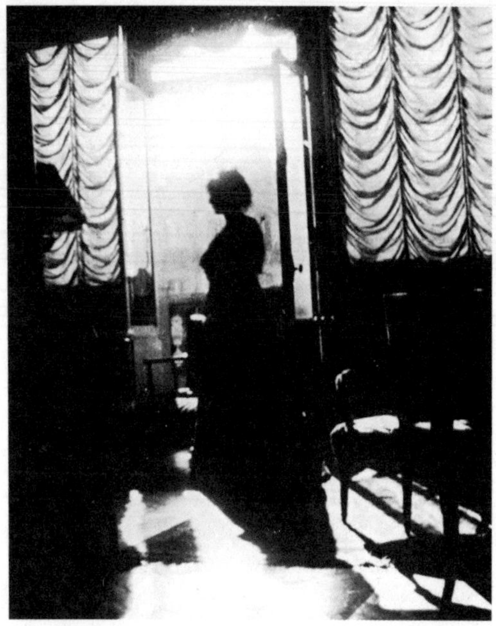

Attributed to Ernest Rouart (1874–1942)
Julie Manet rue de Villejust, c. 1900–01
Paris, Musée Marmottan Monet

She performed good works and, on Sunday in Levallois, she took catechism for the young women at the Petits Chiffonniers club.[433] She took the steps leading to confirmation: the Mass was held on December 4, 1899. "After that we left the archdiocese. I was very happy at what had taken place within me. The thought I had not been confirmed had been weighing on me for so long."[434] Julie and Jeannie were at Mass every day. Julie's path in life, unlike that of her parents, was defined by her faith.

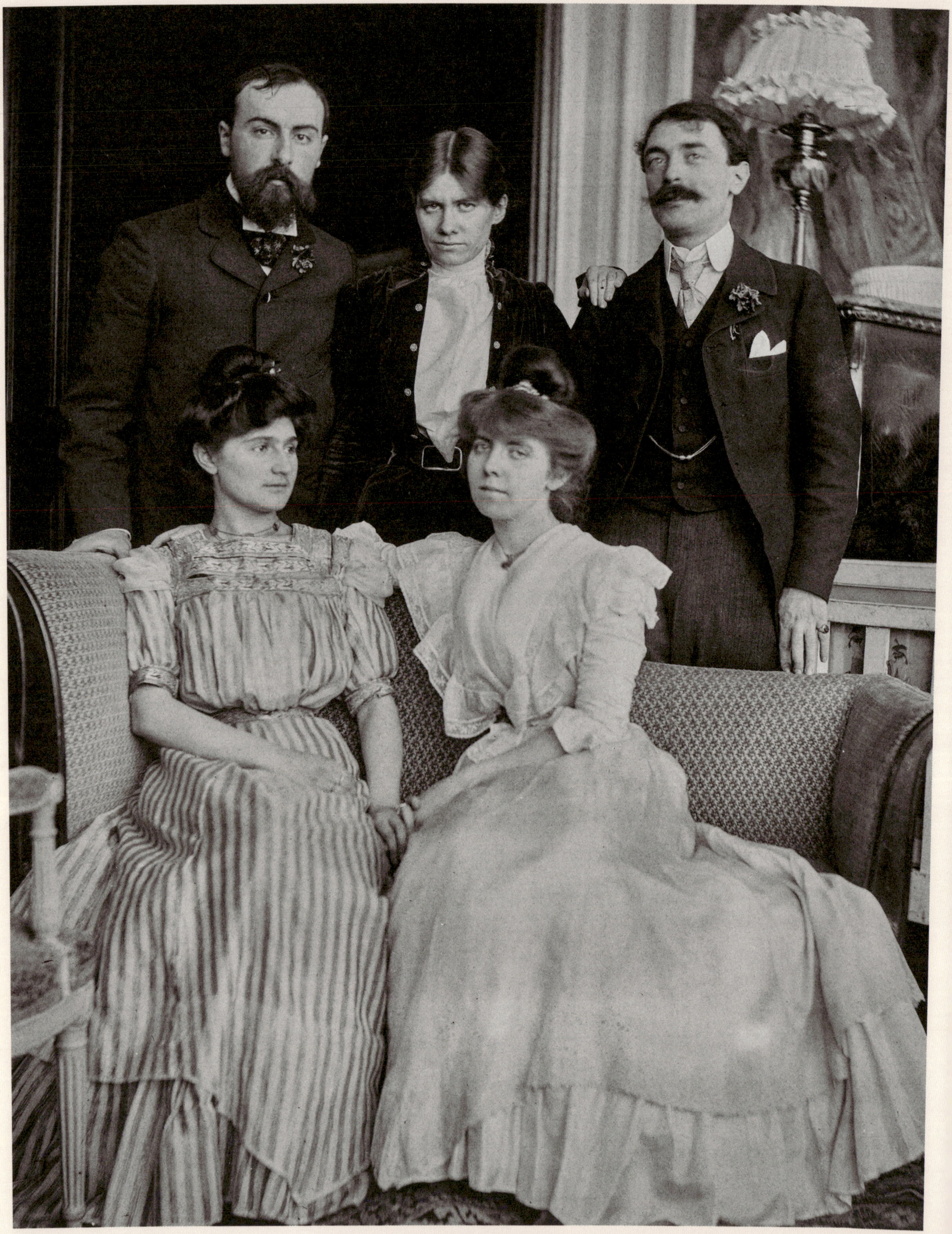

"THE CARACO TRIBE"

1899–1900

"ARRANGED MARRIAGES ARE ODIOUS"[435]

The question of marriage was bound to come up, and did so, unsurprisingly, when Julie reached her majority. The word appears in December 1897 and was soon on everyone's lips.

The "Flying Squadron" was at the forefront. Julie evoked the early stages in her diary, which she stopped keeping after December 26, 1899. Jeannie took over and noted the events of the following months, which would lead them both to the altar on May 31, 1900. This diary is being published for the first time on the occasion of the exhibition at the Musée Marmottan Monet, and numerous excerpts inform this chapter, adorning it with Mlle Gobillard's melodious prose.

How could they dare dream of marriage without undermining the trio, without betraying the "squadron" and bringing about its demise. Such was the question that tormented the demoiselles Manet and Gobillard. The answer was unanimous. None of them dared believe in her own happiness, each hoped that her sister/cousin would be happy, their separation being perceived as a necessary sacrifice, a proof of love.

Julie wrote:

> **They think I am incapable of understanding feeling, or love, that I will not suffer if I remain an old maid, that on the contrary I hate marriage, and obviously, I let them believe it. Sometimes I wish I could express myself more and I think that it would make Paule and Jeannie think I was unhappy about my life with them if I expressed the slightest idea about marriage.[436]**
>
> **. . . I thought of the emotion I would feel if Paule and Jeanne were to marry; they would be hard days to live through, but I want those days to come. The idea that Paule may not marry upsets me . . . Well, she still has time, she is not yet 30. Maman married after 30.[437]**

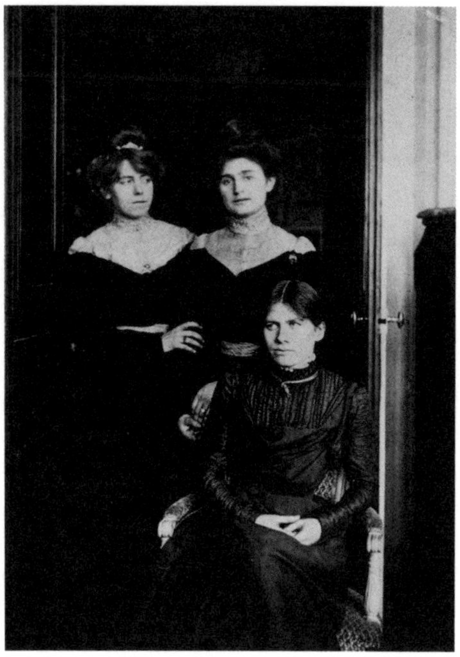

Facing page
The fiancés Julie Manet–Ernest Rouart and Jeannie Gobillard–Paul Valéry, with Paule Gobillard (top middle), rue de Villejust, March 23, 1900
Private collection

Above right
Jeannie Gobillard, Julie Manet and Paule Gobillard (seated), rue de Villejust, c. 1900
Paris, Musée Marmottan Monet

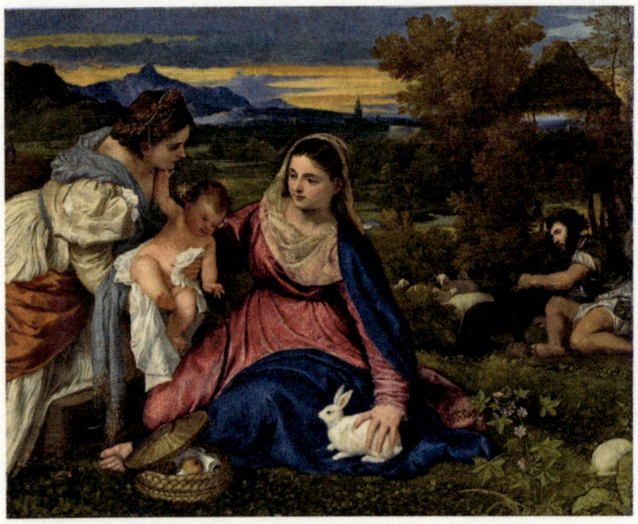

Édouard Manet (1832–1883)
Madonna of the Rabbit (after Titian), 1854
Oil on canvas, 70 × 84 cm
Paris, Musée du Louvre

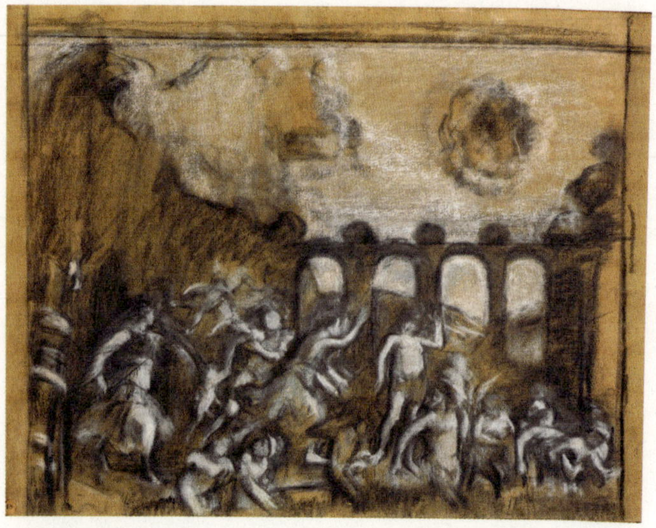

Edgar Degas (1834–1917)
Minerva Expelling the Vices from the Garden of Virtue (copy after Mantegna), 1897
Pastel on canvas, 66 × 81 cm
Paris, Musée d'Orsay, acquired in 1954

Considering the prospects of her sister-cousin's marriage, Jeannie showed the same abnegation: "I was getting used to the idea of being separated from Julie, with my penchant for gloomy imaginings, I pictured the sadness of a wedding, the usurper breaking up friendships, etc. I was getting myself ready."[438] In the end, she reflected: "I envision the thing as a separation which may be absolute, but what I desire is her happiness, because I love her."[439]

Naturally, the circle watching over the "squadron" was also concerned about this matter. There was soon much discussion of the future to be offered to the young ladies. However, Julie never considered that her marriage, or her cousin's, had been arranged. The very idea appalled her:

> It has always struck me that arranged marriages must be odious . . .[440]
>
> Perhaps I am against marriage because I won't tolerate arranged marriages that bring together two poor souls who don't know each other, don't understand each other, and just don't get on. With divorce, marriage has lost its importance. For me it's still sacred, and I think that to avoid these horrible separations which are now made so easily, we must remember. After all, is it not more moral to have too great a weakness for the person we marry than not to love them? If God has established marriage, is it not so that those who get on may come together.[441]

"MONSIEUR DEGAS SAYS HE WANTS TO SEE TO OUR WEDDING"[442]

Even so, Degas, Renoir, and the Mallarmés all undeniably played a role. First of all, these gentlemen organized the introductions. Julie was first. As was the case for Berthe Morisot, the key moment was a copying session at the Louvre. Like mother, like daughter. On November 11, 1897, the Impressionist's daughter registered to copy *The Holy Family* by Veronese, a painter against whom her mother had tested herself at the same age.[443] Jeanne Baudot went with her and chose *The Holy Family* by Titian. On November 23, Paule put her name down for Titian's *Madonna of the Rabbit,* which Édouard Manet had also copied in his day (above).[444] The Louvre was their everyday life, a locus of sociability. Renoir came by regularly to inspect the young ladies' work.[445] Mallarmé came twice, once with Whistler.[446] Arsène Alexandre also paid a visit. They met Zandomeneghi, Helleu, and of course Carolus-Duran, whom they studiously ignored in order to avenge Berthe and Tante Edma.[447] Henner's audacity toward Julie dressed in mourning for her aunt Chevalier[448] came as a surprise. Jeanne Baudot gives the best account:

> She looked very fine in a velvet dress and a big black hat. Henner, who was walking past, noticed her and asked the young man in her company to tell her that he admired her outfit. He had no idea that he was in the presence of Mlle Manet; he was probably disappointed that she failed to respond to this compliment and did not offer to pose for him.[449]

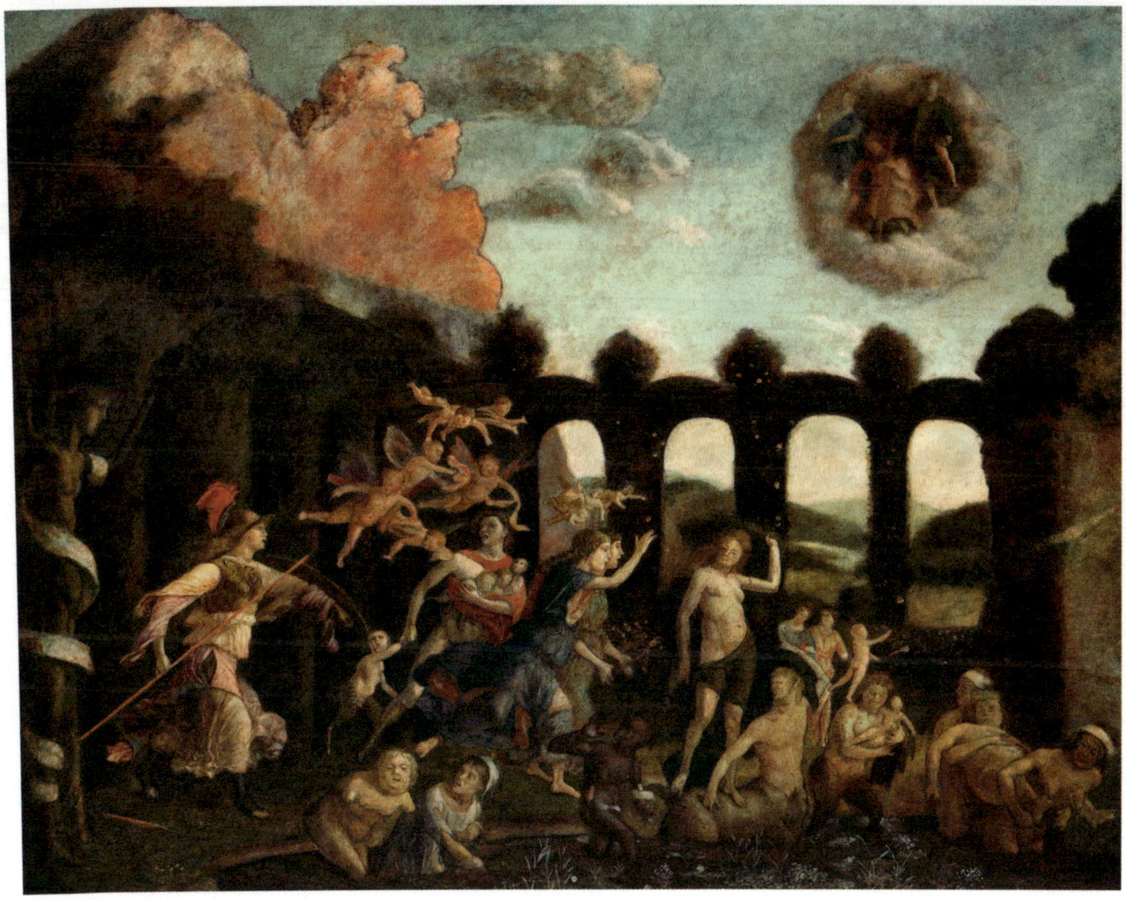

Ernest Rouart (1874–1942)
Minerva Expelling the Vices from the Garden of Virtue (copy after Mantegna), 1897
Oil on canvas, 160.5 × 192.6 cm
Paris, Musée d'Orsay, gift of Clément Rouart and his brothers, the artist's sons, 1975

The event that impressed everybody was the appearance of Degas on Wednesday December 8, 1897: "Met Monsieur Degas at the Louvre, who spent an hour and a half chatting to us about painting," recorded Julie in her diary.

> He looked at Jeanne's copy, which he thought was nicely colored but somewhat spoiled. In front of mine, he added, "She has quite a knack, young Julie; the armor is skillfully done. It's stylish; but still, those bits of white canvas, dearie me, one could say it runs in the family." "Skillful and stylish" pleased me. I'm always afraid that I might lack these qualities, which I think are absolutely essential in a woman. Everything that has been said to me about my copy gives me encouragement.... Monsieur Degas led us into the gallery where the Primitives are hung, to see how his pupil Monsieur Rouart, whom he advised to prime a canvas with green to copy a Mantegna, was getting on. Unfortunately, he had done it in a really bright green.[450]

Degas apparently said to his student: "Now, do you see those young women? Which one would you like me to ask? I assure you that you will not be rebuffed; you are kind, you are wealthy, and you do not look like a rake."[451] Ernest was intimidated, petrified by the arrival of the "squadron." As Jeannie confirmed, he did not say a word to Julie.[452] And yet everyone remembered this as the day their love was born. Several friends have described the encounter. The version of Louis Rouart, Ernest's youngest brother, is very direct: "[Degas] introduced the two young copyists, who a few months later, were married."[453]

In 1874, after the exhibition put on in the former studio of Nadar, whose participants included Julie and Ernest's parents, Berthe Morisot and Henri Rouart, both of them were co-opted by their friend Degas, another—non-Impressionist—creation came into the world, a work in flesh and blood. Ernest[454] Rouart was born on August 24.[455] The fourth of the five children born to Stanislas Henri Rouart

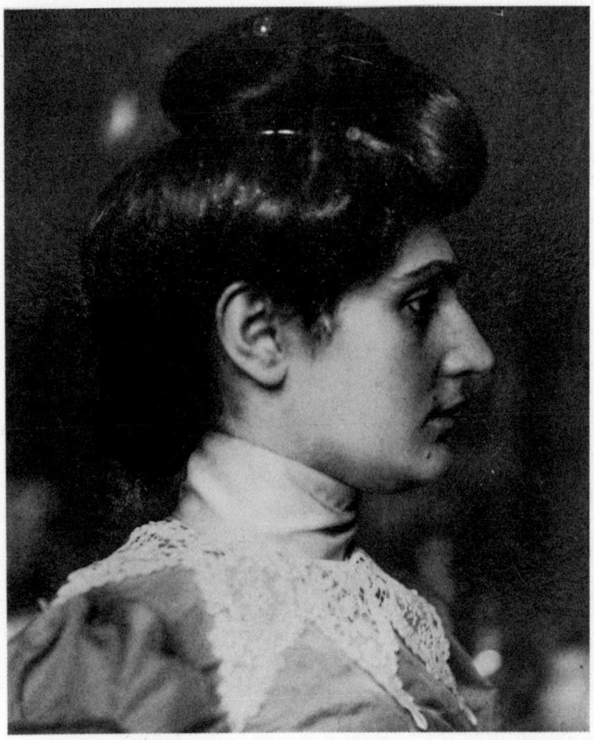

Julie Manet
Paris, Musée Marmottan Monet

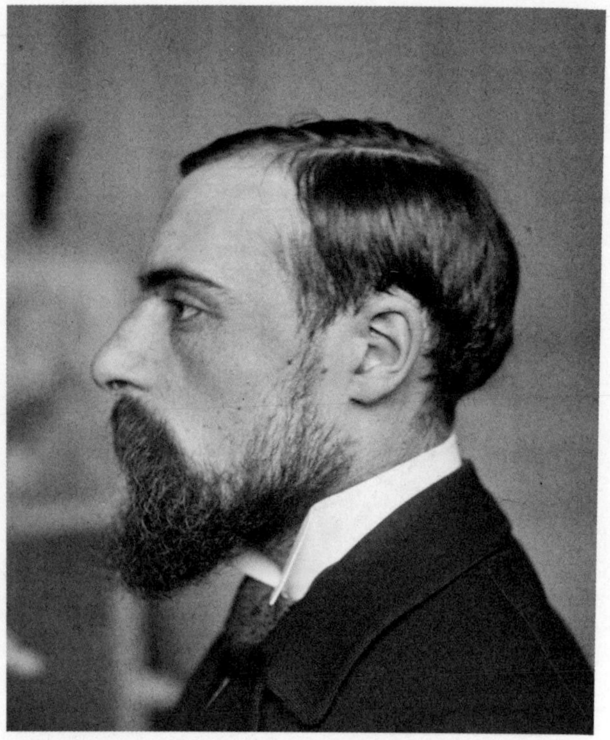

Ernest Rouart
Archives du Mesnil, on permanent loan at the Musée Marmottan Monet

and Hélène Hortense Jacob-Desmalter, he was baptized in the church of Saint-Augustin on December 14, 1874,[456] eight days before the wedding of Berthe Morisot and Eugène Manet, Julie's parents to be. The plan was that he would follow the path laid out by his father. Ernest's name was put down for the Lycée Condorcet, the idea being that he would go on to gain admission to Polytechnique and take the helm of the factory that made the family fortune. In 1886, as his brother later put it, a tragic event "suddenly darkened what was set fair to be a happy childhood." This was the death of his mother, whose sketchbooks he devotedly kept, along with the notes she had made during her final year.[457] "From now on, returning home from school on winter evenings he felt the lack of a welcoming presence in the empty, silent house. Before going to sleep, and on waking in the morning, he suffered from the loss of a presence that seemed divine."[458]

His consolation did not come from his entourage, not from his brothers or his sister, or from his father, although he adored him, let alone from the "dry, ugly, overbearing and mechanically stupid old maid"[459] who was his sole company on Thursdays and Sundays. By all accounts,[460] it was paintings that became his companions. But not just any paintings. The townhouse at 34, rue de Lisbonne built by his father was home to a collection worthy of the Louvre, except that, in addition to treasures of pre-modern art, it also included some of the great masterpieces of the new painting. Over five hundred canvases that stunned those who came to admire them. "It is staggeringly beautiful. From top to bottom the house is full of paintings which, in all the rooms, in the antechambers, in the staircases, line the walls from floor to ceiling. There is not one empty space. It's a profusion of wonders: Corot, Delacroix, Millet, Jongkind, Courbet, Daumier, Degas. I saw so much that I left in a daze."[461]

In this interior, art became Ernest's consolation, a respiration, a need and soon his reason for living. He gave up the idea of Polytechnique and become the sole pupil of his father's friend, Edgar Degas. Obtaining his higher diploma in Oriental languages in 1897[462] changed nothing: he was still determined to be a painter.

Entre Ernest and Julie had plenty of elective affinities. Both grew up surrounded by paintings. Used to living in close contact with her mother's colleagues, Julie witnessed the emergence and the recognition of the new painting (think, for example, of the subscription organized in 1889 for the acquisition of *Olympia*),[463] but she was also a witness to the creative act, to an art that was produced in front of her eyes, and for which she and those close to her were often the models. The paintings that she owned, and that the early twentieth century raised to the rank of masterpieces,[464] speak of her life and her past, illustrate her roots. For Ernest, the love of art also took the creative path, but also (and above all?) the path of collecting. Like his father and his master,[465] he was constantly seeking out art. In his entourage people studied, appraised, and purchased, and they adopted artworks the way one would a child. Each painting became a member of the family. Collecting was an art of living. Both Julie and Ernest assigned to painting filial and therefore vital value. Both orphaned early in life, they felt for friends and family and for the deceased a veneration that only consolidated their natural penchant. The purpose of the first invitation sent out by Degas's student on January 27, 1898, was none other than to reveal to the copyists the marvels of the rue de Lisbonne. There Julie admired a host of masterpieces, notably the figures by Corot, whom Ernest venerated. Her kin were not far away: her father was represented from behind by Uncle Édouard and a canvas by her mother was exhibited. Monsieur and Madame Eugène Manet were also part of the celebration. Was this a sign? Julie took to dreaming:

> In these recent times I sometimes have the sweet dream of giving myself to a being who would share my tastes, with whom I would work on this art of painting, who would venerate Maman's work, and to whom I would describe all the charms of that unique mother. Having children that it would be so interesting to bring up. Helping the wretched: seeing loved ones having a similar life and working together to come closer to God and try to show him gratitude for his great Goodness and to be one in a feeling of infinite love for the Creator. Dare I speak the name of the one who plunges me into these dreams?[466]

Mallarmé did the same with Jeannie and whispered the name of Paul Valéry. "I need a Paul—will Paul come?" wrote the poet.[467] The allusion struck home: the words set Jeannie dreaming, and loving without having even seen or known. On several consecutive Tuesdays she apologized for not being present, deferring the encounter with the spiritual son of Mallarmé, his authentic disciple; the man she already loved.

Born in Sète on October 30, 1871, raised after his father's death by his mother and brother, Valéry was educated in Montpellier. After obtaining his degree in literature in 1881 he studied at the law faculty. In 1890 he made two decisive encounters, with Pierre Louÿs and André Gide. They

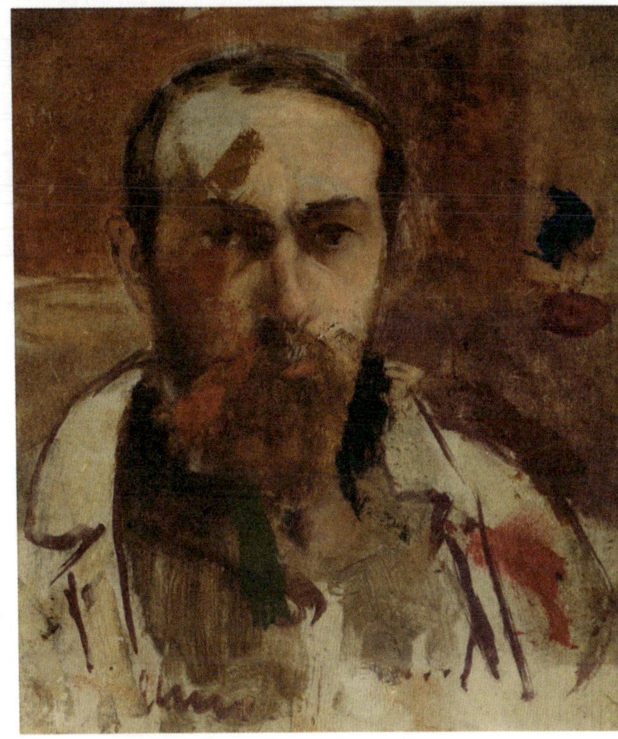

Ernest Rouart (1874–1942)
Self-Portrait, 1908
Oil on wood, 17.2 × 14.4 cm
Private collection

opened up for him the doors to a new world, introducing him into the Rouart circle and enabling this Southerner to approach the living artist he admired more than any other: Degas. Above all, he was introduced to Symbolist literary circles, especially to Mallarmé, with whom he began a correspondence in 1890, and whom he met in 1893, shortly after his arrival in Paris. Despite his *Introduction à la méthode de Léonard de Vinci* and *Soirée avec Monsieur Teste* (a volume he had been hoping to dedicate to Degas),[468] which came out in 1895 and 1896 respectively, the young man was going through a period of doubt and published only episodically. Between 1893 and 1900 Valéry "was no longer a student, but not quite yet a writer." Living at the Hôtel Henri IV, at 13, rue Gay-Lussac, in a space no bigger than a maid's room, he was struggling to carve out a future for himself. Lacking both position and fortune, he had to renounce a position as attaché at the Louvre because it was unpaid.[469] In 1895 he was number eighteen of the twenty candidates admitted to the post of *rédacteur* after the exam organized by the Ministry of War. "He would have been ranked higher were it not for his somewhat strange style."[470] His examiner was indeed disconcerted by his writing, about which he bluntly commented: "He is a vulgar decadent, a Paul Varlaine [*sic*] in prose that the administration has no use for."[471] It was

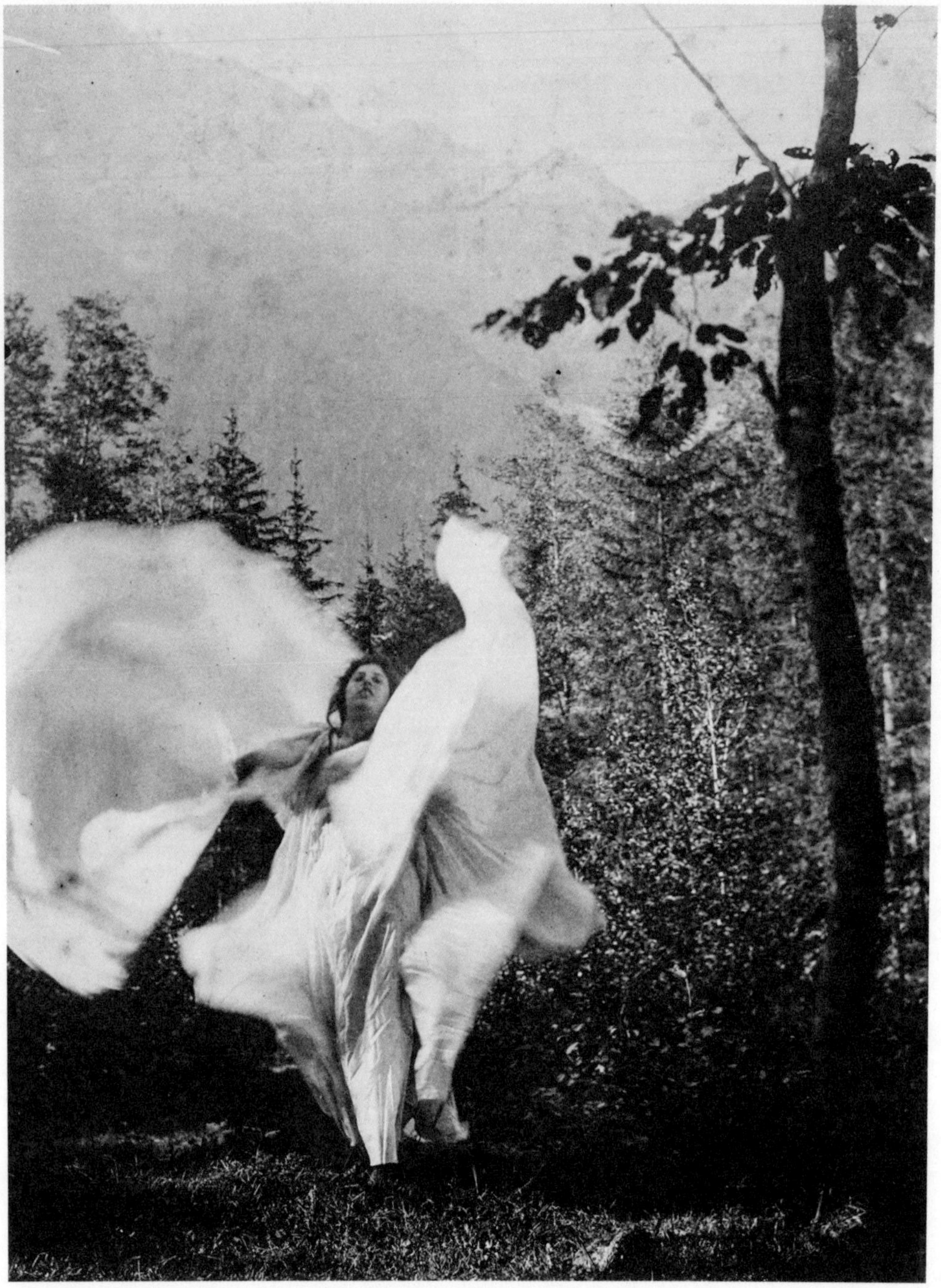

Yvonne Rouart dancing in a dress lent to her by Loïe Fuller, n.d.
Paris, Musée d'Orsay

not until April 30, 1897, he was made a trainee *rédacteur*.[472] Clearly, art and war did not make good bedfellows.

The first thing Jeannie Gobillard and Paul Valéry had to share was tears. On September 9, 1898, Stéphane Mallarmé died suddenly at the age of fifty-six. The funeral was held on Sunday September 11 at Valvins. Julie wrote: "Writers, but also peasants, with whom M. Mallarmé was so friendly, were gathered together . . . Roujon . . . said a few simple, poignant words on behalf of his elderly friends . . . Paul Valéry spoke next in the name of the younger generation, but he was so overcome that he couldn't continue."[473]

These were the distressing circumstances in which Jeannie met him: "The first time that I saw him (apart from imagining him through his name . . .). It was a day of superb scenery but terrible sadness: the day of Monsieur Mallarmé's funeral—we emerged, desolate, from the little church of Samoreau and I met eyes even more desolate, Valéry's eyes. The air or the forest brought me his name. I repeated it aloud and Julie replied: Yes, that's him."[474] In dreaming of Paul Valéry, Jeannie too was placing herself in the register of filiation and fidelity to the past: "[Valéry] brought us back something of the lost atmosphere of Monsieur Mallarmé.[475] . . . I can sense the intervention of the delightful friend who brought us together. Perhaps, in departing, Monsieur Mallarmé bequeathed us to each other."[476]

"THE FORCE OF DESTINY"[477]

From the end of 1898 to the beginning of 1900, the great question was how and when Ernest Rouart and Paul Valéry could be made to declare their passion. The evening of the marriage contract for Yvonne Lerolle and Eugène Rouart, organized chez Degas on December 22, 1898, was a turning point. As the youngest Gobillard recalled: "Paule and I [were] very moved for J[ulie] at the idea of seeing E. Rouart, and we did not doubt his feelings for a moment."[478]

Julie wrote in her diary:

> At the entrance, Ernest gave me his arm and led me in to greet Yvonne . . . I really liked Ernest this evening. He put his shyness aside a little, and, considering our similar tastes and the same milieu, could he not be the one for me? Yes—I can certainly say that this though crossed my mind during the party. "So, I have straightened Ernest out for you," Monsieur Degas said to me. "Now it's up to you to carry on."[479]

Then it was Jeannie's turn. Julie wrote:

> We saw a lot of people we know. . . . I was quite astonished to find Valéry there, and had only one idea—that we should find an opportunity of bringing him and Jeannie together. Ever since that day when Monsieur Mallarmé mentioned him as a possibility for Jeannie, I have been mulling over the idea and wondering how I could orchestrate a meeting between them.[480]

As Jeannie recalled:

> A first time Julie said to me—Look Valéry!—conversation with Mr Degas after which Valéry conducted me to the buffet behind Julie on Ernest's arm.[481]

As Julie noted:

> I was ecstatic, and who knows what it may lead to? Following Valéry and Jeannie on the arm of Ernest Rouart, the thought crossed my mind that maybe we were both on the arm of the person with whom we would spend the rest of our lives, but nothing was less certain, of course.[482]

Retrospectively, Jeannie recognized this evening as the turning point.

> That day, Paule played my hand by talking to him, and she won. That is what I owe her. Will a whole life be enough to acknowledge it?[483]

At Paule's invitation, Valéry was soon calling at the rue de Villejust two Thursdays per month. Jeannie began to describe these visits as "Valéryan stations." The first meeting took place on February 9,[484] shortly after the funeral of Suzanne Butler, which Paule and Julie attended in Giverny. What other subject could there be than painting? How else could they get to know each other? One must always begin at the beginning: "We showed him the paintings by the light of a candle."[485]

In June 1899, Julie's situation had progressed sufficiently for her to note, after a dinner at Degas's home:

> I have finally managed to speak to him—he's not a bit as shy as he was when we met him at the Louvre last year, and I am extremely pleased to have got to know him a bit more. I really like him, yes, I must say I really do. On our way home, in an open carriage, I thought about it and told myself that Ernest is the one for me.[486]

When summer came they all went about their business and the suitors were seen only twice. The trio was with Valéry again at Valvins on July 14. During that brief stay the writer renamed the "Flying Squadron" the "Caraco Tribe" and got out his pencil to draw the young ladies. In September the "Caracos" saw Ernest again in Autun, at the home of Eugène and Yvonne Rouart, whom they admired dancing in the manner of Loïe Fuller (p. 64). A previously unpublished letter that Yvonne wrote to Julie years later gives an idea of the strength of the bonds between them, about which so little is known:

> Life moves on and one of my frequent regrets . . . shall I tell you (between you and me, keep this to yourself) is to spend it so far from you. There is nothing exaggerated, passionate, self-interested or impure about this feeling, but I am often rather sad to be alone and when I ask myself whom I would like to spend 2 or 3 hours

> with, 2 or 3 times a week, the answer is "with Julie." Whatever we are saying, reading, visiting, exploring, I have spontaneous feeling of harmonies falling into place between us, which is very rare.[487]

Julie and Jeannie were now completely absorbed in their future:

> On returning [from the holidays] Julie and I slept together, as always, and I remember our conversation in the morning was so light-hearted. I had dreamed of him and she too had dreamed of him.[488]

With a certain lucidity, Jeannie envisioned the second part of the year as the end of an era, "already the memory of our life à trois."[489]

> I took the trouble to enjoy myself this autumn and I have completely savored our charming independence as something that will come to an end.[490]

A few events in particular marked the year's end: a tour of the Alexis Rouart collection on December 12, then a performance of *Iphigénie* at the Théâtre de la Renaissance on the 15th. Christmas was spent with the Mallarmé ladies, Doctor Bonniot, whom Geneviève married in 1901, and Valéry. The "Valéryan stations" were an object of growing curiosity at rue de Villejust. Blanche Pontillon popped by, and the visit of their cousin, Lucien Boursier, whose first wife Juliette Berthe had painted, as well as their daughter Thérèse, put Jeannie in a rage.

> I came up to Valéry, very close, in order to say in a low voice: "This is the family. Her sister complimented Berthe just once, having mistaken for her signature that of a horrid Dame Morizot. Women painters."[491]

All families have their old quarrels. More interestingly, even surprisingly, coming from Jeannie:

> When he came here, Valéry gave me a notion that I did not have, a notion of us, of my own tendencies, of our interior, made up of those who are no longer here. For me the Valéry of those days, on the outside, is inseparable from the big white salon with light decoration and old furniture. From the little room after that without our mysterious portraits. I could feel that something of Monsieur Mallarmé was coming back to life in us, our mothers. And the delightful relation, bequeathed for them all, established a transformation of time, of their souls in ours. During these hours, too, I came awake. I recognized myself and I knew that I must be his. I felt the force of destiny so strongly.[492]

"MONSIEUR DEGAS DIDN'T PUSH HIM INTO THIS? HE WAS THE ONE ASKING?"[493]

On Sunday January 7, 1900, events speeded up for Julie. "Ernest Rouart has asked for her hand in marriage," recorded Paule. And Jeannie noted:

> God gave me the strength that I asked of him and I answered, as I thought: "Well indeed, I am very happy. . . . what I want is for her to be happy . . . She deserves it." . . . And then Paule, divinely, in a moment I shall never forget, sat on the stepladder that was there and said to me: "But Jeannie, you may also soon be getting what you desire. Tell me, Jeannie, my little kitten," and she pulled me onto her older sister's lap, "do you not love Valéry?"[494]

On January 10, during a performance of the *Mastersingers of Nuremberg* at the Opéra Garnier, Paule's admirer showed his feeling for the brides to be:

> It may indeed be that this divine light of love illumined us, for Redon, seeing us from the forestage somewhere, came up to laugh with us, slightly apart from the strange parade of that evening's audience. He told us, "You are charming. You are a symbol."[495]

Jeannie wrote this (previously unpublished) description of Ernest's proposal:

> On Saturday [January 13, 1900], she [Julie] was ravishing. That day we had decided to take her round to Monsieur Degas's house. We would meet Ernest, we would invite him to come round and see the paintings at home. Ernest would come back and after a few weeks, would duly make his proposal. How inexperienced we were! Good lord. Julie wore the brown outfit that makes her look so much like Aunt Berthe and off we went, cleaving the air. We knocked at the door of Mr. Degas's studio. "Hello, ladies, you are expected." Complete darkness. However, I could see that Ernest was pale behind the screen. "Take a seat. Paule, Jeanne, do sit down. Julie, take the armchair. Ernest, the banquette. Is that it?" Then, to our stupefaction. "Mademoiselle Julie Manet, do you take Monsieur Ernest Rouart in marriage?" Julie laughed nervously. Paule looked alarmed. "But, Monsieur Degas, she is not ready, she knows nothing." At that moment a ray of moonlight hit Ernest's face as he awaited the sentence, pale and impassive. Like an inexpressible Redon. The silence no less expressible. I could sense that there was only one thing for it; to talk, Dreyfus, powder word, Boers, anything, it all

came out. In the end, Paule leaned toward Julie and I heard, with more stupefaction, I heard Julie's answer. Monsieur Degas didn't push him into this? He was the one asking? Oh yes, indeed, yes, without doubt. And we thought she was so nervous, so unsure and so opposed to marriage! Vain to try to describe our astonishment, Ernest's handshake, Zoé's[496] face! I tried to be bold. Julie, who you could sense was getting away, was charming, radiant, saying just one thing: "I don't understand."[497]

Jeannie recorded:

> On Monday [15 January 1900] . . . the three of us went to the cemetery and Aunt Berthe's soul was waiting for us there and under the big cypress tree I wept and I said, "Aunt Berthe, you entrusted her to me. I do not know if I have always been as kind with her as I should, but I have loved her. I have loved her and now I am bringing her back to you. I am bringing her back so that you may give her away. . . . It was one of those moments when a special grace makes you beautiful. Veils the ugly corners of the soul and, as you weep, you bask in that beauty which is not of this world but is surely divine.[498]

Julie informed her friends. Monet's congratulations came at once. In Grasse, Renoir waxed lyrical:

> Bravo a thousand times bravo!!!
> My dear Julie,
> Now that is truly good news and it fills my wife and I with joy. Now I can tell you that he was the fiancé we dreamed of. My wife mentioned this to Degas on the way back from a dinner at your home. Our desire is now a reality: once again, Bravo!!!
> And to chase away the only cloud over your happiness, like that of the mountain, I send you this old saying:
> When happiness enters a house
> Count three times
> My wife and I send you all our love and I am ordering a new morning coat.
> Renoir.[499]

"THEY OUGHT TO INVENT DECLARATION MACHINES"

The "Caraco Tribe" was invited at once to Henri Rouart's Friday dinner. Jeannie recorded:

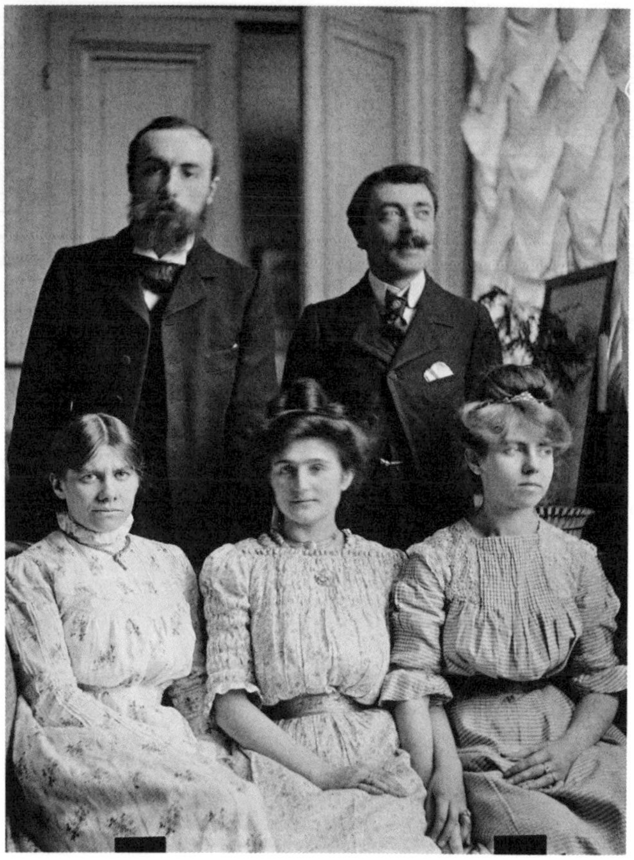

From top to bottom and left to right: *Ernest Rouart, Paul Valéry, Paule Gobillard, Julie Manet, and Jeannie Gobillard rue de Villejust*, c. 1900 Archives BS, Paris, Musée Marmottan Monet

> Monsieur Degas approached us. "Monsieur Degas, I am in the middle of singing praises," ventured Jeannie. "You are right: you will not say any more than we already think. Ah Jeannie, Jeannie. We are watching over you." And he raised a finger.[500]

It was not so much that Valéry was hesitant, but he was afraid:

> One day, a long time ago, already, he went to see the Mallarmés. He was so sad, talking about his solitude, of soon being thirty (although he was only 27), that Geneviève asked him: "But Valéry, this charming interior where you are going, does it mean nothing to you? Are you not thinking of one of them?" "Yes," he replied, and changed the subject. So do you see Jeannie, the only thing holding him back is his situation. He feels that it is not sufficient.[501]

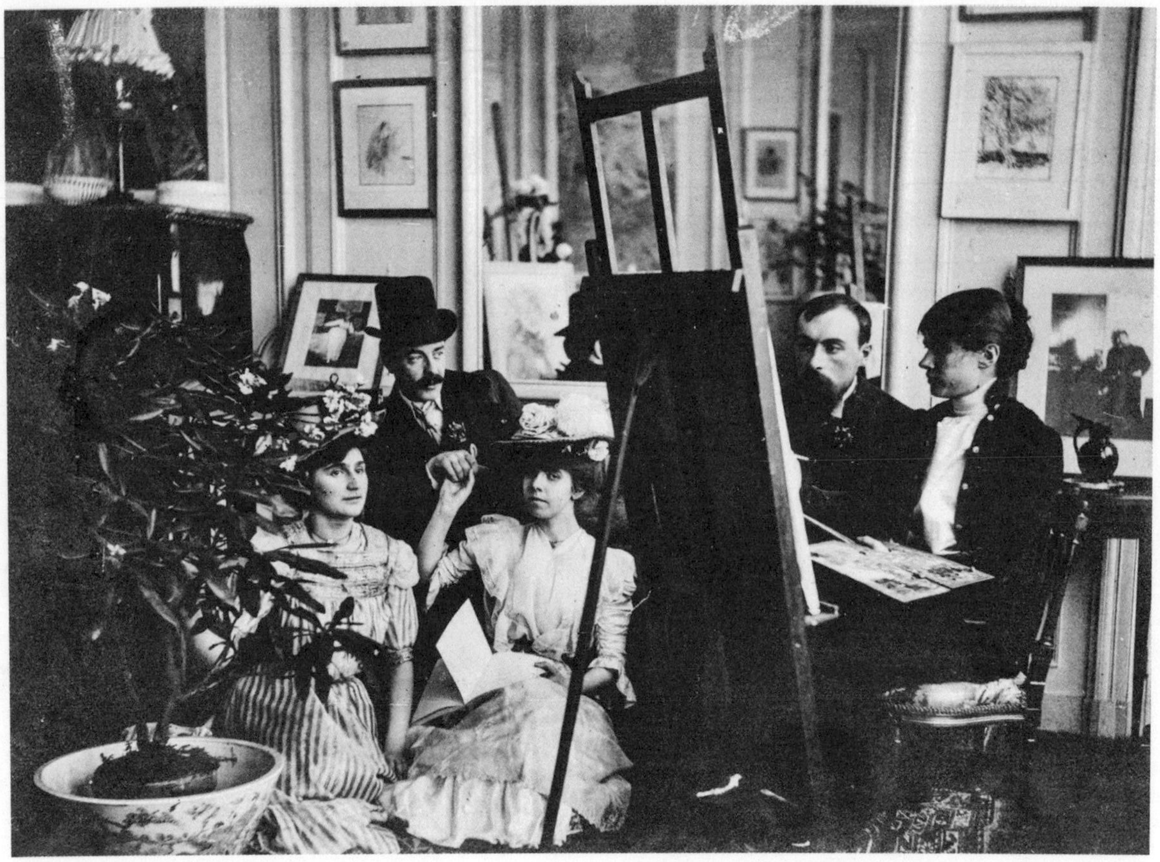

Julie Manet, Paul Valéry, and Jeannie Gobillard (left), Ernest Rouart and Paule Gobillard painting (right), rue de Villejust, March 23, 1900
Private collection

The annual salary of less than 2,000 francs[502] that he received from the Ministry of War was insignificant when compared to the Rouart fortune, and his room at five francs a day[503] was unworthy of the splendors of the rue de Lisbonne. One was just a modest employee, as was Mallarmé, the other was a *grand bourgeois* at whose table they talk "of how great fortunes are made and lost, a question of no value for those who do not have even the basic wherewithal," noted Jeannie.[504] On January 28, 1900, Geneviève Mallarmé summoned Paul and Paule to clarify the situation: "step by step, we came to confessions, to all the grave but indispensable questions, our little fortunes, life *à trois*, you see?" concluded Jeannie.[505]

It took many more interventions by the brothers Rouart, by their friend Gide, and by Doctor Bonniot[506] for Valéry to find the strength to declare his feelings. He did so, naturally, on a Thursday:

On February 22, 1900, arriving late at the dinner to which the Rouarts were now admitted, Paul went into a separate room, where Jeannie got him to speak his mind:

"And now . . . I am going to be perfectly ridiculous." (He went to take a look in the living room). "They have shut us away you know" (And here he came over all youthful and all the time serious like an actor.) "Sit down—no" (But I did sit down, then I got up, feeling a sense of ridicule known to the generations.) (Then, straight out, now the gravitas of a man). "Well then, will you be my wife?" (My wife!) If the inflection of the voice had not been so gentle, caressing, almost supplicating and deliciously questioning I would have recoiled, frightened to have come straight to that point like that, and then, for a second, it felt again as if we were playing and I answered: "You have taken my flag." "I cannot give it back to you" (then I do not know what he answered but I avoided the glow of the lamp and rolled myself in the velvet curtain, the big red crusader's curtain. In that dark clothing I was more at ease.) He, stood facing me, and said, "What I really do not want is to be literary, that any exchange between us should sound like words from books." . . .

"Have I answered you?" I asked him again.
"But . . . it seems to me that you have replied very well" (and then, pauses and many more pauses, and he ventured):
"I would like to be very indiscreet!"
"Do."
"Thank you, you are kind, doesn't this go back to Valvins?" And me: "No . . . much before. Before, but you hardly knew me; I had not spoken to you much." . . . After another pause, he says: "Touch my hand" . . . It was the first time our hands touched since we knew each other and about each other. I shall not forget that impression and indeed that is my only strong emotion from that moment.[507]

And she continued:

> The dinner at which I was a spectator, since in a sense I was not being part of it, was charming in its special intimacy. The big sister presiding over these four children who had declared their feelings was delightful and all the more so, perhaps, in that they talked about very different matters, leaving to float in the atmosphere, on the clusters of the chandelier, in the shiny corners of the frames, the wonderful unstated knowledge, playing with it, sometimes; for example, when Valéry said "They ought to invent declaration machines."[508]

"THE MINUTE OF GREAT THINGS"

> Do we not wake up together with the same breath, Julie and I? And is not this fact that it happens at the same moment due at least in part to our friendship? Perhaps. Why let chance have it all? Some habits, picked up in childhood, of thinking similar things, of understanding each other without speaking, of owning together the same toy, of admiring the same painting, of listening to the same music together, did they not decide the minute of great things? Because we have cried to each other at moments of horror and death, were we not bound to live both together![509]

This time of engagement was lived in unison, as Jeannie noted:

> How happy we are the two of us together when we talk about them. We go arm in arm in the street and we tell each other about our fiancés. It is not always easy, in fact, and it takes all our long experience of understanding each other without saying things.[510]

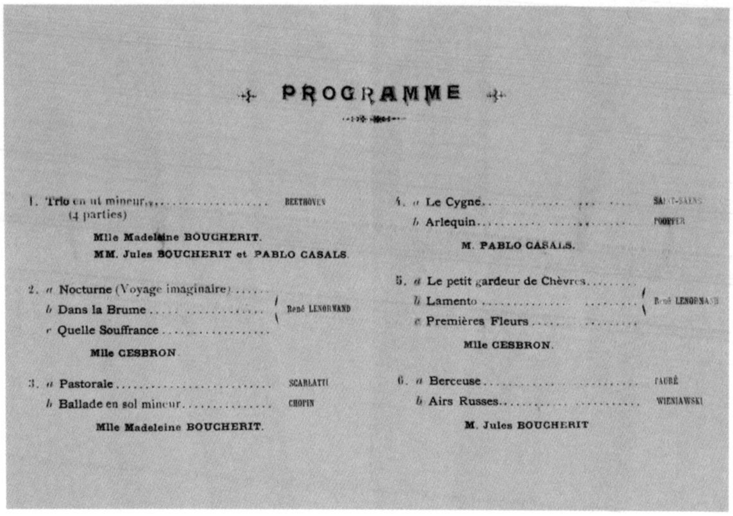

PROGRAMME

1. Trio en ut mineur (4 parties) ... BEETHOVEN
Mlle Madeleine BOUCHERIT.
MM. Jules BOUCHERIT et PABLO CASALS.

2. *a* Nocturne (Voyage imaginaire) ...
b Dans la Brume ... René LENORMAND
c Quelle Souffrance ...
Mlle CESBRON.

3. *a* Pastorale ... SCARLATTI
b Ballade en sol mineur ... CHOPIN
Mlle Madeleine BOUCHERIT.

4. *a* Le Cygne ... SAINT-SAËNS
b Arlequin ... POPPER
M. PABLO CASALS.

5. *a* Le petit gardeur de Chèvres ...
b Lamento ... René LENORMAND
c Premières Fleurs ...
Mlle CESBRON.

6. *a* Berceuse ... FAURÉ
b Airs Russes ... WIENIAWSKI
M. Jules BOUCHERIT

Program for the evening of Julie and Jeannie's marriage contracts, May 26, 1900
Private collection

From now on they were always with their Messieurs, or very nearly. They even managed to contravene the prohibitions of the convent in Versailles where the future spouses went on a retreat from April 25 to May 1.[511] They met in the bedroom:

> We sat in pairs on the beds. Paule, in the only armchair, made jokes. . . . Two gentlemen on beds in a convent! These sisters give the residents too much freedom, says Valéry. . . . It is a comedy set-up, concludes Jeannie.[512]

These marriages were not seen as a separation. If the trio had been a bird, it would have belonged to the species of inseparables. You do not separate those who cannot be kept apart. Their entourage knew it and accepted it. Valéry, who was not afraid to admit that he would have liked to marry all three of them,[513] was well aware of this. The photos taken at the time are eloquent in this respect. They posed as a group. Paul and Jeannie, Julie and Ernest face Paule, who is painting in the living room in the rue de Villejust (p. 68). Time passed, models changed, painting remained and, soon, words were reborn.

These couples were constructed in accordance with the fusional family line that respected the bonds and relations that had always united these young women. Julie continued to financially support those she loved. The dowry of 30,000 francs inherited from Berthe was paid to Jeannie, who considered it as at once a gift and something due:

> This morning Julie gave me a little star of diamonds that will be a lodestar of our friendship. She wears a similar one. She also gave me a very big gift of money and I find that delightful and almost natural,

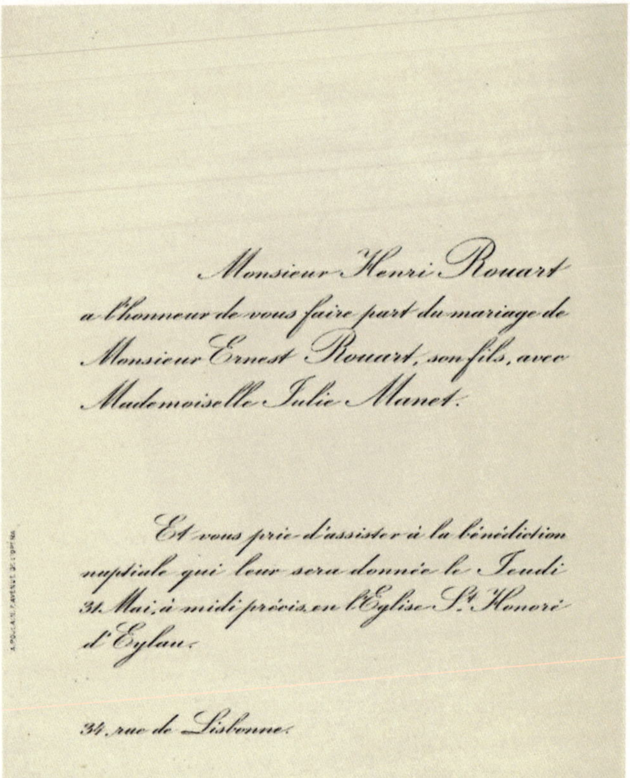

Monsieur Henri Rouart
a l'honneur de vous faire part du mariage de
Monsieur Ernest Rouart, son fils, avec
Mademoiselle Julie Manet.

Et vous prie d'assister à la bénédiction
nuptiale qui leur sera donnée le Jeudi
31 Mai, à midi précis, en l'Eglise St Honoré
d'Eylau.

34, rue de Lisbonne.

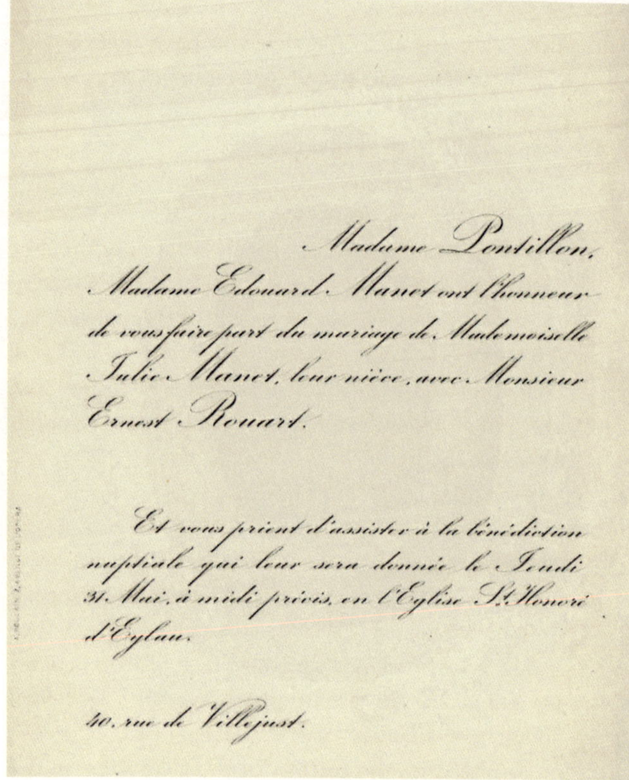

Madame Pontillon,
Madame Edouard Manet ont l'honneur
de vous faire part du mariage de Mademoiselle
Julie Manet, leur nièce, avec Monsieur
Ernest Rouart.

Et vous prient d'assister à la bénédiction
nuptiale qui leur sera donnée le Jeudi
31 Mai, à midi précis, en l'Eglise St Honoré
d'Eylau.

40, rue de Villejust.

The two notices for the wedding of Ernest Rouart and Julie Manet, May 1900
Private collection

> **so obvious does it seem to me that I would have done the same if our positions were reversed. Our coalition, which was at times a conspiracy, is so strong![514]**

There is no denying that the gulf in wealth was immense. Witness their marriage contracts.[515] The Rouart couple started out in life with a capital of 1,446,500 francs. Julie was the wealthier of the two and brought 1,125,660 francs (145,660 francs in personal property, including 40,000 francs of paintings, and 980,000 francs in property); Ernest owned 321,500 francs in separate property. His father, Henri, also gave him an annual income of 6,000 francs, and sent regular monthly payments starting at this date.[516] There's no harm in having plenty of possessions! The capital of the Valérys was estimated at 93,500 francs, including 60,000 francs for Paul's personal possessions; apart from her dowry, Jeannie brought two pianos, an upright and a grand.

It had no doubt already been agreed that the Valérys—that is, Jeannie and the two Paul(e)s—would move into the fourth floor in the rue de Villejust as soon as Aunt Edma had vacated the apartment.[517] Julie and Ernest stayed on the fifth floor. Once again, and as always with the Morisots, the men lived with their wives. Should we be surprised that the soirée celebrating the marriage contract was held at the home of these demoiselles around a musical program performed by Jules and Magdeleine Boucherit and Pablo Casals (p. 69)? A double wedding ceremony was prepared, with the betrothed sharing witnesses: Gabriel Thomas and Émile Mayniel accompanied them both. On May 29 the civil weddings followed each other at the town hall of the 16th arrondissement: Paul and Jeannie at 4 pm,[518] Ernest and Julie at 5 pm.[519] And they stayed together after that. Henri Rouart organized a dinner that evening to celebrate the marriage of "our children," as he wrote to Valéry's mother. The religious ceremony was held shortly afterwards, on May 31, at the church of Saint-Honoré-d'Eylau.[520] The wedding photograph was also double, and taken at the gentlemen's new home in the rue de Villejust (p. 71).

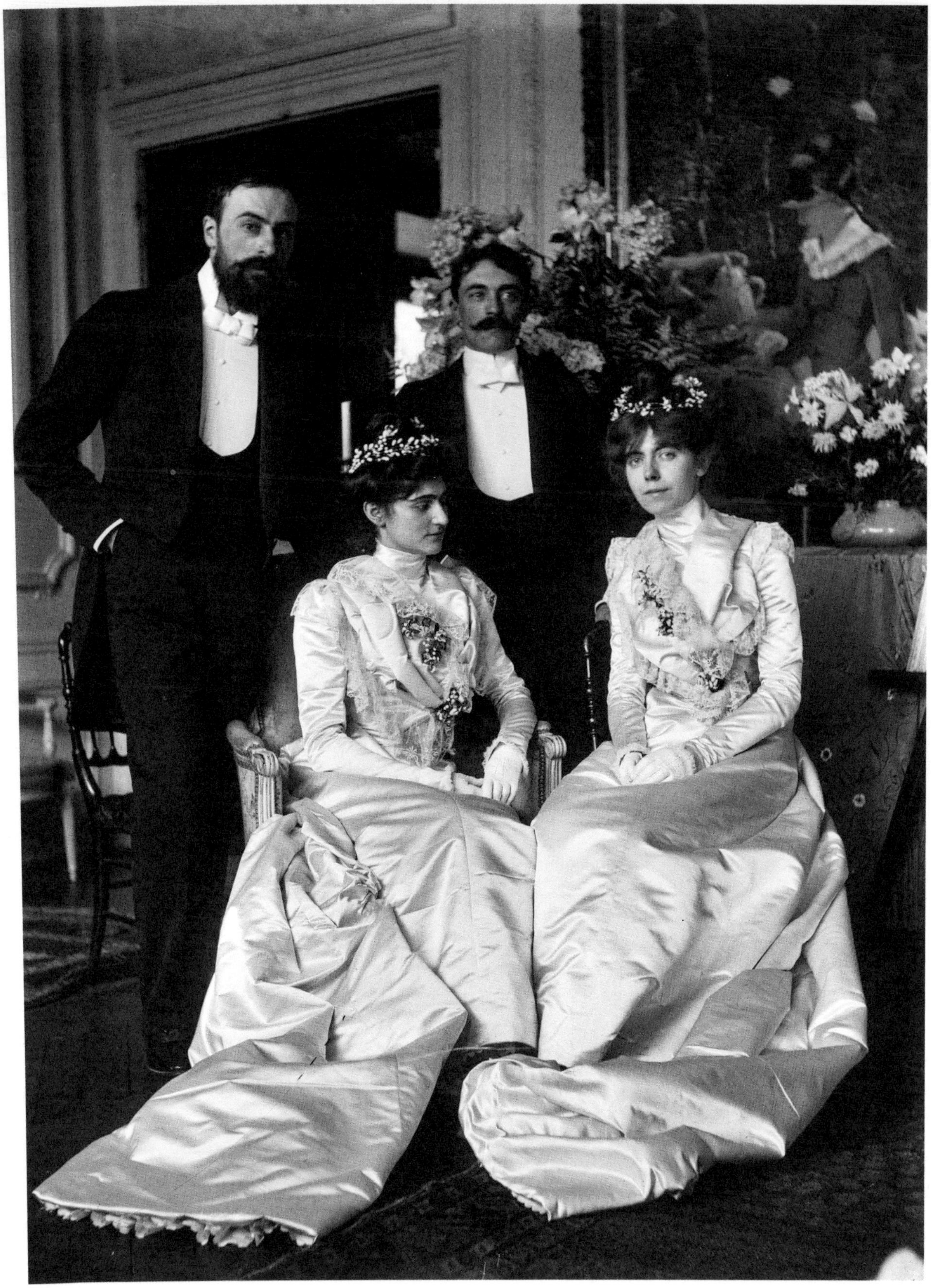

Ernest Rouart, Julie Manet, Paul Valéry, and Jeannie Gobillard in the rue de Villejust on the day of their marriage, May 31, 1900
Archives du Mesnil, on permanent loan at the Musée Marmottan Monet

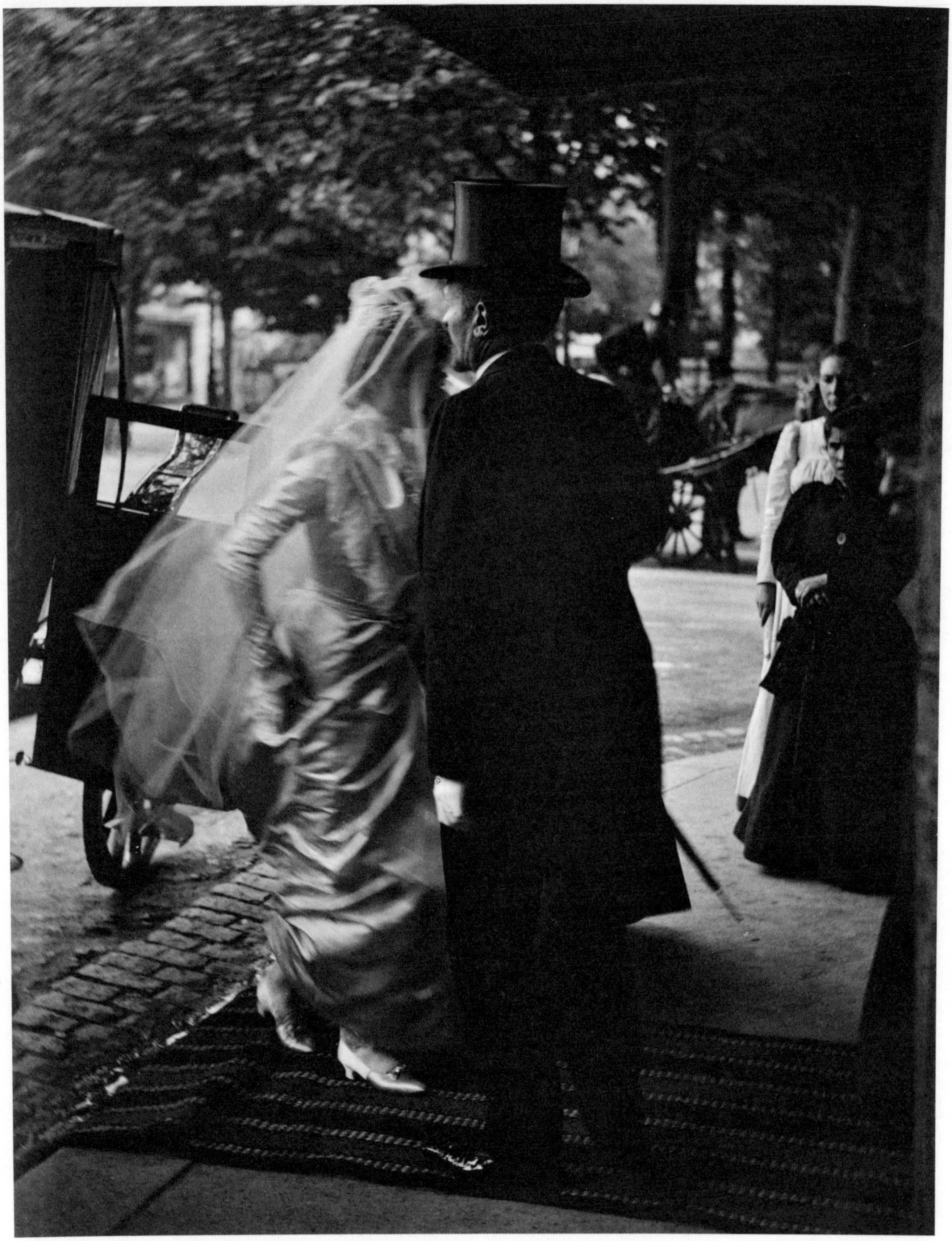

Julie Manet in wedding dress and Gabriel Thomas, her witness, May 31, 1900
Archives BS, Paris, Musée Marmottan Monet

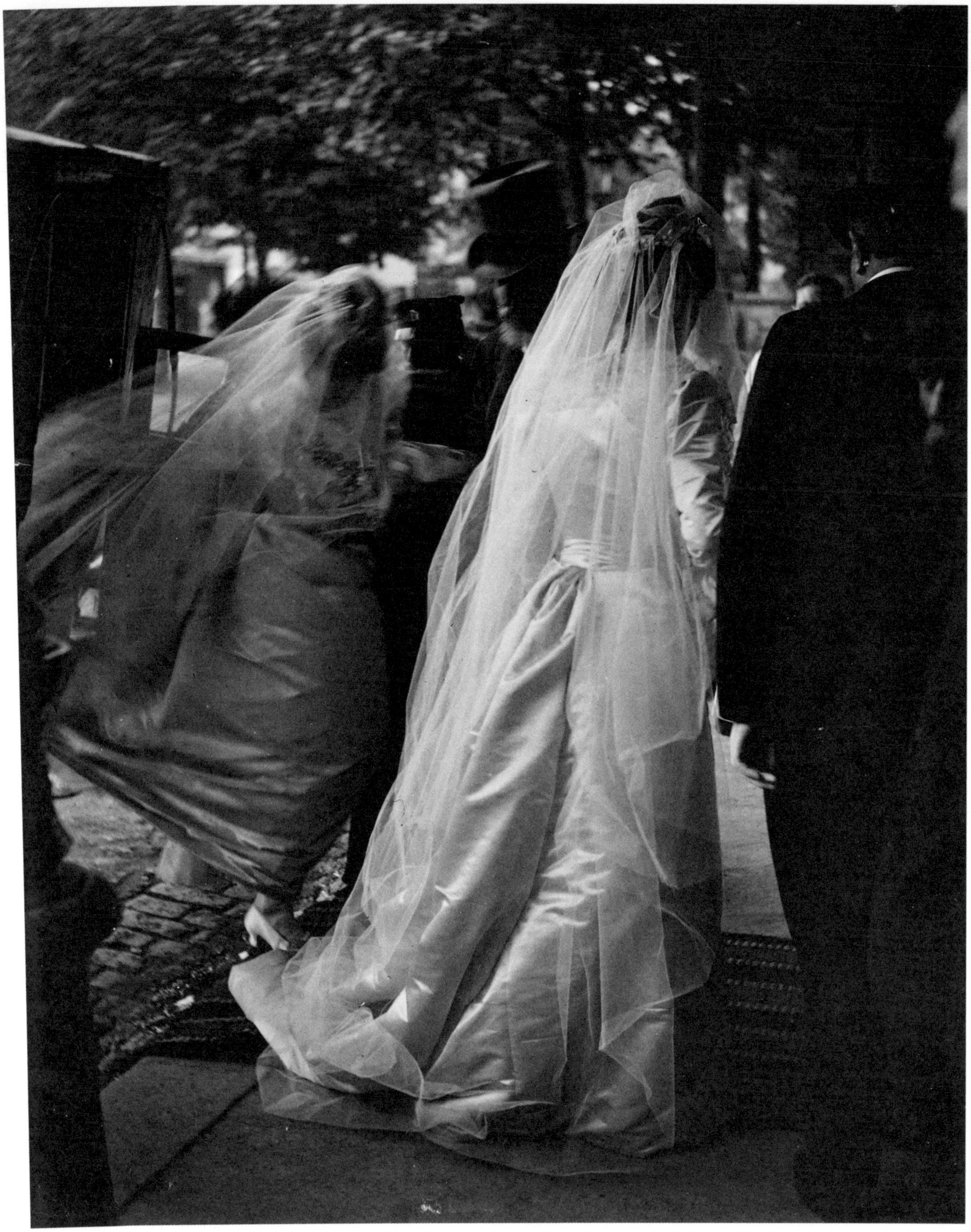

The brides Jeannie Gobillard (left) and Julie Manet (right) and their witnesses Émile Mayniel (front left) and Gabriel Thomas (back turned), May 31, 1900
Archives BS, Paris, Musée Marmottan Monet

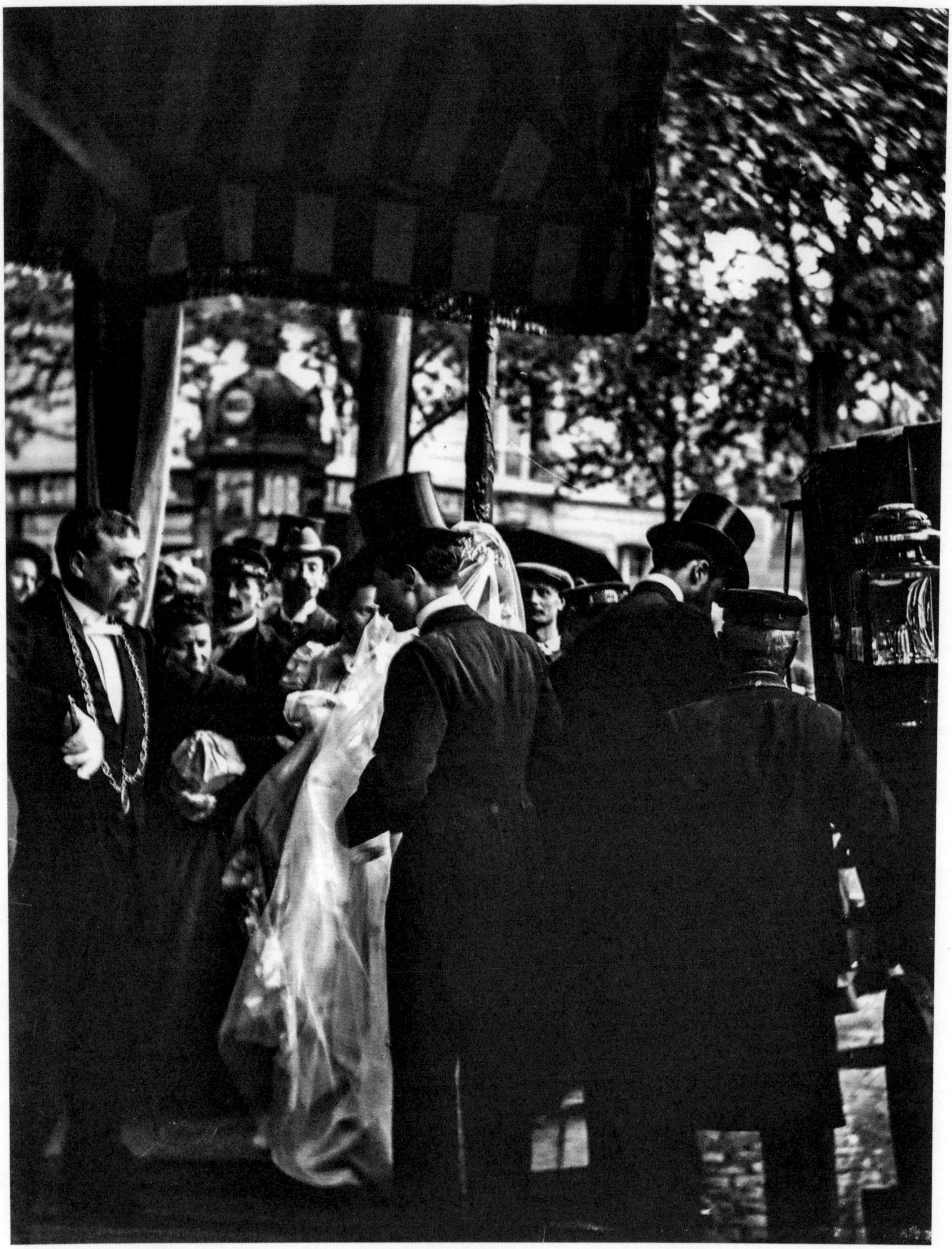

Jeannie Gobillard and Paul Valéry (center) and Ernest Rouart (back right), May 31, 1900
Archives BS, Paris, Musée Marmottan Monet

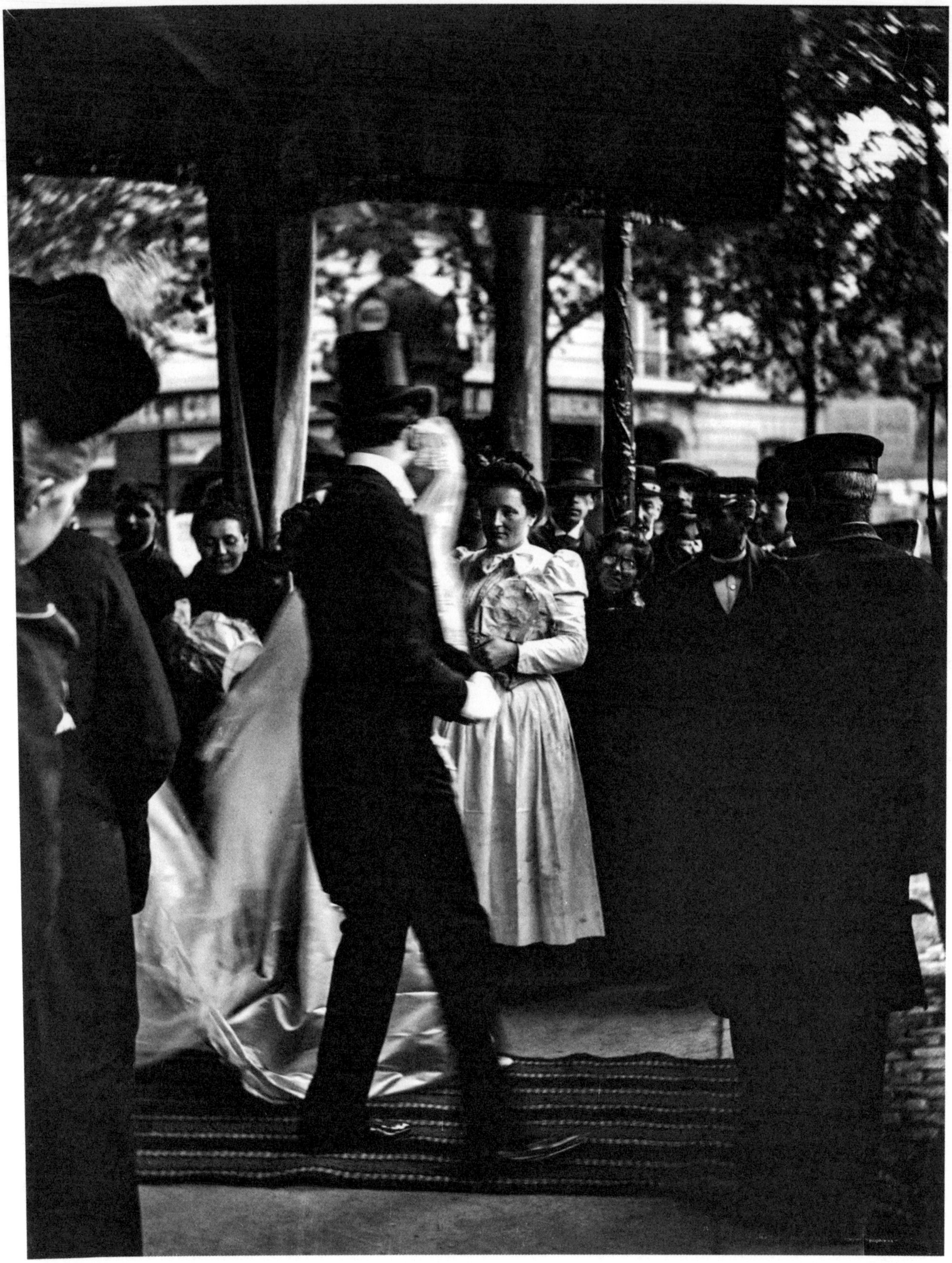

Jeannie Gobillard and Paul Valéry, May 31, 1900
Archives BS, Paris, Musée Marmottan Monet

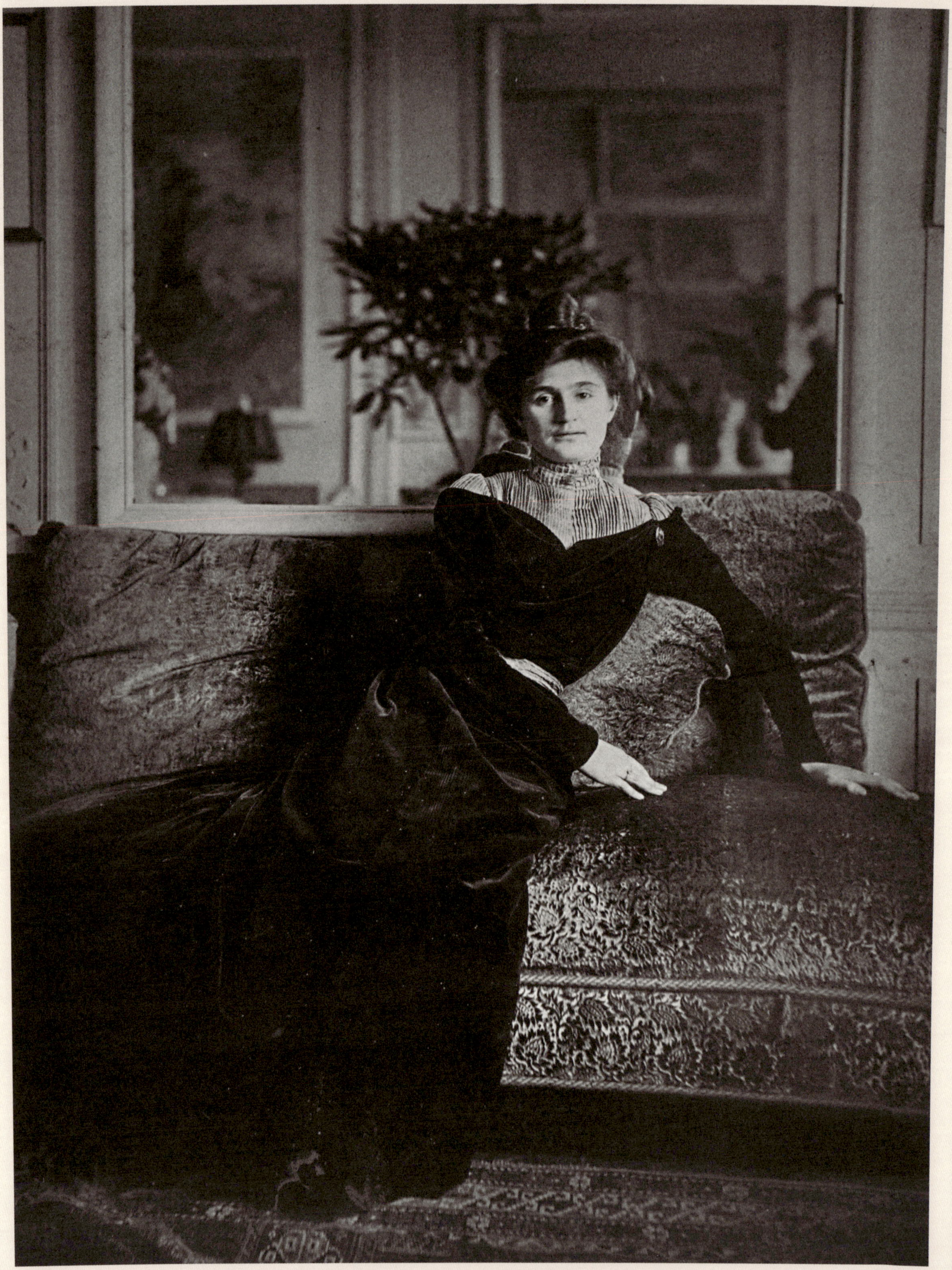

THE REMAINS OF THE DAY

1900–1911

INTERIORS

After the wedding, a new life was put in place in the rue de Villejust. It took a little time, but soon everyone was comfortably settled in. The Valérys resided temporarily at 57, avenue Victor Hugo, allowing time for Edma to vacate the third floor and find new quarters in Passy at 7, square Alboni.[521] Jeannie and Paule, as Julie had done before them, decorated the walls with family paintings, inviting the past to the table of the present. Here, a pastel of their mother by Degas, executed in 1869 (p. 165), there, portraits of Jeannie and Julie in their tenth year painted by Berthe Morisot,[522] and further along, likenesses of a young woman, Paule: their sister, their surrogate mother and their guardian angel. She is immortalized in the loveliest time of life in *Girl with a Dog*[523] and *Paule Gobillard Drawing*,[524] a pastel by her teacher. Her portrait in red chalk by Renoir (p. 91) could also be seen in a photograph that made Julie's "cousin" interior famous (right). The portrait of the Demoiselle Patronne executed by Redon in 1901[525] took pride of place in the living room, where it made a strong impression. After all, the artist sent his model a reproduction of *The Night Watch* accompanied by a simple note: "At Rembrandt's feet and your own."[526] Ernest was not best pleased and found "the business of the . . . at Rembrandt's feet . . . rather rum."[527] This reaction did not discourage the admirer; one of his finest letters to Paule begins, humorously and tenderly: "Your quasi-companion is well."[528]

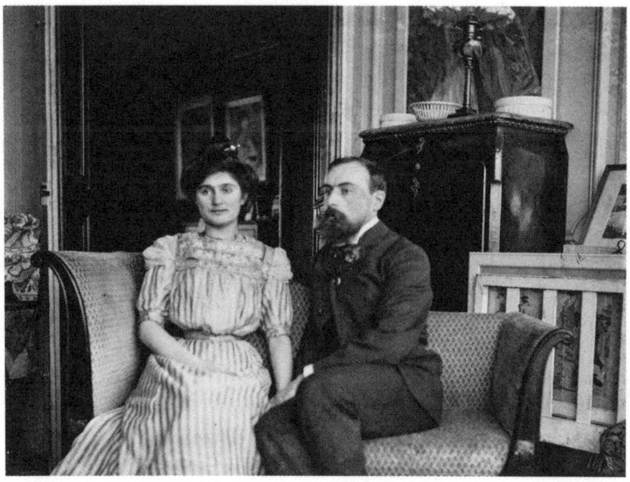

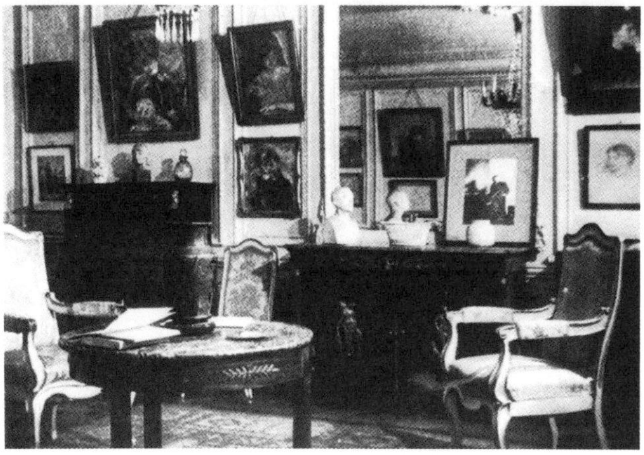

Julie Manet and Ernest Rouart rue de Villejust, c. 1900
Archives du Mesnil, on permanent loan at the Musée Marmottan Monet

Jeannie and Paul Valéry's living room on the third floor in the rue de Villejust, n.d.
Private collection

Facing page
Ernest Rouart (1874–1942)
Julie Manet rue de Villejust and Ernest Rouart (reflected in the mirror), c. 1900
Paris, Musée Marmottan Monet

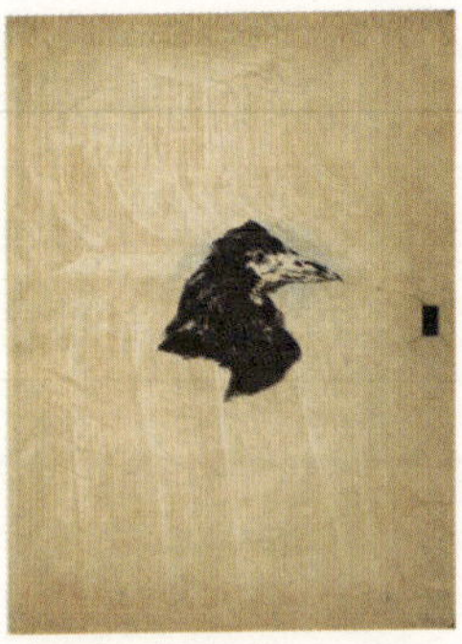

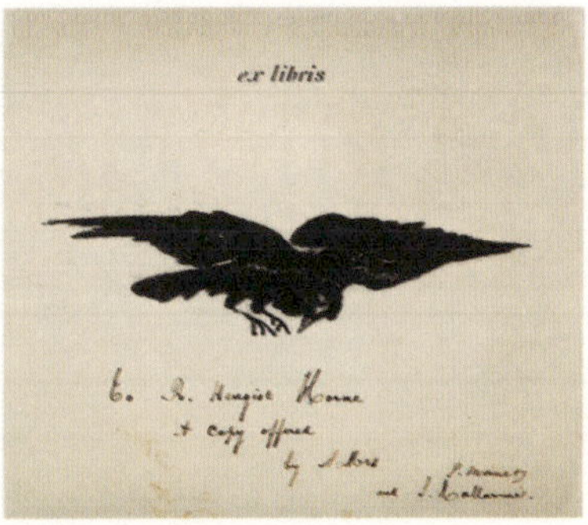

Edgar Poe, Stéphane Mallarmé (trans.), Édouard Manet (ill.),
Le Corbeau, 1875
Printed monograph, 25.7 × 29 cm (ex-libris), 55 × 35 cm (ill.)
Private collection

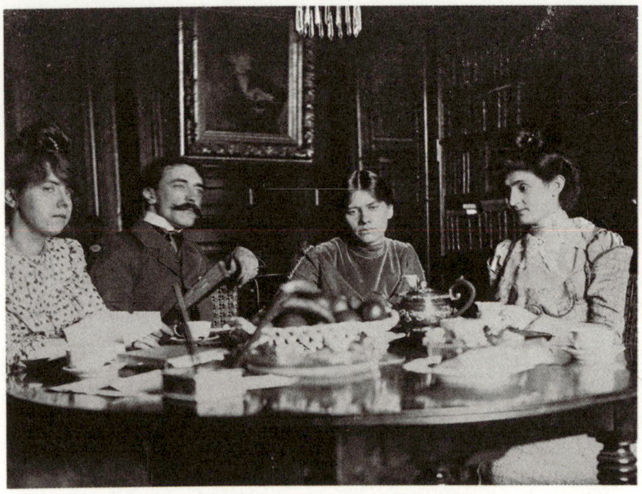

Attributed to Ernest Rouart (1874–1942)
Jeannie Gobillard, Paul Valéry, Paule Gobillard, and Julie Manet in the dining room in the rue de Villejust, c. 1900–01
Private collection

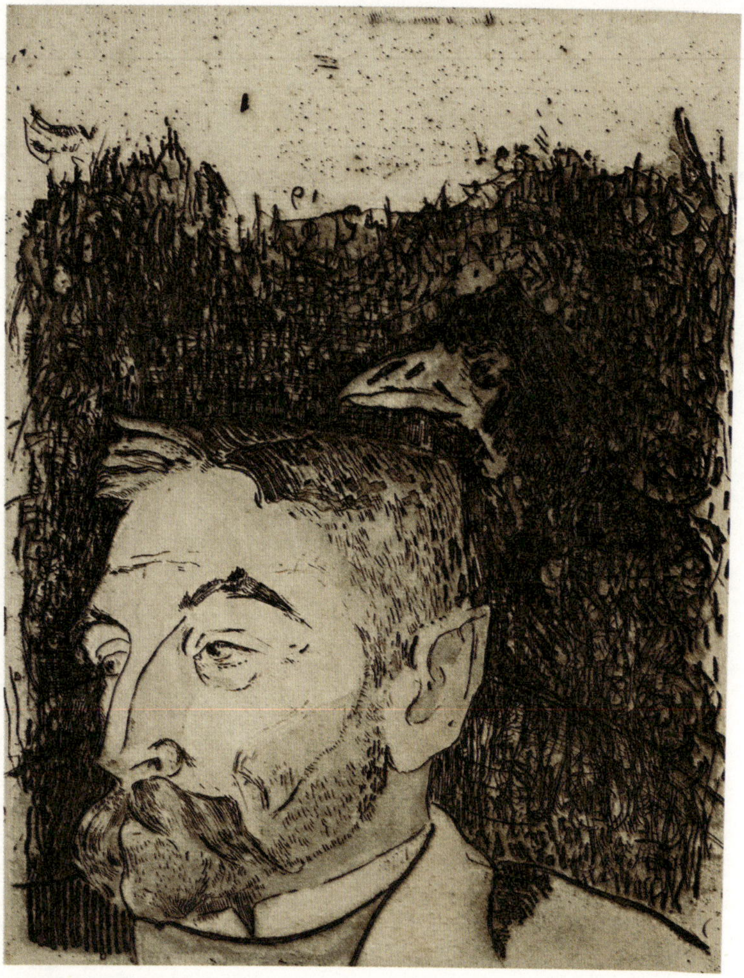

Paul Gauguin (1848–1903)
Portrait of Stéphane Mallarmé "with the Raven," 1891, print from 1919
Etching, 18.4 × 14.4 cm
Private collection

This evocation of the fourth floor would not be complete without the tutelary figure of Mallarmé. In the evening of his life, Valéry would pose next to the photograph of himself with Renoir and Mallarmé, captured on the floor above (the same image was kept by Julie and Ernest Rouart). It was given to him by the photographer, Degas.[529] For a long time, Mallarmé's translation of *The Raven* by Edgar Allan Poe (above), with illustrations by Manet,[530] stood on the piano, like the poetic materialization of a filiation with numerous branches, colored by the bonds of blood and spiritual heritage.

The apartment on the fifth floor was already well equipped, although this did not dispense Ernest from making improvements. He had a library delivered and suggested that a large table be removed—nothing very major.[531] The big question was Le Mesnil:

The property is delightful, it is droll, this low little château against those big chestnut trees of the terrace, that old courtyard, that pigeon loft, the kitchen garden—all that is very French. In this wonderful weather the ensemble exudes a charm that makes you want to stop and spend a few moments of your life musing here. What fun it would be do up the interior of Mesnil, one could do such pretty things. When could I live there?[532]

As soon as they were betrothed, Julie took Ernest on a reconnaissance trip to Gargenville.[533] She was living her dream: Le Mesnil became her home. She would always refuse to let it, not even to Raoul Pugno, Jeannie's mentor.[534] The renovation of this old manor in brick and white stone with slate roof would be the focus of all the couple's

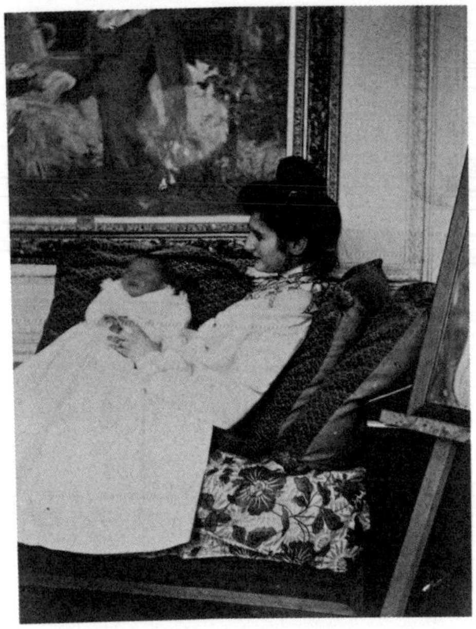

Attributed to Ernest Rouart (1874–1942)
Julie Manet-Rouart and her son Julien in the rue de Villejust, c. 1901
Paris, Musée Marmottan Monet

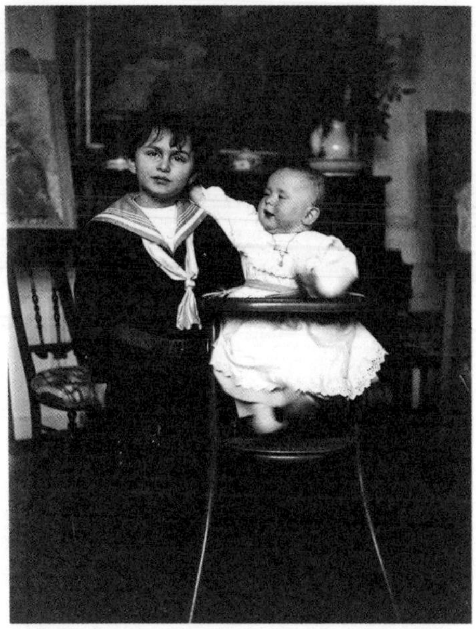

Julie Manet (1878–1966) or Ernest Rouart (1874–1942)
Julien Rouart and her brother Clément rue de Villejust, c. 1906
Archives du Mesnil, on permanent loan at the Musée Marmottan Monet

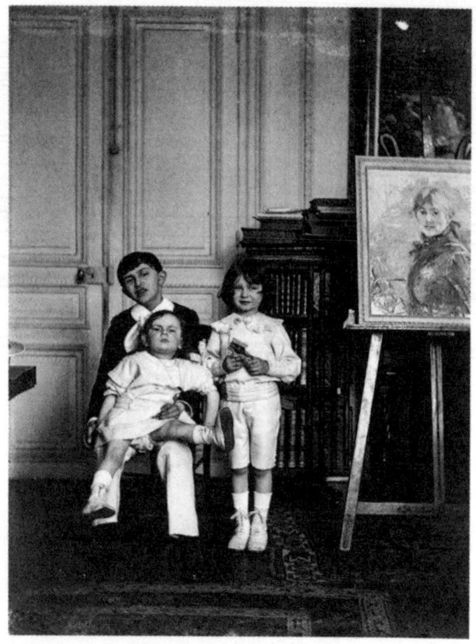

Julie Manet (1878–1966) or Ernest Rouart (1874–1942)
Julien, Clément, and Denis Rouart in the rue de Villejust, c. 1910
Archives du Mesnil, on permanent loan at the Musée Marmottan Monet

efforts. Henri Rouart was alarmed at the scale of the work (although we have no document to determine what this meant). As he wrote, "Your transformations are truly frightening, but as long as it makes you happy, I can say nothing."[535]

On the first floor were the living room, dining room, and studies that Ernest set out to decorate. These were communal rooms. On the upper floor were six bedrooms and several bathrooms. In her survey of the place Julie made an inventory of the furniture.[536] Her bedroom, which she would soon fit out on the first floor, was Empire throughout, with a bed, a full-length mirror, a commode decorated with copper, a console, a mahogany knitting machine, a chaise longue and two chairs upholstered in brocaded silk, two armchairs in cut silk, a big old-rose carpet, a little candle and two copper candlesticks. The only things missing from this list are the artworks, which came and went according to circumstances, not only wars but also the arrival of fresh works—because at Le Mesnil people painted!

MOTHERHOOD

The manor really came into its own with the birth of the children, which was not long coming. The first of the young Rouarts, Henri Julien Eugène, came into the world on March 24, 1901.[537] Degas sent his congratulations without delay: "Here is a new Ernest in the line. My love to the farouche Julie and to yourself."[538] Renoir did likewise: "My dear Julie, Paule was kind enough to tell us the great news that the trumpet of fame had indeed already brought us."[539]

Two others followed soon afterwards: Clément Alexis was born on January 31, 1906 (above).[540] Renoir wrote:

> **We were a little worried about the delay in this event. Indeed, because of this delay my wife announced a boy. We are therefore very happy to know that in spite of the difficult moments it has ended in joy all around. We congratulate the mother and hope that it may continue. One more.[541] We now await the others.[542]**

Their third and last son, Denis Charles Ernest, was born on October 17, 1908.[543] Faithful as ever, Renoir responded: "All our compliments to Julie."[544] Paul Valéry witnessed the birth certificate of each of the three children, describing himself as a *rédacteur* at the Ministry of War in 1901, then, having moved into the private sector—he was now private secretary of the founder of Havas, André Lebey—as a man of letters.

Jeannie, too, became a mother during these same years. Yves Claude François, her older son, was born on August 14, 1903,[545] while Agathe Anne Julie Paule was the quasi-twin of Clément by virtue of her birth on March 7, 1906.[546] Only François Marie Antoine was born in another period of both family and political life: on July 17, 1916.[547]

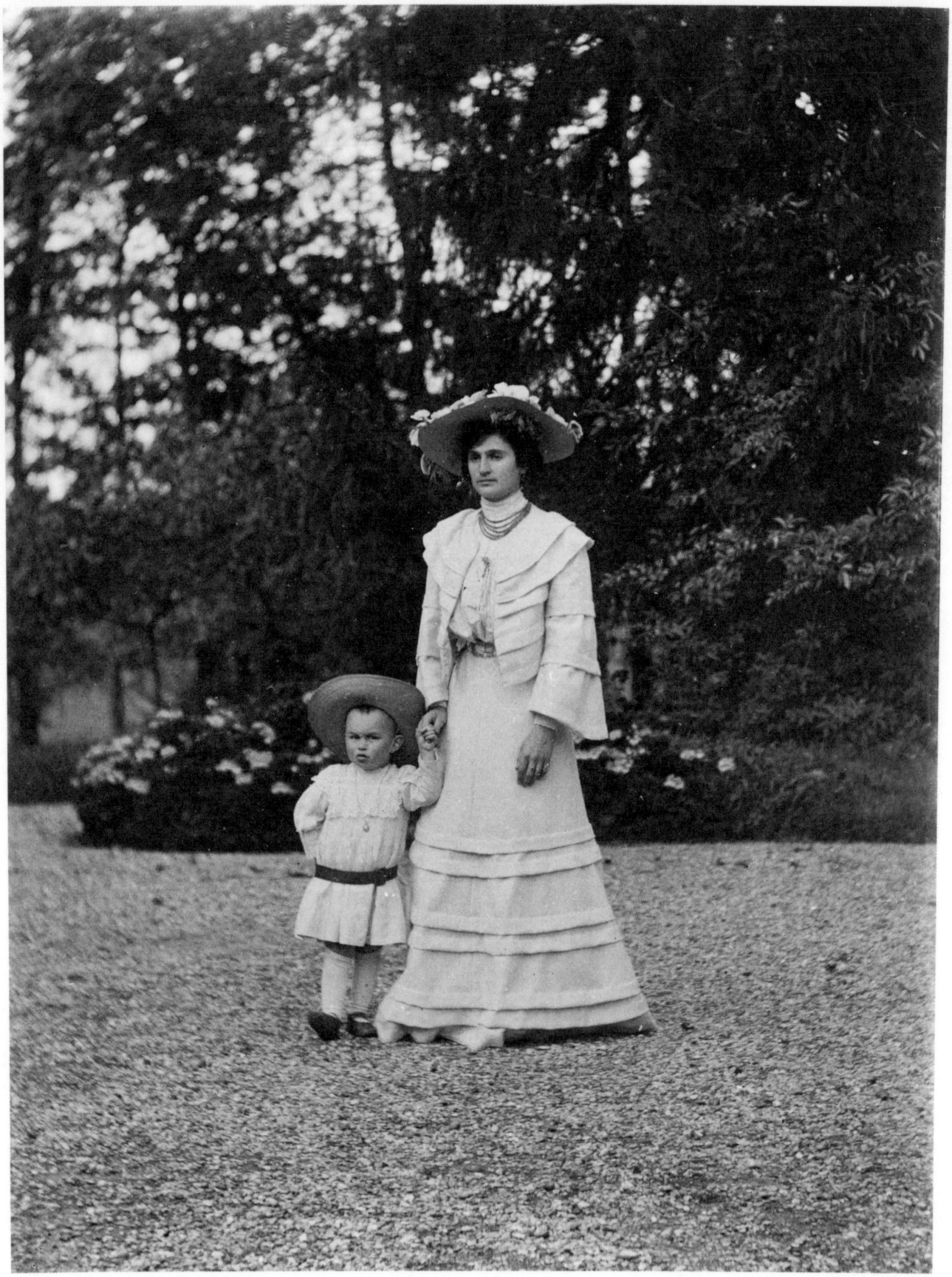

Attributed to Ernest Rouart (1874–1942)
Julie Manet-Rouart and her son Julien, c. 1902–03
Archives BS, Paris, Musée Marmottan Monet

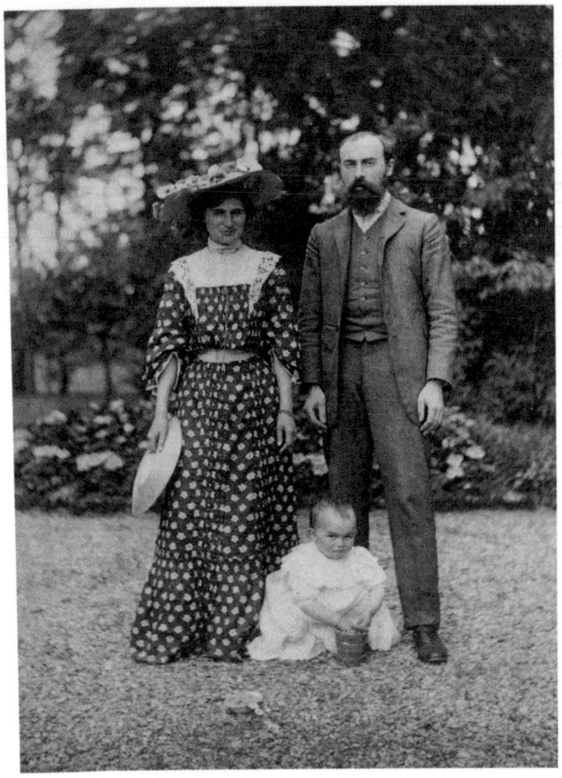

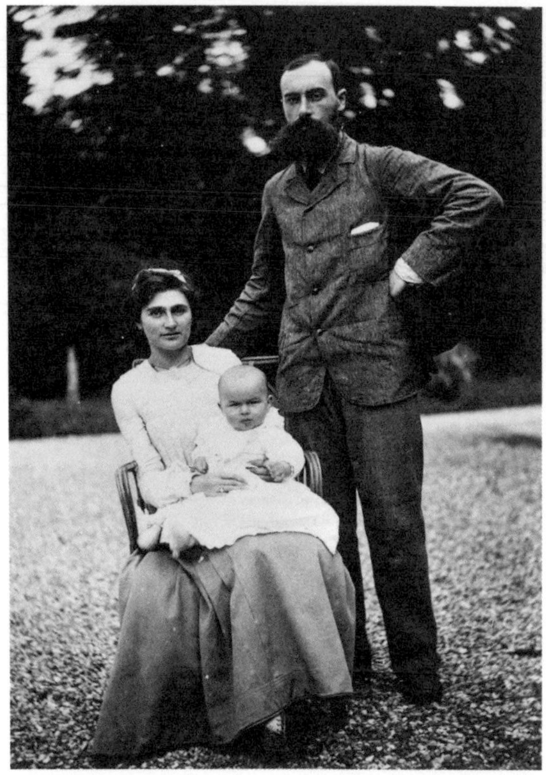

Julie Manet-Rouart, Ernest Rouart, and their son Julien, c. 1902
Paris, Musée Marmottan Monet

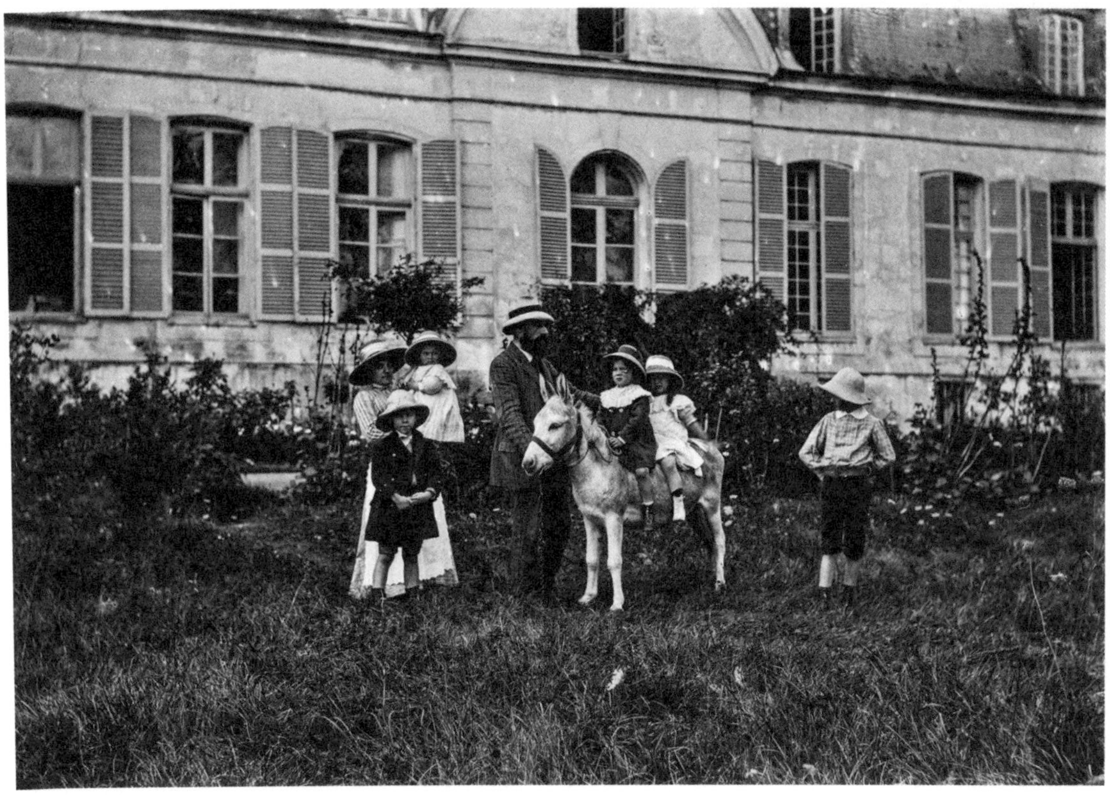

At Le Mesnil, Ernest Rouart with his children and nephews, n.d.
Archives BS, Paris, Musée Marmottan Monet

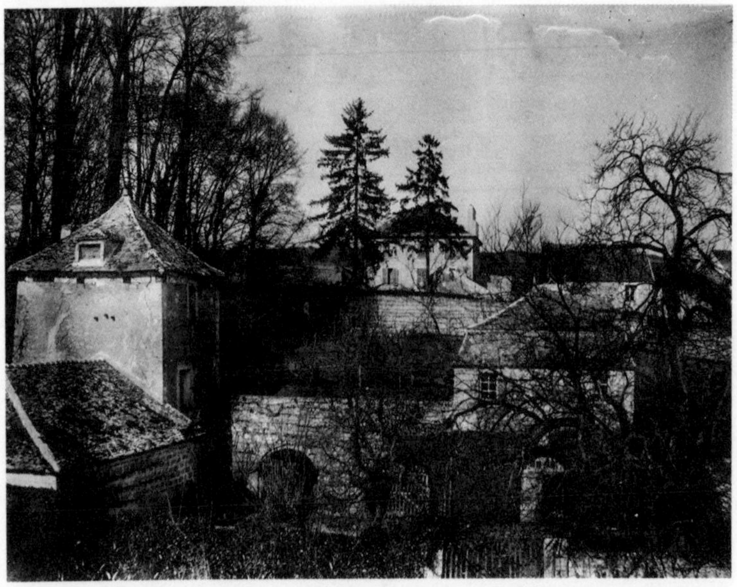

Le Mesnil, view of the dovecote, n.d.
Archives BS, Paris, Musée Marmottan Monet

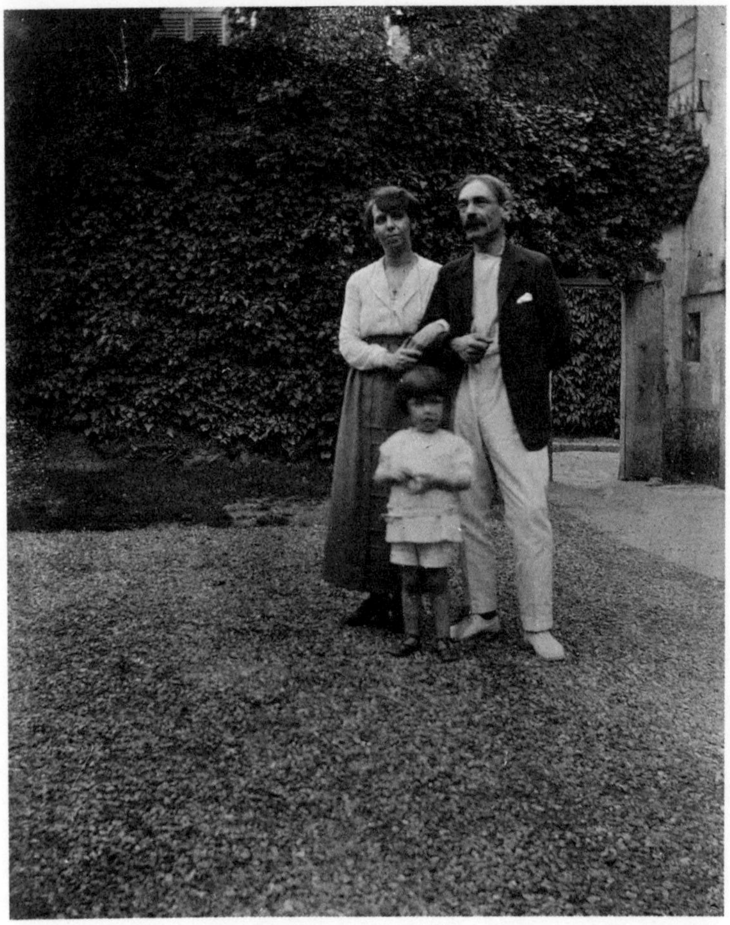

Jeannie Gobillard-Valéry, Paul Valéry, and their son Claude at Le Mesnil, c. 1905
Archives BS, Paris, Musée Marmottan Monet

The following year Paul Valéry published *La Jeune Parque* and entered the firmament of French poets.

Like the rue de Villejust, Le Mesnil was a family home where the sister-cousins and their kin were welcome. Julie was soon dividing her time between Paris and Juziers, where she spent all the summers, allowing her boys to enjoy fresh air and freedom of movement. This was her choice.

And so, after years of freedom, Julie and Jeannie followed the conformist example of their aunt, Edma, who, after her wedding, abandoned her aspirations. Exit Berthe's determination. The two cousins stood back and offered themselves entirely to their husbands and their children. They were wives and mothers. Jeannie gave up her life's dream of entering the Conservatoire and only opened her piano when she felt she had the right: since Valéry worked doggedly away in his study in the rue de Villejust, silence was effectively de rigueur. Julie became the kind of young woman who paints lampshades, the kind she had already described in her diary. But without bitterness; out of choice. She decorated the crockery at Le Mesnil (p. 177), and not without talent. Always holding a brush, she never stopped painting but pursued her practice as an enlightened amateur. She did not view it with her mother's rigor, but more with the modesty of her father-in-law, Henri Rouart, who henceforth signed his letters "Ton père ami."[548] "I hope you are able to work a little. It is such fun."[549] By copying, sometimes pastiching her mother's work, she preserved the connection. To make her own *œuvre* would, on the contrary, be to risk becoming detached from her, orchestrating a second, symbolic death. Julie thus renounced the chance to enter the world of serious artists, without being asked. She said goodbye to hypothetical success, to a possible career. She stopped exhibiting at the Salons, maintained her mother in the firmament of her admiration and left the field to Ernest, a professional painter. Julie kept to the shadows.

This was the tacit contract around which the first years of M. and Mme Ernest Rouart were organized. It was the period when Ernest exhibited most frequently. He was at the Salon de la Société Nationale des Beaux-Arts in 1899 and returned in 1903, 1906, and 1907.[550] In 1908 he featured in the Salon de l'Union Artistique in Toulouse.[551] But it was at the Indépendants that he appeared most regularly, every year from 1903 to 1911. When his wife was far away, Ernest complained: "I can only really find pleasure in my studio. I do not want shows or amusements, even less than usual. What I need is a home where I can sit myself down after working."[552]

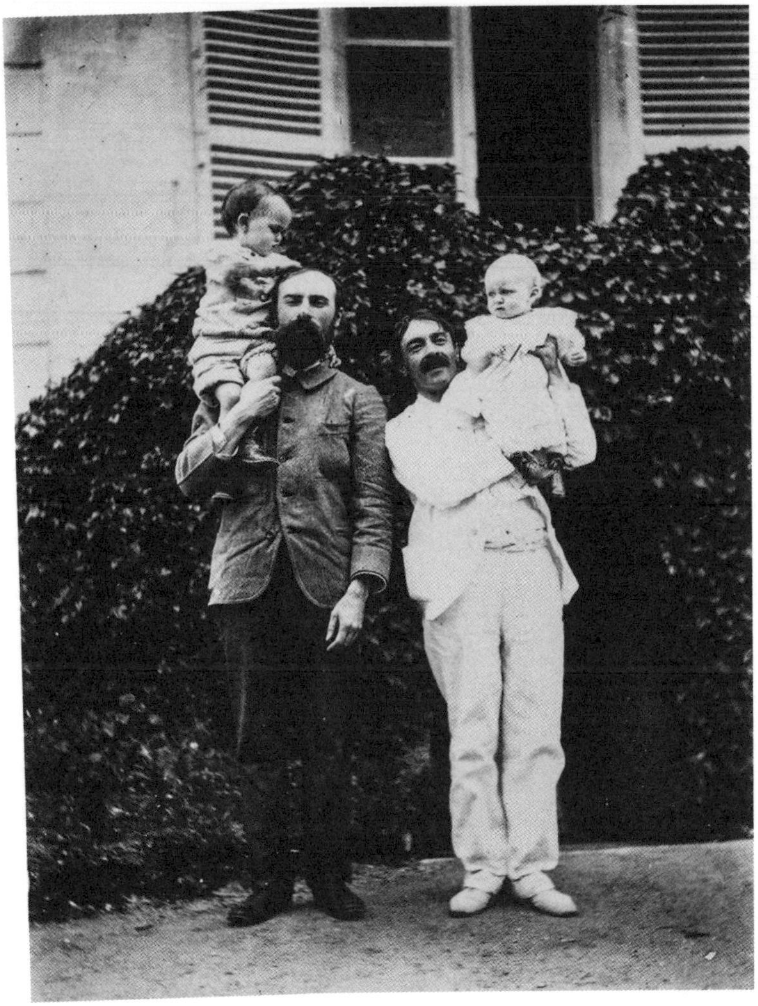

Attributed to Julie Manet (1878–1966)
Ernest Rouart and his son Julien, Paul Valéry and his son Claude, at Le Mesnil, c. 1904
Archives BS, Paris, Musée Marmottan Monet

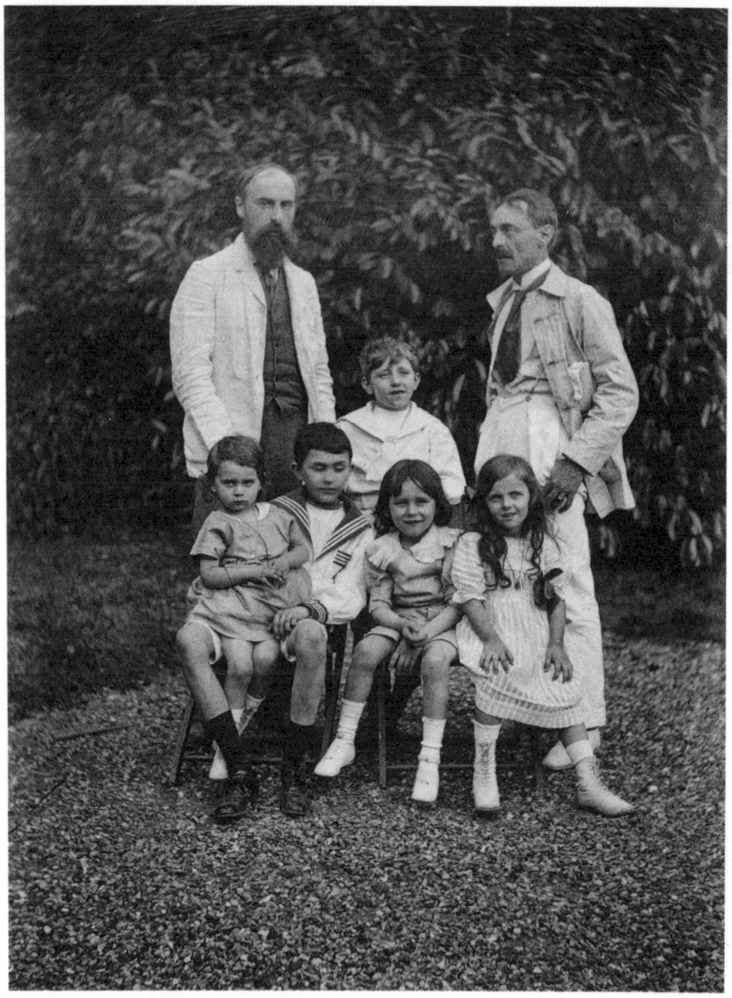

Attributed to Julie Manet (1878–1966)
Ernest Rouart, Paul Valéry and their children, c. 1910
Archives BS, Paris, Musée Marmottan Monet

As one might expect, the couple's correspondence is punctuated with talk about art. Ernest writes:

> Today I went with Louis to see the Gustave Moreaus[553] but I cannot tell you anything about it except that at the end I had it up to here and that I did not see it all, because there is so much. It is deadening, you come out of it without the memory of a single painting, a composition, or even a handsome form, a fine piece. And yet there are a few copies that he made in Italy that are very fine: one after Poussin and others after Carpaccio, Titian, etc.[554]

Ernest's passion for the art of the great masters gave form to his daily life. "This afternoon I went to the Louvre to see the Antiques, not the paintings. I am waiting for you to do that."[555] He took this opportunity to revive their debate over the primacy of the female nude:

> I was looking for a few ideas for draperies for pagan themes. I didn't find much of what I was looking for, but I did recognize once again that truth which you deny: that man is at least as beautiful as woman.... In any case, I affirm that one can do things that are just as beautiful with male nudes as with female nudes: the Greeks, Poussin, and Gauguin are proof of that. What do you have to say to this collection of names?[556]

Berthe, why did you never paint men? In addition to his assiduous frequentation of the Louvre and of museums in general, Ernest was stimulated daily by the presence of Degas—whom he met both in the rue de Lisbonne and the rue Victor Massé. Like his master, he seemed to want to pierce the secrets of the ancients, favoring a technical and practical approach to art, to the detriment of his own inventiveness. He was fired by the artists he admired,

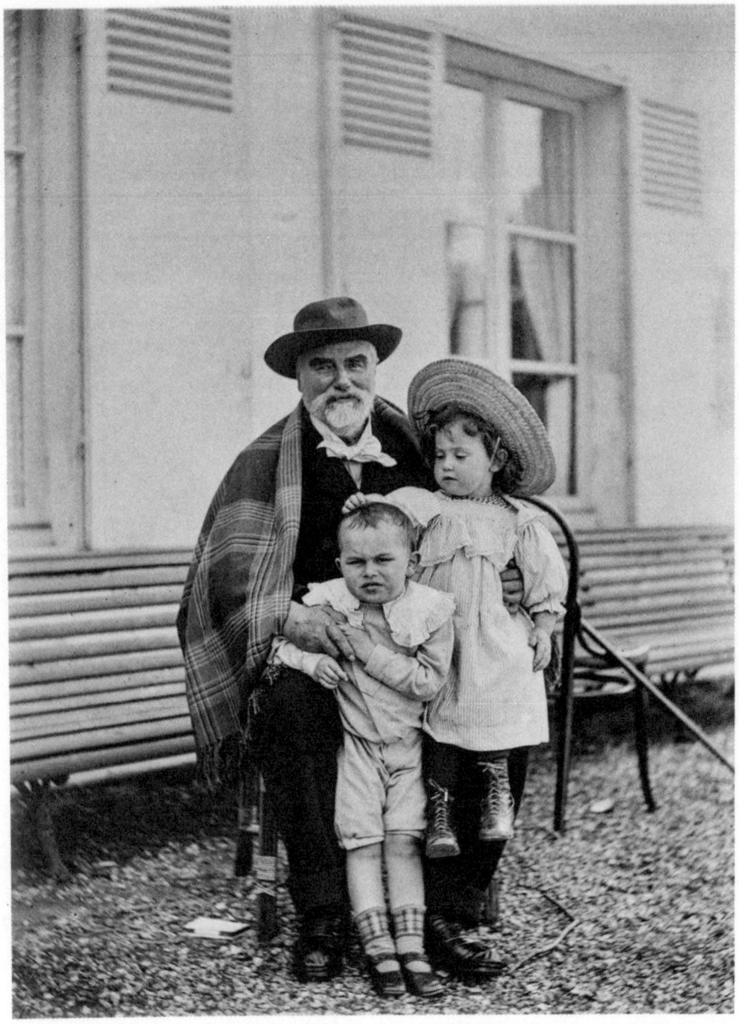

Attributed to Julie Manet (1878–1966)
Henri Rouart and his grandchildren Julien and Hélène at La Queue-en-Brie, c. 1902–04
Archives BS, Paris, Musée Marmottan Monet

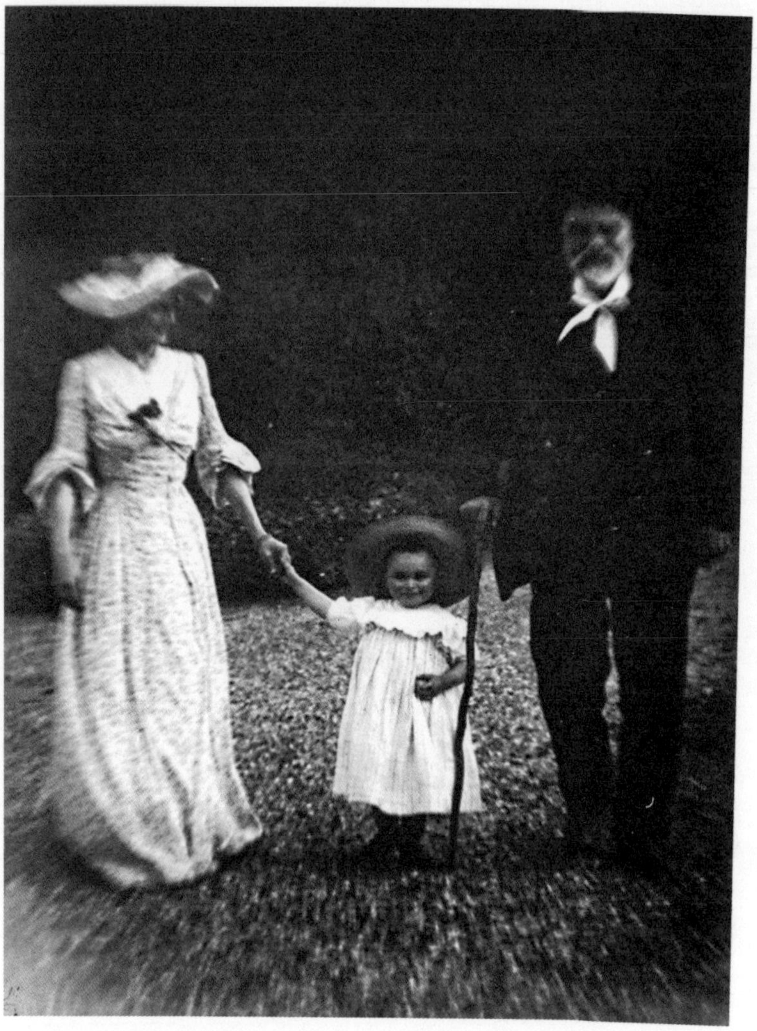

Julie Manet-Rouart, Julien Rouart, and Henri Rouart at La Queue-en-Brie, c. 1902–04
Paris, Musée Marmottan Monet

muting his own creativity. In this respect, like Julie, he retreated into the background, staying in the shadow of the greats. His aspirations were conventional, even backward-looking, since Ernest's ambition was to produce works worthy of the Salon. That at least is what his words suggest: "I have a lot of subjects for paintings in mind but I have to limit myself to the ones I can execute properly on a large scale."[557]

Because Ernest's studio was housed in the Rouart mansion, the painter divided his everyday life between the rues de Villejust and de Lisbonne, in a coming and going between his father and his wife, which seemed enough to make him happy.

In addition to the impromptu lunches around the patriarch, the Rouarts met *en famille* on Friday evenings. Otherwise, each had their day. The ever-present Claire Fontaine, a distant relation who had become Henri Rouart's live-in companion, lived in the house.

His uncle Alexis, Henri's brother, was often present. The family of the late Mme Henri Rouart was among the regulars. Its members were his niece, Thérèse or "Aunt Lefuel" to her relations, her husband Henri and their children Yvonne and Hector,[558] the future director of the Musée Marmottan. Degas, who was loved as a brother or father, depending, was one of the permanent guests.[559] Henri's children and children-in-law were the most eagerly awaited. Ernest and Julie were faithful visitors. As Julien, their oldest child recalled:

> When my parents went round to see Henri Rouart, I would go down to the lower floor to the Valérys where

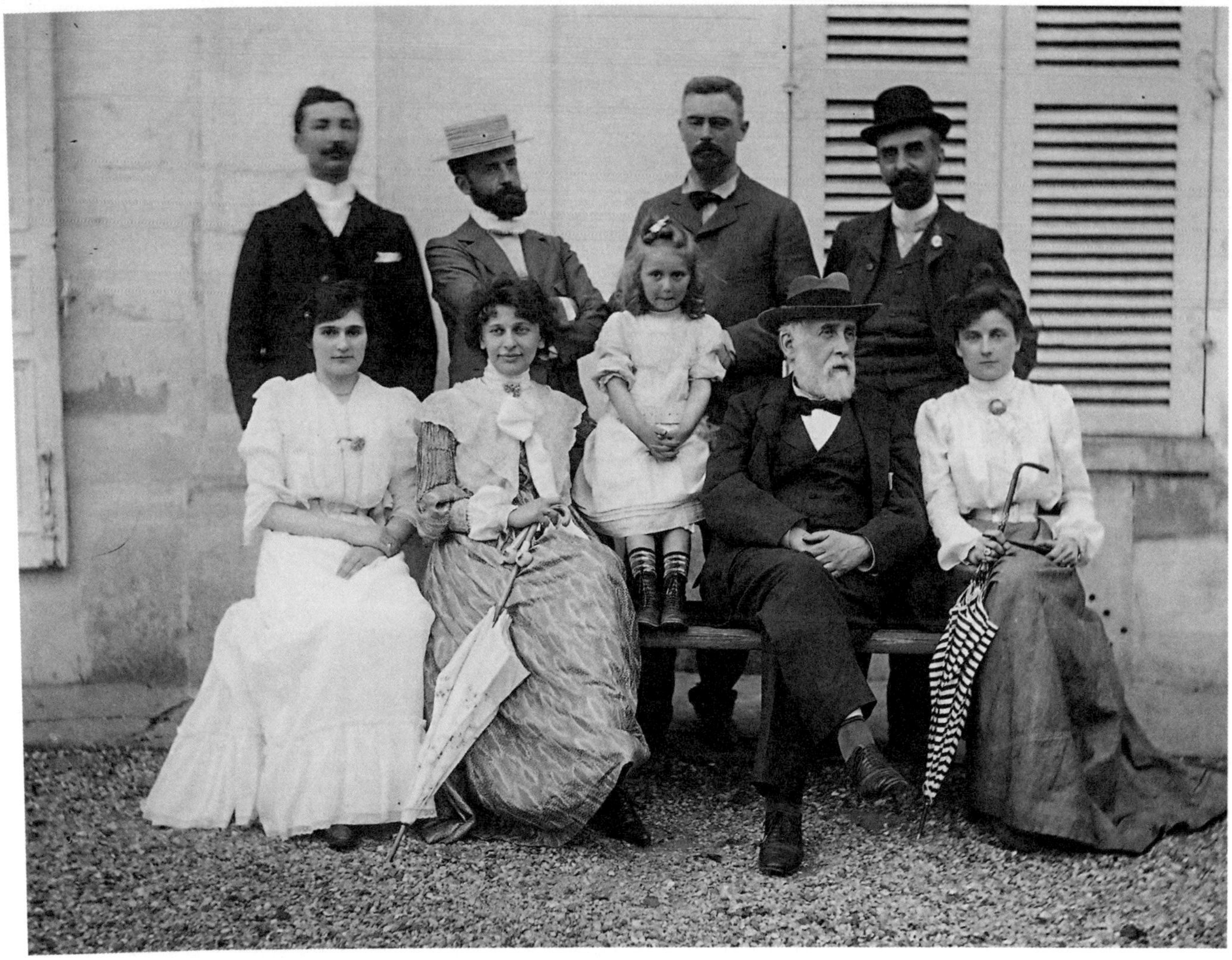

Ernest Rouart (1874-1942)
From top to bottom and from left to right: *M. de Saint-Maurice, Pierre Lalo, Paul Poujaud, Alexis Rouart, Julie Manet-Rouart, Valentine Lamour-Rouart, Madeleine Rouart, Edgar Degas and Mme de Saint-Maurice, at La Queue-en-Brie*, June 1900
Paris, Musée Marmottan Monet

I found Paul Valéry, his wife Jeannie Valéry, Paule Gobillard, Claude, and Agathe. Paul Valéry told stories, it could just as well be bits from the *Thousand and One Nights* as any old thing that he made up as he went along.[560] It was like a kind of feuilleton.

The other Parisians in the family met in the rue de Lisbonne: there was the oldest of the Rouart sons, Alexis, and his wife Valentine Lamour, as well as Louis and Christine Lerolle, whom he had married in February 1901. The years 1900–1901 witnessed the fusion of the Lerolle-Escudier-Rouart and Manet-Rouart-Valéry clans. The première of *Pelléas et Mélisande*, the opera composed by Claude Debussy after a work by Maurice Maeterlinck, which was performed on April 30, 1902 at the Opéra Comique, brought together nearly all the members of this tentacular tribe. There were those who had supported the composer through the development of his art: Henry Lerolle and his wife Madeleine Escudier-Lerolle, Jeanne Escudier-Chausson, widow of the composer Ernest Chausson, who had been so close to Debussy. Arthur Fontaine and Marie Escudier-Fontaine were of course at their side. And also seen were Ernest Rouart and Julie Manet-Rouart, Paul Valéry and Jeannie Gobillard-Valéry, Alexis Rouart and Valentine Lamour-Rouart, and no doubt Louis Rouart and Christine Lerolle-Rouart, Pierre Louÿs, who had introduced Debussy to Maeterlinck, and André Gide. To Eugène and Yvonne—whose beauty inspired the character of Mélisande—the latter wrote: "I saw all your people, which made me feel your absence even more."[561]

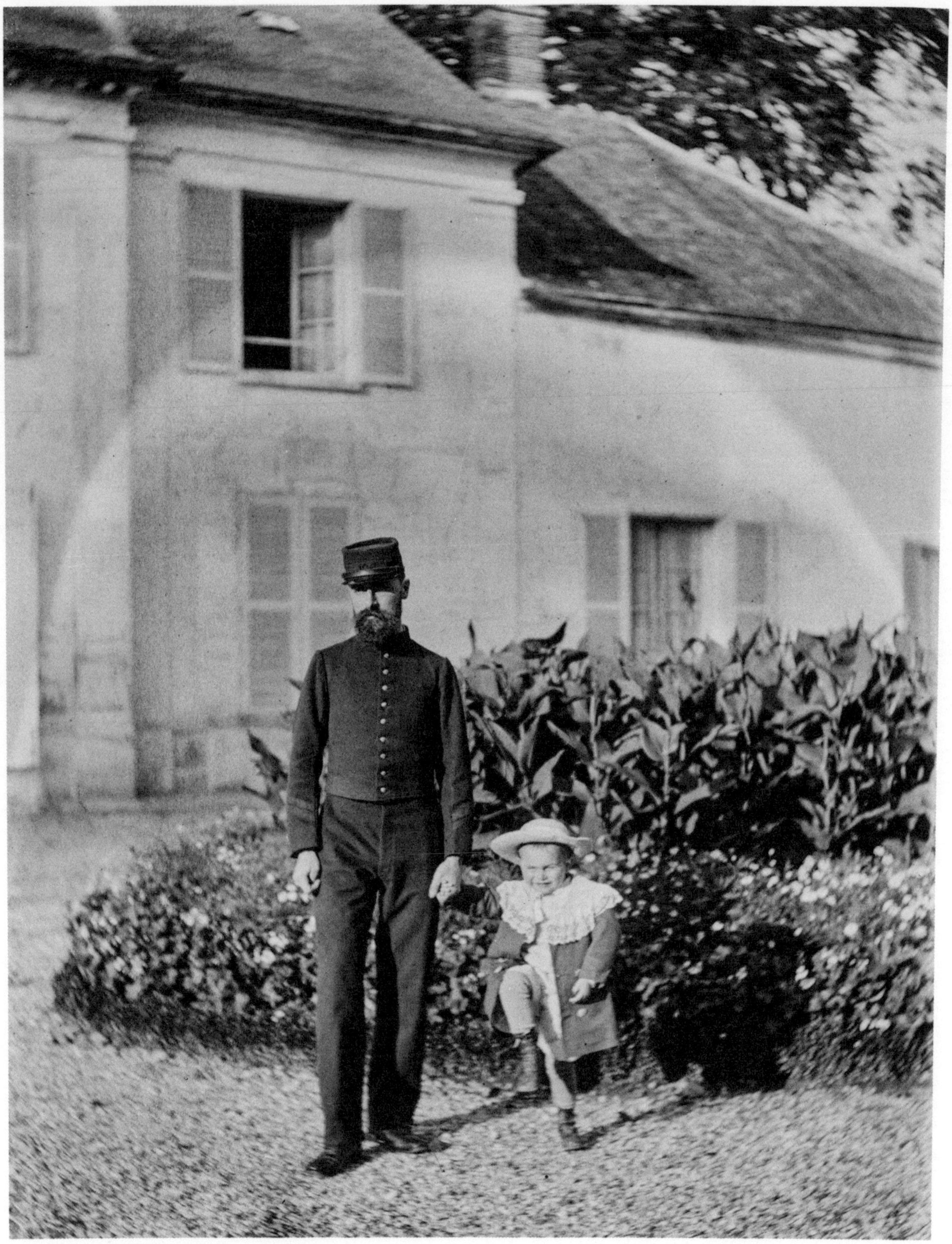

Attributed to Julie Manet (1878–1966)
Ernest Rouart in uniform and his son Julien, 1904
Archives du Mesnil, on permanent loan at the Musée Marmottan Monet

Being a muse does not necessarily give you a right to happiness.[562]

The Rouart family joined together for great occasions. In an unpublished interview, Julien Rouart recalls his childhood memories:

> At my grandfather's house there was a kind of respect for hierarchy, you could say. He really was the *pater familias*. . . . They made my grandfather into a slightly Olympian figure. He leaves me with the memory of a man whom I held in awe.

This was the case at major receptions, for example:

> Among the solemn occasions . . . January 1 every year: we went to see him and we took turns to come in front of him; he gave us our gift and Claire Fontaine, the live-in companion, introduced us: *this is Julien*, and he was given a toolbox. This is . . .

Above all, they went to visit Henri Rouart at his property in La Queue-en-Brie (p. 84 and 85).

> I went to see him in La Queue-en-Brie with my parents, generally in late fall, having spent most of the summer at Le Mesnil. . . . The main thing was the family atmosphere. The Alexis-Rouarts and the Louis-Rouart spent a large part of their summer holidays there, I believe. . . . The atmosphere was stuffy, rather ceremonious, I had the impression I was entering quite a solemn world. Henri Rouart was rather remote and distant for us grandchildren. He was quite intimidating and we didn't have the impression that we could speak to him directly.

After dinner—and if the patriarch did not suffer an attack of gout: "People gathered in front of the house to go and walk around the park. He would set off with daughters-in-law beside him, his sons, and then we grandchildren, we followed behind. It really was a kind of court."[563] We know the photographs of Degas posing on the property of his childhood friend like a member of the family (p. 85). But while it is true that he dropped in, it was always fleetingly. From La Queue-en-Brie, Henri Rouart wrote: "Yesterday I received a visit from my brother and Degas, who had had his arm twisted to come along, it being such a long time that he'd seen any fresh air he was all gray."[564] Julien confirms: "Degas went, but I don't think I saw him. I know that he did not stay very long. He came and he left. He hated the countryside, and he said so." Nor, it seems, did he have much time for children:

> At the time, he was fairly deaf. He got irritable when you talked to him and he couldn't hear properly. Whenever he came to the house he would ask, "How old is he? . . . And him?" He didn't seem to take an interest in the children, and I even believe that the children irritated him. Clément, who was more boisterous than the others, wanted to show Degas something, I cannot remember what, a little statuette he was holding or something, and in doing that he annoyed Degas who took his hand and twisted it. Clément who was, I think, one of the only ones to approach Degas like that, held a grudge after that.[565]

No surprises there.

THE WAY OF THE LORD

In 1904–05 the three Rouart brothers, Louis, Alexis, and Ernest, began to grow closer. Alexis, who had just founded his musical publishing house, A. Rouart,[566] asked Ernest to decorate a score by Aman Comès inspired by a poem by Valio, *Inconstance!*[567] As Julie wrote to inform Ernest when he was doing his twenty-eight days of military service[568] in October 1904 (p. 86): "*Inconstance* has come out. Paul Valéry brought a copy back from Alexis's place yesterday. You are quite extraordinary to have put my face on such a song."[569]

For his part, Louis, whose writerly qualities have been frequently emphasized,[570] embarked on a literary and artistic career, putting his name to the first articles about the work of Berthe Morisot. The exhibition put on at Galerie Druet in February 1905 led to a first paper, published in the journal *L'Occident*[571] under the pseudonym Georges Dralin.[572] In 1907, he published another text in response to the artist's major retrospective at the Salon d'Automne in *Art et Décoration*, "Berthe Morisot (Mme Eugène Manet) 1841–1895."[573] In this way he was helping to obtain posthumous recognition for the work of an artist who, in the early twentieth century, was in sore need of it, as can be seen from the letter sent by the president of the committee to rue de Villejust[574] to thank the family for lending three paintings by "Monsieur Morissot" [*sic*] to the Franco-British exhibition organized in London the following year.[575]

But the brothers' growing closeness did not end there and was most fully expressed in their shared commitment to a brand of Catholic patriotism, initially anti-Dreyfusard and then exacerbated by the law separating Church and state in 1905. The brothers were involved in this movement that culminated in the birth of the "Catholic intellectual," one aim

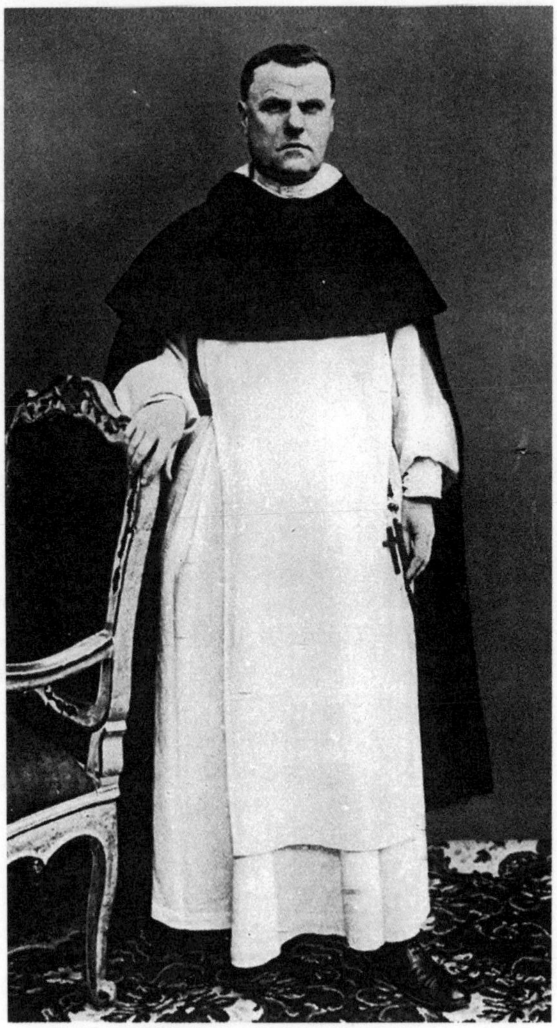

Père Janvier at the time of the conferences at Notre-Dame

of which was to combine spiritual power and social action.[576] Dominicans played a key role in all this, foremost among them Henri Lacordaire (1802–1861), who modernized the order. As the most brilliant preacher at Notre-Dame, his pulpit was specially raised for his Lenten Conferences, helping him to embody theology at its most brilliant and modern. Lacordaire contributed to the emergence of a liberal Catholicism. His successor at Notre-Dame, Père Janvier (above), was more conservative and remained close to Action Française until the movement was condemned by the pope in 1926. He brought artists and intellectuals together in favor of a lay Catholicism. He began to frequent the Rouarts in 1906[577] and invited Louis and Ernest to his conferences in 1907. Louis took him as his confessor,[578] while Ernest sought regular audiences[579] and even introduced him to Valéry, who was interested in everything but no believer.

> **Father, I intend to come and see you on Easter Tuesday at about half past two with my cousin Paul Valéry whom I mentioned to you the other day.[580]**

Finally, Henri Rouart himself invited Père Janvier to dine at the rue de Lisbonne on Thursday May 21, 1908, on the occasion of one of his granddaughters' profession of faith.[581]

Alongside Père Janvier, Louis, Alexis, and Ernest worked to revive the Dominican Third Order. This originally emerged in the thirteenth century as the secular branch of religious congregations. One of its most illustrious figures was Saint Catherine of Siena (1347–1380). With the closing down of unauthorized congregations required by the separation of Church and state, the restoration of the Third Order was particularly significant. Père Janvier later recalled the circumstances:

> **In 1910, when the governments of M. Waldeck-Rousseau and M. Combes had expelled us from our houses and scattered us around the city of Paris, a young man asked me to establish a Third Order for the male sex.[582]**

He founded the Brotherhood of the Holy Sacrament of the Third Order of Penance of Saint Dominic.

> **The first assembly was held in the little room that served as my oratory, on the sixth floor in rue Mirabeau, no. 17, in Auteuil. Eight young men received the habit.[583]**

Consisting of a white tunic, a leather belt, and a scapular, this habit was worn only twice: for the vesture, on which occasion it was blessed, and, if the brother requested it, at his funeral. On that evening the brothers chose their religious names: Ernest would be Frère Antonin, Alexis would be Frère Vincent Ferrier, and Louis would be Frère Thomas d'Aquin.[584] Gabriel Thomas joined them in 1912; becoming Frère Pie.[585] By mid-1914, the Third Order united forty believers. Several family members would occupy the position of prior, notably Alexis, who assembled the community in the 8th arrondissement:

> **He organized for the members of the Brotherhood a welcome full of affection. At the meeting he held in his father's handsome mansion in the rue de Lisbonne, we chanted vespers and complines, then we spoke open-heartedly about how to instill ever more elan into our religious group.[586]**

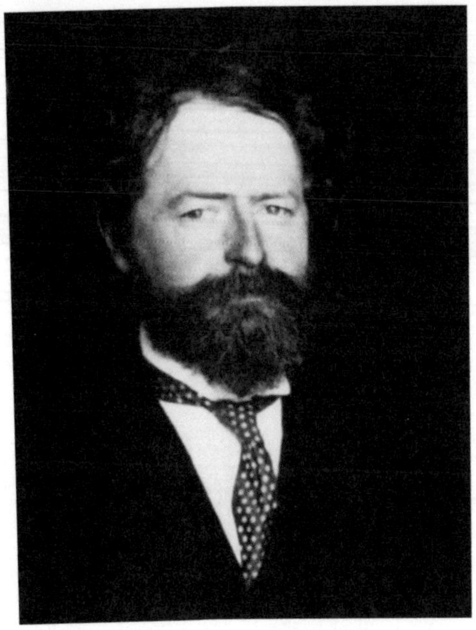

Louis Rouart

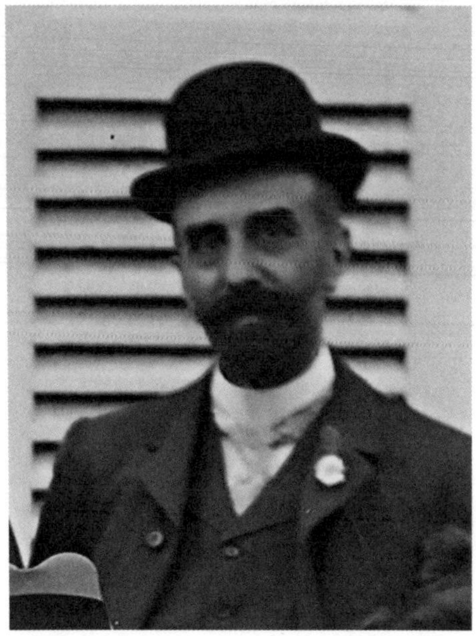

Alexis Rouart

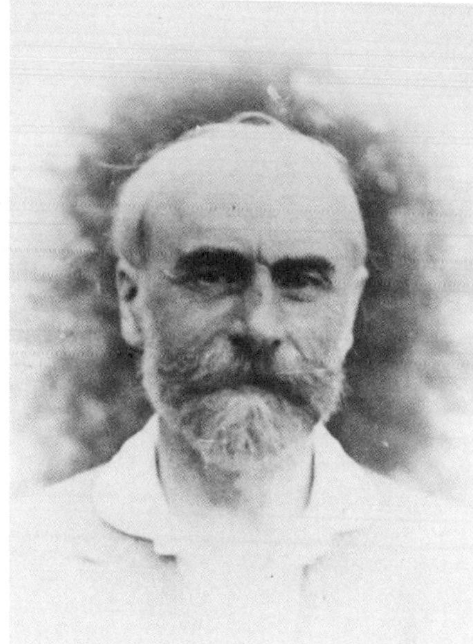

Ernest Rouart

For his part, in 1911 Louis founded a Librairie de l'Art Catholique, which published many Catholic authors, including Claudel and Jammes, as well as a short work on the Dominican Third Order.[587] His aim was also to regenerate Christian imagery and to this end he invited Ernest, who declined, to collaborate. To Louis, who had no fear of contradictions in his mixture of Catholic enthusiasm and Don Juanism, Ernest was exactly as he appeared: faithful and discreet, in his love for God and for Julie. "Denis asks why people always think Papa is a priest."[588] His wife was certainly not displeased with the idea. Julie saw his entry into the Third Order for what it was, a veritable conversion, and spoke of the anxieties she had felt at the moment of their wedding:

> **When, at the time, I used to pray for your conversion I had no hope that you would become a tertiary of Saint Dominic (the older I get, the more I understand the grace God has accorded us by attracting us to that order).[589]**

For many years, Julie had adopted the foundations of the tertiaries' profession of faith, which meant practicing the "real, active, and charitable fraternity cultivated by the Church."[590] On April 5, 1909, in a letter to the wife of Maurice Denis, she spoke of one of her initiatives, a tombola organized on behalf of the widow of the painter Victor Vignon who, she told her correspondent, "has only 60 centimes a day to live on":

> **Degas, Mlle Cassatt, d'Espagnat, Albert André, Dufresnoy, Lacoste, and Laprade have promised me works. Monet and Renoir are giving a sum of money, I would be very happy if your husband also agreed to cooperate with this tombola, for the more interesting things it contains, the easier it will be for me to place the tickets. Naturally, I am giving a canvas by my mother.[591]**

It was therefore no surprise when, on December 1, 1911, Julie joined the women's community of the Third Order, took the cloth, and chose her name. Sœur Rose de Limawas was born.[592]

It was with this sustaining faith that Ernest and Julie were to witness the deaths of friends and family: Aunt Suzanne, the widow Manet,[593] on March 8, 1906; Uncle Alexis Rouart, on January 2, 1911;[594] and the patriarch, Henri Rouart, who passed away on January 2, 1912.[595] The death of Henri Rouart was more than the end of a chapter; it was the end of a world, that of the first collectors of Impressionism.

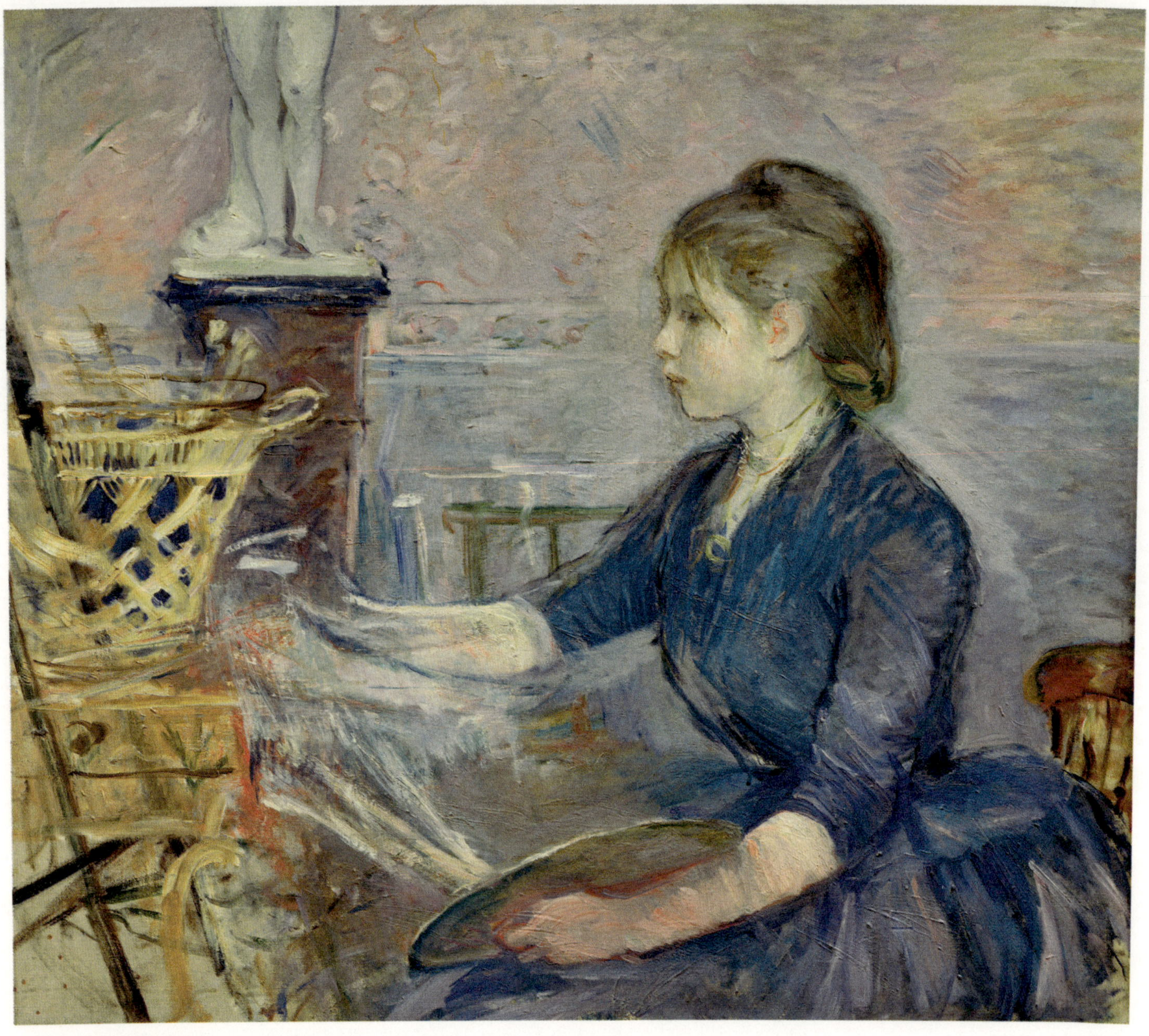

Berthe Morisot (1841–1895)
Paule Gobillard Painting, 1887
Oil on canvas, 86 × 94 cm
Paris, Musée Marmottan Monet

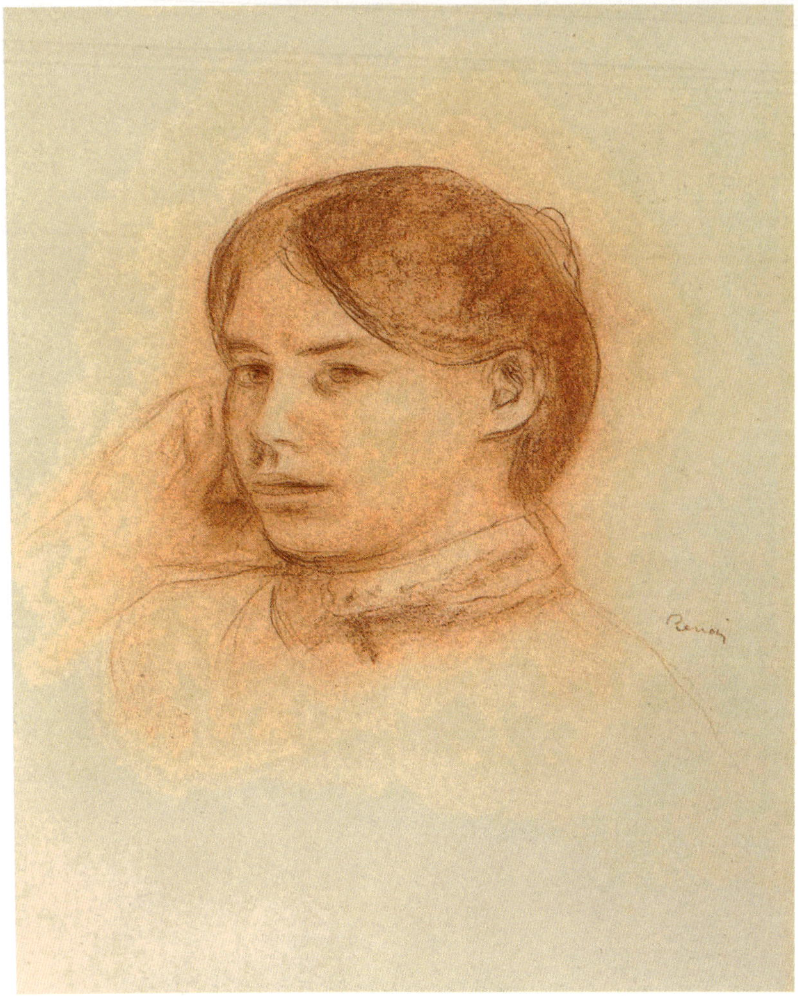

Pierre-Auguste Renoir (1841–1919)
Portrait of Paule Gobillard, n.d.
Red chalk on paper, 41.6 × 34.3 cm
Private collection

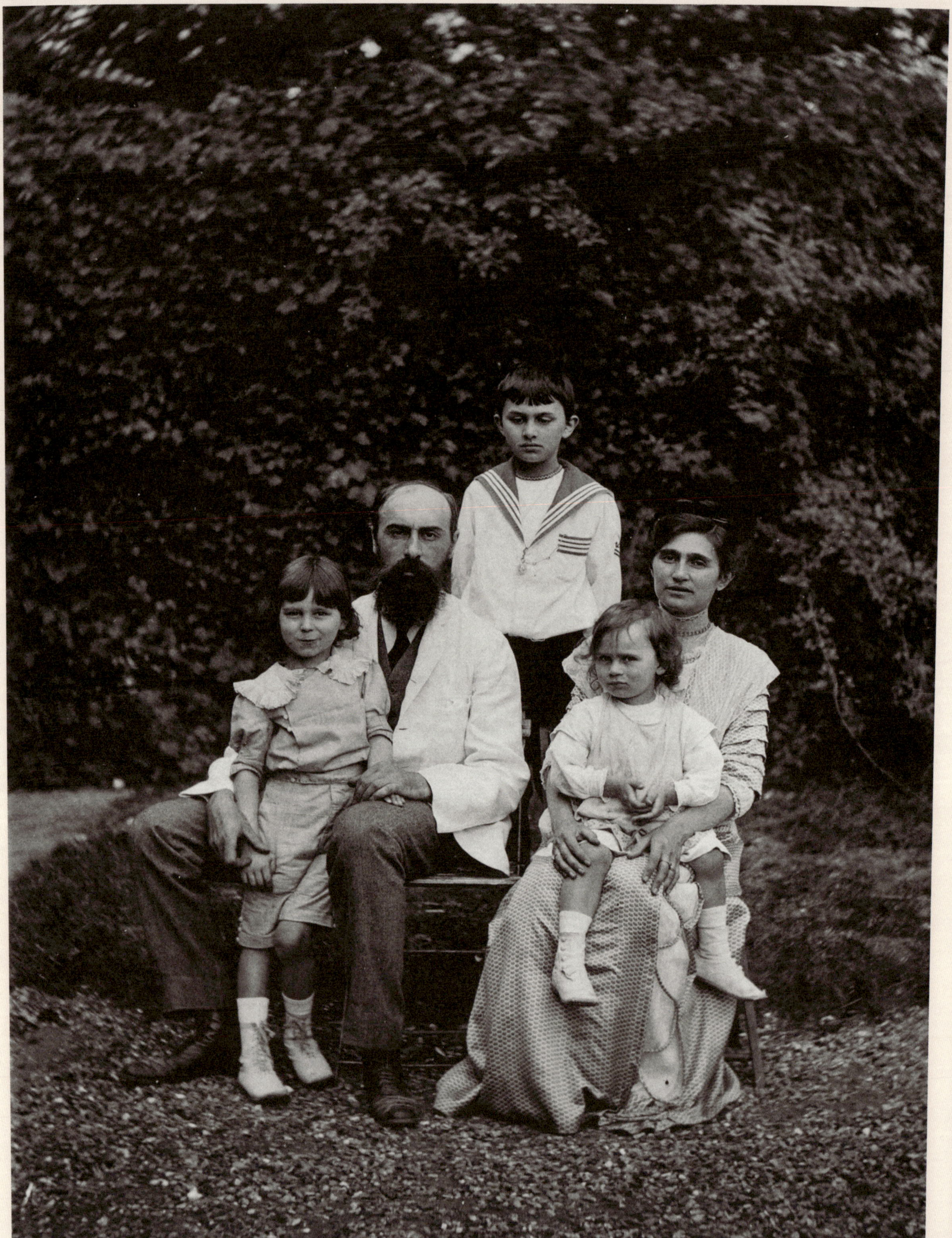

MONSIEUR AND MADAME ERNEST ROUART

1912–1918

"OBVIOUSLY, IT WAS THE FUNERAL OF A *GRAND BOURGEOIS*"[596]

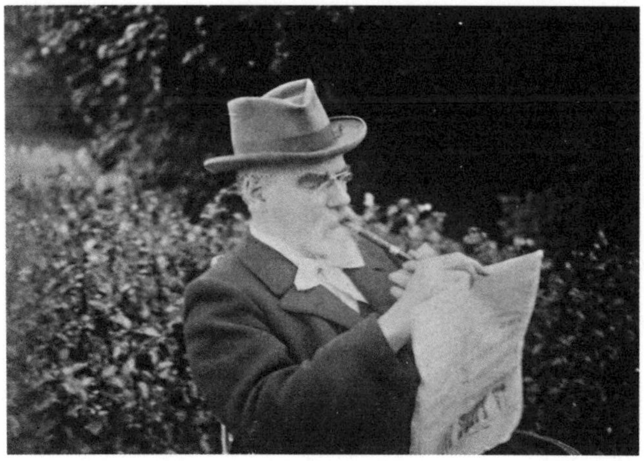

On January 3, 1912, Stanislas Henri Rouart breathed his last. His grandson Julien, who went on to become a psychoanalyst, recalled:

> I was eleven years old. The death of my grandfather was an event that made a deep impression on me. It has remained very vivid in my memory, although it could easily have been quite secondary.

At the time, everyone, without exception, sensed his stature as a patriarch. He left an indelible mark on the current generation and, for the coming generation, representing the founding figure of a dynasty: the Rouarts.

> I remember the visit I paid just before his death, like a kind of farewell visit. The whole family paraded through and I saw him in his bed. He didn't say anything to me, he was no doubt in a coma. He died of uremia.[597]

The funeral was organized with all the expected splendor, as Julien recalls:

> Obviously, it was the funeral of a *grand bourgeois*. My father and my uncles were in morning coats for the funeral. The religious ceremony was at Saint-Augustin, the burial at Père-Lachaise. I had forgotten, but my mother reminded me of the fact: I had asked to follow the cortège with the men, on foot, from Saint-Augustin to Père-Lachaise. There were coaches for the ladies."[598]

All the pomp was both a homage and reflection of the deceased's status.

Then came the time of the succession and of the division between Henri's five children of his considerable fortune. Questions of financial investments and property were settled before the summer.[599] "At one point I recall that there was talk about our branch taking the whole of the rue de Lisbonne, but my mother was very attached to the rue de Villejust," says Julien. The Morisot way was to live at one's wife's home! Which is why the mansion went to Alexis—apart from Ernest's studio, which he kept. The future of the collection was debated and, for lack of agreement, soon went up for

Facing page
Ernest Rouart, Julie Manet-Rouart, and their three children, c. 1910
Archives BS, Paris, Musée Marmottan Monet

Above right
Henri Rouart, n.d.
Private collection

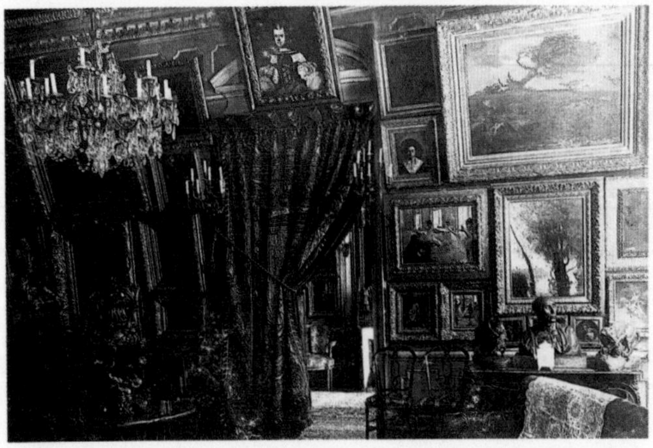

View of the Henri Rouart's living room at 34 rue de Lisbonne

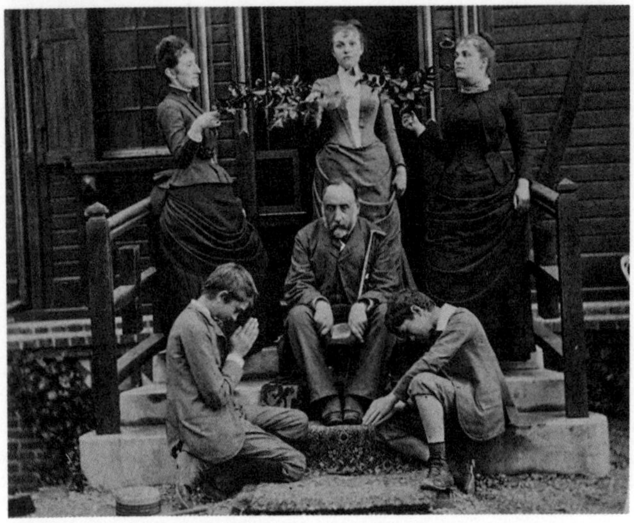

Walter Barnes (1844–1910) and Edgar Degas (1834–1917)
The Apotheosis of Degas, 1885
Los Angeles, J. Paul Getty Museum

sale. "I didn't want this sale to happen," Ernest insisted.[600] For many members of the family, it was a wrench. To disperse a museum-worthy collection was to destroy the work of its creator, Henri Rouart; it was to tear a page out of a history book, one telling of the early days of Impressionism; it was to turn one's back on a conception of life that raised art to the rank of supreme value. For the old friend, the brother of the heart, Degas, it was unthinkable. Ernest and Julie were worried. What if the news proved fatal to him? Ernest agonized: "I really do feel sorry for him. I don't dare tell him that we will sell the paintings, and yet he has to know."[601] And, on the subject of the painter's almost daily visits:

> **He [Degas] spoke to me a great deal . . . about the rue de Lisbonne, about La Queue, Le Mesnil, asked me how we would manage it, Alexis and I, so that we could live in the r[ue] de Lisbonne. But he did not talk to me about the paintings and I did not whisper a word. The other day he said to Durand-Ruel: "Well, the Rouarts are keeping the paintings, they're not selling the collection." Durand didn't set him straight on that, you can be sure. I find this false situation most uncomfortable and there are moments when I want to tell him everything. I think that when he finds out, it will be the final blow for him.[602]**

For Ernest, too, it was "most unpleasant to see the moment coming closer when all that will go."[603] Since the sale is discussed in another essay, let us briefly recall the contradictions surrounding this event. On one side, it was the auction of the century, on the other the "triumph of Papa Rouart's taste,"[604] as Renoir put it to Paule Gobillard. It totaled 5,736,231 francs.[605] *Dancers Practicing at the Barre*[606] fetched a record price for a living artist.[607] This was *The Apotheosis of Degas* as staged by Walter Barnes (left). But that image shows despondency more than triumph. Indeed, in the sales room the artist himself made his famous comment that "The man who painted this picture is no imbecile, but the one who bought it at this price is a fool." Ernest and Julie were anxious. Renoir tried to reassure everyone: "Degas must go on grumbling out of principle, otherwise he would no longer be Degas. But I am delighted to have the joy of witnessing in my lifetime the apotheosis of this artist who is unique, and *magnifique*."[608]

MOBILIZATIONS

On May 29, 1913 the succession was closed. The sum received by each child was 1,282,668 francs.[609] Acting jointly, the descendants also bought some of the works at the auction. Most of the ones chosen by Ernest and Julie were exhibited in the studio in the rue de Lisbonne,[610] as memories of a bygone time from which Ernest drew little benefit. The photographs taken by Julie and Ernest during their holiday at Perros-Guirec immortalize the last carefree moments (p. 95, 96, and 97).

World War I changed everything. If Valéry avoided mobilization by virtue of his age,[611] Ernest was called up from August 3, 1914 to January 9, 1919.[612] Julie, who was worried about Degas, wrote to her husband on August 7:

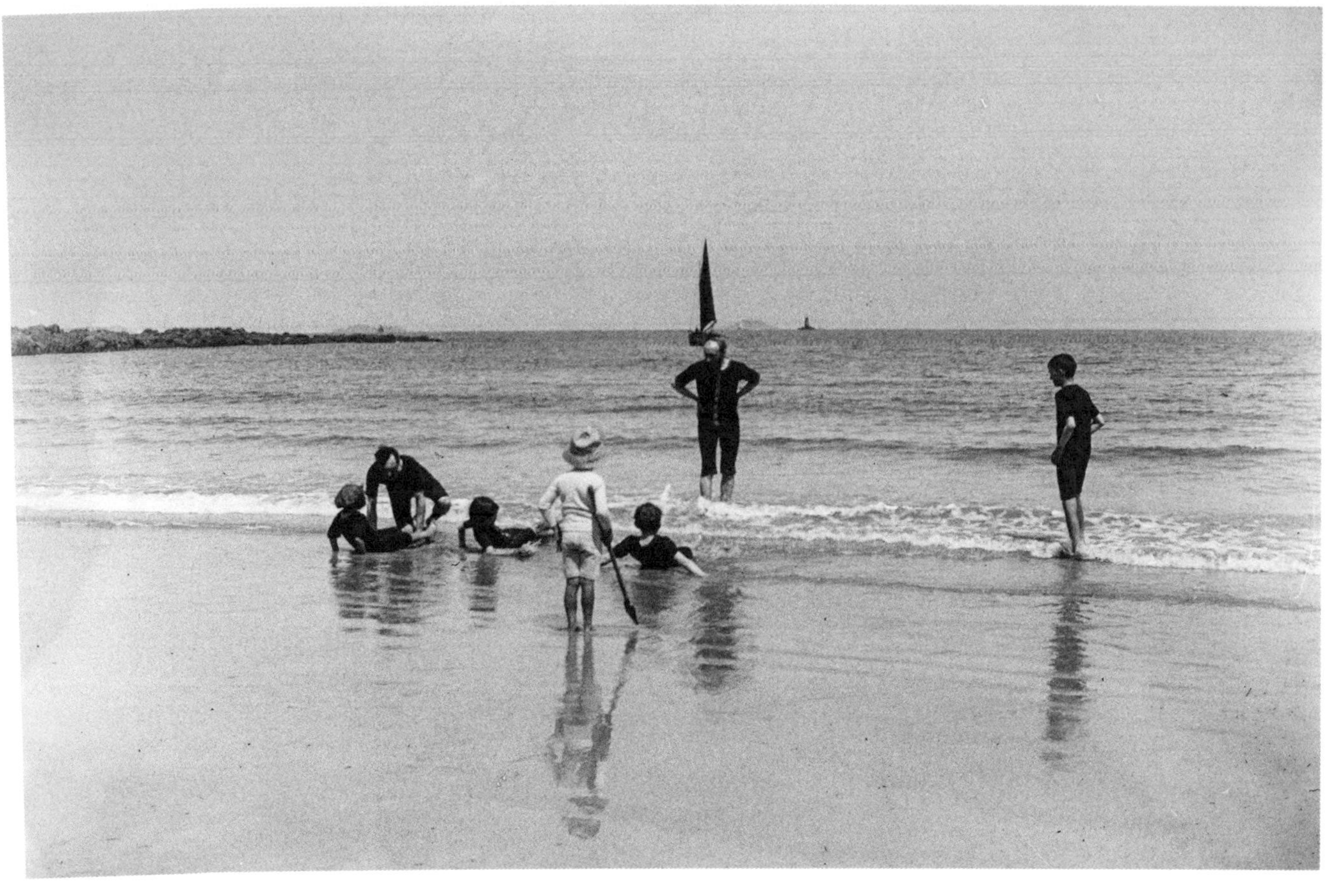

Attributed to Julie Manet (1878–1966)
Paul Valéry, Ernest Rouart, and their children on the beach at Perros-Guirec, 1913
Archives du Mesnil, on permanent loan at the Musée Marmottan Monet

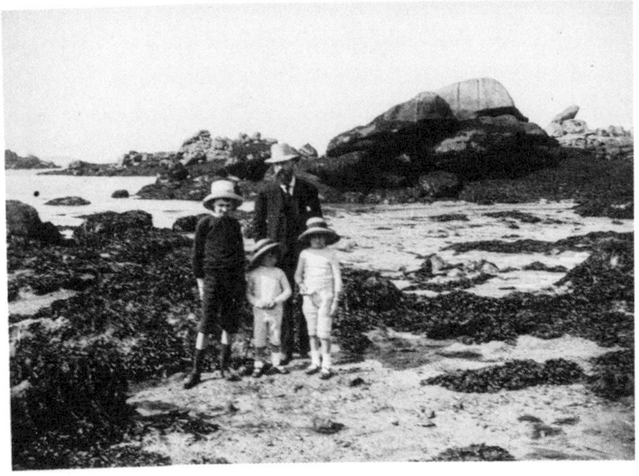

Attributed to Julie Manet (1878–1966)
Ernest Rouart and his three sons at Perros-Guirec, 1913
Archives du Mesnil, on permanent loan at the Musée Marmottan Monet

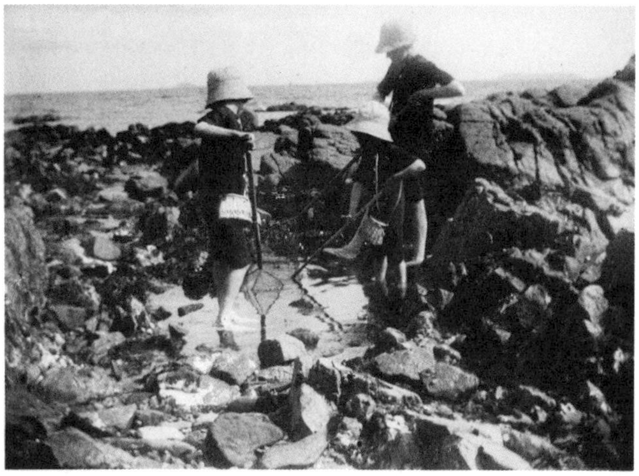

Attributed to Julie Manet (1878–1966)
Julien, Clément, and Denis Rouart at Perros-Guirec, 1913
Archives du Mesnil, on permanent loan at the Musée Marmottan Monet

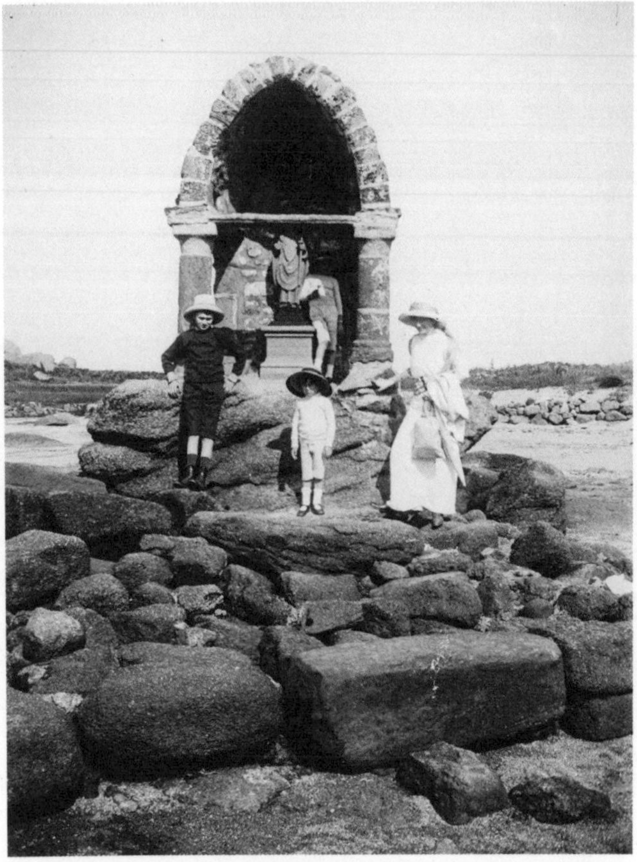

Attributed to Ernest Rouart (1874–1942)
Julie Manet-Rouart and her three sons in front of the Saint Guirec chapel on the Ploumanac'h beach at Perros-Guirec, 1913
Archives du Mesnil, on permanent loan at the Musée Marmottan Monet

> I do indeed regret that I did not speak to you about M. Degas . . . I was wondering if Père Janvier was in Paris and I had been thinking a bit about asking if he wouldn't mind going to see how M. Degas was getting on and having a chat with him.[613]

Julie was all the more worried because she had just left Paris to follow Ernest to Brittany. She settled with her children in Lorient in late 1914–15.[614] More than ever, Degas needed real support. She mentioned this directly to the canon of Notre-Dame de Paris:

> Father, If you have a little time, might I ask you to be so kind as to go and see M. Degas to see how he is and, at the same time, to try to steer his thoughts toward God. I have long been concerned about him from that point of view. A few months ago he was talking to me about death, which is on his mind all the time, and he told me that he envisaged it with indifference and that I was very fortunate to believe in another life. He is not opposed to religion, but, never having had recourse to it, does not realize that he needs it. I wonder how he is getting on at this time and I think that could be a pretext for your visit. He lives at 6 boulevard de Clichy and can generally be found there from 2 to 4 o'clock, for he is in the habit of walking all morning and all the late afternoon.[615]

What a pity that we do not know what happened next.

From 1916 to the end of the war, Ernest served at the camouflage workshops in Châlons-sur-Marne, a section that had recently been created by the French army to meet the needs of trench warfare.[616] There, over two hundred men and women, painters, sculptors, set painters, and avant-garde artists conceived deceptive patterns that would help deceive the enemy. Art, too, had its war.

Julie returned to the capital. The little one attended private schooling with Lacascade and Saint-Dominique and Lacordaire, and Julien was at the Lycée Janson de Sailly, where he took his first *baccalauréat*. His mother proudly informed Ernest of their oldest child's progress: "What I tell him about the artists we knew interests him. In his last lesson with M. Michel, he spoke up for Mallarmé. I think he was rather happy to tell one of his friends that I owned unpublished quatrains by Mallarmé."[617]

Based only two hundred kilometers away, Ernest was reunited with his family whenever he had leave. They made sure to take family photographs at these rare moments of togetherness. The conscript posed in his uniform (p. 98). They tried to get back to something like a normal life. They went walking with their Rouart cousins in the Bois de Boulogne. Julie wrote: "Yesterday Alexis was admiring the lake which reminded me of Maman's paintings. Sitting at the pier, I saw Maman with her canvases taking the boat and the man with the glass eye who said she had Corot's voice."[618]

Nor did they forget their cousin Gabriel Thomas, administrator of the Eiffel Tower, whom they met with regularly at Bellevue. An active member of the Third Order, Frère Pie ordered new works from his friend Maurice Denis. Having conceived *Eternal Spring*[619] for Gabriel's dining room, Denis painted, among other things, *Magnificat* for the bedroom (p. 119) and a *Baptism of Christ* (p. 118),[620] and began working on religious paintings for the upper floor. Julie wrote a fairly precise description:

> On the different doors of the third floor are beatitudes by Denis which look very good. Three of them pleased me a great deal: *Blessed Are the Poor*; Franciscans, the poor in brownish tones on a [illegible word] ground that reminded me of Varèse's

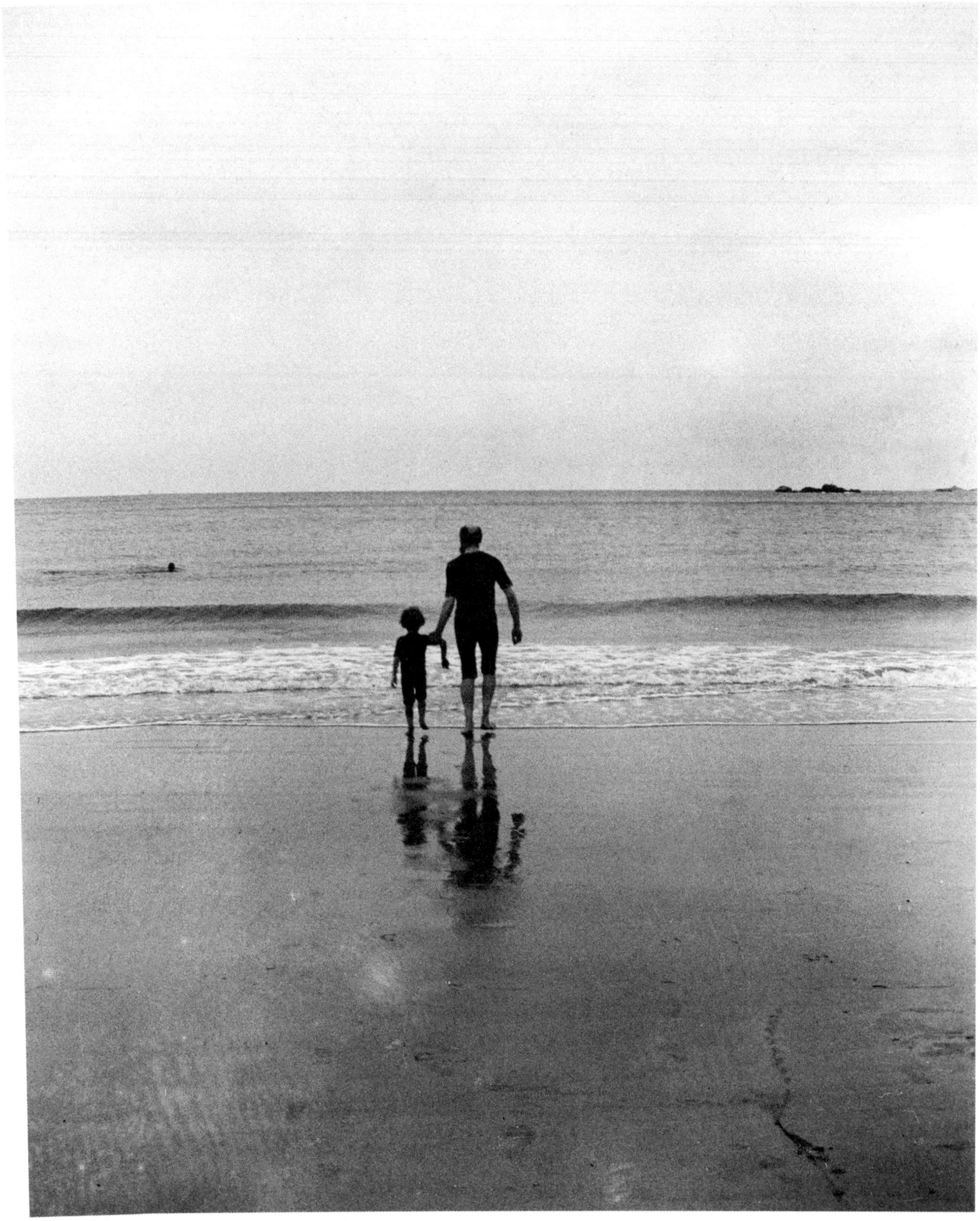

Attributed to Julie Manet (1878–1966)
Ernest Rouart and his son Denis on the beach at Perros-Guirec, 1913
Archives du Mesnil, on permanent loan at the Musée Marmottan Monet

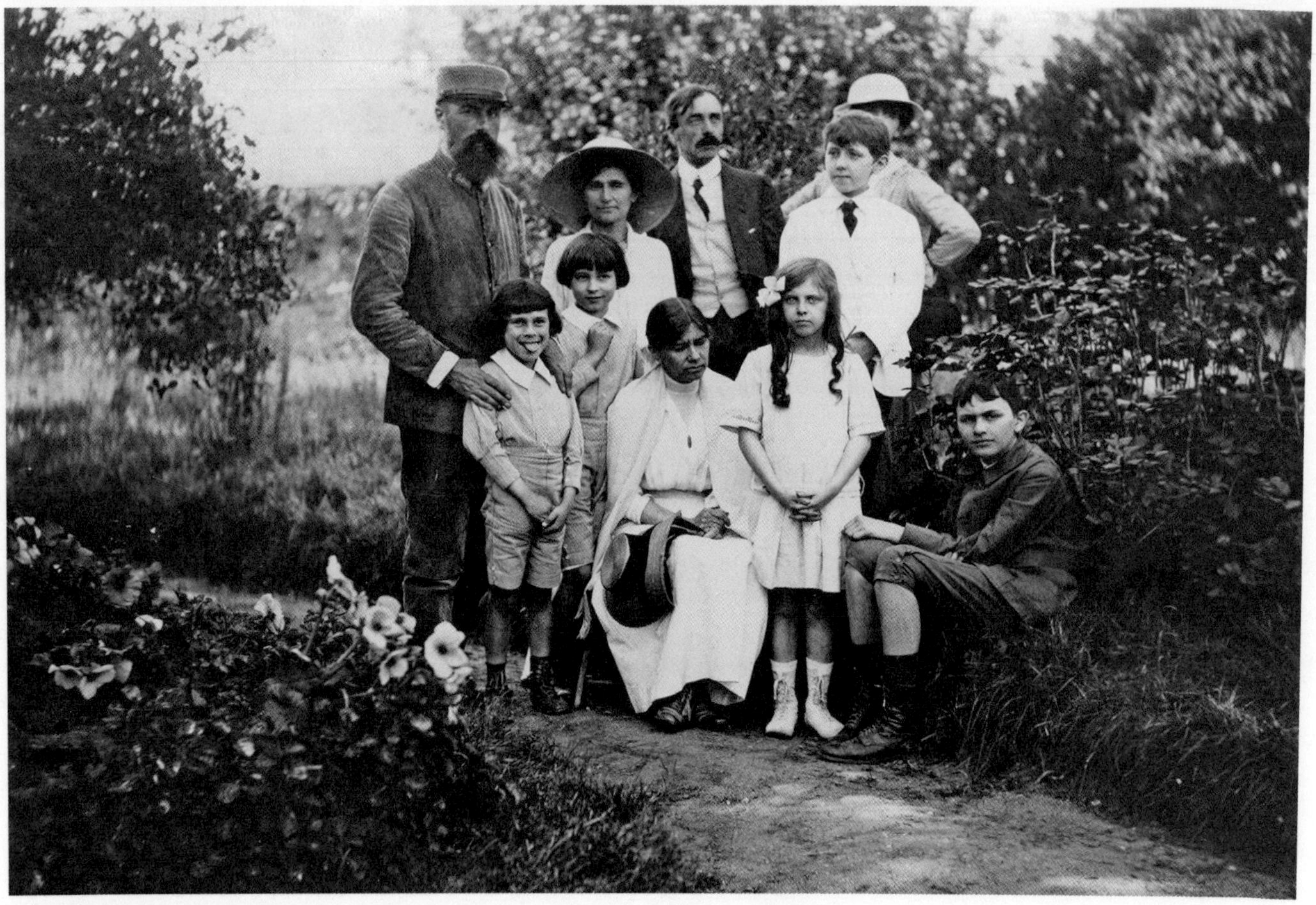

Paule Gobillard (seated at the center), the Manet-Rouart and Gobillard-Valéry couples and their children, c. 1917
Archives BS, Paris, Musée Marmottan Monet

landscapes. *Blessed Are Those Who Hunger and Thirst for Righteousness;* among the figures, St. Louis against a ground of Lake Maggiore against which stands out a gilded [illegible word] that also reminded me of the lake, then *Blessed Are the Meek;* light figures against the forest of Saint-Germain. And as I looked at this I thought of the fecundity of religious subjects.[621]

Gabriel, who financed the publication of handsome books, immediately put his young cousin and her husband, Frère Antonin, on the list of subscribers[622] for *La Vie de saint Dominique,* prefaced by Père Janvier and illustrated by Maurice Denis.[623]

Valéry attended the meetings of the Third Order held to discuss the theological work of Saint Thomas Aquinas, a moment that he not unhumorously described as a "somme théologique" (*somme* meaning both summa and snooze).[624] Religion amused him, to say the least. He implored his friend Denis, who had taken up residence in Perros-Guirec: "Christians, pray for me. Pagans, make a light libation of seawater in my name."[625] During a public reading of his poem *La Jeune Parque,* he dreamed of this event right under Père Janvier's nose. Was Julie aware of this mischievous humor when she described Valéry's first steps in society?

I have only very incompletely related Paul's evening with the Mqse de Clermont-Tonnerre. It seems that this took place in a garden just about under the windows of P[ère] J[anvier], whom Paul in his imagination pictured attending the soirée. Colored glasses hung from the trees, and the women had brought the cushions from a pavilion where the dance was held so they could sit down, and it was in this darkness that de Miomandre[626] recited *La Jeune Parque.*[627]

Two visions of the world and of the spirit thus coexisted in the rue de Villejust: on one side, Valéry's, which was godless and undogmatic, curious about everything; on the other, that of Ernest, Julie, and Jeannie: Catholic, fervent, austere. These divergences did not upset the family equilibrium, even if there were times when they became flagrant. Julien's success at the first *baccalauréat* in 1917 was one such occasion. To congratulate her son, Julie organized a pilgrimage to Lisieux, where the body of Saint Thérèse of the Child Jesus and the Holy Face had just been exhumed a second time[628] for her coming beatification. Uncle Paul advised his nephew to read *Souvenirs d'enfance et de jeunesse* in which the author of the *Vie de Jésus*, Ernest Renan, describes how he lost his faith. This caused quite a stir and was talked about all through the summer, which Paule, Julie, Jeannie, and the children spent with Valéry's mother at Le Mesnil.

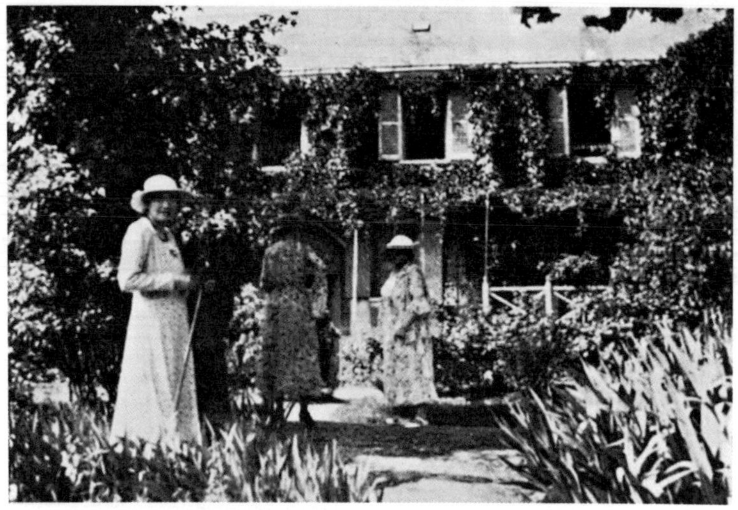

Julie Manet in Giverny, n.d.

"THE LAST MAN OF TASTE"

Before returning to Paris in the autumn, they travelled to Giverny. "We may perhaps go and see Monsieur Monet. Maman is writing to him at this moment,[629] Julien wrote to his father on September 16, 1917 (above right). Ernest congratulated Julie on this: "I am glad you are going to see Monet. One should not abandon old friends and one must try to see them as often as possible."[630] Julien Rouart would remember him well:

> The Impressionist I knew best was Claude Monet because we used to go to Giverny from Le Mesnil. It wasn't very far. There was almost an annual visit to Giverny, and Claude Monet also came to our home. Claude Monet was very nice, not at all solemn. I saw him in the summer. He was always wearing a kind of suit in light tussah. I took photographs of him, I must have an album. They were very badly taken, done with my first camera. He was quite happy to let me photograph him. We used to go walking in that magnificent garden. We went into his studio, we saw his paintings, which he was pleased to show us. [Toward the end of the war] we saw the big studio he had had built. His driver had made big stretchers for him, and this was the beginning of the *Water Lilies* canvases. It was new to him.[631]

Writing about her other son, Julie noted that "Denis is doing watercolors in his album. He did Monet painting on the edge of his pond."[632] After briefly mentioning "the decorations," she dwells, instead, on another piece of news: "Monet has gone to do Reims Cathedral." Ernest replied at once: "I hear that they said in the newspapers some time ago that Monet was going to paint Reims Cathedral. This is an event."[633] Reading them, there seems no doubt that Monet had seriously considered painting the ruins of this cathedral, which had been bombarded in 1914. But he abandoned the idea. The only response he could find to the horrors of war was the hope conveyed by nature in full bloom. An Eden of painting.

On September 27, 1917, a few days after Berthe Morisot's daughter paid her visit to Monet, Degas passed away. Ernest's last meeting with his master had been deeply upsetting, as Julien would recall long afterwards: "When he was on leave he went to see Degas who was so diminished that he did not recognize him. That affected my father deeply."[634]

Ernest was unable to leave Châlons to attend the funeral. "When war starts, hell opens"![635] Among those who could be present, *Le Figaro* mentions his brothers Alexis and Louis, Bartholomé, Monet, Lerolle, and the Durand-Ruels.[636] The paper does not mention Valéry, whose hour of glory was yet to come, or the ladies of the family, and yet there is every indication that they were there. The poet wrote this touching account to his cousin:

> I do not know what will become of Degas's riches. The museum he dreamed of! In the end, he did very decently with the press. His glory will start the work for which he gathered the materials. He was a great artist but also, beside that, the last link connecting today's France to an entire civilization that is as lost to us as the Etruscans. The last man of taste. He was

placed in a vault that is very much his. As naked, as elementary as possible. Not even a name on the pediment.[637]

Ernest wrote at once to his wife:

If you hear something about what we are to do with Degas's studio, keep me informed. I suppose the heirs are going to hold a sale, which worries me as to the fate of all his works. Well, we shall see what we shall see.[638]

Everything having to do with Degas was communicated to Ernest. Valéry wrote:

On this point, I can inform you that Vollard-Bernheim are going to publish a Degas album at 100 francs for an ordinary copy. I leafed through this collection at the home of the amiable Fénéon. Numerous reproductions of admirable things. 4 color reproductions rather awful. But the drawing is still there, despite the blur and the crush of the prints. And there are lots of them. Nothing from the early days in fine pencil. But nudes, nudes, and nudes from the broad, brutal times, elegant atrocities. I would be very much inclined to use on that the five louis I have earned from *La Jeune parque* ! (3 years of work – 514 lines – 100 francs), unless I frame the check. Let that be an example to anyone who wants to write poetry. This album cannot be left lying on the table and for me that will be an argument against acquiring it. I don't even know where to hide my friends' books![639]

Ernest was concerned about the only woman who ever put up with Degas: his maid: "Do you know if in any of his moments Degas left something to Zoé?"[640] Julie answered:

I know nothing about Zoé. All the foreigners deeply regret that you weren't asked to sort things out. D'Esp[agnat] is one of them. I regret it, too, for Degas's work, but not for you.[641]

They soon learned that nothing had been planned for Zoé and set about remedying this:

It really is rather appalling that none of Degas's heirs thought to have something put in the will for her, but we should not be too surprised, given the way they each acted on their own. I am in favor of Lafond's idea,[642] to club together among friends of Degas to give her something. He must have mentioned it to Alexis. You can find out about that when you see him.[643]

The sale was indeed held, in the middle of the war. The artist's oeuvre and personal collection were so considerable that it took no less than sixteen days—spaced between March 26, 1918 and April 7, 1919—to empty the studio. As the first auction dedicated to his master's collection approached, Ernest confided:

What memories, indeed, they bring back, these paintings bought by poor old Degas; touching memories. I can never think of them without feeling deeply stirred up. It was at these encounters, these meetings that our marriage gestated, and the conversation in the avenue Victor Massé[644] was simply the consequence of that—somewhat rushed, perhaps, but natural.[645]

It was, in a way, Ernest and Julie's life that was being auctioned. Ernest dreamed of being able to attend, as if for a final homage. He told Julie he was working on it:

I told Duval about the sale of our poor Degas's collection. He said right away that we should go up to Paris for it. Personally, I think I could get my leave to coincide with that time. If you hear of other details please do let me know. What I shall most regret, perhaps, will be seeing all those watercolors by Delacroix, by Ingres, which he assembled with such love, disappear. It's sad to think of all that being scattered. It would have been so interesting for everyone, so consoling for his memory to form an ensemble from his collection and a certain number of his works, judiciously chosen. That, indeed, is what he dreamed of doing and never got round to carrying out when he was alive. Oh well, it was not to be. In spite of it all, I cannot keep from regretting it, for him, for his memory, much more than for me, where it would, I fear, have been a source of bother and difficulties with that very uninteresting family. All the denigrations, the false appreciations of the young generations of artists will not, I hope, keep him from being given the place in painting that he merits. All these injustices are repaired sooner or later.[646]

On February 12, Ernest warned Julie:

I see that you would very much like to go to Lourdes during the holidays but that would be rather difficult for me as I would have things to do in Paris. The Degas sale first of all, and a lot of research in my papers.[647]

Unfortunately, the leave he was hoping for was not granted. War is a cruel mistress.

PROGRESS IN SAVAGERY AND VANDALISM

Ernest soon had other preoccupations. On January 30, 1918, Paris was hit by eighty German aerial bombardments, posing a threat to the capital and its population. Julie and Ernest discussed the measures they should take. When she asked him about the paintings, Ernest who, after four years of military service, had witnessed many daily horrors, was detached:

> You ask me for instructions for Corots. I really do not see what we could do. There are only cellars that could protect them from bombs, but then they would be damaged by humidity. I think the best thing, then, would be to leave them where they are, abandoning them to the grace of God.[648]

And he continued in the same register:

> I share your opinion about insurance against airplanes. We should take it out for the house but for the paintings it would be extremely costly and would not give us back the paintings we lost.[649]

Julie suggested rolling them up and having them transported outside Paris. Again, he was reluctant:

> The more I think about it, the more dodgy it sounds. You're taking quite a risk to roll them up. The operation would be less dangerous if one did it with only a few paintings, and even then you would need to choose ones that are not threatened by this treatment. If they have the slightest tendency to peel away from the canvas, they are lost. Know, in any case, that you should always roll with the paint on the outside, because there is less risk of it breaking, which is always a worry with pictures that are already old and very dry and as thickly laid on as some of ours.[650]

Safes were no more convincing:

> For the armored strongboxes in banks, I wonder if it would be very good for the paintings. If these boxes are made in freshly worked cement, there is a fear of moisture with all the drawbacks that brings.[651]

The artillery fire was incessant. On January 30 they hit the headquarters of the Crédit Lyonnais in the rue de Choiseul. On March 8, it was the turn of the rue Laffitte, so intimately bound up with the beginnings of Impressionism (p. 102).

The situation grew worse in late March. Equipped with a long-range cannon, a thirty-meter monster from the Krupp factory, posted a hundred and fifty kilometers from the capital at Laon, the German army bombarded Paris. The first shots from Big Bertha rained down on March 23. At 3 pm the French authorities sent out an official communiqué:

> Since 8 o'clock in the morning, every quarter of an hour, 240 shells have reached the capital and the suburbs.[652]

The following week, the church of Saint-Gervais was pulverized during the Good Friday service, killing ninety-two people and wounding sixty-eight others. It was the most deadly bombardment of World War I. Looking back, Julien Rouart recalled:

> My father who was mobilized at that time, and who was in Châlons, very close to the front, insisted that we leave. And that is when we went to my mother's cousins, the de Vaissière cousins, who had a château in Sarthe.[653]

Julie and the children thus took refuge in Vassé. Berthe Morisot's daughter left her paintings behind, for which she would never forgive herself. Abandoning her apartment was a wrench. To leave her interior was to imperil her ecosystem. Preserving her paintings and drawings was vital. By early April she was already thinking of going back to Paris to have them stored safely away. For the first time, husband and wife disagreed. Ernest's position was firm: art might give life meaning, but only life was sacred. With respect to Julie, he considered that to take useless risks was to disregard her duty as a mother. To begin with, he tried to console her:

> I understand that it was hard for you to leave your house, your paintings and all the memories you have there, but in spite of it all, I am happy that you left. This is not bravura on my part . . . Your duty was to leave with your children, whatever you might think, and all fathers will share my opinion.[654]

He returned to the point a few days later:

> I understand that you regret not having taken away the portrait of your mother and a few small pictures, but just think how difficult it would have been to transport them by hand with all the other packages you had.[655]

Nothing could convince him to approve this planned trip; on the contrary, "If it was your duty to stay in Paris, I could understand this, but that is not the case and I believe, for my part, that it is your duty to leave."[656] The disquiet grew from day to day. On April 5 he wrote:

> The canon is now spewing day and night and the victims are always people housed in the upper floors

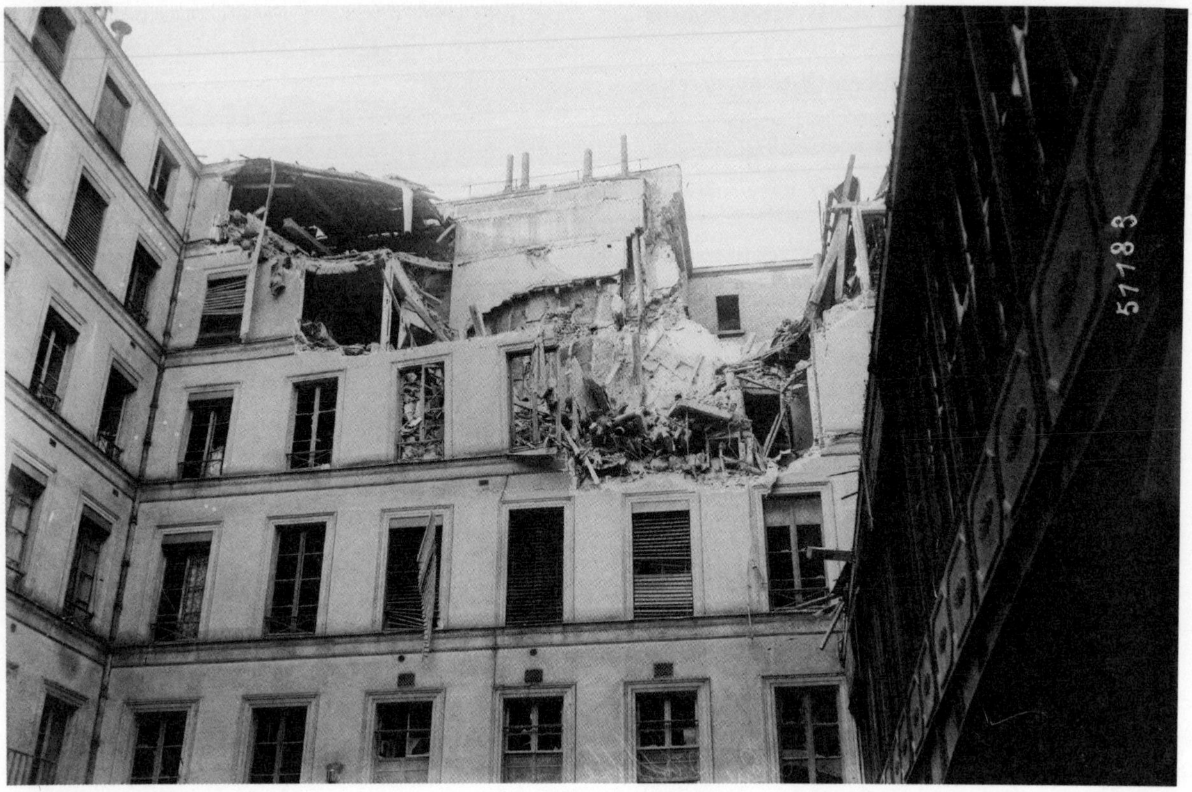

Damage at Rue Laffitte from the aerial bombardments of March 8, 1918

of buildings."[657] Why hurry to the last floor of the rue de Villejust? On the 17th, he implored: "I beg you, do not dream of going to Paris for the moment, whether for the paintings or for something else . . . We cannot expect to make everything we have safe.[658]

By late April, the situation was so serious that the army requisitioned the family manor. "We cannot prevent them from requisitioning Le Mesnil as we are not living there,"[659] noted Ernest, conceding that "it is not very pleasant to see an infirmary being organized"[660] in your own home. On April 23, he wrote again:

> It is distressing for me to know that you are yourself exiled far from the places and memories that are dear to you because of all the memories attaching to them.
>
> In spite of it all, I think I was right to make you go and I cannot be at ease with the idea of seeing you come back to Paris, if only for two days. Do you think it will be possible to take a trunk? Are you now allowed to travel with luggage? You would do well to find out.[661]

Julie was unbending. She planned to make a return trip to put the pictures in crates that she had ordered in March.[662] Ernest raged:

> "Do what you will for the picture crate, but who will carry it for you to the Société Générale. I think it would be rather difficult to get the portrait of your grandparents in there now. This idea of travelling to Paris torments me."[663]

Always ready to help, the next morning he wrote:

> You could perhaps have them taken to Madame Pécourt"[664]—now the occupant of the first floor in the rue de Villejust.
>
> As for the canvases you would like to roll up and take away, I think it's rather risky as I was explaining yesterday and a lot of clutter for you and heavy to carry. To soothe you completely would have taken a complete move of the paintings which was no longer possible. In spite of it all, we cannot hope to confront all these events.[665]

Resigned, he dreamed of meeting Julie on a hypothetical leave:

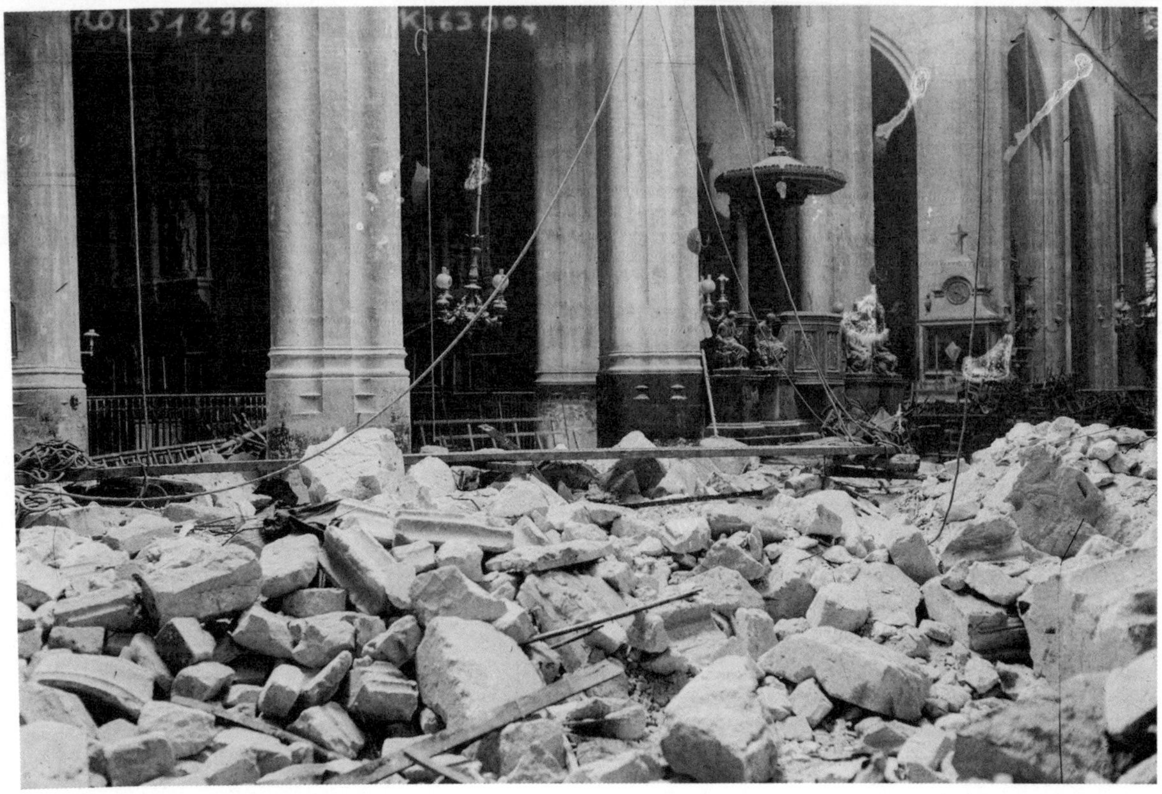

Interior of the church Saint-Gervais in Paris, after the bombardment of Mars 29, 1918

> If we have the happiness of being together again we could see the Degases together but I fear that this letter has arrived too late."[666]

He was no longer able to attend the auction on May 6, the last one organized before the end of hostilities.

In such circumstances, there was no question of Julie and the children moving back to Paris After much hesitation, they opted for Brittany. Julien recalled:

> I took . . . the second bac in Rennes, where we had gone in the last year of the war, when there was Big Bertha, in Paris, a long-range cannon.[667]

Jeannie, Paule, and the Valéry children also left for Brittany. Paul, who stayed in Paris, could not resist the temptation to take a witty swipe at the Breton clergy.

> As for Paul's allegation about curates, don't let it trouble you. If you have chosen that city, it is because you felt it was better, so you have acted wisely and I approve you.[668]

More than ever, Ernest and Julie drew strength from their faith.

> Truly, it is only religion that helps me endure [this ordeal] and also the feeling of duty which we must not shirk.[669]

As he told her:

> I continue to go to Mass every morning. . . . When will we be able to go there together and resume our pious exercises side by side? I make up for it in thought as much as I can, but I cannot keep from missing your dear presence which has always been salutary for me, and which, for example, has done much to guide me along the right path and to direct my eyes toward heaven. I do wish I had taken that path earlier and more completely. It seems to me that I have thus wasted the finest years of our union. And it is alas just when this union has become more complete and more intimate by a more perfect communion of ideas and feelings that we are forced to live apart from each other in a time with no foreseeable end. May God help us and sustain us.[670]

And so it turned out. The armistice was signed on November 11, 1918.

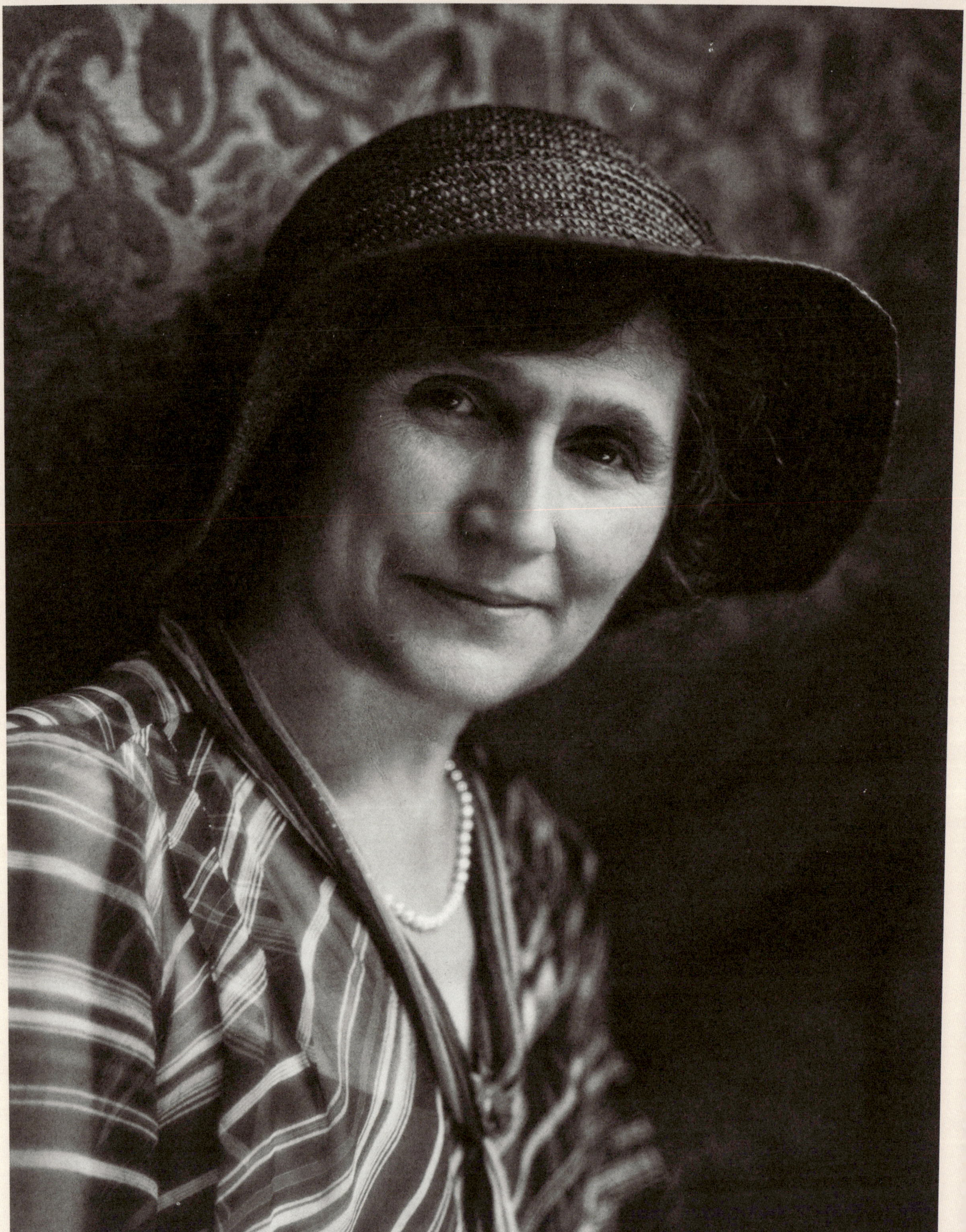

LET MEMORY COME ALIVE!

1919–1941

"SHE COULD EASILY HAVE DEVOTED HER LIFE TO HER MOTHER'S MEMORY"[671]

Julie dreamed of offering her mother, the first woman Impressionist, the recognition she had lacked at her death. That was her mission, her vocation, as Julien, her older son, would recall: "The catalogue of Berthe Morisot's oeuvre took over part of my mother's life. Indeed, at the time of the 1914 war she contacted Vollard [p.107], who suggested it to her. He said, 'I take a very long time to do things, sometimes thirty years.'"[672]

Jeanne Baudot also remembered bumping into her friend when she was visiting the gallerist "to talk with Vollard about the catalogue of her mother's work."[673] Having published two volumes of Renoir's work, with 1,741 illustrations, in 1914, Vollard now began work on Morisot's catalogue raisonné.[674] As he warned, it was a long-term undertaking: "For several years, there was a photographer who came to photograph all the Berthe Morisots we had at home."[675] In her letters to Ernest, Julie refers several times to this man, Étienne Delétang, who had been working for Vollard since 1904 and, in that capacity, had photographed the work of Degas (1904), Gauguin (1904–07), and Cézanne (1907–12), as well as Renoir, Redon, and Cassatt. Julie received him in the rue de Villejust and warned her husband of her intention to have him come to Juziers: "I am going to write to Vollard so that Delétang can come and photograph the paintings we have here."[676]

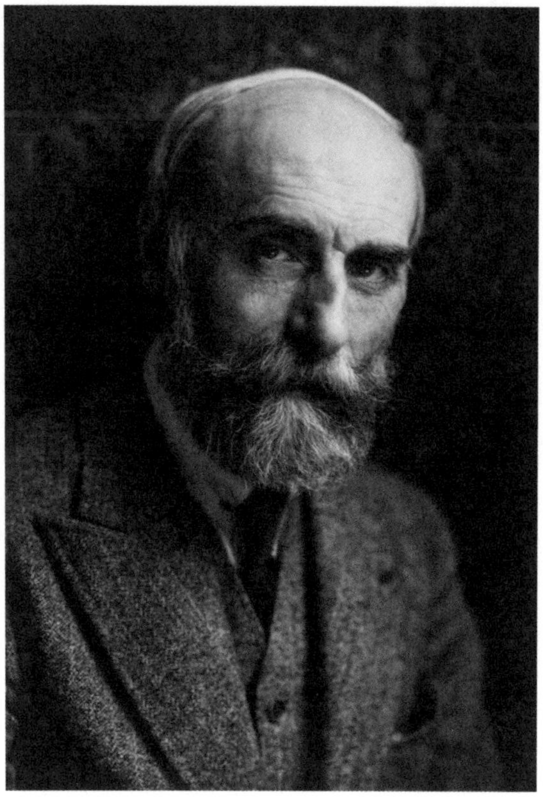

Portrait of Ernest Rouart, 1932
Paris, Bibliothèque Nationale de France

Facing page
Portrait of Julie Manet-Rouart, 1932
Paris, Bibliothèque Nationale de France

Judging from her letters, she had something to do with the photographer's visit to her neighbor Monet:

> Did I tell you that Delétang came to fetch something else the other day? He is delighted with his trip to Giverny and he is going back to photograph the Decorations. What will Durand and Bernheim say when they find out that it was Vollard's photographer who did that?[677]

In all, Delétang photographed three hundred and sixty Morisots.[678] But Julie's big concern was the text. She suggested that it be entrusted to her cousin Valéry, who appears to have agreed, judging by the lines that follow, concerning another of Julie's conversations with Vollard:

> He liked the idea of a biography by Paul for the catalogue. When I told him that I had the feeling artists' lives were always deformed, he replied: I am the only person who says things exactly as they are, and they insist that I am joking.[679]

Point noted! Julie set about gathering elements that might help Valéry. To document the life of a mother lost at the age of sixteen is a wager. True, the correspondence was a help, and not to be ignored. Julie loved to peruse it, as a way back into her family world.[680] But even so, information was missing. She therefore started searching, looking for witnesses. She was delighted with a visit to Aunt Edma:

> I asked her about Maman's youth and she told me things that interested me greatly. In fact, Guichard was Maman's one true master. Paul could establish that. She modelled for a year with the sculptor Aimé Millet. Fantin [Latour] and another student of Guichard. It was also through Guichard that she got to know Corot.[681]

Paul was able to confirm this. Although at the forefront, Julie remained in the shadow. She did not write, did not sign. Jacques-Émile Blanche was writing his childhood memories. *Les Dames de la Grande-Rue*,[682] which he dedicated to Julie, relates Berthe Morisot's early years in Passy. This was as much toadying as testimony, and certainly very social, but it could still speak truth. As for Julie, she was Berthe Morisot's daughter, not her biographer. An heiress, not a historian. She thus promised and supported whatever could help gain recognition for her mother's work, and make it part of history. Let memory come alive!

The death of Renoir on December 3, 1919, fanned the flame of memory. Monet, the last survivor, confirmed this. To Jeannie's condolences—she knew how close the two men were—he replied:

> How I thank you for your good and very affectionate letter, how grateful I am to you for this delicacy. Renoir's death is a great sorrow for me; with him goes part of my own life, and I keep picturing those days of youth, of struggle and hope. It is a hard blow for the old man that I am. And yet I go on and keep on painting and seeking.[683]

The tribe in the rue de Villejust was closer than ever to old Monet. The Rouart and Valéry children (p. 108 left), who, with the exception of the little François Valéry, still in shorts, were children no more, remembered the master in their twenties. In a letter to her uncle Ernest, Agathe Valéry regretted having missed him:

> All those cars at Le Mesnil this Wednesday! Monet's visit left us with many regrets. You must have been surprised to see him arrive.[684]

Julien remembered their days in Giverny in around 1923:

> At about this time he [Monet] was operated for his cataract. I recall that he was operated on by an ophthalmologist from the hospitals by the name of [Charles] Coutela, to whom he had recommended me. Coutela had supported me for a competition or for an exam. I saw Claude Monet after his operation. He said he had seen a magnificent blue. He showed us a few canvases he had made at the beginning of his cataract, in which there was a lot of yellow. He always added yellow because, in fact, he couldn't see yellow. But there were fools who told him it was very good. He said, "I have kept a few of them but I have destroyed a great many."[685]

Although the Impressionists had gone, the "Thursdays" continued. Julie received the new generation of artists in the rue de Villejust.

> My mother organized meetings, often on Thursday evening, once a month or more often, at which there were Paul Valéry, painters, Albert André, Charles Lacoste, painters from those times, Vuillard . . .[686]

Although Vuillard was not an habitué, we have several notes confirming his presence:

> My dear Rouart, You are very kind to ask me. I shall come on Thursday with great pleasure.[687]

Julien remembered him:

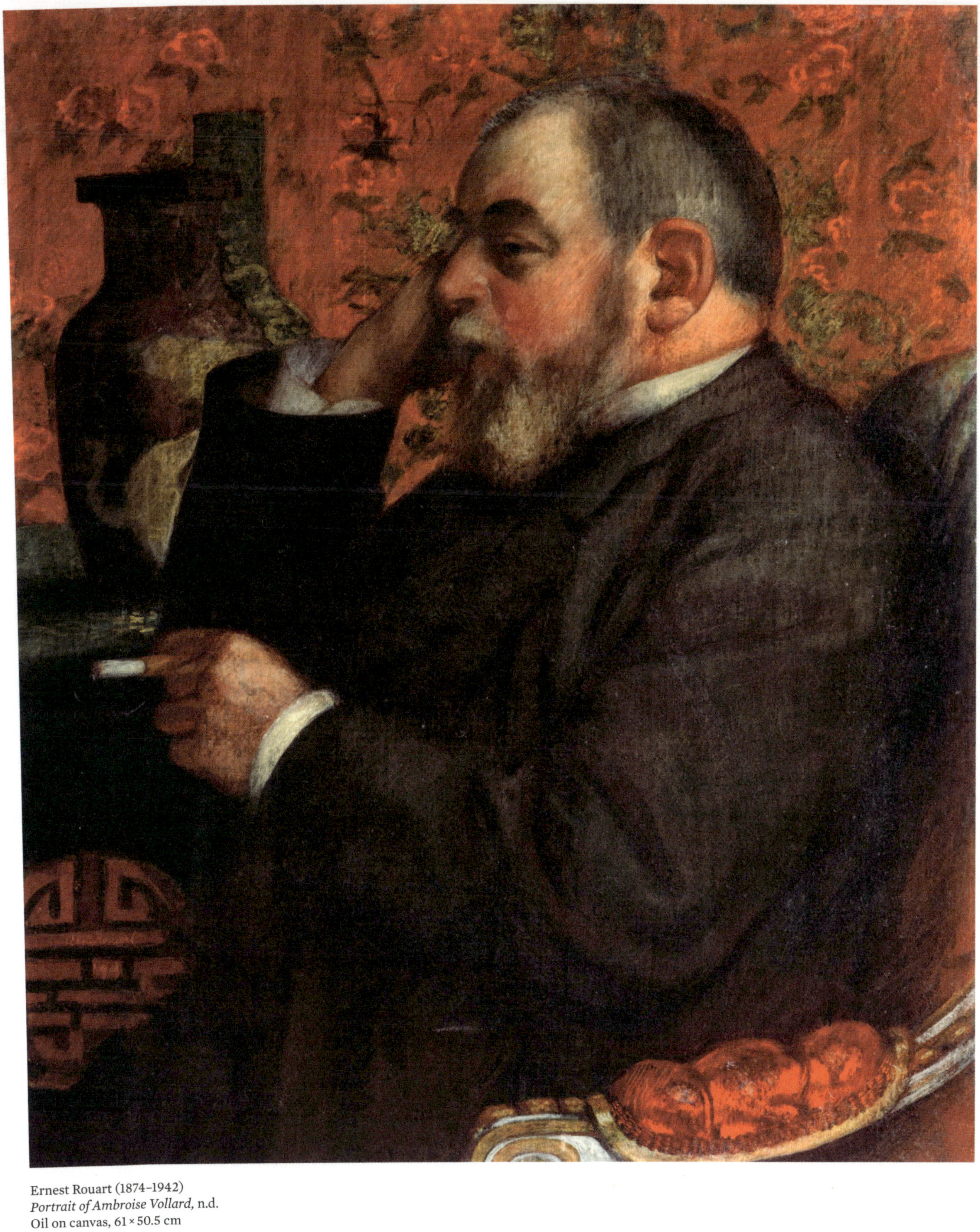

Ernest Rouart (1874–1942)
Portrait of Ambroise Vollard, n.d.
Oil on canvas, 61 × 50.5 cm
Private collection

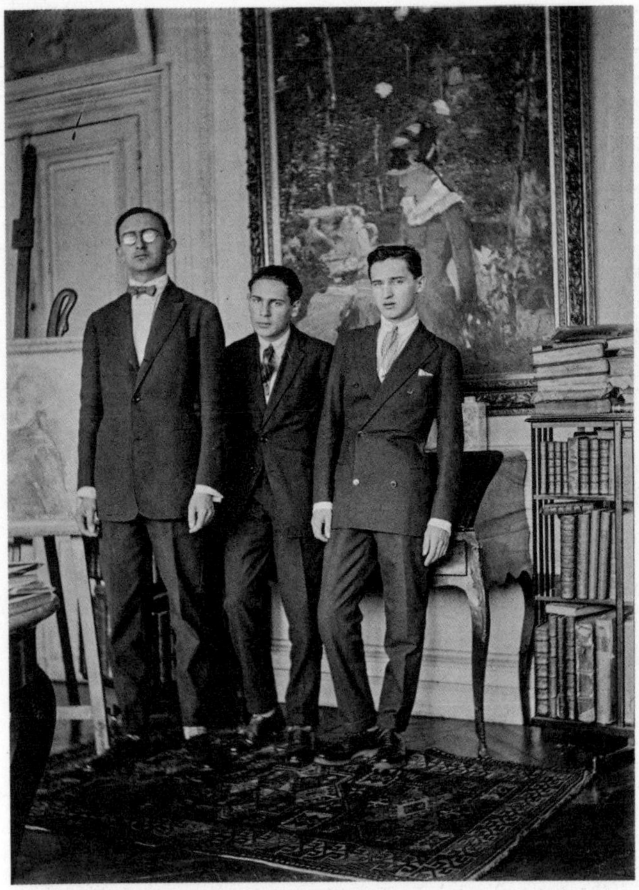

Attributed to Julie Manet (1878–1966)
Julien, Clément, and Denis Rouart rue de Villejust, c. 1925
Archives du Mesnil, on permanent loan at the Musée Marmottan Monet

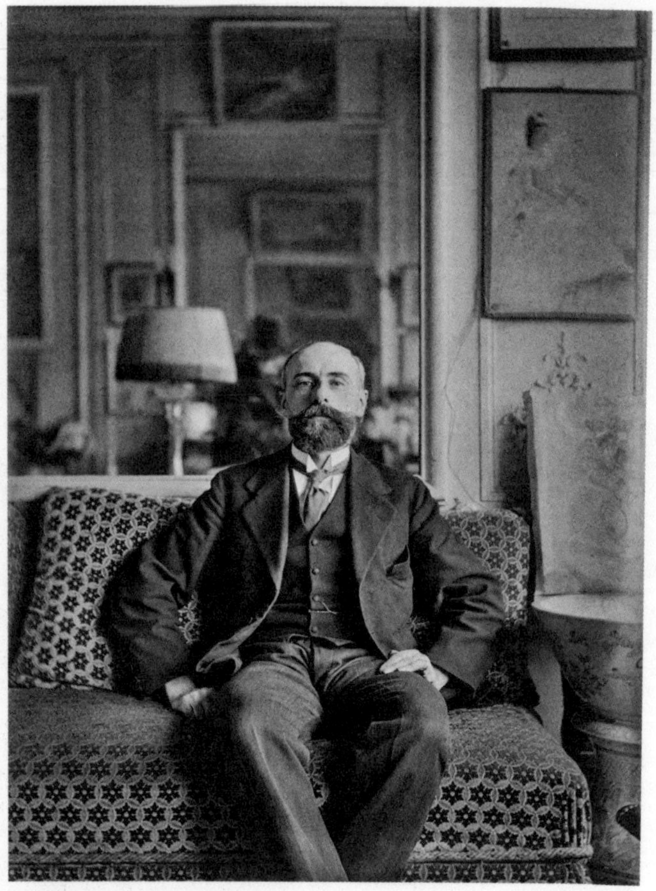

Attributed to Julie Manet (1878–1966)
Ernest Rouart in the living room in the rue de Villejust, n.d.
Archives BS, Paris, Musée Marmottan Monet

> Yes, I knew Vuillard. I remember a man who did not speak a great deal, but was very composed, a big beard, very much the painter, and seeming very gentle, very calm. But what he said about painting, I don't recall.[688]

Other artists frequented the rue de Villejust, including Georges d'Espagnat, who was close to Valéry and made several portraits of him (p. 109).

"I AM FAR FROM CONFUSING RELIGION AND ART"[689]

> The 1914 war, the danger or war, perhaps heightened religiosity, the belief in divine protection, well, something like that. . . . At that moment, precisely, the religious influence was very strong [in my family]; I still went to confession from time to time. I remember confessing to Père Janvier, who was certainly put forward by my family, who rolled his Rs terribly when he said to me "tu n'es pas heurrrrrreux."[690]

The Third Order, where he was a member of the council,[691] held a key position in Ernest's life. His entourage shared the commitment. The function of prior remained in the family for a decade. His brother Alexis (Frère Vincent Ferrier), prior from 1919 to 1921, was succeeded by two cousins: Henri Rouart[692] (Frère Raymond) from 1921 to 1925, then Gabriel Thomas (Frère Pie) from 1925 to 1928. The profession of faith of the painter George Desvallières (Frère Marie Albert) on May 30, 1914, then the induction into the order of Maurice Denis (Frère Jean-Dominique) on January 12, 1919, consolidated the presence of painters and illustrates the engagement on the part of artists in favor of a reinvigorated Catholic art. They militated for the renewal of Christian art and, in 1919, created a school to "provide churches, and especially churches devastated by the war, with religious works that are at once aesthetic,

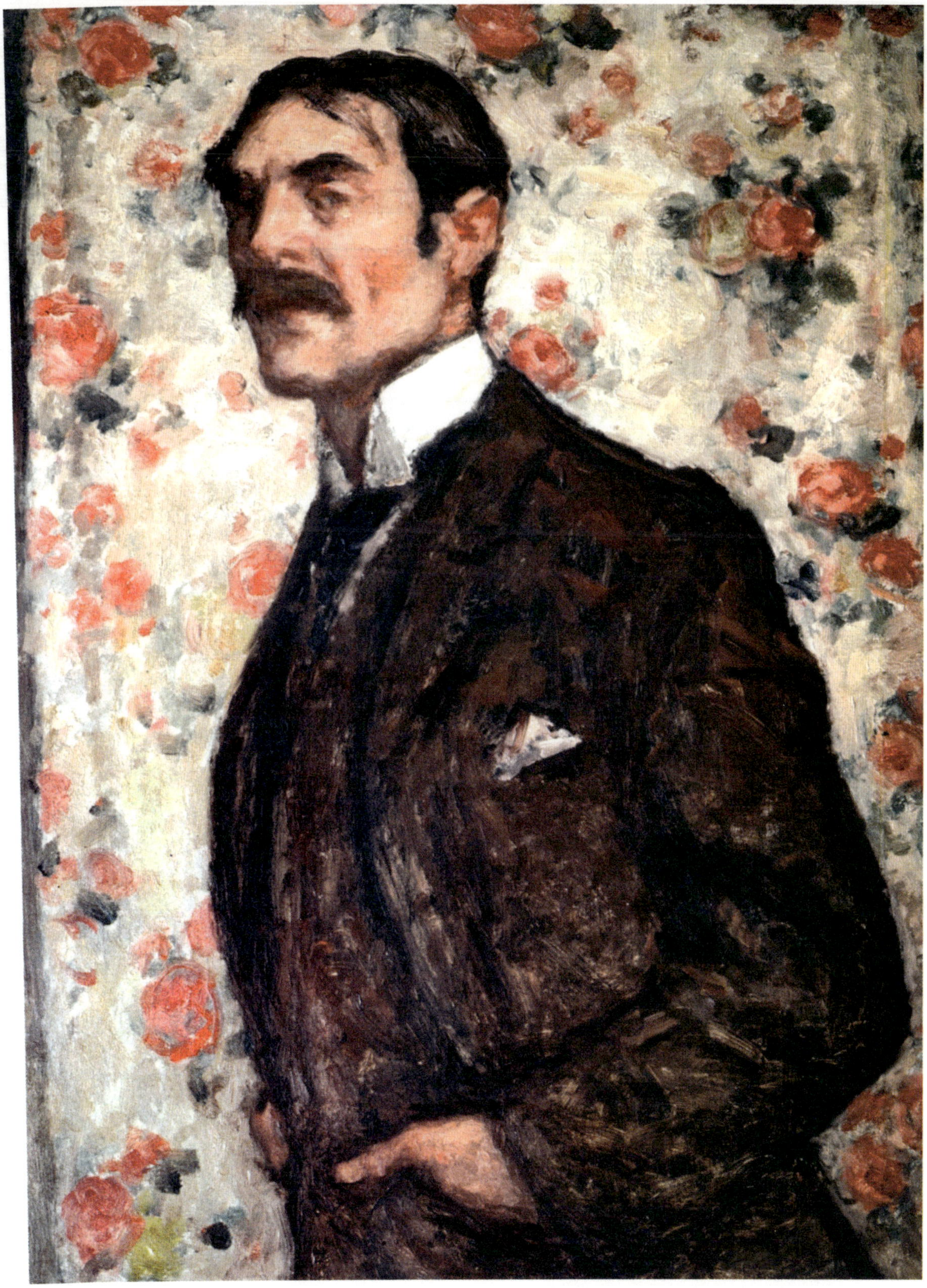

Georges d'Espagnat (1870–1950)
Portrait of Paul Valéry, c. 1910
Oil on canvas, 73 × 59.8 cm
Private collection

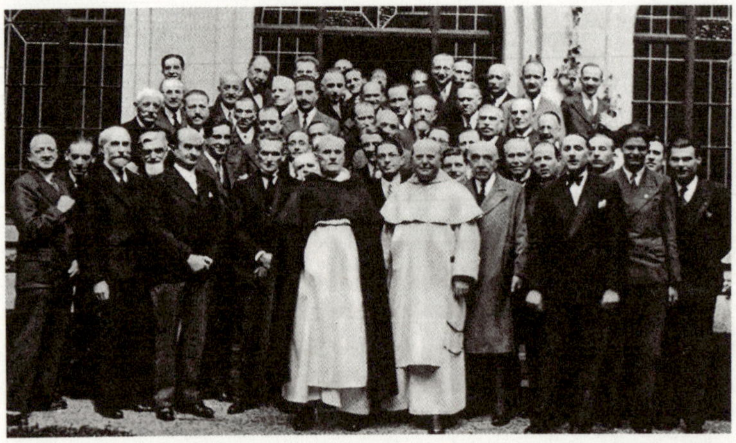

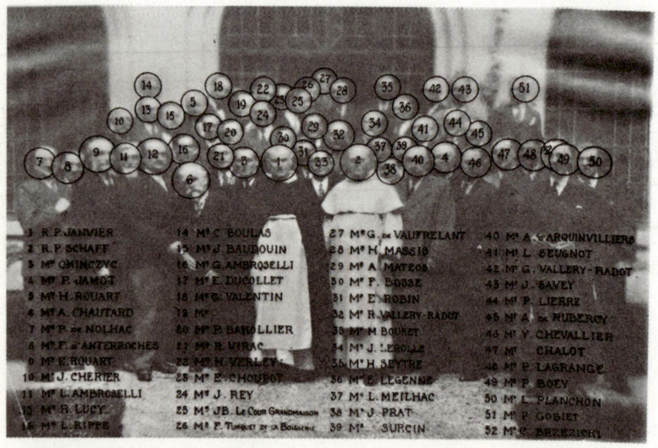

Third Order of Saint Dominic: a group of friars surrounding Père Janvier and Père Schaff after a meeting, 1935, and the corresponding sheet of tracing paper specifying the identity of the friars

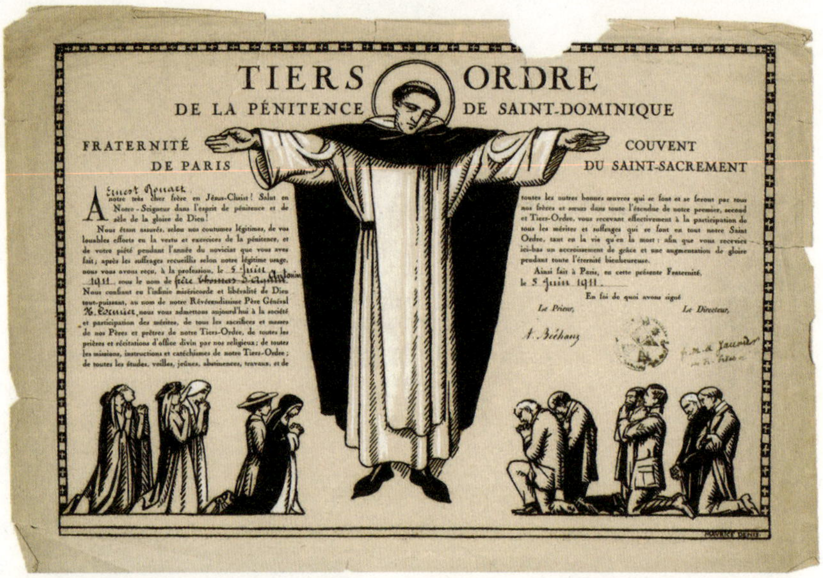

TIERS ORDRE
DE LA PÉNITENCE DE SAINT-DOMINIQUE
FRATERNITÉ DE PARIS
COUVENT DU SAINT-SACREMENT

Maurice Denis (1870–1943)
Diploma of the Brotherhood of the Third Order of the Penitence of Saint Dominic, awarded to Ernest Rouart (Frère Antonin)
Archives du Mesnil, on permanent loan at the Musée Marmottan Monet

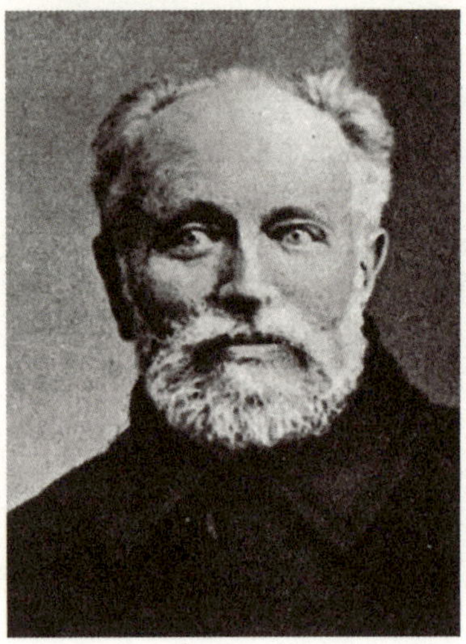

Gabriel Thomas

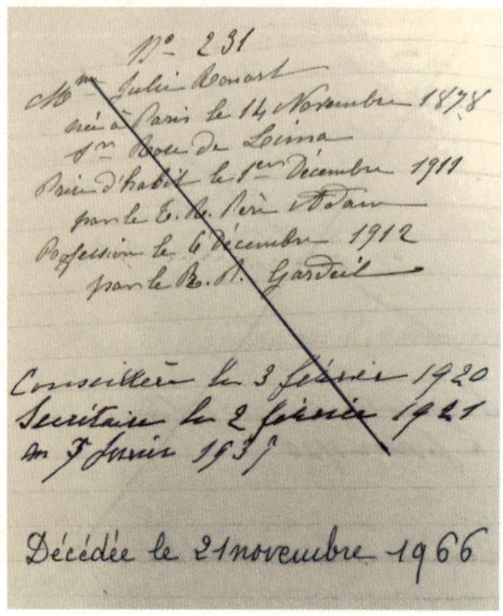

No 231

Décédée le 21 novembre 1966

Page from the list of members of the Brotherhood of the Annunciation showing member no. 231, Mme Julie Manet
Archives de la Province Dominicaine de France

traditional, and modern."[693] Such were the Ateliers d'Art Sacré. In *Nouvelles théories sur l'art moderne, sur l'art sacré*, published by Louis Rouart, Maurice Denis set out his credo:

> I proscribe academicism because it sacrifices emotion to convention and artifice because it is theatrical or dull. . . . I proscribe Jansenism because it is the death of art, coldness and tedium. . . . I proscribe realism because it is prose and I want "music above all things" and poetry. Finally, I shall preach Beauty. Beauty is an attribute of Divinity.[694]

Ernest manifestly did not share this faith in art. While we do not have his word expressing it, Julie's remark to him enlightens us on this relation to Beauty:

> I do not think as you do that the sensibility and the habit of seeing things on the artistic side (I don't like using that expression) is an obstacle to religiosity, I believe on the contrary that it can help it, but I do not express myself well; I am far from confusing Religion with Art.[695]

Ernest did not confuse them either. Not at all. Is that why he kept his distance from the Ateliers d'Art Sacré that his brothers in faith had just founded? Ernest did not put down his brush, even so. He was working, but had virtually stopped exhibiting. In 1919 he was at the Salon d'Automne,[696] then did not go back until 1936.[697] Fifteen years of absence. Fifteen years of a vow of silence. Ernest took a backseat. He chose the shadows. Like Julie, with Julie.

Should we be surprised that Julie also joined a community, a female Dominican Third Order? The *coutumier* of the Brotherhood of the Annunciation defined their rule in nineteen chapters. One of them, on "Outings and Social Pleasures," recommended:

> Sisters will attend social receptions or shows only to meet the demands of their life in the world: to develop their culture (students, teachers, educators) [and] family obligations (wives or mothers) . . . But let them not forget that, as members of the "Third Order of the Penitence of Saint Dominic," they would do better to abstain from anything that might undermine the spirit of inwardness and mortification.[698]

The tone was set. Julie took the habit on December 1, 1911 and made her profession of faith on December 6, 1912.[699] She would be Sœur Rose de Lima. The saint from whom she took her name (1586–1617) was, after Saint Catherine of Siena, an eminent Dominican tertiary. From the age of twenty, this young Peruvian took refuge in a hermitage located at the end of her parents' garden,

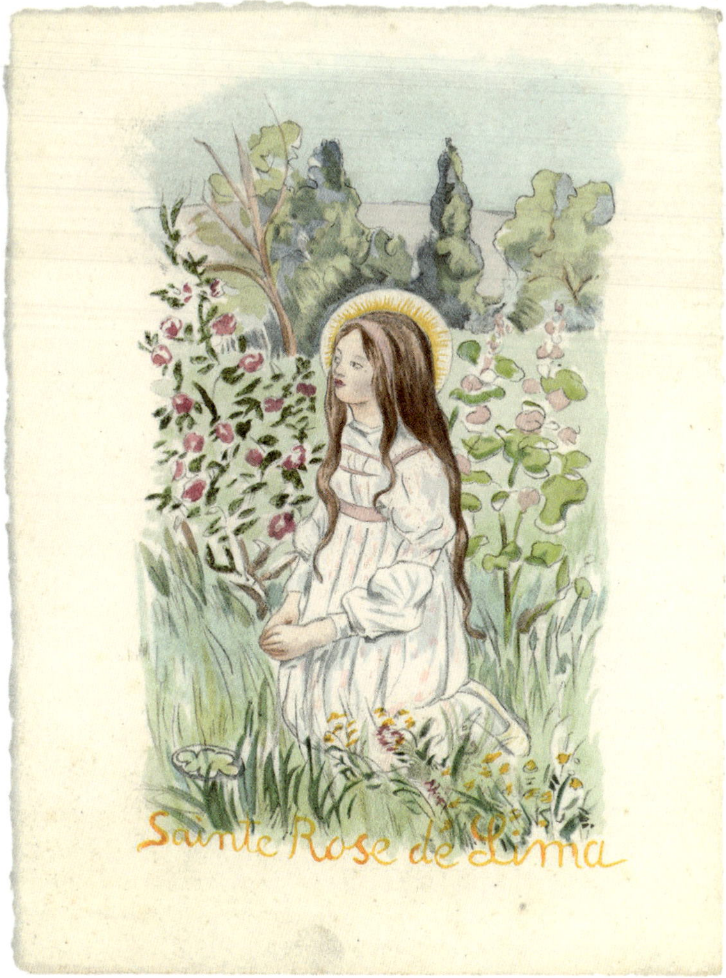

Julie Manet (1878–1966)
Saint Rose of Lima, c. 1938
Photoengraving, 19.3 × 14 cm
Archives du Mesnil, on permanent loan at the Musée Marmottan Monet

where she remained until her death. Rose lived a life of extreme penitence and mortification, eating only bread and water and sleeping on a bed made of pieces of wood tied together with rope, the gaps filled with fragments of crockery and tiles with the sharp bits pointing upwards. Sanctification, mortification. Devoted to the service of Indians and natives, she became the patron saint of Lima, Peru, the Americas, and the Philippines.

We do not know exactly what it was that drew Julie to Rose of Lima, of whom she made a charming illustration (above). Julie was an exemplary tertiary, charitable and attentive to the poor. Her good works were innumerable, as can be seen from the list of beneficiaries found in her accounts notebooks which, to venture an anachronism, are like random, catch-all inventories *à*

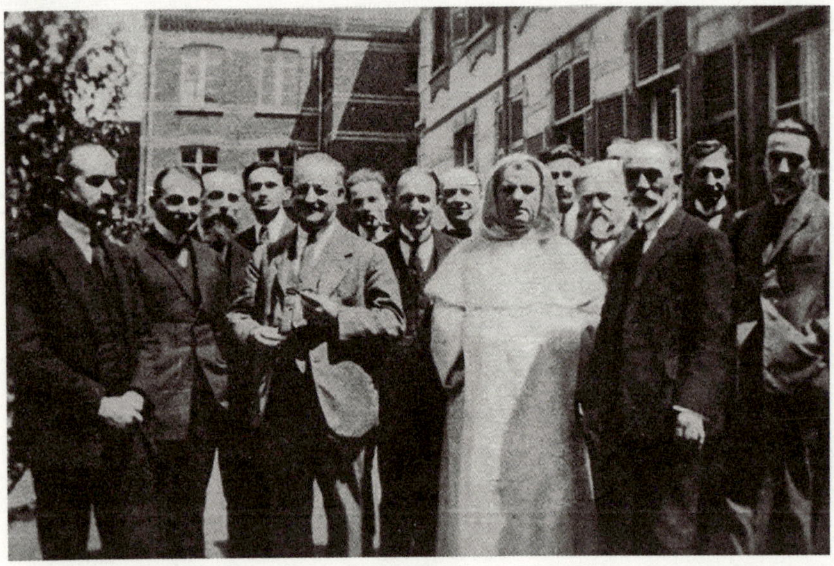

Retreatants surrounding the Père Janvier at Le Saulchoir
Ernest Rouart is third from left

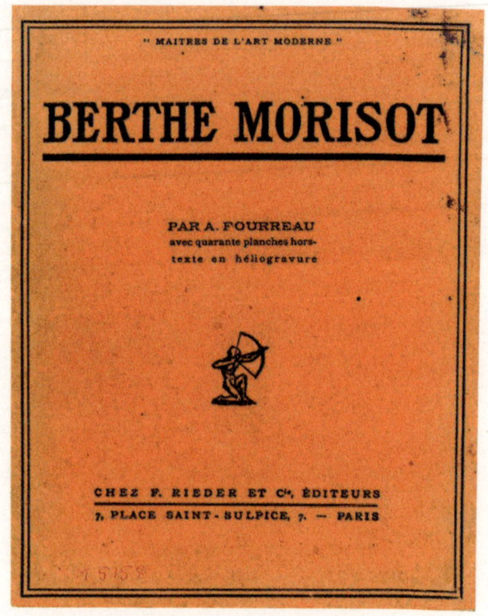

Cover of the first monograph on Berthe Morisot by Armand Fourreau, 1925
Paris, Musée Marmottan Monet

la Prévert (p. 113). She was devoted and soon occupied a key position in the Brotherhood. Not much later, her cousin Jeannie joined under the name of Sœur Marie-François.[700] Made a member of the council in 1920, from 1921 to 1937 Julie acted as secretary, writing the minutes of the council meetings[701] and keeping up the register of attendees.[702] Every year a pilgrimage united the sisters at Lourdes, a place that she had long loved. With the exception of the summer holidays, Julie devoted at least a day a week to the Third Order. Sœur Rose de Lima was not an abstraction.

"TO MADAME ERNEST ROUART, THE PIOUS GUARDIAN OF A GLORIOUS AND CHERISHED MEMORY"[703]

The life of service chosen by Ernest and Julie after the war is manifest in their relation to art. Sharing it with others and showing it. Julie continued to work in the service of her mother. After the death of Aunt Edma in 1921, a few discoveries were made. Julie wrote about this to Ernest:

> **This morning Blanche showed me letters found at her mother's home. Several by Corot; in one, he tells her to work hard in the country and to forget Papa Corot a bit, since nature is better. Then one from my uncle Édouard, others from Jules Ferry, from the Duc de La Rochefoucauld asking if wrong head has really sat his exam (you can tell this is a father-in-law). Two to mother from Puvis de Chavannes, one of them from Versailles at the moment of the Commune urging Maman to persuade her parents to leave Paris. One from Mallarmé written to Aunt Edma to warn her that there were articles that we should not read in an issue of *La Revue Blanche* that they were going to be sending to me containing an article about Maman. A word from "papa to mama," he said. Congratulations from Degas for Jeanne's marriage.[704]**

Uncle Tiburce being the last survivor of that generation, they turned to him. Aunt Edma's daughters also took part in their way. Jeanne confirmed this with regard to her sister Blanche:

> **I completely agree about giving the posthumous correspondence to Uncle Tiburce, but on the condition that we sort through it, for there is a risk that he will come across judgments about him which, although fifty years old, would not please him at all in the letters from Aunt Bertha.[705]**

Tiburce then wrote his recollections of his sister's childhood, forging the story of the artist's early years for the decades to come. The manuscript has been lost, but excerpts are quoted by Armand Fourreau, who published the first biography of Berthe Morisot in 1925 (above).[706] Unfortunately, we have no letters about the genesis of this work, except for the printed dedication that accompanied it, which speaks volumes:

To Madame Ernest Rouart, the pious guardian of a glorious and dear memory.[707]

Piously, Julie watched over her family. She wrote to the parish priest of Aspremont, where Uncle Tiburce lived. The abbé Bianchi reported on the visit:

> Worthy Madame Rouart, you did well to write to me after having prayed. Armed with your good letter or, rather, your greetings, I was able to approach your uncle who I thought still had a little strength and, while expressing your interest in him, I was able to deftly slip in the urgings of the Holy Ghost that you have granted him. For this first time he asked only that I recognize his serious state, his imminent end, the formalities for his burial in Nice[708] and Extreme_Unction when the time comes; then to reply to you and to tell you about his galloping decline, not hoping, he said, that you could leave Paris to come and see him one last time. That is all, but he listened attentively to my exhortations and showed no refusal of any kind to receive the help of Religion on another day, for I understood myself that for a first visit his weakness could not bear a longer extension. And so the two of us are thus reassured and the Sacred Heart in its blessed month will not allow to escape this soul that is indeed adorned with an intelligence that is not ordinary: we will continue to keep an interest in him, indeed, in our prayers at Holy Mass. And also, if you manage to come to Aspremont in the days to come, it would be, from what I gather, not only a boon for his soul but also for his material assistance, perhaps too for a funeral that is a little honorable, less costly if you like at church but still rather a worry as regards the undertaker for the formalities of the transport to Caucade cemetery in Nice. In the eventuality that you might wish this concern to fall to you, you can see how precious your presence would be, for Mlle Alice Gamby does not look to me able to manage.[709]

Julie hurried there and gave assistance to Alice, Uncle Tiburce's daughter-in-law. Jeannie and Paule stayed in Paris with Valéry, who was putting the finishing touches to his speech of induction at the Académie Française. A few days before Valéry joined the circle of "Immortals,"[710] Julie was there to give her uncle to God. Tiburce passed away on June 13, 1927.[711] The next day Paule wrote:

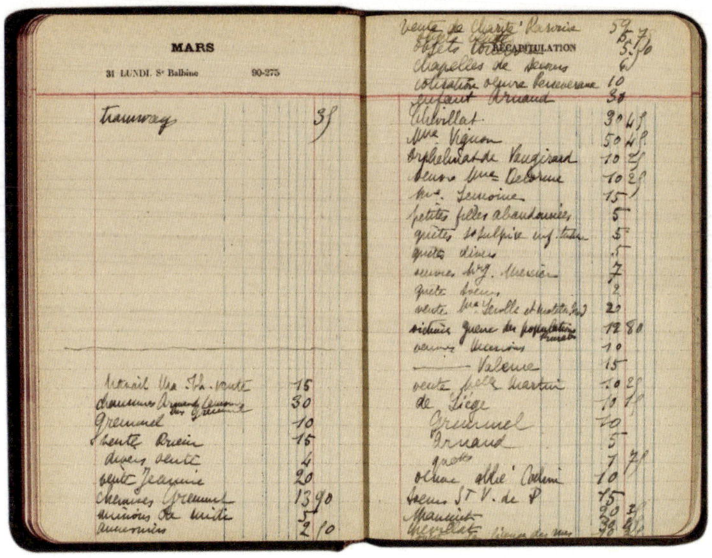

Page from Julie Manet's diary for the year 1919: list of good works
Archives du Mesnil, on permanent loan at the Musée Marmottan Monet

> My dear Julie, I am thinking of you, not knowing how you are occupied and what occupies you the most. Your evening yesterday cannot have been much fun. Ernest had Clément bring down your letter this morning. Did Uncle Tiburce recognize you any better? What regrets you would have had if you had not gone. Never would I have thought that you would arrive right on the eve of his death. Is the paperwork complicated [?] I think that the ceremony will be held tomorrow in the little church of Aspremont where I used to go in the morning. . . . You have such extraordinary energy, I can picture you doing everything. . . . I do not know if Alice will go through the papers of the father-in-law. I know that after having heard the story of his adventures in Africa, I told him he should write his memoirs. It is fortunate that you have his memories of Aunt Berthe.[712]

Fortunate indeed.

A new era was beginning in the rue de Villejust, now better known as the home of a poet than as that of a painter. All the light was now drawn to the fourth floor, a fact that never troubled the inwardness that defined the soul of those above. It was a natural movement of the stars that disturbed neither the harmony of the place nor the understanding between its occupants.

The townhouse in the rue de Lisbonne was now rented. Ernest was forced to leave his studio, although he fought this as long as he could. Like Julie, he was attached to history and the places embodying it. Invoking a lease granted him in the past, the painter even took the case to the Court of Appeal. On November 12, 1929, the judgment was issued and the expulsion order given.[713] Ernest retreated to the rue de Villejust, where the couple had a studio built at the end of Berthe Morisot's garden (it is still there today). Were they thinking of Saint Rose de Lima's hermitage? Facing north, this plain construction offered Frère Antonin the space he needed to work in his cloister.

A DECADE OF CENTENARIES

Ernest was an avid museum-goer. The newspapers recorded his and Julie's presence at the main Parisian openings. The couple were of course there for the opening ceremony of the Musée Marmottan, whose curator was their grand-cousin by marriage,[714] Hector Lefuel.[715] It was above all as an organizer of exhibitions that Lefuel distinguished himself in the 1930s. As France prepared to celebrate the centenary of the birth of his painter forebears, Ernest contributed to the organization of these major retrospectives. The Manet exhibition put on at the Orangerie des Tuileries in 1932 was the first in the series, and Ernest threw himself into it. His son, Julien, recalled that "on this occasion he was offered the Légion d'Honneur and, what do you know, he turned it down."[716] What a contrast with his friends who thirsted for glory! That was the case with Maurice Denis, who was elected to the Académie des Beaux-Arts the same year. Gabriel Thomas, died shortly before this triumph acclaimed by his neighbor at the Académie Française:

> My dear friend and now colleague, I am delighted, and here are diverse compliments from myself and my wife, and for you and your wife. And for us, the Institut, who are greatly in need of . . . and . . . ! I dare not fill in these blanks. I shake your hand, Paul Valéry.[717]

Ernest was quick to contact his brother in the Third Order:

> My dear friend,
> We were very happy to learn of your election to the Institut and we send you our sincere congratulations with all our heart, with warm regards to yourself and Madame Denis.
> Cordially,
> Ernest Rouart[718]

With Ernest, humility and reticence reigned, with the risk that he might forget himself. Busy with his homages, he devoted himself to his father and to the Henri Rouart exhibition put on at the Galerie Rosenberg in 1933.[719] And Ernest was discreet in his service: the catalogue preface was entrusted to the inevitable Valéry, in the hope that his illustrious pen would scatter a little glory on those it honored.

Julie was devoted to her mother. Although in 1931 Vollard gave up the idea of publishing the Berthe Morisot catalogue and instead sold the iconographic rights to Éditions des Beaux-Arts,[720] she continued to work on this publication that was close to her heart. Striving to be as exhaustive as possible, she tracked down the privately owned Morisots and, in a little notebook, noted the names of some fifteen collectors and the titles of the works in their possession, placing these between two sketches in keeping with the family tradition. Each art lover had their own sheet, although Paule and Jeannie, who opened the list, were naturally treated as one. Among those that followed were Michel Monet, who had inherited his father's collection in 1926, Guillaume Lerolle, Donop de Monchy, Louis Rouart, Pierre Renoir, Durand Ruel, and Mme Doucet.[721] In 1933, a new monograph on Berthe Morisot was published by Monique Angoulvent, the daughter of her childhood friend, Léon Angoulvent.[722] The new generations were beginning to take over. Julie, for her part, continued to keep notes. In London, where the Knoedler Gallery exhibited her mother's work in 1936, she located two new canvases. In one of her notebooks [723] she copies in color pencil *The Sewing Lesson* and *The Cup of Tea* (p. 115), which belonged to Lady Cunard. The hanging plan for the main room at the Knoedler Gallery—a plan recalling its drawn variant—and the review of the 1896 exhibition are also worth mentioning. Julie no doubt kept the memories entrusted to her by Alice Gamby:

> Yes, your mother was right to paint. Her first picture[724] was bought by Alfred Stevens when he went to her house, where your Uncle Tiburce just happened to be. She told me that what really made her happy was that it was a painter who bought it.[725]

Alice's reports were not always reliable. For example, she had Berthe Morisot living at Juziers, which had never been the case:

> Naturally there is no better place for working and doing your mother's biography than Le Mesnil, where she lived. During the last days of his life my father-in-law spoke to me often about his sisters and his mother, whom he loved, and yet he resisted coming to live near her, even though she told him it was his duty to come and take the place of his father [Edme Morisot].[726]

For all that, the family memory was all that Julie had to work with.

The memory of another artist occupied all the floors of the rue de Villejust, that of Degas. In 1929, after a meeting with Vollard, Valéry offered to write an essay about him,

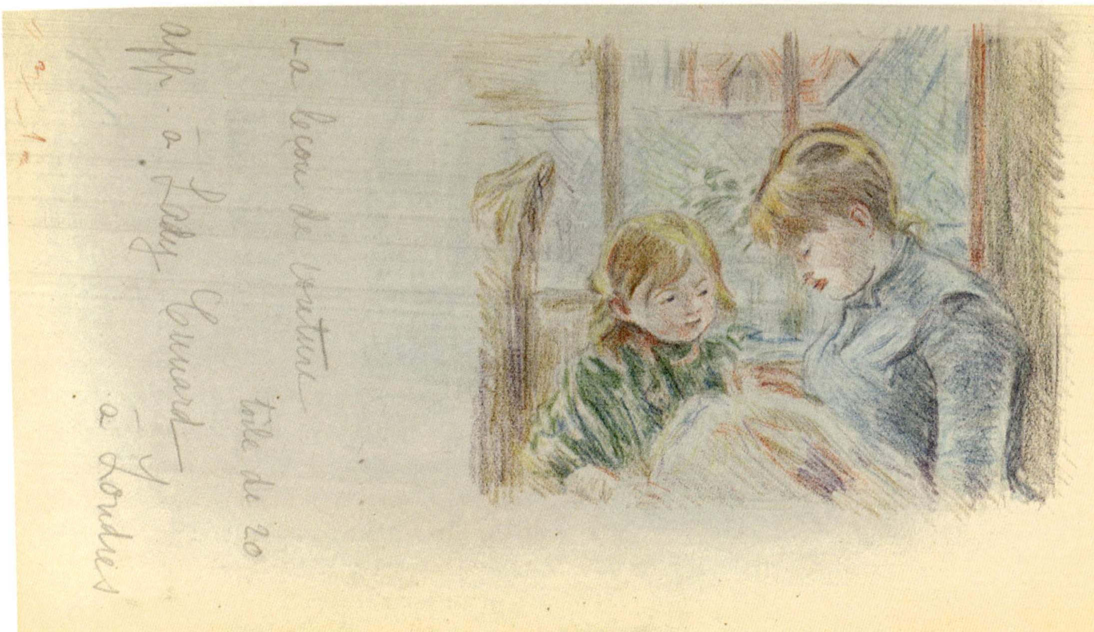

Julie Manet (1878–1966)
Page from a sketchbook: *The Sewing Lesson* (after Berthe Morisot), c. 1936
Archives du Mesnil, on permanent loan at the Musée Marmottan Monet

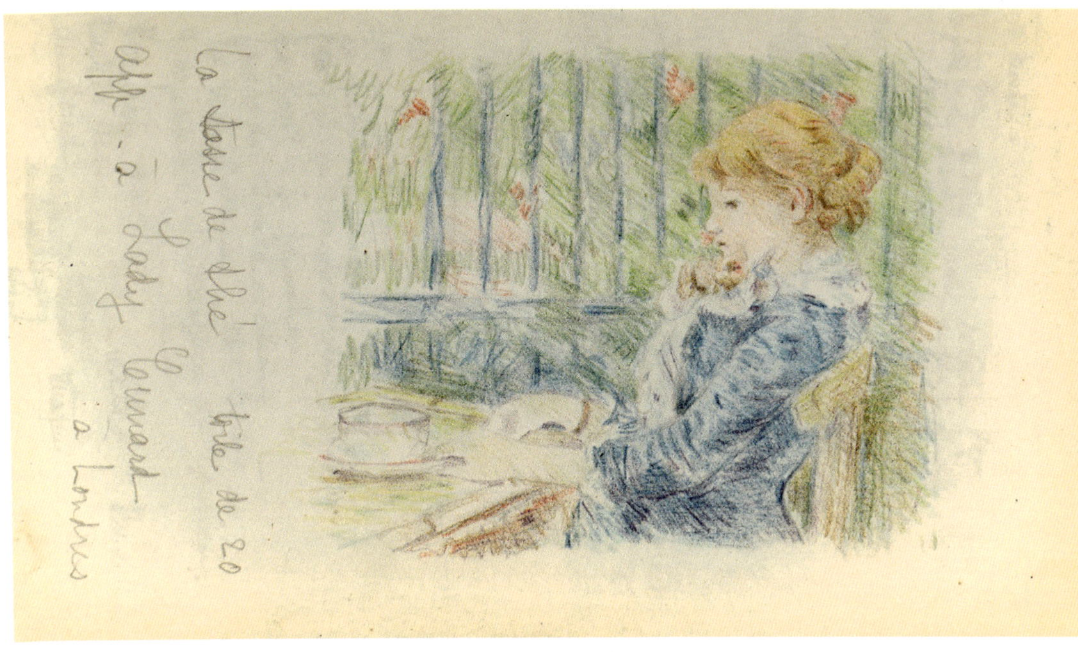

Julie Manet (1878–1966)
Page from a sketchbook: *The Cup of Tea* (after Berthe Morisot), c. 1936
Archives du Mesnil, on permanent loan at the Musée Marmottan Monet

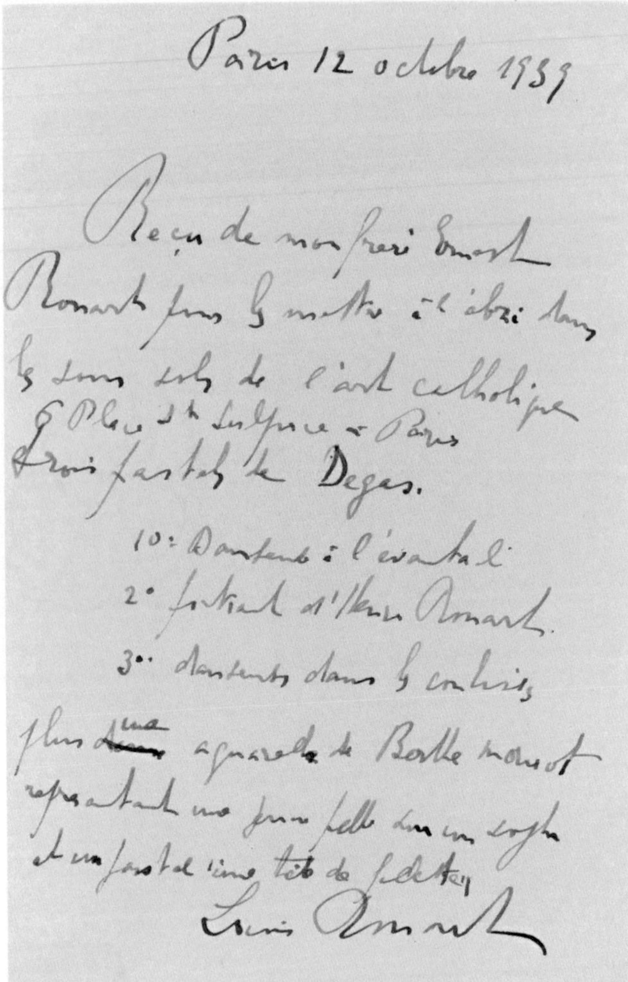
Paris 12 octobre 1939

Reçu de mon frère Ernest Rouart pour les mettre à l'abri dans les sous sols de l'art catholique 6 Place St Sulpice à Paris trois pastels de Degas.

1° Danseuse à l'éventail

2° portrait d'Henri Rouart.

3° danseuses dans les coulisses

plus une aquarelle de Berthe Morisot représentant une jeune fille dans un sopha et un pastel une tête de fillette

Louis Rouart

Receipt signed by Louis Rouart attesting the depositing of works from the collection of Ernest and Julie Rouart for safe storage, October 12, 1939
Archives du Mesnil, on permanent loan at the Musée Marmottan Monet

which he titled *Degas Danse Dessin – DDD* [Degas Dance Drawing]. The genesis of this piece is well known and the unpublished family correspondence confirms what we know already: that Ernest made a key contribution to this project. Jeannie wrote to her pseudo-brother-in-law thus:

> You have not responded to his [Paul's] invitation [de Paul] to share a few memories of Degas and Julie has not refreshed my memory (she knows how imprecise it is) about the decoration scene. Paul was hoping that you would provide him with a few pages of his Degas, at which he is working away.[727]

Julie's nudges became frequent: "And those memories of Degas, have you forgotten them?"[728] And, later:

> Paul is typing out his memories of Degas having decided, I believe, to get him done. You have such a precise memory, you should send him the anecdote about when Mallarmé was snubbed by him, and any other from yourself or from Ernest. That could help him. Quite naturally, he will have cause to talk about his friendship with M. Rouart.[729]

It was Ernest who orchestrated the Degas centenary exhibition at the Orangerie. Paul Jamot, honorary curator of paintings at the Louvre, a member of the Third Order since 1924, and a prior from 1928 to 1935, was also involved in the project. In the year he took the habit he was also invited to the rue de Villejust to see Ernest's Degases. It was Jamot who wrote the preface for the catalogue, while the entries were written by curators at the Louvre. In this very singular context, amidst the abundant homages, when Degas's art was unanimously acclaimed, and with everyone rushing in to comment on his work, Ernest took up the pen for the first time and published an open letter in the newspaper *Le Soir*:

> Organizer of the Degas exhibition that opens on Friday? Yes . . . You could say, as I was of the Manet exhibition. It is the privilege of age and of the friendship of M. Henri Verne, director of the national museums. Here at last is the finishing touch to the panorama of French painting undertaken six years ago at the Orangerie. The public will observe all the things that united the debutants of 1863—the integration of life into their art—and everything that divided them: technique and sensibility. Degas was at one with his comrades for ten years: exhibitions, struggles, insults . . . But in his traditional technique, created under the rude discipline of M. Ingres, do not go looking for the brisk flourishes of Manet or the shimmering colors of Renoir, any more than his vision as agreeable as that of an enchanting animal. In the spectacle of women at their labor, of dance seen from the side of effort, of Parisiennes surprised at their toilet, Degas was close to the realism of his literary friends, Duranty more than Zola. In 1872, he wrote to my father from New Orleans to describe a woman who had "that degree of ugliness without which there is no salvation." Much more than any lengthy discussion, does not this confidence reveal the nature of Degas's art. Cruel? Pessimistic? Misogynistic? Speak the truth. He was true. And I would like this exhibition to allow the public to discover, at last, all the treasures of intelligence and modest tenderness that there were in that Parisian *grand bourgeois* who has been turned into a specialist of snide asides, into a tough old beast stingy with smiles, even tight-lipped ones.[730]

Ernest did what only a son feels duty-bound to do: to come to the defense of a guilty father. He defended the man, not the artist. His text is preceded by a few disturbing lines:

Painter and collector, son-in-law [*sic*] of the great realist painter Degas, M. Ernest Rouart tells us.[731]

Mistake or Freudian slip, this introduction says a great deal about the author's motivations.

Should we be surprised that Ernest's younger son followed the path set out by his father, that he studied art history and defended a thesis on "Degas and Technique" on February 27, 1939 at the École du Louvre?[732] Degas was on all minds, at the heart of concerns. This state of affairs did not change with the war. In 1918 the rue de Villejust was busy protecting his works. As of October 12, 1939, its occupants placed the most precious pastels—*Dancer with a Fan* (p. 271),[733] *Henri Rouart* (p. 279),[734] *In the Wings* (p. 303)[735]—in the basements of the Librairie de l'Art Catholique founded by Ernest's brother Louis.[736] Alice Gamby wrote to Julie about this:

> Your paintings are probably in the Banque de France, I thought you had left everything in the rue de Villejust, the portrait of your mother on the easel who would protect you from the beyond: you have had the courage *petite biche* as your mother called you to proceed together with your husband, to piously store away all these memories.[737]

Julie drew up the inventory of the paintings placed in the Musée des Beaux-Arts in Pau, at the home of M. Chapuis, 4, rue Crétet, Paris, and of the "50 pastels watercolors and drawings and a bust" entrusted to the Valérys in the rue de Villejust.[738] In May 1940 a considerable part of their collection was put away safely in the Musées de France storerooms at the châteaux of Chambord, Brissac and Sourches.[739]

A note from Jeannie enlightens us about this period:

> Downheartedness must not cohabit with danger. Surrounded by difficulties, let us be strong. The secret of strength is confidence, general and individual confidence. We must trust in the will of God in events that give us such an opportunity to become detached. There is nothing more we can do. It is for us to do it well, giving the fullness of ourselves to religious, social, and family life, giving all we can give. Spectacular deeds are for those who defend us. We who are on the margins of this frame of heroism, we can, however, become heroic, a little. I am talking to those tertiaries, whose patriotism must be linked to a life of sanctification that depends wholly on our progress in charity, and that God increases in us. As soon as he sees us disposed to valorize it, and prepared to expel the deliberate venial sin that opposes it. . . . The state of war is one of those moments. It is "forbidden" to tertiaries to remain mediocre. On the contrary, they must attain spiritual intrepidness. It is time.[740]

Julie wholly shared her cousin's point of view, as can be seen from the draft of a letter intended for Paul Reynaud,[741] Président du Conseil:

> Monsieur Président du Conseil,
> Forgive me for taking one of your moments at this time, but I am encouraged to do so by the answer you made to me when I addressed my best wishes for your government. Has not the time come when Paris and France should turn toward God?
> I am, with all my consideration and admiration, yours,
> J. Manet Rouart.[742]

Immersed in an ultra-Catholic, patriotic milieu close to Action Française, in which notions such as the nation and duty were raised to the rank of supreme values, Ernest and Julie continued to do their work in France during the Occupation. How could they not celebrate the centenary of Berthe Morisot, who was born in 1841? How could they view the year 1941 through any other prism than that of filial memory, when they had made that their sole horizon? Like so many other French people, Julie and Ernest did not see the world as it was, nor the tragedy that was unfolding in it. Once again, they were absorbed in their mission: living in the past, serving it in real time, at the risk of failing to see the present. The exhibition for Berthe Morisot's centenary took place in a collaborationist France. The institutions played their part and the Orangerie Nationale des Tuileries exhibited two hundred and eighty-seven works by the Impressionist. The lenders, old friends, responded faithfully: Paule Gobillard, Jeannie Valéry, Blanche Pontillon-Forget, Louis Rouart, Octave Thomas, Michel Monet, Mme Jacques Doucet, M. Faure, and the Vicomtesse de Gastines, as well as those who preferred to remain anonymous. Paul Valéry did his bit and wrote the preface in honor of the woman who, after forty years of marriage to her niece, had become his Aunt Berthe.[743] Louis Rouart, too, came forward; he had ceased to write but took up his pen again to state his deep admiration. The centenary of the artist by whom he acquired numerous works impelled him to publish his "biography" of Berthe Morisot.[744] It too appeared in 1941. "By going so far into the details of the past, one makes the present bearable."[745]

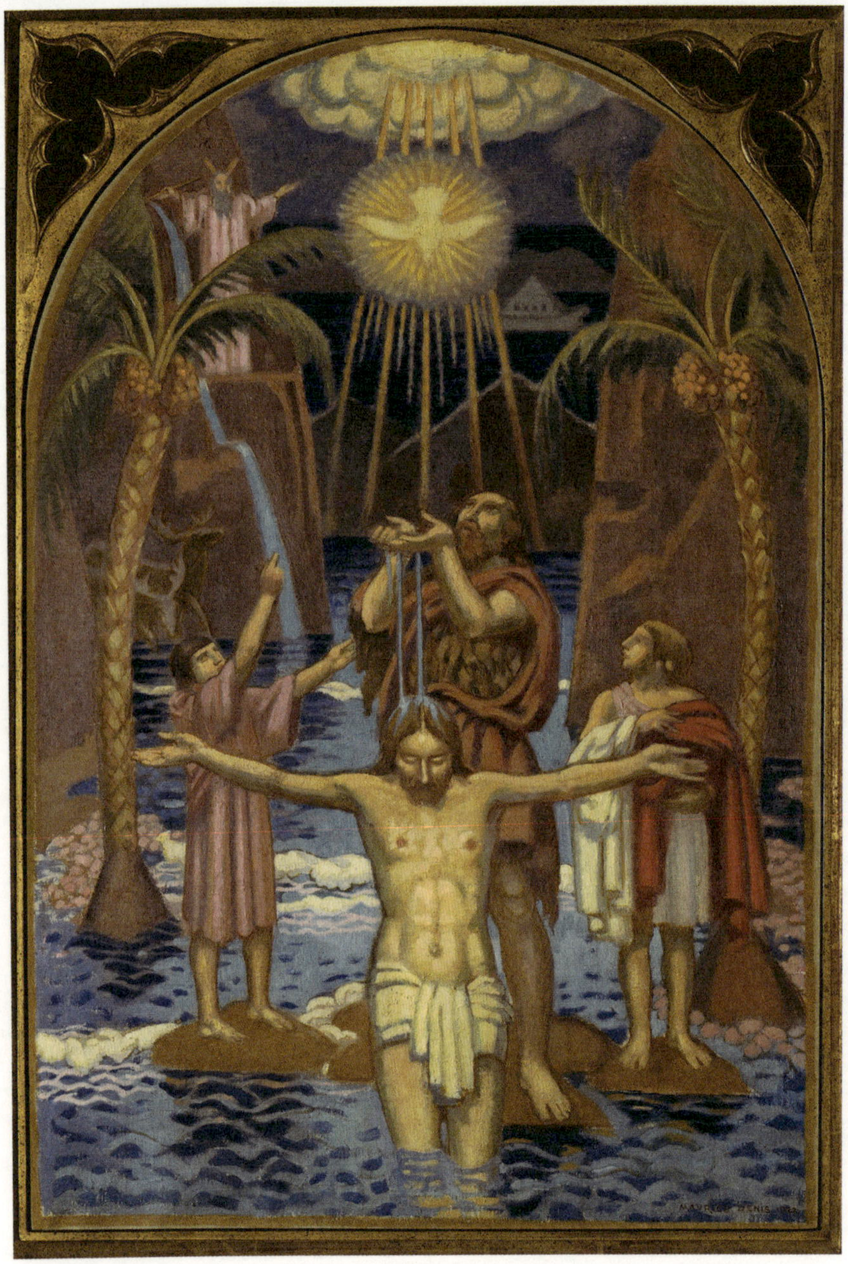

Maurice Denis (1870–1943)
Baptism of Christ or *Baptism in the Jordan* (sketch for the mosaic in the church of Saint-Paul in Geneva), 1922
Oil on canvas, 86 × 57.5 cm
France, private collection

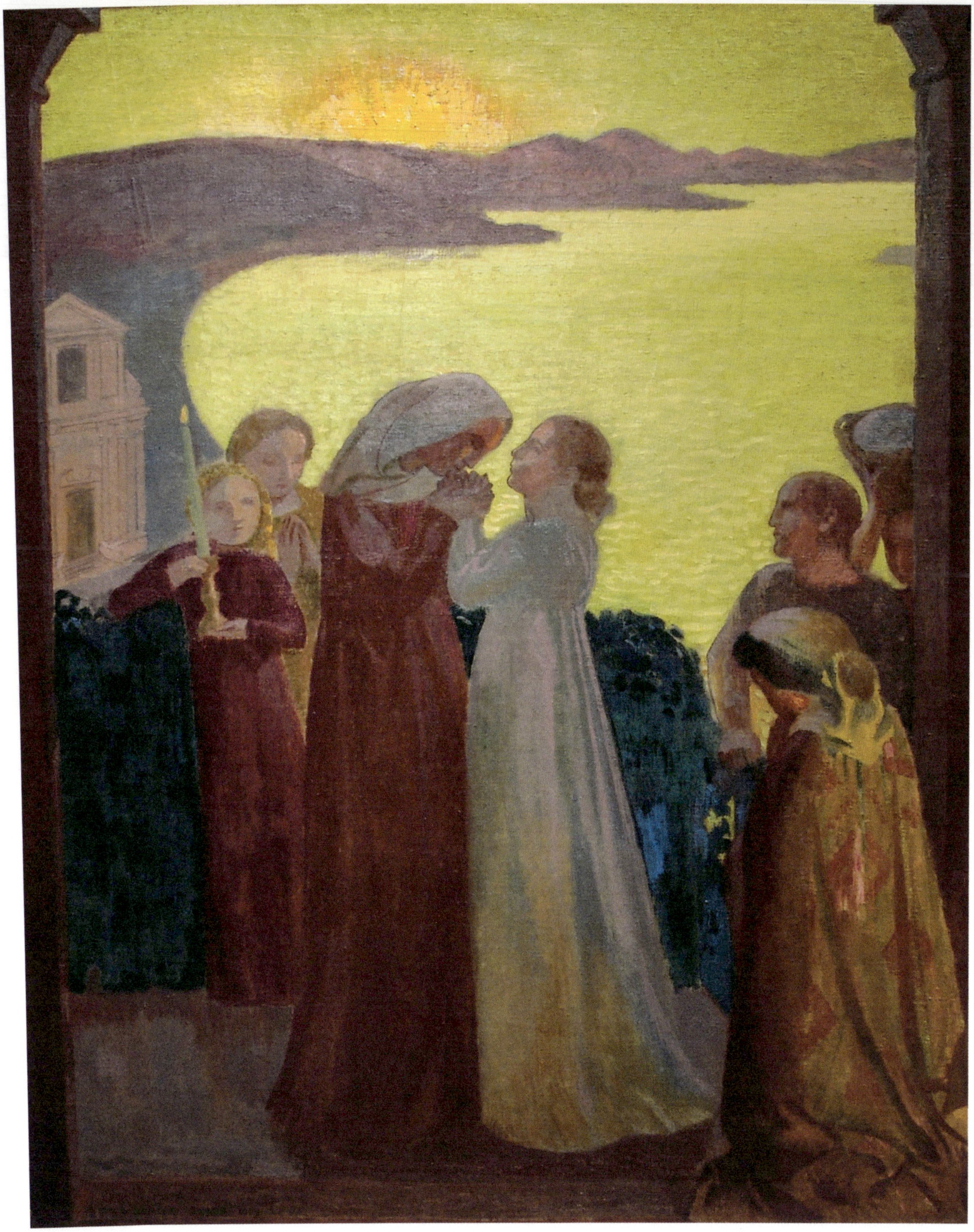

Maurice Denis (1870–1943)
Magnificat, 1909
Oil on canvas, 130 × 104 cm
Private collection

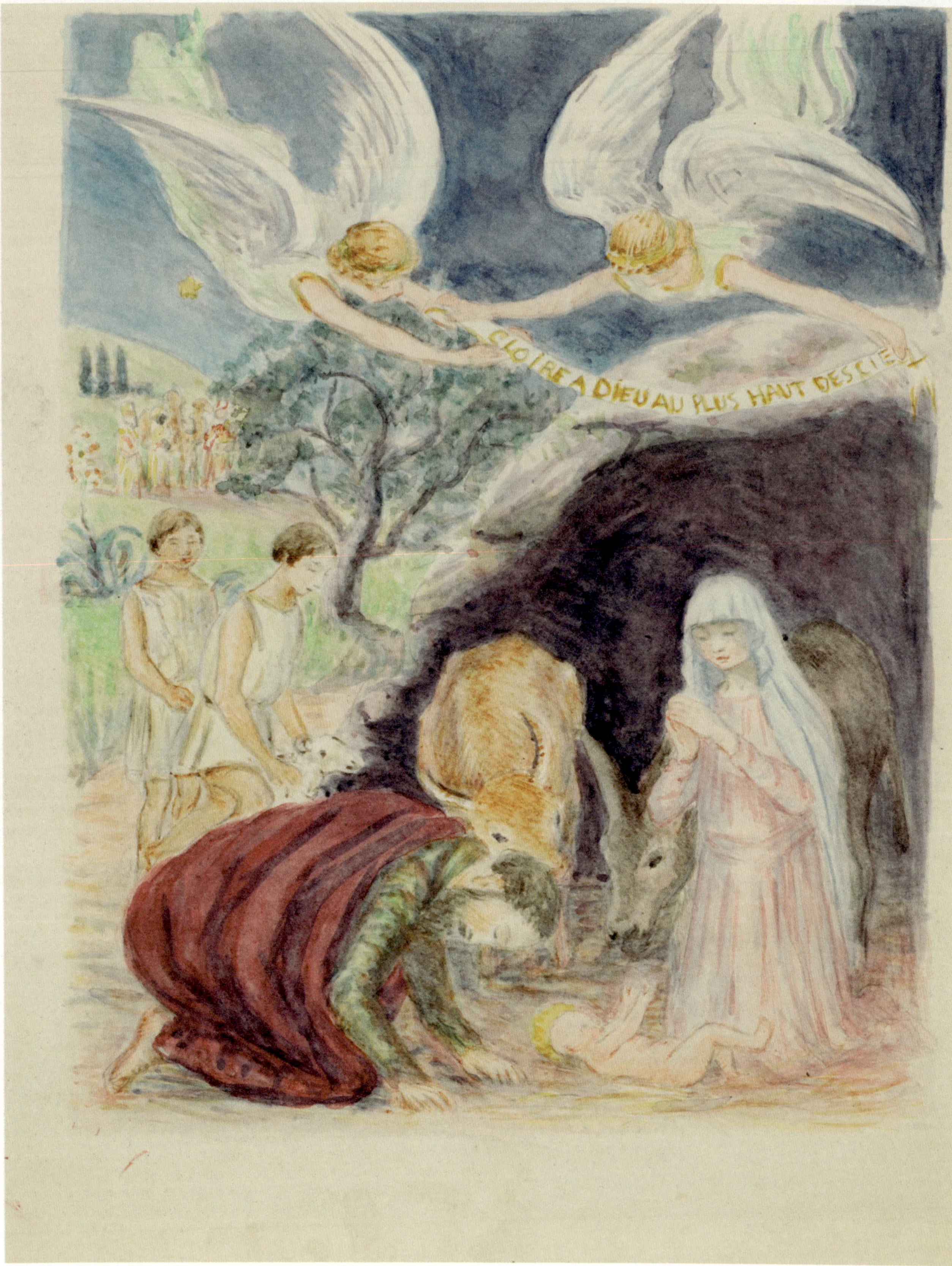

Julie Manet (1878–1966)
Nativity, illustration from Jean-Michel's catechism book, c. 1941
Watercolor and pencil on paper, 23 × 18.5 cm
Private collection

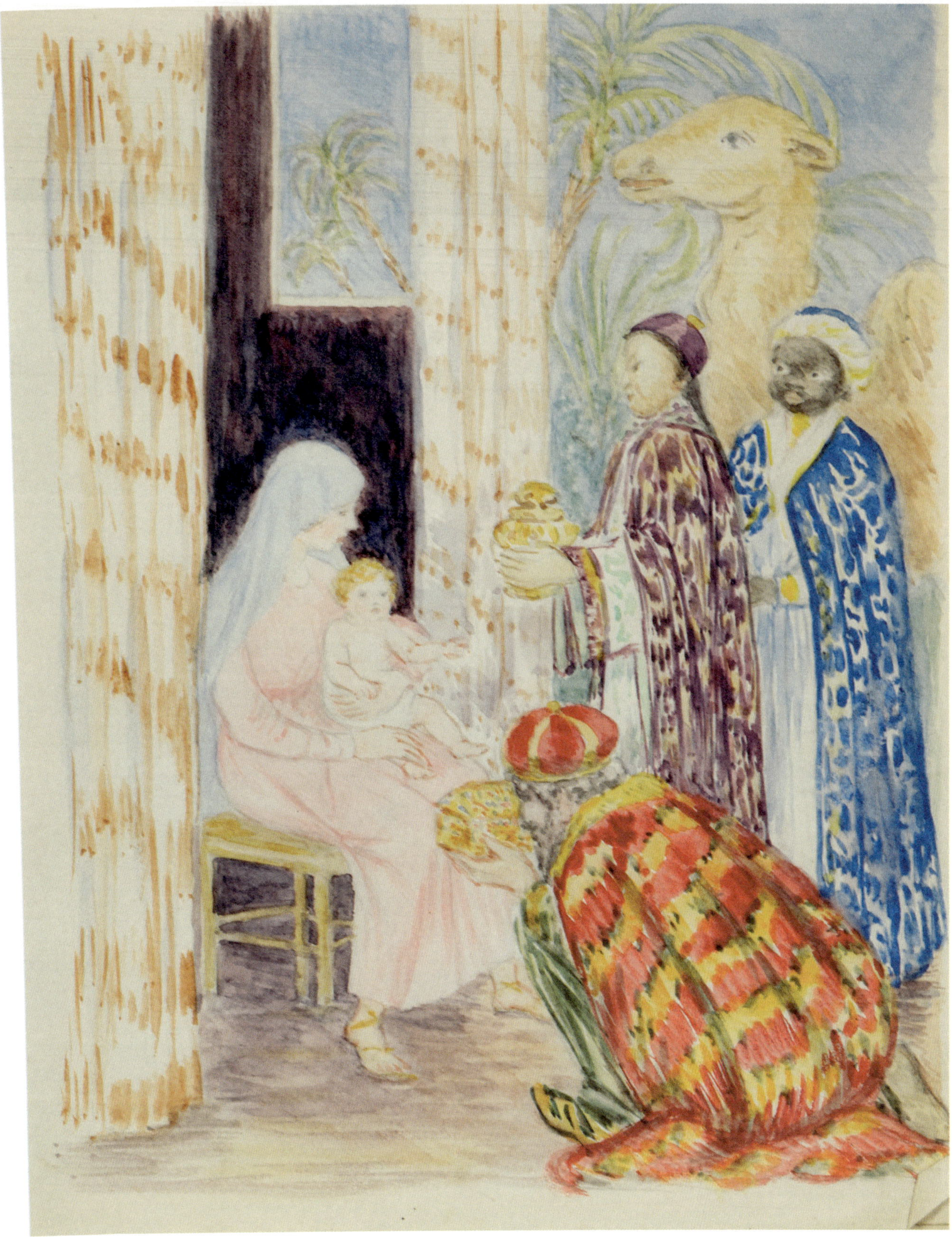

Julie Manet (1878–1966)
The Adoration of the Magi, illustration from Jean-Michel's catechism book, c. 1941
Watercolor and pencil on paper, 23 × 18.5 cm
Private collection

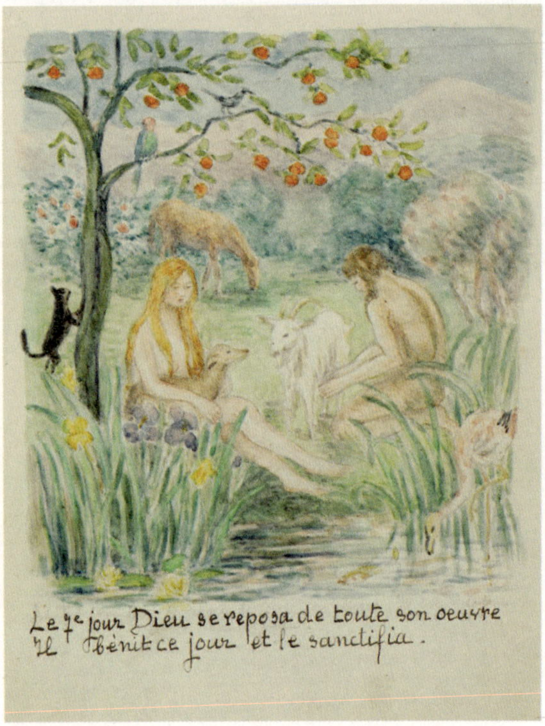

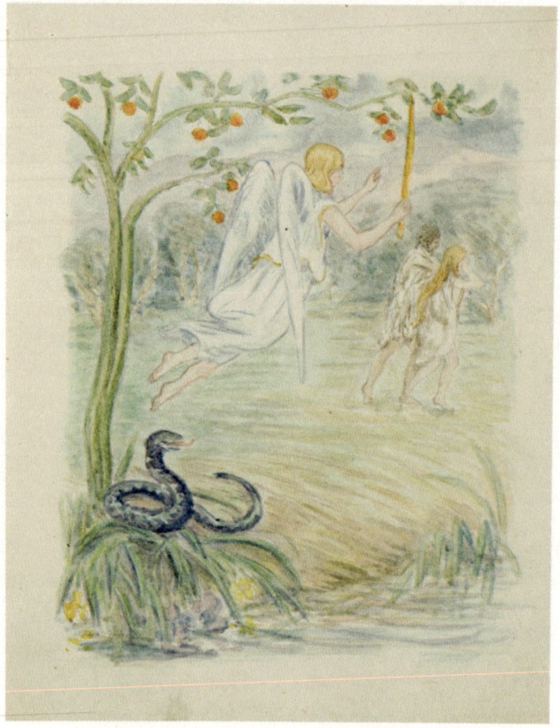

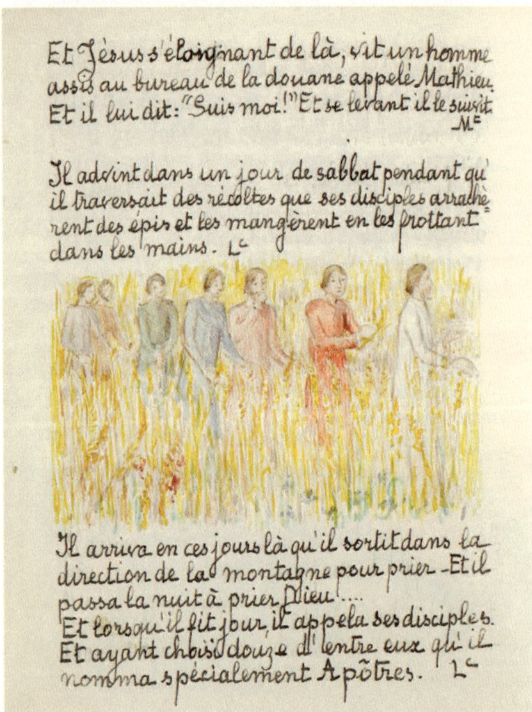

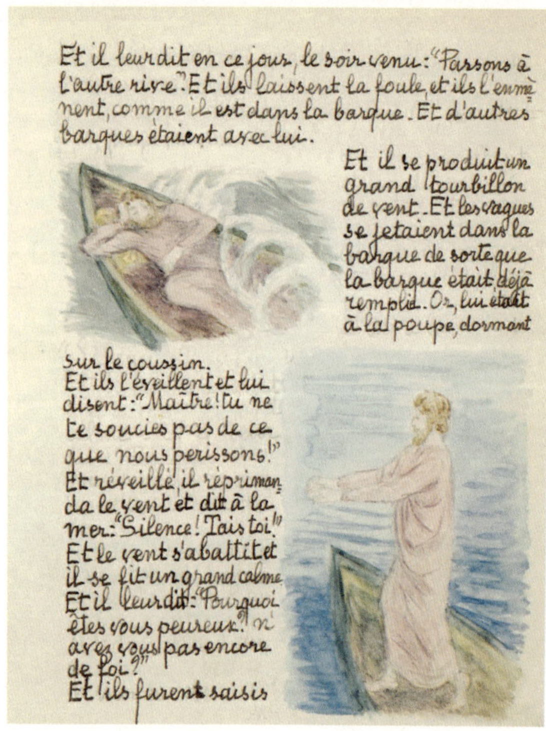

Julie Manet (1878–1966)
Adam and Eve in the Garden of Eden
Adam and Eve Banished from the Garden of Eden
The Ears of Wheat
Stilling the Storm
Illustrations from Jean-Michel's catechism book, c. 1941
Watercolor and pencil on paper, 23 × 18.5 cm (each)
Private collection

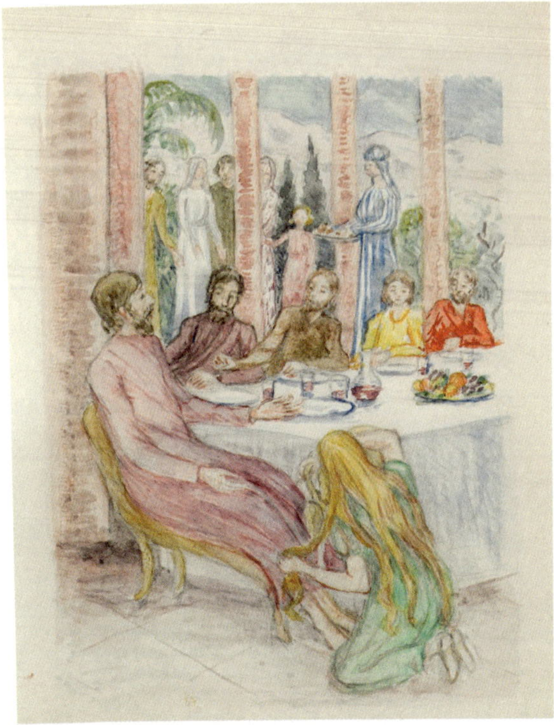

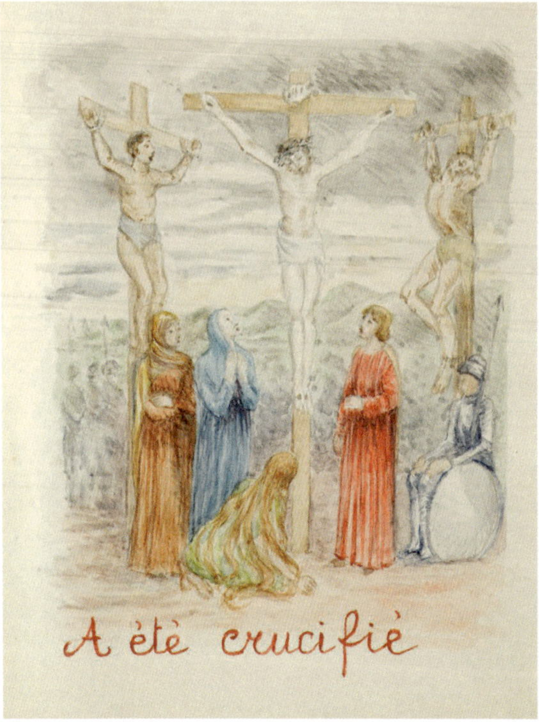

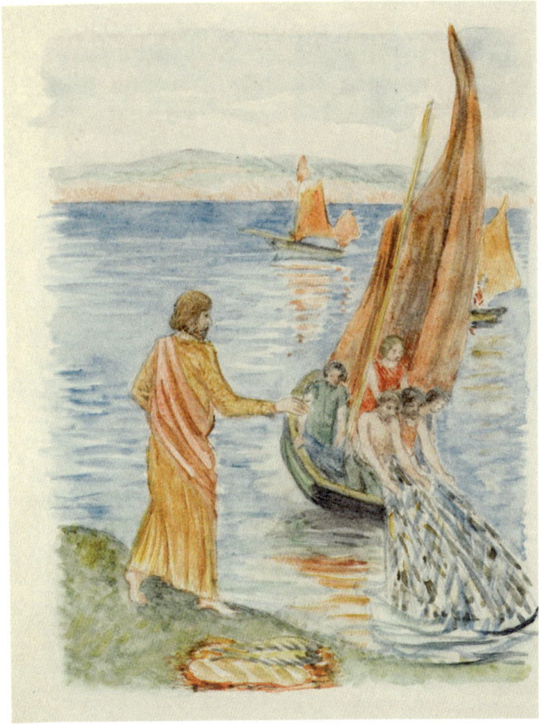

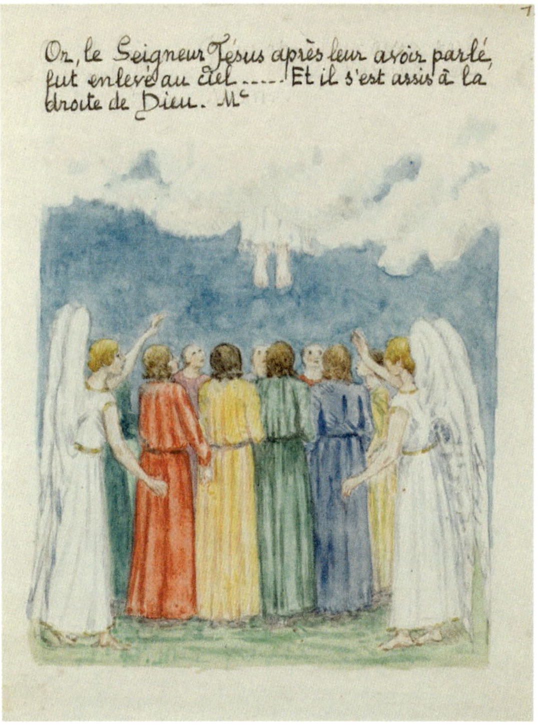

Julie Manet (1878–1966)
The Anointing at Bethany
The Crucifixion
The Miraculous Draft of Fishes
The Ascension
Illustrations from Jean-Michel's catechism book, c. 1941
Watercolor and pencil on paper, 23 × 18.5 cm (each)
Private collection

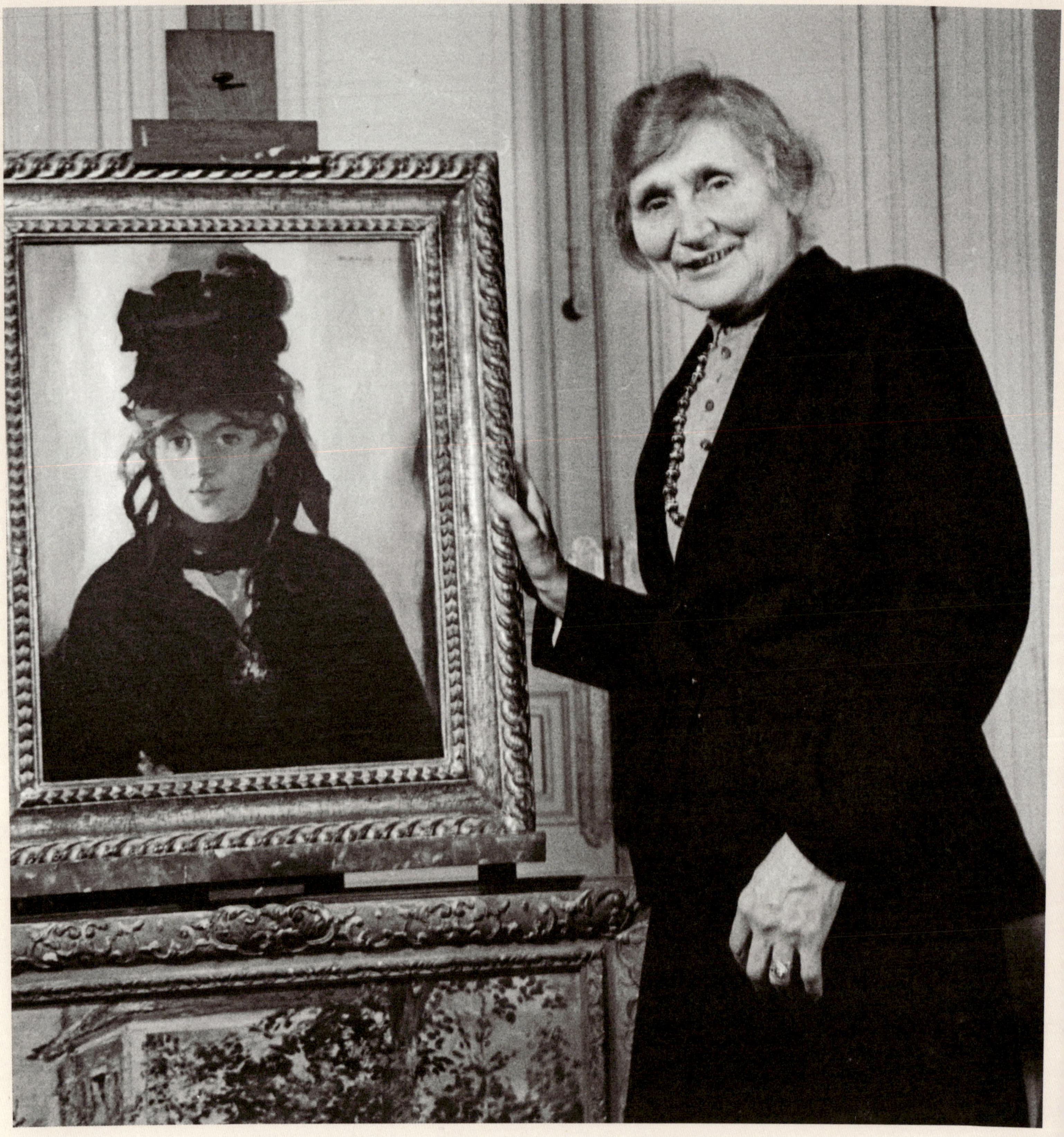

"AND SO ENDED THE EXISTENCE OF THE RUE DE VILLEJUST"

1941–1966

"SHE MUST BE BLESSING YOU FROM UP IN THE SKY FOR ALL YOU DID FOR HER"[746]

A life had passed. Now death was taking its place in the rue de Villejust. The 1940s were a decade of adieux. Berthe Morisot's niece, Blanche Pontillon, immortalized at birth in *The Cradle* (right), was one of the first to go. Julie provided her first cousin with care in these final moments. She had her at home in the rue de Villejust, where she breathed her last on July 8, 1941.[747] From the Montée du Rêve, a poetic address in Beaulieu-sur-Mer, the deceased's brother, Edme Pontillon, wrote at once:

> I had been expecting this sad end, my dear Julie, ever since I received Jeannie's card. I must confess that, knowing the truth, I sometimes came to wish for the end of that vain and atrocious struggle. Present at the tragedy in my mind, how many times did I thank God that this poor martyr who was constantly tried by life[748] did at least have the consolation of being surrounded right up to the last moment with the affection of her family.[749]

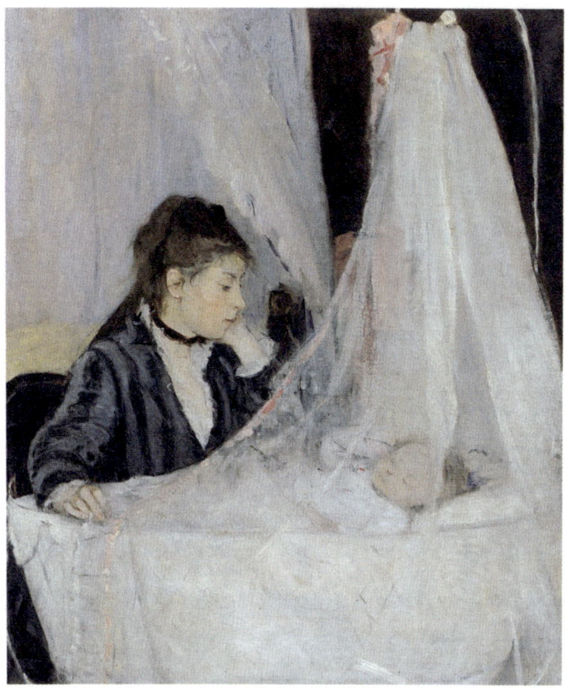

Berthe Morisot (1841–1895)
The Cradle, 1872
Oil on canvas, 56 × 46.5 cm
Paris, Musée d'Orsay

Facing page
Julie Manet in front of the portrait of her mother by Édouard Manet, n.d.

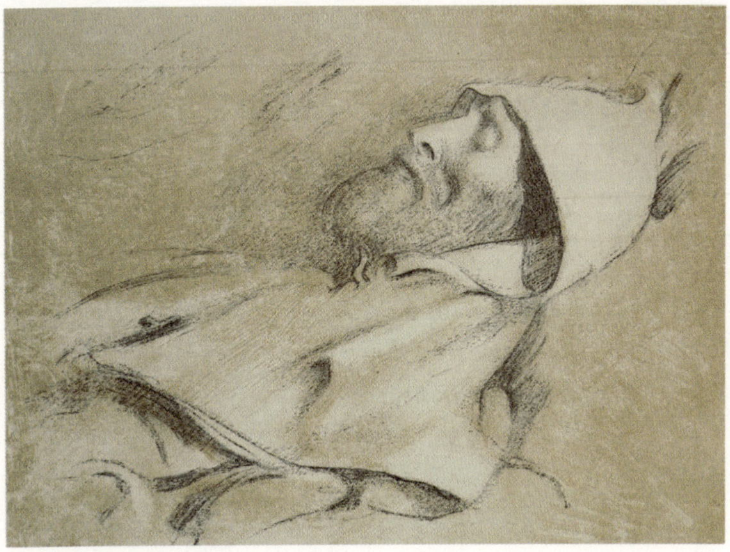

Maurice Denis (1870–1943)
Funerary Portrait of Gabriel Thomas, 1932
Lithograph in brown on paper, 32.4 × 43.4 cm
Private collection

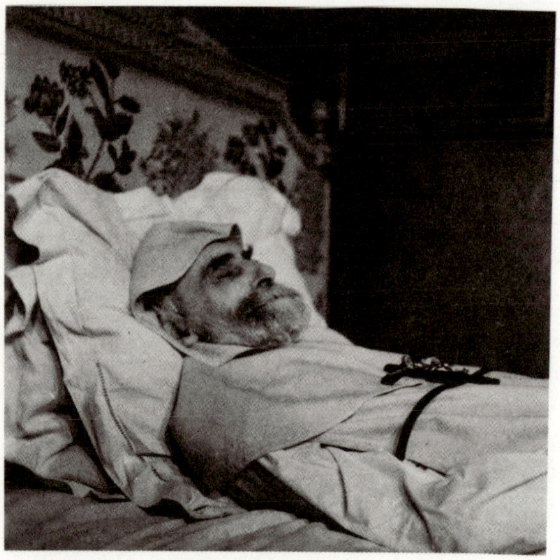

Funerary Portrait of Ernest Rouart, 1942
Archives du Mesnil, on permanent loan at the Musée Marmottan Monet

Jeannie also wrote:

> **You have lived the saddest days from much closer up even than I did. No doubt, your impression is a different one. In contrast to the regret I feel at having communicated with Blanche much less since the beginning of the war, the thought of the emptiness that opened up beside you after the months of shared existence is what concerns me now . . . Truly, you gave her the most total hospitality.[750]**

And Paule:

> **She must be blessing you from up in the sky for all you did for her during the last months of her life, so that she was surrounded by the most affectionate care. Jeannie has spoken to me often of Ernest's charity towards her, charity that he has always shown to all.[751]**

So be it.

Seven months later, on February 27, 1942, it was Ernest's turn.[752] Julie described his last hours to their son Denis.[753] "I did not believe that he suffered as you tell me,"[754] he admitted to his mother. Ernest's death was seen through the prism of an absolute Christian faith, as a return to God, beyond pain. A friend of the couple spoke of "The gentle, beautiful death that he had, with you [Julie] beside him helping [him] up to the last moment, what a great happiness for you!"[755] Her words must be understood in this way, as the words of a believer. In a letter to Maurice Denis, Julie evokes his unfailing generosity and his devotion to family interests. "Not having had the time to manage his own canvases, devoting himself entirely to the organization of the exhibition of my mother's works, for which he perhaps did not sufficiently spare himself and managed to overcome all the difficulties. He went about this with the same passion as he did organizing the Manet and Degas exhibitions, even hanging some of the canvases himself."[756] Ernest sacrificed his remaining strength on the altar of his ancestors. That is the image given by these few lines. He had always served others, and religion was surely not unrelated to this choice. A doyen of the Dominican Brotherhood of the Third Order, he wished to be buried in his white habit. Their cousin Gabriel Thomas made the same choice, as is evident from a moving lithograph by Maurice Denis (above left). There is no painting of Ernest, but there is a photograph (probably by Julie) representing him before he was placed in the coffin (above right). Looking at this pious image, we forget that he is resting on Berthe Morisot's Louis XVI bed, which the painter used in one of her most delicate odes to youth: *Getting Up* (p. 127). What a contrast between that painting and the image of a recumbent monk! "Charity is the immortality of the humble," noted Berthe Morisot.[757] It was as such that Ernest Rouart—Frère Antonin for the Dominicans—was making ready to go to his Father's House. For all eternity.

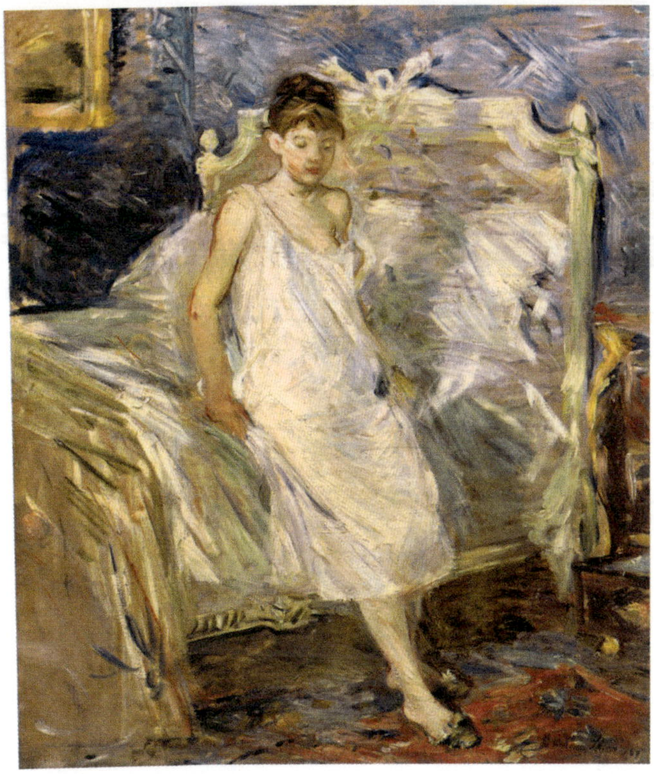

Berthe Morisot (1841–1895)
Getting Up, c. 1885–86
Oil on canvas, 65 × 54 cm
Private collection

"PAUL THINKS I HAVE THE WARRING SPIRIT OF MY GRANDFATHER MANET."[758]

One might imagine a plain, moving ceremony. A moment of meditation and grief elevated by faith in the resurrection that nothing could distract. The reality was more complex. Julie insisted on having Ernest buried in the vault in the cemetery at Passy, next to his parents and his uncle. And to be with them after that.

Eugène Manet had bought the plot after the death of his brother Édouard, putting it in the name of the painter's widow, Suzanne Leenhoff. Naturally, the discoverer of the tomb, Eugène, was buried there in 1892, followed by his wife, Berthe Morisot, in 1895. Suzanne was buried there in 1906. If the Manet-Leenhoff-Morisots of the Impressionist generation managed to maintain their links despite all the bones of contention and unspoken grievances, it was quite different for their children. Brought up with the idea that she was the one and only descendant of the Manets, Julie gradually lost sight of Suzanne's son, Léon (p. 23), whom many considered the natural son of the painter of *Olympia*.[759] In the interview he granted to his cousin Jean-Marie Rouart, Julie's oldest son, Julien Rouart, indicated that Léon was perfectly unknown to those of his generation: a painted figure. An excerpt from this exchange is eloquent:

> **Léon Leenhoff, he's the one in the Manet painting where there's a young man in front of a table, and in several other paintings, I believe.**
>
> **Leenhoff was the son of Édouard Manet's wife, Suzanne Leenhoff, who was Dutch, and who was his piano and music teacher.**
>
> **[Suzanne Leenhoff] had this son, according to what people said, and some people, journalists and writers, thought Léon Leenhoff was Manet's son. In any case, he never recognized him as a son, and he made him his sole legatee. He survived and the family had no dealings with him. His mother rejected the idea that he might be Manet's son.[760]**
>
> . . .
>
> **[After Suzanne's death] Léon Leenhoff disappeared from the scene, and things remained like that. I did not know him. My mother never tried to find out what had happened to him.[761]**

Not much is known about what happened after 1900. Time and distance had done their work. A few facts do enlighten us, even so. Julie did not attend Léon's wedding with Marie Fanfillon, celebrated in Paris on July 20, 1895,[762] and she did not frequent the couple. When Marie died,[763] Léon went about getting him buried in the family vault. The historian Adolphe Tabarant, who published a thoroughly documented book in 1947,[764] evokes this difficult time:

> **On August 11, 1917, his wife having died in the villa in Sarcelles, at 12, rue Verte, the notice bore [the name of]: Mme Koëlla-Leenhoff. Followed by this indication: "The inhumation took place on August 14, in the strictest privacy, provisionally in the city cemetery, pending transfer to Édouard Manet's family vault in Passy."[765]**

Given that only "Manets from the direct line" could be buried in Passy, Julie officially opposed the transfer. The report she prepared for Ernest informs us about the procedure she applied:

> **I think that for your part you will be eager to know how my initiatives ended. . . . I went to see [the lawyer] M. Bouts who told me to go to the bailiff . . . and he advised me to oppose not only the exhumation but also the inhumation, telling me that I owed it to my parents' memory. This conformity of**

thought with my own pleased me, and I told him how helpful his advice often was. He truly is very precious to us. I therefore took the tram to Passy but M. [Merlier?] was not there and I had to deal with an old clerk who didn't know much and insisted to me that Léon Leenhoff could do whatever he wanted with my parents. I thought that was a bit rich and, thanks to the advice of the house of Borniol and Mr Bouts, I held firm in my idea of opposition. He told me then that he could notify only Leenhoff and not the Prefecture, unless I can find a paper naming me as the holder, and he therefore advised me to go there, which I did on the Passy-Hôtel de Ville tram. At the prefecture they told me that they surely had nothing other than at the cemetery but that I could perfectly well send my opposition, which would be passed on to the cemetery. Before leaving I asked Charlotte[766] to take to the bailiff a letter containing the paper from the cemetery, 25 francs, which he is asking for to lodge the two oppositions, one to the Prefecture and one to Léon Leenhoff, and telling him to lodge these oppositions as soon as possible. They must be sent in your name and they do not need our signatures. I was thinking we could do without Léon's, but that was not the opinion of the clerk or of Paul [Valéry]. I am naturally expecting trouble because I have provoked it. Paul thinks I have the battling spirit of my grandfather Manet. When I was leaving Mass, I was thinking exactly what you told me about M. Bouts and that is what made me act, I think it would be a serious dereliction of my duties towards Papa and Maman.[767]

Tabarant says that "in the name of the Manet-Morisot family, M. Ernest Rouart will object by bailiff to the admission of Mme Koëlla, née Fanfillon, into the vault."[768] As we have seen, the initiative came down to Julie alone, who went from being the instrument to the protagonist of a family conflict.[769] On September 23, 1917, Ernest returned to the matter:

> You haven't told me what happened to your objection via bailiff to Léon K. Perhaps you have not heard. I hope that you will gain satisfaction on this side and I regret not having been able to help you in your dealings.[770]

If the diplomatic Tabarant found "the opposition totally justified, as the Koëlla line cannot legally lay claim to the Manet line,"[771] his interpretation was erroneous. As the only descendant of the licensee, Mme Suzanne Leenhoff, Manet's widow, Léon was the exclusive owner of the tomb, which had been signaled to Julie, as we have seen above.

Was it the fate he was dealt by the "Rouart-Manets" on this unfortunate occasion, the time taken to administer the case, or the difficulties due to the war that dissuaded him from transferring his wife's body to Passy? We do not yet know, but it is certain that Marie Fanfillon does not rest there.

KOËLLA VERSUS ROUART-MANET

The result was an irremediable break. No doubt in order to cut off all contact and clarify a personal situation that had become untenable, after this date Léon now began using only his legal patronym of Koëlla, a name that his entourage had never pronounced until his marriage, and that remained unknown to many.[772] Léon died childless in Vernon on September 3, 1927.[773] There is no evidence any steps were taken to bury him in Passy as was his right. It is still not known where his grave is.

It is in this very particular context that we should place Ernest Rouart's funeral. The account by his oldest son, Julien, then forty years old, is richly instructive about the spoken and unspoken truths that cement and separate generations. Truth, history, and family memories do not always get along.

> When my father died in 1942, my mother always thought that this tomb belonged to him, and that she would be buried there, and her husband, etc.
>
> When we came to bury my father, we realized that the tomb was not in my mother's name, although she was paying for its upkeep, and that it was claimed by one Monsieur Koëlla, a descendant of the Leenhoffs . . . I do not know how he came to be called Koëlla, I never knew the precise filiation, nor I believe did my mother, but this gentlemen had to be found.

Obviously, Julie could not fail to know. Since Léon had no direct heir, the vault in Passy went to the collateral branch of the Koëllas. Perfect strangers who shared neither Léon's past nor Julie's. And so the filiation that this family cobbled together, their refusal to allow Suzanne's son the slightest place, led to this paradox: perfect strangers were made the legitimate heirs of Manet's tomb. Without their authorization, the City could not agree to any burial, not even Ernest's.

While waiting to settle this question, Julie acted as Léon once had for Marie Fanfillon. On March 3, 1942 she went ahead with a provisional burial in the Tayssèdre vault that Père-Lachaise cemetery provided for that purpose.[774] On March 1, Blanche Hoschedé-Monet evoked the prospect of the funeral:

> **My dear Julie, Although I phoned you yesterday, I want to tell you again how much I feel with you all in your pain! I had the presentiment of this misfortune and I have not stopped thinking of our dear friend. I cannot believe that this has happened. I cannot tell you strongly enough how very sorry I am not to be able to be with you on Tuesday [March 3] but I am becoming truly infirm and can no longer walk or use my hands.[775]**

All the evidence is that the funeral was a strictly private occasion, as the family did not publish a death notice in the press. Was Julie hoping to organize a proper ceremony after solving the question of the vault?

In any case, she began looking for Léon's heirs, determined to buy the tomb back from them. Hoping to do this, she contacted the great niece of Suzanne Leenhoff, Marthe Mezzara-Dufet.[776] The woman lived in Casablanca and did not answer until May 12, 1942.

> **Madame,**
>
> **You are receiving this answer to your letter very late indeed, and I apologize but I have been in Morocco these last three weeks with my daughter. I have asked someone in Paris to open my mail and to copy out the contents for me on an interzone card. Hence I found out this morning about your missive telling me of your loss and your concern about that tomb. I am saddened to see you distressed and upset that I cannot at this moment provide you with the information you ask me for. As soon as I get back I shall look through my father's papers[777] to find a more recent address for the heirs of Léon Koëlla Leenhoff. I do not know if my father stayed in contact with them. I do not believe so. It should not be impossible to track them down. I can assure you, Madame, that I will go about this with all my heart when I get back, for I understand how painful this situation must be for you.**
>
> **. . . Rest assured, as soon as I have any information whatsoever I shall inform you.[778]**

Julien's memories tell us what happened next:

> **We looked everywhere [for Léon's heir] and in the end we found him. I know that he had lived in Évreux. I went to Évreux with my mother. This was in the middle of the war. The whole center of Évreux was smashed. We went to the notaries. My mother found a few bits of information and, in the end, she was able to get in touch with this Monsieur Koëlla, who was a worker in the suburbs of Paris.**
>
> **We offered to pay for the repossession of the tomb, and he said, "But this tomb is important to me, for my little family." He would not hear of selling it. He was trying a kind of blackmail, and that is where my mother was rather clever, because she got the tomb listed.[779]**

It would seem that discussions of a possible sale went quite far, far enough for Julie to realize that it was impossible, since a funeral plot held in perpetuity can be sold only between heirs. That is what we may gather from this undated draft of a letter Julie sent to the artworks, museums, and exhibitions department of the Bureau des Beaux-Arts:

> **Mademoiselle,**
>
> **As I told you by telephone a few days ago, I would like to know if Monsieur Poli[780] has seen the note I sent him last summer concerning the tomb of Édouard Manet, which is also the tomb of my parents Mr and Mme Eugène Manet.**
>
> **It so happens that as the plot was acquired in the name of Mme Édouard Manet, it is the indirect heirs, who not only do not belong to the Manet family, but nor even to his own family, who own this tomb, which they are not particularly set on keeping and would readily sell; but the law allows them to do this only to persons of their own family.**
>
> **That is why I thought that the Beaux-Arts might perhaps intervene (call for) to take possession of this tomb of artists: my uncle Édouard Manet and my mother Berthe Morisot (widow of Eugène Manet). Naturally, I would bear all the costs. I am perfectly prepared to come up with what is considered a fair sum for the current owner, and my children and I would take charge of the tomb's maintenance, as we have up to now.**
>
> **My only purpose would be to take it out of the hands of strangers who might have work done on it.[781]**

Contrary to Julien's affirmation, the tomb was not listed and remains private property. Julie, who completely lost touch with the Koëllas, did manage to obtain a plot close to that of her parents.[782] The tombstone, featuring a monumental cross in low relief, bears the family name Rouart-Manet. Ernest's body was transferred there on July 15, 1943.[783]

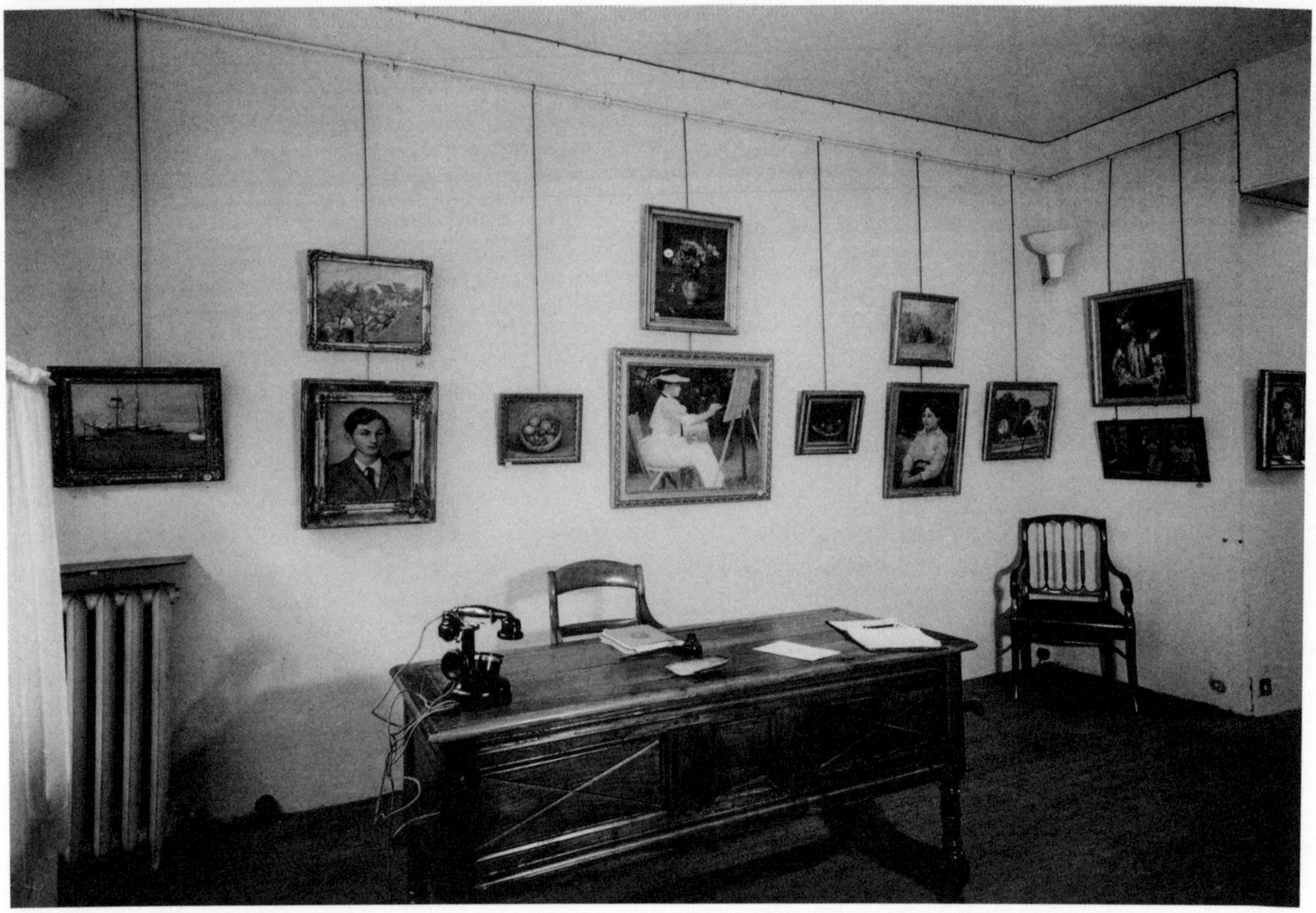

Exhibition of canvases by Ernest Rouart at the Galerie Berri-Raspail, June 1942
Paris, Musée Carnavalet

IN MEMORIAM

Julie also took charge of celebrating the work of her dear departed. On April 4, 1942, the arts page of *Le Figaro* published a homage to the painter Ernest Rouart written by Maurice Denis, a fine article whose publication no doubt compensated for the absence of a death notice. From now on, Julie made it her duty to organize her husband's posthumous exhibition, a project of which she informed Denis at once.

> I do not know if I told you that I wanted to put on the exhibition that I was always asking him to do [and] that he was thinking about, but that events always caused us to put off. I have brought back the canvases from Le Mesnil, I am assembling them here. Yesterday, Louis [Rouart] helped me make a selection of drawings, pastels, and watercolors. I hope to have the gallery sorted out by the end of the week.[784]

On June 27 an insert in the artistic journal *Comœdia*[785] announced the Ernest Rouart exhibition at the Galerie Berri-Raspail.[786] The exhibition brochure had a preface by Paul Valéry, an excerpt from which, "In Memoriam Ernest Rouart," was reprinted in *Le Figaro* on July 7.[787] On the same day, Léon-Paul Fargue published a very positive review in the daily newspaper *Aujourd'hui*.[788] A series of photographs kept at the Musée Carnavalet recall the hanging (above). The faithful Blanche Hoschedé-Monet attended the inauguration and congratulated her old friend:

> My dear Julie, Since getting back I have wanted to say how happy I was to see you all again, but also how one could sense the presence of your dear husband. I would have been so happy to tell him of my joy at seeing his work, of which I had no idea. I wish we could have chatted a little, the two of us . . . and that was not possible, as of course you had so much attention.[789]

As the closure approached, Jeannie was worried for her sister-cousin:

> **I really suffer for you to see the [exhibition] ending. So much of Ernest's presence in those canvases, and of all his life. Which is in large part your own. You will be able to see them again, but not so piously assembled. It is another adieu to something, for the moment. I am thinking of you both.[790]**

The canvases were not sold, which angered the other painter in the family, Paule. Even so, the curator of the museum in Albi, Charles Bellet, was charmed by one canvas, *At the Races*,[791] which Julie happily offered the museum at his request.

In October, the homage continued at the Salon d'Automne, where the committee vice-president,[792] Georges d'Espagnat, orchestrated a new retrospective. As always, Julie was in the thick of it. To Maurice Denis, in charge of the preface, she wrote:

> **I spent the first days of this week in Paris preparing Ernest's paintings for the Salon d'Automne. I added to Espagnat's selection the little painting of the street,[793] which Paule told me you liked.[794]**

For Julie, the arrival of grandchildren was the greatest joy. Now the "Mamaïta" of Jean-Michel, Yves, Françoise, and Micheline, Julie watched over the children of her son Clément and her daughter-in-law Victoria. They were growing up in the rue de Villejust, in Berthe Morisot's old first-floor apartment. Space being at a premium, Jean-Michel moved in on the fifth floor, where he lived with his grandmother. Agathe, Paul and Jeannie's daughter, was now a mother too and moved in with her husband, Paul Rouart, at number 23.[795]

Two years later, Paul Valéry died on July 20, 1945. His state funeral requires no further commentary here, except to point out its exceptional status[796] as the first one to be organized for a writer since Victor Hugo.

On February 27, 1946, it was the turn of Paule Gobillard. In Nice, Alice Gamby wrote of the dearly departed:

> **My dear Julie, how grateful I am to you for having given me the details of the end of our dear Paule, she goes to be with her mother, for whom she had such great affection. My father-in-law [Tiburce Morisot] has told me how admirably devoted she was when your Aunt Yves was so ill. Then, after her death, a very difficult situation. She was a [illegible word] Jeannie too young to understand. With Paule goes the memory of grandmother Morisot whom she knew, since in 1870 she was already in this world as were Blanche and Jeanne who came to live near her in St. Germain where my f.[ather]-in-law was garrisoned with the 4th chasseurs [p. 14]. You yourself Julie and Jeannie, she knew you as babies. You write to me on Friday March 1 and tell me that her body has been transported to the Church, the burial not being possible before Tuesday.[797]**

The funeral was held on March 5. Paule lies at rest in Père-Lachaise in the Morisot vault.[798] Alice speaks of the event as if she were there:

> **In my mind I was before the Morisot tomb, Paule closes the cycle of deaths: your mother took care of this tomb which was made for your grandmother and grandfather and their 4 children.[799]**

A "Paule Gobillard" retrospective was announced for the Salon d'Automne. Once again, the ladies in the rue de Villejust got to work. Jeannie told Julie:

> **Before leaving Paris, I wrote to [Maurice] Dufrêne[800] as she advised. Three of the canvases not being of the right size, he could not provide the frames and offered what he called the hire-purchase system. His house would provide all the frames providing a third of their total value was purchased from him. Would that be an advantage, I wonder?[801]**

In the same letter, she evokes another important event: on the occasion of the first anniversary of the poet's death, the rue de Villejust was to be renamed rue Paul Valéry. Jeannie told Julie, who did not plan to come back to Paris for the occasion:

> **I am dreading the return, the anniversary day. It is decided, Claude [his older son] telephoned me, that the plaque bearing the name Paul Valéry will be put up on the 20th, with a certain ceremonial, Jaujard speaking in the name of the Beaux-Arts, Duhamel for the Académie [Française], Gérard Bauer for the Société des Gens de Lettres. So ends the life of the rue de Villejust, so much a part of each of you that we cannot fail to feel a discomfort that Paul would have experienced.[802]**

Jeannie wrote to her sister-cousin the day after the event:

> **Today, the street does not know its name. The Paul Valéry plaque unveiled yesterday by the V.[ice] Pres.[ident] of the municipal council, placed on the railings that form the corner with the avenue Foch, next to another on which the name Villejust is struck out, in itself indicates the new baptism. All the old ones were still in place. And so the day I was so dreading has**

passed. . . . Nobody has forgotten to talk about the history of our house, our past . . . which made Charlotte remark that you, of all people, should have been there. Naturally, I missed you as she did.[803]

In August, they continued to prepare for the exhibition of Paule's work that the painter Georges Barat-Levraux[804] was to organize in the name of the committee of the Salon d'Automne:

And here is another pressing matter, today Barat-Levraux (to whom in fact I meant to write, as well as to d'Espagnat, but I forgot to take their addresses) sends me a notice for the Automne on August 2 which he received late. It is before Sept. 10 that we must have communicated the name of the works and the preface that he planned for this exhib. . . . He found Fargue an obvious choice, but Fargue knows nothing about Paule's painting, he will be uncomfortable. I hesitate to put him in that awkward situation, after what he has already done. Agathe gives me at random the names of Marie de Régnier[805] or Laurencin[806] (does she write, this one?) Vaudoyer,[807] Mondor[808] (who I don't think is an obvious choice). Can you think of a real art critic, and who? I think they want a rather big name. They should have attended to that at the beginning of the month, at least. If you have an idea, telephone.[809]

In the end, it was Marie de Régnier, daughter of José Maria de Heredia, who signed the preface with her pen name, Gérard d'Houville.[810]

Jeannie points out: "Barat-Levraux adds that the committee, which has enthusiastically accepted the idea of having this retrospective presided over by the portrait of B. Morisot,[811] would be in favor of also showing the red chalk by Renoir [p. 6]. . . . As he says below, apart from that modification, we change nothing."[812]

The sister-cousins were not alone. The new generation helped with the organization of the homages and collating the last testimony from the time of Impressionism. The Valérys' last-born had tried to help Jeanne Baudot with the writing of her memoirs, which amused Paule shortly before her death:

François has finished correcting (if I can put it like that) Jeanne Baudot's memories of Renoir. He finds her stubborn, very attached to what she has written and, in the end, refusing to cut anything.[813]

By virtue of his function, Denis Rouart's role was particularly important. Trained at the École du Louvre, he became a curator of heritage[814] and was, it is tempting to say, faithful to his father, who throughout his life made it his mission to conserve the work of his kith and kin. Nor was his vocation unconnected to his mother, with whom he shared a certain conception of the past. Witness these lines that one could easily attribute to Julie were it not for his signature:

I believe we can partially compensate for absence through thought, and that the best way of fighting against the absence of a loved one is to think about them a great deal, to live with them in thought. In this way you can deny their absence and live with them almost as much as if they were there. Affection survives and can guide our acts. One can live even for a being who has gone, and tailor our acts to their tastes and desires. It is a way of extending their company even after death. It is in my view the true way to serve a memory, much more than by conventional events.[815]

Should we be surprised that Denis continued Julie's work? His mother had begun to classify her forbears' letters, as can be seen from this missive that she received in 1945: "I wonder if you have got over sorting through your mother's and Mallarmé's correspondence."[816]

Denis took over. He assembled and edited Berthe Morisot's correspondence published at the author's expense[817] in 1950.[818] In 1961, he prefaced the Berthe Morisot catalogue raisonné on which his mother had worked so hard, and that was edited by Marie-Louise Bataille,[819] who took over from Vollard, under the direction of Georges Wildenstein.[820] Four hundred and sixteen paintings, one hundred and ninety-one pastels, and two hundred and thirty-eight watercolors were listed. At last, Julie's work had taken shape. Soon, Clément would publish her journal. She was no longer "alone to recall the life of Papa and Maman."[821] Her sons had taken over. Julie passed away on November 21, 1966. Buried beside her spouse, she rests for eternity in her Dominican habit.

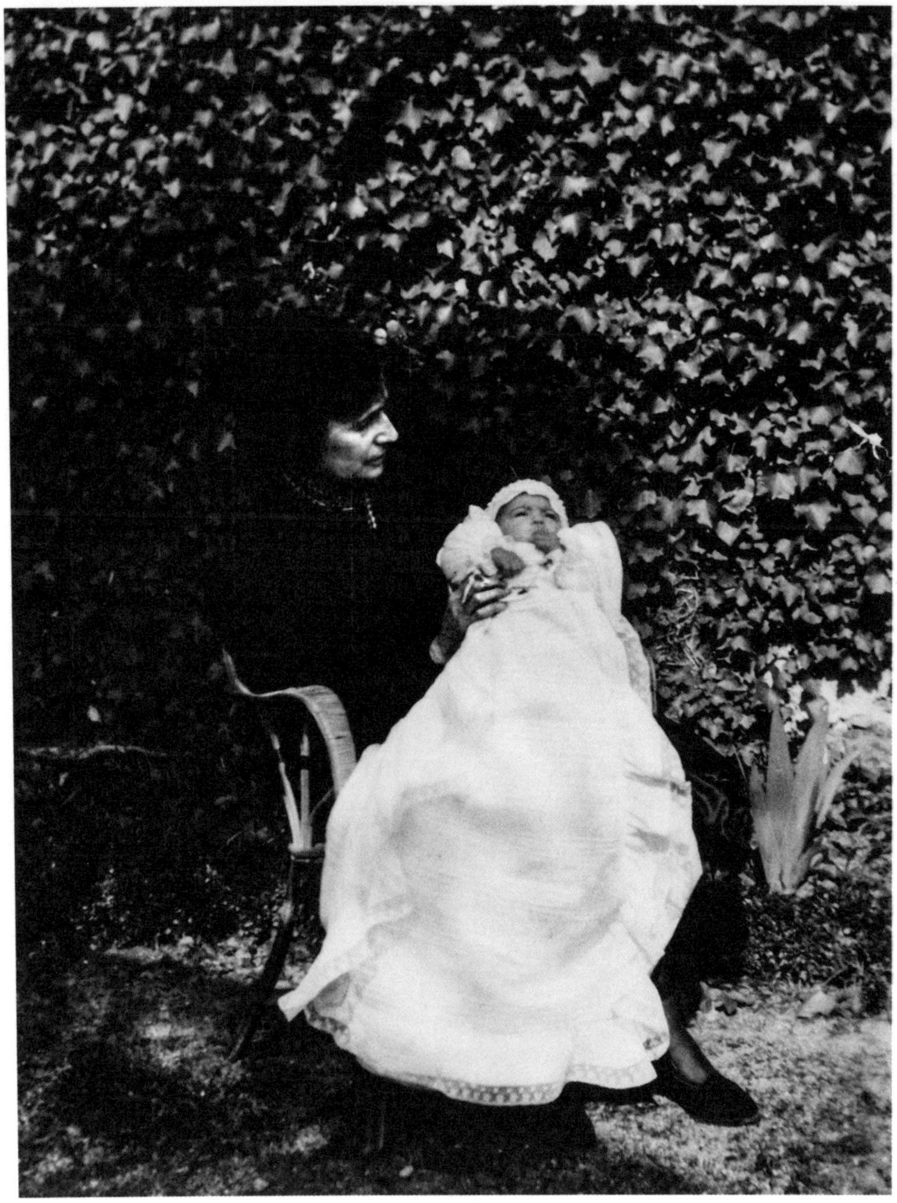

Julie Manet and her grandchild Françoise Rouart, 1942
Archives du Mesnil, on permanent loan at the Musée Marmottan Monet

NOTES

PASSY, A FAMILY PENCHANT

1. Marie Amélie Thomas (March 14, 1832, Paris 16th–June 30, 1844, Paris 16th), Arch. Paris, reconstituted civil records, death, V3E/D 1411.
2. Jean Simon Joseph Thomas (March 19, 1789, Lunéville–November 11, 1880, Paris 16th), death certificate, Arch. Paris, V4E 4696.
3. Cézan 1963, n.p.
4. Marie Françoise Caroline Mayniel (October 24, 1793, Toulouse–January 22, 1870, Paris 16th), death certificate, Arch. Paris, V4E 1973.
5. Cézan 1963, n.p.
6. According to their death certificates, five of Jean Simon Joseph Thomas and Marie Françoise Caroline Mayniel's children died in the 16th arrondissement of Paris (Marie Amélie, Arch. Paris, reconstituted civil records, death certificate, V3E/D 1411; Marie Joseph Charles, Arch. Paris, death certificate, V4E 4657; Marie Joséphine Cornélie, Arch. Paris, death certificate, V4E 4675; Marie Joséphine Clémentine, death certificate, Arch. Paris, V4E 10037).
7. Marie Joséphine Clémentine Thomas (August 26, 1814, Écouen–December 15, 1897, Paris 16th), death certificate, Arch. Paris, V4E 10037.
8. Arch. Paris, reconstituted civil records, marriages, V3E/M 200.
9. Arch. Paris, reconstituted civil records, weddings, V3E/M 231, and marriage certificate, reconstituted civil records, 5Mi1 2184.
10. Félicie Louise Cosnard (August 23, 1829, Paris 16th–January 8, 1905, Neuilly-sur-Seine), birth certificate, Arch. Paris, reconstituted civil records, V3E/N 551; death certificate, Arch. Dép. des Hauts-de-Seine, E_NUM_NEU_D1905; Claude Cézan recalls that Louise Cosnard's family owned all the land between the Trocadéro and the Seine and were among the most prominent landowners in the neighborhood.
11. Marie Joseph Charles Thomas (November 22, 1820, Écouen–April 16, 1873, Paris 16th), death certificate, Arch. Paris, V4E 4657.
12. According to the address appearing on the religious wedding certificate of Marie Joseph Charles Thomas and Félicie Louise Cosnard (Arch. Paris, reconstituted civil records, 5Mi1 2184).
13. From 1854 to 1863, according to the addresses appearing on the civil certificates (birth certificate of Marie Gabriel Thomas, Arch. Paris, reconstituted civil records, 5Mi1 800; birth certificate of Marie Madeleine Thomas, Arch. Paris, V4E 1913; birth certificate of Marie Eugénie Marthe Thomas, Arch. Paris, V4E 1927).
14. Birth certificate, Arch. Paris, reconstituted civil records, 5Mi1 800.
15. If, in around 1863, Mr. and Mrs. Joseph Thomas moved, it was for the nearby street of La Muette no. 4 first of all (birth certificate of Marie François Albert Charles Thomas, Arch. Paris, V4E 1970) and then the rue de La Tour no. 119 (death certificate of Marie Joseph Charles Thomas, Arch. Paris, V4E 4657).
16. Marie Joséphine Cornélie Thomas (October 5, 1819, Paris 12th–December 15, 1876, Paris 16th), birth certificate, Arch. Paris, reconstituted civil records, 5Mi1 209; death certificate, Arch. Paris, V4E 4675.
17. Edme Tiburce Morisot (March 11, 1806, Paris 3rd–January 24, 1874, Paris 16th), birth certificate, Arch. Paris, reconstituted civil records, 5Mi1 134; death certificate, Arch. Paris, V4E 4675.
18. The Morisots' address appears on numerous documents. The brochure for the Salon of 1864 has them at 12, rue Franklin, while later brochures have them at 16, rue Franklin.
19. Birth certificate, Arch. Dép. du Nord, NMD 1126/1341.
20. Birth certificate, Arch. Dép. du Nord, D [1838], NMD [1839] (1838–1839).
21. Birth certificate, Arch. Dép. du Cher, 3E 2538.
22. Birth certificate, Arch. Dép. de la Haute-Vienne, 3 E 85 / 180.
23. Marriage certificate, Arch. Paris, V4E 1948.
24. Marriage certificate, Arch. Paris, V4E 1966.
25. Birth certificate, Arch. Paris, V4E 1970.
26. Birth certificate, Arch. Paris, V4E 4644.
27. Paule Gobillard (December 3, 1867, Quimperlé–February 27, 1946, Paris 16th), birth certificate, Arch. Dép. de la Finistère, 1 MI EC 289/7; death certificate, Arch. Paris, 16D 176.
28. 1872, Tokyo, Bridgestone Museum of Art (CMR 24).
29. He owed 17,791.55 francs according to the account of the estate of M. Morisot established in the post-mortem inventory of Mme Morisot, AN, MC/ET/XL/512.
30. I shall make no attempt here to detail the artist's training, work, and career. For more on these matters, see the general bibliography.
31. 1864: no. 1394, *Memory of the Banks of the Oise* (CMR 5, location unknown), no. 1395, *Old Track to Auvers* (CMR 6, private collection); 1865: no. 1551, *Study* (not mentioned in the catalogue raisonné, private collection), no. 1552, *Still Life* (CMR 7, private collection); 1866: no. 1412, *Thatched Cottage in Normandy* (CMR 10, Paris, Musée Marmottan Monet); no. 1413, *La Brémondière (Orne)* (CMR 9, location unknown); 1867: no. 1100, *The Seine below the Pont d'Iéna* (CMR 11, private collection); 1868: no. 1819, *Ros-Bras (Finistère)* (CMR 12, private collection); 1870: no. 2039, *Portraits of Mmes*** (CMR 20, Washington, D.C., National Gallery of Art); no. 2040, *The Artist's Sister at a Window* (CMR 18, Washington, D.C., National Gallery of Art); 1872: no. 1142, *Portrait of Mlle E. P.* (BW 419, Paris, Musée d'Orsay); 1873: no. 1090, *Blanche* (BW 422, private collection).
32. Edgar Degas, *Portrait of Madame Théodore Gobillard (Yves Morisot, 1838–1893)*, 1869, oil on canvas (L 213), and *Portrait of Théodore Gobillard (Yves Morisot, 1838–1893)* (p. 154; L 214), both held at the Metropolitan Museum of Art in New York.
33. According to Berthe Morisot's letters, two oils were refused, one in 1872, the other in 1873.
34. Declaration of transfer of the property of Edme Tiburce Morisot, declaration of succession (AN, DQ7 12618 and DQ7 12619).
35. See Mathieu 2019, p. 174.
36. Clément Manet (June 17, 1764, Paris–February 27, 1814, Gennevilliers).
37. See the family tree p. 321.
38. Marguerite Manet (October 25, 1773, Paris–June 22, 1828, Gennevilliers); death certificate, Arch. Dép. des Hauts-de-Seine, E_NUM_GEN240 1828.
39. Félicité Clémence Manet (July 17, 1804, Gennevilliers–?).
40. Émilie Manet (1795, Paris–July 12, 1834, Gennevilliers); death certificate, Arch. Dép. des Hauts-de-Seine, E_NUM_GEN246 1834.
41. Denis François Claude de Jouy (1780–September 22, 1854, Gennevilliers).
42. Anatole Jules de Jouy (March 8, 1815, Gennevilliers–March 9, 1894, Paris), birth certificate, Arch. Dép. des Hauts-de-Seine, E_NUM_GEN49; death certificate, Arch. Paris, V4E 8032.
43. Marie Geneviève Quatremère (January 3, 1825, Paris –November 23, 1847, ?).
44. Post-mortem inventory of Jules de Jouy (ref. 20e), AN, MC/ET/LXXIX/1017.
45. Auguste Manet (August 30, 1796, Paris–September 25, 1862, Paris); birth certificate, Arch. Paris, reconstituted civil records, 5Mi 195; death certificate, Arch. Paris, V4E 986.
46. Eugénie Désirée Fournier (November 12, 1911, Paris–January 8, 1885, Paris); birth certificate, Arch. Paris, reconstituted civil records, V3E/N918; death certificate, Arch. Paris, V4E7322.
47. Birth certificate, Arch. Paris, reconstituted civil records, 5Mi1 734. On Koëlla, see Coppens 2014.
48. Gustave Manet (16 March 1835, Paris 10th–December 18, 1884, Menton), birth certificate, Andriveau fund; death certificate, civil records of the City of Menton, 1884.
49. Ibid., p. 9.
50. According to her declaration of succession, Arch. Paris, DQ7 12455.
51. Eugène Manet (November 21, 1833, Paris–April 13, 1892), birth certificate, Arch. Paris, reconstituted civil records, 5Mi1 395; death certificate, Arch. Paris, V4E7336.
52. Ibid., p. 9; Wojciechowski 2019, p. 240.
53. According to the marriage certificate of Eugène Manet and Berthe Morisot (Arch. Paris, V4E 4661) and her declaration of succession, October 12, 1892 (Arch. Paris, DQ7 12762).
54. Me Charles Victor Amy, active from September 5, 1847 to April 24, 1895, worked first in Passy, then from 1860 to 1888 at 12, rue Franklin, and finally, from 1889 to 1895, at no. 15 in the same street (AN, directory of notaries).
55. Marriage contract, December 21, 1874, AN, MC/ET/XL/487.
56. Laroche-Gisserot 1988.
57. According to the post-mortem inventory of Marie Joséphine Cornélie Thomas, AN, MC/ET/XL/512.
58. At least since December 1874. Address mentioned on the marriage certificate of Berthe Morisot and Eugène Manet and on the death certificate of Marie Joséphine Cornélie Thomas (Arch. Paris, V4E 4675).
59. Death certificate of Marie Joséphine Cornélie Thomas (Arch. Paris, V4E 4675).
60. Letter from Eugène Manet to Berthe Morisot, September 22, 1876, Paris, Musée Marmottan Monet, inv. D.4-1986.2013.24.
61. The doctor Esprit Blanche opened an asylum for the insane using progressive methods in the Hôtel de Lamballe, Passy, in 1846. His son, Émile Blanche, who was close to Morisot, succeeded him in 1852. His own, son, Jacques-Émile Blanche, was also close to the Morisots. On this point, see the bibliography.
62. Letter from Marie Cornélie Morisot to Berthe Morisot-Manet, Tuesday May 23, [1876], Archives BS, 2021.2.185.
63. Maison de Santé PG Ville Évrard, medical record of Théodore Gobillard (June 24, 1876–October 24, 1876) 205R143.
64. Maison de Charenton, Hôpital Esquirol, Saint-Maurice. Register of male patients by date of admission, 1874–85 (Arch. Dép. du Val-de-Marne, 4X 524).
65. Death certificate, Arch. Dép. du Val-de-Marne, 1MI 2484.
66. Marcel Gobillard (March 17, 1872, Mirande–October 25, 1920, Mexico), birth certificate, Arch. Dép. du Gers, 5 E 18096.
67. This address appears on the post-mortem inventory of Marie Joséphine Cornélie Thomas, AN, MC/ET/XL/512.
68. Birth certificate, Arch. Paris, V4E 4676.
69. *Archives Commerciales de la France, Journal bi-hebdomadaire*, June 10, 1877 (BnF, Sciences et Techniques, 4 V 295).
70. Letter from Yves Gobillard to the Grand Chancelier de la Légion d'honneur, January 25, 1877, school record of Paule Gobillard, Archives of the Maison d'Éducation de Saint-Denis. With thanks to Abbé Gabriel Grimaud for sending these documents.
71. Paule attended the school from April 25, 1877 to July 13, 1884 (school record of Paule Gobillard, archives of the Maison d'Éducation de Saint-Denis).
72. Statutes of the Maisons d'Éducation de la Légion d'honneur, 1890, Arch. Dép. de la Marne, 14M24.
73. Letter from Yves Gobillard to Edma Pontillon, December 15, 1878, Paris, Musée Marmottan Monet, inv. D.4-1986.2013.898.
74. Berthe Morisot, *Baby Sitting*, 1878, pastel, 45 × 59 cm, BW 448; *Baby in a Bonnet*, 1878, pastel, 37 × 35 cm, BW 444; *Two Baby's Heads with Bonnet*, 1878, pastel, 45 × 37 cm, BW 445.
75. Birth certificate, Arch. Paris, V4E 4682.
76. Letter from Yves Morisot-Gobillard to Edma Morisot, Saturday 16 [November 1878], Arch. du Mesnil, inv. 2021.1.2712.
77. Letter from Edma Morisot-Pontillon to Eugène Manet, n.d. [November 1878], Paris, Musée Marmottan Monet, inv. D.4-1986.2013.385.
78. Ibid.
79. Birth certificate, Arch. Paris, V4E 4682.

80. Arch. Paris, Catholicity registers of the archdiocese of Paris, register of baptisms, parish of La Madeleine, D6J 4284.
81. Abbé Hurel appears on the handwritten will of Mme Auguste Manet, dated February 12, 1871 and registered on January 8, 1885 (AN, MC/ET/XCIV/1635).
82. Manet 1979, p. 21.
83. RW 294.
84. Letter from Yves Morisot-Gobillard to Edma Morisot-Pontillon, December 15, 1878, Paris, Musée Marmottan Monet, inv. D.4-1986.2013.898.
85. Ibid.
86. Rouart 1950, p. 100.
87. Cézan 1963, n.p.
88. Octave Thomas (1825–1913), former treasurer general for Isère, lived at 15, rue Franklin according to the death certificate of his sister Marie-Cornélie Morisot, December 15, 1876 (Arch. Paris, V4E 4675).
89. Letter from Edma Pontillon to Berthe Morisot, n.d., Paris, Musée Marmottan Monet, inv. D.4-1986.2013.790.
90. Berthe Morisot, *Little Boy in Gray*, 1880 (CMR 89); *Little Boy*, 1880 (CMR 90).
91. Letter from Yves Morisot-Gobillard to Paule Gobillard, n.d., Paris, Musée Marmottan Monet, inv. D.4-1986.2013.900.
92. Ibid.
93. Letter from Edma Morisot-Pontillon (?) to Berthe Morisot, n.d., Paris, Musée Marmottan Monet, inv. D.4-1986.2013.790.
94. Death certificate, Arch. Paris, V4E 4696.

A PLACE OF ONE'S OWN

95. Berthe Morisot, married name Manet, post-mortem inventory, AN, MC/ET/XXX/1293.
96. Berthe sold nineteen shares in the Compagnie du Gaz for 28,500 francs in April 1881 (post-mortem inventory, AN, MC/ET/XXX/1293) and, in December 1881, inherited 15,063,65 francs from her maternal grandfather.
97. Berthe Morisot, married name Manet, post-mortem inventory, AN, MC/ET/XXX/1293.
98. *The Wet Nurse*, oil on canvas, 50 × 61 cm, private collection (CMR 95) and *Child in Profile* pastel, 40 × 30 cm, private collection (BW 453).
99. See the essay in this volume by Dominique d'Arnoult, "Julie the Painter, the Last of the Manets or the Interrupted Apprenticeship," p. 186–271.
100. Address given for 1883 in the school record of Paule Gobillard, Archives of the Maison d'Éducation de Saint-Denis.
101. I have merely touched on the different addresses occupied by Yves Gobillard after 1884. An undated letter written in English by the young Julie held at the Musée Marmottan Monet suggests that she moved to Versailles for a while, before moving to Neuilly, her home for the rest of her life, at an unknown date. According to the 1891 census, Yves and her daughters lived at 89, avenue de Neuilly; that is the address given by Paule Gobillard for the brochure of the 1893 Salon des Indépendants. The village of Vieux-Moulin, near Compiègne, where Berthe Morisot visited her sister in 1885, and the address in Marly-le-Roi, in the rue de Saint-Cyr, where she died, were vacation addresses (death certificate, Arch. Dép. des Yvelines, 2MIEC245).
102. Letter from Berthe Morisot to Eugène Manet, March 7, 1882, Paris, Musée Marmottan Monet, inv. D.4-1986.2013.4.
103. Letter from Eugène Manet to Berthe Morisot, March 1, 1882, Paris, Musée Marmottan Monet, inv. D.4-1986.2013.25.
104. *Eugène Manet and His Daughter in the Garden at Bougival* (p. 2°3; CMR 104); *Child in the Hollyhocks*, 1881 (CMR 108); *Beach at Nice*, 1882, Paris, Musée Marmottan Manet (CMR 117); *The Balcony*, 1882 (CMR 125).
105. On the identification and list of works exhibited by Berthe Morisot, see exh. cat. Washington and San Francisco 1996.
106. Ibid.
107. Ibid.
108. Rouart 1950, p. 112.
109. Post-mortem inventory, AN, MC/ET/XXX/1293, refs. 2e and 32e.
110. Income tax was instituted in 1914.
111. Berthe Morisot, post-mortem inventory, AN, MC/ET/XXX/1293.
112. As indicated on the plan reproduced in CMR 1997, p. 57.
113. Edgar Degas to Eugène Manet, n.d. [1883], Paris, Musée Marmottan Monet, inv. D.4-1986.2013.193.
114. Blanche 1921.
115. Death certificate, Arch. Dép. du Val-de-Marne, 1MI 2484.
116. Letter from Eugénie Manet to Suzanne Leenhoff, May 7, 1883, Paris, Musée Marmottan Monet, inv. D.4-1986.2013.412.
117. Letter from Léon Leenhoff to Eugène Manet, May 12, 1883, Paris, Musée Marmottan Monet, inv. D.4-1986.2013.407.
118. Henri Fantin-Latour, *Édouard Manet*, 1867, oil on canvas, 117.5 × 90 cm, Chicago, The Art Institute of Chicago.
119. Claude Monet, *Manet Painting in Monet's Garden in Argenteuil*, 1874, location unknown (W 342).
120. *Boat at Low Tide, Fécamp*, 1868 (W 117); *La Grenouillère*, 1869 (W 134); *The Wooden Bridge*, 1872 (W 195); the two other, unidentified canvases, are titled *Sailing Boats at Argenteuil* and *Windmill in Holland* in Édouard Manet's post-mortem inventory, reproduced in Rouart and Wildenstein 1975, I, p. 26.
121. Bearing the title *Bridge with Boats on the Seine* in Manet's post-mortem inventory, ibid., unidentified.
122. Bears the title *Environs of Paris* in Manet's post-mortem inventory, ibid., not identified.
123. Berthe Morisot, *The Harbor at Lorient*, 1869, Washington, D.C., National Gallery of Art (CMR 17), and *Hide and Seek*, 1873, private collection (CMR 27).
124. RW 30.
125. RW 36.
126. Works featuring in Édouard Manet's post-mortem inventory reproduced in Rouart, Wildenstein, 1975, I, p. 26.
127. Inv. 6086.
128. L 339 / MS 745; Manet, 1979, p. 145.
129. Berthe Morisot, *Venus at the Forge of Vulcan* (after Boucher), 1884, Paris, private collection (CMR 145).
130. The works are mentioned in several documents, notably in the post-mortem inventories of Eugène Manet in 1892 and Berthe Morisot in 1895; unfortunately, they have not been identified.
131. W 300.
132. See the post-mortem inventory of Eugène Manet, AN, MC/ET/XXX/1263.
133. Letter from Berthe Morisot to Edma Pontillon, n.d. [1884], Paris, Musée Marmottan Monet, inv. D.4-1986.2013.9.
134. RW 237.
135. Édouard Manet, *Girl in the Garden at Bellevue*, 1880, oil on canvas, 151 × 115 cm, location unknown (RW 343).
136. Édouard Manet, *Singer at a Café-Concert*, c. 1879, oil on canvas, 73 × 92 cm, location unknown (RW 310).
137. RW 318.
138. Édouard Manet, *Oysters and Champagne*, c. 1877, oil on canvas, 55 × 35 cm, location unknown (RW 267).
139. See the essay by Marianne Mathieu in this volume, "Monsieur and Madame Ernest Rouart, Collectors and Donators," p. 254–307.
140. Berthe Morisot, *Young Girl in Mourning Clothes in a Garden*, 1883, location unknown (CMR 131).
141. Letter from Berthe Morisot to Sophie Canat, n.d. [May 1883], Paris, Musée Marmottan Monet, inv. D.4-1986.2013.5.
142. Letter from Eugénie Manet to Jules de Jouy, January 24, 1883, Paris, Musée Marmottan Monet, inv. D.4-1986.2013.591.
143. Letter from Eugénie Manet to Jules de Jouy, July 10, 1883, Paris, Musée Marmottan Monet, inv. D.4-1986.2013.587.
144. Letter from Eugénie Manet to Jules de Jouy, February 10, 1883, Paris, Musée Marmottan Monet, inv. D.4-1986.2013.590.
145. Eugénie Manet's words were related by her son Gustave in a letter to Jules de Jouy, June 28, 1883, Paris, Musée Marmottan Monet, inv. D.4-1986.2013.625.
146. Will of Marie Eugénie Fournier, married name Manet, dated February 12, 1871 and registered on January 8, 1885, AN, MC/ET/XCIV/1635.
147. Will and codicil dated June 27, 1883 of Marie Eugénie Fournier, married name Manet, AN, MC/ET/XCIV/1635.
148. Ibid.
149. Suzanne was counting on the proceeds from the sale to reimburse her mother-in-law on January 1, 1889—completely, if the proceeds exceeded 200,000 francs, or by half, if they were no more than 150,000 francs. In fact the net proceeds were no more than 102,402 francs (see Berthe Morisot, post-mortem inventory, ref. 30e (AN, MC/ET/XXX/1293) and minutes of the posthumous sale of Édouard Manet, Arch. Paris, D48E3C72).
150. Berthe Morisot, post-mortem inventory, refs. 2e and 23e, AN, MC/ET/XXX/1293.
151. See Pouly 2012.
152. Ibid.
153. Letter from Eugène Manet to Berthe Morisot and Julie Manet, November 24, [1884], Paris, Musée Marmottan Monet, inv. D.4-1986.2013.28.
154. Berthe Morisot, Mézy notebook, also known as the "black notebook," 1891, Paris, Musée Marmottan Monet, inv. D.4-1986.2014.4.
155. Ibid.
156. A list drawn up by Eugène Manet includes a portrait of Miss Reynolds dating from 1881, Paris, Musée Marmottan Monet, inv. D.4-1986.2013.727.
157. Berthe Morisot, *Miss Reynolds*, 1884, oil on canvas, 73 × 60 cm, private collection (CMR 167), and *The English Lesson* 1884, watercolor on paper, 24 × 30 cm, private collection (BW 698).
158. Berthe Morisot, post-mortem inventory, ref. 51e, AN, MC/ET/XXX/1293.
159. See the general bibliography for other publications on this subject.
160. Letter from C. Chevalier to Berthe Morisot, December 1884, Paris, Musée Marmottan Monet, inv. D.4-1986.2013.787.
161. Letter from Paule Gobillard to Berthe Morisot, n.d., Paris, Musée Marmottan Monet, inv. D.4-1986.2013.73.
162. Letter from Berthe Morisot to Paule Gobillard, Rotterdam, n.d., Jean-Marc Delvaux sale, Paris, Richelieu Drouot, December 9, 2011, lot 47.
163. Based on a family memory kindly communicated by Julie Manet's granddaughter, Mme Françoise Rouart.
164. Berthe Morisot, "beige notebook," between 1885 and 1888, Paris, Musée Marmottan Monet, inv. D.4-1986.2014.1.
165. Berthe Morisot, Mézy or "black notebook," 1891, Paris, Musée Marmottan Monet, inv. D.4-1986.2014.4.
166. Ibid.
167. Words spoken. by Renoir recorded by Berthe Morisot in her "beige notebook," Paris, Musée Marmottan Monet, inv. D.4-1986.2014.1.
168. Ibid.
169. Letter from Berthe Morisot to Paule Gobillard, 1879, in Rouart, 1950, p. 100.
170. Letter from Pierre-Auguste Renoir to Berthe Morisot, n.d. [1888], Paris, Musée Marmottan Monet, inv. D.4-1986.2013.134.
171. Letter from Mallarmé to Berthe Morisot, November 19, 1886, in Mallarmé 2019, no. 749.
172. Letter from Berthe Morisot to Geneviève Mallarmé, n.d. [April 5, 1887], Paris, Musée Marmottan Monet, inv. D.4-1986.2013.281.
173. Rouart 1950, p. 175.
174. Ibid., p. 156–157.
175. Letter from Berthe Morisot to Stéphane Mallarmé, July 22 [1888], Paris, Musée Marmottan Monet, inv. D.4-1986.2013.289.
176. Letter from Mallarmé to Berthe Morisot, July 26, 1888, in Mallarmé 2019, no. 989.
177. Rouart 1950, p. 144.
178. Letter from Berthe Morisot to Stéphane Mallarmé, February 28, 1889, Paris, Musée Marmottan Monet, inv. D.4-1986.2013.296.
179. Mallarmé 2019, no. 1066.

180. Manet 1979, p. 119.
181. See Gobillard 2021, p. 32 and 41.
182. Mallarmé 2019, no. 1054: "This poem turned prose, How all is in reverse, When I for each rose, Should send you only verse."
183. Ibid., no. 1231: "On Pegasus surely mounted/ Wherever your steed flies/Remain, Bibi, Mademoiselle/ Julie with his New Year."
184. Julie Manet's school exercise book, 1888, Arch. BS, 2021.2.218.
185. Letter from Edgar Bèhne to Julie Manet, March 11, 1895, Paris, Musée Marmottan Monet, inv. D.4-1986.2013.845.
186. Letter from Edgar Bèhne to Eugène Manet, May 7, 1889, Paris, Musée Marmottan Monet, inv. D.4-1986.2013.805.
187. Bertinot [n.d.], p. 26.
188. Rouart 1950, p. 141.
189. Letter from Berthe Morisot to Suzanne Leenhoff, n.d., Paris, Musée Marmottan Monet, inv. D.4-1986.2013.17.
190. Letter from Berthe Morisot to Paule Gobillard, n.d., Jean-Marc Delvaux sale, Paris, Richelieu Drouot, December 9, 2011, lot no. 49.
191. Letter from Berthe Morisot to a friend, n.d., Paris, Musée Marmottan Monet, inv. D.4-1986.2013.18.
192. Berthe Morisot, Mézy or "black notebook," 1891, Paris, Musée Marmottan Monet, inv. D.4-1986.2014.4.
193. Letter from Marie-Thérèse Ollivier to Berthe Morisot, March 27, 1889, Paris, Musée Marmottan Monet, inv. D.4-1986.2013.381.
194. *La Liberté*, May 29, 1890, p. 4.
195. *Lucie Léon at the Piano*, 1892 (CMR 320 to 322).
196. Rouart 1950, p. 178.
197. Mallarmé 2019, no. 1326.
198. Ibid., no. 1433: "Here the humble clerk/Attests the melancholy/He feels when spelling/Julie otherwise than Jolie."
199. Letter from Pierre-Auguste Renoir to Berthe Morisot, January 9, 1890, Paris, Musée Marmottan Monet, inv. D.4-1986.2013.135.
200. See the essay by Dominique d'Arnoult in this volume, "Julie Manet Model, a Natural Art of the Pose," p. 186–217.
201. Born in Paris (July 31, 1840–May 25, 1917), the wife of the lawyer Léon Renault (March 26, 1828–July 15, 1921), not to be confused with his contemporary and namesake Charles-Léon Renault (September 24, 1839–May 25, 1933), lawyer, prefect, and politician.
202. Regina Berthe Renault (February 19, 1878–December 5, 1948)
203. Julie Manet's role in *Le Service intéressé*, performed on May 11, 1891, manuscript, Arch. BS, 2021.2.219.
204. Letter from Eugène Manet to Suzanne Leenhoff, n.d., Paris, Musée Marmottan Monet, inv. D.4-1986.2013.394.
205. Letter from Louise Riesener to Berthe Morisot, May 23, 1890, Paris, Musée Marmottan Monet, inv. D.4-1986.2013.82.
206. Berthe Morisot, Mézy or "black notebook," 1891, Paris, Musée Marmottan Monet, inv. D.4-1986.2014.4.
207. Letter from Berthe Morisot to Edma Pontillon, 1879, in Rouart 1950, p. 99.
208. Letter from Berthe Morisot to Stéphane Mallarmé, April 13, 1890, Paris, Musée Marmottan Monet, inv. D.4-1986.2013.301.
209. Ibid.
210. Letter from Stéphane Mallarmé to Berthe Morisot, April 28, 1890, Paris, Musée Marmottan Monet, inv. D.4-1986.2013.302.
211. Letter from Stéphane Mallarmé to Berthe Morisot, May 5, 1890, Paris, Musée Marmottan Monet, inv. D.4-1986.2013.304.
212. Letter from Berthe Morisot to Claude Monet, September 23, [1890], Paris, Musée Marmottan Monet, inv. 6515.
213. Rouart 1950, p. 155.
214. Letter from Stéphane Mallarmé to Berthe Morisot, n.d. [October 11, 1890], Paris, Musée Marmottan Monet, inv. D.4-1986.2013.310.
215. Rouart 1950, p. 152.
216. Ibid., p. 156–157.
217. Ibid., p. 157.
218. Berthe Morisot, post-mortem inventory, March 13, 1895, AN, MC/ET/XXX/1293.
219. Ibid.
220. Letter from Eugène Manet to Jules de Jouy, June 2, 1891, Paris, Musée Marmottan Monet, inv. D.4-1986.2013.604.

JULIE IN THE LIBERTY HAT

221. Letter from Paule Gobillard to Berthe Morisot, n.d. [1892], Paris, Musée Marmottan Monet, inv. D.4-1986.2013.78.
222. Letter from Berthe Morisot to Stéphane Mallarmé, n.d. [March 24, 1892], Paris, Musée Marmottan Monet, inv. D.4-1986.2013.321.
223. Letter from Paule Gobillard to Berthe Morisot, n.d. [1892], Paris, Musée Marmottan Monet, inv. D.4-1986.2013.78.
224. Cabanne 1989, p. 268.
225. Telegram from Berthe Morisot to Stéphane Mallarmé, April 13, 1892, Paris, Musée Marmottan Monet, inv. D.4-1986.2013.325.
226. Berthe Morisot to Sophie Canat, October 7, 1892, in Rouart 1950, p. 173.
227. Manet 1979, p. 110.
228. The role of the deputy guardian was to oversee the action of the guardian. Such a role was created usually only when the person had a considerable fortune.
229. Post-mortem inventory of Eugène Manet, AN, MC/ET/XXX/1263.
230. The archives of the justice of the peace of the 16th arrondissement are in deplorable condition at the Archives de Paris. The period concerning Julie Manet, 1892–95, seems to have disappeared. Arch. Paris, D16U1.
231. Letter from Jules de Jouy to Berthe Morisot, May 5, 1892, Paris, Musée Marmottan Monet, inv. D.4-1986.2013.772.
232. Letter from Adolphe Pontillon to Berthe Morisot, April 20, 1892, Arch. BS, 2021.2.224.
233. Émile Henry Marie Mayniel (June 25, 1843, Paris 2nd–January 13, 1918, Paris 8th), birth certificate, reconstituted civil records, Arch. Paris, V3E/N 1584 ; death certificate, Arch. Paris, 8D 163.
234. See the essay by Marianne Mathieu in this volume, "Passy, a Family Penchant," p. 13–19.
235. Letter from Julien Morize to Berthe Morisot, May 5, 1892, Paris, Musée Marmottan Monet, inv. D.4-1986.2013.732.
236. Letter-card from Stéphane Mallarmé to Berthe Morisot, n.d. [May 3, 1892], Paris, Musée Marmottan Monet, inv. D.4-1986.2013.329.
237. Rouart 1950, p. 169.
238. Letter from Louise Riesener to Berthe Morisot, June 12, 1892, Paris, Musée Marmottan Monet, inv. D.4-1986.2013.84.
239. The correspondence with M. Plessis provides information in the regular maintenance of Le Mesnil.
240. Rouart 1950, p. 169.
241. A half-brother of Émile Henry Mayniel, Alfred Louis Auguste Bergère (1828–1914), married Zoé Marie Jagerschmidt (1842–1905), thereby linking the two families.
242. Berthe Morisot, post-mortem inventory, ref. 26e, AN, MC/ET/XXX/1293.
243. Letter from Berthe Morisot to Stéphane Mallarmé, n.d. [September 26, 1892], Paris, Musée Marmottan Monet, inv. D.4-1986.2013.334.
244. Manet 1979, p. 24.
245. Berthe Morisot to Paule Gobillard, n.d., Jean-Marc Delvaux sale, Paris, Richelieu Drouot, December 9, 2011, lot 52.
246. This address appears on the death certificate of Yves Gobillard (Departmental Archives of Les Yvelines, 2MIEC245).
247. Letter from Julien Morize to Berthe Morisot, June 29, 1892, Paris, Musée Marmottan Monet, inv. D.4-1986.2013.738.
248. Berthe Morisot, Mézy or "black notebook," 1891, Paris, Musée Marmottan Monet, inv. D.4-1986.2014.4.
249. Inv. 6086.
250. L 339 / MS 745.
251. RW 304.
252. Berthe Morisot, *The Black Bodice*, 1878, oil on canvas, 73 × 59.8 cm, Dublin, National Gallery of Ireland (CMR 74).
253. "I keep a few screens that were used for backgrounds, among others representing whaling," Berthe Morisot, "green notebook A", Paris, Musée Marmottan Monet, inv. D.5-1986.2014.2
254. Berthe Morisot, post-mortem inventory, AN, MC/ET/XXX/1293.
255. Declaration of change of ownership following the death of Eugène Manet, October 12, 1892, Arch. Paris, DQ7 12762.
256. Suzanne Leenhoff-Manet to Berthe Morisot, June 16, 1892, Paris, Musée Marmottan Monet, inv. D.4-1986.2013.38.
257. This was the term used by Stéphane Mallarmé in a letter to Berthe Morisot date July 22, 1892, Paris, Musée Marmottan Monet, inv. D.4-1986.2013.332.
258. See the essay in this volume "A Place of One's Own," p. 20–31.
259. Polonius, the father of Laertes and Ophelia, was accidentally killed by Hamlet.
260. Stéphane Mallarmé, "Notes sur le théâtre, Hamlet, Pierrot assassin de sa femme," *La Revue Indépendante : politique, littéraire et artistique*, November 1886.
261. Letter from Stéphane Mallarmé to Berthe Morisot, n.d. [September 6, 1893], Paris, Musée Marmottan Monet, inv. D.4-1986.2013.345. This line, "Good Laertes," is repeated three times in *Hamlet*, in act IV, scenes 5 and 6, but is not spoken by Hamlet himself. It is King Claudius and Queen Gertrude of Denmark, Hamlet's uncle and mother, who speak to Laertes in this way, seeking to persuade him that his desire for vengeance is justified and that he should turn it on Hamlet. My thanks to Julie Pelloie for her research.
262. The *département* of Seine-et-Oise.–*Trans.*
263. Letter from Berthe Morisot to Stéphane Mallarmé, April 26, 1892, Paris, Musée Marmottan Monet, inv. D.4-1986.2013.327.
264. Declaration of change of ownership after the death of Stéphane Mallarmé, March 7, 1899, Arch. Paris, DQ7 12014.
265. See for example the letters from Berthe Morisot to Stéphane Mallarmé, May 27, 1893, Paris, Musée Marmottan Monet, inv. D.4-1986.2013.339, and June 13, 1893, Paris, Musée Marmottan Monet, inv. D.4-1986.2013.340.
266. Letter from Berthe Morisot to Paule Gobillard, n.d. [1893], Paris, Musée Marmottan Monet, inv. D.4-1986.2013.20.
267. Unpublished notes by Jeannie Gobillard, recto-verso manuscript, private collection, Paris. See the essay by Claire Gooden in this volume, "The Diary of Julie Manet," p. 142–157.
268. Exhibition, "Jean-Louis Ernest Meissonier," Paris, Galerie Georges Petit, March 1893.
269. Unpublished notes by Jeannie Gobillard, loc. cit.
270. Yves Gobillard, death certificate, Arch. Dép. des Yvelines, 2MIEC245.
271. Père-Lachaise cemetery, annual list of burials, Arch. Paris, CPL_RA18751879_02.
272. Letter from Jules de Jouy to Berthe Morisot, June 10, 1893, Paris, Musée Marmottan Monet, inv. D.4-1986.2013.774.
273. Letter from Sophie Canat to Berthe Morisot, June 12 [1893], Paris, Musée Marmottan Monet, inv. D.4-1986.2013.752.
274. Census of Neuilly-sur-Seine, 1891, Arch. Dép. des Hauts-de-Seine, D_NUM_NEU_1891.
275. Residence of Paule Gobillard published in the brochure of the Salon des Indépendants in 1895, quoted in Lobstein 2003, p. 758.
276. Letter from Suzanne Leenhoff to Berthe Morisot-Manet, January 17, 1894, Arch. BS, 2021.2.145.
277. Letter to Berthe Morisot, March 1, 1893, Paris, Musée Marmottan Monet, inv. D.4-1986.2013.743.
278. Letter from Julie Manet to Jeannie Gobillard, Valvins, Wednesday evening, Arch. du Mesnil, inv. 2021.1.44.
279. Letter from Julie Manet to Jeannie Gobillard, Friday, Archives of Le Mesnil, inv. 2021.1.46.

280. *Paris-Adresses, annuaire général de l'industrie*, 1893.
281. Manet 1979, p. 26.
282. Receipt for half a year dated December 1, 1893 for the student Julie Manet, Paris, Musée Marmottan Monet, inv. D.4-1986.2013.909; according to Manet 1979, p. 50–51, she may have been enrolled in 1894.
283. *Paris-Adresses, annuaire général de l'industrie*, 1893. The letter referred to in the following note is sent from Wagram, 77.
284. Letter from Minnie Vos to Berthe Morisot, n.d. [1893], Paris, Musée Marmottan Monet, inv. D.4-1986.2013.757.
285. Manet 1979, p. 20.
286. See the essay by Claire Gooden in this volume, "The Diary of Julie Manet," p. 142–157.
287. See the essay in this volume "Passy, a Family Penchant," p. 12–31.
288. Sophie Canat (1836–?) is a relative, for she married Marie Louis Gabriel Thomas, Berthe Morisot's uncle. She married Colonel Canat in her second marriage.
289. Berthe Morisot, *On the Chaise Longue*, 1893, location unknown (CMR 344).
290. Berthe Morisot, *The Two Sisters*, 1894, private collection (CMR 416).
291. CMR 418.
292. See the essay by Dominique d'Arnoult in this volume, "Julie the Painter, the Last of the Manets or the Interrupted Apprenticeship," p. 158–185.
293. Manet 1979, p. 23.
294. Gobillard 2021.
295. Letter from Camille Mauclair to Berthe Morisot, n.d. [1893], Paris, Musée Marmottan Monet, inv. D.4-1986.2013.366.
296. Mallarmé 2019, no. 2087. "Julie, before your eyes so fair/Alight on the page there/And tumbling mermaid locks/Speak first to Monsieur Mauclair."
297. Manet 1979, p. 28.
298. Letter from Jules de Jouy to Berthe Morisot, December 18, 1893, Arch. du Mesnil, inv. 2021.1.2729.
299. March 10 and 11, 1894, see Manet 1979, p. 28.
300. Death certificate of Jules de Jouy, Arch. Paris, V4E 8032.
301. Manet 1979, p. 50.
302. Berthe Morisot, post-mortem inventory, ref. 52ᵉ, AN, MC/ET/XXX/1293.
303. Letter from Suzanne Leenhoff-Manet to Berthe Morisot, Friday March 23 [1894], Arch. BS, 2021.2.146.
304. The power is attached to the post-mortem inventory, March 24, April 10, 11, and 12, 1894, AN, MC/ET/LXXIX/1017.
305. See the essay by Marianne Mathieu in this volume, "Painting as a Legacy," p. 219–233.
306. Letter from Suzanne Leenhoff-Manet to Berthe Morisot, Friday, March 23, [1894], Arch. BS, 2021.2.146.
307. Letter from Suzanne Leenhoff to Berthe Morisot, March 30, 1894, Paris, Musée Marmottan Monet, inv. D.4-1986.2013.46.
308. Letter from Suzanne Leenhoff to Berthe Morisot, August 25 [1894], Paris, Musée Marmottan Monet, inv. D.4-1986.2013.50.
309. Letter from Suzanne Leenhoff to Berthe Morisot, December 24 [1894], Paris, Musée Marmottan Monet, inv. D.4-1986.2013.56; Berthe Morisot, post-mortem inventory, ref. 52ᵉ, AN, MC/ET/XXX/1293.
310. Berthe Morisot, *Young Girl in a Ball Gown*, 1879, oil on canvas, 71 × 54 cm, Paris, Musée d'Orsay (CMR 81).
311. RW 179.
312. Letter from Berthe Morisot to Stéphane Mallarmé, September 1, 1894, Paris, Musée Marmottan Monet, inv. D.4-1986.2013.356.
313. Letter from Jules de Jouy to Berthe Morisot, February 14, 1894, Paris, Musée Marmottan Monet, inv. D.4-1986.2013.776.
314. Berthe Morisot, post-mortem inventory, refs. 2ᵉ and 41ᵉ, AN, MC/ET/XXX/1293.
315. Manet 2017, 53.
316. Mallarmé 2019, no. 1869: "She who under the sky so fast/Attains an exact height/Flowers like a slender lily and cannot prevent/The guardian from being at her feet."
317. CMR 1997, p. 319.

"THE FLYING SQUADRON"

318. Gobillard 2021, p. 139.
319. Ibid., photo 107.
320. The will, a private agreement, unsealed, was deposited with Mᵉ Fermé on March 15 (Departmental Archives of Hauts-de-Seine, 3E/SUR_661).
321. See the essay in this volume, "A Place of One's Own," p. 20–31.
322. Manet 2017, p. 54.
323. Rouart 1950, p. 184–185.
324. Gobillard 2021, p. 140.
325. Manet 1979, p. 75.
326. Mallarmé 2019, nos. 2342 to 2348.
327. Ibid., no. 2343.
328. Letter from Edme Pontillon to Julie Manet, n.d., Paris, Musée Marmottan Monet, inv. D.4-1986.2013.831.
329. Gobillard 2021, p. 140.
330. Letter from Claude Monet to Alice Hoschedé Monet, March 10, 1895, in Wildenstein 1979, vol. III, p. 283, no. 1281.
331. Summary of the book of condolences, private collection. Thanks to M. Yves Rouart.
332. Bailly-Hertzberg 1989, p. 41, letter no. 1117.
333. Letter from Émile Mayniel to Gabriel Thomas, March 6, 1895, Arch. BS, 2021.2.223.
334. Post-mortem inventory of Berthe Morisot, AN, MC/ET/XXX/1293.
335. Manet 1979, p. 53.
336. Exhibition organized toward a centenary monument to Corot, May–June 1895, Palais Galliera.
337. Exhibition of paintings by Claude Monet, May 10–31, 1895, Galeries Durand-Ruel, 16, rue Laffitte, 11, rue Lepeltier.
338. Gobillard 2021, p. 141.
339. See the essay in this volume "Julie in the Liberty Hat," p. 32–43.
340. Gobillard 2021, p. 141.
341. Berthe Morisot, statement of the estate, Arch. Paris, DQ7 12 791.
342. On details of summer 1895, see Julie Manet's diary and the essay by Dominique d'Arnoult in this volume, "Julie the Painter, the Last of the Manets or the Interrupted Apprenticeship," p. 158–185.
343. *Gil Blas*, year 18, no. 5926, February 8, 1896, p. 3.
344. Maurice Bouts, Parisian lawyer, successor of M. Olivier.
345. With thanks to Mme Monique Valéry, who shared the memories engraved in the family memory of Gabriel's generous deposit.
346. See the essay in this volume "Julie in the Liberty Hat," p. 32–43.
347. Acknowledgment of 225,000 francs by Mlle Manet to the advantage of M. Broët: "This sum was used in keeping with the recommendations of the family council to reimburse the sums owed by Mlle Manet to the Crédit Foncier, to M. Bonot, and to M. Main assignee of M. Jolivard, and for the payment of invoices from sundry entrepreneurs." The loan, with a rate of interest of 4%, was taken out for ten years, staring on April 17, 1896, and was accompanied by the mortgaging of the building in the rue de Villejust. Arch. du Mesnil, inv. 2021.1.1145.
348. Presentation of the administrator's accounts of the possessions of Mlle Manet, Paris, May 16, 1898. With thanks to Fabienne Stahl.
349. Manet 1979, p. 198.
350. Gobillard 2021, p. 141.
351. The property notebooks held at the Arch. Paris were not available, making it possible to check this information.
352. Gobillard 2021, p. 141.
353. Post-mortem inventory of Berthe Morisot, AN, MC/ET/XXX/1293: the estimation of Berthe Morisot's works is succinct and the works are assembled in lots.
354. Berthe Morisot, *The Cherry Tree*, 1891, Paris, Musée Marmottan Monet, inv. 6020 (CMR 281).
355. Berthe Morisot, *The Goose*, 1885, private collection (CMR 183).
356. Berthe Morisot, *Young Woman and Child on an Isle*, 1883, private collection (CMR 140).
357. Manet 1979, p. 200.
358. Berthe Morisot, *Young Woman in Gray Reclining*, 1878, private collection (CMR 77).
359. Berthe Morisot, *On the Lake in the Bois de Boulogne*, 1884, private collection (CMR 148).
360. Berthe Morisot, *Large Nude*, 1888, private collection (BW 761).
361. Édouard Manet, *Young Woman in the Garden*, 1880, location unknown (RW 343).
362. L 173.
363. Édouard Manet, *Oysters*, c. 1877, location unknown (RW 267).
364. RW 310.
365. Édouard Manet, *Singer at a Café-Concert*, c. 1879, location unknown (RW 310).
366. According to the post-mortem inventory of Eugène Manet, AN, MC/ET/XXX/1263.
367. She later occupied a room giving onto the street, as recalled by her granddaughter, Mme Françoise Rouart.
368. Manet 1979, p. 74.
369. See Berthe Morisot, *In front of the Mirror*, 1890, Martigny, Fondation Pierre Gianadda.
370. According to a privately owned note by Jeannie Gobillard.
371. For the date, see exh. cat. Paris 1999.
372. See the address on Jeanne Pontillon's marriage certificate, Arch. Paris, V4E 10025.
373. Letter from Julie Manet to Gabriel Thomas, Monday, October 28 [1895], Arch. BS, 2021.2.111.
374. Letter from Edma Pontillon to Gabriel Thomas, November 11, [18]95, Arch. BS, 2021.2.93.
375. Report to M. Gabriel Thomas, guardian of Mademoiselle Manet, from M. Maurice Bouts, lawyer at 13, rue Pasquier, Paris, following the one established on May 2, 1896, Arch. BS, 2021.2.571 to 2021.2.576.
376. Geffroy, 1896.
377. Manet 1979, p. 77–93.
378. Manet 1987, p. 140.
379. James Abbott McNeill Whistler, *Arrangement In Gray and Black No. 1 (Portrait of the Artist's Mother)*, 1871, Paris, Musée d'Orsay.
380. Baudot 1949, p. 35.
381. Mallarmé to Paule Gobillard, n.d., "Little ones and Demoiselle Patronne, will you have me at dinner on Thursday with nothing extraordinary except for my presence" (Jean-Marc Delvaux sale, Paris, Richelieu Drouot, December 13, 2007, lot 114).
382. Odilon Redon, *Portrait of Paule Gobillard*, 1901, pastel, location unknown (W 79).
383. The correspondence between Paule Gobillard and Odilon has been dispersed. Three notes can be cited by way of an example; see Jean-Marc Delvaux sale, Paris, Richelieu Drouot, December 9, 2011, lots 64 to 66.
384. Baudot 1949, p. 7.
385. Ibid., p. 66.
386. Manet 1979, p. 202.
387. Ibid., p. 225.
388. Adolphe Angoulvent (December 12, 1825–September 21, 1890), bank owner and trustee, remarried with Henriette Gabrielle Ferdinande Baligand (November 14, 1847–February 10, 1930).
389. Léon Angoulvent (1876–1954).
390. Fernande Angoulvent (1877–1961).
391. Gabrielle Angoulvent (1879–1939).
392. Éditions Fischbacher, 1898.
393. Manet 1979, p. 151 and 282, student from 1901 to 1910. With thanks to Dominique Lobstein, who confirmed and consulted the file AJ/52/407.
394. Ibid., p. 198.
395. Ibid.
396. Ibid.
397. Rouart 2012, p. 9.
398. In her memoirs Jeanne Baudot makes a passing allusion, as if she was part of the furniture, to "my Catherine, who raised me, who was very old, and always with me" (Baudot 1949, p. 65).
399. Manet 1979, p. 114.
400. After Yves's death, in June 1893, his children spent the summer at Mas Marvent.
401. Manet 1979, p. 128.
402. Pierre-Auguste Renoir to Mesdemoiselles Manet and Gobillard, August 27, 1898 (Jean-Marc Delvaux, Paris, Richelieu Drouot, December 13, 2007, lot 124).
403. Manet 1979, p. 182.

404. Pierre-Auguste Renoir to Mesdemoiselles Manet and Gobillard, August 27, 1898 (Jean-Marc Delvaux, Paris, Richelieu Drouot, December 13, 2007, lot 124).
405. Manet 1979, p. 180.
406. Ibid., p. 186.
407. Jean-Marc Delvaux sale, Paris, Richelieu Drouot, December 9, 2011, lot 38.
408. All the signs are that Julie stopped attending private lessons and that Camille Mauclair would soon stop providing instruction in the rue de Villejust.
409. Manet 1979, p. 123.
410. Ibid., p. 124.
411. According to a handwritten program dating from June 11, 1896 reproduced in Manet 1987, p. 101.
412. Manet 1979, p. 124.
413. Ibid., p. 149.
414. Ibid., p. 151.
415. Ibid., p. 163–164.
416. Baudot 1949, p. 64.
417. A pun on *saindoux*, the French for lard.–*Trans.*
418. Ibid., p. 65.
419. Manet 1979, p. 212.
420. Lobstein 2003, *1896*, no. 696 *Young Girl at the Piano*, no. 697 *Bay of Douarnenez.*
421. Manet 1979, p. 131.
422. Lobstein 2003, *1898*, no. 379 *Girl with Dog*, no. 380 *Dahlias.*
423. Stéphane Mallarmé to Paule Gobillard (Jean-Marc Delvaux sale, Paris, Richelieu Drouot, December 9, 2011, lot 33).
424. After Sister Thérèse de Lisieux, *Story of a Soul* (1898). Thérèse de Lisieux made a lasting impression on Julie Manet. See the essay in this volume "Monsieur and Madame Ernest Rouart, Collectors and Donators," p. 98–99.
425. Manet 1979, p. 66.
426. Ibid., p. 247.
427. Ibid., p. 110.
428. Ibid., p. 159.
429. Ibid., p. 96.
430. Ibid., p. 140.
431. Ibid., p. 125.
432. Parish of Saint-Honoré d'Eylau, Association des Enfants de Marie, deed of consecration, December 11, 1898, Arch. du Mesnil, inv. 2021.1.3108.
433. Manet 1979, p. 226.
434. Ibid., p. 283.

"THE CARACO TRIBE"

435. Manet 1979, p. 137.
436. Ibid., p. 244–245.
437. Ibid., p. 140.
438. Gobillard 2021, p. 39.
439. Ibid., p. 46.
440. Manet 1979, p. 137.
441. Ibid., p. 244–245.
442. Ibid., p. 202.
443. Berthe Morisot, *The Meal at the House of Simon the Pharisee* (after Veronese), 1860, Paris, Musée Marmottan Monet; Berthe Morisot, *Calvary* (after Veronese), 1860, private collection (CMR 3).
444. AMN, register of copyists, microfilm, 20150282/174.
445. Manet 1979, p. 141; *pneumatique* card from Pierre-Auguste Renoir to Julie Manet, December 17, 1897, Paris, Musée Marmottan Monet, inv. D.4-1986.2013.155.
446. Baudot 1949, p. 34–35.
447. On this subject, see Mathieu 2019.
448. Marie Joséphine Clémentine Thomas widow Chevalier, December 15, 1897, Arch. Paris, V4E 10037.
449. Baudot 1949, p. 34–35.
450. Manet 2017, p. 125–126.
451. Ibid., p. 202.
452. Gobillard 2021.
453. Rouart 1956, p. 24.
454. His second given name is Henri.
455. Ernest Rouart, birth certificate, Arch. Paris, V4E 3392.
456. Ernest Rouart, excerpt from the register of baptism, Paris, April 30, 1900, Paris, parish of Saint-Augustin, Arch. du Mesnil, inv. 2021.1.1146.
457. Notebook of Hélène Hortense Françoise Jacob-Desmalter, Madame Henri Rouart, Arch. du Mesnil, inv. 2021.1.2295.
458. Rouart 1956, p. 19.
459. Ibid., p. 19.
460. On Ernest Rouart's visceral love of art, see the bibliography.
461. Diary of Paul Signac, February 16, 1898. Thanks to Charlotte Hellman for her kind permission.
462. Ernest Rouart, Arch. Paris, matriculation register (1887–1921), D4R1 0816.
463. Distel 1990.
464. Berthe Morisot's posthumous reputation took longer to be established.
465. Exh. cat. New York 1997–98.
466. Manet 1979, p. 244–245.
467. Gobillard 2021, p. 31.
468. Haziot 2012, p. 237.
469. Pierre Louÿs to Paul Valéry [c. 1894–95], quoted in exh. cat. Paris 1956, no. 148, p. 25.
470. Letter from P. G. La Chesnais to Paul Valéry, ibid., no. 151, p. 26.
471. Ibid., p. 25.
472. Ibid.
473. Manet 2017, p. 146–147.
474. Gobillard 2021, p. 31.
475. Ibid., p. 32.
476. Ibid., p. 40.
477. Ibid., p. 44.
478. Ibid., p. 31.
479. Manet 2017, p. 156–157.
480. Ibid., p. 156.
481. Gobillard 2021, p. 31.
482. Manet 2017, p. 157.
483. Gobillard 2021, p. 31.
484. Manet 1979, p. 216.
485. Gobillard 2021, p. 32.
486. Manet 2017, p. 154.
487. Card-letter from Yvonne Lerolle-Rouart to Julie Manet, March 27, 1943, Arch. du Mesnil, inv. 2021.1.573.
488. Gobillard 2021, p. 38.
489. Ibid., p. 37.
490. Ibid., p. 39.
491. Ibid., p. 43.
492. Ibid., p. 43–44.
493. Ibid., p. 50.
494. Ibid., p. 46.
495. Ibid., p. 47–48.
496. Zoé Closier, Degas's maid.
497. Gobillard 2021, p. 50.
498. Ibid., p. 53.
499. Letter from Pierre-Auguste Renoir to Julie Manet, January 17, 1900, Paris, Musée Marmottan Monet, inv. D.4-1986.2013.164.
500. Gobillard 2021, p. 56.
501. Ibid., p. 47.
502. Peeters 2016, E.1140.
503. Ibid., Kindle version, position 779.
504. Gobillard 2021, p. 83.
505. Ibid., p. 63.
506. Gobillard 2021.
507. Ibid., p. 75.
508. Ibid., p. 75–76.
509. Ibid., p. 105–106.
510. Ibid., p. 79.
511. Gobillard 2021.
512. Ibid., p. 103.
513. Peeters 2016, E.1668.
514. Gobillard 2021, p. 106.
515. Marriage certificate of Ernest Rouart and Julie Manet, May 25, 1900, with Me Albert Morel d'Arleux, AN, MC/ET/CI1741; marriage certificate of Paul Valéry and Jeannie Gobillard, with Me Amy, AN, MC/ET/XL/812.
516. Letter from Henri Rouart to Julie Manet, June 2, 1903, Paris, Musée Marmottan Monet, inv. D.4-1986.2013.672.
517. Peeters 2016, E.1645.
518. Civil marriage certificate, Valéry-Gobillard, Arch. Paris, V4E10066.
519. Civil marriage certificate, Rouart-Manet, Arch. Paris, V4E10066.
520. Religious marriage certificate Valéry Gobillard and Rouart Manet, Arch. Paris, D6J 9521.

THE REMAINS OF THE DAY

521. Address appearing on the certificate for her daughter Blanche Pontillon's civil marriage with Michel Forget, October 17, 1908, Paris 16th, Arch. Paris, 16M 161.
522. Berthe Morisot, *Little Girl with Blond Hair*, 1881 (CMR 110); Berthe Morisot, *Julie Listening*, 1888 (CMR 233).
523. Berthe Morisot, *Girl with a Dog*, 1887, Los Angeles, Hammer Museum (CMR 213).
524. Berthe Morisot, *Paule Gobillard Drawing*, 1886, pastel (BW 500).
525. Odilon Redon, *Paule Gobillard*, 1900, pastel, location unknown (W 79).
526. Odilon Redon to Paule Gobillard, November 7, 1901, Jean-Marc Delvaux sale, Paris, Richelieu Drouot, December 9, 2011, lot no. 65.
527. Letter from Ernest Rouart to Julie Manet, Arch. du Mesnil, inv. 2021.1.523.
528. Odilon Redon to Paule Gobillard, February 28, 1909, Jean-Marc Delvaux sale, Paris, Richelieu Drouot, lot no. 66.
529. Print bequeathed and annotated by Paul Valéry, Paris, Bibliothèque Littéraire Jacques Doucet, inv. 79.
530. Éditions Richard Lesclide, 1875; quoted in Rouart 2012, p. 25.
531. Letter from Ernest Rouart to Julie Manet, Arch. du Mesnil, inv. 2021.1.523.
532. Manet 1979, p. 223–224.
533. Gobillard 2021.
534. Letter from Raoul Pugno to Julie Manet, August 10, 1902, Paris, Musée Marmottan Monet, inv. D.4-1986.2013.915.
535. Letter from Henri Rouart to Julie Manet, August 27, 1907, Paris, Musée Marmottan Monet, inv. D.4-1986.2013.696.
536. Julie Manet, descriptive summary of the interior, n.d., Arch. du Mesnil, inv. 2021.1.2731.
537. Julien Rouart, birth certificate, Arch. Paris, V4E 100 73.
538. Letter from Edgar Degas to Ernest Rouart, March 27, 1901, Paris, Musée Marmottan Monet, inv. D.4-1986.2013.223.
539. Letter from Pierre-Auguste Renoir to Julie Manet, March 31, 1901, Paris, Musée Marmottan Monet, inv. D.4-1986.2013.167.
540. Clément Rouart, birth certificate, Arch. Paris, 16N 95_A.
541. Renoir is referring to the future birth of Agathe Valéry, on March 7, 1906.
542. Letter from Pierre-Auguste Renoir to Paule Gobillard, March 4, 1906, Jean-Marc Delvaux sale, Paris, Richelieu Drouot, December 9, 2011, lot no. 77.
543. Denis Rouart, birth certificate, Arch. Paris, 16N 100_A.
544. Letter from Pierre-Auguste Renoir to Paule Gobillard, March 4, 1906, Jean-Marc Delvaux sale, Paris, Richelieu Drouot, December 9, 2011, lot no. 82.
545. Claude Valéry, birth certificate, Arch. Paris, 16N 89_A.
546. Agathe Valéry, birth certificate, Arch. Paris, 16N 95_A.
547. François Valéry, birth certificate, Arch. Paris, 16N 116_2.
548. "Your father-friend." On Julie's practice and her exchanges with Ernest Rouart, see the essay by Dominique d'Arnoult, "Julie the Painter, the Last of the Manets or the Interrupted Apprenticeship," p. 158–185.
549. Letter from Ernest Rouart to Julie Manet, June 15, 1901, Paris, Musée Marmottan Monet, inv. D.4-1986.2013.648.
550. 1899, no. 1277 *The Red Hat* (on this subject, see Manet 1979, p. 236); 1903, no. 1032 *Nausicaa* (painting); 1906, no. 2167 *Nude Woman* (print); 1907, no. 2301 *Reclining Nude* (print, soft varnish).
551. No. 304 *Woman in the Bath* (print), no. 303 *Nude Woman at Her Toilette.*
552. Letter from Ernest Rouart to Julie Manet, n.d. [November 1901], Arch. du Mesnil, inv. 2021.1.522.
553. The Musée Gustave Moreau did not open until 1903, but Moreau's executor, Henri Rupp, began organizing visits while waiting for the state to accept the

bequest, which it did in 1902. The date of 1901 is therefore perfectly plausible.
554. Letter from Ernest Rouart to Julie Manet, n.d. [November 1901], Arch. du Mesnil, inv. 2021.1.521.
555. Letter from Ernest Rouart to Julie Manet, n.d. [November 1901], Arch. du Mesnil, inv. 2021.1.526.
556. Ibid.
557. Letter from Ernest Rouart to Julie Manet, n.d. [November 1901], Arch. du Mesnil, inv. 2021.1.521.
558. Hortense Marie Thérèse Guillaume (October 18, 1857, Paris–after 1906) Mrs. Louis Henri Lefuel (August 16, 1846, Versailles–December 6, 1904, Paris). Their children were Yvonne André Hortense Lefuel (July 1, 1883, Corbeil–November 30, 1937, Lausanne) and Hector André Louis Henri Lefuel (December 14, 1885, Paris–March 29, 1937, Lausanne).
559. The family correspondence contains regular references to the Lefuels, notably an undated letter from Ernest Rouart to Julie Manet, Arch. du Mesnil, inv. 2021.1.523: "at the rue de Lisbonne this evening only Henri Lefuel and Yvonne were there for dinner because Hector is sick." Letter from Henri Rouart to Julie Manet: "Ernest left yesterday in the morning . . . At the station he met the Lefuels who were on their way to stay here." Years later, on July 28, 1931, the Lefuels were invited to the wedding of Clément Rouart, Julie and Ernest's son, and Victoria Rapin, Arch. du Mesnil, inv. 2021.1.375 to 2021.1.398.
560. Interview with Julien and Jean-Marie Rouart.
561. This quotation and the passage preceding it are based on Haziot 2012, p. 270–271.
562. See Bona 2012.
563. These quotations are from an interview recorded by Julien and Jean-Marie Rouart and compiled from a transcript kept at the Musée Marmottan Monet.
564. Letter from Henri Rouart to Julie Manet, October 10, 1902, Paris, Musée Marmottan Monet, inv. D.4-1986.2013.671.
565. See above, note 45.
566. Arch. SACEM: https://musee.sacem.fr/index.php/Detail/objects/50691.
567. https://catalogue.bnf.fr/ark:/12148/cb42920035c.
568. This was a period of exercise imposed on the army reserve corps.
569. Letter from Julie Manet to Ernest Rouart, October 26, 1904, Arch. du Mesnil, inv. 2021.1.62.
570. Her grandson, Jean-Marie Rouart, presents a poignant but uncompromising portrait his book *Une jeunesse à l'ombre de la lumière* (Rouart 2000).
571. *L'Occident*, no. 39, February 1905, p. 105–106.
572. On Louis Rouart's many pseudonyms, see Haziot 2012, p. 240.
573. Rouart 1908.
574. Arch. du Mesnil, inv. 2021.1.1147.
575. London, Franco-British Exhibition, May 14–October 31, 1908.
576. On this point, see Serry 2004.
577. The Archives de la Province Dominicaine de France (APDF) hold the correspondence of Père Janvier. The oldest communication exchanged with Ernest dates from December 14, 1906. Unless otherwise indicated, the letters quoted here and information deduced therefrom are found in section V 303.
578. Letters from Louis Rouart to Père Janvier, December 20, 1906 and May 23, 1907, APDF, section V 303.
579. Letter from Ernest Rouart to Père Janvier, October 29, 1907, APDF, section V 303, and Père Janvier to Ernest Rouart, Arch. du Mesnil, inv. 2021.1.1063.
580. Letter from Ernest Rouart to Père Janvier, March 28, 1907, APDF, section V 303.
581. Letter from Henri Rouart to Père Janvier, May 7, 1908, APDF, section V 303.
582. Janvier 1936, p. 12.
583. Ibid.
584. Ibid.
585. List of members of the brotherhood who usually attended the meetings, APDF, ref. 102.
586. Janvier 1936, p. 17.
587. Louis 1917.
588. Letter from Julie Manet to Ernest Rouart, June 13, 1917, Arch. du Mesnil, inv. 2021.1.13.
589. Letter from Julie Manet to Ernest Rouart, May 29, 1917, Arch. du Mesnil, inv. 2021.1.67.
590. Chronicle of the Fraternité du Saint-Sacrement du Tiers-Ordre de la Pénitence de Saint Dominique, APDF, ref. 101.
591. Letter from Julie Manet to Madame Maurice Denis, April 5 [1909], Arch. Dép. des Yvelines, no. 166J58, Ms9568.
592. Inscription register no. 2, APDF, ref. 002.
593. Suzanne Leenhoff, death certificate, Arch. Paris, 7D 127.
594. Alexis Hubert Rouart, death certificate, Arch. Paris, 8D 138.
595. Henri Rouart, death certificate, Arch. Paris, 8D 141.
596. Conversation between Julien and Jean-Marie Rouart.

MONSIEUR AND MADAME ERNEST ROUART

597. Conversation between Julien and Jean-Marie Rouart.
598. Conversation between Julien and Jean-Marie Rouart.
599. The declarations concerning the post-mortem transfer of ownership of bank and property investments were drawn up on April 11, 1912 (no. 613) and June 12, 1912 (no. 987), Arch. Paris, DQ7 31810 and DQ7 31814.
600. Letter from Ernest Rouart to Julie Manet-Rouart, Monday July 8 [1912], Arch. BS, inv. 2021.2.23.
601. Letter from Ernest Rouart to Julie Manet-Rouart, Friday July 5 [1912], Arch. du Mesnil, inv. 2021.1.2322.
602. Letter from Ernest Rouart to Julie Manet-Rouart, Wednesday July 10 [1912], Arch. du Mesnil, inv. 2021.1.2323.
603. Letter from Ernest Rouart to Julie Manet-Rouart, Wednesday [1912], Arch. du Mesnil, inv. 2021.1.2325.
604. Letter from Pierre-Auguste Renoir to Paule Gobillard, December 16, 1912, Jean-Marc Delvaux sale, Paris, Richelieu Drouot, December 9, 2011, lot 83.
605. Proceedings of the sale, *Du 7 December [1912] Réquisition afin de ventes de tableaux, dessins et pastels provenant de la succession de M. Henri Rouart du 9 décembre vente des dits tableaux etc. du 8 juillet 1913 décharge du produit de la vente*, Me F. LAIR – DUBREUIL, auctioneer in Paris, in Arch. Paris, D42E3 124.
606. Edgar Degas, *Dancers Practicing at the Barre* 1876–77, New York, The Metropolitan Museum of Art.
607. Julien Rouart spoke at length about this episode in an interview: "The big event was the sale of the Degas painting *Dancers Practicing at the Barre* which, I recall, made, in the money of the day, 435,000 francs. It was the first time an Impressionist painting made that figure, and it was even in the newspaper headlines. I recall that when I got to school the next day my classmates looked at me with amazement. I had become someone else for them, especially as I was quite shy, withdrawn, and I was rather surprised. I couldn't fathom it."
608. Letter from Pierre-Auguste Renoir to Paule Gobillard, December 16, 1912, Jean-Marc Delvaux sale, Paris, Richelieu Drouot, December 9, 2011, lot 83.
609. Succession of Henri Rouart, declaration of transfer of property, April 11, 1912 (no. 613), June 19, 1912 (no. 987), May 29, 1913 (no. 828), Arch. Paris, DQ7 31810, DQ7 31814 and DQ7 31831.
610. As remembered by Julien Rouart, see conversation.
611. Signorile 2015.
612. Ernest Rouart, service number 407, military recruitment for Seine, register of recruitment service numbers (1887–1921), Arch. Paris, D4R1 816.
613. Letter from Julie Manet-Rouart to Ernest Rouart, Friday August 7, 1914, Arch. du Mesnil, inv. 2021.1.2326.
614. The name and address are indicated on the letter head of Julie Manet-Rouart's letters to Père Janvier, September 3, 1914, APDF, section V 303; the cost of the say in Julie's accounts notebooks, "Agenda 1915," Arch. du Mesnil, inv. 2021.1.3804; see also the conversation between Julien and Jean-Marie Rouart.
615. Letter from Julie Manet-Rouart to Père Janvier, September 3, 1914, APDF, section V 303.
616. On this subject, see Coutin 2012.
617. Letter from Julie Manet-Rouart to Ernest Rouart, June 18, 1917, Arch. du Mesnil, inv. 2021.1.17.
618. Letter from Julie Manet-Rouart to Ernest Rouart, Monday morning [June 4, 1917], Arch. du Mesnil, inv. 2021.1.69.
619. Maurice Denis, *Eternal Spring*, 1908, Saint-Germain-en-Laye, Musée Maurice-Denis.
620. This was a sketch for a mosaic for the church of Saint-Paul in Geneva whose decorative program Maurice Denis oversaw from 1915 to 1925.
621. Letter from Julie Manet-Rouart to Ernest Rouart, June 24, [1917], Arch. du Mesnil, inv. 2021.1.75.
622. Letter from Julie Manet-Rouart to Ernest Rouart, June 30, [1917], Arch. du Mesnil, inv. 2021.1.81.
623. Lacordaire 1919.
624. Conversation between Julien and Jean-Marie Rouart.
625. Letter from Paul Valéry to Maurice Denis, n.d., Arch. Dép. des Yvelines, 166J68, Ms 12281.
626. Francis de Miomandre (1880–1959), French writer and translator, winner of the Prix Goncourt in 1908.
627. Letter from Julie Manet-Rouart to Ernest Rouart, June 25–26, 1917, Arch. du Mesnil, inv. 2021.1.76.
628. On August 9 and 10, 1917, three thousand stood for nearly two whole days in the cemetery.
629. Letter from Julien Rouart to Ernest Rouart, September 16, 1917, Arch. du Mesnil, inv. 2021.1.2331.
630. Letter from Ernest Rouart to Julie Manet, September 21, 1917, Arch. du Mesnil, inv. 2021.1.2330.
631. Conversation between Julien and Jean-Marie Rouart.
632. Letter from Julie Manet-Rouart to Ernest Rouart, October 17, 1917, Arch. du Mesnil, inv. 2021.1.2329.
633. Letter from Ernest Rouart to Julie Manet-Rouart, October 16, 1917, Arch. du Mesnil, inv. 2021.1.2328.
634. Conversation between Julien and Jean-Marie Rouart.
635. Portuguese proverb.
636. *Le Figaro*, Sunday September 30, 1917, p. 3.
637. Letter from Paul Valéry to Ernest Rouart, [October 19, 1917], Arch. du Mesnil, inv. 2021.1.2332.
638. Letter from Ernest Rouart to Julie Manet-Rouart, October 3, 1917, Arch. du Mesnil, inv. 2021.1.2333.
639. Letter from Paul Valéry to Ernest Rouart, October 27, 1917, Arch. du Mesnil, inv. 2021.1.2336.
640. Letter from Ernest Rouart to Julie Manet-Rouart, October 20, 1917, Arch. du Mesnil, inv. 2021.1.2334.
641. Letter from Julie Manet-Rouart to Ernest Rouart, October 22, 1917, Arch. du Mesnil, inv. 2021.1.2339.
642. Paul Lafond (1847–1918), etcher and keeper of the Musée des Beaux-Arts in Pau and a friend of Degas.
643. Letter from Ernest Rouart to Julie Manet-Rouart, October 27, 1917, Arch. du Mesnil, inv. 2021.1.2335.
644. See the essay in this volume, "The Caraco Tribe," p. 59–70.
645. Letter from Ernest Rouart to Julie Manet-Rouart, February 8, 1918, Arch. du Mesnil, inv. 2021.1.2344.
646. Letter from Ernest Rouart to Julie Manet-Rouart, February 10, 1918, Arch. du Mesnil, inv. 2021.1.2345.
647. Letter from Ernest Rouart to Julie Manet-Rouart, February 12, 1918, Arch. du Mesnil, inv. 2021.1.2349.
648. Letter from Ernest Rouart to Julie Manet-Rouart, February 3, 1918, Arch. du Mesnil, inv. 2021.1.2359.
649. Letter from Ernest Rouart to Julie Manet-Rouart, February 12, 1918, Arch. du Mesnil, inv. 2021.1.2349.
650. Letter from Ernest Rouart to Julie Manet-Rouart, February 10; 1918, Arch. du Mesnil, inv. 2021.1.2361.
651. Letter from Ernest Rouart to Julie Manet-Rouart, March 16, 1918, Arch. du Mesnil, inv. 2021.1.2360.
652. *Excelsior*, 9th year, no. 2686, Sunday March 24, 1918.
653. Conversation between Julien and Jean-Marie Rouart.
654. Letter from Ernest Rouart to Julie Manet-Rouart, April 4, 1918, Arch. du Mesnil, inv. 2021.1.2351.
655. Letter from Ernest Rouart to Julie Manet-Rouart, April 12, 1918, Arch. du Mesnil, inv. 2021.1.2352.
656. Letter from Ernest Rouart to Julie Manet-Rouart, Saturday April 13, 1918, Arch. du Mesnil, inv. 2021.1.2353.

657. Letter from Ernest Rouart to Julie Manet-Rouart, Monday April 15, 1918, Arch. du Mesnil, inv. 2021.1.2354.
658. Letter from Ernest Rouart to Julie Manet-Rouart, April 17, 1917, Arch. du Mesnil, inv. 2021.1.2355.
659. Letter from Ernest Rouart to Julie Manet-Rouart, April 19, 1918, Arch. du Mesnil, inv. 2021.1.2346.
660. Letter from Ernest Rouart to Julie Manet-Rouart, April 18, 1918, Arch. du Mesnil, inv. 2021.1.2356.
661. Letter from Ernest Rouart to Julie Manet-Rouart, April 23, 1918, Arch. du Mesnil, inv. 2021.1.2357.
662. Diary 1918, accounts notebook March 27–28, Arch. du Mesnil, inv. 2021.1.3805.
663. Letter from Ernest Rouart to Julie Manet-Rouart, April 23, 1918, Arch. du Mesnil, inv. 2021.1.2357.
664. Letter from Ernest Rouart to Julie Manet-Rouart, April 24, 1918, Arch. du Mesnil, inv. 2021.1.2362.
665. Letter from Ernest Rouart to Julie Manet-Rouart, April 24, 1918, Arch. du Mesnil, inv. 2021.1.2362.
666. Letter from Ernest Rouart to Julie Manet-Rouart, April 29, 1918, Arch. du Mesnil, inv. 2021.1.2340.
667. Conversation between Julien and Jean-Marie Rouart.
668. Letter from Ernest Rouart to Julie Manet-Rouart, April 26, 1918, Arch. du Mesnil, inv. 2021.1.2363.
669. Letter from Ernest Rouart to Julie Manet-Rouart, April 25, 1918, Arch. du Mesnil, inv. 2021.1.2347.
670. Letter from Ernest Rouart to Julie Manet-Rouart, April 19, 1918, Arch. du Mesnil, inv. 2021.1.2346.

LET MEMORY COME ALIVE!

671. Conversation between Julien and Jean-Marie Rouart.
672. Ibid.
673. Baudot 1949, p. 47.
674. On this subject, see exh. cat. New York, Chicago, and Paris 2006–07.
675. Conversation between Julien and Jean-Marie Rouart.
676. Letter from Julie Manet to Ernest Rouart, July 22, 1917, Arch. du Mesnil, inv. 2021.1.96.
677. Letter from Julie Manet to Ernest Rouart, October 14, 1917, Arch. du Mesnil, inv. 2021.1.2329.
678. Isabelle Cahn, in exh. cat. New York, Chicago, and Paris 2006–07, p. 282.
679. Letter from Julie Manet to Ernest Rouart, June 28, 1917, Arch. du Mesnil, inv. 2021.1.79.
680. Manet 1979, p. 110.
681. Letter from Julie Manet to Ernest Rouart, July 1 [1917], Arch. du Mesnil, inv. 2021.1.82.
682. Blanche 1921.
683. Letter from Claude Monet to Jeannie Gobillard-Valéry, December 7, 1919, Jean-Marc Delvaux sale, Paris, Richelieu Drouot, December 9, 1911, lot no. 46.
684. Letter from Agathe Valéry to Ernest Rouart, n.d., Arch. du Mesnil, inv. 2021.1.620.
685. Conversation between Julien and Jean-Marie Rouart.
686. Ibid.
687. Letter from Édouard Vuillard to Ernest Rouart, February 14, 1922, Paris, Musée Marmottan Monet, inv. D.4–1986.2013.411.
688. Conversation between Julien and Jean-Marie Rouart.
689. Letter from Julie Manet to Ernest Rouart, September 5, 1917, Arch. du Mesnil, inv. 2021.1.2365.
690. "You are not happy?" Conversation between Julien and Jean-Marie Rouart.
691. Council of the Brotherhood of the T.O. of the Men of the T.S. Sacrament, APDF, 108.
692. The son of Alexis Hubert Rouart (1839–1911).
693. George Desvallières and Maurice Denis, quoted in Chavence 1920, p. 3.
694. Denis 1922, p. 283–284.
695. Letter from Julie Manet to Ernest Rouart, September 5, 1917, Arch. du Mesnil, inv. 2021.1.2365.
696. *Young Girl in a Garden*, painting, no. 2209.
697. Ernest Rouart exhibited again, and modestly, in 1936, 1937, 1938, 1940, and 1941.
698. *Coutumier* of the Brotherhood of the Annunciation of the Third Order of Saint Dominic, APDF, R044-R046.
699. Alphabetical list APDF, 010.
700. Register of inscriptions, APDF, 002.
701. Minutes of the council meetings, 1918–1932, APDF, R022.
702. Alphabetical list, APDF, R009.
703. Fourreau 1925, p. 2.
704. Letter from Julie Manet to Ernest Rouart, Wednesday August 3 [1921], Arch. du Mesnil, inv. 2021.1.140.
705. Letter from Jeanne Pontillon to Blanche Pontillon, July 11 [1921], Paris, Musée Marmottan Monet, inv. D.4–1986.2013.896.
706. Fourreau 1925.
707. Ibid., p. 2.
708. The tomb of Tiburce Morisot has not been located, but it seems most likely that he was buried at Aspremont.
709. Letter from Abbé Blanchi to Julie Manet, June 3, 1927, Arch. du Mesnil, inv. 2021.1.1339.
710. Elected to the chair of Anatole France in 1925, Paul Valéry was received on June 23, 1927.
711. Marie Charles Tiburce Morisot, death certificate, Arch. Dép. des Alpes-Maritimes, 02 E 0461.
712. Letter from Paule Gobillard to Julie Manet, Tuesday [June 14, 1927], Arch. du Mesnil, inv. 2021.1.196.
713. Decree of November 12, 1929, in *Dalloz, recueil hebdomadaire de jurisprudence en matière civile*, 1929, p. 353.
714. See the essay in this volume "The Remains of the Day," p. 76–91.
715. *Le Figaro*, June 30, 1934, p. 2.
716. Conversation between Julien and Jean-Marie Rouart.
717. Letter from Paul Valéry to Maurice Denis, January 31, 1932, Arch. dép. des Yvelines, 166J 68 / Ms 12287.
718. Letter from Ernest Rouart to Maurice Denis, February 2, 1932, Arch. Dép. des Yvelines, 166J 58 / Ms 9544.
719. "Henri Rouart," Paris, Galerie Paul Rosenberg, March 20–April 12, 1933.
720. Cahn 2006.
721. "Catalogue raisonné notebook," Arch. du Mesnil, inv. 2021.1.2299.
722. Manet 1979, p. 56.
723. "London notebook," 1936, Arch. du Mesnil, inv. 2021.1.3818.
724. Berthe Morisot, *Portrait of Mme Boursier and Her Daughter*, 1874, Brooklyn, Brooklyn Museum (CMR 34).
725. Letter from Alice Gamby to Julie Manet, Nice, August 6, Arch. du Mesnil, inv. 2021.1.707.
726. Letter from Alice Gamby to Julie Manet, Saturday June 17, 1939, Arch. du Mesnil, inv. 2021.1.648.
727. Postcard from Jeannie Gobillard to Ernest Rouart, Thursday 24, Arch. du Mesnil, inv. 2021.1.312.
728. Letter from Jeannie Gobillard to Julie Manet, n.d., Arch. du Mesnil, inv. 2021.1.272.
729. Letter from Jeannie Gobillard to Julie Manet, August 9, Arch. du Mesnil, inv. 2021.1.292.
730. Rouart 1937.
731. Ibid.
732. Paris, Bibliothèque de l'École du Louvre, Br11327 RRC.
733. L 545 / MS 196.
734. L 1177 bis / MS 1166.
735. L 715 / MS 2063.
736. Receipt signed by Louis Rouart, Paris, October 12, 1939, Arch. du Mesnil, inv. 2021.1.629.
737. Letter from Alice Gamby to Julie Manet-Rouart, n.d., Arch. du Mesnil, inv. 2021.1.697.
738. Paintings belonging to M. and Mme Ernest Rouart, undated handwritten inventory, Arch. BS, 2021.2.217.
739. AMN, on the national museums during World War 2 and the evacuation of artworks (series R), AN, 20144792/99, 20144792/220, 20144792/221, 20144792/223, 20144792/227, 20144792/270, 20144792/274.
740. Note by Jeannie Gobillard, n.d., Arch. du Mesnil, inv. 2021.1.315.
741. Paul Reynaud was prime minister from March 22 to 16 June, 1940, a function which he combined with that of Foreign Minister and then Minister of War.
742. Draft of a letter from Julie Manet-Rouart, Sunday June 2 [1940], Arch. BS, 2021.2.102.
743. Exh. cat. Paris 1941.
744. Rouart 1941.
745. Du Camp 1867, p. 261.

"AND SO ENDED THE EXISTENCE OF THE RUE DE VILLEJUST"

746. Letter from Paule Gobillard to Julie Manet-Rouart, La Bretonnière Sunday morning, Arch. du Mesnil, inv. 2021.1.199.
747. Blanche Pontillon, death certificate, Arch. Paris, 16D 163.
748. The widow of Pierre Forget (1869–?), Blanche Pontillon-Forget had lost her son Gérard Forget (1909–1929) and her daughter Christine Forget (1912–1930). Her last living son, Michel Forget, embarked on a military career at the time of her death. He died for France at Cao Bang (Indochina) in 1951.
749. Postcard from Edme Pontillon to Julie Manet-Rouart, July 9, 1941, Arch. du Mesnil, inv. 2021.1.584.
750. Letter from Jeannie Gobillard-Valéry to Julie Manet-Rouart, August 9 [1941], Arch. du Mesnil, inv. 2021.1.280.
751. Letter from Paule Gobillard to Julie Manet-Rouart, La Bretonnière Sunday morning, Arch. du Mesnil, inv. 2021.1.199.
752. Ernest Rouart, death certificate, Arch. Paris, 16D 165.
753. Denis Rouart, an attaché at the Musée National d'Art Moderne (former Musée du Luxembourg), serving in the air force, was imprisoned at the camp of Saint-Hervé in Hennebont, Morbihan (Brittany), shortly after the Occupation. Family letters show evidence of attempts to obtain his liberation. See the draft of a letter by Ernest Rouart [drawing on verso], n.d., Arch. du Mesnil, inv. 2021.1.524; on the conditions of prisoners of war, see Bougeard and Cariou, 2015.
754. Letter from Denis Rouart to Julie Manet-Rouart, n.d., "Samedi," Arch. du Mesnil, inv. 2021.1.485.
755. Letter from Mme Libersen to Julie Manet-Rouart, March 12, 1942, Arch. du Mesnil, inv. 2021.1.1391.
756. Letter from Julie Manet-Rouart to Maurice Denis, March 11 [1942], Arch. Dép. des Yvelines, 166J58 [Ms 9565].
757. Berthe Morisot, Mézy notebook, also known as the "black notebook," 1891, Paris, Musée Marmottan Monet, inv. D.5–1986.2014.4.
758. Letter from Julie Manet-Rouart to Ernest Rouart, Friday August 31, 1917, Arch. du Mesnil, inv. 2021.1.3132.
759. See the essay in this book, "A Place of One's Own (1881–1892)," and particularly the section "Léon versus Julie," p. 23.
760. Conversation between Julien and Jean-Marie Rouart.
761. Ibid.
762. July 20, 1895 is the date Julie resumed her diary after her mother's death. That day's entry evokes her arrival at the home of Mme Renault in Saint-Enogat. There is no reference to Léon's wedding, held at about the same time.
763. Marie Eugénie Mathilde Fanfillon, died August 11, 1917, city of Sarcelles, record of deaths, Arch. Dép. du Val d'Oise, 4 E 1262.
764. Tabarant 1947.
765. Ibid., p. 483
766. Charlotte Lecoq, Paul and Jeannie Valéry's cook.
767. Letter from Julie Manet-Rouart to Ernest Rouart, Friday August 31, 1917, Arch. du Mesnil, inv. 2021.1.3132.
768. Tabarant, 1947, p. 483.
769. See the essay in this volume, "A Place of One's Own (1881–1892)," and particularly the section "Léon versus Julie," p. 23.
770. Letter from Ernest Rouart to Julie Manet-Rouart, Sunday September 23, 1917, Arch. du Mesnil, inv. 2021.1.3131.
771. Tabarant 1947, p. 483.

772. Officially registered as the "son of Koella and Suzanne Leenhoff," Léon was presented as Suzanne's brother and not her son. The use of the name Leenhoff served to hide the reality. On this point, see ibid. and Coppens, 2014.
773. Léon Edouard Koëlla died on September 3, 1927 in Vernon; death certificate, Arch. Dép. de l'Eure, D (1927) (2 E 8791). His burial place is not known.
774. Père-Lachaise cemetery, daily register of burials, Arch. Paris, CPL_RJ19411943_01.
775. Letter from Blanche Hoschedé Monet to Julie Manet-Rouart, erroneously dated Giverny February (actually March) 1, 1942, Arch. du Mesnil, inv. 2021.1.3243.
776. Marthe Ida Mireille Mezzara (1889–?) wife of Michel André Dufet (1888–1985).
777. Charles Antoine Mezzara (1858–?), son of the sculptor Joseph Mezzara (1820–1901). He was the teacher of Ferdinand Leenhoff, marrying his sister Mathilde and thereby becoming the brother-in-law of Suzanne Leenhoff and Édouard Manet.
778. Marthe Ida Mireille Mezzara to Julie Manet-Rouart, Casablanca May 12, 1942, Arch. du Mesnil, inv. 2021.1.1393.
779. Conversation between Julien and Jean-Marie Rouart.
780. M. Vincent Poli, head of the artworks, museums and exhibitions department at the Direction Générale des Beaux-Arts.
781. Draft of letter by Julie Manet to the artworks department, n.d., Arch. du Mesnil, inv. 2021.1.187 (for the sake of clarity, the transcription excludes the crossings-out).
782. Passy cemetery, 2nd division, cadaster 202, no. 23PA1942.
783. Père-Lachaise cemetery, daily register of burials, Arch. Paris, CPL_RJ19411943_01.
784. Letter from Julie Manet-Rouart to Maurice Denis, April 20 [1942], Arch. Dép. des Yvelines, 166J58 [Ms 9564].
785. *Comœdia*, June 27, 1942, p. 6–8.
786. Retrospective exhibition, "Ernest Rouart," Galerie Berri-Raspail, 99, boulevard Raspail, June 20–July 9, 1942.
787. Valéry 1942.
788. Fargue 1942.
789. Letter from Blanche Hoschedé-Monet to Julie Manet-Rouart, Giverny June 13, 1942, Arch. du Mesnil, inv. 2021.1.3268.
790. Letter from Jeannie Gobillard-Valéry to Julie Manet-Rouart, Friday [July 1942], Arch. du Mesnil, inv. 2021.1.298.
791. Ernest Rouart, *At the Races*, oil on canvas, 47.2 × 37.4 cm, Albi, Musée Toulouse-Lautrec, inv. MOD. 381.
792. Thanks to Manon Baroni, Archives du Salon d'Automne.
793. Ten works appear in the brochure of the Salon d'Automne in 1942: no. 1760, *The Mozart Sonata*; no. 1761, *In the Street* [mentioned here in the letter]; no. 1762, *At the Piano*; no. 1763, *Two Young Girls*; no. 1764, *Young Girl Sewing*; no. 1765, *Nude Study*; no. 1766, *Nude Study*; no. 1767, *The Dovecote at Le Mesnil*; no. 1768, *The Dovecote*; no. 1769, *Garden Scene*; no. 1770, *Effect of Spring*.
794. Letter from Julie Manet-Rouart to Maurice Denis, September 18 [1942], Arch. Dép. des Yvelines, 166J 58 [Ms 9566].
795. On this point see Rouart 2012.
796. French and foreign newspapers alike noted the solemnity of this funeral held on July 25 on the Trocadéro esplanade. Paul Valéry was buried three days later in the marine cemetery in his home town of Sète.
797. Letter from Alice Gamby to Julie Manet-Rouart, n.d. [March 1946], Arch. du Mesnil, inv. 2021.1.711.
798. Plot acquired in perpetuity in 1827. Vault no. 17 Chemin de la Bédoyère (no. 33007), transferred in 1893 to the neighboring tomb, no. 31 (no. 30363). Daily register of burials, Père-Lachaise cemetery, Arch. Paris, CPL_RJ19441946_01.
799. Letter from Alice Gamby to Julie Manet-Rouart, 31 March [1946], Arch. du Mesnil, inv. 2021.1.701.
800. Cabinetmaker and interior architect Maurice Dufrène (1876–1955) was vice president of the Salon d'Automne in 1942.
801. Letter from Jeannie Gobillard-Valéry to Julie Manet-Rouart, July 12 [1946], Arch. du Mesnil, inv. 2021.1.273.
802. Letter from Jeannie Gobillard-Valéry to Julie Manet-Rouart, July 12 [1946], Arch. du Mesnil, inv. 2021.1.273.
803. Letter from Jeannie Gobillard-Valéry to Julie Manet-Rouart, Sunday [July 21, 1946], Arch. du Mesnil, inv. 2021.1.264.
804. Georges Barat-Levraux (1878–1964), painter.
805. Marie de Régnier (married name, 1875–1963) was the daughter of José Maria de Heredia and herself a poet, novelist, and dramatist, publishing under the name of Gérard d'Houville.
806. Marie Laurencin (1883–1856), painter.
807. Jean-Louis Vaudoyer (1883–1963), art historian and writer.
808. Henri Mondor (1885–1962), doctor, surgeon, and historian.
809. Letter from Jeannie Gobillard-Valéry to Julie Manet-Rouart, August 20, [1946], Arch. du Mesnil, inv. 2021.1.287
810. Salon d'Automne 1946, p. 115.
811. Berthe Morisot, *Paule Gobillard Drawing*, pastel, 73 × 60 cm, location unknown (BW 500).
812. Letter from Jeannie Gobillard-Valéry to Julie Manet-Rouart, August 20 [1946], Arch. du Mesnil, inv. 2021.1.287
813. Letter from Paule Gobillard-Valéry to Julie Manet-Rouart, Saturday July 8 [1944], Arch. du Mesnil, inv. 2021.1.237.
814. He was curator at the Musée des Beaux-Arts de Nancy from 1946 to 1969.
815. Letter from Denis Rouart to Julie Manet-Rouart, Thursday September 2, Arch. du Mesnil, inv. 2021.1.486.
816. Letter from Berthe Noufflard to Julie Manet-Rouart, September 9, 1945, Arch. du Mesnil, inv. 2021.1.1410.
817. My thanks to M. Yves Rouart for this detail.
818. Rouart 1950; an English edition came out in 1986.
819. This was the historian Marie-Louise Bataille (1889–1966), who happened to be the namesake of one of Morisot's models, seen for example in *On the Chaise Longue* (p. 161, CMR 344).
820. Bataille and Wildenstein 1961.
821. Manet 1979, p. 66.

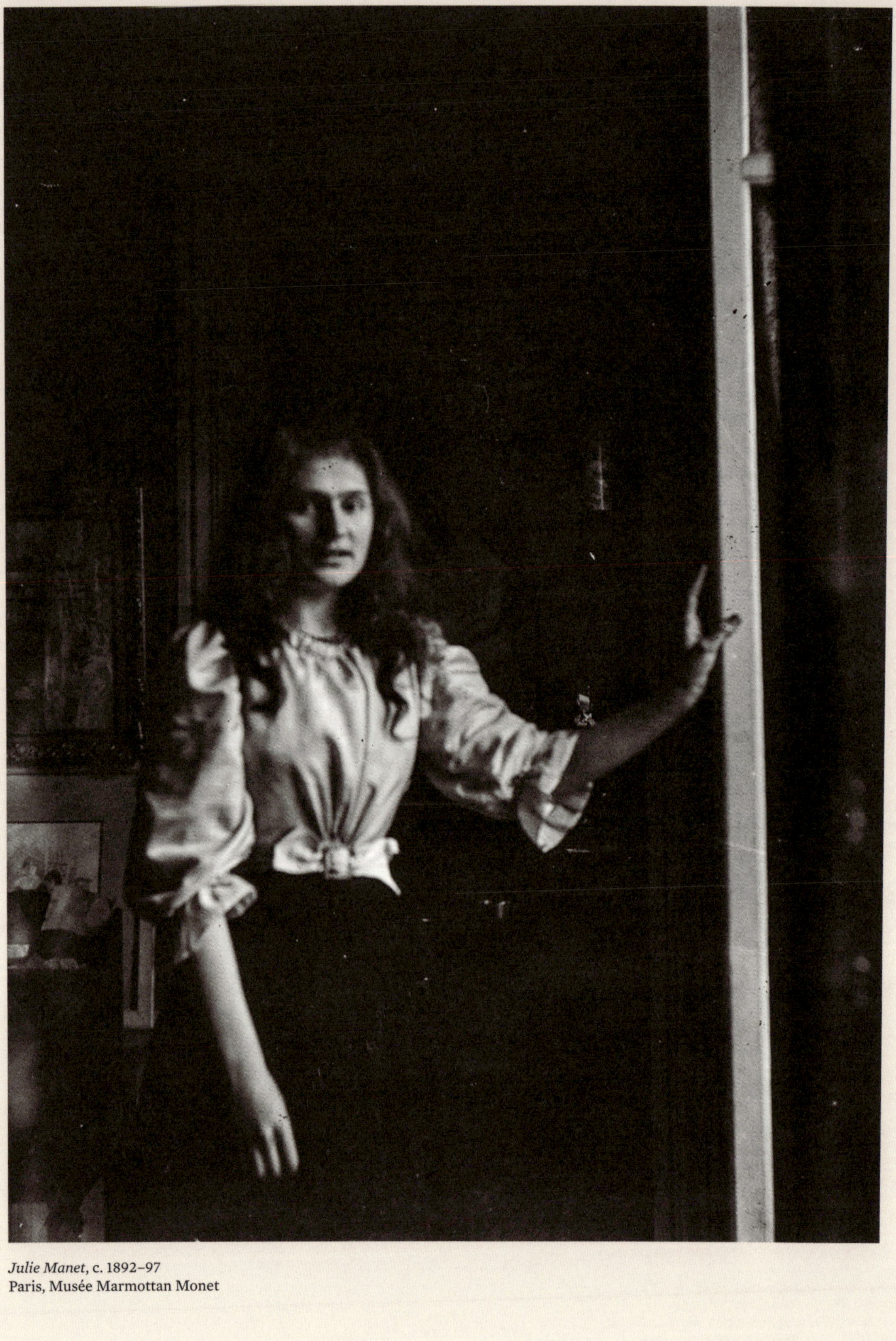

Julie Manet, c. 1892–97
Paris, Musée Marmottan Monet

THE DIARY OF JULIE MANET

FROM EDUCATIVE PRINCIPLE TO SELF-ASSERTION

CLAIRE GOODEN

AN EDUCATIONAL PRACTICE

> Study your character as you examine your conscience in order to present yourself at the tribunal of penance; examine your inclinations, your tastes, and your thoughts when you present yourself to your judgment and your mind. If you want to get to know others well, you must begin to know yourself well! To do this easily, there is a very good habit to acquire: it is to write down every night before going to bed, a diary of your thoughts and actions during the day that has just passed.[1]

Thus the Comtesse de Bassanville, author in the second half of the nineteenth century of numerous works on good manners and etiquette for young women, encouraged the latter to keep a diary to improve their morality and style. According to Philippe Lejeune, a specialist in the field,[2] the practice seems to have been established at the beginning of the July Monarchy to then spread gradually throughout the nineteenth century, up until today when it is not uncommon for pre-adolescent girls to be offered small notebooks with locks.

The education of girls based on the transmission of family morality developed during the Second Empire, a period of new and lasting stability for the bourgeoisie, then recovering from the fears caused by the revolutionary days of 1848. The new regime also enabled the clergy to considerably strengthen its influence, especially in the field of education. This education, which was given to children at a young age in the home, was taught by the mother, sometimes assisted or replaced by a teacher or a tutor. Many educational books and volumes of religious writings aimed specifically at girls and young women[3] appeared, setting out the attitude and duties of the Christian woman. Because it developed character and heart, and favored the examination of conscience at the same time as it was a good exercise in writing, the model of the diary was thus proposed from the time of the first communion, around the age of ten or eleven.[4] Once they had completed their education, adolescents continued this training alone when, at the age of fourteen or fifteen, they entered the pre-marital period, to finally abandon it definitively, the majority of them at least, on the eve of their marriage.[5] Although they were not strictly speaking "intimate" because generally written "to order," encouraged by the family institution and thus intended, if not to be censured, at least to be reread, the diaries which have come down to us are nevertheless a precious contribution in that they reveal, in addition to the way of life of a particular social class, the effects of an inculcated model.

As a result of rigorous research into previously published diaries, in the Bibliothèque Nationale's[6] file of individual biographies, and thanks to unpublished manuscripts sent to him by private individuals, Philippe Lejeune compiled a non-exhaustive chronological list of some one hundred diaries kept by girls born between 1820 and 1889.[7] Julie Manet's diary was included in this inventory. Written between 1893 and 1899, known since 1979—the date of their first publication—the pages composed by Berthe Morisot's daughter are today considered a work in their own right, a precious evocation of the time of Impressionism. They can also be read for what they are: one of the most enlightening accounts of an educational practice with literary overtones for young girls from good families. Writing so as to learn to know oneself.

FIRST ENCOURAGEMENTS

In accordance with the practices and customs of her milieu and time, the education received by Julie Manet was mainly carried out at home with tutors.[8] When she was ten years old, one of her teachers, writing to her father Eugène Manet, outlined his program and encouraged her to take up the pen:

> Take as the basis of the lessons what the pupil has [around her]; that is to say, she should send me an account of what she observes; I shall send it back as we go along with corrections and annotations. These essays can be about her reading or her excursions, or descriptions of the house, the garden, an enumeration of its flowers, about which I shall give her botanical explanations, etc.[9]

In fact, we know from a letter from Berthe Morisot to Stéphane Mallarmé that "Julie [was] writing her memoirs and learning to play the mandolin" as early as November 1888.[10] Was it in reference to this exercise that one of Morisot's friends wrote to her in September 1890 that she was "happy . . . to know that Bibi is satisfied with her diary"?[11] In the absence of further information, it is difficult to say. However, Morisot must have encouraged this practice, which she saw as an exercise in style rather than a moral apprenticeship, one that would build character. Indeed, in the summer of 1884, she wrote to her sister Edma, who had given her the diary kept by her eldest daughter, Jeanne Pontillon:

> You are very kind to have sent me Jeannot's style which I find very pleasant and which touches me greatly. . . . She is a lovely girl, and what an excellent idea she had to record her thoughts every day; nothing forms one's style more effectively. And by this I mean not the habit of turning out fine phrases but of putting one's thoughts into words. It even seems to me that we ought to be very lenient, to condone lack of correctness, provided that the feeling is real and that the ideas are personal. Correctness should come naturally from exercise and constant effort, especially when one begins this study at an early age. . . . Lastly, let Jeannot develop at her ease.

To which she added:

> Paule [Gobillard] also seems to possess a certain facility of style that I urge her mother to cultivate.[12]

Berthe Morisot also devoted herself punctually, in small notebooks, to this exercise about which she declared:

> I would like to relive my life and write it down. . . . What I would like is to find the moments when I have [illegible word] and to free up a course of action, a rule, a faith. But this is beyond my powers, so why doodle? Because a whole life that is coming to an end must try to summarize itself and writing forces one to find phrasing eluded by daydreaming.[13]

Julie's diary

Like most women of the period, Julie Manet's mother, as well as her cousins[14] (and no doubt her female friends), kept a diary. The activity was encouraged, passed on as an inheritance and practiced from mother to daughter. Under the impetus of her entourage, Julie followed the custom. Nothing remains of her first memoirs mentioned by Berthe Morisot. This may be because the conventional exercise of learning to write was a normal part of a pedagogical project and as such no trace of it was kept either in Julie's or the family's archives. At any rate, it was much later, on Thursday, August 24, 1893, on the eve of her fourteenth birthday, that Julie began a diary, "her diary," which she kept seriously and regularly—at least during the final two years—until December 1899, two weeks before her engagement. From being a little girl, she became a young girl and started writing with complete autonomy:

> I have often wanted to keep a diary, so I think I'll start one now. I suppose I might have left it rather late, but the longer I wait the later it will be—and, after all, I'm still only 14.[15]

She had no shortage of role models. Coinciding with the development of the practice and the first publications in this genre, Julie could count on some remarkable journals.

Initially published posthumously in the spring of 1893,[16] *The Journal of Eugène Delacroix* is one of the most important texts in art history. In this fascinating commentary on nineteenth-century French society, the artist expounded his ideas—on the arts, his work, individuals, but also on the philosophical questions of life—with great freedom. As early as July, Julie admitted:

> Delacroix's journal looks very interesting, I intend to read it.[17]

Initiated into art by her milieu, the young girl was receptive to good painting and admired Delacroix, whom she often quoted in her diary. His role was all the more important as it seems that the artist was the source of her desire to partake of this exercise:

> It seems to me that he is right to think it good to write a diary. I remember Maman reading me passages of this journal and it was what started me off scribbling these pages, pointlessly as it turns out. After all I don't see much benefit from it. Although now perhaps I would still be a little more stupid if I didn't write. I often suffer from not being more intelligent.[18]

Sought after for what they conveyed of attitudes and moral values, reading and writing thus contributed to Julie's education. However, her literary background was not intended to prepare her for an exam, but rather to open her eyes to what a girl of her background should know. Like her mother before her and many of her contemporaries, she made, for example, Marie Bashkirtseff's diary,[19] published in 1887, one of her bedside books and the subject of reading reports:

> I read a few pages of Marie Bashkirtseff's diary this morning, as I didn't have time to finish it on the journey. It's really very interesting to read the diary of an intelligent young woman with an open mind; she is curious, not at all snooty as I had believed from what I had heard others say of her.[20]
>
> . . . I have just read a hilarious description of Carolus-Duran in Marie Bashkirtseff's memoirs; you can just visualize that show-off son of a wine merchant who became such a dauber.[21]

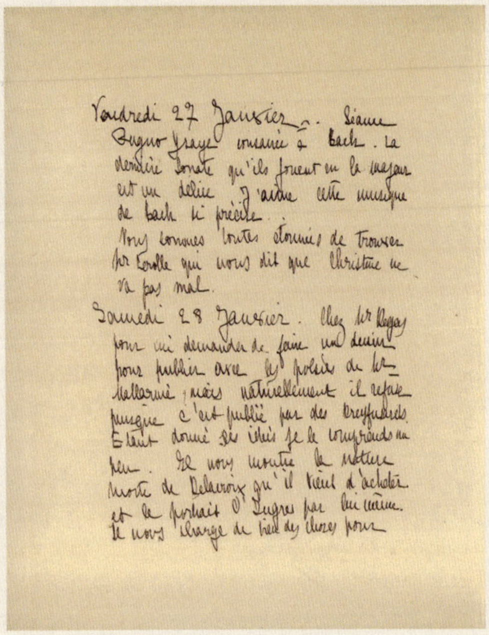

Vendredi 27 Janvier. Séance
Pugno-Ysaÿe consacrée à Bach. La
dernière sonate qu'ils jouent en la majeur
est un délice. J'adore cette musique
de Bach si précise.
Nous sommes toutes étonnées de trouver
Mr Corolle qui nous dit que Christine ne
va pas mal.
Samedi 28 Janvier. Chez Mr Degas
pour lui demander de faire un dessin
pour publier avec les poésies de Mr
Mallarmé, mais naturellement il refuse
puisque c'est publié par des dreyfusards.
Étant donné ses idées je le comprends un
peu. Il nous montre la nature
morte de Delacroix qu'il vient d'acheter
et le portrait d'Ingres par lui-même.
Il nous charge de bien des choses pour

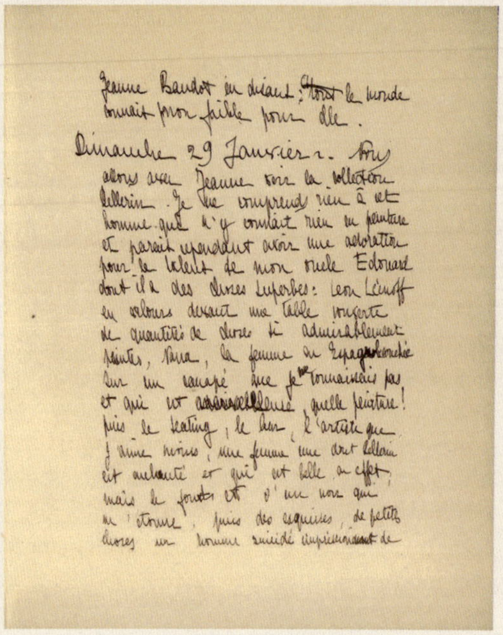

Jeanne Baudot en disant : tout le monde
connait mon faible pour elle.
Dimanche 29 Janvier. Nous
allons avec Jeanne voir la collection
Pellerin. Je ne comprends rien à cet
homme qui n'y connaît rien en peinture
et paraît cependant avoir une adoration
pour le talent de mon oncle Edouard
dont il a des choses superbes : Leon Leenhoff
en velours devant une table couverte
de quantités de choses si admirablement
peintes, Nana, la femme en Espagnole couchée
sur un canapé que je ne connaissais pas
et qui est [illegible], quelle peinture !
puis le Skating, le Bar, l'artiste que
j'aime moins, une femme dont Pellerin
est enchanté et qui est belle en effet,
mais le fond est d'un noir qui
m'étonne, puis des esquisses, de petites
choses, un homme suicidé [illegible] de

Pages from the original manuscipt of Julie Manet's diary, reproduced in the edition from 1987

Upon discovering her diary, many teenage girls turned Marie Bashkirtseff into a kind of "fin-de-siècle myth" and started writing their own. Like Julie, they all had to see in it what they were and what they did not always dare to admit to themselves:

> **Unlike most books (according to hearsay),[22] this one is best understood by a young girl who can enter the mind of the person telling you about her life and thoughts and who can even compare it with her own thoughts.[23]**

To spare Bashkirtseff's family, depicted with scant indulgence, and to erase the boldness in the account of her flirtations, two thirds of the first edition were however largely censored and truncated. Thus, although Julie was "infuriated" by the fact that "living at the time when Manet and all the Impressionists were painting, she never mentions them at all,"[24] it must be emphasized that Marie Bashkirtseff was indeed amazed by the art of Manet. Visiting his posthumous exhibition at the École Nationale des Beaux-Arts in 1884, Bashkirtseff alluded to *Olympia*, which, from being a "reclining woman" in her handwritten manuscript, became a "sketched woman" in the published version, thereby preserving decency, but making it difficult to identify the painting.[25] It is hence clear what other influence she may have had to endure.

THE REDISCOVERED TYPESCRIPT OR THE EDITION IN QUESTION

Just before being published, Julie's diary would also be copy-edited and amended. It was at the instigation of Julie's second son, Clément Rouart, that the diary was published for the first time in 1979, by Éditions Klincksieck. Since then, it has been published in four additional editions, the most recent of which,[26] in English, is the most extensively annotated by Jane Roberts. Since the original manuscript is now lost, it is difficult to say whether these works faithfully reflect the authentic one. The original is known only through the photographs of two sheets reproduced on the title page and in color in the 1987 edition, the only remnants of this document in which Julie's very round and perfectly decipherable handwriting is recognizable (above). Rosalind de Boland Roberts and Jane Roberts, in the introductory essay to

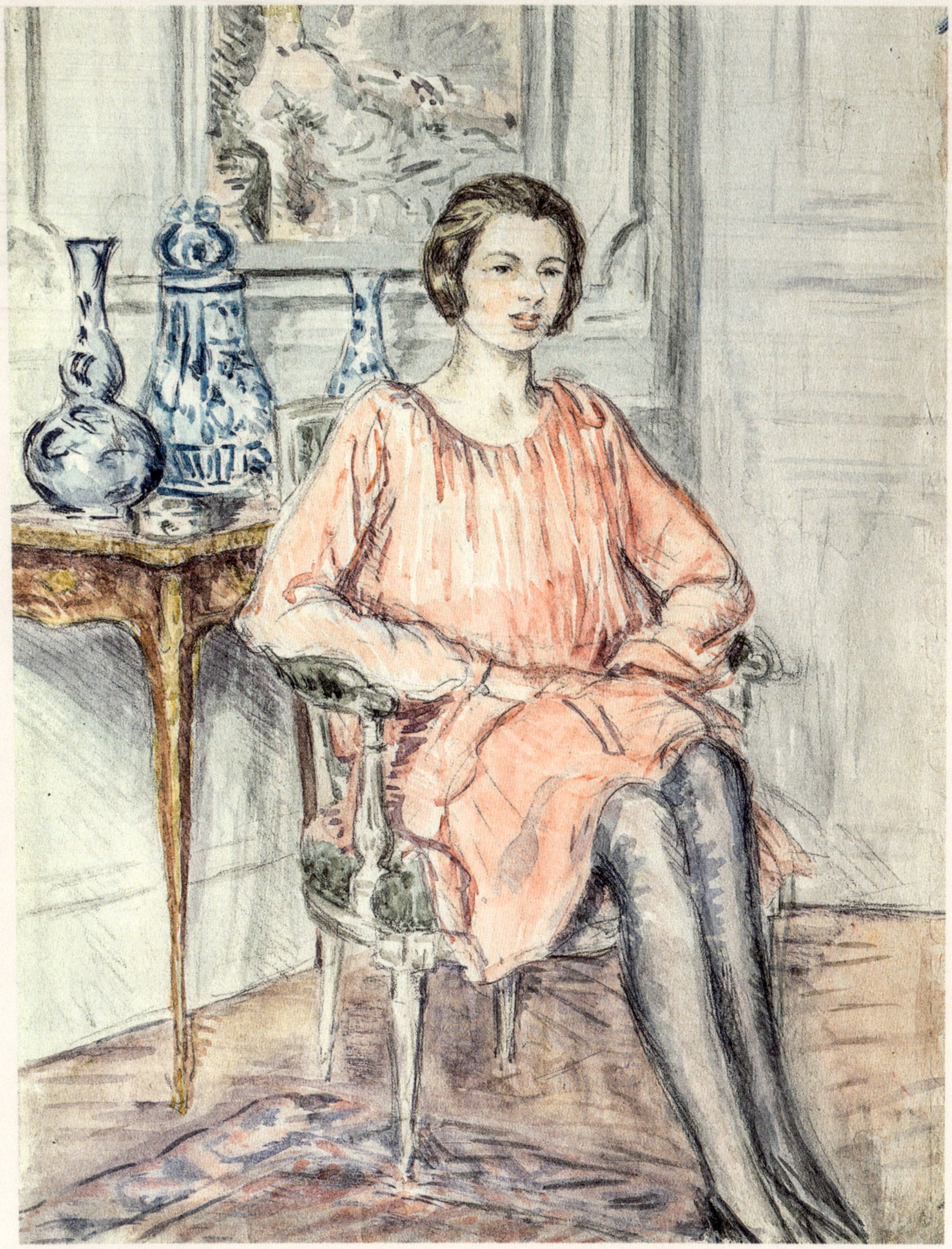

Julie Manet (1878–1966)
Portrait of Annie Conan, n.d.
Watercolor on paper, 31.5 × 24 cm
Paris, Musée Marmottan Monet

this same edition, give us a further clue as to the manuscript's appearance, "no neat leather-bound volume with lock and key; just untidy notes scribbled in old exercise books, often in pencil, the presentation as spontaneous as the contents."[27]

According to family memory, a typescript, taken from this diary, was given to Annie Conan, Clément Rouart's sister-in-law and the wife of Denis Rouart (above). Rediscovered during the preparation of this book, this document sheds new light on the genesis of the publication of the journal and on certain editorial choices.

The study of this "unpublished" source calls for some comments, first on its elaboration, then on its content. Its elaboration first. It seems that this typescript was realized in two stages. The first one, the most substantial, concerns the transcription from Julie's trip to Brittany in 1894 to the year 1899. This set consists of folios numbered from 1 to 256 and classified by year in six folders with fasteners. A second set, obviously dealt with later, transcribes the beginning of the diary. It concerns the period from Thursday, August 24, 1893 to Monday, March 19, 1894. Numbered by hand from 1 to 20, these loose sheets, probably initially kept in an envelope bearing the handwritten note "beginning of Julie's diary 1893–94," were later grouped together in a simple folder annotated "1893." Folios 18 to 20, corresponding to the year 1894, were pinned and placed in the folder for the year 1894. Thus, everything leads us to believe that the reconstitution of the diary was progressive, punctuated by discoveries, a hypothesis that is not incompatible with the description given by Jane Roberts.

Now for content and editorial choices. The typed text of the typescript is accompanied by numerous handwritten annotations, attributed to Annie Conan (p. 149). All these corrections, suggestions, and deletions confirm that this document was the object of editorial work in view of its first publication. What do they consist of? First, some of the anti-Semitic language, stemming from the Dreyfus Affair, has been removed or replaced[28] Secondly, some lines were censored to spare the sensitivities of Julie's entourage. The Angoulvent family, for example, of whom Monique,[29] a contemporary of Clément Rouart and a future reader of the diary, was the author of a monograph on Berthe Morisot. Thus, when Julie, carried away, wrote that they "know nothing . . . read nothing and blush when one speaks of birth" their name disappears, courteously replaced by an "X."[30] In the same way, the day of October 21, 1897 is reduced to the following lines:

> And it's sad and wrong to say, but I think we are equally bored by each other. Fernande and Gabrielle are always the same; people who change so little are so annoying. I'm really horrid not to enjoy my friends' company more, but I was expecting to do so, hence I'm disappointed.[31]

The Gobillard-Valéry cousins were also spared, by truncating the part of the typescript that is critical of Marcel:

> And that fool M. is always a new bore for her; I pity Paule and Jeannie for having a brother so little like them. I sometimes think that it is better that Tante Yves is no longer of this world, for what new sufferings she would have experienced dear poor Tante Yves![32]

Some lines were deleted as a way to silence family discord.[33]

Finally, while all the modifications previously mentioned are few, the most important part of the typescript that has been expunged related to Julie's religious practice and deep faith. It concerns several pages[34] recounting in great detail the course of her retreats, the transcription of sermons, and the teaching she tried to gain from them. We can suppose that the editor wanted to prioritize the descriptions of the period of Impressionism above any other consideration. As a result, the proposed simplifications place the edited version halfway between a girl's diary and a historical account, at the expense of a faithful and complete portrait of its author. It does not allow us to take the full measure of Julie's powerful and precocious faith,[35] a point that deeply distinguished her from her mother.

A comparative survey carried out between the typescript and the first edition of the journal quickly showed that the modifications suggested in the margin were, for the most part, incorporated. The typescript was thus the source for the Klincksieck edition, a work which would become the exclusive basis of the later editions.

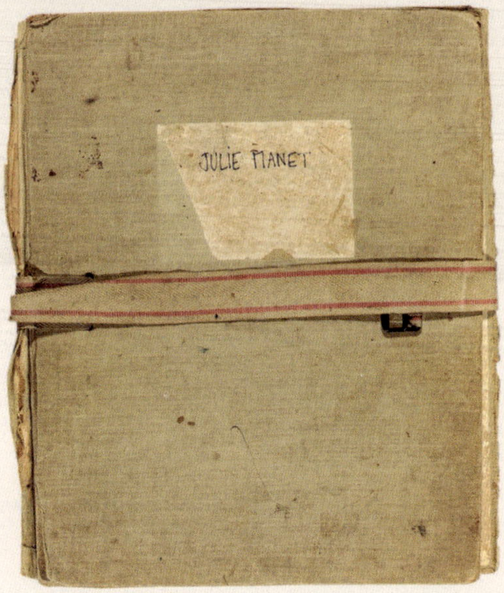

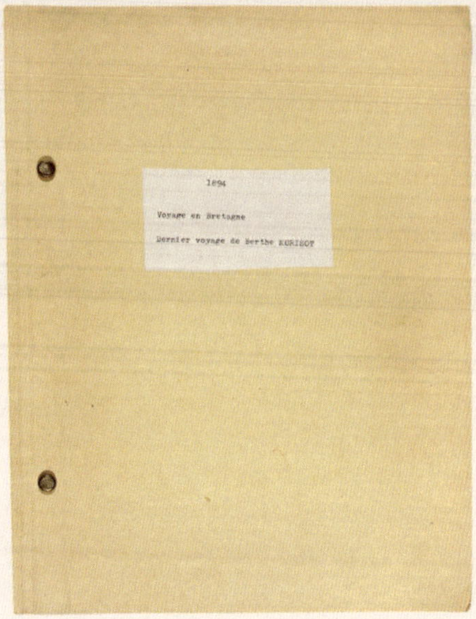

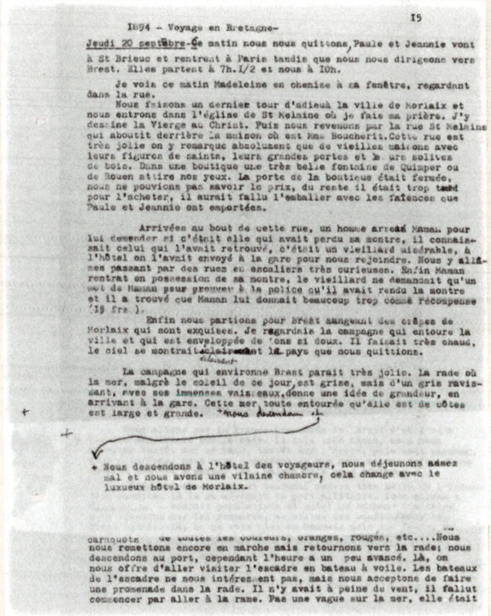

15

1894 – Voyage en Bretagne–

Jeudi 20 septembre–Ce matin nous nous quittons, Paule et Jeannie vont à St Brieuc et rentrent à Paris tandis que nous nous dirigeons vers Brest. Elles partent à 7h.1/2 et nous à 10h.

Je vois ce matin Madeleine en chemise à sa fenêtre, regardant dans la rue.

Nous faisons un dernier tour d'adieu à la ville de Morlaix et nous entrons dans l'église de St Melaine où je fais ma prière. J'y dessine la Vierge au Christ. Puis nous revenons par la rue St Melaine qui aboutit derrière la maison où est Mme Boucherit. Cette rue est très jolie on y remarque absolument que de vieilles maisons avec leurs figures de saints, leurs grandes portes et leurs solives de bois. Dans une boutique une très belle fontaine de Quimper ou de Rouen attire nos yeux. La porte de la boutique était fermée, nous ne pouvions pas savoir le prix, du reste il était trop tard pour l'acheter, il aurait fallu l'emballer avec les faïences que Paule et Jeannie ont emportées.

Arrivées au bout de cette rue, un homme arrête Maman pour lui demander si c'était elle qui avait perdu sa montre, il connaissait celui qui l'avait retrouvé, c'était un vieillard misérable, à l'hôtel on l'avait envoyé à la gare pour nous rejoindre. Nous y allâmes passant par des rues en escaliers très curieuses. Enfin Maman rentrat en possession de sa montre, le vieillard ne demandait qu'un mot de Maman pour prouver à la police qu'il avait rendu la montre et il a trouvé que Maman lui donnait beaucoup trop comme récompense (15 frs).

Enfin nous partions pour Brest mangeant des crêpes de Morlaix qui sont exquises. Je regardais la campagne qui entoure la ville et qui est enveloppée de tons si doux. Il faisait très chaud, le ciel se montrait éclairant le pays que nous quittions.

La campagne qui environne Brest parait très jolie. La rade où la mer, malgré le soleil de ce jour, est grise, mais d'un gris ravissant, avec ses immenses vaisseaux, donne une idée de grandeur, en arrivant à la gare. Cette mer toute entourée qu'elle est de côtes est large et grande. + nous descendons à

+ Nous descendons à l'hôtel des voyageurs, nous déjeunons assez mal et nous avons une vilaine chambre, cela change avec le luxueux hôtel de Morlaix.

carnquots de toutes les couleurs, oranges, rouges, etc....Nous nous remettons encore en marche mais retournons vers la rade; nous descendons au port, cependant l'heure a un peu avancé. Là, on nous offre d'aller visiter l'escadre en bateau à voile. Les bateaux de l'escadre ne nous intéressent pas, mais nous acceptons de faire une promenade dans la rade. Il n'y avait à peine de vent, il fallut commencer par aller à la rame. Pas une vague sur la mer, elle était

Typescript of Julie Manet's diary, typed and annoted by Annie Conan-Rouart
Archives BS, Paris, musée Marmottan Monet

JULIE BY HERSELF

All these editions offer a unique testimony of Julie Manet's daily life. If readers wish to follow Julie Manet's itinerary in detail for the period in question (1893 to 1899), they may refer to one of the five editions mentioned above and supplement their reading with the biographical essay that Marianne Mathieu devotes to the young woman in the present catalog. It is especially interesting for our study to examine the diary's rhythm and to identify certain passages which, from starting out as a family or social chronicle, gradually give way to the author's ideas, drifting toward a diary of moral and intellectual life as much as toward self-discovery. To do this, we must rely on the 1979 edition, the most complete to date, as the later transcriptions have in fact been, to varying degrees, expunged of certain days, either because they were considered unworthy of interest, or because the subject evoked may have been perceived as sensitive.

First of all, the rhythm. After having carried out a quantified comparison, period by period, of the typescript and different published versions, it appears that Julie kept her diary according to a specific and relatively homogeneous rhythm until the end of 1897. Indeed, with a few exceptions,[36] the young diarist initially wrote regularly and for the most part during the months of July, August, September, and October. What happened during the months when her writing stopped? We would be tempted to tackle the question in reverse and to consider that, initially, for Julie the exercise was similar to a travel journal. Away from Parisian life and her social and family obligations, she wrote during the summer, when her classes were interrupted, first at the Mallarmés' home in Valvins, then in Brittany and when she visited Touraine and its châteaux, sojourned in the Sarthe, or in the countryside at Essoyes with Renoir. As she meticulously reported on daily events through the narrative of her walks and visits, she was given the opportunity to continue working on her spelling and style. As a travel companion, her pen was trained and practiced, seeking the most appropriate expression. This is illustrated by certain anecdotes, told with slight variations both in her diary and in her correspondence, such as the episode of the theft of which she and her mother were victims in the Bois de Boulogne.[37]

A complementary practice to photography, to which Julie dedicated herself as an enlightened amateur,[38] the writing to which she devoted herself during her various sojourns could also be considered a means of remembering. It was a memory noted from day to day, a recording of data, an archive of her trips.

After her first meeting with her future husband Ernest Rouart on Wednesday, December 8, 1897—which was also recounted by her relatives[39]—Julie said nothing about her impressions. Was it due to modesty? It must be noted that from then on, and until the last day, her entries became more regular, almost daily. Not one month of the year was omitted, a precious chronicle of what her life was like during the two years preceding her marriage. In her diary, which is yet to be published, her cousin Jeannie Gobillard easily evoked this "moment of life . . . transitory and important, where God must find his place."[40] In fact, Julie then entered a moment of waiting, the pre-marital period. Ernest's name appeared for the first time on November 3, 1898; he would be mentioned about fifty times during the final year, becoming one of the main characters of Julie's personal narrative. As she shared her thoughts on marriage,[41] she also gradually got to know her suitor and confided in him, with all the restraint expected of young women of her rank:

> I really liked Ernest[42]
>
> . . . Ernest is a very good fellow[43]
>
> . . . Ernest . . . is so polite and thoughtful . . . constantly trying to help others . . . He is totally wonderful, just perfect. . . . I thought about it all and told myself that Ernest is the one for me.[44]
>
> . . . I thank God for having allowed me to have these days in Autun, meeting Ernest as I never dared to dream[45]
>
> . . . handsome young man. I no longer have the slightest hesitation in saying that he is definitely the one I would like to marry.[46]

In the final two years, her diary also increasingly became a "chronicle" of Julie's social and worldly life, as she intensified her social engagements, lunches, dinners, concerts, and exhibition visits. Mixing with good society, she conformed to its customs:

> Tonight we have our first dance class since it seems that you have to know how to dance.[47]

Learning how to behave in her environment, she was also preparing herself, probably unconsciously, to become a good wife:

> I don't know how to cook at all, and I find that lacking in a woman.[48]

While asserting her personality, which led her to develop her ideas and her critical faculties and to share her aesthetic or political opinions, she extended her examination of conscience and tried to improve virtuous aspects. There were many moments of introspection strongly linked to religion, when Julie emphasized her desire to improve herself:

> Right now I feel very disheartened, I have no love for life and at the same time I would be very unhappy to leave it not having done my duty yet . . . will I ever do it? I would like to, and I hope so, God help me. I should only think of this.[49]
>
> . . . I don't do my duty, I don't devote myself to anyone, I don't care enough for the poor. I want to change. I resolve to do so.[50]
>
> . . . Now I have lived more, I have sinned more, I have more faults for which I must make amends, I have no parents to guide me, I must guide myself, I must do my duty[51]
>
> . . . I am sad and discouraged, I have had enough of everything. It's awful to be like this, it proves that I lack courage, patience . . . Ah, it's horrible to be like this, Holy Mary give me strength.[52]

The important role that religion played in her life is also revealing about an era that saw the emergence of numerous female religious congregations and testifies to the control of the clergy over women's education. Marie-Françoise Lévy[53] also indicates that it was in the nineteenth century that a new devotion appeared, the Marian movement, which was accompanied by prayer recommendations for young girls. Pursuing the idea of improving virtue, Julie was no exception:

> Sunday, June 5 [1898]: I went to Madame Quesnoy's then on to a meeting of the Enfants de Marie to which, as from today, Jeannie and I belong as novices. The reception ceremony was inspiring: calm and very religious. I put myself under the protection of the Holy Virgin, asking her to look after me; and made the resolution, as a Child of Mary, to be a better Christian and to help others more. It's about time I began helping the poor and serving other people. I shall be 20 soon, so I ought to start.[54]

Progress in style, perfection in self-discovery, and moral guidance—we see how the model that had been instilled in her was working. A relentless witness to her relapses and aberrations, Julie Manet's diary became the discreet repository of her efforts leading toward perfection. It also testified to her character, one of modesty, propriety, and discretion. She barely dared admit that she felt like "[having] fun this coming year . . . to take pleasure."[55] In this context, intimacy had no place and the relationship with the body was taboo. In an interview recorded and discovered during the preparation of this exhibition, Julien Rouart confided that his mother "used some sort of oratorical precautions, strange euphemisms, distant metaphors to designate everything relating to the body." This is verified in her diary. When nudes and bodies are described, they are those of painting; and when Julie evoked her own body, it was to denigrate it:

> It's the first time I put on a low-cut dress, it intimidates me and I feel very ugly.[56]

Chastity also in the way she appeared in the world, when she sketched a self-portrait of her temperament:

> It has been said while doing my graphology that I had contained passion, and I can judge the accuracy of this remark. It is even the excess of this contained passion that generates coldness in me. I prefer to show myself as ice than to make people suspect that I harbor sentimentality, and to hide it I am forced to resort to a complete disguise. This game which, to my nature, seems like simple modesty sometimes gets on my nerves and I would like to relieve myself of it, but despite my determination, I remain the same and acquire no exuberance.[57]

However, the positive and structuring aspect of this type of education must be emphasized. Admittedly resigned to her social role, Julie also found in writing a means of support to cope with suffering and death. Thus, on April 17, 1895, she reflected on the death of her mother, which had occurred a few weeks earlier:

> Oh, what sorrow! Since I last wrote in my diary, I lost Maman. She died at half past ten on Saturday, March 2. . . . Oh God! Help me to bear this loss, sustain me . . . Yes, dear God, you are infinitely good; make sure Maman is happy at your side.[58]

This is the only passage in which the young girl, now an orphan, transcribed an event not on the day it happened, but in retrospect. After the few weeks of immense shock and sadness that followed her mother's death, the fact of writing down her sorrow went beyond a natural gesture, it was a need, perhaps a vital one. The diary did not stop, it continued and was kept up until the end, through this or that anecdote, this or that visit, the memory of her mother. It thus also became a remedy for solitude, a memory tool.

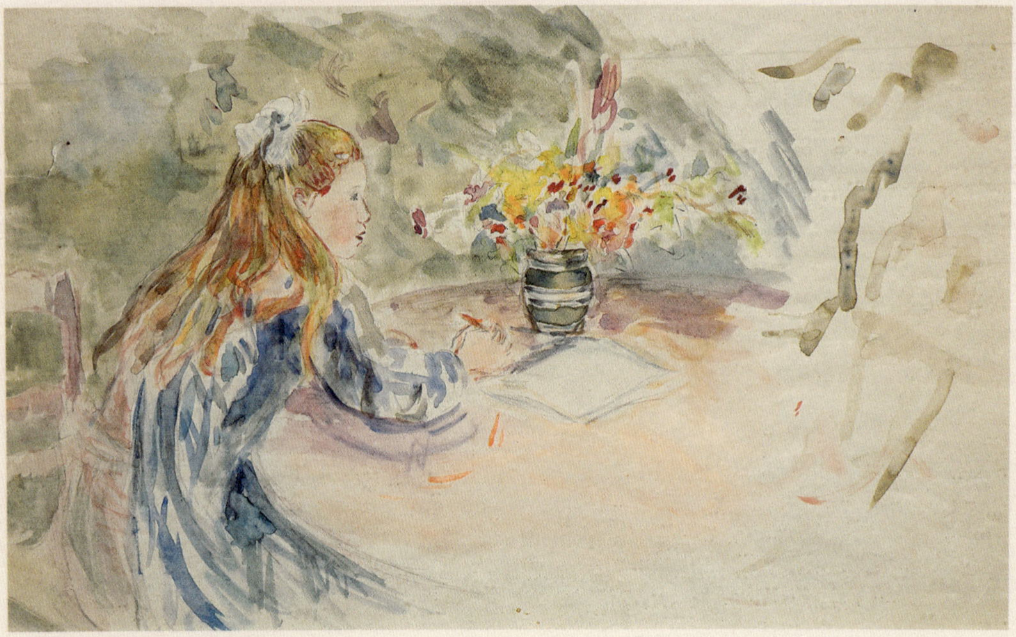

Julie Manet (1878–1966)
Young Girl Writing, n.d.
Watercolor on paper, 18 × 30 cm
Paris, Musée Marmottan Monet

The last words of Julie's diary were addressed to Rose Caron, an opera soprano who played the role of Leonore in Beethoven's opera *Fidelio*, which Julie had just attended. "She is infinitely a woman,"[59] she concluded, as if to turn the page of her life as a young girl, foreshadowing the wife she would become a few months later.

What became of her writing? Did it continue as a family and social chronicle or did it end? Jane Roberts tells us in the 1987 edition that "[Julie] had resumed her diary shortly after her marriage, but it was no longer the day-to-day journal of a young Parisian girl in the 1890s, and more an introspective reflection on life as she became an increasingly devout and fervent Catholic."[60] No trace exists of the rest of the diary mentioned. But it is a fact that writing was part of Julie's life, as testified by the abundant correspondence that has come down to us and the portraits that Ernest did of her with pen in hand (p. 155 and 199). As was the custom at the time, the exercise had its place in the schedule of the young housewife, to whom it offered the opportunity to cultivate the virtues of humility and self-effacement. Daily events were no longer meticulously recorded in notebooks, but gave way for the young woman's meditations, reflections, and thoughts jotted down on loose sheets of paper:

> Wednesday morning: the need to for us to experience a deep inner peace . . . as many occupations at home as outside from which inner agitation arises . . . Useless agitation . . . To put ourselves in communion with God for the day. Resolution to do meditation or to do it better (p. 153).[61]

In search of a course of action and code dictated by her faith and by strict morals, Julie would try all her life to perfect herself:

> Prayer: lack of attention, forgetting to put myself in the presence of God . . . Charity: love not joyful enough, lack of gratitude . . . How can I have peace if I am worried about my children? . . . Resolutions: make a fervent act of faith every morning that continues at Mass and throughout the day.[62]

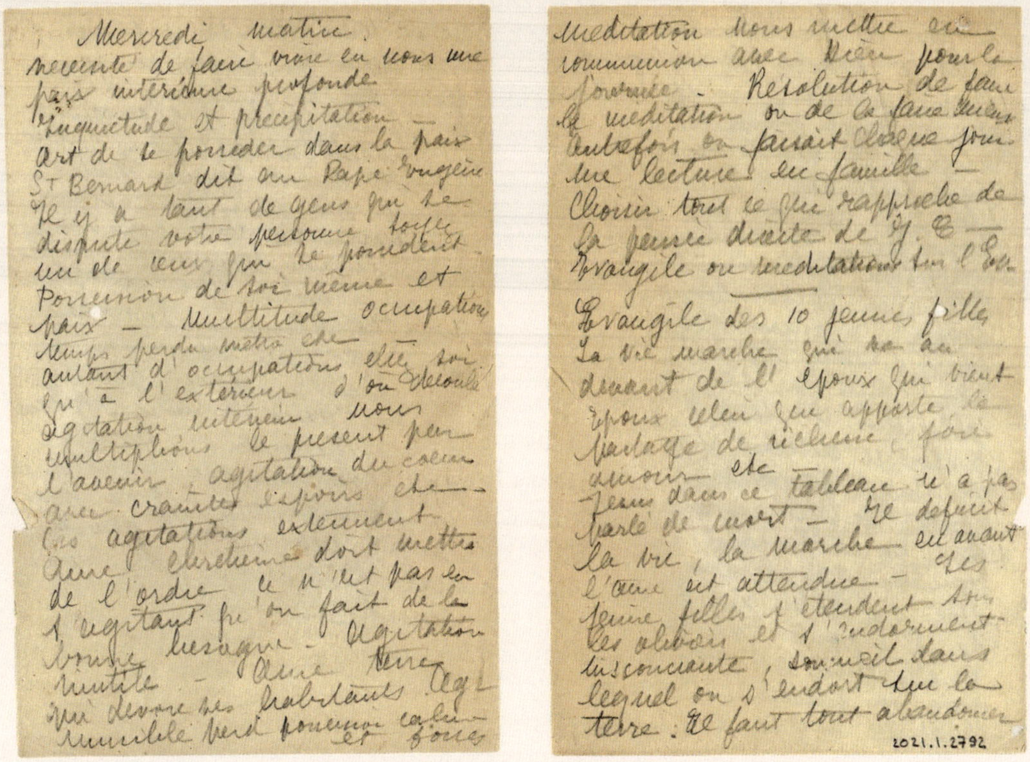
Mercredi matin
nécessité de faire vivre en nous une
paix intérieure profonde
inquiétude et précipitation —
art de se posséder dans la paix
St Bernard dit au Pape Eugène
Il y a tant de gens qui se
disputent votre personne soyez
un de ceux qui se possèdent
Possession de soi même et
paix — multitude occupation
temps perdu mettre etc
autant d'occupations elles soi
qu'à l'extérieur d'où découle
agitation intérieure nous
multiplions le présent par
l'avenir agitation du cœur
avec craintes espoirs etc —
les agitations extérieures
âme chrétienne doit mettre
de l'ordre ce n'est pas en
s'agitant qu'on fait de la
bonne besogne — Agitation
inutile — Âme terre
qui dévore ses habitants
paix possession calme et force

méditation nous mettre en
communion avec Dieu pour la
journée. Résolution de faire
la méditation ou de la faire mieux
autrefois on faisait chaque jour
une lecture en famille —
Choisir tout ce qui rapproche de
la pensée directe de J. C. —
Évangile ou méditations sur l'Év.
Évangile des 10 jeunes filles
La vie marche qui va au
devant de l'Époux qui vient
Époux celui qui apporte le
partage de richesse, force
amour etc
Jésus dans ce tableau n'a pas
parlé de mort — Il définit
la vie, la marche en avant
l'âme est attendue — Les
jeunes filles s'étendent sur
les oliviers et s'endorment
insouciante, sommeil dans
lequel on s'endort sur la
terre : Il faut tout abandonner
2021.1.2792

Julie Manet (1878–1966)
Notes on loose paper, line of conduct and resolutions, n.d.
Archives du Mesnil, on permanent loan at the Musée Marmottan Monet

JULIE VERSUS JEANNIE: FRAGMENTS AND DIVERSITY OF APPROACHES

As we have said, although Julie Manet complied rigorously with the exercise of keeping a diary, a companion of her education, she was not an isolated case in the nineteenth century. As the sheet of paper dated April 2, 1893 and attributed to Jeannie Gobillard reveals,[63] her cousin also devoted herself to this apprenticeship.

In parallel with this exhibition, the Musée Marmottan Monet is publishing another section of this diary, which has remained unpublished until now.[64] In this one, some sheets dated 1894–95 show her way of approaching it. Less seriously than Julie, Jeannie first recorded her occupations, meetings, and travels in a very factual and messy way, like note-taking:

> **June: Julie and Tante Berthe on their balcony . . . / The Pontillons in Maurecourt / A painting I did on a hot day . . . July: The evenings after dinner J. in a white dress . . . Amsterdam street, mosquitoes, the piano.[65]**

Even significant events, such as the account of her aunt's last days, were depicted in a laconic manner:

> **8 J.[anuary]: Julie sick . . . February: Julie still sick / Tante B. and Julie sick . . . 5 March: Tante B's friends who come . . . Julie in a black dress . . . my sorrow.[66]**

Perhaps these pages were a simple memento intended to serve as a basis for later more advanced and more literary writing, because, it must be said, Jeannie excelled in this field, to the point that she surpassed her cousin. The continuation of her diary especially allows us to evaluate her narrative talent.

Unlike Julie, who participated in the exercise day after day, Jeannie took up her notebook again at the beginning of 1900 to reflect retrospectively upon the year gone by and certain past events in a hundred pages or so. We quickly understand the reason for this:

> Tonight I am alone; and I want to tell this paper, habitual prattler of useless phrases, the reason for my awakening to everything.[67]

Paul Valéry, her future husband, had just declared himself. Jeannie took up her pen to describe, as well as the last moments of her life as a young girl, the meeting, the waiting, the doubt, and all the moments shared with her loved ones and especially with the one she called her "tyrant." Her diary became the confidant that she would be able to call upon when she wanted to remember events or thoughts, the receptacle of memories intended for her "selves" who would read this:[68]

> And now, I think I am obliged to write down as badly as possible, by the way, a time that will escape me like the others, even if it means being able to recapture something here by the sheer physical force of the moment when I will have written because . . . I have the ridiculous habit of remembering and of wanting to measure things that cannot be measured. And then the anguish of the future.[69]

It is interesting to note that certain dates are found in the diaries of both cousins. At a time when it was customary to circulate one's personal writings and to submit them to a rereading, it is not impossible that Jeannie may have relied on Julie's diary to go back over certain episodes, like July 14, 1899 in Valvins at the Mallarmés', recounted with very slight variations in each of their diaries. Julie recalled a dinner at Madame Mallarmé's where "we are extremely cheerful, we talk, we laugh, we smoke, Valéry having brought ladies' cigarettes, he now calls us, Jeannie and me, the caracos [*sic*] or the caraco [*sic*] tribe,"[70] while Jeannie recounted it as follows:

> Shall I speak here of that walk in the forest, of the episode that brought to light the name of the caracos and the tribe . . . ? No, only to say that beneath this forest I felt that his soul had taken root in mine . . . The dinner was cheerful: we drank, we smoked.[71]

Very quickly, however, we can distinguish the traits of their characters and their way of approaching the exercise: very factual and disciplined writing for one, a means of giving free rein to her thoughts and feelings for the other. Thus, on the subject of a portrait that Jeannie did of Paul Valéry in Valvins, Julie wrote: "Jeannie drew a picture of him that he took away with contentment,"[72] while Jeannie shared her doubts and disillusionment: "He took it with an air of indifference. He the barbarian: having drawn Paule and Julie without pretending to look at me."[73]

As a good student, full of piety, Julie saw fit to evoke her travel reading when, on September 4, 1899, she took the train with her cousin on her way back from Autun:

> On my way home, I read a book I started a long time ago on the authenticity of the Gospels and the life of Jesus Christ by Father Bougaud. It's very good. How moving this life of Jesus is, how sweet this Christ is![74]

For her part, Jeannie paid attention to the journey's little anecdotes and let herself be carried away by her reverie:

> So the three of us were very cheerful and we slept comfortably on the benches of the return train, very much watched over by a gentleman who looked at us through the corridor window, which made Julie and me, the most awake, laugh. And on the [bass] of the wheels' motion I sang again in my mind about the whole trip, and many other things, with the confidence of a child and also a great apprehension of the return, which was going to tarnish all this freshness regained.[75]

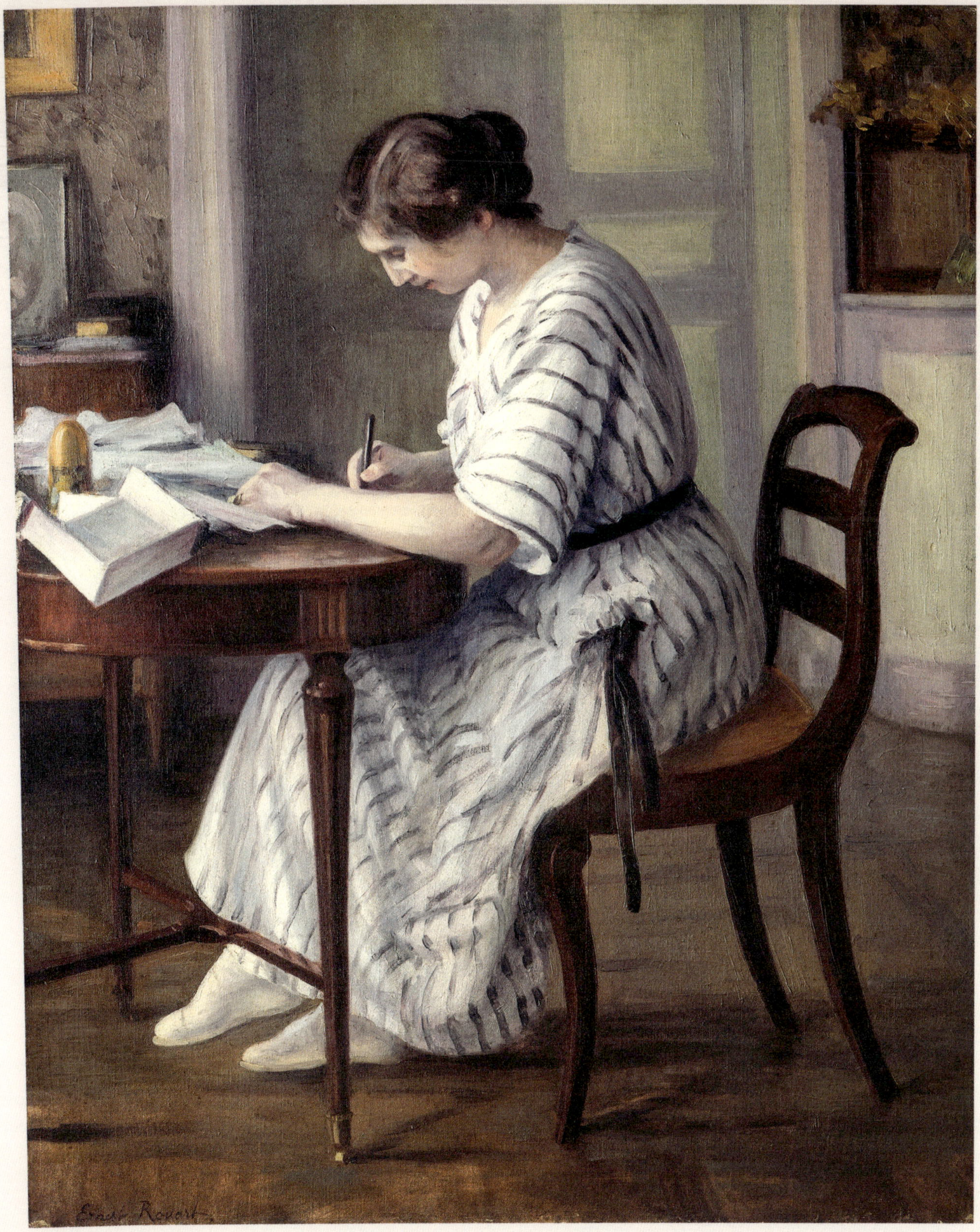

Ernest Rouart (1874–1942)
Julie Manet Writing, n.d.
Oil on canvas, 73 × 92 cm
Private collection

Jeannie's narrative touched on the intimate so frequently that the diary became what she pointedly called a "confidant." Turning away from the strict chronicle, going further than Julie ever dared to do, the young girl revealed her feelings, depicted her sensations:

> I took a bath, on this day, a vulgar characteristic that brings me alone to note my singular emotion, of a new physical order.[76]
>
> . . . While I was playing the moon, I missed that I was being listened to with love. . . . Finally, to feel it! Then there was Schumann and there, no longer only his profile, but his eyes, his eyes so beautiful and charming that fix on me. My playing is enlivened by him. It is a march of triumph and his gaze slides between my fingers, on the keys, and gives them fever and life.[77]
>
> . . . I venture, from the side, a glance. . . . And then, from the side, another glance. Is it mine reflected? No . . . his! This glance is enormous: it shines. I burn, it penetrates me.[78]

Or again:

> We were spiritual only after having felt the ardor of our flesh. I was in tune with him. . . . My emotion, my joy is such that I cannot swallow anything. I am only feathers, shivers, flashes, fluids.[79]

Sentences became heightened, the writing became lyrical, until evoking the carnal act:

> We are now touching on something that I know and don't know and that scares a part of me. I know it's inevitable. My thinking approaches it, guesses my feelings, and suddenly escapes. Yes, I want to flee, to flee in my virgin house and block my ears to my crazy ideas. . . . I will speak only to your soul, Paul, because it cannot be seen.[80]

Less modesty than in Julie's case, but sometimes just as much religiosity, especially when it came to making virtuous progress:

> A resolution to make room for God. Prayer and work. Prayer of meditation. Sacrifice for Jesus, the one who sacrificed himself, eternal gratitude to Paule. There are some good things in the retreat: to strive for perfection with a devotional, vocational aim, a little perfection that is very domestic and without pride. To seek Jesus and to seek him where he is found among the poor, among those who suffer . . . To set oneself apart from the profession of uselessness in which all women find themselves, not to be religious like everyone else.[81]

A sort of sequel to Julie's diary, Jeannie's one continued beyond December 26, 1899 to the day of her marriage to Paul Valéry on May 31, 1900. She took up the pen, drew a long portrait of her fiancé,[82] and recorded her memories, every detail, until the last moments:

> I am in [a shirt] with my hair down my back, my feet . . . in big black stockings and I am breathing in all the fragrance of our existence [as three]. And now I'm writing in the middle of the . . . preparations. . . . And I will stop to put on the ridiculous livery.[83]

After her marriage, and as was the custom, the diary continued but in another form, family tradition dictating that Jeannie pursue the exercise in simple account notebooks.

Although the two cousins' diaries conformed to a conventional practice, they were nonetheless a means of expression of the individual domain and of self-discovery; "and something occurs that is literature all the same. Absolutely literal, candor, fragmentation, repetition."[84]

NOTES

1. Bassanville 1847, p. 16–17.
2. See Lejeune 1993.
3. Marie-Françoise Lévy lists two hundred and fifty-six works of this type for the period (Lévy 1984, p. 12).
4. Lejeune 1993, p. 20.
5. Ibid., p. 11.
6. See on this subject Lejeune 1984.
7. With one exception: the diary of Lucile Duplessis, the oldest known diary dating from before 1789. Lucile Desmoulins (née Duplessis), a figure of the French Revolution alongside her husband Camille Desmoulins, was guillotined on April 13, 1794, one week after her husband. In the form of single sheets or small notebooks scattered in various collections, her diary, kept from 1788 to 1793, was published in 1995: Desmoulins 1995.
8. On the subject of Julie Manet's education, see the essay by Marianne Mathieu in this volume, "Julie in the Liberty Hat," p. 32–43.
9. Letter from Edgar Bèhne to Eugène Manet, May 7, 1889, Paris, Musée Marmottan Monet, inv. D.4-1986.2013.805.
10. Letter from Berthe Morisot to Stéphane Mallarmé, Thursday, November 8, 1888, Paris, Musée Marmottan Monet, inv. D.4-1986.2013.293.
11. Letter from W. Laptchinsky to Berthe Morisot, September 25, 1890, Paris, Musée Marmottan Monet, inv. D.4-1986.2013.720.
12. Letter from Berthe Morisot to her sister Edma, retranscribed in Rouart 1950, p. 122.
13. Berthe Morisot, Mézy notebook 1891, also known as the "black notebook," Paris, Musée Marmottan Monet, inv. D.5-1986.2014.4.
14. In addition to the diaries of Jeanne Pontillon and Paule Gobillard mentioned by Berthe Morisot in the letter to her sister Edma cited above, it is worth noting the single sheet of paper, dated April 1893 and attributed to Jeannie Gobillard, which we also mention at the end of this essay. Judging by the way it was written, it can be assumed that it belonged to a diary.
15. Manet 2017, p. 39.
16. Delacroix 1893–95.
17. Letter from Julie Manet to Jeannie Gobillard, Sunday, July 16 [1893], Arch. du Mesnil, inv. 2021.1.49.
18. Manet 1979, p. 190–191.
19. The daughter of a Ukrainian marshal of nobility, Marie Bashkirtseff (1858–1884) was a painter and sculptor, trained at the Académie Julian. She kept a personal diary from the age of fifteen until her premature death from tuberculosis at the age of twenty-five. Despite the recognition she enjoyed, and more than her pictorial oeuvre, it was this diary of a young girl, a masterpiece of its kind, that ensured her fame.
20. Manet 2017, p. 112.
21. Ibid., p. 117. For a discussion of this judgment, the reader may also refer to Mathieu 2019.
22. It is interesting to note the bracketing of "according to hearsay," as if Julie wanted to emphasize that the scope of her reading was limited.
23. Manet 1979, p. 138.
24. Ibid., p. 131.
25. Cosnier 2001, p. 117.
26. Manet 2017a. For the other editions, refer to the bibliography.
27. Manet 2017, p. 1.
28. Contemporaneous with the Dreyfus Affair, which deeply divided French society at the end of the nineteenth century, Julie Manet's diary bears witness in certain passages to the anti-Dreyfus political positions of her milieu. Some anti-Semitic remarks featuring in the typescript, reflecting widespread and accepted thinking at the time, were removed from the 1979 edition (with "Jews" becoming "those people"). Later editions sometimes made further cuts (mainly in the 1987 and the 2017 English edition); the remarks of a single day, September 20, 1899, when Julie indicated that she was sending "the modest sum of six francs to *La Libre Parole* for the workers of La Villette in the name of six young girls for the repatriation of Jews to Jerusalem," are not transcribed in the 2017 French edition.
29. Monique Angoulvent (1910–1996). See on this subject Marianne Mathieu's essays "The Flying Squadron," p. 44–57, and "Let Memory Come Alive," p. 104–123.
30. Manet 1979, p. 179.
31. Typescript of Julie Manet's diary, fol. 99.
32. Typescript of Julie Manet's diary, November 12, 1897, fol. 102.
33. Having deserted military service, Marcel cut the ties with his sisters and would no longer be part of everyday life in the rue de Villejust, as evidenced by the memories of Julien Rouart, Julie Manet's oldest son, who confided, in an interview with his cousin Jean-Marie Rouart: "It was through [Jeanne Pontillon] that we knew of family tales, which were something we never talked about: in particular the brother of Paule Gobillard and Jeannie Gobillard, who had been rejected by the family because he had deserted during his military service. He was struck with infamy. We did not talk about it, it was extraordinary. . . . I was more than 20 years old."
34. For the dates March 29, 1898, April 6–7, 1898, March 13, 14, and 15, 1899.
35. See the essay by Marianne Mathieu's in this volume, "The Remains of the Day," p. 76–91.
36. For the months of March 1894, 1895, and 1896, as well as some days from January to March 1897.
37. On September 7, 1893, Julie and Berthe were drawing near a lake in the Bois de Boulogne. They were robbed of their belongings by a thief who ran away. This "man in black with a horrible yellow face" as described in her diary becomes a "man . . . not badly dressed but with an ugly face" in the letter she sent the next day to her cousin. The story also became more precise, "Maman's bag" with "a purse with only 6 francs 50 in it" became a "black silk bag" in which there was "a purse with 4 frs 50c." (Manet 2017, p. 30), and letter from Julie Manet to Jeannie Gobillard, n.d. [September 8, 1893], Arch. du Mesnil, inv. 2021.1.43).
38. See the essays in this volume by Marianne Mathieu, "Julie in the Liberty Hat," p. 32–43, and Dominique d'Arnoult, "Julie the Painter, the Last of the Manets or the Interrupted Apprenticeship," p. 158–185.
39. This encounter, as well as the engagement and marriage, are recounted in the essay in this volume, "The Caraco Tribe," p. 58–75.
40. Gobillard 2021.
41. Manet 2017, p. 181.
42. Ibid., p. 157.
43. Ibid., p. 170.
44. Ibid., p. 174.
45. Manet 1979, p. 254.
46. Manet 2017, p. 187.
47. Manet 1979, p. 150.
48. Ibid., p. 139.
49. Ibid., p. 154.
50. Ibid., p. 159.
51. Ibid., p. 160.
52. Ibid., p. 156.
53. Lévy 1984.
54. Manet 2017, p.139.
55. Ibid., p.128.
56. Manet 1979, p. 148.
57. Ibid., p. 278.
58. Manet 2017, p. 55–56.
59. Ibid., p. 287.
60. Manet 1987, p. 190.
61. Note by Julie Manet, Arch. du Mesnil, inv. 2021.1.2792.
62. Note by Julie Manet, Arch. du Mesnil, inv. 2021.1.2794.
63. On this subject, see the essay in this volume by Marianne Mathieu, "Julie in the Liberty Hat," p. 32–43.
64. Gobillard 2021.
65. Ibid., p. 119.
66. Ibid., p. 140.
67. Ibid., p. 30.
68. Ibid., p. 74.
69. Ibid., p. 39.
70. Manet 1979, p. 241.
71. Gobillard 2021, p. 34–35.
72. Manet 1979, p. 241.
73. Gobillard 2021, p. 36.
74. Manet 1979, p. 254.
75. Gobillard 2021, p. 38.
76. Ibid., p. 60.
77. Ibid., p. 62.
78. Ibid., p. 65.
79. Ibid., p. 68.
80. Ibid., p. 80.
81. Ibid., p. 82.
82. Gobillard, 2021.
83. Ibid., p. 109.
84. See Lejeune 1993, p. 48.

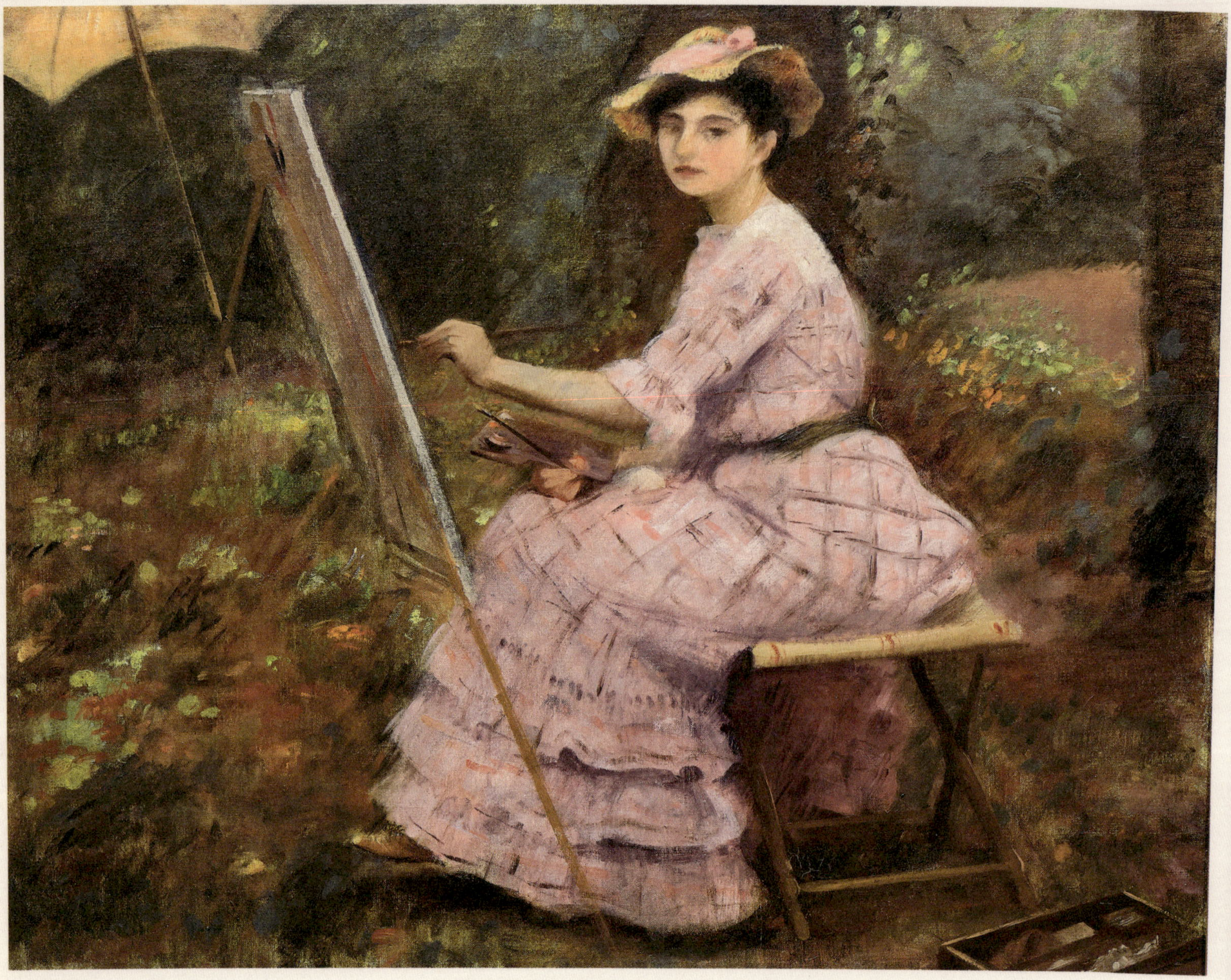

JULIE THE PAINTER

THE LAST OF THE MANETS OR THE INTERRUPTED APPRENTICESHIP

DOMINIQUE D'ARNOULT

The daughter of two artists, Berthe Morisot and Eugène Manet,[1] and niece of artist Édouard Manet, Julie Manet desired during her adolescence, marked by their bereavements,[2] to get closer to them through painting. "The thought that I could lose my parents seemed an awful thing to me," she wrote, "I lost my father at thirteen, my mother at sixteen. I often reproached myself for not showing them enough affection, especially to my father whom I loved very much but who intimidated me."[3] Her young life as a painter is revealed throughout her diary from the age of fourteen to twenty-one, albeit only partially due to lacunae. It is now enriched by a surplus of correspondence[4] and a large number of unpublished works by her.[5] It was a painter's diary, that of Delacroix, which prompted Julie Manet to start her own;[6] the private writings that she left behind are also a painter's diary. Moreover, her journey allows us to draw attention to the training of young artists in the wake of the Impressionist generation.

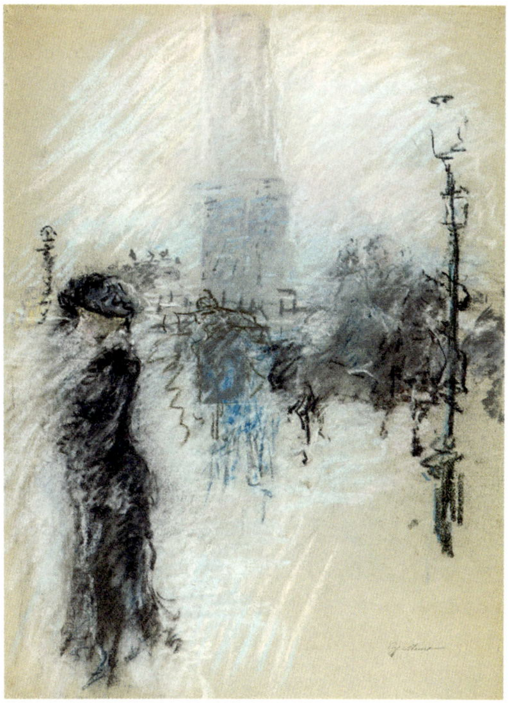

Eugène Manet (1833–1892)
Scene of Parisian Life, c. 1870
Pastel on paper, 60 × 45 cm
Private collection

"THE EDUCATION THAT I'VE RECEIVED"[7]

OBSERVING AND DESCRIBING

Her mother believed that literature was, as much as painting, the way for a woman to achieve fame. "Why shouldn't there be as much chance of success in a literary future as in an artistic one?" She exhorted the young girls of her family to read "good classic French as much as possible," in order to avoid any risk "of silliness, sentimentality, and affectation." She encouraged them to "express [their] thoughts" by writing a diary. She advised her sister Edma,

Facing page
Ernest Rouart (1874–1942)
Julie Manet Painting, 1905
Oil on canvas, 70 × 82.7 cm
Private collection

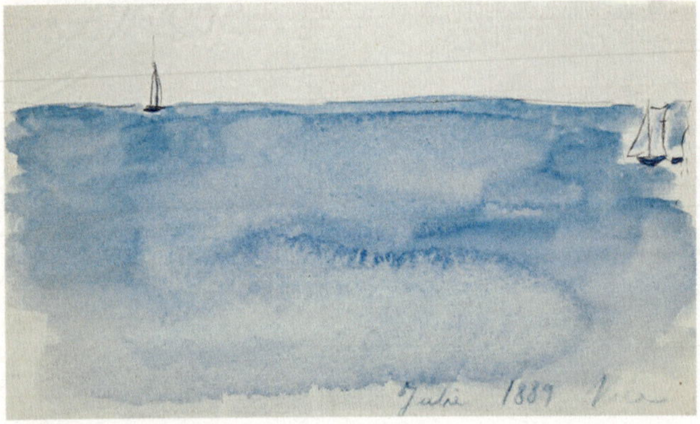

Julie Manet (1878–1966)
Nice, 1889
Watercolor on paper, 10.3 × 16.6 cm
Private collection

the mother of a fourteen-year-old girl, Jeanne, to "be very lenient," to "condone lack of correctness, provided that the feeling is real and the ideas are personal."[8]

The education of ten-year-old Julie followed this orientation and was based on the observation and literary description of her surroundings, as devised by Edgar Bèhne, one of her teachers during the family's sojourn in Nice in the winter of 1889–90, one of whose letters is enlightening.[9] "Julie is writing her memoirs,"[10] her mother wrote from Nice to Mallarmé. Bèhne provided Julie with knowledge relating to what she chose to describe around her—if it concerned flowers, details of botany. As for her artistic education, it was equal parts music, with "pieces" played on the mandolin, and drawing through "copies." Her parents were concerned about her excessive sensitivity. They talked about it to Bèhne, who wrote to them on their return to Paris:

> **And has Mademoiselle Julie's impressionability diminished? Nervous sensitivity is a chance for artistic success, and consequently for others' enjoyment, but may engender suffering for oneself. This will pass little by little, thanks to the countryside and your good care.[11]**

The Exposition Universelle of 1889 offered Julie an infinite field of investigation, but to be discovered in small "tours" only, according to the recommendation made to her mother "not to tire the child."[12]

The education she received gave Julie a literary skill similar to painting.[13] Her youthful writings, correspondence, and diary were peppered with descriptions composed like colorful paintings. She excelled at sketching landscapes in a few words. Her descriptions were real *ekphrasis* of mental landscapes, of which she specified the composition, colors, luminous effects, and atmosphere. Julie walked, saw, and wrote as a painter.

DRAWING AND PAINTING

The young girl brought back from her Mediterranean sojourn a watercolor, delightfully signed, dated, and located "Julie 1889 Nice" (left), a pure expression of her poetic sensibility. In Paris, she drew and painted in the garden of the townhouse in the rue de Villejust or in the living room, as part of a "girl's education at home," according to Edma, who added to her sister Berthe: "Julie is only a distraction and a rest from your work, which is very interesting, by the way."[14] Julie was eleven years old and painted the garden of Mézy during the summer of 1890. "Have you done any beautiful little paintings?" asked her aunt, Suzanne Leenhoff-Manet.[15] Her tendency to draw and paint with her left hand is confirmed in the portraits where, twice, her mother depicted her at the easel, drawing flowers[16] in 1891 and the following year painting indoors. Much attention and finesse would have overcome the prejudice left-handed people faced at the end of the nineteenth century.[17] This peculiarity might have troubled her parents, but not a word was ever said about it.

At the Musée des Beaux-Arts de Tours, October–November 1892, copying the masters

Staying in Tours, on the hillside of the Saint-Symphorien district, at the Trianon[18] guest house had been one of Eugène Manet's last wishes in the spring of 1892.[19] Mother and daughter stayed there in the fall, for almost two weeks, before going to stay with relatives at the Château de Vassé. From the Trianon's gardens, the view embraced the city of Tours and, below, they only had to cross the Loire River to reach the museum. There they chose paintings to copy:[20] Berthe, a detail of François Boucher's *Apollo Revealing his Divinity before the Shepherdess Isse*;[21] Julie, one of the two Mantegna paintings, *The Agony in the Garden*, as the fourteen-year-old letter writer told her cousin Paule in a letter in which she tried to convince her to join them and paint together:[22]

> **The country is delightful. Today, we strolled on the banks of the Loire to an area where there are houses, on a hillside, with gardens planted with vineyards, pruned trees, arbors. The trees are of a very pretty color; there are a lot of fir trees. The sky is blue as in the Midi and the whole landscape resembles it. On our walk we saw houses built from large rocks, they have**

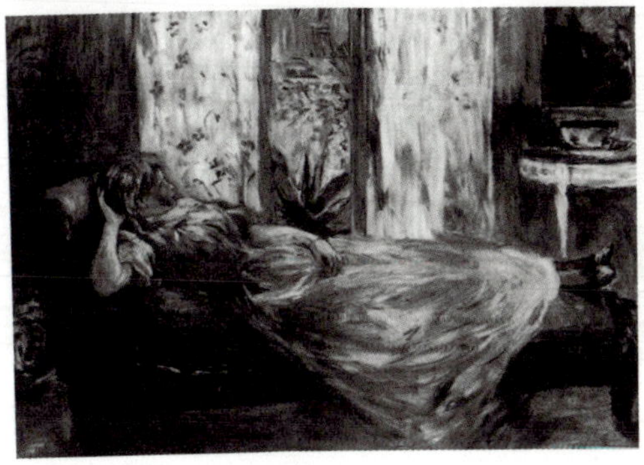

Berthe Morisot (1841–1895)
On the Chaise Longue, 1893
Oil on canvas, 55 × 73 cm
New York, collection of Mr. & Mrs. David Schwartz, 1957

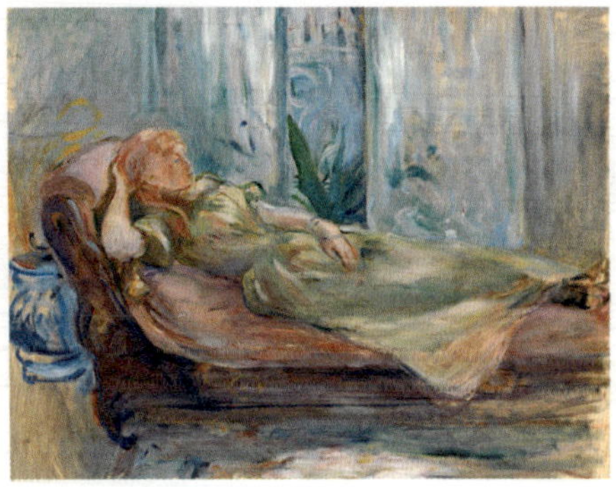

Berthe Morisot (1841–1895)
Girl on the Chaise Longue, 1893
Oil on canvas, 45.9 × 55.1 cm
Saint-Denis de La Réunion, Musée Léon-Dierx

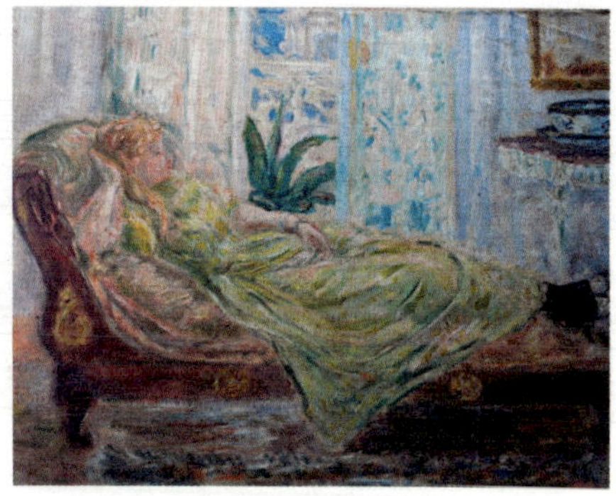

Julie Manet (1878–1966)
Girl on the Chaise Longue, 1893
Oil on canvas
Private collection

lovely little windows, balconies, and terraces. Then at the top of the hill a kind of small tower or big chimney, stands out against the sky.

The Loire is quite high up. It's very beautiful. . . . Once we arrived at Tours we took a carriage with a white silk interior, torn everywhere . . . We passed under a triumphal arch in greenery on which was written in pink flowers: "To Léon Bourgeois."[23] . . .

You must come here. You'd paint lovely landscapes. . . .

We went to the Museum, there are two lovely Mantegnas, and a Boucher, a Delacroix, a Vender Meulen, and a few other things. We are going to copy tomorrow. Maman is going to do a part of the Boucher, where he has nymphs in the water surrounded by reeds, with glorious large woods in the background.

I'm going to copy one of the Mantegnas, which depicts Jesus Christ praying in the garden of the olive trees. In the foreground are the sleeping disciples, and in the background, the city of Jerusalem.[24]

This morning we saw two painters at the museum copying a very ugly painting. They couldn't bring themselves to do anything other than a small square that depicted a door.[25]

Berthe Morisot became so involved in the execution of her copy that she made herself ill, as Julie wrote:

> Maman is not well today, she has a stomachache. I think it's from painting a lot at the museum yesterday.[26]

The copy after Boucher concentrated the affects and memories of discussions with Eugène Manet about the eighteenth-century spirit, and with Édouard Manet about his drawings for *L'Après-midi d'un faune*.[27] It required extracting the manner of the painter of the Graces while finding the *sprezzatura* of her own gesture. Berthe added a sheet to her daughter's letter:

> I have twice wanted to do landscapes, but I won't do any, we are going to the museum tomorrow. Julie is looking forward to copying a beautiful Mantegna. Tell your mother goodbye from me, I will write to her soon. I have some rest here, have I some rest?[28]

Julie's copy of Mantegna does not seem to have been conserved.

Painting the same motif, side by side

Throughout her youth, Berthe Morisot had painted alongside Edma, until her older sister's marriage and her move to Lorient separated them. The two young women painted in the living room of their parents' house, with its threshold to the garden.[29] Once married, Berthe painted with Eugène at her side. She listened to his suggestions, as Julie recalled:

> My father was very interested in my mother's painting, and he often worked with her, advising her to paint in a light and hazy way.[30]

After her husband's death, Berthe repeated this practice with Julie.

In the rue Weber apartment, Paris, Girl on the Chaise Longue

While her mother worked from a model sent by Renoir, Marie-Louise Bataille,[31] and left several versions of her composition,[32] Julie painted a small study of the same subject, from a slightly different point of view, with her easel

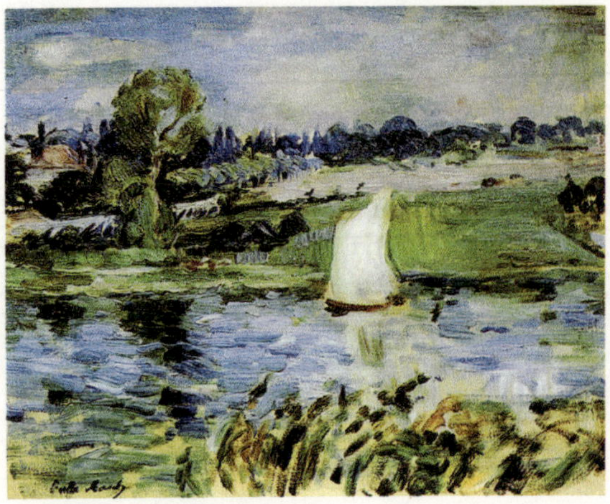

Berthe Morisot (1841–1895)
Sail on the River (The Little Boat)
Oil on canvas, 28.4 × 34.9 cm
Private collection

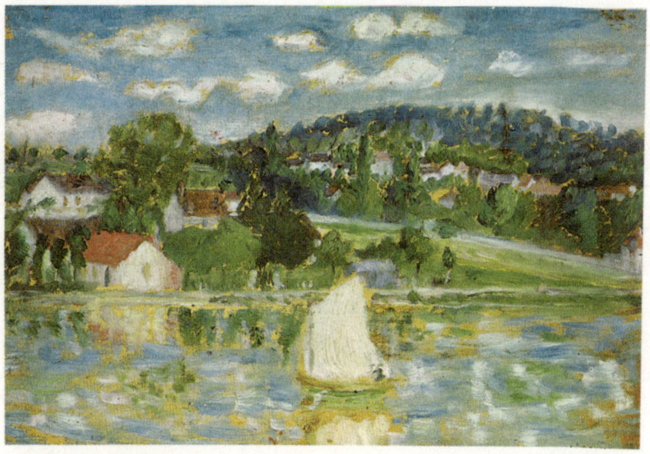

Julie Manet (1878–1966)
Sail on the River, 1893
Oil on canvas, 24.5 × 33 cm
Private collection

to the left of her mother's so that both were free to move, Julie painting with her left hand (p. 161).

> **Reclining in a yellow dress in foulard on the Empire sofa, slippers on her feet, in front of the open window behind which one can see an aloe and through which the warm rays of the sun penetrate, a young girl with blond hair is resting.**[33]

This is how Julie remembered the moment of the sitting, the suspended sensuality of July with the aloe on the balcony reminiscent of the gardens of Nice, when she described her mother's painting at the retrospective exhibition devoted to her in 1896. Her study can be compared with the version of Berthe Morisot's painting in the New York collection. The young painter remembered these sessions when she had a model sit for her alone a few years later.

Landscape from the inn window in Valvins

Later in the summer, from August 25 to September 4, 1893, mother and daughter joined the Mallarmé family in Valvins, on the banks of the Seine. The poet had found them a room that could meet their expectations and serve as their studio:

> **I have questioned all the inns. The one nearby will do quite nicely as I will now detail: because, with regard to two ladies, one of whom, Julie, is a decorator (although I haven't mentioned this), it offers a room with two beds overlooking the river, and meals, for fourteen francs, per day, instead of sixteen. One is not wrong to confide in dreamers who, alone, are practical: and see how, with these details, I have already concocted a charming dream for myself.**[34]

From the window, they painted the writer's sailing skiff: "Today, Maman and I both began studies of the view from our windows and of Monsieur Mallarmé's boat."[35]

Their painting days began early, were interrupted for lunch, and resumed in the afternoon, which they called "the day," with another motif. Three sessions were necessary for Julie, two for her mother.[36] The comparison of the two paintings confirms the novice's general tendency to try to render details. On the other hand, in Berthe Morisot's painting, distances are lacking, perhaps because of the recent decline in her eyesight.[37]

At the Bois de Boulogne, preparatory drawing for the painting

According to her diary, on her return to Paris, Julie continued to paint from September 5 to October 14, 1893. Before resuming classes, she and her mother drew with colored crayons in the Bois de Boulogne, which was not without risk:

> **Maman and I were sitting very close to each other, with her bag between us on the ground and Laertes in front. All of a sudden a suspicious-looking man in black with a horrible yellow face approached us, stroked Laertes, then, with a hideous bony hand, grabbed the bag and ran off in the direction of the Pré-Catelan.**[38]

These drawings could later be used for works painted in oils at the apartment or in the small studio in rue Weber, as in the case of two paintings, *Woman and Girl beside a Lake* by Berthe (p. 163), of which a preparatory drawing exists,[39] and the same motif painted by Julie (p. 163). In the first, the strolling woman is captured in three-quarter profile, while Julie drew her in profile and avoided depicting the child's face.

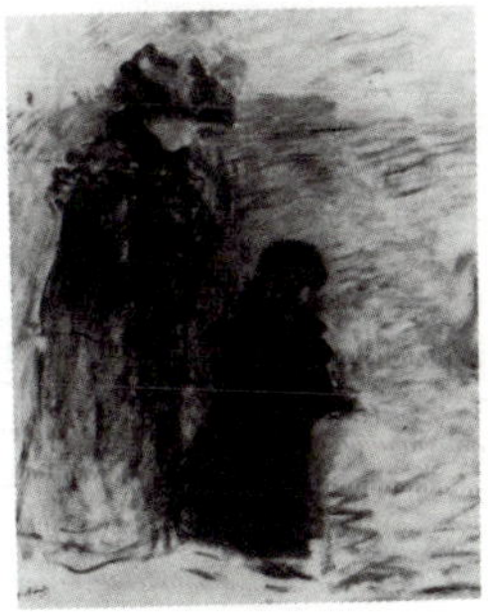

Berthe Morisot (1841–1895)
Woman and Girl beside a Lake, 1893–94
Oil on canvas, 61 × 50 cm
Private collection

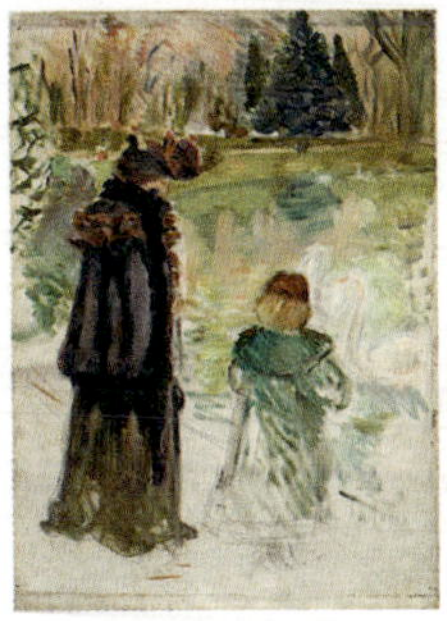

Julie Manet (1878–1966)
Woman and Girl beside a Lake, 1893–94
Oil on canvas, 53 × 35 cm
Private collection

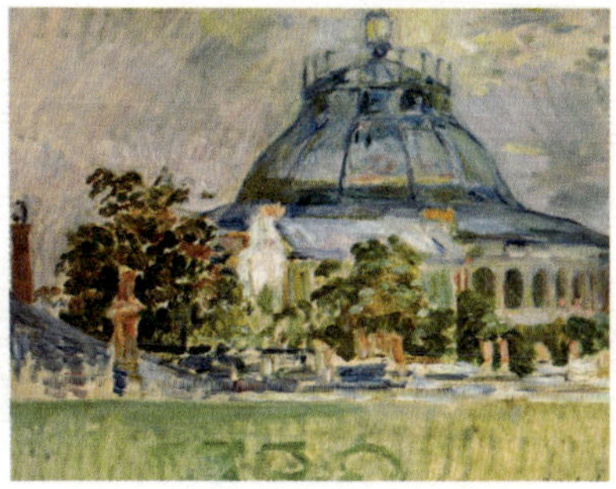

Berthe Morisot (1841–1895)
The Dome of the Arena in the Rue Pergolèse, 1893
Oil on canvas, 33 × 41 cm
Private collection, with the kind permission of the Galerie Hopkins, Paris

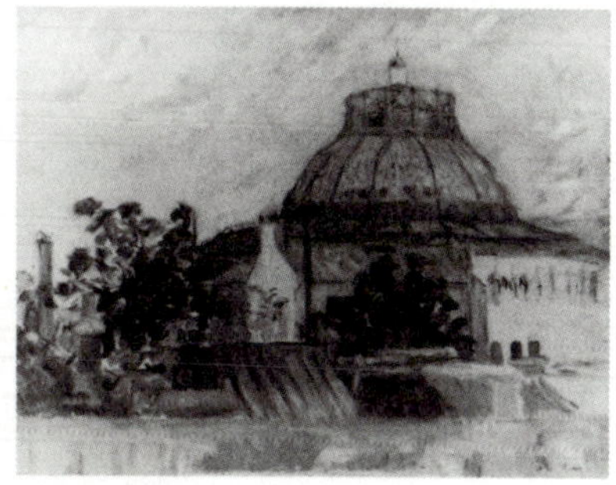

Julie Manet (1878–1966), previously attributed to Berthe Morisot (1841–1895)
The Dome of the Arena in the Rue Pergolèse, Sunset, 1893
Oil on canvas, 33 × 41 cm
Private collection

From the window of the rue Weber apartment, the view of the rooftops

From September 12 to 14, 1893, Berthe and Julie would work on painting the view from the apartment in rue Weber. Julie noted in her diary: "They are going to demolish the Dome of the rue Pergolèse: we must hurry to paint it; so I bought two small canvasses[40] specially with Octavie."[41] As in Valvins, from their hotel room, they painted the view of the bullring built for the 1889 Exposition Universelle. The "Grande Plaza de Toros of the Bois de Boulogne," as it was called, might have evoked the memory of Berthe's trip to Madrid in 1872, as well as the bullfighting scenes in Édouard Manet's paintings. Julie worked on it for three days, as she did on *Sailing on the River in Valvins*.[42] Her diary, as well as the context of painting as a duo, allow us to question the attribution to Morisot of two paintings, of identical formats, depicting the *Dome of the Arena in the rue Pergolèse*.[43] Certain particularities of the drawing, brushwork and color make it possible to assign one of the canvases to Julie (above[44]).

THE COPIES AFTER ONCLE ÉDOUARD

The copy (p. 234) after the portrait of her grandparents, *M. and Mme Auguste Manet*, painted by Édouard Manet (p. 235), seems to relate to a duty of memory, to be a filial and pictorial exercise for Julie and her cousin Jeannie Gobillard. "I started mine [the copy] in the spring, but it's not making much progress," Julie noted on October 13, 1893.[45] Painting activity would be interrupted when Madame Jammès[46] resumed her classes. The copy after Édouard Manet encouraged Julie to paint broadly, one of the qualities of execution that she would seek to acquire in painting as in violin playing.[47] In Théodore Duret's collection put up for sale she admired, next to *Young Girl in a Ball Gown* (1879) painted by her mother,[48] portraits of the latter by Édouard Manet, "a small portrait of Maman in three-quarter profile, dressed in black with a bouquet of violets and wearing a small hat, her face against the light. I adore this portrait—the brushwork is so good and the blacks are quite magnificent, as are the whites in the other portrait [*The Rest*]. Oncle Edouard was such a master of the paintbrush!"[49] Her copies of *The Rest* (p. 237),[50] *The Café-concert*, *Polichinelle*,[51] and *Nina de Callias* (p. 280–281), among others, were her own initiative. Julie would set a precedent for women artists in the family. Decades later, in 1933, they would exhibit together their copies of Manet[52] following the exhibition dedicated to him.

Julie felt responsible for the heritage of the Manet brothers when her uncle godfather, Jules de Jouy,[53] died, following on from the deaths of her father and her "Oncle Édouard":

> **My dear old Oncle Parrain, the last of the Manets. Now I really am the only descendant of the three Manet brothers; all that's left are one poor young girl and two widows to mourn them.[54]**

The portrait of this godfather by Édouard Manet (p. 17) returned to her,[55] as well as drawings and sketches.[56]

Julie learned from the proximity of Manet's works, from those painted alongside Berthe Morisot, of which other examples would be found, as her description of *Jeanne Marie Doing Marthe's Hair* suggests:

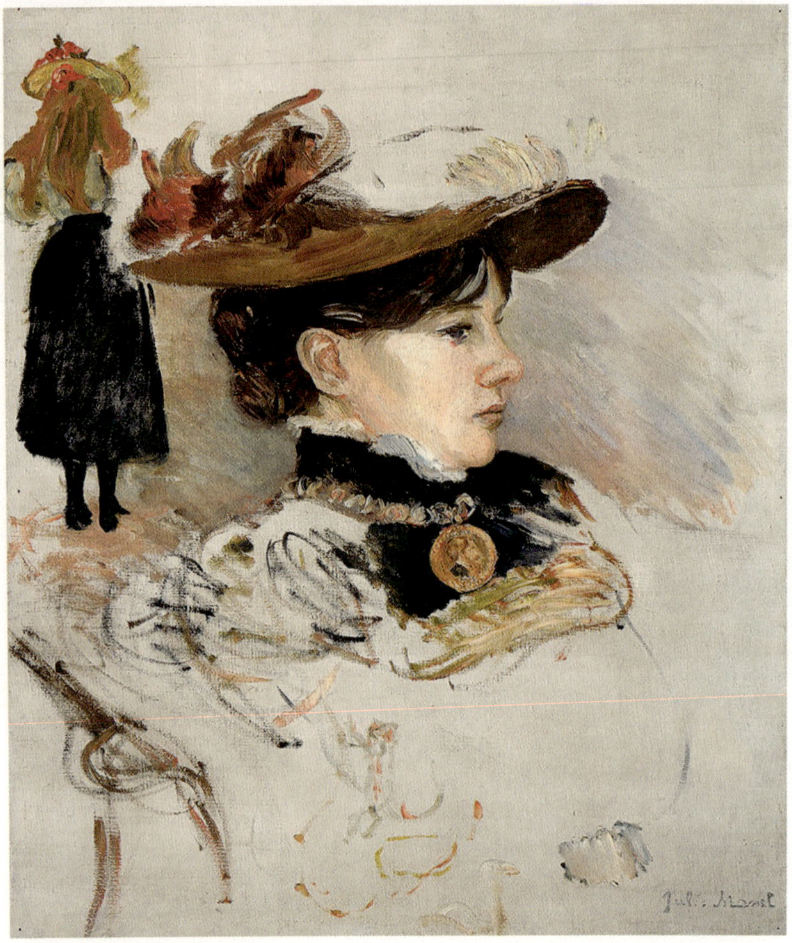

Julie Manet (1878–1966)
Portrait of Paule Gobillard, c. 1894
Oil on canvas, 59.5 × 49.5 cm
Private collection

What a beautiful light, colorful canvas! I remember working alongside Maman in the studio in the rue Weber when she did it.[57]

During this period, she trained her eye during friendly visits to the studios of Renoir, Monet—"these pictures by Monsieur Monet certainly are an excellent lesson in painting"—and, soon after, Edgar Degas.[58]

PORTRAIT OF PAULE GOBILLARD

Paule Gobillard (1867–1946) was to become one of the family's renowned painters. She probably advised and encouraged Julie in the execution of her portrait, signed in the lower right "Julie Manet" (above). The painting can probably be dated to 1894 or early 1895, as suggested by the age of the models, shortly after the death of their mother Yves, following which they became close to Berthe and her daughter. While Jeannie Gobillard's silhouette from behind is completely painted, the main subject's clothing is deliberately unfinished, leaving large areas of the canvas visible, in a manner reminiscent of Morisot and Degas. Also from Degas is the pose of the face, "almost in profile," taken precisely by Julie from the pastel portrait he did of Paule's mother, Madame Théodore Gobillard, in 1869 (p. 165). A third person appears in Paule's portrait, a man with a blond beard, painted in profile on a miniature attached to her neck by a heavy chain.[59] Perhaps this was a family medallion portraying Édouard Manet, included in the composition for his decisive influence on Paule's painting vocation?

FINAL SHARED SUBJECTS, SUMMER 1894

During this sojourn with her mother and her cousins, Julie painted for only a few days, from August 12 to 18, and noted: "We spent the afternoon painting in the garden,"[60]

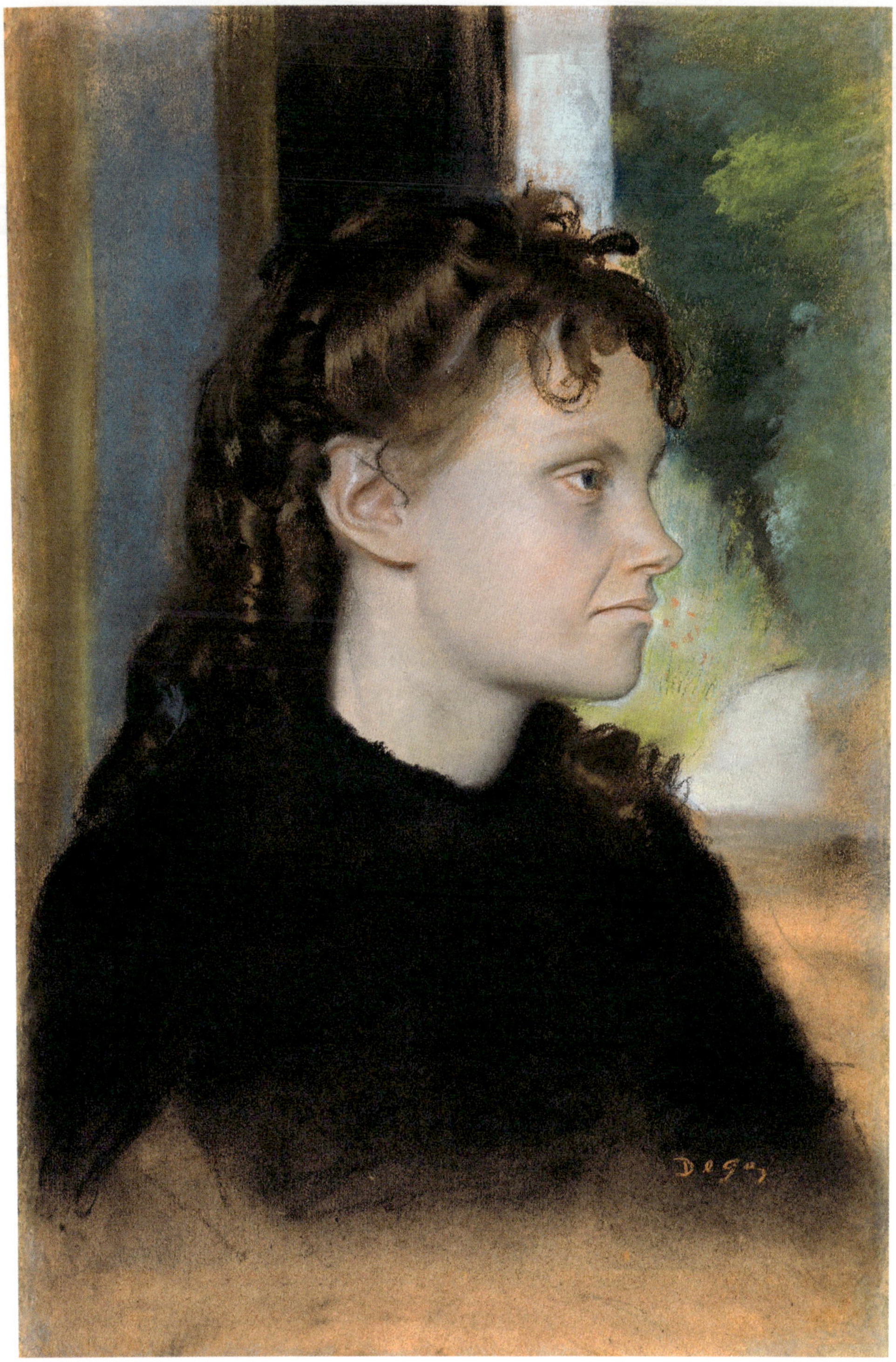

Edgar Degas (1834–1917)
Portrait of Madame Théodore Gobillard (Yves Morisot, 1838–1893), 1869
Pastel on paper, 48 × 30 cm
New York, The Metropolitan Museum of Art, Joan Whitney Payson bequest, 1975

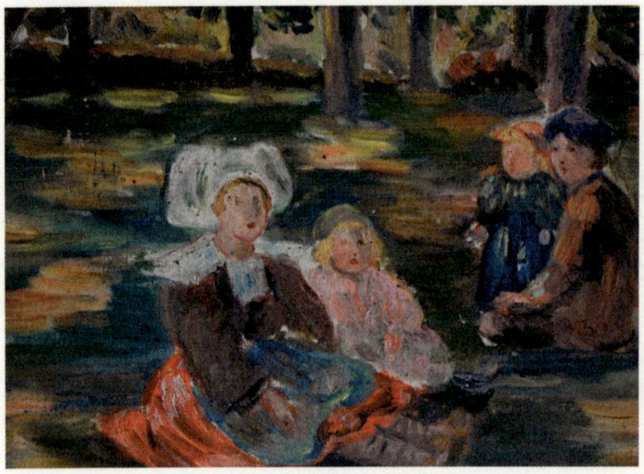

Julie Manet (1878–1966)
Children on the Grass in Brittany, 1895
Oil on canvas
Private collection

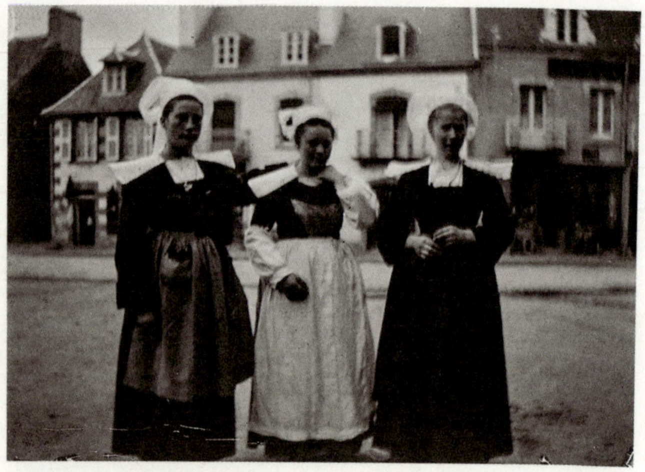

Julie Manet (1878–1966)
Waitresses Joséphine, Julia Guillou, future manager of the Hôtel des Voyageurs, and Anna on the Grand-Place in Douarnenez, today Place Julia, August 30, 1895
Archives BS, Paris, Musée Marmottan Monet

a garden known by two of Berthe's paintings, *La Roche-Plate at Portrieux*, and a sketch painted in oils showing her daughter and Jeannie in conversation on a bench.[61] Once back in the Parisian studio, Berthe would work from the sketch to paint a larger painting[62] for which she would use two professional models. Julie, no longer required as a model, painted a version of the scene that stands out for its tall format and composition, placing the model's red hair, seen from behind, in the center of the painting.[63] Another day in Portrieux: "It's really pretty to have the sea behind the wheat, fields of all kinds, houses,"[64] she noted in passing as she painted.

"What are you seeking right now?"[65] Edma asked Berthe Morisot about her painting. It is a pity that the answer is unknown. For Julie Manet, mimicry and absorption could not take the place of learning. Moreover, she did not mention any advice she received from her mother. Nevertheless, she had listened to what her mother had instilled in her: "real feeling," "personal ideas." She sought her own way of doing things through deeply thinking about the works of her mother and of her uncle Édouard Manet. She loved a broad manner and solidity in painting.

HER TRAINING ALONGSIDE RENOIR

Julie Manet. . .
"an unfathomable enigma"

Renoir wrote to Monet, on the death of their friend Berthe Morisot:

> **This poor little thing [Julie Manet] is very weak and worries us a great deal. She, with her courage, is an unfathomable enigma . . . The poor woman [Berthe Morisot] thought of everything and did not lose her mind for a moment. She bid farewell to all her friends without forgetting anyone, recommending Julie to them, a few moments before she died. But I see that I am going astray. I'm working as hard as I can, and I'm forcing myself not to think too much. Fortunately, everything is going well for the moment at home.**[66]

He often saw Julie:

> **It shakes her up a bit, that's all we can hope for at the moment.**[67]

He played a decisive role in her life, and the following summer he pulled her out of her slump by inviting her to share his family vacation in Brittany. More than a guide in painting, Renoir was first of all a model of balance in her life. He charmed Julie and her cousins with his attention, his conversations, the walks where he sharpened their eye for the landscape, and he introduced them to various skills, cooking, and sports. With Julie's mother, he had looked at the *Bathers*

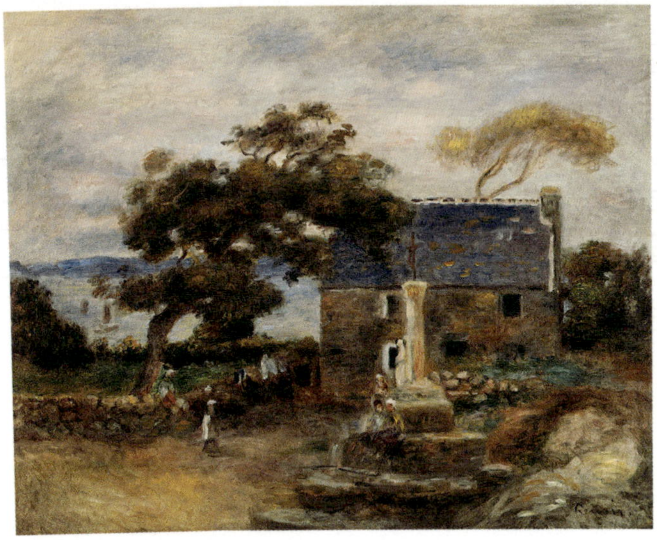

Pierre-Auguste Renoir (1841–1919)
Tréboul near Douarnenez, 1895
Oil on canvas, 55.2 × 66 cm
Private collection

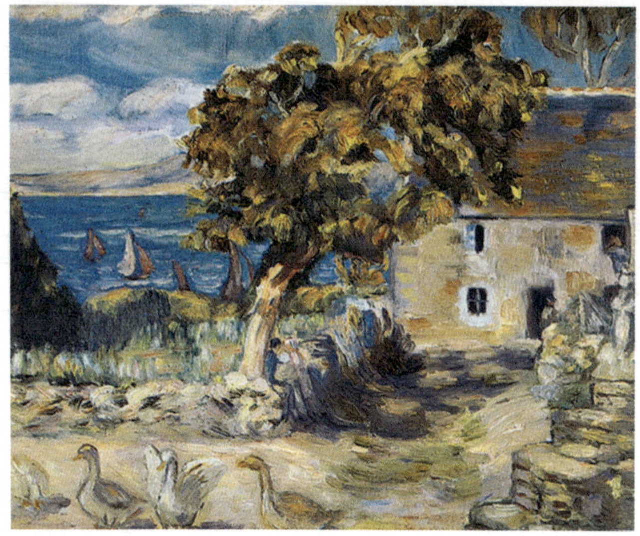

Julie Manet (1878–1966)
Tréboul near Douarnenez, 1895
Oil on canvas
Private collection

of Girardon's bas-relief, and he taught the young Manets to swim.[68] Once back in Paris, Julie would write:

> **Monsieur Renoir has been so kind and charming all summer; the more one sees of him, the more one realizes he is a true artist, witty and extraordinarily intelligent, but also genuinely kind and sincere.[69]**

In 1895, with Renoir, Julie could continue Corot's practice passed on by Berthe Morisot, devoting herself, better than from her window, to painting outdoors, day after day, from nature.

BRITTANY, SUMMER 1895 (AUGUST 8–OCTOBER 4)

In Pont-Aven, staying at the famous Hôtel des Voyageurs from August 10 to September 2, Julie and her cousins lived a resort life with Madame Renoir and her one-year-old son, Jean. Pont-Aven was now attracting tourists and banked on its exoticism. At the end of their sojourn, the young women took with them only "a few paintings, different head studies of a rather funny little girl." Julie regretted:

> **I would have liked to do something else with her. I saw a Velázquez with these light bonnets and these big ruffs.[70]**

A study may depict this little girl, sitting with her friends in the undergrowth (p. 166 left). Julie seems to pastiche, by synthesizing them with *Luncheon on the Grass* by Oncle Édouard and her mother's *Children on the Grass*.[71] Before leaving Pont-Aven, Julie took photographs of the hotel waitresses (p. 166 right), "They are all very pretty," she wrote, "Julia[72] is the prettiest, then comes Joséphine. It seems to me that we are the common people and are served by princesses."[73] These photographs would later be used for a painting in the studio.[74]

Near Douarnenez, from September 3 to October 3, Renoir found them a house in Tréboul, while he lived nearby in a farmhouse with his family. Julie listened to him defend the artisanal aspect of painting to a detractor of *Olympia*. A "cracked" painting, however beautiful it may be, "proves that it's a bad picture," "painting is a craft that must be learned; a good picture has to be well painted."[75] Painting and watercoloring became daily tasks. Julie had never worked so hard.

"The view from our house"

> **We went up to St Jean where our house is. It is very nice, all white inside with green doors; we have a room for the three of us. There is a small garden full of flowers; it is very well located, in front is a small square with a crucifix, a Virgin with the infant Jesus, then a walnut tree, an old house, and behind the sea and the coast close the horizon.[76]**

Everyone painted this view.

> **After lunch I began the view we have from our house [above right]. Paule and Jeannie paint from above and Monsieur Renoir does it in the morning.[77]**

This diary passage helps to clarify the history of a painting by Renoir, *Tréboul near Douarnenez* (p. 167),[78] which features the "crucifix" and the "old house" with the "walnut tree" described by Julie. "The crucifix and the house on the square" reminded her of the "Mantegna of Tours."[79] To judge the pertinence of the surprising connection she makes between these two compositions, one need only compare Renoir's painting, the point of view after a photograph of the site, and the Mantegna. Julie grasped the global nature of the composition and the common hierarchy of the different planes. The young painter imbued the elements of the landscape with mysticism. On another occasion, she evoked Palestine (which she had never visited):

> **I did a watercolor of the view we have of Douarnenez. On our way back, in the setting sun, whose light here, which lends everything a golden and pinkish hue, is particularly beautiful, we found a great resemblance (and this is not the first time that it has happened) between Brittany and what one imagines of Palestine. I saw a Christ praying on this arid mountain covered with gorse, heather, and rocks with the pine tree in front and, in the background, this city lit with fire with the church tower standing out against the pink sky. There the trees in the shade let us glimpse the sea, in their summits a spot of gold, the last ray of the sun which sets in the bottom of waves in the residence of the delicious Thetis.[80]**

The bay of Douarnenez was a mythical place for three generations of women in the family: their maternal grandmother, Cornélie, then Berthe and Edma, who had been dazzled by it in 1866,[81] and now Julie, Jeannie, and Paule. Julie would paint it several mornings in a row on a larger canvas[82] than her usual studies. She exhibited it at the Salon des Indépendants in Paris the following May, with the title *Bay of Douarnenez*.[83] She thus perpetuated Berthe Morisot's habit of exhibiting the works she had painted the previous summer at the Salon du Louvre. Renoir's opinion had encouraged her to do so:

> **Monsieur Renoir came to fetch us. He said that I knew how to get the houses just right. Such a compliment from a great master gave me pleasure but perhaps it's just vanity on my part? However, it does seem to me that one should be able to be pleased when someone who really knows tells you, after you have worked very hard, that the result is not completely wanting. Certainly, I know I have many faults—I want to work hard at everything this year.[84]**

Among the many picturesque descriptions, the following one evoked a study that has been conserved:

> **Worked . . . on the Saint-Jean houses, the bell and the sea in the background.[85]**

With its vivid colors and long brush strokes that link it to the art of Renoir, the study differs from earlier works.

PARIS, WINTER 1895–1896

Thanks to the catalog of the 1896 Salon des Indépendants, where Julie Manet's *Young Girl at the Piano* was presented,[86] we know that the young painter had already tried her hand at the interior scene and the motif that Renoir had just illustrated with a work representative of his "pearl period."[87] Julie made no mention in her diary, which was incomplete from the beginning of December 1895 to March 2, 1896, of the painting she exhibited. For lack of a professional model, she used her cousin Jeannie Gobillard sitting for long hours at her piano in the living room. She portrayed her in profile, left hand on her hip, right hand on the keyboard, her gaze focused on the score open on the music stand.[88]

At the same time as she was dealing with her own presentation to the public, Julie was preparing the retrospective exhibition of her mother's work which opened at the Galerie Durand-Ruel on March 1, 1896. Mallarmé was in charge of the catalog, while Monet, Renoir, and Degas oversaw the hanging. Degas was responsible for the display of the watercolors, using an eight-leaf folding screen that he had ordered for the occasion. Julie numbered the works and described each painting in an illuminating way.[89]

AUGUST 15, 1896

In the summer, around mid-August, the Seine at Valvins made her "think of those landscapes, so extensive and full of atmosphere, by Van der Meulen."[90] She returned to painting, practicing still life and devoting herself to the study of red. She had already congratulated herself for her ability to use "Saturn red" in watercolor, for the burned trees in the forest of Fontainebleau.[91] This time she used "a lot" and all "kinds . . . to make gladioli, roses, queen daisies, and other red flowers in a patterned earthenware bowl."[92] Painting became social entertainment when Julie painted on glass, in three small pictures, for Geneviève Mallarmé's magic lantern, the *Adventure of Miss Voss*, [93] her English conversation teacher, who was also a friend of the Mallarmés.[94]

BEGINNINGS IN PORTRAITURE

Renoir had shown her portraits of models whose clothing he had himself concocted, "a ravishing hat of white chiffon with a rose on it (which he had made himself!) and a white dress with a green belt."[95] Her mother, Berthe Morisot, proceeded in a similar manner by lending her costumes to her models. Julie's interest in portraiture was sparked by visits to Degas's studio,[96] where she had seen his portrait of Oncle Édouard and that in "pastel of Tante Suzanne on a blue sofa," as well as the clay portrait of Zandomeneghi. In December, in Paris, Renoir got Julie Manet to refocus on painting, through portraiture. He sent her models:

> **I am sending you a very nice little girl who poses very well for her age. Try her if you like.**
> **Kind regards, Renoir**
> **I pay her 7 francs a day and lunch**
> **Ask her if she likes it. You'll have to pay for the train as well.**[97]

Echoing these undated letters from Renoir, we read this note from Julie on December 7, 1896:

> **We worked from a little girl that Monsieur Renoir sent us.**[98]

ESSOYES 1897, "A SUMMER WITH MONSIEUR RENOIR" (EARLY SEPTEMBER–OCTOBER 19, 1897)

Renoir welcomed Julie and her cousins to Essoyes, in his new country house, during the summers of 1897 and 1898. From the beginning of September[99] to October 19, 1897, a period that the young painter would call "a summer with Monsieur Renoir," then after the summer break, at the Louvre, Renoir lavished his time on Julie, correcting her, giving her advice and guidance.

Legitimate but rejected: renewed ambition

In the spring of 1897, Julie Manet's desire to exhibit, not at the Salon des Indépendants, but at the Salon National des Beaux-Arts, met with the jury's rejection. One of the works she presented, *Little Girl with a Mandolin,* perhaps painted after a model sent by Renoir, struck her as feeble when she went to collect it.[100]

Comparing herself to Mademoiselle Baudot, a painter her age to whom she had been introduced by Renoir, she noticed that this artist was far superior to herself, both in maturity and in painting. She also compared herself to Marie Bashkirtseff, whose diary she read during her stay in Essoyes.[101] The young Julie did not like the painting of the brilliant student from the Académie Julian, but knowing the artist's entourage she excused her, because she "was taught among bad painters, in a family that understood nothing about art." This was also partly the excuse that she would find for Jeanne Baudot when the latter would fail in her copy in the Louvre, her background being "a family that does not understand anything about the art which one likes."[102] While, on the other hand, Julie's environment forced her to succeed:

> **I am lucky to have been brought up in such an artistic environment; one would really have to be a silly goose not to love beautiful things. If she were in my place, I'm sure that Jeanne [Baudot] would do a painting much better than I would. In short, let's not complain.**[103]

Renoir, to whom she opened up about her difficulty in evaluating herself, replied that it was "ridiculous not to be able to distinguish what is good from what is bad." With regard to the dahlias she had just painted, he told her that they were "splendid," but advised her to "leave them turned to the wall for a week or so" and then she would be able to judge them for herself.[104] He would state:

> **In life, it's the same as in art, everything is a matter of comparison.**[105]

How did Julie rate her talent? Was she just above "a silly young lady who paints fans and lampshades"?[106] Four days later, having regained her courage:

> **Decidedly I thought I was going to become more virtuous. But no, I want to be more than a silly young lady who paints fans.**[107]

We witness the first manifestation of her personal struggle to come: virtue (duty) against painting (vanity). For the time being, she had not lost hope of being admitted by the juries:

> **After spending a summer in Monsieur Renoir's company, I am sure that in life everyone should know how to do a little of everything, and especially be skillful at whatever they undertake. Monsieur Renoir repeats this idea constantly and eventually it sinks in. He has a great deal of influence over the young people who admire him, and says such philosophical things, so charmingly, that I automatically believe them.**[108]

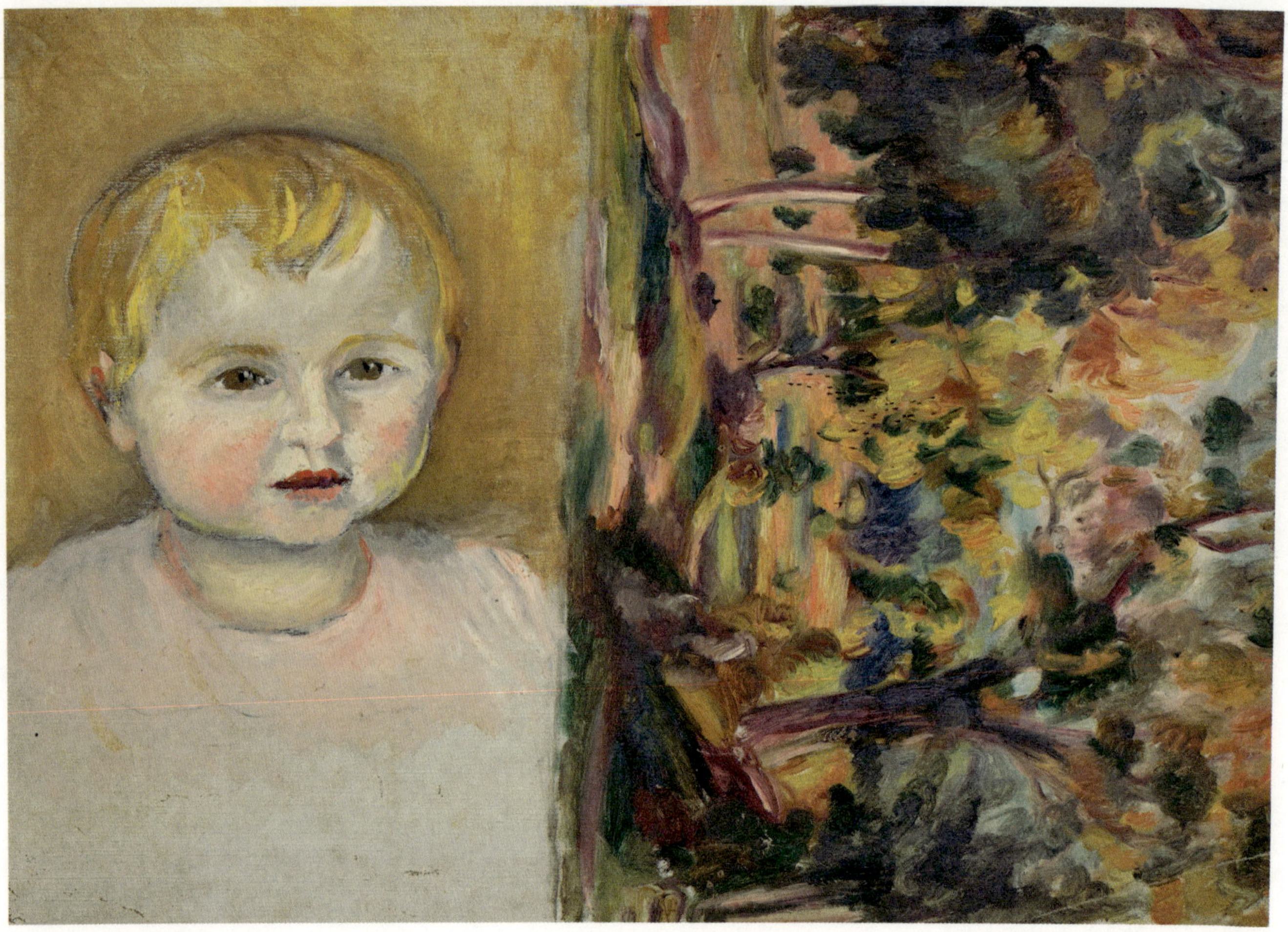

Julie Manet (1878–1966)
Portrait of Jean Renoir; Landscape at Essoyes, 1897–1898
Oil on canvas, 35.7× 46 cm
Private collection

COULD THE IMPRESSIONIST PAINTERS BE TEACHERS?

No matter that she was surrounded by artists, Julie continually complained about the lack of guidance, the absence of advice. Jeannie told her "something rather true":

> At the point where I am with the education I have received, complete supervision would perhaps confuse me. I would not like to be corrected, for example, I would never dare to continue something that had been corrected for me, it would bother me.[109]

Claude Monet had also told her: "You have to find yourself." And Julie decided:

> So let's slave away alone, observing what real artists do and thinking about what Maman did.[110]

Years later, Julie still searched for lessons between the pages of her mother's notebooks and reread entire chapters she had copied from a handwritten "Traité de peinture" by Léon Riesener.[111] She found it more beneficial for Renoir to tell her to scrape and redo her "Dina with a Basket" than to receive his compliments. She dreaded the return to Paris, where she would not have the benefit of his advice "as here," in Essoyes.

Renoir put her back to work, with flower painting sessions interspersed with walks and bicycle lessons. She attempted drawing correction, with Dina "well proportioned" in the painting that she started again.[112] She worked relentlessly—"I'm completely obsessed with painting"—and exhibited two paintings at the next Salon des Indépendants, including *Dahlias Painted in Essoyes*. A study shows her manner and reveals how she executed, as an exercise, like Renoir, several independent subjects on the same canvas.[113] She regretfully left the "golden countryside":

> What folly to leave such beautiful countryside. The road from Essoyes to Polisot was marvelous. The golden yellow trees, the green meadows, the gray, pink, velvety hillside grounds, the red peach trees, an extravaganza of tones. What a beautiful autumn. Jean and the little Trotteuse or the Roussette or Nini, Madame Renoir's new maid, mingling their red hair with the faintest of the leaves. What wonderful landscapes.[114]

Julie sketched a portrait of the young Jean she refers to, a blond child captured from the front, in one of her characteristic paintings resulting from Renoir's teachings (p. 170).

Julie and the Impressionist masters at the Louvre

At the instigation of Renoir, who was to supervise their copies, Julie, Paule, and Jeannie went to the Louvre on November 11, 1897 to pick up their copy permissions. They made their selections: Julie Manet copied Veronese's *Holy Family*; [115] Paule Gobillard, Titian's *The Madonna of the Rabbit*,[116] a painting copied by the young Édouard Manet[117] (p. 60); Jeanne Baudot also chose Titian, copying his *Virgin and Child*.[118]

Julie worked at the Louvre for around ten sessions,[119] from November 16 to December 18, and again on January 4. Renoir visited four times. He approved the choice of Veronese, "good for copying," and took care of Julie:

> Indeed, one would have thought I was his pupil rather than Jeanne [Baudot], and I couldn't understand it . . . I had somehow imagined him to be far more of a teacher to her; but now I see that he doesn't really have a teacher's attitude toward her.[120]

The next day in his studio, he advised her to start "with a simple sketch to give oneself an idea of the overall effect and only then paint in the figures," which is to say in a single session, as he explained:

> Ingres always painted a torso in one go, even if he had to do it again the following day.[121]

He reassured her: once she had nearly finished her copy, he would come by "just to tell [her] it was awful, so that [she] could start the whole thing again."[122] He then pointed out some mistakes and noted that Julie had made it bigger than the original, which "should be avoided . . . although it is quite good." "I was rather pleased, as I had no idea how I was getting on," Julie wrote.

On December 8, Degas came to their room in the Louvre and talked to them about painting for an hour and a half. He advised Paule, whose copy he thought had started off very well, not to use too many colors:

> In *The Madonna of the Rabbit*, the fabrics and the mountains should be done with the same blue as the sky; the flesh passages and the orange fabric with the same color. "That's what gives a painting harmony," he said.[123]

As for Julie, she received a flattering appraisal:

> "She has quite a knack, young Julie; the armor is skillfully done, it's stylish; but still, those bits of white canvas, dearie me, one could say it runs in the family." "Skillful and stylish" pleased me. I'm always afraid I lack these qualities, which I think are absolutely essential in a woman. Everything that has been said to me about my copy gives me encouragement.[124]

Julie and Paule had left sections of the canvas unpainted, as in the *Portrait of Paule Gobillard* (p. 164). Degas then led them into the gallery where the pre-Renaissance artists were hung to see his pupil Ernest Rouart, who, under Degas's instructions, was priming a canvas with green to copy a Mantegna. "Unfortunately, he had done it in a really bright green," Julie noted with surprise.[125]

Renoir explained the challenge of copying from the Old Masters, with this new opinion of Julie's painting as a "whole":

> "It's very good, you only have to finish, it renders the painting while possessing your particularities. It's done as if you had seen it from afar, and clearer; I assure you it's very good, I like it better than the Veronese."
> Never have I received so many compliments.[126]

The challenge had been that of copying the detail of the *Two Nymphs* painted after François Boucher by Berthe Morisot in the Musée de Tours,[127] with "the particularities" of its making, and this same "clearer" rendering of the whole.

While copying, Julie had seen "a lot of people" at the Louvre, both painters (Whistler, Zandomeneghi, Helleu, Henner) and men of letters (Mallarmé, Arsène Alexandre), as well as Madame Henry Lerolle.

A rediscovered canvas that shows evidence of the lesson of the copy after Veronese is identifiable with the *Young Girl with a Dog* exhibited by the young painter at the following Salon des Indépendants, with its inscription "Julie Manet" on the reverse side.[128] It probably depicts Martha in a green velvet dress, with Laërtes on her lap.[129] A preparatory version exists (p. 180).

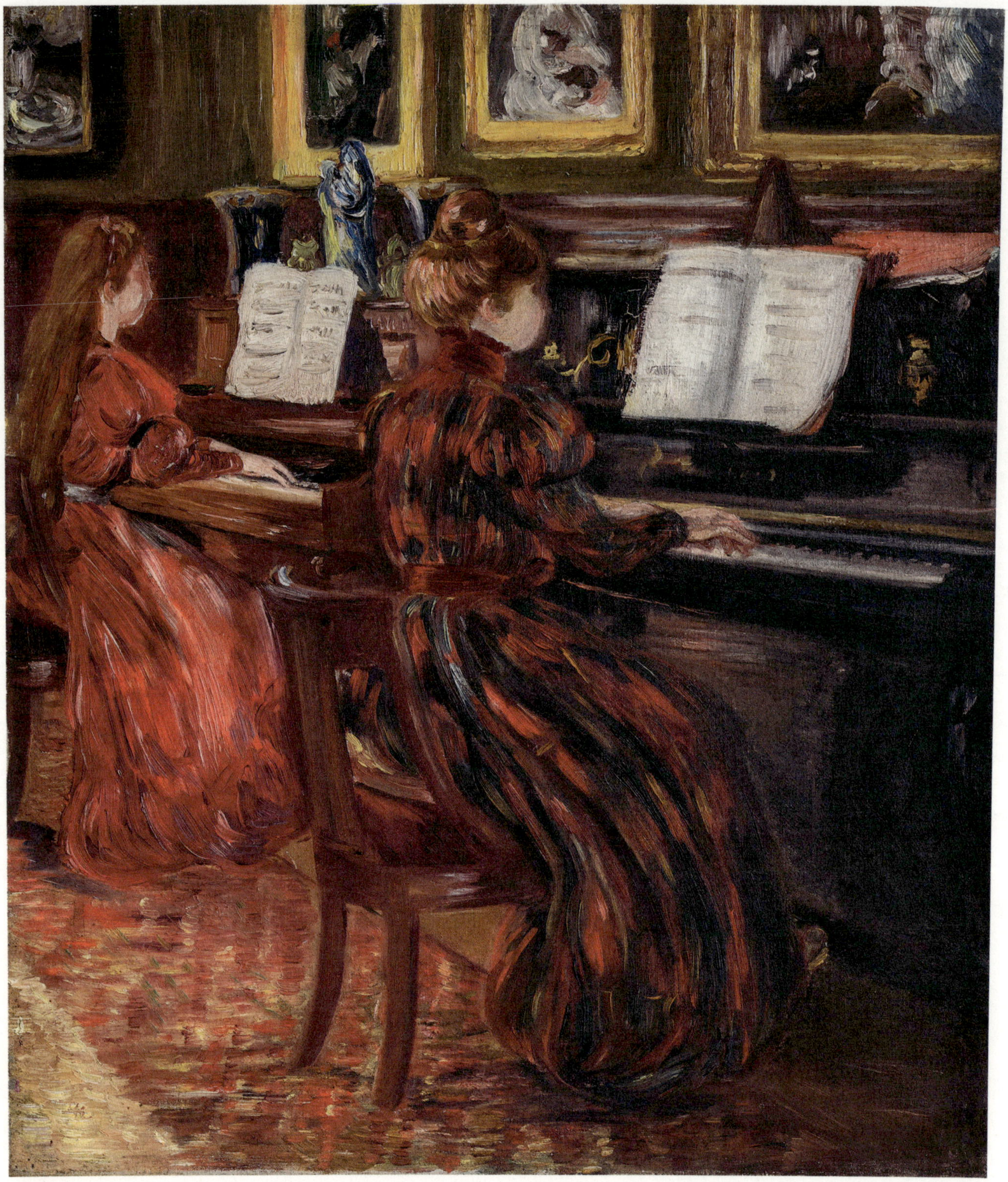

Julie Manet (1878–1966)
The Piano Duo, c. 1898
Oil on canvas, 55 × 46 cm
Private collection

ESSOYES 1898, THE LONG-AWAITED LESSONS (SEPTEMBER 7–OCTOBER 23)

For Julie Manet, "the only distraction from grief is the one that brings your thoughts close to that grief: work, for me painting."[130] Nevertheless, in 1898 she was determined to enjoy herself, as if out of "duty." But in an intimate prayer to her mother, she vowed to paint as Berthe Morisot would have wanted her to, to "be your daughter well."[131]

After the success of her copy, Renoir, during his second sojourn at Essoyes, from September 7 to October 23, 1898, provided Julie with the tools useful to her ambition, by giving her theoretical lessons and technical advice. He organized the girls' days in the following way: in the morning, model drawing, and landscape in the afternoon; or, in the morning, studies by the river, and in the afternoon, in the meadows:

> I regularly work four to five hours on painting, about two hours of playing the violin, and then in the evening I write and read.[132]

Renoir provided the instructions that Julie awaited: painting a small landscape in one go; painting lightly to begin with; and still lifes to "learn to paint quickly."[133] He then gave her the next two lessons.

The lesson on the Landscape by the River *(September 24, 1898)*

Renoir advised her "not to place the horizon line too high in a canvas, but in the middle as the point that attracts the eye, and not to start the foreground too close." Thus "the river looks more like it is flowing and sinking into the trees at the end."[134]

The lesson on a Still Life with Partridges *(October 2, 1898)*

During another "excellent lesson" on a "still life of partridges" that she showed him on October 2, 1898:[135]

> He [Renoir] said that when one begins a still life, or any other thing, one must look at the values carefully in relation to each other and sketch the composition in very lightly, while observing closely what is black, gray and white. "There is only black and white in painting," said Monsieur Renoir. Then he added that one must give white its intensity from the value of what is around it, and not by using white paint.

We recognize in this statement the lesson that Nicolas de Largillierre had received from his Antwerp masters and that he had conveyed to his young pupil, Jean-Baptiste Oudry, by asking him to paint a bouquet of white flowers on a light ground, which required that one proceed "always by comparison, and never otherwise."[136]

Renoir corrected Julie on the drapery of the tablecloth on which the partridges rest (see his related study[137]), which he explained lacked "the luminous place" of the fold. One must look "in the works of a great painter, the whites are beautiful and simple because he knows how to give them their place. Look at the whites of Titian, the whites of Corot." As for the partridges in her still life, "[they] weren't simple enough, velvety enough; they lacked color because there were too many of them," Renoir said, adding that the peaches were very good. Renoir also said "that it is very good to make houses precisely, to learn to make the white of the walls shine in the sun." Julie would remember this when she painted the walls of the dovecote at the Château du Mesnil.

The painter gave her the book by Georges Lafenestre (1837–1919) on Italian painting.[138] The book, "dutiful reading,"[139] was tedious until she read about "the techniques of old master painting. Fresco painting, egg tempera or glue-based paint were replaced by oil painting in the tenth century by the monk Theophilus and rediscovered by Cennino Cennini and also later by the Van Eyck brothers."[140] Following her reading of Lafenestre, Julie wanted to return to the Louvre to see the Italian pre-Renaissance painters and to look at "how the landscapes of the different painters are placed in the canvases."

Painting with oil rather than with turpentine

As for the medium, "Monsieur Renoir [said] that he thinks true painting is done with thick oil rather than thinned with turpentine and that should only be used for quick sketches. I've been trying oil for a month and find it gives great consistency."[141] It is a matter of the proportion of turpentine and oil with which painters dilute their colors. Painters, often for reasons of economy, dilute their colors to make them more fluid. This makes it possible to obtain glazes, or to give the impression of a fresco. But as the layers follow one another, it is necessary to reduce this proportion to then paint only with oil. These are the first principles that one teaches a painter, and it is surprising that Julie had to wait so long to be informed of them.

RED ON RED: *THE PIANO DUET*

The Piano Duet, depicting Jeannie and a friend playing together (p. 172), may date from the winter of 1898–99. As previously mentioned, Jeanne Clément may be sitting at the second piano.[142] Julie had already had the idea of using pianists as models in her home. In Renoir's painting *Yvonne and Christine Lerolle at the Piano*, she had admired the drapery, Christine's resemblance, and the evocation, in the background, of two paintings by Degas.[143] In her composition, she avoided having to capture the resemblance of the features, but concentrated on the attitude of the pianists, achieving an effect of atmospheric perspective, or soft focus, through the more allusive treatment of the pianist in the background. She depicted the bottom of the paintings hanging on the walls of the living room, including a portrait of her with a cat by Renoir (p. 209). Placed on the music stands of the two upright pianos, one ebony-colored, the other light oak, the sheets of music evoke drawing sheets and easel canvases. In this rare variation on the motif of the "young girl at the piano," in addition to the composition portraying two figures at the pianos, the singularity lies in the tension that it manages to render, the focus of the pianists concentrating on their music, bathed in the sonorous universe by the treatment of the red on red.

A *Virgin* is depicted on the left piano. Julie spoke of it as "a very pretty earthenware Virgin" bought in Renoir's company by Paule, who gave it to her as a Christmas present.[144] She kept it all her life, placed in one of the two niches that framed the double door of the living room at the Château du Mesnil.

1899

In the early days of 1899, she worked assiduously. Paule Gobillard and Julie sought out Renoir's advice when they brought their work to the studio. He was direct:

> **"What you are doing is full of qualities, but there is a certain awkwardness that prevents it from being completely good" and he says that this is perhaps due to the fact that we are working together without being able to get the model to pose according to our own separate ideas. For him, the awkwardness in our drawing of movements stems from this. He advises us not to do something elaborate at the same time as each other, and to draw a lot.**

Julie received compliments for *Yvonne Wearing a Hat*, and Jeannie's "red jacket":

> **I was quite surprised, finally he seems to find that I can continue to paint; so much the better, it is amusing, but I am afraid that he is too indulgent.[145]**

The blonde *Yvonne* had posed "in a blue ball gown and the little brown maid [Antoinette] putting roses on her skirt." A few days later, the young painter added her cousin Edme appearing through the half-open door, which "makes it very comical" (p. 182). That day she painted "from 9 o'clock to 4 o'clock, then 3½ hours of violin."[146]

Her paintings display sincerity, as well as daring and awkwardness. It was probably during this period that, following Renoir's advice to have the model pose separately for each of them, she confronted the female nude, no doubt for the first time,[147] in a reminiscence of *Allongée*—the same Empire daybed, the same slippers, here thrown on the floor. Against the background of an upholstery screen, she has the model strike a pose reminiscent of those in *Olympia* and *Nina de Callias* by Édouard Manet (p. 280–281).

She painted the *Portrait of Jeanne Baudot* (p. 184) inspired by the attitude of eighteenth-century portrait busts, in particular those by Nattier, Drouais, and Perronneau, whom she admired, and interpreting the manner of Renoir. She had a predilection for the broad brush stroke, not without a certain heaviness, but she imparted an expressive force to some of her compositions. It would be interesting to compare her portrait with the one of the same model painted by Paule Gobillard the same day.[148] Édouard Manet still came to her mind when at the concert she heard *La Rédemption* by César Franck:

> **Ah, here is scope, broad beauty, solidity. One senses in Franck the great artist who, in his new interpretation remains classical, as one senses in my Oncle Édouard. It is an art which rises, which goes up toward God and not the dull art which crawls on the earth.[149]**

Julie qualified the long-awaited opinion of January 30 that she could "continue to paint."[150] She showed Renoir her *Portraits of Jeannie at the Piano and Paule Listening to Her* (p. 183), and received "advice, that of redoing a few small things."[151] It seems that she did not exhibit in the spring of 1899. Her mind was elsewhere. "[I] . . . told myself that Ernest Rouart is the one for me," she wrote on her way home from a dinner at Degas's on June 6.[152] A new state of mind was emerging in her entourage. In February, Paul Valéry was received for the first time on a Thursday, the day when the household welcomed guests, in the apartment in the rue de Villejust.[153] In this salon, filled with seriousness, but circumspect about the conventions of the "world," he charmed by his conversation. Some of his views were similar to Julie's:

> **He [Valéry] sees the ridiculousness of these literati who want to do everything: "For, after all,' he says, 'literature, music, painting, what is it."[154]**

It seems that Julie no longer thought of professionalizing her practice; she spoke of "the painting she loves so much" as "an occupation" should she remain a spinster.[155]

Julie spent another two weeks in Renoir's circle in Saint-Cloud, from July 28 to August 12, 1899. She listened to the master but did not paint. Conversation strayed over general topics.

> **This evening Monsieur Renoir, speaking of music, violin, and piano, said: It must be very difficult in violin playing as in painting to find the right tone at the first attempt. . . . I consider that an art is inferior when there is a secret: in the painting of Rubens as in that of Velazquez there is nothing hidden, nothing underlying, it is painted from the outset.[156]**

The question of secrecy in painting was a way to foil Degas.

THE "GRAND TOUR" IN RENOIR'S FOOTSTEPS IN PROVENCE (OCTOBER 9–NOVEMBER 7, 1899)

Renoir encouraged the cousins to take a trip to Provence and sent them a letter on September 27.[157] They would follow his advice: from Lyon, go to see the museum; enjoy the landscape by train (low speed) or by boat (on the Rhône); see St. Chamas, etc. They chose to go down the Rhône by boat. Sitting in the front, Julie took out her sketchbook and watercolors. It would be the same in Vienne, Valence, Avignon, Villeneuve, in the garden of the Maison Fragonard perfumery in Grasse, at the Pharo in Marseille, in Martigues. The style, which had become telegraphic, reproduced the sustained rhythm. Their intention was to also paint with oils:

> **Then, we took our paint boxes out of the crate; the colors are mush, everything overtaken by emerald green. In spite of these disasters, the green, and the mosquitoes, we settle down to paint in front of the Flavien arch which, as you contemplate it, appears more and more beautiful. At sunset it becomes superb, the ochres and the golds of the stone are transformed into fiery reds; the lions [of the cornice] stand out clearly against the sky and the walls of old Miramas shine surrounded by a rosy glow that turns into lilac. Then the fires die out, an enveloping charm hovers in the atmosphere.[158]**

On her return, except for a portrait of a "bland model," Julie would not report on her work until the abrupt end of her published journal.

Renoir would send her warm congratulations on the announcement of her marriage to Ernest Rouart:

> **Now I can tell you that he was the fiancé of our dreams. A thousand times bravo!!! . . . I shall order a new suit.[159]**

He would not attend the wedding.

AN ART AT THE SERVICE OF THE FAMILY

"I see Rouart's son so happy . . . good thing to get married . . . ," Degas confided,[160] speaking of a union he had encouraged. Julie Manet would be an artist all her life. A sketch executed on the day of her wedding[161], celebrated as a double ceremony with that of Jeannie and Paul Valéry, announced her new style, tinged with humility. She devoted herself to her new family and gave priority to the work of her husband, Ernest Rouart, as Eugène Manet, her father, had done when he married Berthe Morisot. Henceforth, her diary ceased. Her correspondence, works, and conserved documents continued to give echoes of her artistic activity. Only a few years after her marriage, the letter writer's tone changed. No more composed, colorful descriptions, but arguments reflecting marital discussions, or long, dense, precise missives, dedicated to everyday life.

From the beginning of their marriage, Julie would lead Ernest Rouart to paint *en plein air*, which, as a "disciple of Monsieur Degas,"[162] he did not do. It was as a *plein air* painter that he portrayed her when he painted her portrait (p. 158). Henri Rouart, her father-in-law, wrote to her from his property in La Queue-en-Brie:

> **And during the good weather I am cross I no longer see the two of you working around me, it's so nice.[163]**

The following year, in Brittany, at Kertugal, the couple painted together: "Poor Ernest, who has turned into a landscape painter, ends up running in the rain,"[164] she wrote to her father-in-law, who replied: "I'm glad you can paint."[165]

The freedom of not so long ago, when she traveled with her cousins like a "Flying Squadron," was hard to maintain when it came to looking after the apartment or anticipating a train ride home. Was Ernest caught up in some military obligation? She left for Italy with her son Julien, aged one and a half, accompanied by Paule Gobillard. They stayed in Varese, and while her cousin visited Verona and Venice, she tried her hand at painting a mountain landscape. Her father-in-law, always supportive, wrote to her:

> **I pay you my compliments for doing landscapes. This will allow you to pass time in Italy, and since you have good weather, you are right to make the most of it.[166]**

She painted portraits of her children in pastel and oil, landscapes and outdoor scenes in watercolor, and later drew a group portrait in red chalk.[167] She continued to sign "Julie Manet." Her notebooks would be covered with pencil and colored pencil drawings. In the summer of 1904, she painted her son Julien in the garden of his grandfather's property in La Queue-en-Brie. As a counterpoint, she took a large number of photographs of her models painted in oil or pastel: she painted Julien—"I wanted to finish the portrait of Julien, but it was too windy to paint outside"[168]—and did a portrait of "Zizie" in pastel, then photographed them together. She developed her photographs herself.[169]

> **Where did you put the Mesnil plates? Henri doesn't know where they are . . . How long do you leave proofs in water?[170]**

She used photographic framing when she painted Julien, aged about three, drawing on a chair that served as her table in the dining room of the rue de Villejust (p. 185). Degas had got Mallarmé and Renoir to sit for a double photographic portrait in her home in 1895, which required nine oil lamps and fifteen minutes of posing time.[171] How long did it take Julie for this session in which she photographed "Zizie" with Clément in her arms and Julien by her legs, who, at five years old, could not hold the pose? Later, in 1911, she did an oil painting of the young Augustin Rouart (1907–1997), son of Louis Rouart and Christine Lerolle.

Julie no longer exhibited, it seems, unlike her husband, Ernest, who was admitted in 1903 to the Salon de la Société Nationale des Beaux-Arts and then to the "Engraving" section, and her cousin Paule Gobillard, who copied after Boucher in the Louvre in 1905,[172] and whose single life left her free to pursue a professional activity.

DECORATIVE ARTS AND ILLUSTRATIONS

Invited to come to Renoir's studio, Julie visited him as she had done in the past with Paule and Jeannie.[173] She had always shared his taste for the decorative arts. Around 1907 she painted furniture and a chest of drawers.[174] She also painted a Louis XV period table with curved legs which served as a work desk for Paul Valéry in the rue de Villejust.[175]

Alexis Rouart would seek Julie out as an illustrator, asking her "for something for a postcard."[176] In 1917, Ambroise Vollard, who encouraged many painters to take up etching and lithography, thought "later [to ask her] to do illustrations for something like the lives of saints. He had the idea that a little book on flowers would be right for me," she wrote to Ernest, adding:

> **He also told me that, in collaboration with [Pierre] Bonnard, he was doing a life of the mean Saint Monica, who nevertheless ascended to heaven.[177]**

This project seems to have had no follow-up. On the other hand, Julie, having joined the community of the Blessed Sacrament, made her contribution to religious imagery through the Librairie de l'Art Catholique directed by Louis Rouart, by executing drawings intended to be reproduced in photoengraving (p. 111)[178]. She deployed this talent for illustrating with watercolors on the pages of a handwritten notebook "Le Livre de Jean-Michel," a catechism skillfully conceived by the theologian from Bible excerpts, intended to accompany her grandson who was going to make his communion (p. 120–123).

PLATE PAINTING

Julie's line became meticulous when, in 1936, at the Berthe Morisot exhibition organized at the Knoedler & Co. Gallery in London, she drew with colored pencils, in a notebook, two paintings that she may have discovered at the time, *The Sewing Lesson* and *The Cup of Tea* (p. 115).[179] This meticulousness was also employed in the painting of plates. This practice was linked to the memory of those painted by Degas, which she and Ernest Rouart admired in Alexis Rouart's collection.[180] Her husband died in 1942. An earthenware plate decorated with columbines, signed on the reverse "J M," testifies to her beginnings in this domain[181]. It seems that Paul Valéry shared this activity: this attribution is suggested by the marine decoration, featuring a lobster and various fish, on a large piece, which is comparable by its manner to a painting by him, *Shellfish* (around 1931).[182] Julie executed a series suggesting that she possessed an entomology book she drew on for butterflies, a spider, and other insects (p. 177).

At the age of eighty, Julie Manet received photographers in her rue de Villejust apartment, where some of Berthe Morisot's renovations could still be seen, not to mention her paintings. But was this view an express request on her part, or did it stem from the photographer's attention to the artist she still was: in several shots, one of her own paintings fills the foreground, as if to say that, next to her mother's much admired work, here was an artist not to be neglected. Among her relatives, she could count on the unfailing support of Yvonne Lerolle-Rouart, who lectured her shortly before her death:

> **And aren't you betraying your mission, your great mission to painting? You know what I think about this: you are not free and have no right to despise the immense, exceptional gifts you possess.[183]**

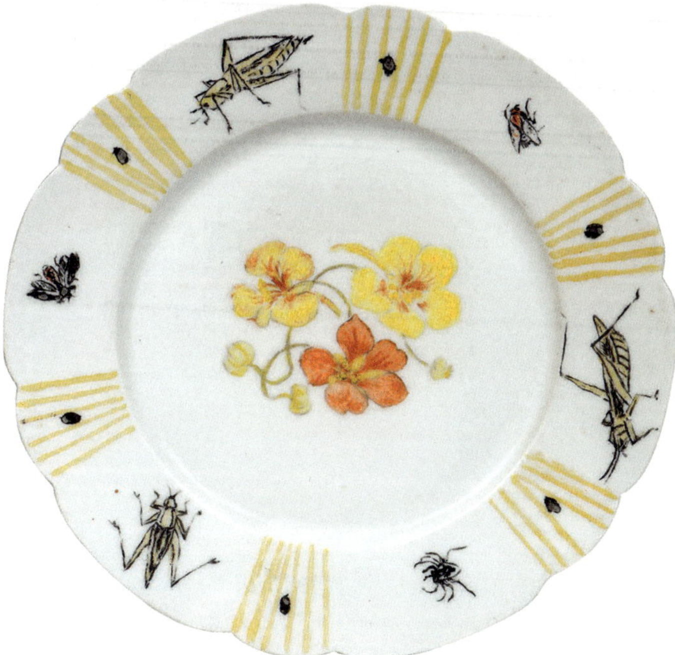

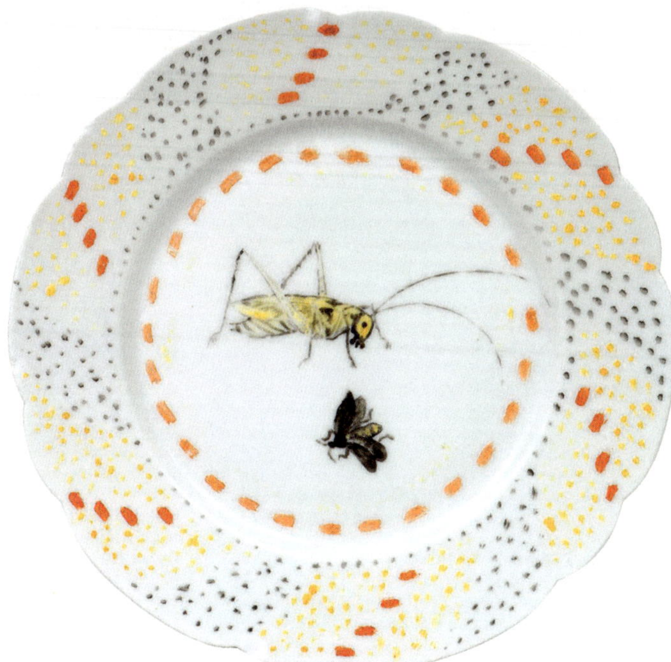

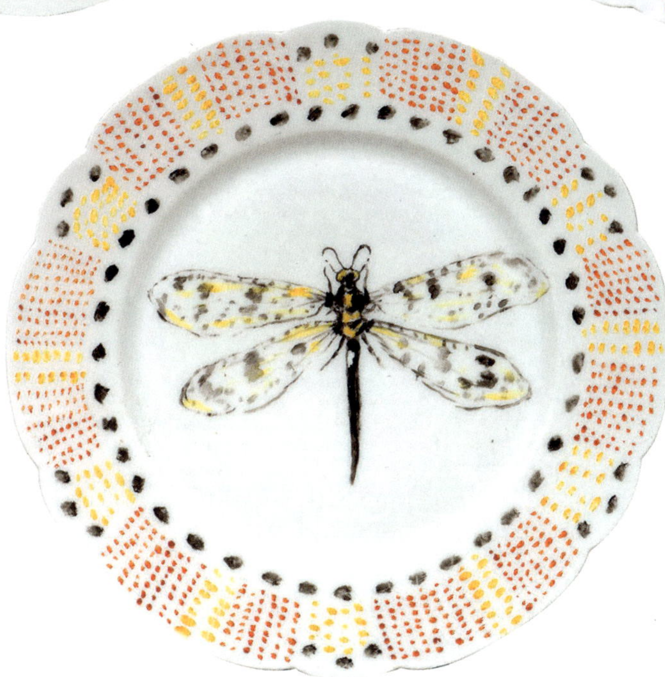

Julie Manet (1878–1966)
Painted plates
Private collection

NOTES

1. Concerning Eugène Manet, the painter, let us cite a dozen paintings stored or rolled up, mentioned in a list of paintings established by his hand, in 1886: "Canvases stored in the rented room at Jennings' / 1886": [Package] No. 9 "Marine by Eugène [Manet]"; [Package] No. 10 "[Landscape] Gennevilliers Eugène [Manet]"; "Rolls of canvases . . . V. Paintings by Eugène [Manet]"; VII. "Canvases by Eugène [Manet]" (Paris, Musée Marmottan Monet, inv. D.4-1986.2013.727). Each roll contains three or four paintings. Eugène Manet was also a pastelist.
2. See the biography of Julie Manet by Marianne Mathieu in this volume.
3. Julie Manet, "Souvenirs d'Édouard Manet," typescript, 2 sheets, n.d. [c. 1960], Arch. BS, inv. 2021.2.479.
4. The Musée Marmottan Monet holds an important collection of letters, documents, and family notebooks, as well as recent loans from Julie Manet's descendants. This collection completes the correspondence published in 1950 by Denis Rouart, the youngest of Julie Manet's three sons (Rouart 1950).
5. Unless otherwise indicated, the works by Julie Manet or attributed by the author to Julie Manet are in private collections.
6. Manet 2017, October 1, 1898, p. 368–369: "I remember Maman reading me passages of this journal [of Delacroix] and it was what started me off scribbling these pages, pointlessly as it turns out."
7. Ibid., October 14, 1897, p. 253.
8. Letter from Berthe Morisot to her sister Edma Pontillon, Bougival, n.d. [summer 1884], in Rouart 1950, p. 122.
9. Letter from Edgar Bèhne to Eugène Manet, Nice, May 7, 1889, Paris, Musée Marmottan Monet, inv. D.4-1986.2013.805. Edgar Bèhne had just published *Le Nouveau Petit Poucet, conte raisonnable* (1885).
10. Rouart 1950, p. 141.
11. Letter from Edgar Bèhne to Eugène Manet, Nice, May 22, 1890, Arch. BS, inv. 2021.2.312.
12. Letter from Edgar Bèhne to Eugène Manet, Nice, May 7, 1889, cited in note 9. The Exposition was held from May 5 to October 13, 1889.
13. Her parents had initiated this talent: "It is a delight for us that your descriptions are so picturesque, so vivid. We almost feel as though we are there; perhaps we would not have as much pleasure by ourselves and would not see such beautiful things so well," letter from Edgar Bèhne to Eugène Manet and his wife, May 22, 1890, Arch. BS, inv. 2021.2.312.
14. Letter from Edma Pontillon to Berthe Morisot, n.d. [c. 1890?], Paris, Musée Marmottan Monet, inv. D.4-1986.2013.70.
15. Julie, then on vacation with her mother, visited Monet in Giverny: "Have you done any beautiful little paintings? When I come back from The Hague, I'll come and see you and you'll show me them" (letter from Suzanne Leenhoff to Julie Manet, The Hague, July 28, 1890, Paris, Musée Marmottan Monet, inv. D.4-1986.2013.419).
16. See the essay in this volume "Julie Manet Model," p. 186–217.
17. Bertrand 2018: "The worst period for left-handed people was the 19th century."
18. Letter from Adèle Pascal to Berthe Morisot, April 13, 1892, Arch. BS, inv. 2021.2.74.
19. "Eugène wants to go to Touraine with Pissaro, it's the end" (letter from Berthe Morisot to Stéphane Mallarmé, April 4, 1892, Paris, Musée Marmottan Monet, inv. D.4-1986.2013.326).
20. Berthe Morisot had copied at the Musée du Louvre, under the direction of Joseph Benoît Guichard in 1858, after Veronese, *The Feast in the House of Simon the Pharisee* (CMR 3, Paris, Musée Marmottan Monet, inv. 6023), then in 1865, after Rubens (Reff 1964, p. 556, note 7).
21. Berthe Morisot, *Two Nymphs Embracing*, Paris, Musée Marmottan Monet, inv. 2020.1.1, painted after François Boucher, *Apollo Revealing his Divinity before the Shepherdess Isse*, 1750, oil on canvas, Tours, Musée des Beaux-Arts, inv. 1794-1-1.
22. Letter from Julie Manet to Paule Gobillard, Trianon, (property of Adèle Pascal), Saint Symphorien, Tours, Wednesday, October 19 [1892], private collection, from a photocopy kindly provided by Bruno Chenique.
23. Léon Bourgeois (1851–1925), politician, minister of the Third Republic, Minister of the Interior in 1890, in charge of Public Instruction and Fine Arts in 1892.
24. Andrea Mantegna (Isola di Carturo, 1430/1431–Mantua, 1506), *The Agony in the Garden*, 71.1 × 93.7 cm, Tours, Musée des Beaux-Arts, inv. 1803-1-24.
25. Letter from Julie Manet to Paule Gobillard, Trianon, (property of Adèle Pascal), Saint Symphorien, Tours, Wednesday, October 19 [1892], private collection, from a photocopy kindly provided by Bruno Chenique.
26. Letter from Julie Manet to Paule Gobillard, Tours (Trianon), Tuesday, November 1 [1892], Paris, Musée Marmottan Monet, inv. D.4-1986.2013.418.1, supplemented by inv. D.4-1986.2013.19.
27. Manet 2017, August 1, 1897, p. 235. Thinking back to her mother's copy, five years later Julie wrote that the two nymphs reminded her "of the first line of *L'après-midi d'un Faune* by Monsieur Mallarmé—The faun: These nymphs I would perpetuate. / So clear / Their light carnation . . ." (Mallarmé 1876, trans. Roger Fry).
28. Letter from Berthe Morisot to Paule Gobillard, Tours (Trianon), n.d. [November 1, 1892], Paris, Musée Marmottan Monet, inv. D.4-1986.2013.19, complementary to inv. D.4-1986.2013.418.1. Contrary to what she wrote, Berthe Morisot painted two landscapes in Tours: the view from one of the museum's windows of the square, its statues, the Loire, and the Saint-Symphorien hillside, and another view of the city from the same hillside, respectively *Paysage de Tours* (CMR 325, repr.) and *Vue de Tours* (CMR 323, not repr.).
29. See Kang 2018.
30. Julie Manet, "Souvenirs d'Édouard Manet," cited in note 3.
31. Pierre-Auguste Renoir would have painted from this model *Young Girls at the Piano*, 1892, oil on canvas, 116 × 90 cm, Paris, Musée d'Orsay, RF 755.
32. Berthe Morisot, *On the Chaise Longue*, 55 × 73 cm, coll. Mr. & Mrs. David Schwartz, New York (CMR 344; p. 161 left). A preparatory pastel and other versions in oil are known; the larger one approaches the portrait, with its tighter framing around the bust and a more accomplished treatment of the facial features: *Young Girl Reclining*, 1893, 65 × 81 cm, New York, private collection (CMR 343). Another version is held at the Musée Léon-Dierx (Saint-Denis-de-La-Réunion): *Girl on the Chaise Longue*, 1893, oil on canvas, 45.9 × 55.1 cm, inv. 1947.01.82 (p. 161 center).
33. Manet 2017, March 4, 1896, p. 169.
34. Letter from Stéphane Mallarmé to Berthe Morisot, August 10, 1893, Paris, Musée Marmottan Monet, inv. D.4-1986.2013.342.
35. Manet 2017, August 25, 1893, p. 40.
36. Ibid., August 27, 1893, p. 10; ibid., August 28, 1893, p. 13.
37. Letter from Suzanne Leenhoff-Manet to Berthe Morisot, Gennevilliers, February 18, 1893, Paris, Musée Marmottan Monet, inv. D.4-1986.2013.42: "It's annoying to need glasses, you'll get used to them."
38. Manet 2017a, September 7, 1893, p. 45–46.
39. Berthe Morisot, *Woman and Girl beside the Lake*, 1894, oil on canvas, 61 × 50 cm, location unknown (CMR 418, repr.).
40. With regard to the Parisian suppliers of Berthe Morisot's and then Julie Manet's painting canvases: several of Julie Manet's canvas stretcher frames of various types are stamped with "P. Aprin / marchand de couleurs fines et de toiles à tableaux / 43, rue de Douai" active from 1880 to 1898, according to the "Guide Labreuche." This mark was already found in 1881–82 on the reverse of Morisot's painting *The Port of Nice*, 1881 or 1882 (CMR 114). On the other hand, the mark of "Tasset, fabricant de couleurs fines, 1 rue Pierre Fontaine, Paris, 9e," a friend of Edgar Degas with whom he exhibited his photographs, is found on a painting by Julie Manet, *In the Garden*, painted at the same time as that by Berthe Morisot (CMR 399) in 1894.
41. English edition, Manet 2017a, September 12, 1893, p. 48.
42. Ibid., September 13, 1893: "at the end of the day worked on the Dome"; and the next day "like these past two days, worked on the Dome," p. 28.
43. In this catalogue: p. 163, 3rd image, stamp of the signature on the lower right-hand side (CMR 354, repr.; sale, London, Sotheby's, March 26, 1986, no. 107): "a preparatory pastel for this painting exists"; Julie Manet, previously attributed to Berthe Morisot: p. 163 4th image, stamp of the signature on the lower right-hand side (CMR 355).
44. CMR 355.
45. Manet 2017a, October 13, 1893, p. 50.
46. Cours de Madame Jammès, formerly Cours Evelart-Deleury, 54, Faubourg Saint Honoré (six-monthly invoice), Paris, Musée Marmottan Monet, inv. D.4-1986.2013.345.
47. "Blanche plays well but lacks breadth in her style. . . . I plan to practice the violin more . . . and learn to play with more gusto." (Manet 2017a, October 18, 1893, p. 50).
48. Berthe Morisot, *Young Girl in a Ball Gown*, oil on canvas, 71.5 × 54 cm, Paris, Musée d'Orsay, inv. RF 843, LUX 326.
49. Manet 2017a, March 17, 1894, p. 57–58.
50. In this catalogue : p. 236 and 238, and Julie Manet, after Édouard Manet, *Portrait of Berthe Morisot*, oil on canvas, private collection.
51. Julie Manet, after Édouard Manet, *Café-concert*, n.d., watercolor on paper, 22 × 25 cm; Julie Manet, after Édouard Manet, *Polichinelle*, n.d., watercolor on paper, 28.5 × 15.5 cm, Paris, Musée Marmottan-Monet, respectively inv. 6167 and inv. 6179.
52. *Autour de Manet* exhibition, Galerie des Beaux-Arts, 140, rue du Faubourg Saint-Honoré, November 25–December 6, 1933: Madames Julie Rouart-Manet, Madeleine Valéry, and Mademoiselle Paule Gobillard exhibited "copies after Manet" ("The loveliest copies in the loveliest setting," *Paris-Soir*, November 30, 1933, p. 3).
53. Anatole Jules de Jouy (1815–1894), lawyer to the Paris appeal court.
54. Manet 2017a, November 2, 1894, p. 64.
55. Letter from Suzanne Leenhoff-Manet to Berthe Morisot, May 31, 1894, Paris, Musée Marmottan Monet, inv. D.4-1986.2013.48.
56. Letter from Suzanne Leenhoff-Manet to Berthe Morisot, January 16, 1895, Paris, Musée Marmottan Monet, inv. D.4-1986.2013.59.
57. Manet 2017a, March 4, 1896 (description of the paintings of the retrospective exhibition), p. 106; see Berthe Morisot, *La Coiffure*, 1894, oil on canvas, 55 × 46 cm, Buenos Aires, Museo Nacional de Bellas Artes (CMR 365, repr.).
58. Manet 2017a, at Renoir's studio, September 8,1893, p. 46; at Monet's studio, October 30, 1893, p. 52.
59. Among the estate jewels bequeathed by Édouard Manet's mother to his widow "the medallion and the gold chain, containing the hair of my poor son," Madame Auguste Manet, will dated June 27, 1883 and deposited January 8, 1885, AN, MC/ET/XCIV/1635.
60. Manet ed. 2017a, August 12 and 18, 1894, p. 60–61.
61. CMR 397 and 398.
62. Berthe Morisot, *In the Garden*, oil on canvas, 50 × 61 cm, Paris, private collection (CMR 399).
63. Julie Manet, *In the Garden*, dimensions unknown, 1894, private collection.
64. Manet 2017, August 16, 1894, p. 54–55.
65. Letter from Edma Pontillon to her sister Berthe Morisot, n.d. [c. 1890], Paris, Musée Marmottan Monet, inv. D.4-1986.2013.70.
66. Letter from Pierre-Auguste Renoir to Claude Monet, March 16, 1895, Artcurial sale, December 13, 2006, no. 258, 8vo.
67. Ibid.
68. "I've been bathing all week—we are absolutely mad on swimming. I can float on my back now and turn over in the water, but I would like to be able to dive and really swim properly. It's extremely pleasant to take a dip, surrounded by this beautiful coastline after having had the sun on one's back all morning, painting." Manet, 2017a, September 22, 1895, p. 77–78. The image of the three cousins frolicking in the water irresistibly

evokes *The Diana Basin* (François Girardon), which Renoir had used as inspiration for his *The Great Bathers* (1884–87, Philadelphia Museum of Art). This bas-relief had been the source of exchanges between Renoir and Morisot, who sketched it on a double page of one of her notebooks (Berthe Morisot, "green notebook A", 1885–86, fol. 21 verso–22 recto, Paris, Musée Marmottan Monet, inv. D.5-1986.2014.2).
69. Manet 2017a, October 4, 1895, p. 79.
70. Ibid., September 1, 1895, p. 116.
71. Édouard Manet, *Luncheon on the Grass*, 1863, oil on canvas, 207 × 265 cm, Musée d'Orsay, inv. RF 1668; Berthe Morisot, *Child on the Grass in England*, 1875, oil on canvas, 41 × 51, private collection (CMR 48).
72. Julia Guillou (1848–1927), the "good hostess."
73. Manet 2017a, August 30, 1895, p. 76.
74. Julie Manet, *Young Woman with an Apron*, private collection.
75. Manet 2017a, August 23, 1895, p. 113–114.
76. Ibid., September 2, 1895, p. 117.
77. Ibid., September 4, 1895, p. 119.
78. D 1904, repr.
79. Manet 2017, September 7, 1895, p. 120.
80. Ibid., September 17, 1895, p. 122.
81. Rouart 1950, p. 15. See Wojciechowski 2019, p. 236, note 32.
82. Manet 2017, September 14–18, 1895, p. 121–123.
83. Paris, Salon des Indépendants 1896, Julie Manet, no. 697 (Lobstein 2003).
84. Manet 2017a, September 26, 1895, p. 79.
85. Ibid., September 7, 1895, p. 120.
86. Paris, Salon des Indépendants 1896, Julie Manet, no. 696 (Lobstein 2003).
87. Renoir, *Young Girls at the Piano*, mentioned in note 31.
88. See also Julie Manet, *Jeannie Gobillard at the Piano*, n.d., oil on canvas (Manet 1987, p. 166, repr.).
89. Manet 2017, March 4, 1896, p. 147–176.
90. Ibid., August 17, 1896, p. 178.
91. Ibid., September 4, 1893, p. 23.
92. Ibid., August 28, 1896, p. 181.
93. *Lanterne magique de Geneviève Mallarmé*, Vulaines-sur-Seine, Musée Départemental Stéphane-Mallarmé, inv. 2203.2-4. Among the company, the pianist Misia Natanson, the Angoulvent family, Madame Marchand.
94. See in this book, Marianne Mathieu, "The Flying Squadron," p. 44–57.
95. Manet 2017a, November 17, 1895, p. 83.
96. Ibid., November 20 and 29, 1895, p. 83–85 and 85–88.
97. Letter from Renoir to Julie Manet, n.d., Paris, Musée Marmottan Monet, inv. D.4-1986.2013.157; and letter from Renoir to Julie Manet, n.d., Paris, Musée Marmottan Monet, inv. D.4-1986.2013.156.
98. Manet 2017, December 7, 1896, p. 221.
99. Letter from Renoir to Julie Manet, August 5, 1897, Paris, Musée Marmottan Monet, inv. D.4-1986.2013.154: "I have a crazy need to paint . . . Should you forget, the name of the railway station is Bar-sur-Seine . . . In case you arrive at an ungodly hour, go to the Hotel de la Fontaine in Bar-sur-Seine."
100. Manet 2017, September 16, 1897, p. 245.
101. Bashkirtseff 1890.
102. Manet 2017, November 18, 1897, p. 266.
103. Ibid., November 18, 1897, p. 266.
104. Ibid., September 16, 1897, p. 245.
105. Ibid., September 22, 1897, p. 247.
106. Ibid., September 16, 1897, p. 246.
107. Ibid., September 20, 1897, p. 247.
108. Ibid., October 28, 1897, p. 260.
109. Ibid., October 14, 1897, p. 253.
110. Ibid.
111. "I am thinking these days of vigorous coloring while trying steer clear of the hardness that is one of my faults. I think of the things about painting written by Riesener that are so pretty, so much of a painter, a colorist. And I think of thoughts about painting scattered in a notebook among Maman's drawings. What beautiful lines hatched from this celestial painting!" Manet 2017, p. 224, December 15, 1896. Berthe Morisot had copied "about 135 pages" of Léon Riesener writings (Viallefond 1955, p. 39). These notes appear to be lost.
112. Ibid.
113. Breuille 1992, p. 315.
114. Manet 2017, October 19, 1897, p. 255–256.
115. AN, AMN, Musée du Louvre (LL series), copyist register, Italian school, Spanish school, English school (1893–1920), cote 20150337/468: "Caliari (Paolo known as Veronese), no. 1190 Holy Family," "1897 November 11 / Mlle Manet / [no.] 72 / 6." Paolo Veronese, *Virgin and Child between St. Justine and St. Georges, with a Benedictine monk*, sixteenth century, oil on canvas, 100 × 99 cm, Paris, Musée du Louvre, Department of Paintings, INV. 139.
116. AN (see above, note 115): on November 11, 1897, the day when Julie copied, it was Monsieur Winter who copied this painting (card [no.] 662); November 25 it was "Madame de Blacas" (card [no] 705 / 23).
117. Édouard Manet, copy of *The Virgin and Child with Saint Catherine and a Shepherd*, known as *The Madonna of the Rabbit*, after Titian (p. 60). Reff dates Manet's copy as 1852 or 1854 according to his other copies recorded in the copyist registers (Reff 1964, p. 556). Paule Gobillard could not have seen this copy sold by Manet to the baritone and collector Jean-Baptiste Faure in January 1875.
118. Baudot 1949, p. 34– 35.
119. Manet 2017, 16, 17, 18, [sessions n.d.], November 27, December 3, 8, 17, 18, 1897; January 4, 1898, p. 263–277 (in part).
120. Ibid., November 16, 1897, p. 264.
121. Ibid., December 3, 1897, p. 269.
122. Ibid., November 17, 1897, p. 265..
123. Ibid., December 8, 1897, p. 270.
124. Ibid.
125. AN (see, note 105), "Mantegna (Andrea) No. 1376 *La Sagesse victorieuse des Vices* / 1897 November 5 / Monsieur Rouart / [no.] 214 /2 – taken away without registration." Andrea Mantegna, *Triumph of the Virtues*, 1475–1500, tempera on canvas, 106 × 192 cm, Paris, Musée du Louvre, Department of Paintings, INV. 371.
126. Manet ed. 2017, December 17, 1897, p. 273.
127. See note 21, p. 178.
128. Paris, Salon des Indépendants 1898, Julie Manet, no. 379, *Young Girl with a Dog*; no. 380, *Dahlias* (Lobstein 2003).
129. Manet 2017, April 1, 1898, p. 311: "As J. M. [Michelin] is no longer coming, I finish this painting of Martha, which amuses me. And to mix things up, I've added Laertes."
130. Manet 2017, February 4, 1898, p. 286–287.
131. Ibid., March 1, 1898, p. 293.
132. Ibid., September 19, 1898, p. 365.
133. Ibid., September 29, 1898, p. 368.
134. Ibid., September 24, 1898, p. 366.
135. Ibid., p. 370–372.
136. Oudry 1749.
137. 1898, private collection.
138. Lafenestre [1885].
139. Manet 2017, October 5, 1898, p. 373.
140. Ibid., October 20, 1898, p. 381.
141. Ibid.
142. Ibid., September 4, 1898, p. 357: "Paule and I can paint with Jeanne B. [Baudot] and if Jeanne C. [Clément] comes to Paris this winter it will be lovely for Jeannie to play the piano with her."
143. Ibid., October 25, 1897, p. 258.
144. Ibid., December 8, 1896, p. 221. See Renoir, *Virgin and Child after a Faience*, c. 1900, oil on canvas, 40 × 27 cm, private collection (D 1761, repr.), painted from another piece of earthenware.
145. Manet 2017, January 30, 1899, p. 410.
146. Ibid., January 4, 6–7, 9, 11, 1899, p. 404–405.
147. *Half-Length Reclining Woman*, n.d., private collection.
148. Paule Gobillard, *Portrait of Jeanne Baudot*, repr. in exh. cat. Paris 2004.
149. Manet 2017, March 5, 1899, p. 426.
150. Ibid., January 31, 1899, p. 410.
151. Ibid., April 22, 1899, p. 438.
152. Ibid., June 6, 1899, p. 449.
153. Ibid., February 9, 1899, p. 416.
154. Ibid., February 22, 1899, p. 421.
155. Ibid., July 27, 1899, p. 474.
156. Ibid., August 7, 1899, p. 480–481.
157. Letter from Renoir to Julie Manet, September 27, 1899, Paris, Musée Marmottan Monet, inv. D.4-1986.2013.163.
158. Manet 2017, p. 535–536.
159. Letter from Renoir to Julie Manet, January 17, 1900, Paris, Musée Marmottan Monet, inv. D.4-1986.2013.269.
160. Halévy 1960, p. 130–131, cited in Loyrette, 1991, p. 660.
161. Paris, Musée d'Orsay.
162. Manet 2017a, September 4, 1899, p. 186.
163. Letter from Henri Rouart to Julie Manet-Rouart, August 30, 1900, Paris, Musée Marmottan Monet, inv. D.4-1986.2013.646.
164. Letter from Julie Manet-Rouart to Henri Rouart, August 13, 1901, Paris, Musée Marmottan Monet, inv. D.4-1986.2013.655.
165. Letter from Henri Rouart to Julie Manet-Rouart, August 26, 1901, Paris, Musée Marmottan Monet, inv. D.4-1986.2013.656.
166. Letter from Henri Rouart to Julie Manet-Rouart, September 29, 1902, Paris, Musée Marmottan Monet, inv. D.4-1986.2013.670.
167. *Paul Valéry Surrounded by his Children*, n.d., red chalk on paper, private collection.
168. Letter from Julie Manet-Rouart to Ernest Rouart, October 6, 1904, Arch. du Mesnil, inv. 2021.1.52.
169. Letter from Julie Manet-Rouart to Ernest Rouart, October 6, 1904, Arch. du Mesnil, inv. 2021.1.52.
170. Letter from Julie Manet-Rouart to Ernest Rouart, Tuesday [October 1904], Arch. du Mesnil, inv. 2021.1.50.
171. Loyrette 1991, p. 584–585.
172. AN, AMN, Musée du Louvre (série LL), copyist register, French school (1893–1906), 20150282/179: "Boucher (François) No. 31 *Venus Demanding Arms from Vulcan for Aeneas* / 1905 June 15 / Mademoiselle Gobillard / [no. carte] 401 / 5."
173. Letter from Julie Manet-Rouart to Ernest Rouart, October 17, 1904, Arch. du Mesnil, inv. 2021.1.56; letter from Renoir to Julie Manet-Rouart: "I'm still in my studio. Don't hesitate to pass by whenever you like." Paris, Musée Marmottan Monet, inv. D.4-1986.2013.168 and D.4-1986.2013.170.
174. Letter from Henri Rouart to Julie Manet-Rouart, October 21, 1906, Paris, Musée Marmottan Monet, inv. D.4-1986.2013.686.
175. Sorbonne, Paul Valéry's desk (MO 77). Gift of the Valéry family.
176. Letter from Julie Manet-Rouart to Ernest Rouart, n.d. [October 1904], Arch. du Mesnil, inv. 2021.1.51.
177. Letter from Julie Manet-Rouart to Ernest Rouart, June 28 [1917], Arch. du Mesnil, inv. 2021.1.79.
178. BnF, Department of Prints, AA-3, "Julie Manet illustrateur."
179. Respectively, CMR 147 and CMR 126.
180. Manet ed. 2017, December 12, 1899, p. 556; Jamot, 1924.
181. n.d., private collection.
182. Paul Valéry, *Shellfish*, c. 1931, in Valéry, 1938, repr. p. 210 (fig. 140).
183. Letter from Yvonne Lerolle-Rouart to Julie Manet-Rouart, December 28, 1939, Arch. du Mesnil, inv. 2021.1.564.

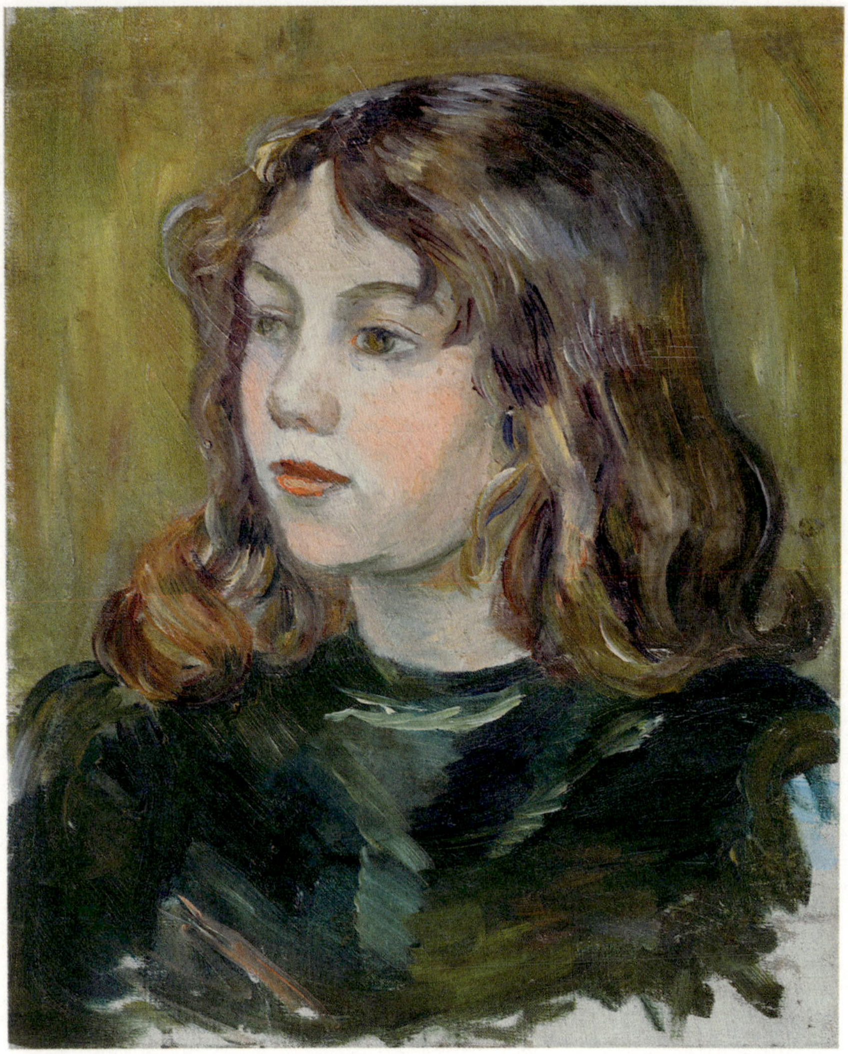

Julie Manet (1878–1966)
Martha in a Green Velvet Dress, 1898
Oil on canvas, 41 × 33 cm
Private collection

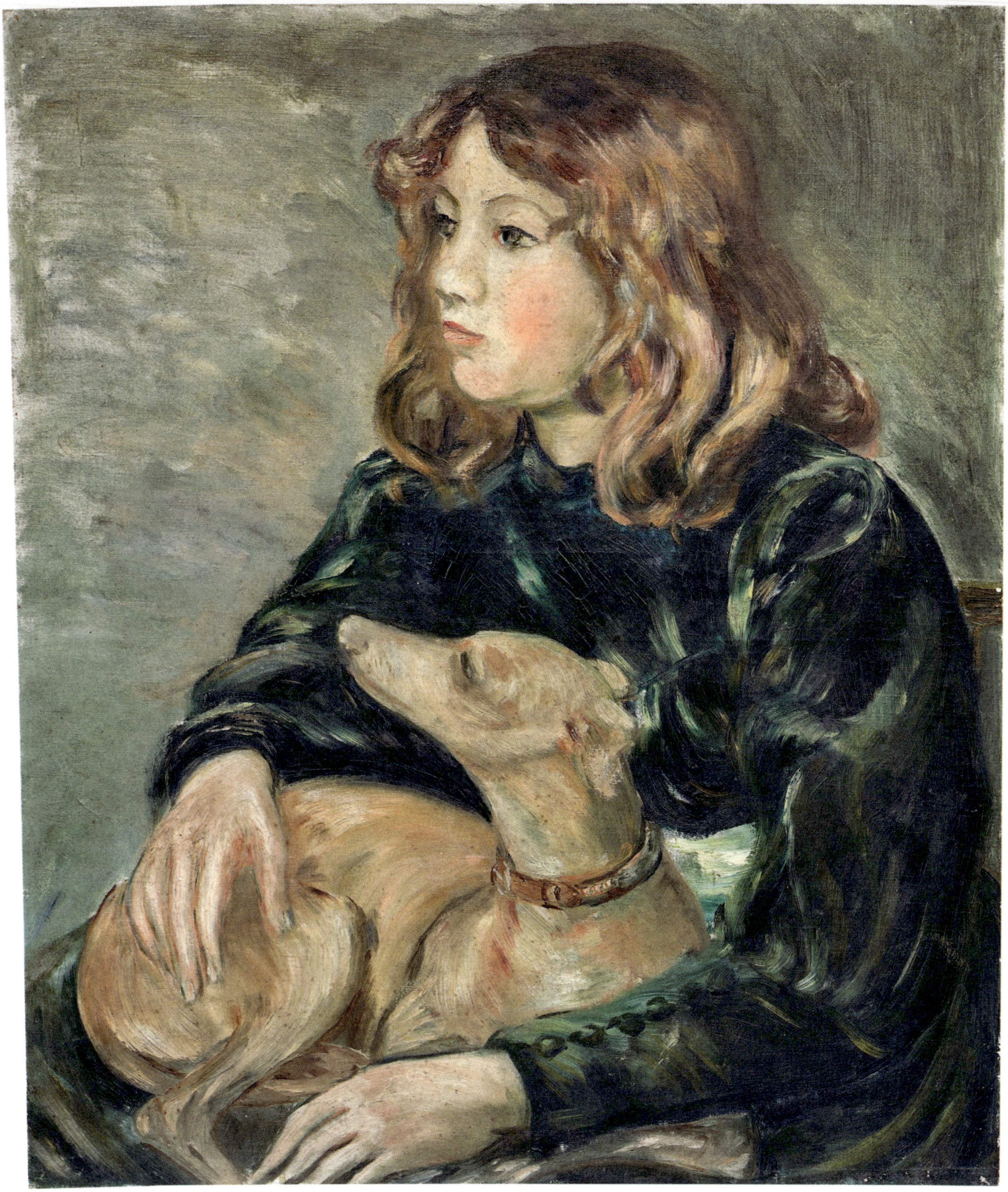

Julie Manet (1878–1966)
Young Girl with Dog, 1898
Oil on canvas, 61 × 50 cm
Private collection

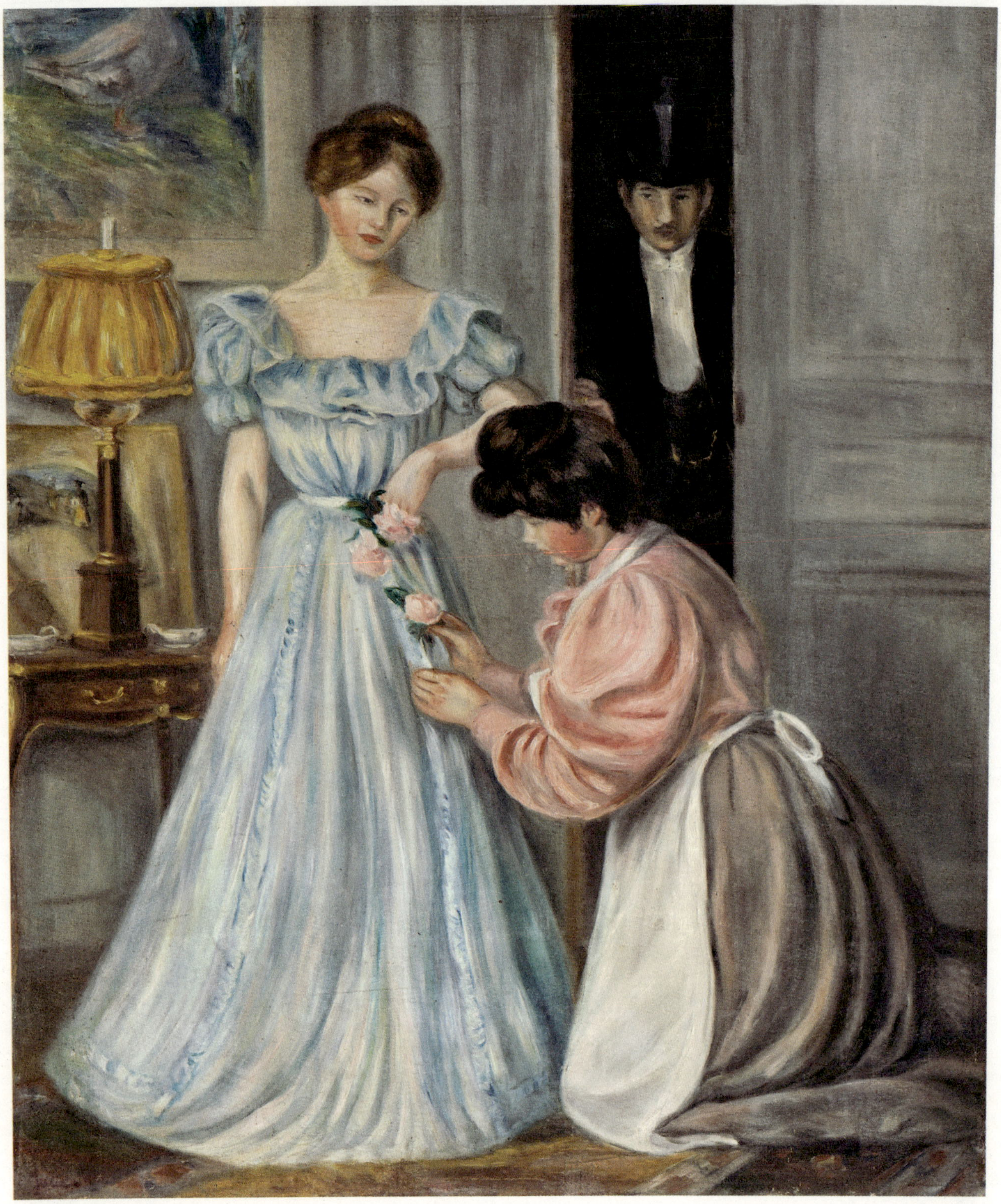

Julie Manet (1878–1966)
Before the Ball, January 1899
Oil on canvas, 100 × 81 cm
Private collection

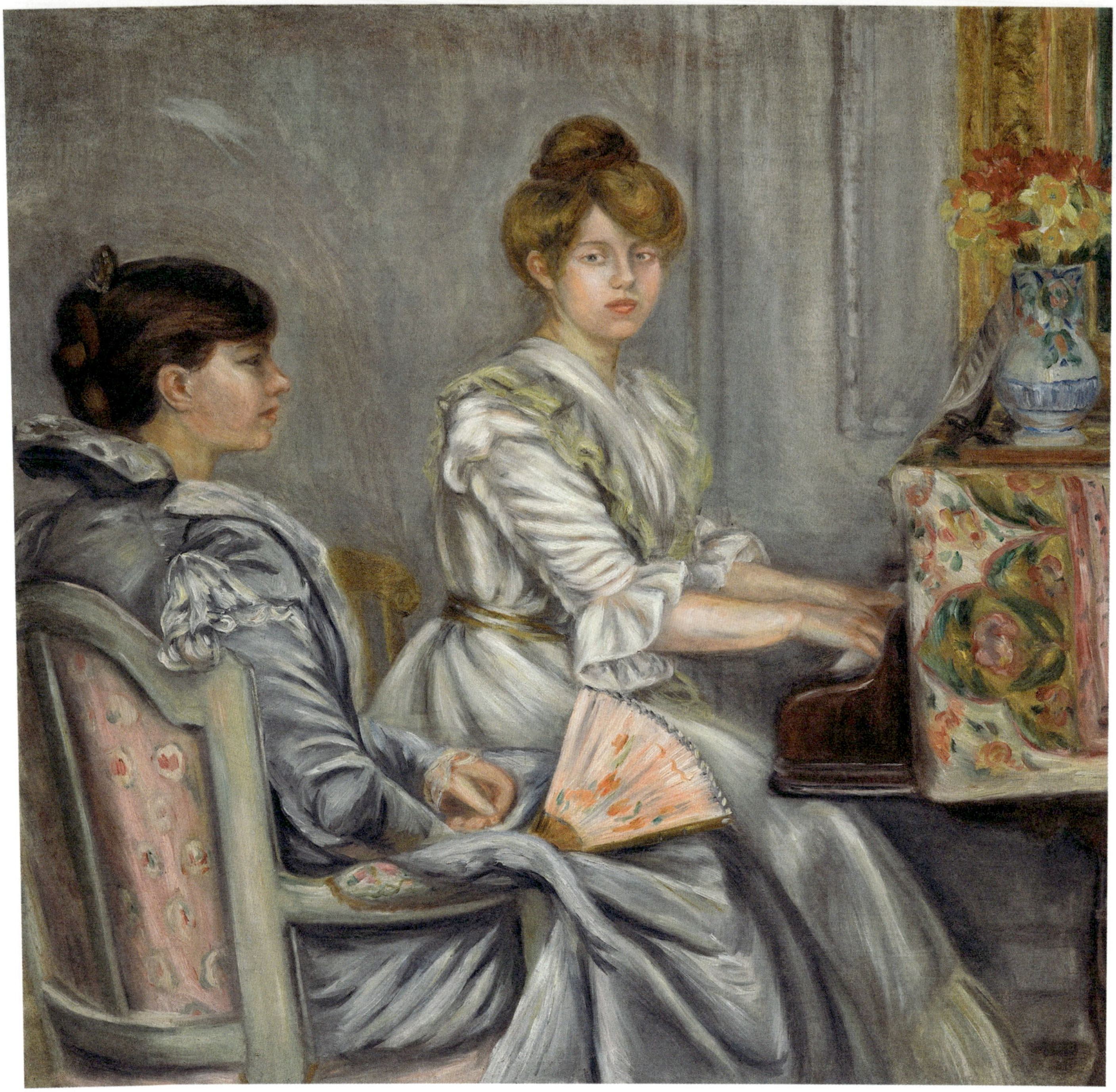

Julie Manet (1878–1966)
Portraits of Jeannie at the Piano and Paule Listening to Her, 1899
Oil on canvas, 90 × 90 cm
Private collection

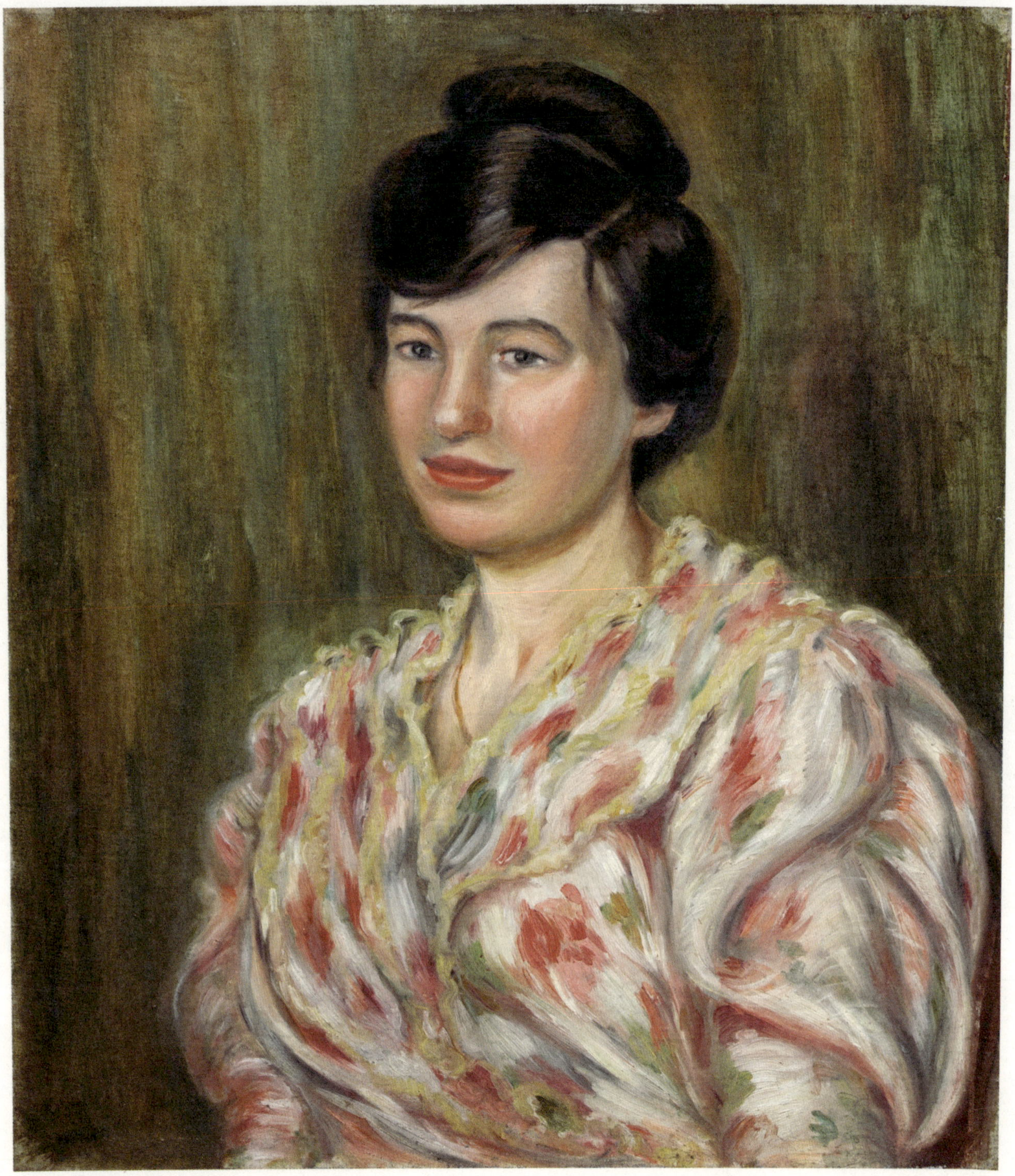

Julie Manet (1878–1966)
Portrait of Jeanne Baudot, January–February 1899
Oil on canvas, 55 × 46.5 cm
Private collection

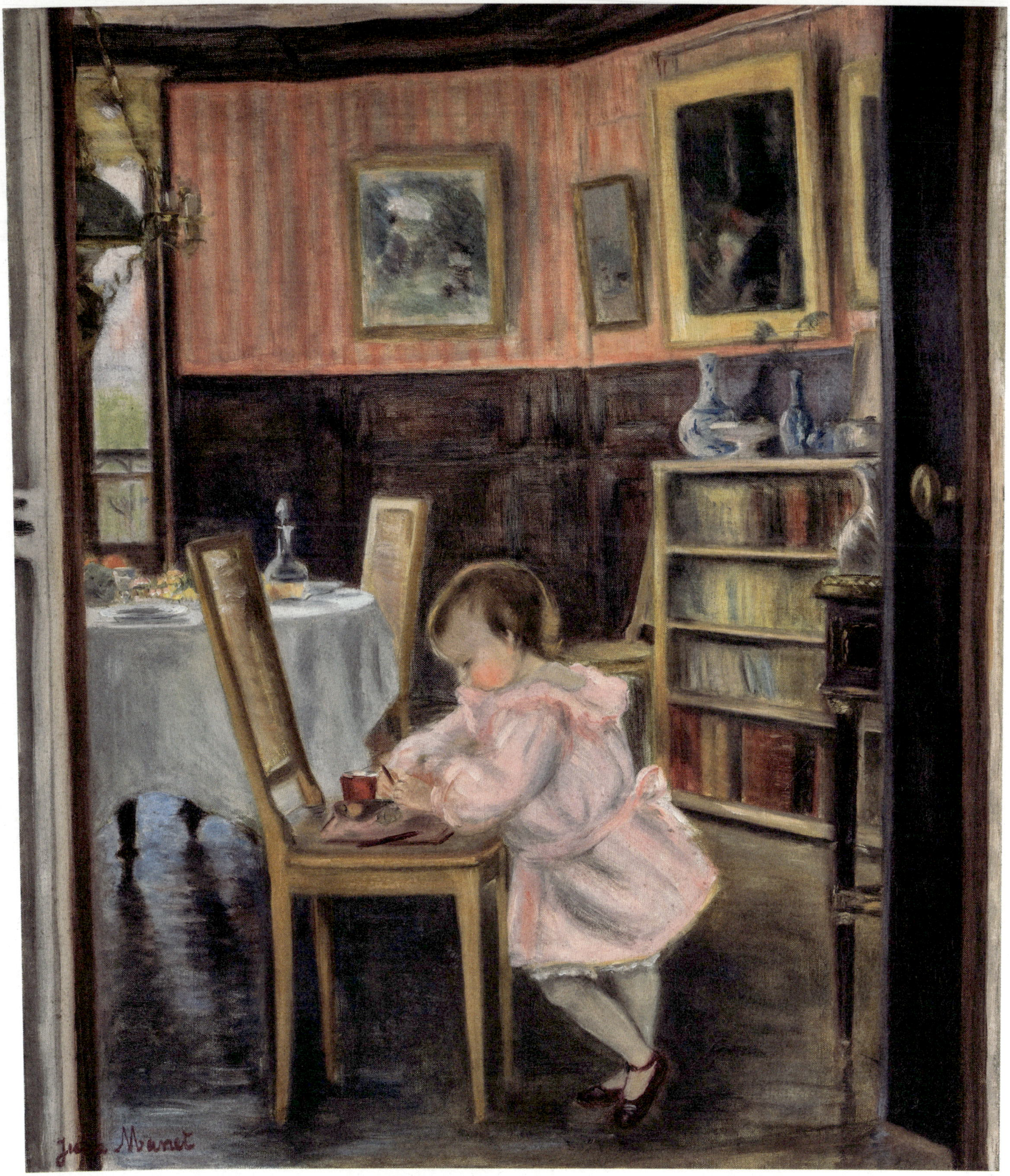

Julie Manet (1878–1966)
Julien Rouart Painting in the Dining Room in the rue de Villejust, c. 1904
Oil on canvas, 65.5 × 54.5 cm
Private collection

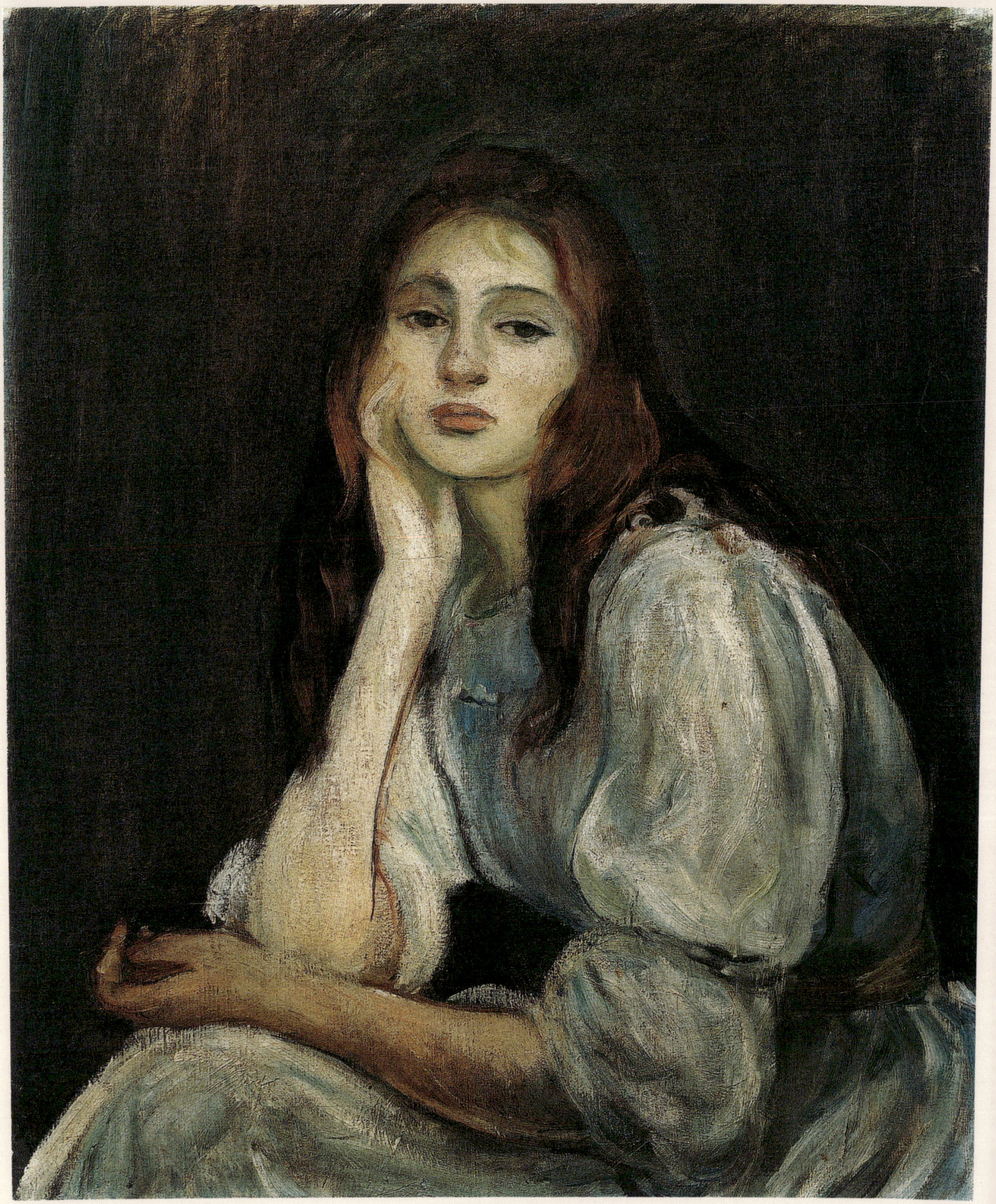

JULIE MANET MODEL

A NATURAL ART OF THE POSE

DOMINIQUE D'ARNOULT

Julie Manet posed for about thirty portraits[1] during the first forty years of her life. During the Impressionist period, Édouard Manet, her uncle, Berthe Morisot, her mother, Armand Guillaumin, Pierre-Auguste Renoir, and, in the next generation, Paule Gobillard, her cousin, and Ernest Rouart, her husband, painted "after" Julie, according to the usual expression used by portrait painters. Guillaumin's pastel has disappeared. Some projects remained unfinished: Marie Cassatt had proposed to paint Julie as a child with her mother;[2] Edgar Degas had the intention of depicting the Eugène Manet family, as shown in one of his letters which has remained unpublished. The preserved group of paintings presents a remarkable unity. Julie Manet posing was at the center of her portraitists' research and experimentation. Her beauty, her focused expression, her apparent calm, although she described herself at twenty-one as a self-restrained passionate person,[3] suited them.

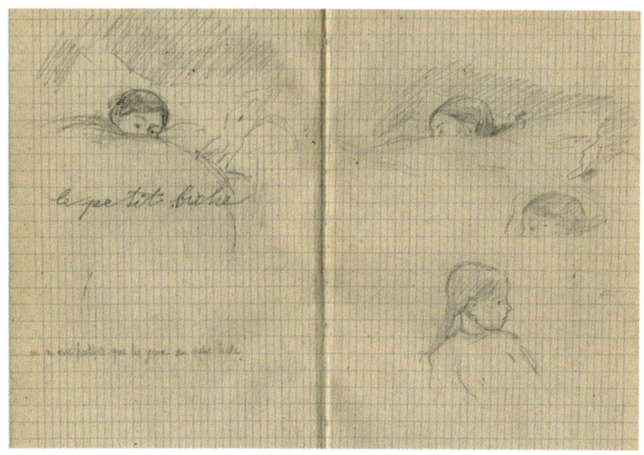

Berthe Morisot (1841–1895)
Page from a sketchbook: *The Little Doe*, 1885–86
Pencil on paper, 17.3 × 23 cm
Paris, Musée Marmottan Monet

ÉDOUARD MANET

Édouard Manet was the first to paint Julie as a baby, in an oil sketch "executed in an hour" (p. 21).[4] Julie would keep this painting and bequeath it to her grandchildren as "My baby portrait."[5] Another time, Manet sketched with an amused brush the child sitting on a watering can in the Rueil garden (p. 188).[6] Julie was then four years old:

> **I see him vaguely in Rueil where he spent his last summer in '82. But I remember going to the garden where his friend Abbé Hurel told me that he would baptize me a second time if I kissed him and I didn't want to kiss him. I had to pose for the sketch on the watering can, I think Maman was sorry he didn't continue it.[7]**

Facing page
Berthe Morisot (1841–1895)
Julie Daydreaming, 1894
Oil on canvas, 65 × 54 cm
Private collection

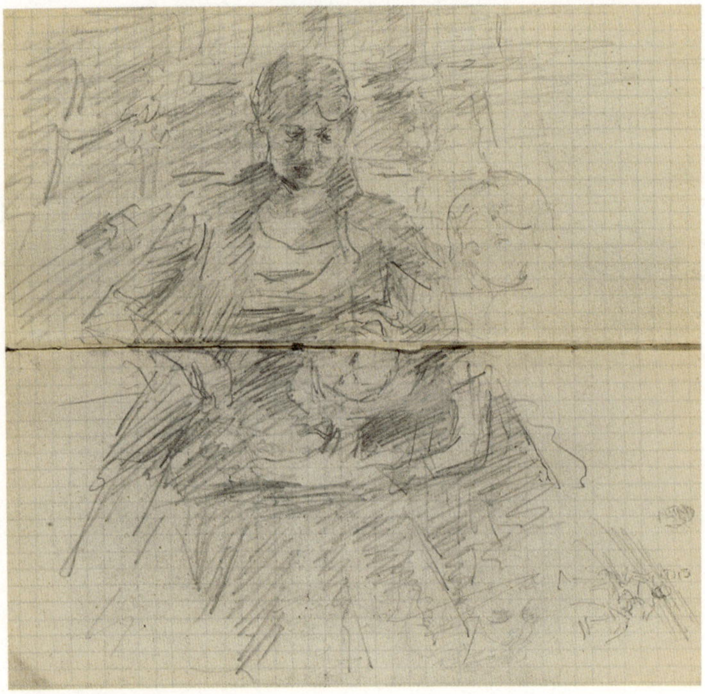

Eugène Manet (1833–1892)
Page from the notebook: *Berthe Morisot and Her Daughter Julie*, c. 1882
Pencil on paper, 16 × 18 cm
Paris, Musée Marmottan Monet

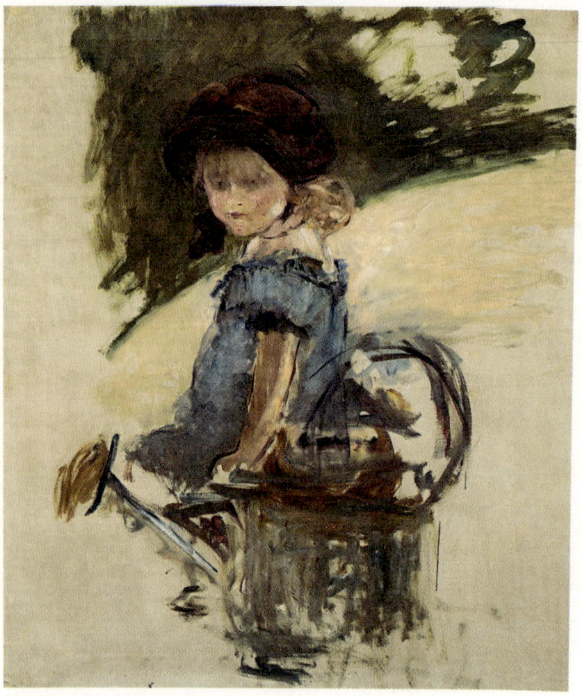

Berthe Morisot (1841–1895)
Julie Manet on the Watering Can, 1882
Oil on canvas, 100 × 81 cm
Private collection

Unfinished as it was, Berthe Morisot copied this painting into her notebook (p. 190 left).[8] It was hung in a prominent position in the living room at Le Mesnil, where Paule Gobillard depicted it decades later.[9]

BERTHE MORISOT, EXCESSIVE AMBITION

More than three quarters of Berthe Morisot's oeuvre post-dated the birth of her daughter, while the time spent with Julie—fourteen years—covered only half of Berthe's career as a painter. The exhibition catalog by Alain Clairet, Delphine Montalant, and Yves Rouart (CMR) lists the oil paintings: four hundred and twenty-three, of which three hundred and twenty-eight were painted after Julie's birth in 1878. Among them, about ninety were devoted to her, which is to say more than a quarter. The same proportion is found in the corpus of the retrospective exhibition in 1896, about one hundred and ten items, of which thirty-one depict Julie to varying degrees.

The omnipresence of Julie as a child in her mother's canvases was unprecedented. She was an integral part of her oeuvre. The child embodied all aspects of it; she was sometimes a motif, sometimes a distant yet recognizable figure. She stimulated the painter's reflection on the place of the figure in the landscape. Berthe then sought to "capture something of what is happening," "an attitude of Julie."[10] Later, Julie would also be Berthe's model and the subject of portraits in the strict sense of the term.[11]

WHAT A MODEL CHILD?

Right from her first months, Julie was kept at a distance in the arms of a nurse, a distance that left her mother free to paint her. Morisot reined in her pride and cast an uncompromising gaze upon her baby—"the head like a paving stone," "Poor Julie, all she has are her big cheeks and her pretty complexion,"[12] or let her delight explode, describing her as a "little cat":

> I'm sure you'll like our little cousin when you get to know her, she loves to laugh and play so much! She's like a little cat who's always in a good mood. She's as round as a ball, with little eyes that sparkle and a big mouth that grins. She makes little faces from the other world and will be a real comedian.[13]

In the end, because of Julie's reluctance to maintain a pose, Berthe was most often forced to make do with her model:

> **I worked in my room and too much; with a model like Bibi, one can only go very slowly if one doesn't want to risk compromising everything. It had worked and it doesn't work anymore. I don't despair of putting it back together, but it will take longer than you think.[14]**

DRAWING AND PAINTING AN ATTITUDE

Berthe captured the first idea of the child, in the form of a sketch drawn in her notebooks or painted in watercolor (p. 187).[15] The child was at the beginning of the process of the painting's development; the landscape came as an addition. A paradoxical aspect of her mother's art of the figure is highlighted in Julie's later descriptions of it. In a small figure, a detail can be "well done":

> **The figure of the woman in blue is full of graceful movement, her hand (even though the figure is tiny) is beautifully executed, taking an orange from a basket.[16]**

Another paradox is that a figure can have "something naive at the same time as knowledgeable.[17]

Elsewhere, Julie can appear twice in a painting, in the center as a portrait and in the background as a secondary character:

> **I am next to her [Jeannie], but I am also represented as a small figure in white carrying a basket in the background.[18]**

Ambiguity reached its apex in *The Mozart Sonata*, an 1894 painting that required five preparatory drawings:

> **This painting is very successful. From a distance you think you can see the figures' features, when you get closer there is nothing.[19]**

The polysemy of the word "figure" is welcome when it can designate the character or the face.

THE PORTRAITS

The list of "Canvases stored in the rented room at Jennings' premises" by Eugene Manet in 1886 includes the first true portraits of Julie:[20]

> **Portraits of Julie at 3 and 4 years old.**
>
> **1. on a chair**
>
> **2. on a bench[21]**
>
> **3. Eugène and Julie[22]**
>
> **4. Portrait of Julie[23]**
>
> **5. Portrait of Paule[24]**

After the double portraits of Julie with her nurse, with Angèle, with her maid Pasie, and with Miss Reynolds, Berthe finally depicted herself with the child in 1882, a painting named by Julie "Portrait of my mother with me."[25] Eugène Manet may have contributed to convincing Berthe to portray herself as a mother: a drawing by his hand shows a first notion of this portrait, probably the subject of exchanges with Berthe (p. 188 left). He also sketched his daughter in his notebooks, which show the sureness of his line. Berthe represented him drawing on his lap with the child in *Eugène Manet and His Daughter in the Garden*, in 1883 (p. 190).[26]

One of the most faithful and rare portraits is undoubtedly the modeled head of Julie, in 1886. Berthe remembered taking sculpture classes with Aimé Millet in 1863 to 1864 and attending the studio of her friend Adèle d'Affry, Duchess Colonna, known as "Marcello." She sought Rodin's technical assistance in casting this head (p. 206), on the advice of Claude Monet,[27] who encouraged her to exhibit the bronze in 1887 at the Galerie Georges Petit. This head would remain among the model's descendants. It would only be cast later.[28]

In the spring of 1889, Berthe embarked on a project for an "Album" in which she wished to capture different moments of Julie's childhood,[29] a project pondered after her attempt at color lithography for the illustration of Mallarmé's poem *White Water Lily*.

Returning to painting, Berthe Morisot then portrayed Julie at the easel in *Girl Drawing* (1891) and *Girl Painting* (1892),[30] in a pose similar to that of the young, accomplished amateur, Caroline Luise painted by Liotard (1746–1747)[31]. The young artist's expression is striking for her candor and naturalness. Seen from a distance, her eyes as if reddened, Julie appears just after the death of her father, *On the Bench at Le Mesnil*,[32] wearing the black wide-brimmed hat that is present in other small paintings from the period of her youthful mourning, in 1892 to 1893. Her face remains vague or sketched in with a few strokes, as in *Little Girl Playing with Her Dog* in 1892[33] or the large *Julie Manet in the Liberty Hat* (p. 41), an unfinished canvas named by Julie "Sketch with a large hat."[34]

In *Julie Daydreaming* (p. 186), Julie is no longer in mourning. With this painting, Berthe achieved her most accomplished portrait. The title under which Julie bequeathed it makes it a manifesto of her mother's thoughts, which she expressed in her notebook:

> **You get restless, wiggle around, no longer understand that nothing is worth two hours spent lying on a deckchair. The dream is life—and the dream is truer**

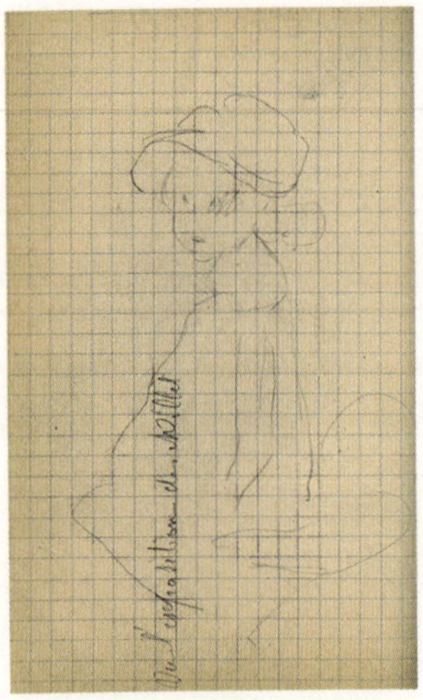

Berthe Morisot (1841–1895)
Page from a sketchbook, 1885–88
Black pencil on paper, 15 × 10.3 cm
Paris, Musée Marmottan Monet

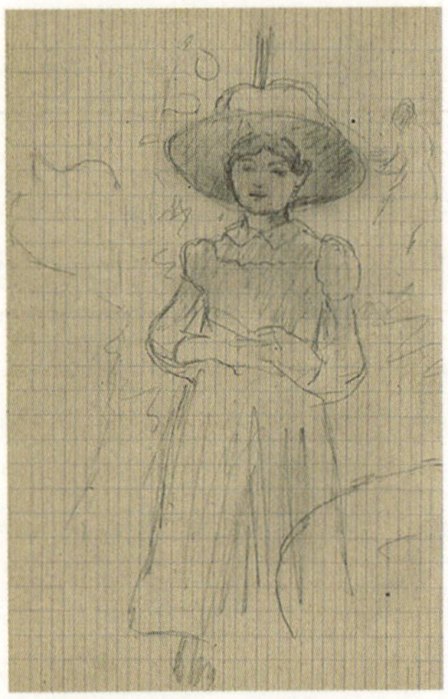

Berthe Morisot (1841–1895)
Double page from the "green notebook B," c. 1888–89
Black pencil on paper, 17.3 × 23.2 cm
Paris, Musée Marmottan Monet

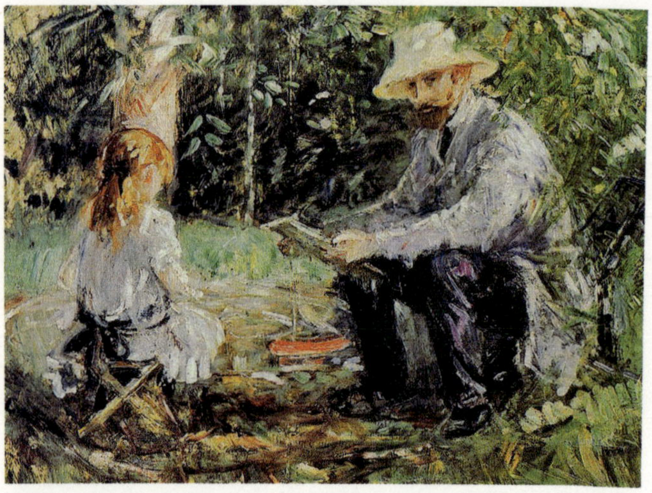

Berthe Morisot (1841–1895)
Eugène Manet and His Daughter in the Garden, 1883
Oil on canvas, 60 × 73 cm
Location unknownn

> **than reality, you are really you—if you have a soul, it is there.**[35]

Berthe Morisot's portraits and figures of Julie Manet show another nature, human, in motion, floral, expressive, treated as an intimate landscape, a private territory that must nevertheless be delivered to the public.

AN EDGAR DEGAS PROJECT

An unpublished and undated letter from Edgar Degas to Berthe reveals that he had begun work on a portrait of the Eugène Manet family:

> **Tuesday evening**
> **Dear Madame**
> **Now your excellent husband has eluded me for Thursday. Tomorrow, Wednesday, I must go to your house, a little for him. For I want to put him in your place in the portrait and it would be very good if I could draw, in the first instance, his proportions in relation to his daughter. So, please give me leave, and trust in my unbearable friendship.**
> **Degas.**[36]

Degas had envisaged a first composition, probably during a sitting with Berthe and Julie. As with his *Portrait of Madame Théodore Gobillard (Yves Morisot, 1838–1893)* in 1869,[37] no doubt he had executed a sketch or preparatory drawing, the first idea for a "portrait" that was to include Berthe, Julie, and Eugène.[38] Eugene had cancelled the following Thursday's sitting, and Degas seemed to request his presence at the sitting scheduled for Berthe and Julie the day after his letter, on Wednesday. The project came to nothing.[39] One could become lost in suppositions about the reasons for this failure.

For the *Portrait of Madame Théodore Gobillard*, he had transferred a preparatory drawing to canvas.[40] In the portrait of Julie in 1887, Renoir used a similar procedure.

PIERRE-AUGUSTE RENOIR

At the request of her parents, Julie posed for Renoir in 1887 in a portrait that he called "Mademoiselle holding a cat in her arms," conserved at the Musée d'Orsay under the title *Child with Cat* (p. 209). The sessions took place at the Morisot family home in the rue de Villejust. Julie is seated on the Restoration period chaise longue on which Ernest Rouart would pose her thirty years later with her three sons (p. 197). In addition to this item of furniture, one recognizes the flowered wallpaper that covered the walls of the apartment. The cat appeared in 1886 on Julie's lap in *The Lesson in the Garden* by Berthe Morisot.[41]

Five preparatory drawings[42] given by Renoir to Berthe Morisot trace the composition's development. He begins by capturing Julie from the front in two sketch drawings[43] and in another more accomplished drawing (p. 208).

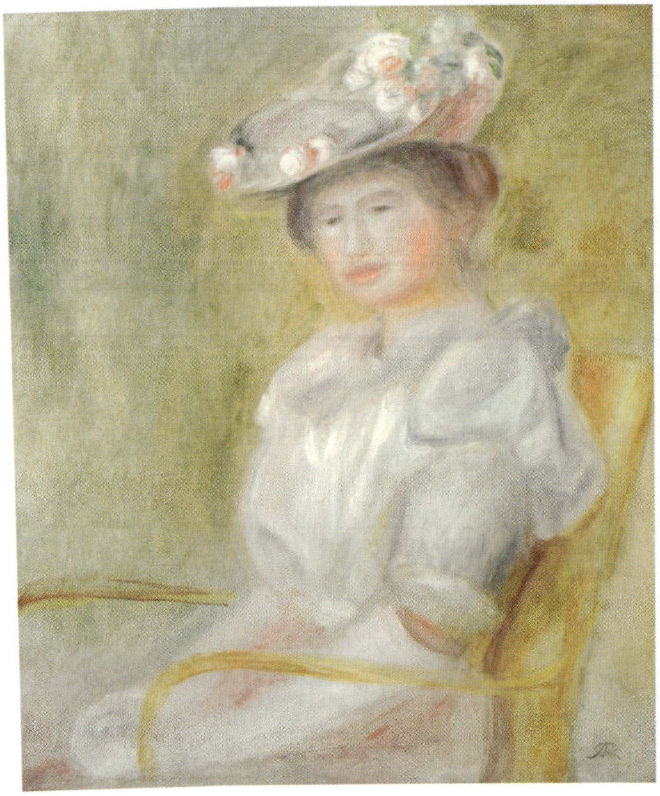

Pierre-Auguste Renoir (1841-1919)
Presumed Portrait of Julie Manet, n.d.
Oil on canvas, 71 × 58.5 cm
Private collection

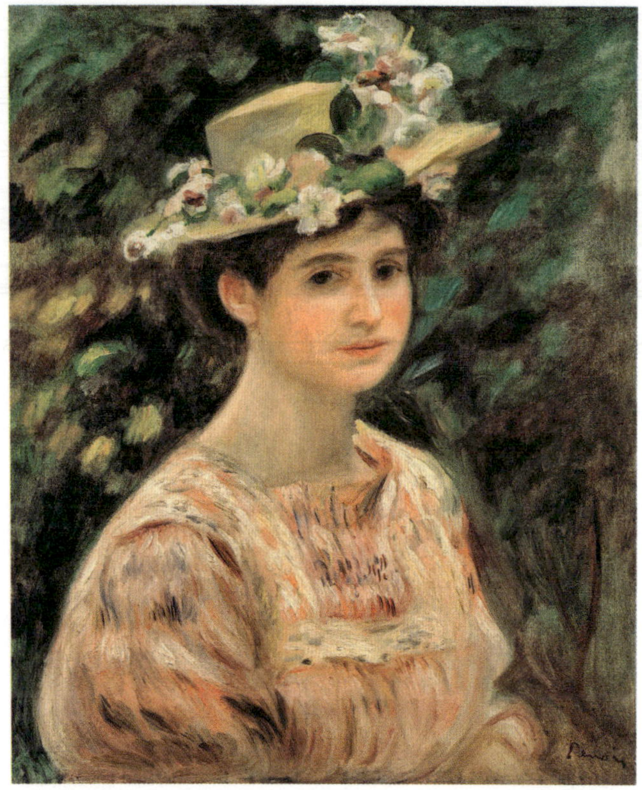

Pierre-Auguste Renoir (1841–1919)
Julie Manet in a Pink Dress and a Hat with Apple Blossom, 1899
Oil on canvas, 54 × 44.4 cm
Location unknown

The melancholy of the expression may have led Renoir to try another slightly three-quarter pose, here with the chin slightly raised (p. 211). Its dimensions are close to those of the final work (p. 209), a similarity made clear by the 1963 testimony in which Julie Manet revealed the process Renoir employed:

> He first primed his canvas with a layer of whitewash. Once the background was dry, he transferred his drawing to a tracing paper to which he applied some red chalk on its reverse side. Then he placed it on the dry canvas, with the red chalk underneath, and went back over the lines with a hard pencil. This is how he was able to transfer the precise contours of the face and the collar onto the prepared canvas, starting from the last preparatory drawing, which left no room for spontaneity.[44]

For Renoir, it was the drawing, more than the painting, which allowed resemblance to be obtained, according to comments he made reported by Jeanne Baudot:

> When Julie Manet was a little girl, her parents asked Renoir to paint her portrait and Paule Gobillard noted the artist's reply: "You can't paint a portrait. The first portraitist who comes along and takes 25 sous from you will do your nose, your eyes, your mouth. As soon as a painter gets involved, there is nothing more, no more likeness. The family is impossible to satisfy. It never understands the color of hair or eyes, not seeing the tone given by the reflections, the surroundings, and the different lights of the day. Degas, on the other hand, clearly set out his conditions. He said, either to the mother or to the husband: 'I am willing to do something after your daughter or your wife, nothing more.' Renoir agreed to the request of Monsieur and Madame Eugene Manet, resulting in the portrait, full of candor and tenderness entitled: "L'Enfant au chat."[45]

Renoir indeed adjusted the "reflections," which is to say, he colored his shadows with the nearest hue, which he lightened, a technique he borrowed from the old masters. He worked on his portraits in the *Ingresque* manner that Berthe Morisot was so fond of. As for the difficult passage from drawing to painting, Julie recounts:

> Renoir had painted his portrait "piece by piece," one day my head and a bit of the background, another day

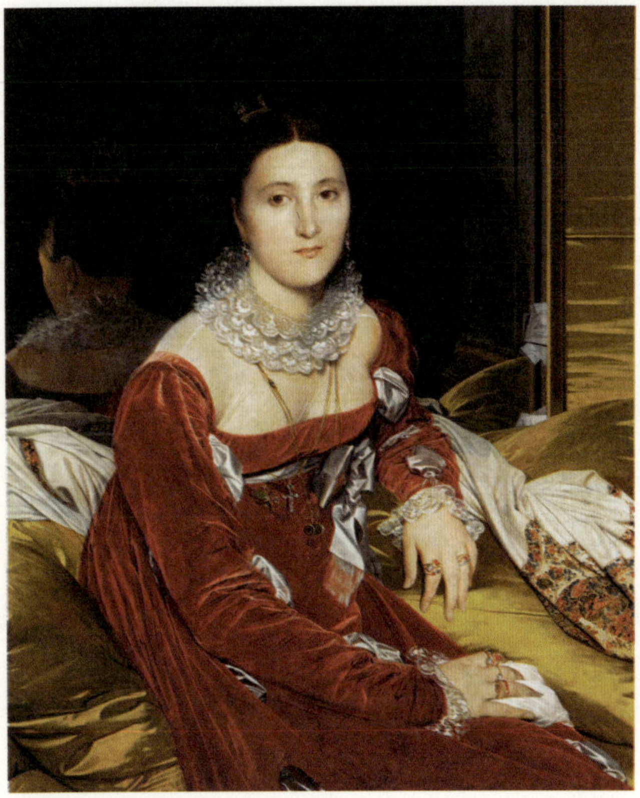

Jean Auguste Dominique Ingres (1780–1867)
Portrait of Madame de Senonnes, 1814
Oil on canvas, 106 × 84 cm
Musée d'Arts de Nantes

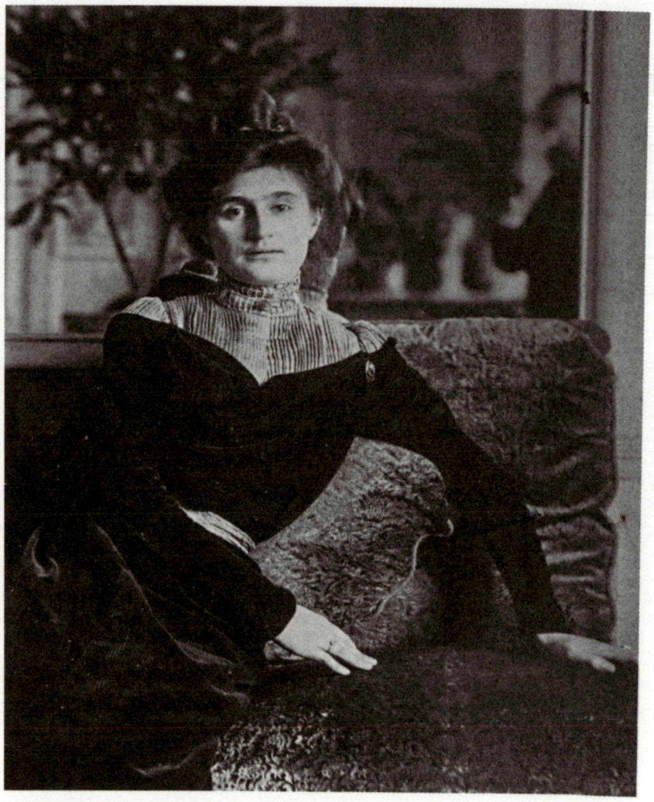

Ernest Rouart (1874–1942)
Julie Manet rue de Villejust and Ernest Rouart (reflected in the mirror), c. 1900, detail
Paris, Musée Marmottan Monet

my dress and the cat, separating the areas of color. In order to delay the drying during the execution, he left the canvas overnight in the dampness of their cellar. Renoir's *Ingresque* manner allowed him to achieve the transparent and soft effect he was looking for. Unfortunately, the undercoat began to crack shortly after the painting was completed.[46]

In the midst of the First World War, Julie Manet-Rouart considered selling her paintings to the Galerie Durand-Ruel, including her portrait called "the girl with the cat," according to an unpublished letter to her husband.[47] In the end, she preferred to keep her portrait all her life.

"THE GIRL WITH THE BEAUTIFUL PAN HAIR"

The portrait dated 1894 (p. 214) illustrates Renoir's affectionate gaze upon Julie, "the girl with the beautiful Pan hair" from his letter of 1890.[48] He had celebrated the mythological deity in a decor painted for his friends the Bérards at the Château de Wargemont.[49] Renoir reprised the pose of the face turned slightly to the right of his first portrait. In mourning for her father, Julie wears a black dress illuminated by a large collar in the style of Velázquez, a reminder of "his ruffs, so light, consisting of white and black, in the paintings in the Madrid Museum."[50]

It was these contrasts that Renoir used the same year when he asked Berthe Morisot to pose with her daughter.[51] He began the portrait in rue Weber with a pastel sketch (p. 43), but eventually preferred to have Berthe and Julie come to his studio in rue de Tourlaque. In the meantime, Julie left the black dress behind, while her mother continued to wear mourning attire, following the customary practice: "For the death of her parents, it is expected that the daughter dresses in black for a year or six months."[52] Julie posed this time from the front, wearing a snowy hat continued by her mother's hair.

Renoir had tried to paint the young woman with one of her cousins, in *Pinning the Hat (Berthe Morisot's Daughter and Her Cousin)*, painted in pastel and then in oil,[53] and *The Two Sisters*.[54] After Berthe's death, during the sojourns that Julie and her cousins spent with his family,[55] the painter planned in 1897 and 1898 to paint the young woman with her cousins, Jeannie and Paule Gobillard.[56] It was then that he executed engravings after *Pinning the Hat*. They were more of a fantasy figure than a portrait and could therefore be marketed.[57]

Julie Manet in a Pink Dress and a Hat with Apple Blossom[58] (p. 191 right), according to Julie's description in her diary, was painted in Saint-Cloud during five sittings, from Saturday, July 29 to Thursday, August 3, 1899:[59] the first time, he started "something after me" (the word "portrait" is not mentioned). On the Monday it was now a "portrait" and was already "very nice"; on Thursday it was finished ("the mastery of the figure, of the foliage's surface is marvelous"). The hat is an artificial assembly concocted by Renoir because in July apple trees are no longer in bloom. Roses are, however, and a study of a seated young woman (p. 191 left)[60] whose hat is decorated with them may be a first attempt at *Julie in a Pink Dress*. The features of the young woman are similar to those of Julie in the pastel sketch of the double portrait in the Musée du Petit Palais (p. 43). The young woman seated in the garden is wearing a white collared dress, which was Julie's customary style, and long gloves—complementary accessories to the hat. Renoir gave the portrait of *Julie in a Pink Dress* to Durand-Ruel.[61] These two paintings would later be found with the dealer Ambroise Vollard.

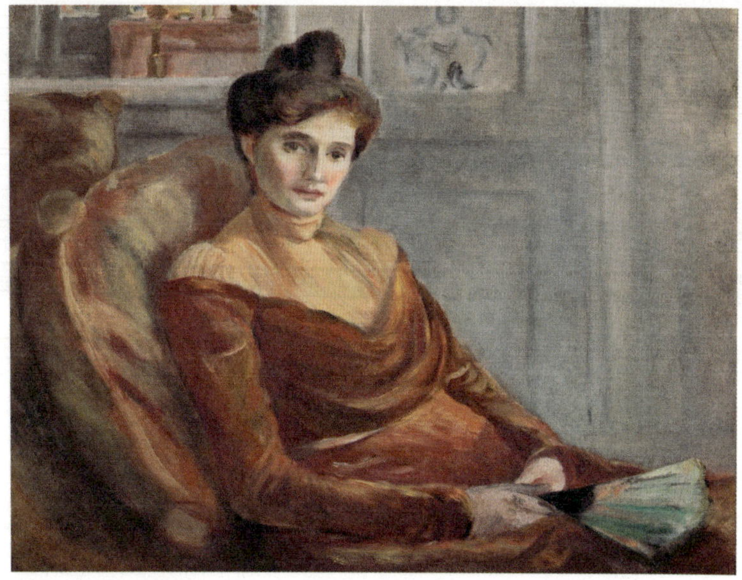

Paule Gobillard (1867-1946)
Julie Resting in Rue de Villejust, c. 1900
Oil on canvas, 37 × 45 cm
Private collection

PAULE GOBILLARD

Paule Gobillard (1867–1946), Julie's older cousin by about ten years, received her artistic education from her aunt, Berthe Morisot, who portrayed her in 1884 and as a painter at the age of twenty, in 1887.[62] After Berthe's death, Paule and her sister Jeannie were at Julie's side. Paule, in charge of her sister's and her cousin's education, as "Demoiselle Patronne" as Mallarmé called her, temporarily abandoned her plans to pursue a professional career as a painter. She accompanied Julie to Renoir's studios, copied with her in the Louvre, and, like her, received advice and guidance.[63] She exhibited and remained attached to Renoir, with whom she also painted in Cagnes. Léon-Paul Fargue, a familiar figure and member of the Académie Mallarmé, would devote several pages to her following his tribute to Paul Valéry, evoking, among the "golden circle" of the rue de Villejust, "her noble and brilliant destiny, steady and meticulous," "a great past, dominated by the Impressionists of the highest order, a past of fine work, of profound manners, and beneath their sweetness, a past of groups."[64]

In rue de Villejust, Paule and Julie painted each other and on April 22, 1899, could show their work to Renoir: Julie produced the *Portraits of Jeannie at the Piano and Paule Listening to Her* (p. 183), and Paule, a *Portrait of Julie in a Red Velvet Dress*:

> Paule showed Monsieur Renoir the portrait of me in a red velvet dress she has just finished and I showed him my study of Jeannie at the piano with Paule listening to her [p. 183]. He gave us a few tips and told us to correct things here and there. Monsieur Renoir is really rather encouraging.

The description of the dress in which Julie indulges a few days earlier could identify the portrait painted by Paule (above):

> A red velvet dress with a lace guimpe placed on pink and a chinchilla border. This dress is very good; Monsieur Renoir said he would like to paint it. It reminded me of the dress of Madame Senonnes by Ingres.[65]

The predilection for Ingres and his *Portrait of Madame de Senonnes* (p. 192), shared with her mother during the trip to Nantes in 1893, was common to the artists of Julie's milieu:

> We hasten to go to the museum to see the portrait of Madame de Senonnes by Ingres. It is a masterpiece.

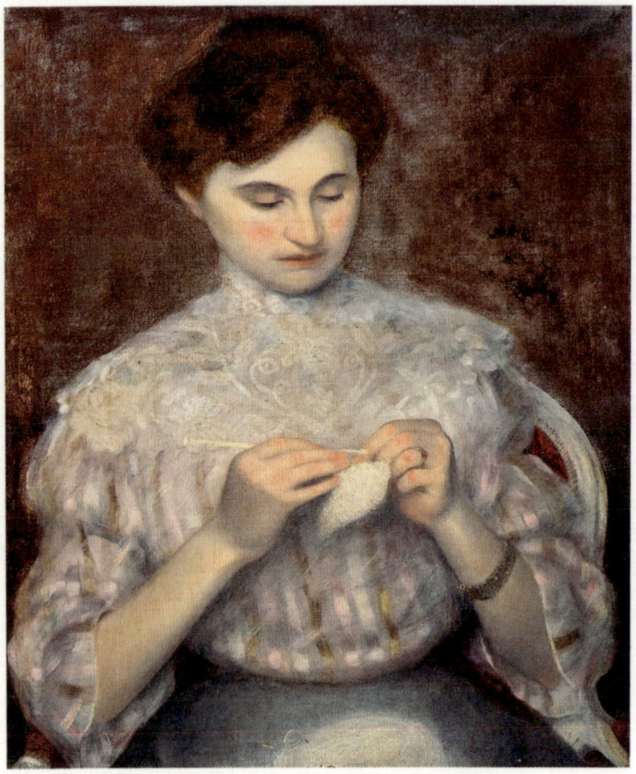

Ernest Rouart (1874–1942)
Julie Doing Crochet, c. 1901
Oil on canvas, 62 × 50 cm
Private collection

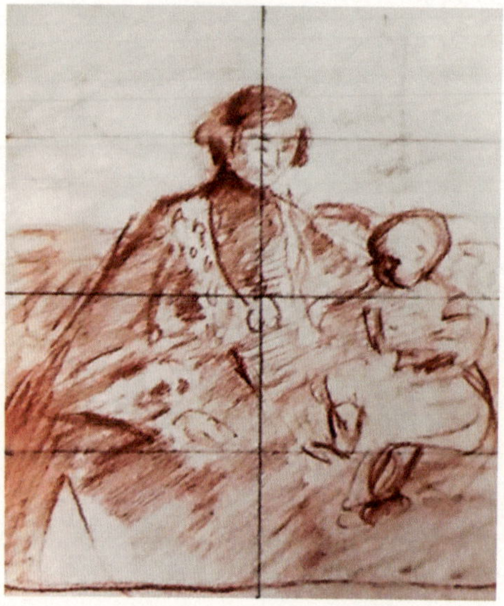

Ernest Rouart (1874–1942)
Sketch of Julie and One of Her Son
Red chalk on paper
Private collection

> **It's a pleasure when it has been some time since one has seen painting to look at a marvel like that. . . . This portrait is extremely well done and at the same time loses nothing of the freshness and lightness of the first brushstrokes.**[66]

The composition inspired Julie's pose in a photograph that Ernest took of her (p. 192 right). This red velvet dress, with its pictorial references, can be found in the undated portrait *Julie Resting in Rue de Villejust* (p. 193),[67] where it is painted in a muted tone, and where the young woman, with a hollowed face and her dress transformed, is holding a closed fan in her lap, in the apartment in the rue de Villejust. Ernest Rouart, whom Degas had introduced to Julie and her cousins at the Louvre in the fall of 1898, had married Julie in May 1900.[68]

Her hands are no longer idle in Paule's depiction of Julie in the garden at Le Mesnil, where she shows her engaged in minor sewing tasks.[69] In the *Portrait of Paul Valéry's Mother and of Julie Manet-Rouart*,[70] Julie, her clothing draped, head resting on her hand in a familiar attitude, is reading to Paul Valéry's mother, Fanny Valéry Grassi (1831–1927), at the Château du Mesnil. The painting was in Paul Valéry's study, in his apartment on the fourth floor of the rue de Villejust, above that of Julie and her husband.

ERNEST ROUART, TIMELESS PORTRAITS

Ernest Rouart (1874–1942) renounced the path of the École Polytechnique opened by his father Henri Rouart in order to train as a painter. He was enrolled at the Académie Julian, as the 1893 list of students reveals,[71] but his name was not associated with any teacher, unlike those of the other students. He was trained "under the tutelage" of his father's friend, Edgar Degas.[72] Ernest also obtained a diploma from the École des Langues Orientales in 1897.[73] Léon-Paul Fargue pictured him again "preparing his canvases, grinding his colors, manipulating acid and handling the tip like a craftsman, meditating for a long time on the means and the ends of his art, as a philosopher who takes pleasure in high solitude and in the silence of labor. He hid from all this, working for his conscience and signing his paintings only at the last minute when he was pressed a little harder to send them to the Salon." He remembered that "he had never lived except for his family and for painting."[74]

JULIE AND DEPICTIONS OF *OTIUM*

Ernest Rouart first painted Julie *en plein air*, converted by her to this practice of painting from nature, in the symbolic place of *otium*, the garden, the setting for moments devoted to painting, reading, or daydreaming. In *Julie Painting* (p. 158), it seems that Ernest wanted to emphasize the fact that Julie painted with her left hand, as Berthe had done. In May 1904, when Julie expressed her wish to Ernest that he finish a portrait of her, was it this one or another?

> Today I tried to do a pastel of Zizie . . . I hear your big head is a big hit in Alexis's store. I still regret that you couldn't finish my portrait.[75]

In *Portrait of Julie in a Yellow Dress*,[76] with its frontal pose, the painter endeavored to capture his model's straight-browed gaze and, in the middle of the cherry season, her curious hat. His *Portrait with an Umbrella*[77] highlights Julie's elegance, seated in a fresh ruffled dress, with a wide ribbon at the waist, while a child stands alongside in an alley of the park.

Ernest Rouart's description of Degas's work speaks clearly of his own research:

> What he [Degas] needed to be satisfied was that his work was complete, not in the perfection of the details, but in the overall impression it should give: first in the construction and in the coordination of the various elements of which it was composed, which is to say, in the accurate relationships of the drawing's lines, of the values, and of the colors among themselves.[78]

He achieved this "coordination of the various elements" in the bust portrait of *Julie Doing Crochet* (p. 194),[79] which he agreed to sign.

JULIE AND HER CHILDREN

The painter reflected on majestic compositions of the mother and her first son Julien. A sketch in red chalk, squared, outlines a mid-length portrait reaching the knees, with the face looking forward, the fabric of the dress widely spread out in the lower part, and the child royally seated to the left of Julie, toward whom he turns (p. 194 right). This project led, after several months of reflection, to a picture painted in the ancient technique of egg tempera, entitled at the 1942 exhibition *The Artist's Wife and Child*.[80] Julie is wearing family jewelry: the bracelet shown in the bust portrait, and three rings representative of her family history. One recognizes the onyx ring passed on by her mother, who had received it from Madame Manet *mère*, according to the wish expressed in her will:

> I give to my daughter-in-law Madame Eugène Manet [Berthe Morisot] . . . The Ring with an engraved Onix [*sic*] that Eugène brought back for me from Italy. My other ring with a number R. M. containing hair of my poor husband will be given in the jewels of my granddaughter Julie Manet.[81]

The dress illustrates her taste for timeless clothes, which she herself sometimes created, a taste shared with her husband. She wrote to him:

> I haven't done anything since yesterday except sewing—my dress is not progressing—and a little music earlier with Valentine. I wanted to finish the portrait of Julien but it was too windy to paint outside.[82]

And later:

> Don't worry about my dress, I'll get it done in November.[83]

The sharpness of the design and the coloring evoke the atmosphere of Japanese prints, as does the patterned fabric, the pink silk lining of the sleeves, the belt's sashes, wide like an *obi*. Julie was not concerned about appearing fashionable, as this other letter suggests:

> I did several boring errands yesterday. At the furriers, it was impossible to make them understand what I want, because they think it won't be fashionable.[84]

The series of portraits of Julie as a mother served as a family album in paintings, for personal use. Photographs taken during the sitting for the paintings can sometimes be used to date works, such as the intimate moment depicted in *Julie with Plait* (p. 196),[85] probably painted in the rue de Villejust during February 1906, judging by the inscription on the reverse of the photograph taken at the same time: "Clément at one month." At Le Mesnil, Ernest painted Julie with Clément on her lap and Julien playing in the foreground.[86]

A photograph[87] allows us to place the large *Portraits of Madame Ernest Rouart and Her Three Sons* (p. 197), showing Julie sitting on a chaise longue surrounded by her three sons, in rue de Villejust. The photograph captured Ernest, in his soldier's uniform, seated on this chaise longue, set slightly to the back, and surrounded by

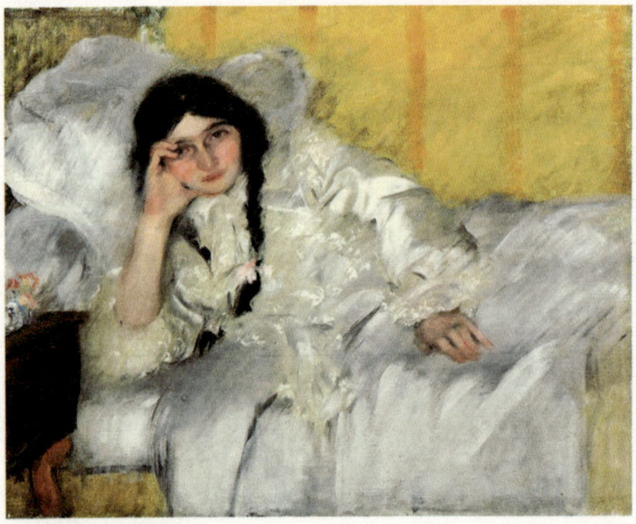

Ernest Rouart (1874–1942)
Julie with Plait, 1906
Oil on canvas, 61 × 73.5 cm
Private collection

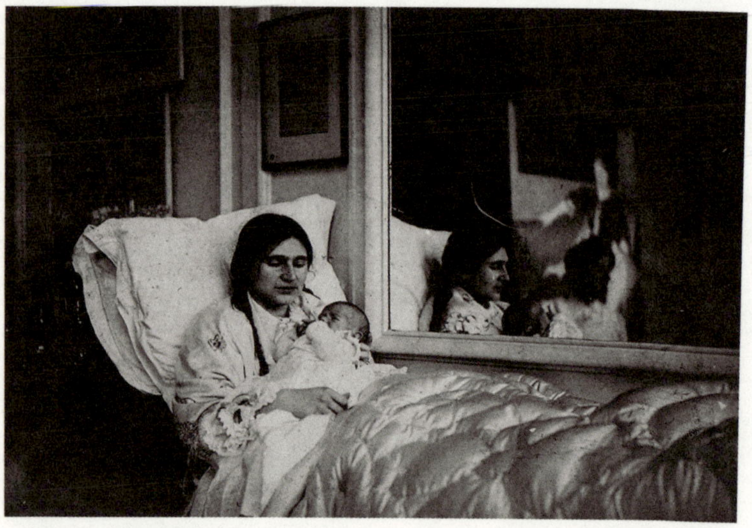

Attributed to Ernest Rouart (1874–1942)
Julie Manet-Rouart at the Birth of her son Clément, Rue de Villejust, 1906
Private collection

his sons. Berthe Morisot used the piece of furniture many times as a setting for her subject, as in *Embroidery*.[88] Emblematic of the Morisot-Manet family apartment for the painting's composition, the chaise longue allows the four heads to be arranged in a movement oriented by the direction of Julie's gaze, from left to right, accompanied by the graceful curve of its asymmetrical headboards. The eyeline goes from Clément, standing up, to Julie, then to Denis, the tip of whose collar coincides with the center of the painting, and from there to the gaze of Julien, the eldest son, focused on a book. Four people think about each other without their eyes meeting, as in the group portrait of the Nabis painters executed by Vallotton in the spirit of Rembrandt.[89] Rouart was indeed the disciple of Degas, who "attached enormous value to the composition, to the general arabesque of the lines, then to the rendering of the form and the modeling, to the accent of the drawing, as he called it."[90]

Beyond the composition, the harmonious colors lend coherence. One thinks of Degas's reflection, transcribed by Berthe in her notebook:

> **Degas says: orange colors, green neutralizes, violet shades.**[91]

The secret language of the painting permeates the furniture, the porcelain coffee service from Limoges, Berthe Morisot's childhood town, Julie's high-waisted dress, inspired by the one in the *Portrait of Madame de Senonnes* (p. 192)—"The dress is short-waisted, she is sitting with great grace"[92]—no jewelry.

The painting remained unfinished, *a fortiori* unsigned, as Clément's sailor collar on the left was not completed.

PORTRAITS OF JULIE THE LETTER-WRITER

Julie no longer posed and Ernest captured her absorbed in her letter-writing activity, or drawing (p. 198 left) in a watercolor dated "August 20, 1916," like the page of a newspaper. It was a family tradition of the cultivated bourgeoisie: Henri Rouart, thus, had painted Madame Rouart at her desk.[93] The natural pose of Julie writing was the subject of two portraits with very different color treatments.

In *Julie Manet Writing* in a white striped dress (p. 155),[94] the face, leaning over the paper, receives the light by reflection. On the table, a powder box—to dry ink before the blotter was invented—and a set of writing paper. Julie is wearing a loose striped summer dress, belted with a black velvet cord, like the tie knotted on the pocket. She is bathed in the morning light that comes from the window opposite her, probably at Le Mesnil. The painter has endeavored to render her concentration, her quietude, her effort. The coloring of the surroundings follows from the stripes of the dress, purple and mahogany. One thinks of the teaching of Degas, who recommended using few different colors.[95] A portrait of a man, painted in an oval, is placed on the dresser.

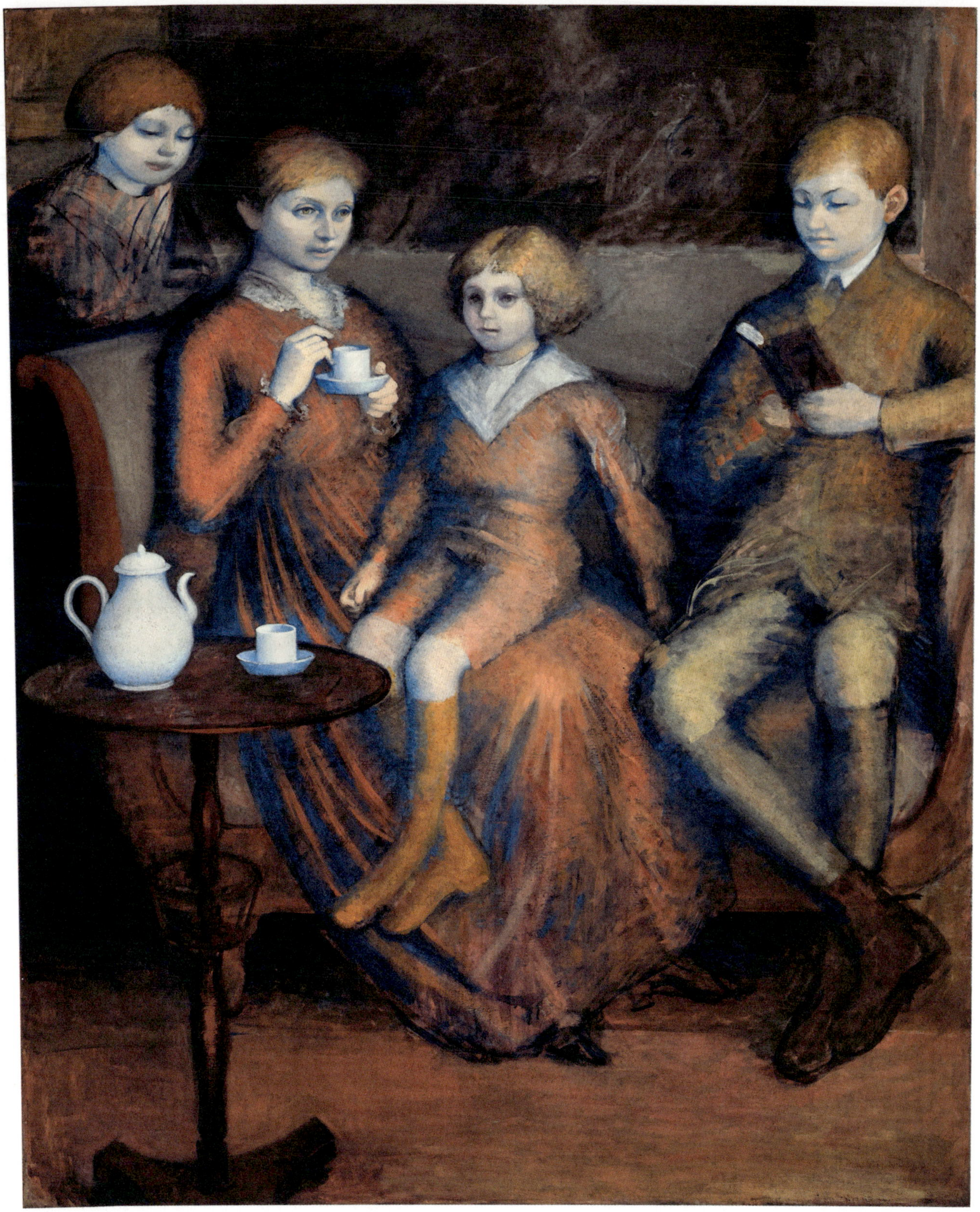

Ernest Rouart (1874–1942)
Portraits of Madame Ernest Rouart and Her Three Sons, c. 1913
Oil on canvas, 162 × 130 cm
Private collection

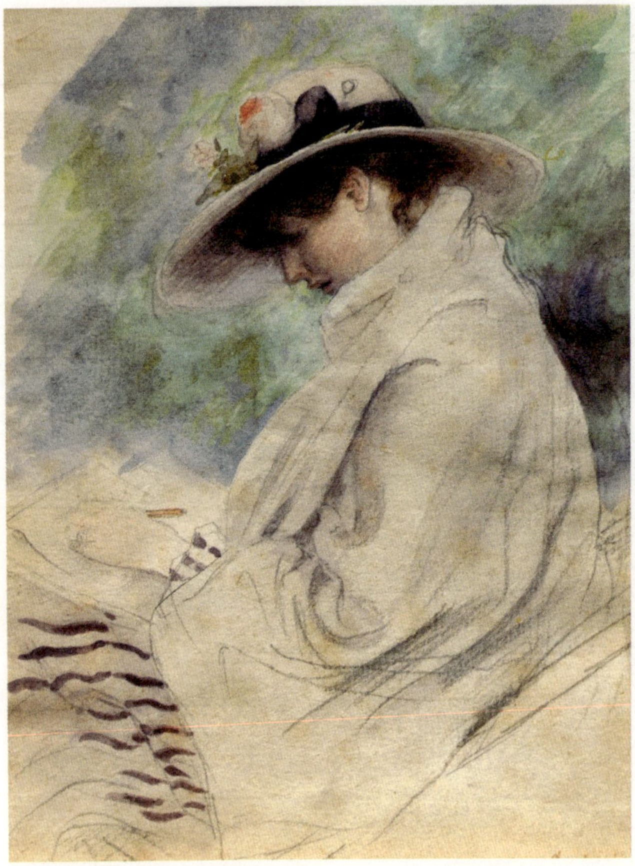

Ernest Rouart (1874–1942)
Julie Manet Drawing, August 20, 1916
Watercolor on paper, 16.5 × 11.5 cm
Private collection

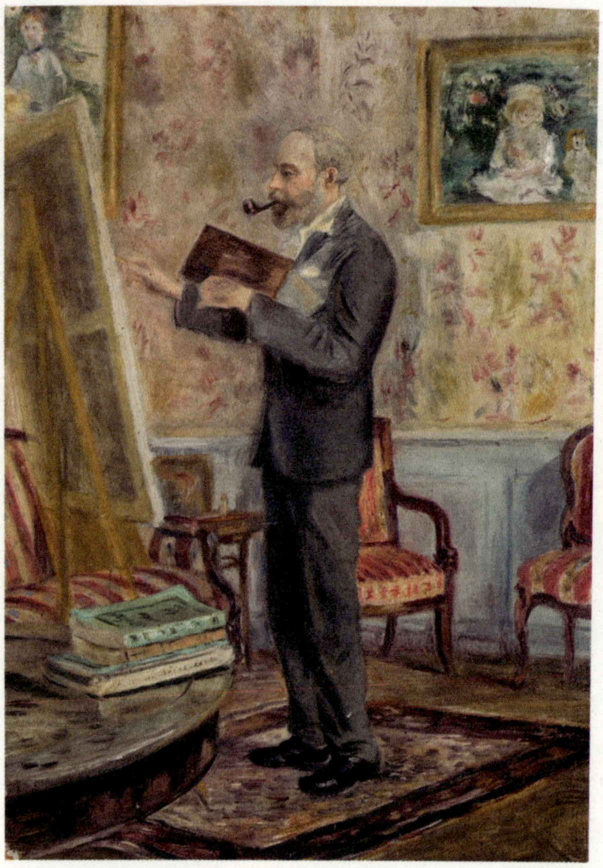

Attributed to Julie Manet (1878–1966)
Portrait of Ernest Rouart, n.d.
Oil on canvas, 55 × 38 cm
Private collection

In *Julie Manet Writing* (p. 199), Ernest painted her against the light, with the light coming from the back of the painting, from the right window. With her head in her left hand, leaning against a mahogany desk, Julie is writing with her right hand, wearing a brown dress of the same hue as the shadow. On the mantelpiece, a bouquet gathers together some end-of-summer flowers: zinnia, gladiolus, rose, and carnation. The cheerfulness of the summer light is reflected on the writing pages, which the shadow tints with all the colors of the background against which Julie stands out. A green reflection streaks across the white of the forearm.

It was undoubtedly Julie who portrayed Ernest Rouart with the attributes of the painter and the thinker, the palette and the book clutched to him, in a portrait showing him at the easel, pipe in mouth, in the Le Mesnil living room (above). The 1942 retrospective exhibition would show this "lost paradise," his oeuvre, "but all the life so intimate and united of Le Mesnil, so happy, your true atmosphere,"[96] Agathe would write. And Jeannie:

> So much of Ernest's presence in these paintings, and of his whole life. That is to say, of yours, in large part. You will be able to see them again, but not grouped so piously. It is still a farewell to something, for the moment.[97]

The heiress of the Morisot-Manet and Rouart collections[98] saw her life exhibited in paintings in 1896 and 1942. Her portrait, *Child with Cat* by Renoir (p. 209), was exhibited in Paris in 1888, 1928, and 1933, and in London in 1953. It has been on display at the Musée d'Orsay since 1999. By Renoir again, the one painted in 1894 is in the Musée Marmottan Monet; as is her portrait in blue jersey painted by Berthe Morisot in pastel (p. 207). Several are in private collections. Most of those that were painted for two reasons, for oneself and as family portraits, and executed by a painter in the family, have remained among her descendants. They depict a moment of grace.

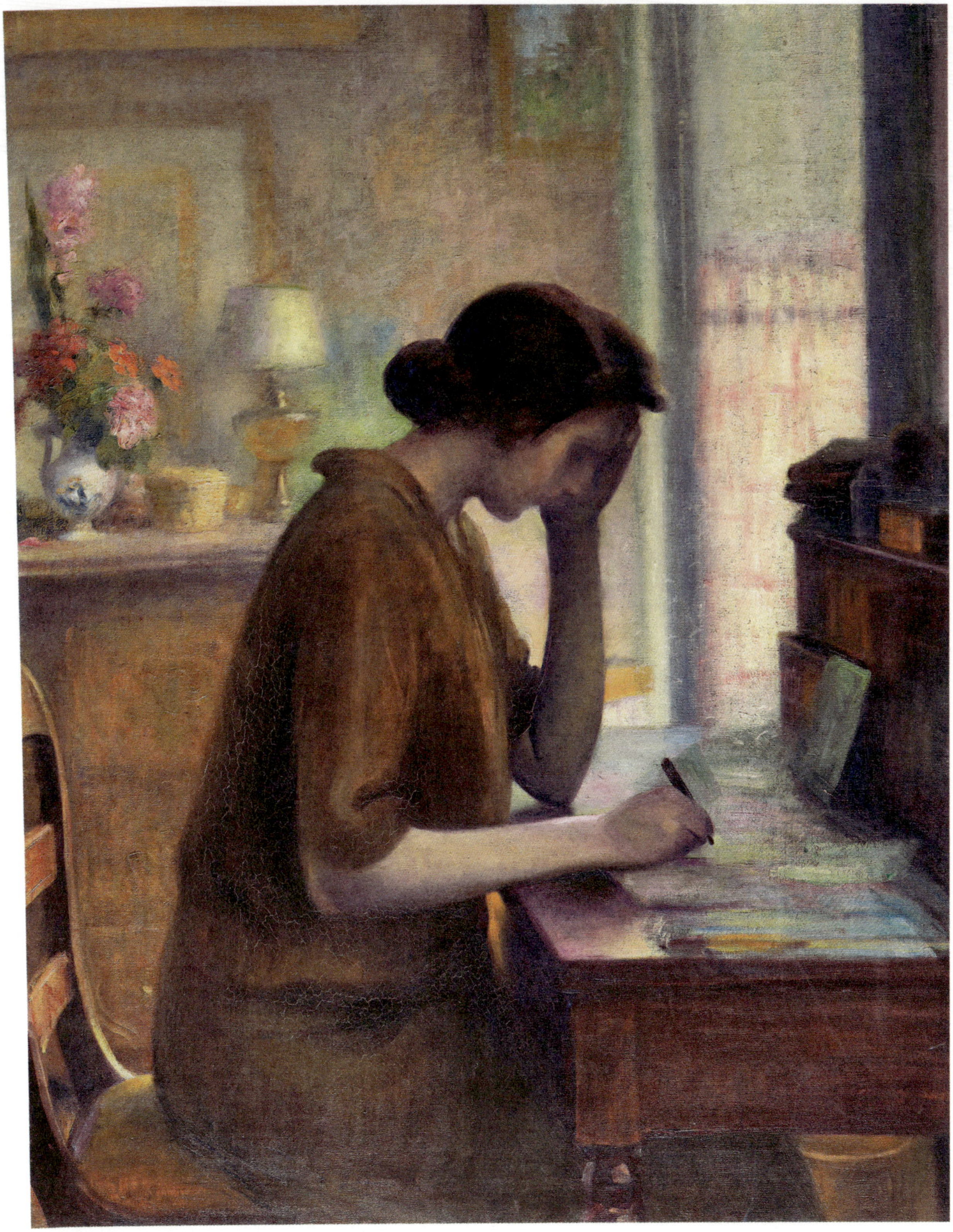

Ernest Rouart (1874–1942)
Julie Manet Writing, n.d.
Oil on canvas, 116.7 × 89.2 cm
Private collection

NOTES

1. The last portrait of Julie, painted in her twilight years, is the work of an American artist whose identity remains to be discovered (Manet 1987, repr. p. 191). Special thanks to Yves Rouart.
2. Letter from Eugène Manet to Berthe Morisot, n.d. [March 1882]: "I met Mademoiselle Cassatt yesterday at the Exhibition who seems to me to want a closer relationship. She asked to do Bibi's portrait and yours. I told her gladly on the condition of reciprocity" (Rouart 1950, p. 111.)
3. Manet 2017, November 14, 1899, p. 544–545.
4. Detail added by Berthe Morisot in a note on the back. Édouard Manet, *Portrait of Julie Manet as a Baby* [1879 or 1880], oil on canvas, 36 × 33 cm, private collection (Rouart and Wildenstein 1975, no. 298; through an inconsistency in the catalog, the painting is dated 1879 and the child is said to be "fifteen months old").
5. See note 11: letter of intent for a bequest to her four grandchildren, handwritten manuscript, c. 1960, Arch. BS, inv. 2021.2.221.
6. RW 399.
7. Julie Manet, "Souvenirs d'Édouard Manet," typescript [n.d., c. 1960], Arch. BS, inv. 2021.2.479.
8. Berthe Morisot, sketchbook, known as the "beige sketchbook," 1885–88, Paris, Musée Marmottan Monet, inv. D.5-1986.2014.1.
9. Paule Gobillard, *Living Room of the Château du Mesnil* [n.d., c. 1920], oil on canvas, 35 × 45 cm, private collection.
10. Berthe Morisot, Mézy notebook, also known as the "black notebook," 1891, Paris, Musée Marmottan Monet, inv. D.5-1986.2014.4.
11. Julie, when giving her grandchildren some of her paintings by her mother, distinguished her "portraits" from other works featuring her for which she did not use this term: "I, the undersigned Julie Manet, residing in Paris (16th) 40 rue Paul Valéry, widow of Ernest Rouart, bequeath to my grandchildren: the following paintings by their great-grandmother Berthe Morisot, 1 . . . My portrait in white entitled: Julie rêveuse 1894 no. 374 of the catalog [Bataille and Wildenstein] [CMR 379]; Portrait de ma mère avec moi 1882 no. 126 of the catalog [BW] [CMR 127]; 2 . . . Sous l'Oranger 1889 no. 237 in the catalog [BW] [CMR 241]; Mon portrait au pastel 1889 no. 552 in the catalog [BW]; 3 . . . Le Mandoline 1889 no. 238 in the catalog [BW] [CMR 242]; Fillettes sur une fenêtre au Mesnil no. 293 in the catalog [BW] [1892, CMR 302]; 4° . . . La Broderie 1889 no. 246 in the catalog [BW] [CMR 250], Sur le banc au Mesnil 1892 no. 304 in the catalog [BW] [CMR 308]. . . . To all four of you, by Édouard Manet . . . My baby portrait," Julie Manet, letter of intent for a bequest to her four grandchildren, manuscript, c. 1960, Arch. BS, inv. 2021.2.221.
12. Letter from Berthe Morisot to her sister Edma, 1879, in the collection of Julie Manet's transcriptions of Berthe Morisot's letters, Arch. BS, inv. 2021.2.579.
13. Letter from Berthe Morisot to Jeanne Pontillon, 1879 (Rouart 1950, p. 100).
14. Letter from Berthe Morisot to Eugène Manet, March 1882 (Rouart 1950, p. 108).
15. Inv. 6030.
16. Manet 2017, March 4, 1896, p. 148 (Berthe Morisot, *Luncheon on the Grass*, 1875, 60 × 74 cm, private collection, CMR 47).
17. Ibid., p. 149–150 (Berthe Morisot, *Interior*, 1872, private collection, CMR 26).
18. Ibid., p. 159 (Berthe Morisot, *The Garden at Portrieux*, 1894, 38 × 55 cm, private collection, CMR 398).
19. Ibid., p. 172 (Berthe Morisot, *The Mozart Sonata*, 1894, 46 × 56 cm, private collection, CMR 382).
20. Eugène Manet, "Toiles remisées dans la Chambre louée Chez Jennings, 1886," "[Rouleau] VI, 4 Portrait de Julie," Paris, Musée Marmottan Monet, inv. D.4-1986.2013.727.
21. CMR 170?
22. CMR 104 (p. 191)?
23. CMR 110?
24. CMR 162?
25. CMR 127, location unknown. Julie Manet, letter of intent to bequeath to her four grandchildren, handwritten manuscript, c. 1960, Arch. BS, inv. 2021.2.221. See note 11.
26. CMR 138.
27. Nivet and Michel 1990, p. 312. See exh. cat. Lille and Martigny 2002, no. 106, p. 342.
28. Letter from Denis Rouart to Alan Dubois, September 28, 1968, Museum of Fine Arts conservation archives, St. Petersburg, cited in Lesko, 1994.
29. See Bailly-Hertzberg 1979, p. 218.
30. Berthe Morisot, *Girl Drawing*, 1891, oil on canvas, 74.5 × 69.5 cm, United States, private collection (CMR 274); Berthe Morisot, *Girl Painting*, 1892, oil on canvas, 40 × 32 cm, location unknown (CMR 296).
31. Jean-Étienne Liotard, *Portrait of Caroline Luise de Hesse-Darmstadt*, 1745–46, pastel on parchment, Karlsruhe, Staatliche Kunsthalle.
32. Berthe Morisot, *On the Bench at Le Mesnil*, 1892, oil on canvas, 38 × 55 cm, private collection (CMR 400).
33. Berthe Morisot, *Girl with Her Dog*, 1892, oil on canvas, 27.5 × 36 cm, private collection (CMR 310).
34. Julie Manet, "Painting belonging to Monsieur and Madame Ernest Rouart," [c. 1940], "Paintings deposited at Monsieur Chapuis 4 rue Cretet in Paris" [fol. 2 recto], "Esquisse au grand chapeau," Arch. BS, inv. 2021.2.217.
35. Berthe Morisot, Mézy notebook, also known as the "black notebook," 1891, Paris, Musée Marmottan Monet, inv. D.5-1986.2014.4 (transcribed in Québec, Philadelphia, and Paris 2018–19, p. 271–278).
36. Letter from Edgar Degas to Berthe Morisot [n.d.], Paris, Musée Marmottan Monet, inv. D.4-1986.2013.232.
37. Edgar Degas, *Portrait of Madame Théodore Gobillard*, 1869, oil on canvas, 55.2 × 65.1 cm, New York, The Metropolitan Museum of Art, inv. 29.100.45.
38. Edgar Degas, *Eugène Manet*, 1874, oil on canvas, 65 × 86 cm, private collection.
39. Such a portrait is not known. The search for a possible preparatory drawing has been unsuccessful for the moment.
40. Rouart 1950, letter from Yves (Madame Théodore Gobillard) to Berthe Morisot, June 26 [1869], p. 31–32.
41. "Papa in a straw hat and I lightly dressed and in a wide-brimmed straw hat that they had brought back from Jersey and with a cat on my lap"; Berthe Morisot, *The Lesson in the Garden*, 1886, oil on canvas, 73 × 92 cm, private collection (CMR 205).
42. White 1985, three reproduced drawings, p. 175.
43. Pierre-Auguste Renoir, *Study for Child with Cat*, 1887, charcoal and pencil, 58.4 × 43 cm, private collection, ibid., repr. top left, p. 176.
44. White 1985, p. 175.
45. Baudot 1949, p. 16.
46. "Interview with Madame Ernest Rouart," Paris, summer 1963, cited in White 1985, p. 175.
47. Letter from Julie Manet-Rouart to "Sergent Ernest Rouart, section de camouflage / G. A. C. / Secteur 5," October 28, 1917, Arch. du Mesnil, inv. 2021.1.2327.
48. Letter from Renoir to Berthe Morisot, January 9, 1890, Paris, Musée Marmottan Monet, inv. D.4-1986.2013.135.
49. Pierre-Auguste Renoir, *The Festival of Pan*, 1879, 60 × 72 cm, private collection, Minnesota Marine Art Museum (D 240).

50. Manet 2017, August 7, 1899, p. 481.
51. Pierre-Auguste Renoir, *Berthe Morisot and her Daughter, Julie Manet*, 1894, oil on canvas, 81.3 × 65.4 cm, private collection.
52. D'Acq 1881, p. 189–201, p. 190, cited in Nonnis Vigilante 2005.
53. Pierre-Auguste Renoir, *Pinning the Hat*, 1893, pastel, 63.5 × 50 cm (Kansas City, The Nelson Atkins Museum, inv. 2015.13.20); idem, 1893, oil on canvas, 65 × 54 cm (Zürich, Emil Bührle Foundation).
54. Pierre-Auguste Renoir, *The Two Sisters* [1894–1895 or 1890], oil on canvas, 55 × 46 cm where Dauberville recognized Julie Manet and Paule Gobillard (D 998).
55. See the essay in this volume by Dominique d'Arnoult, "Julie the Painter, the Last of the Manets or the Interrupted Apprenticeship," p. 158–185.
56. Manet 2017, January 8, 1898, p. 27.
57. Pierre-Auguste Renoir after himself, *Pinning the Hat*, 1st plate, 1897, lithography printed in bister, 78.8 × 57.7 cm (sheet) and 60 × 49.2 cm (print); id., 2nd plate, c. 1898, lithography printed in color, 82.6 × 61.8 cm and 60 × 49.2 cm; idem., variant III, 2nd state, etching on vellum paper, 25.6 × 18.9 cm and 12 × 8.6 cm.
58. D 2223.
59. See Manet 2017, from July 29 to August 3, 1899, p. 476–478. The irrefutable testimony of the model contradicts the "circa 1896" dating put forward by Dauberville.
60. D 2201, dated by Dauberville "1898."
61. Manet 2017, August 3, 1899, p. 478.
62. Berthe Morisot, *Portrait of Paule Gobillard*, 1884, oil on canvas, 73 × 60 cm, private collection (CMR 162); Berthe Morisot, *Paule Gobillard Painting*, 1887, oil on canvas, 86 × 94 cm (CMR 212), Paris, Musée Marmottan Monet, inv. 6500.
63. See the essay in this volume by Dominique d'Arnoult, "Julie the Painter, the Last of the Manets or the Interrupted Apprenticeship," p. 158–185.
64. Fargue 1946, p. 48 and 50.
65. Manet 2107, December 28, 1898, p. 401.
66. Manet 2017, September 23, 1893, p. 86.
67. Exh. cat. Paris 2004, repr. p. 103.
68. See the essay in this volume by Marianne Mathieu "The Caraco Tribe," p. 58–75.
69. Paule Gobillard, *Julie Manet and her Cousin Jeannie in the Garden at Le Mesnil*, c. 1906, oil on canvas, dimensions unknown, signed on the back bottom right "Paule Gobillard 1906?," private collection, repr. in Manet 1987, p. 144; Paule Gobillard, *Portrait of Julie Manet and her son Julien*, n.d., watercolor, dimensions unknown, private collection, repr. in ibid., p. 164.
70. Paule Gobillard, *Portrait of Paul Valéry's Mother and Julie Manet-Rouart* [c. 1920], oil on canvas, 60 × 70 cm, Sorbonne (Université), Bibliothèque littéraire Jacques Doucet, inv. MO 81.
71. "List of students enrolled at the Julian Academy," in exh. cat. New York 1989.
72. See exh. cat. Nancy, Yerres, 2014–2015.
73. Arch. Paris, D4R1 816, "Rouart, Ernest Henri, matricule 407."
74. Fargue 1946a, p. 58 (repr. of Fargue 1942); new edition in exh. cat. Nancy and Yerres 2014–15, p. 69–70.
75. Letter from Julie Manet to Ernest Rouart, May 5 or 6, 1904, Arch. du Mesnil, inv. 2021.1.50.
76. N.d., private collection.
77. N.d., private collection.
78. Valéry 1965, p. 219–220.
79. Signed bottom right, in red paint "Ernest Rouart."
80. Exh. cat. Paris 1942, no. 18, *The Artist's Wife and Child* (egg-based paint). Work photographed in the exhibition (photo Papillon, June 1942, Musée Carnavalet, Histoire de Paris, inv. PH45031).
81. Will of Madame Manet *mère*, January 14, 1885, AN, MC/ET/XCIV/1635.
82. Letter from Julie Manet-Rouart to Ernest Rouart, October 6, 1909, Arch. du Mesnil, inv. 2021.1.52.
83. Letter from Julie Manet-Rouart to Ernest Rouart, October 28, 1917 [post office stamp on the envelope], Arch. du Mesnil, inv. 2021.1.52.
84. Letter from Julie Manet-Rouart to Ernest Rouart, Friday morning [October 14, 1904], Arch. du Mesnil, inv. 2021.1.55.
85. Exh. cat. Paris 1942, no. 12 *Young Woman in Bed*.
86. Ernest Rouart, *Portrait of Julie at Le Mesnil with Julien and Clément*, n.d. [c. 1907], oil on canvas, private collection.
87. Julie Manet, photograph, *Ernest Rouart in his soldier's uniform and his children* [from left to right:] Clément Rouart, Denis Rouart, Julien Rouart, n.d. [1916], in exh. cat. Paris 2004, repr. p. 76.
88. CMR 250.
89. Félix Vallotton, *The Five Painters*, 1903, oil on canvas, 145 × 187 cm, Winterthur, Kuntsmuseum.
90. Valéry 1965, p. 222.
91. Berthe Morisot, "green notebook A", Paris, Musée Marmottan Monet, fol. 24 recto.
92. Manet 2017, September 23, 1893, p. 86.
93. Henri Rouart, *Portrait of Madame Rouart*, n.d., oil on canvas, 66 × 47 cm, private collection.
94. Signed bottom left "Ernest Rouart."
95. Manet 2017, December 8, 1898, p. 270.
96. Agathe Valéry to Julie Manet, n.d. [1942], Arch. du Mesnil, inv. 2021.1.613.
97. Jeannie Gobillard-Valéry to Julie Manet-Rouart, n.d. [July 1942], Arch. du Mesnil, inv. 2021.1.298.
98. Cabanne 2003, p. 251–259. See also Marianne Mathieu, "Painting as a Legacy," p. 218–253.

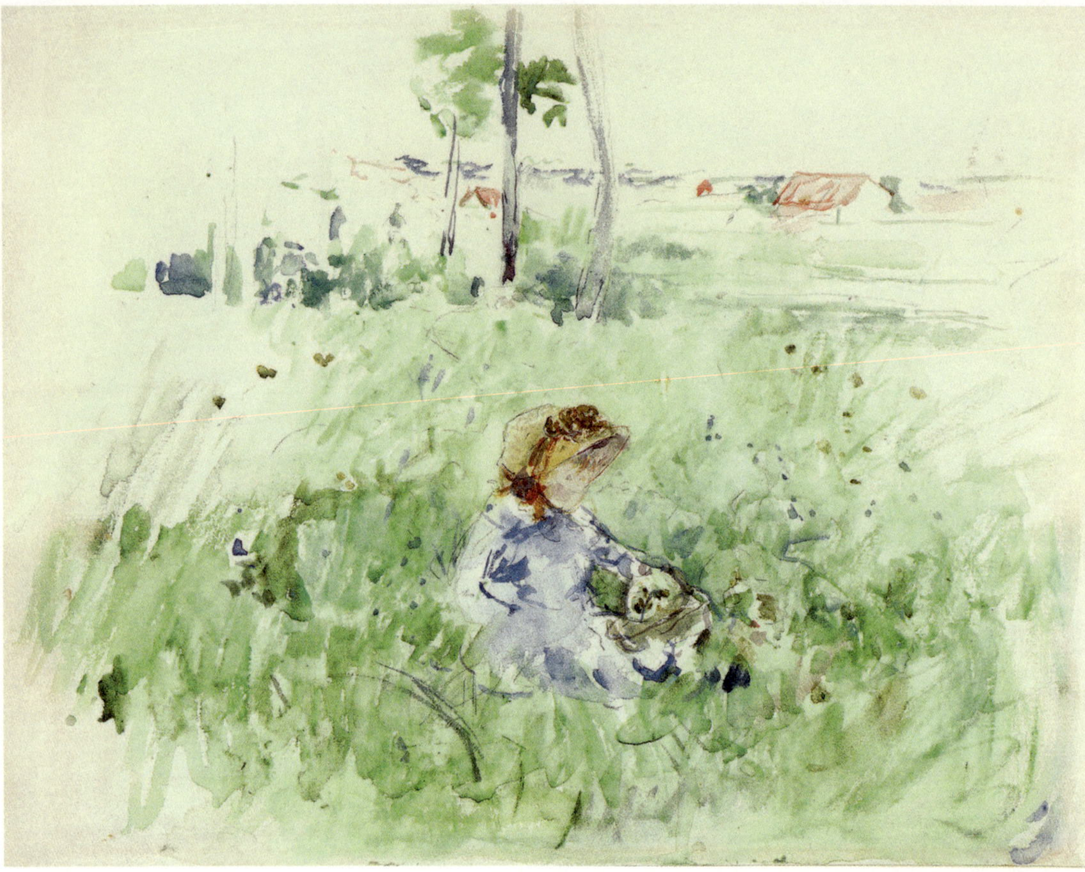

Berthe Morisot (1841–1895)
Young Girl Sitting in the Grass, 1882
Watercolor on paper, 26 × 32 cm
Paris, Musée Marmottan Monet

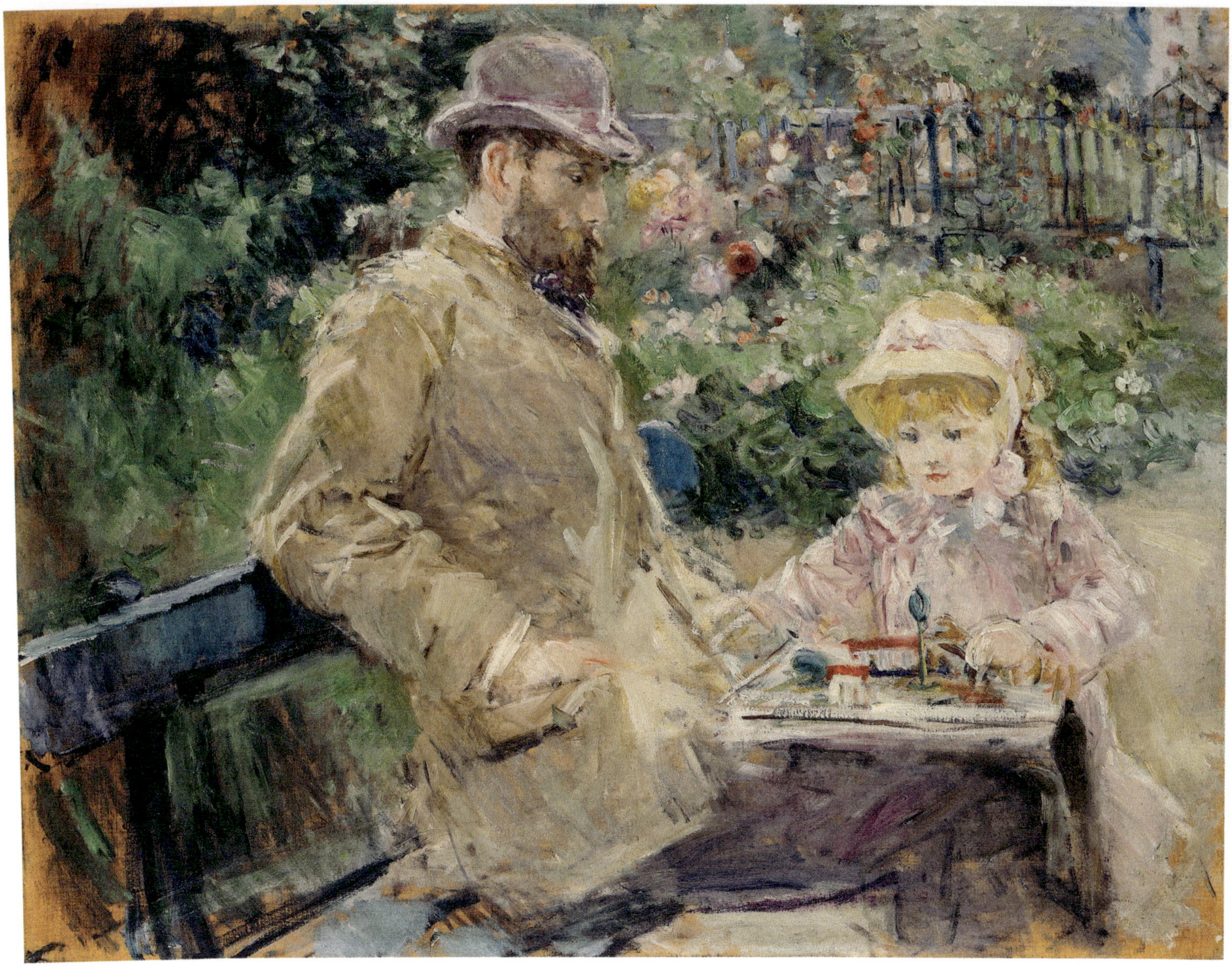

Berthe Morisot (1841–1895)
Eugène Manet and Her Daughter in the Garden at Bougival, 1881
Oil on canvas, 73 × 92 cm
Paris, Musée Marmottan Monet

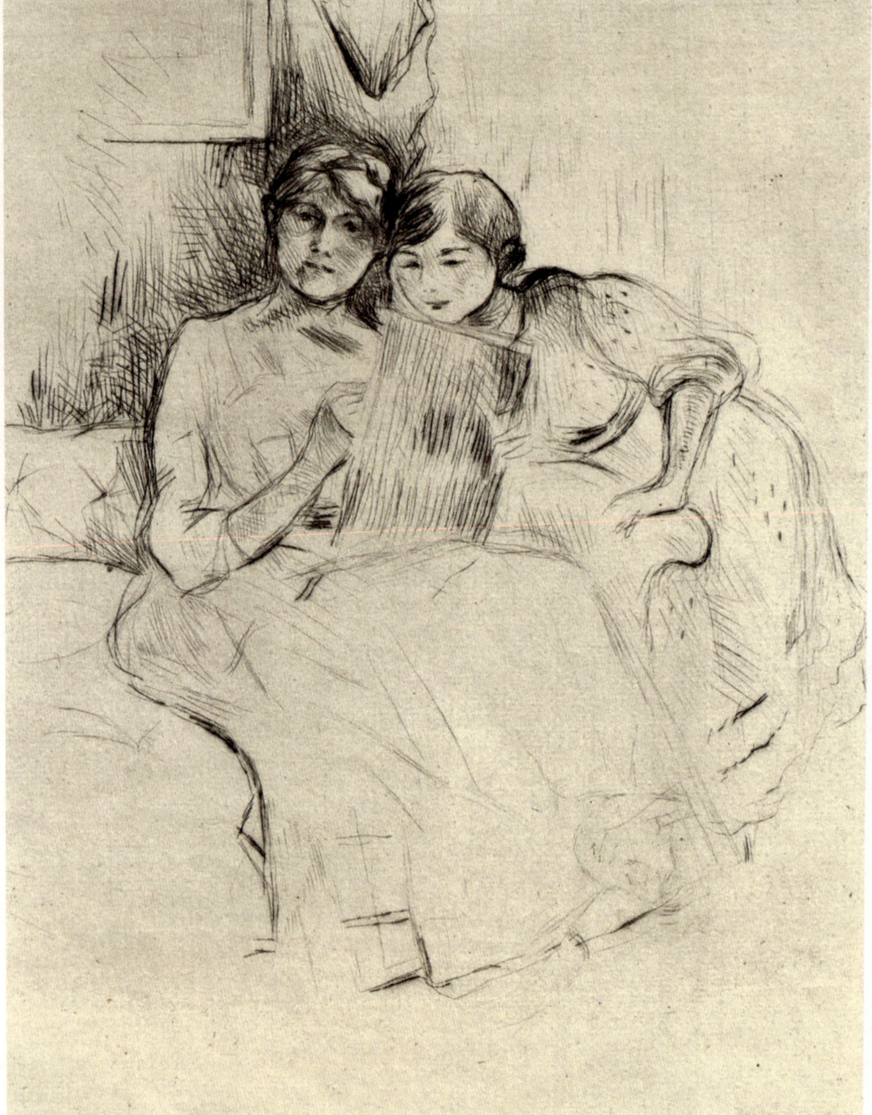

Berthe Morisot (1841–1895)
Portrait of the Artist and Her Daughter, also known as *The Drawing Lesson*, 1889
Drypoint, 20.5 × 15.5 cm
Private collection

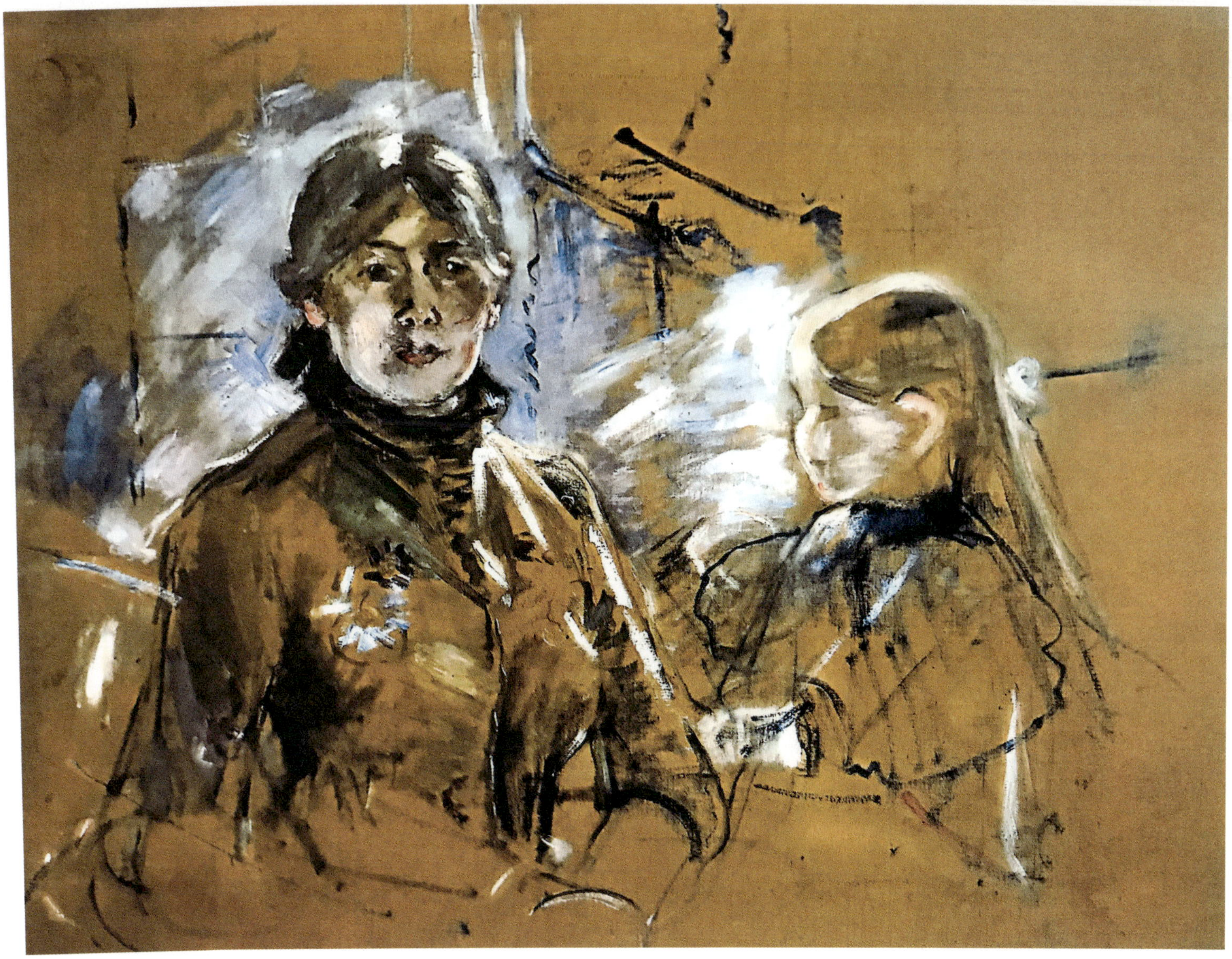

Berthe Morisot (1841–1895)
Portrait of Berthe Morisot and Her Daughter, 1885
Oil on canvas, 72 × 91 cm
Private collection

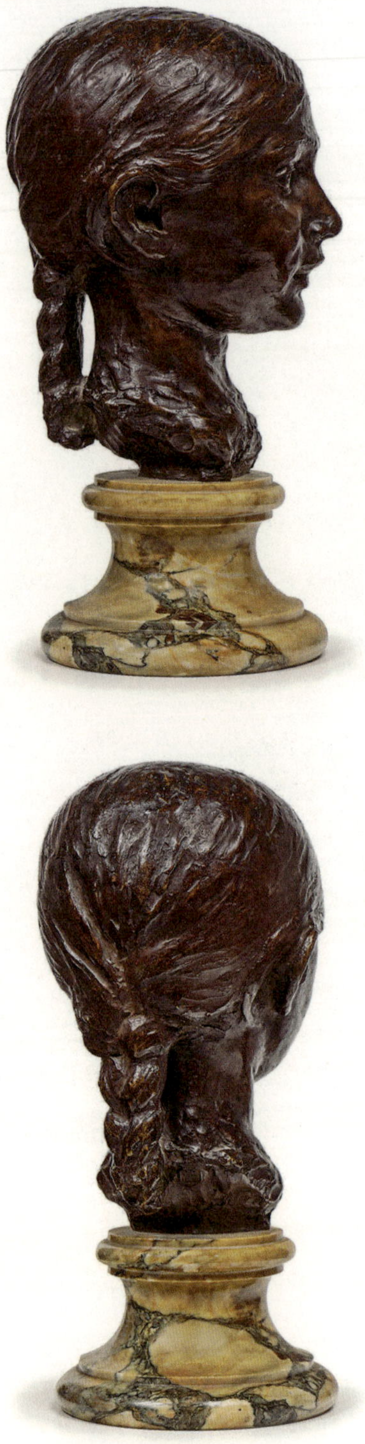

Berthe Morisot (1841–1895)
Bust of Julie Manet, 1886
Patinated bronze and marble, H. 36 cm
(with base)
Private collection

Berthe Morisot (1841–1895)
Little Girl in a Blue Dress, 1886
Pastel on canvas, 100 × 81 cm
Paris, Musée Marmottan Monet

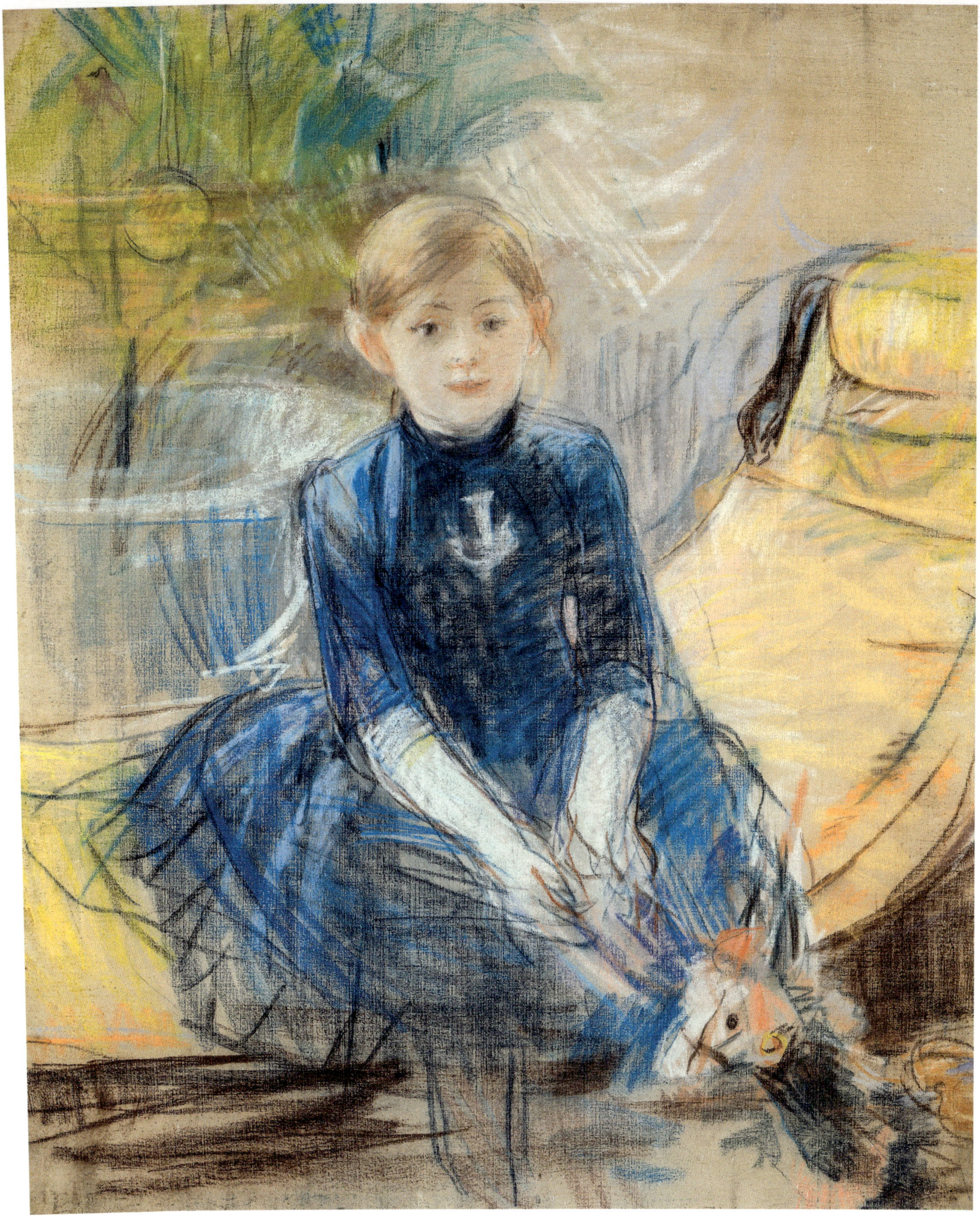

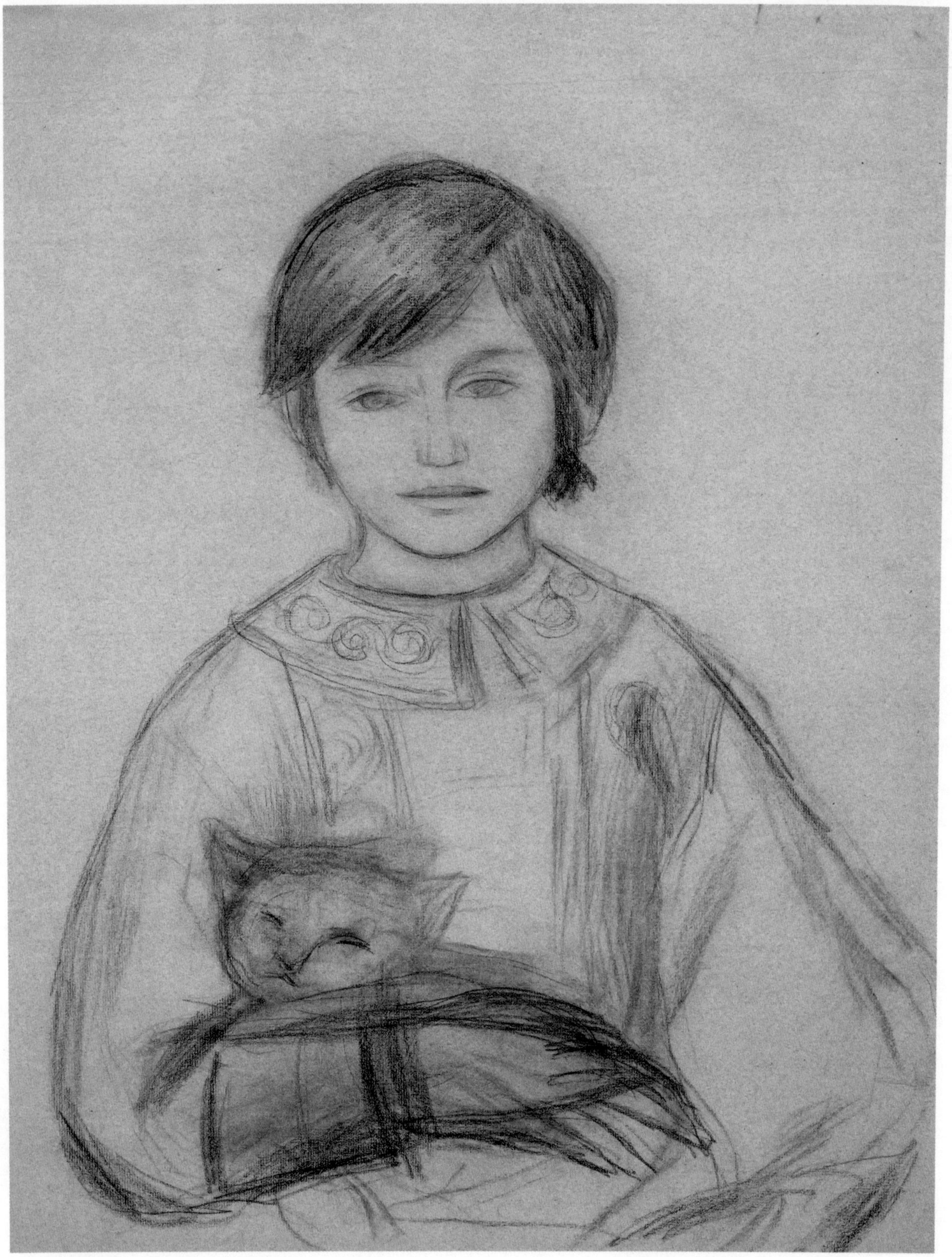

Pierre-Auguste Renoir (1841–1919)
Julie Manet or *Child with a Cat* (preparatory drawing), c. 1887
Charcoal and pencil on blue paper, 62 × 47 cm
Private collection

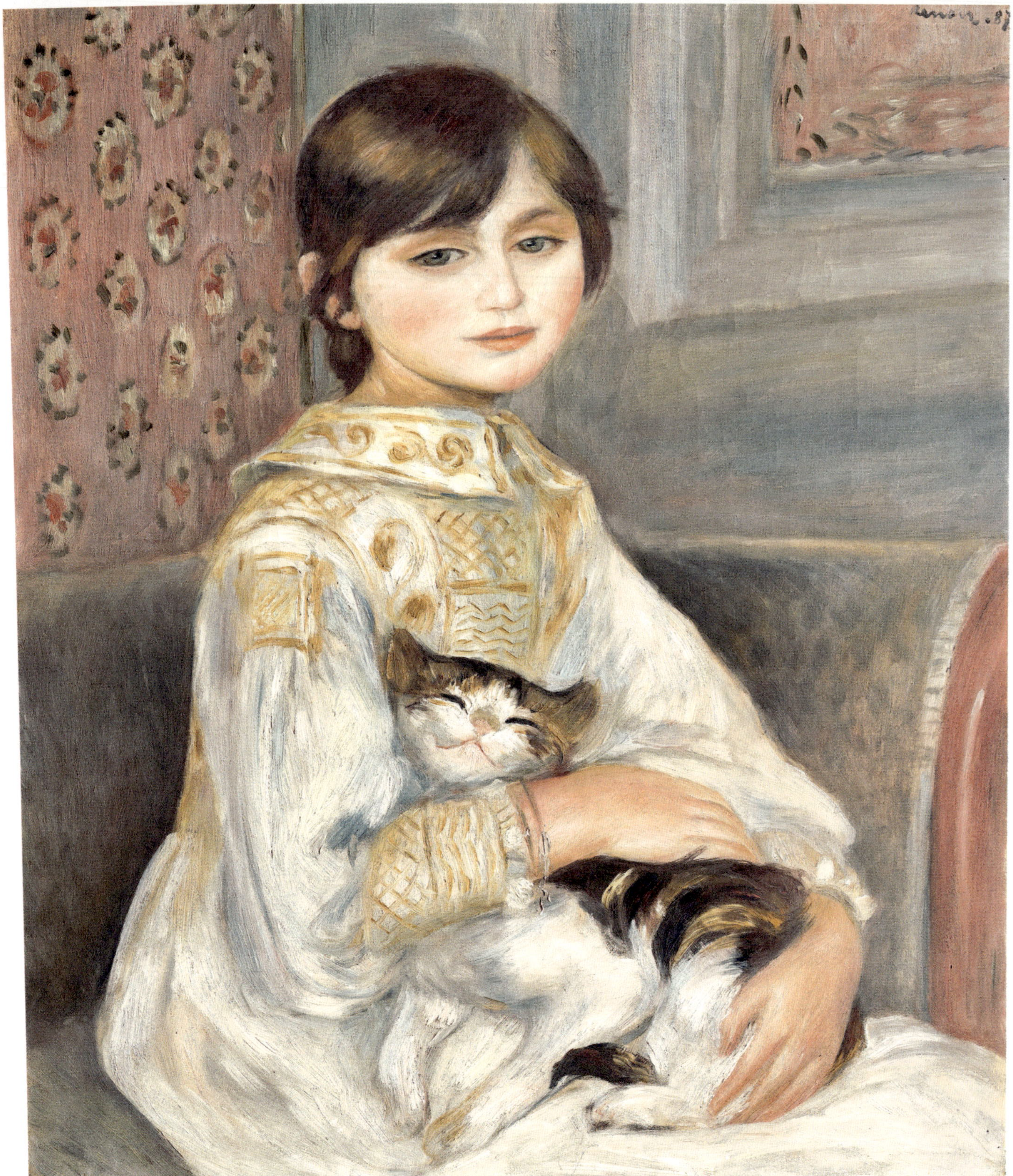

Pierre-Auguste Renoir (1841–1919)
Julie Manet or *Child with a Cat*, 1887
Oil on canvas, 65.5 × 53.5 cm
Paris, Musée d'Orsay, accepted by the state in lieu of estate tax, 1999

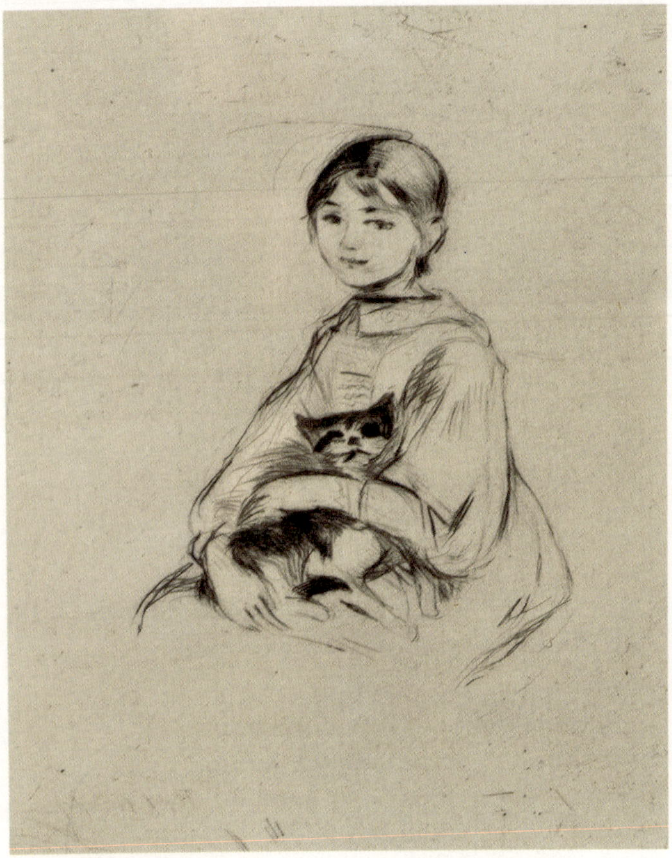

Berthe Morisot (1841–1895)
Julie Manet or *Child with a Cat* (after Pierre-Auguste Renoir), 1889
Drypoint, 13.5 × 10.7 cm
Paris, Musée Marmottan Monet

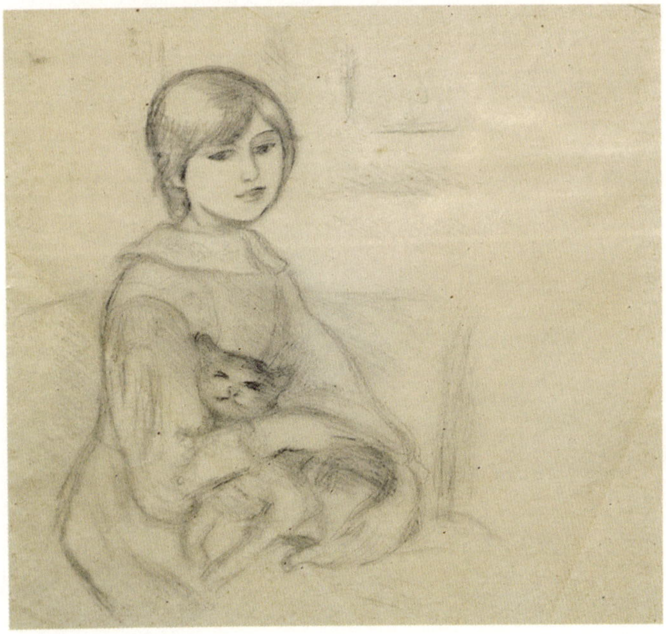

Julie Manet (1878–1966)
Julie Manet or *Child with a Cat* (after Pierre-Auguste Renoir), n.d.
Black pencil on tracing paper, 17 × 18 cm
Paris, Musée Marmottan Monet

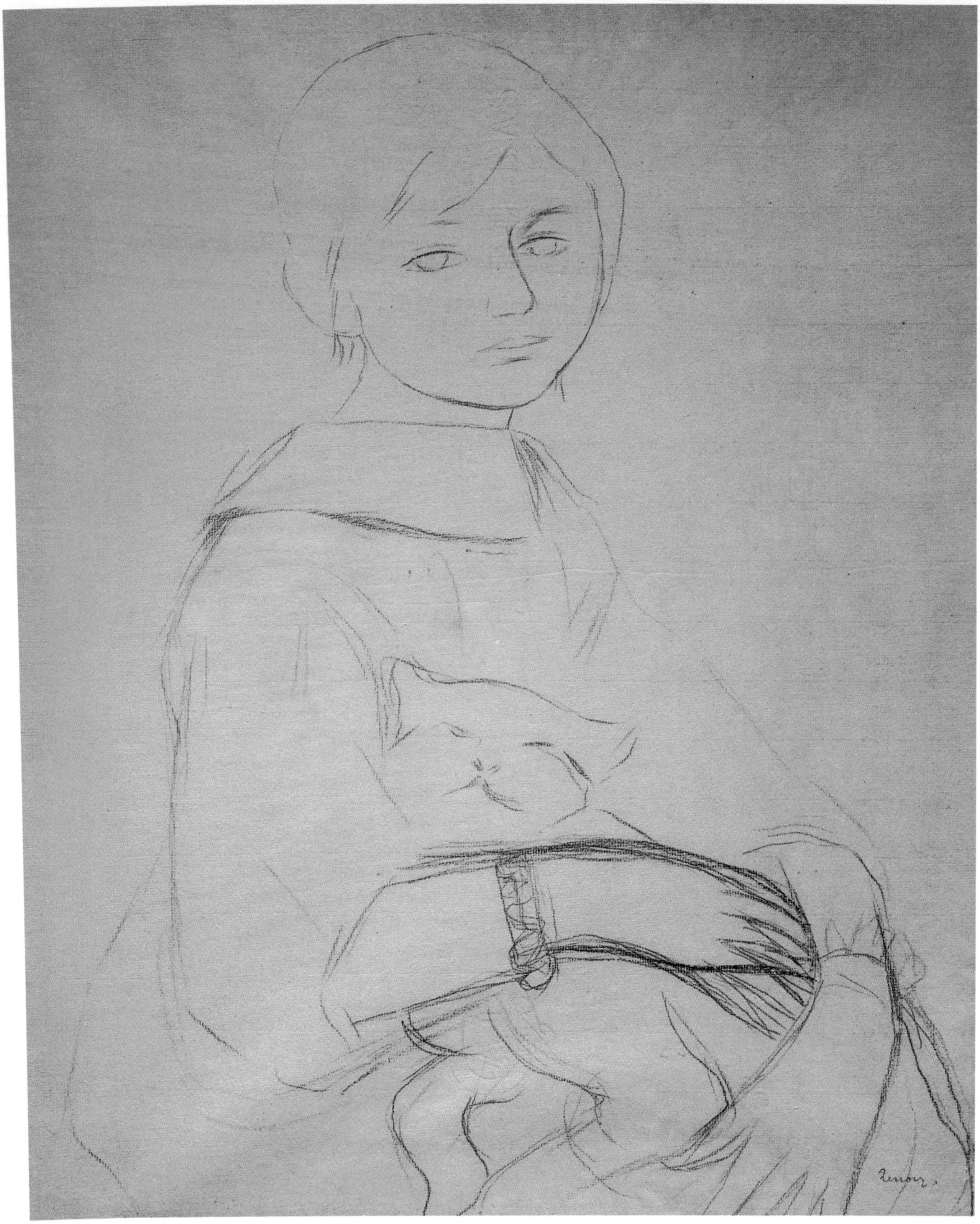

Pierre-Auguste Renoir (1841–1919)
Julie Manet or *Child with a Cat* (preparatory drawing), c. 1887
Pencil on paper, 61 × 47.5 cm
Private collection

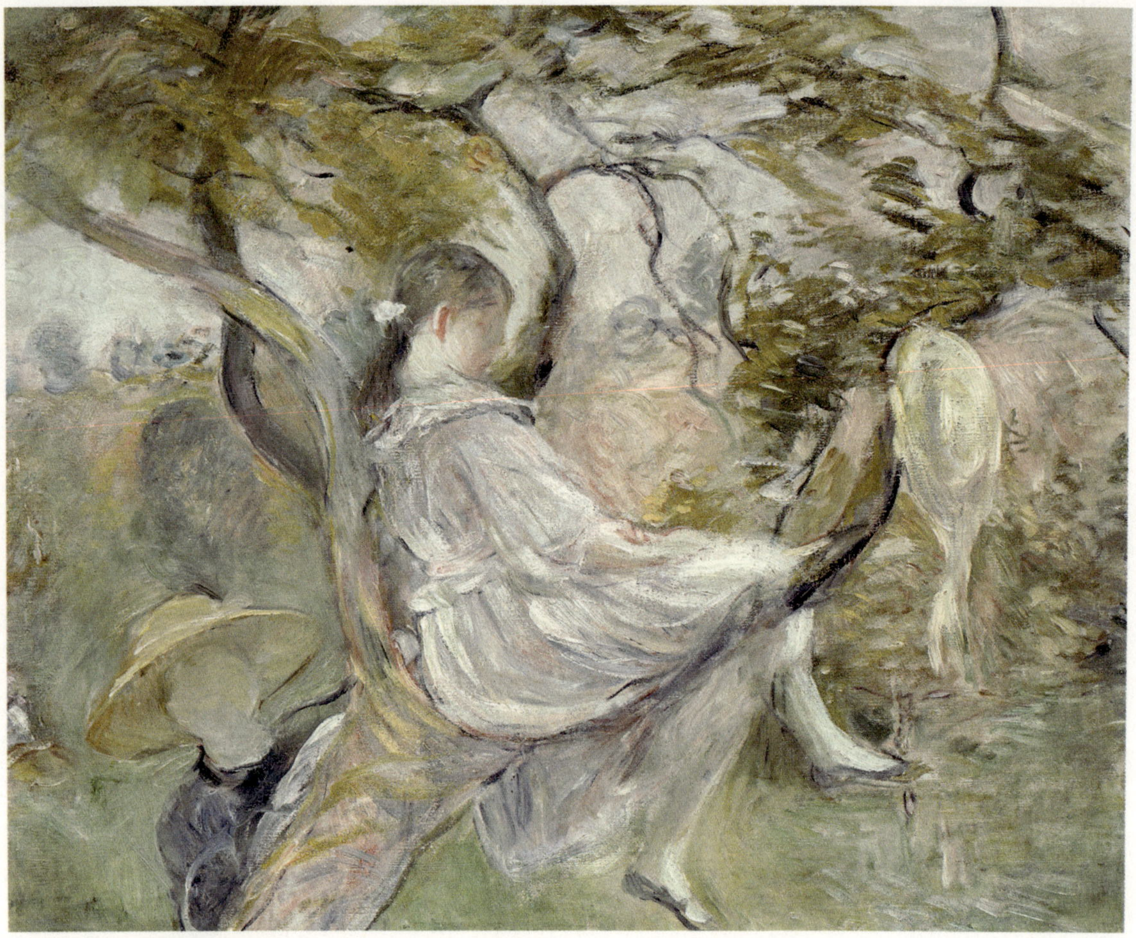

Berthe Morisot (1841–1895)
In the Apple Tree, 1890
Oil on canvas, 48 × 56 cm
Paris, Musée Marmottan Monet

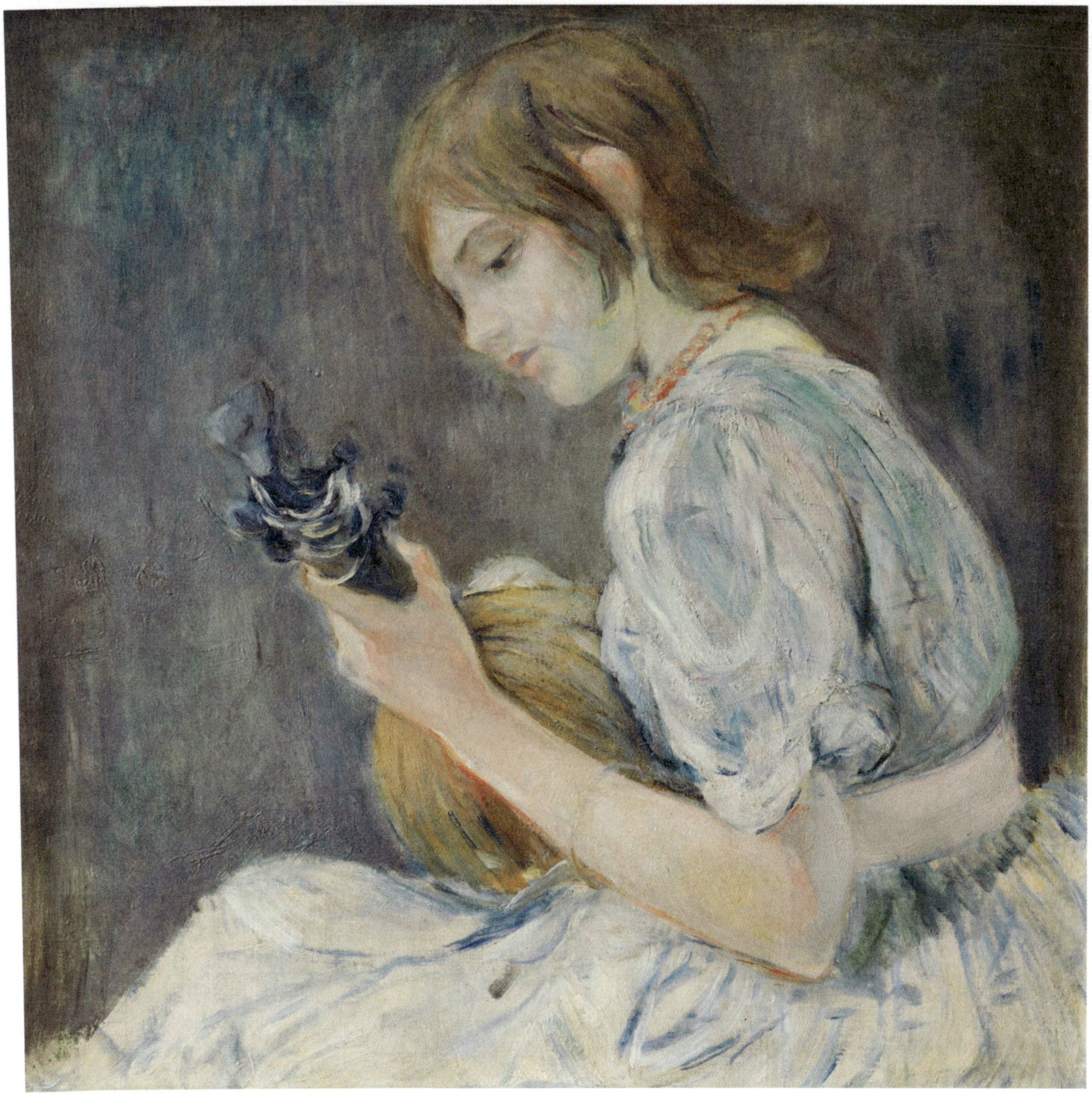

Berthe Morisot (1841–1895)
The Mandolin, 1889
Oil on canvas, 55 × 57 cm
Private collection

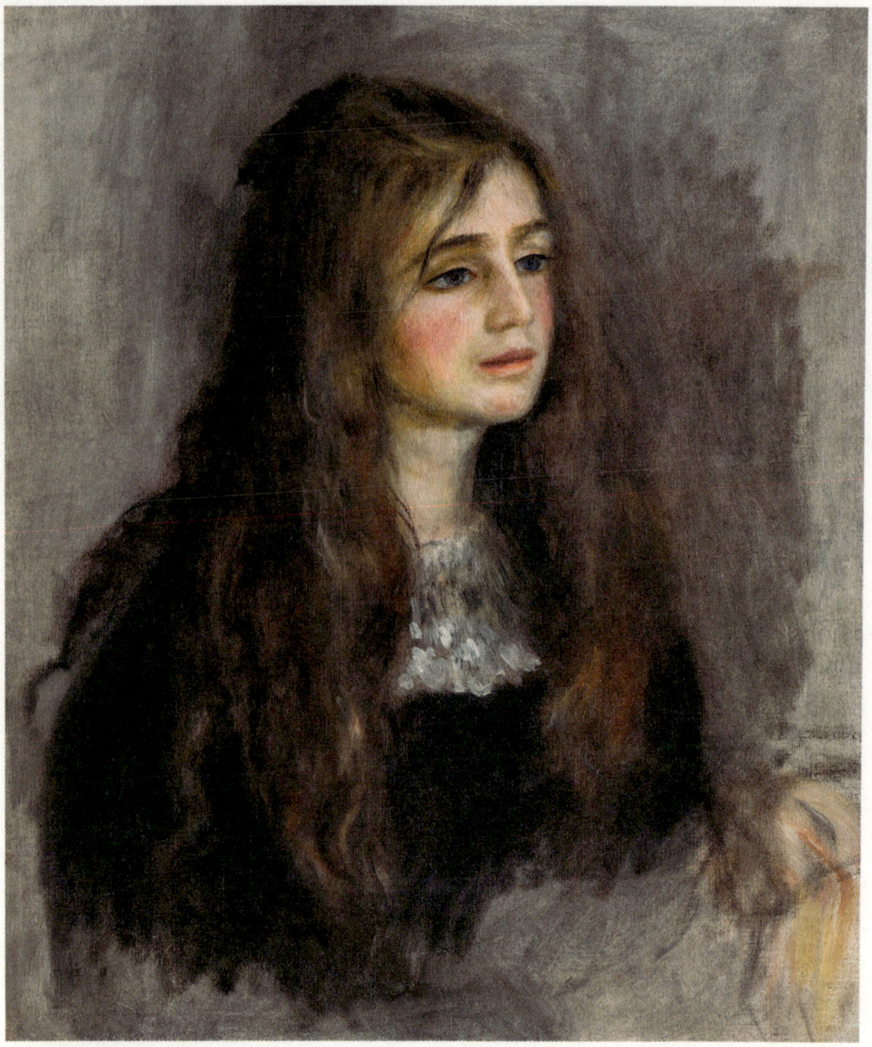

Pierre-Auguste Renoir (1841–1919)
Portrait of Julie Manet, 1894
Oil on canvas, 55 × 46 cm
Paris, Musée Marmottan Monet

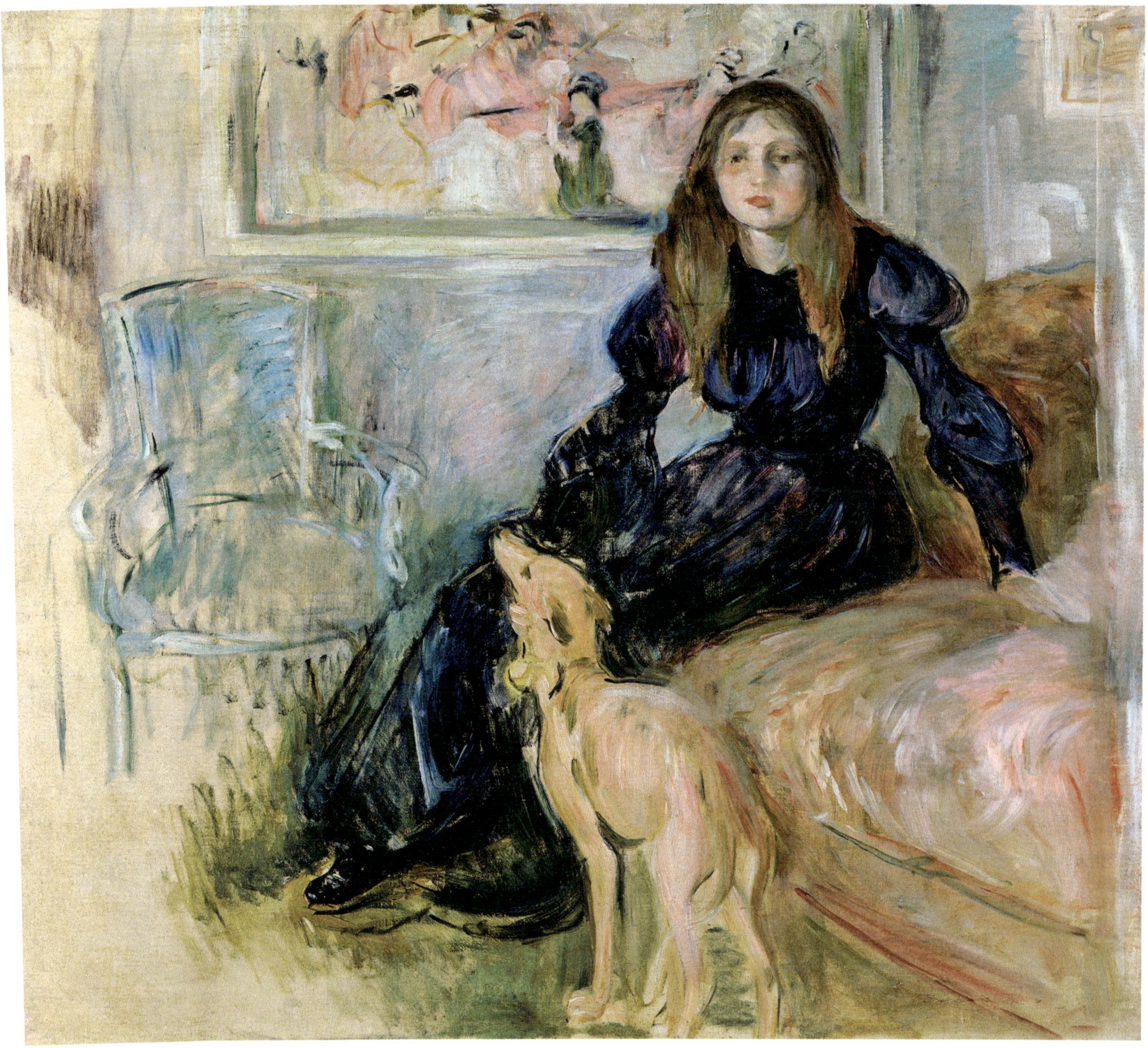

Berthe Morisot (1841–1895)
Julie Manet and Her Greyhound Laërtes, 1893
Oil on canvas, 73 × 80 cm
Paris, Musée Marmottan Monet

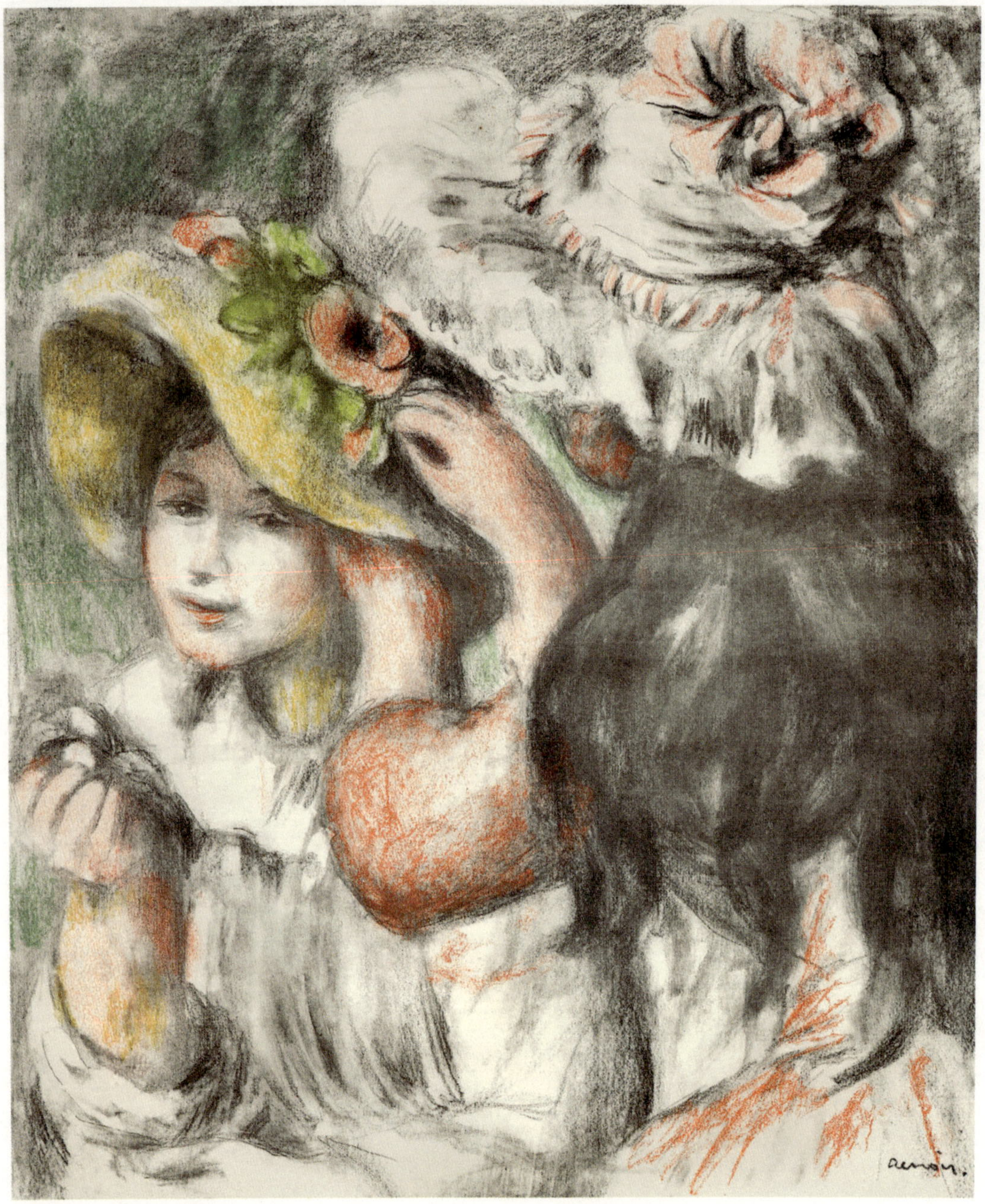

Pierre-Auguste Renoir (1841–1919)
Pinning the Hat, 1898
Lithograph in seven colors on laid paper, 60 × 49 cm
Private collection

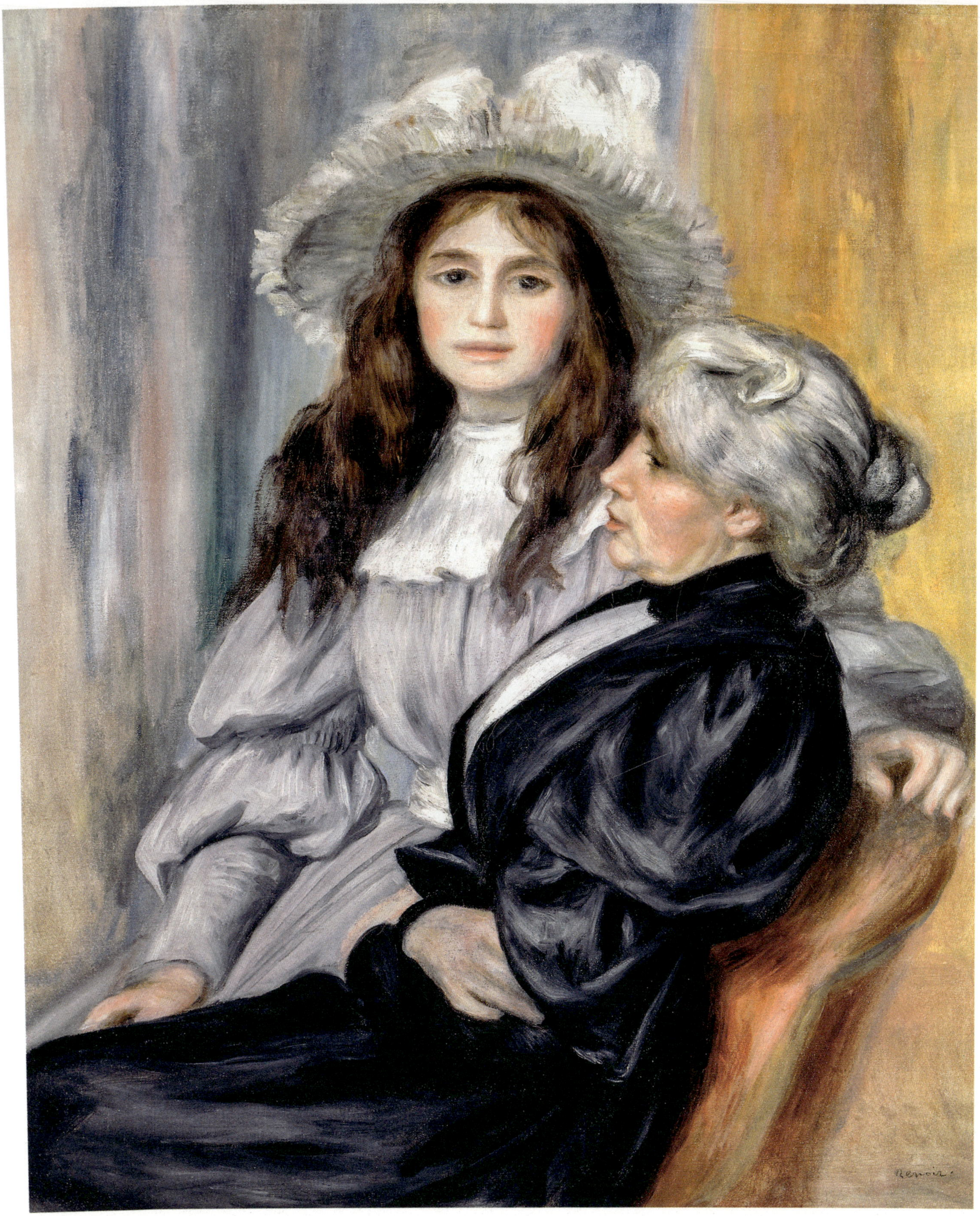

Pierre-Auguste Renoir (1841–1919)
Portrait of Berthe Morisot and Her Daughter Julie Manet, 1894
Oil on canvas, 81 × 65.5 cm
Private collection

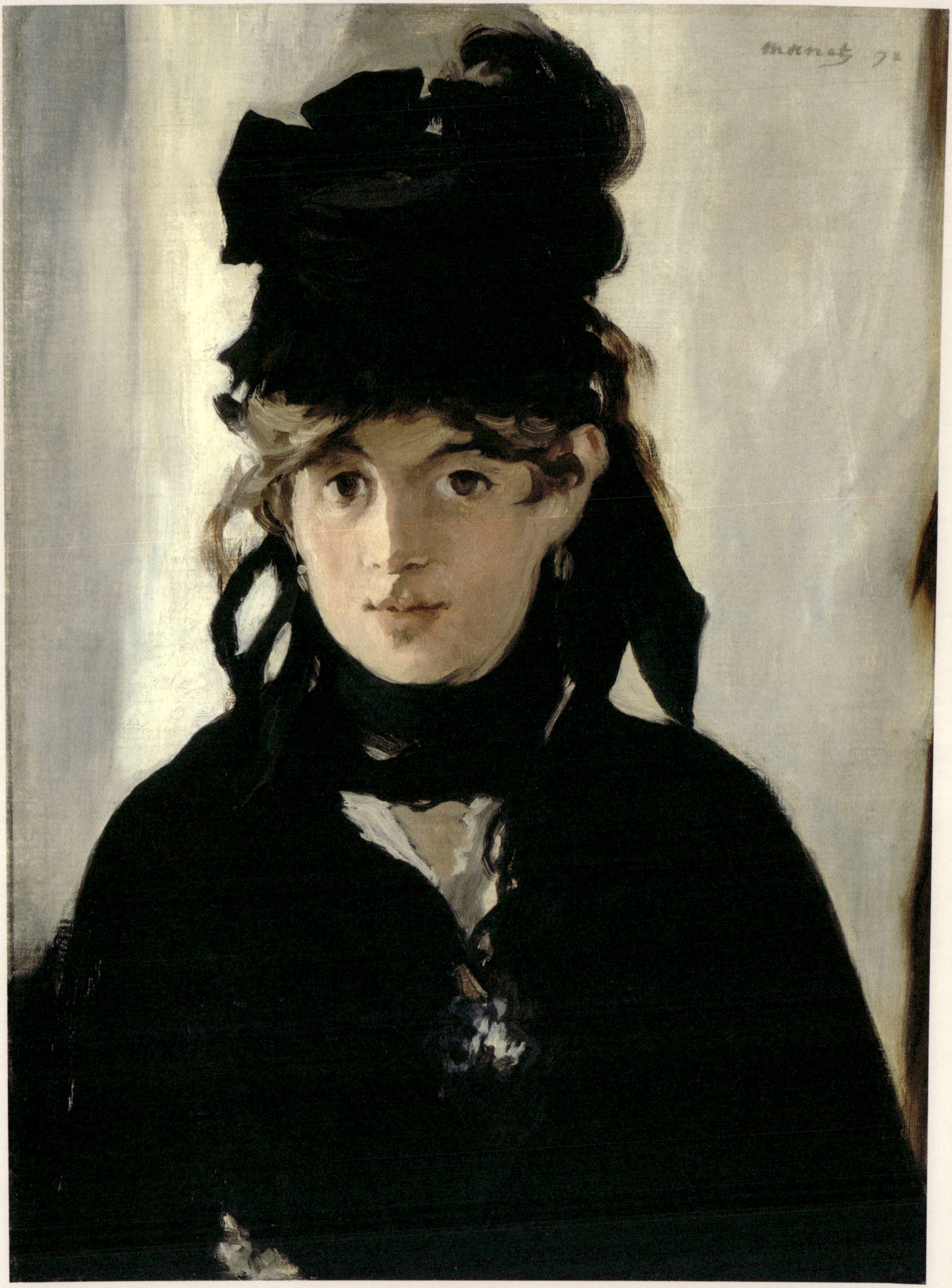
manet 72

PAINTING AS A LEGACY
1862-1895

MARIANNE MATHIEU

Much has been said about Berthe Morisot's situation: a key painter of Impressionism who—because she was a woman and bourgeois—was deprived all her life of a painter's status and—outside of enlightened circles—of recognition. The inventory drawn up at her death bears witness to this fact. Her work was described as follows:

> twenty-four canvases and unfinished sketches valued at fifty francs, twenty-six canvases, sketches, frames, drawings, various cartoons from the studio valued at one hundred francs [then] in the studio on the fourth floor, a memorial family portrait, seventy canvases of unfinished sketches, cartoon, record, the whole valued at two hundred francs, a watercolor and a pastel valued at twenty francs.[1]

The artist's name appears only twice: "two watercolors Berthe Morizot valued at 40 francs" and "a painting of a character and Love[2] (by Mad[emoiselle]. Morizot)," a mention intended to clarify an earlier title suggesting that this copy after Boucher was by another artist.[3] Ten lines—all in all—list the work of a lifetime. Its total value: 360 francs![4] Needless to say, this was a far cry from the inventories of studio collections and stocks carried out in accordance with professional standards, such as the one Monet drew up on the death of Pissarro in 1903: three hundred and forty-five works, numbered, titled, and valued at a total of 456,100 francs.[5]

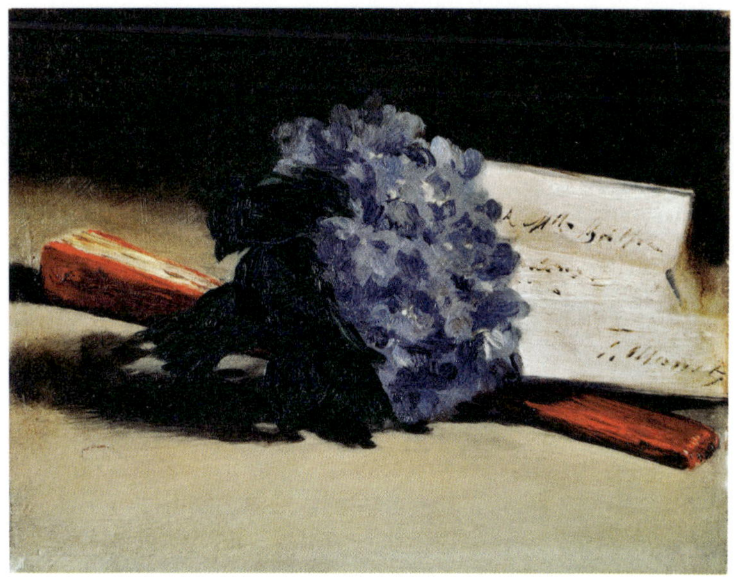

Édouard Manet (1832–1883)
The Bouquet of Violets, 1872
Oil on canvas, 22 × 27 cm
Private collection

Facing page
Édouard Manet (1832–1883)
Berthe Morisot with a Bouquet of Violets, 1872
Oil on canvas, 55.5 × 40.5 cm
Paris, Musée d'Orsay

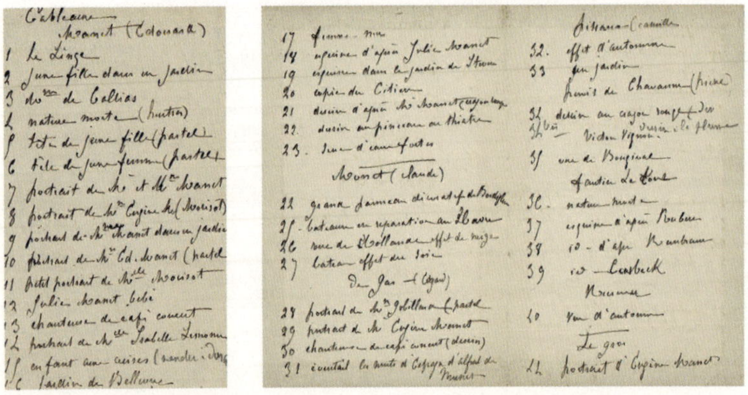

Berthe Morisot (1841–1895)
Inventory of 42 paintins, drawings, and engravings that belonged to her, c. 1885
Archives BS, Paris, Musée Marmottan Monet

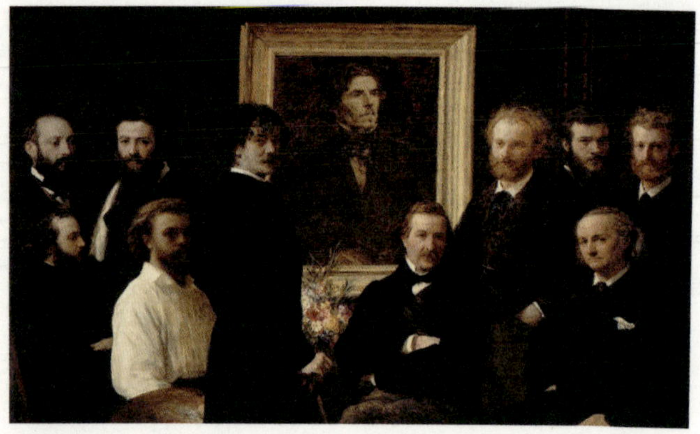

Henri Fantin-Latour (1836–1904)
Homage to Delacroix, 1864
Oil on canvas, 160 × 250 cm
Paris, Musée d'Orsay

Which of Berthe Morisot's works did Julie Manet inherit? One could say all of them, with the exception of the rare pieces sold or offered during the artist's lifetime.[6] The succession documents do not allow us to list them. Julie would make it her mission to compensate for this lack of information and to establish an exhaustive list of her mother's creations in the form of a catalogue raisonné, which was published five years before Julie Manet's death in 1961.[7] To give birth to an artist and recognize her work.

The works by other artists that Julie inherited are better documented. Three handwritten lists drawn up around 1885–86 by her parents offer a unique testimony to the genesis of their collection. The "History of the paintings of Ed. Manet belonging to me"[8] drawn up by the Impressionist in her notebook lists thirteen paintings. Another document, unpublished to this day, also written by Berthe Morisot during the same period, lists on three pages, forty-two works, twenty-three of which were by Manet (above). These notes are not, however, exhaustive. The absence of a gift—oh so famous—*The Bouquet of Violets* (p. 219) dedicated to Mademoiselle Berthe Morisot by Manet as a thank you for her posing sessions for *Berthe Morisot with a Bouquet of Violets* (p. 218), which was acquired by the critic Théodore Duret, is proof of this. Lastly, the list of "Paintings stored in the room rented from Jennings[9] 1886"[10] drawn up by Eugène would also be mentioned. The Manets that entered the rue de Villejust are known thanks to the inventories established after his death and the minutes of the artist's posthumous sale. They were very well documented by Adolphe Tabarant, whose book *Manet et son œuvre* remains one of the most well-informed publications to this day. As we shall see, however rich these sources are, they sometimes contradict each other. Finally, only some of the graphic works—summarily mentioned and often presented in batches when cited—can be identified. It is therefore a glimpse of the collection that Julie received as an inheritance that is proposed here.

GENESIS OF A COLLECTION (1862–1883)

As sensitive to the arts as Berthe Morisot's father was, a senior civil servant trained as an architect, founder in 1846 of the Société Archéologique et Historique du Limousin[11] with the mission of creating a departmental museum of antiquities[12] while he was prefect of Haute-Vienne, Edme Tiburce Morisot did not have a collector's soul. No artwork appears in the estate inventory in 1874,[13] nothing old and nothing more recent. Although he encouraged his daughter in her vocation as a painter and although the Morisots frequented Édouard Manet, the leader of the Batignolles school, Berthe was categorical:

> **My father and mother would never have had the idea of using a 1,000 or even a 500 bill to buy this kind [of painting].[14]**

Berthe Morisot thus inherited no artistic patrimony—at most a portrait by Évariste Fragonard (1780–1850) of a lady from Marie-Cornélie Morisot's family.[15] No works were listed in the list of assets attached to her marriage contract. The same was true for her husband, Eugène Manet.[16]

However, the young couple already possessed some pieces. Henri Fantin-Latour and his entourage were the best represented, for example Alphonse Legros (1837–1911), a painter and engraver born in Dijon, who, like Fantin, attended the Petite École de Dessin in Paris and then the studio of Horace Lecoq de Boisbaudran. As a

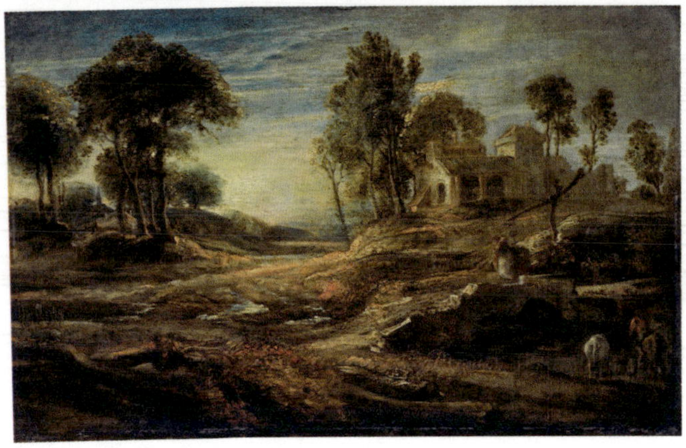

Peter Paul Rubens (1577–1640)
Landscape with a Drinking Trough, n.d.
Oil on panel, 29 × 43 cm
Paris, Musée du Louvre

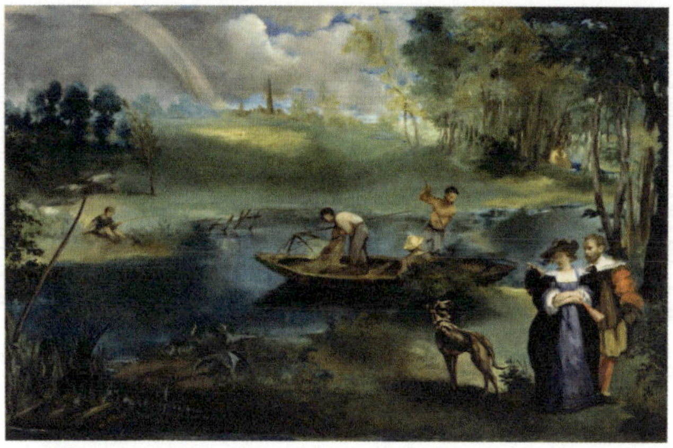

Édouard Manet (1832–1883)
Fishing, c. 1862–63
Oil on canvas, 76.8 × 123.2 cm
New York, The Metropolitan Museum of Art, Purchase, Mr. and Mrs. Richard J. Bernhard Gift, 1957

testimony of mutual friendship and admiration, Fantin, in the *Homage to Delacroix* (p. 220), depicted Alphonse Legros alongside Louis Cordier, Edmond Duranty, James Whistler, Champfleury, Charles Baudelaire, Albert de Balleroy, Félix Bracquemond, and Édouard Manet. Before leaving Paris for London, where he settled in 1863, Legros painted a half-length portrait of "Eugène Manet," a canvas signed and dated at the top left "A. Legros 1862" (p. 241),[17] then, around 1863, one of his brother Édouard.[18] Which of these two paintings corresponds to the *Portrait of E. M.* (no. 303) presented at the Salon des Refusés not far from *The Luncheon on the Grass*[19] for which Eugène was one of the models? The critic Fernand Desnoyers noted without further details:

> **Monsieur Legros has a large painting at the Reçus[20] and a small portrait at the Refusés. This portrait is very good; but it must frighten the members of the Jury by pursuing them like remorse. Why was it thrown out? The Jury remains silent.[21]**

In the absence of a more precise description, it is not possible to determine which of the portraits of Édouard or Eugène Manet by Legros was exhibited.

Several copies of the masters painted by Fantin-Latour belonged to the couple. The copy of *Painter Painting a Portrait*[22] by the Dutchman Joos van Craesbeeck (1605–1660) appears in the inventory of Berthe Morisot's paintings[23] as well as in the catalog of Fantin-Latour's complete works established and written by Madame Fantin-Latour in 1911,[24] where it was followed by the annotation "To Eugène Manet." A sketch after Peter Paul Rubens (1577–1640) was also mentioned by Berthe Morisot.[25] Madame Fantin-Latour indicated that a landscape[26] after the master belonged to E. Manet.[27] The only Rubens of its kind held in the Louvre, *Landscape with a Drinking Trough* (above), is in all likelihood the painting that served as a model for their friend. Édouard Manet was inspired by this same landscape for the bucolic setting of *Fishing* (above), a painting from 1862–63 that we will discuss again later. Berthe Morisot also mentioned in her inventory a sketch after Rembrandt[28] and a still life[29] that we cannot identify at the present time. In her catalog, Madame Fantin did not attribute any copy of Rembrandt to the couple; on the other hand, she gave Eugène Manet *The Two Bellins*,[30] probably inspired by Jean-Baptiste Belin de Fontenay, also known as Blin de Fontenay (1653–1715), a specialist in paintings of flowers and fruit. The work does not appear in Berthe's inventory.

The young couple's "trousseau of paintings" seems to echo those years spent pacing the Louvre. For Berthe Morisot, as would later be the case for her daughter, this museum was the scene of great encounters, and even of budding love affairs. It was alongside Rubens, whom she copied in 1868, under the auspices of the master's models—Henri IV and his queens, Marguerite de Valois and Marie de Médicis—that Berthe Morisot was introduced to the already famous Édouard Manet by Fantin-Latour and Félix Bracquemond[31] in that same year. From then on, Berthe Morisot joined their circle. Manet, Edgar Degas, and Pierre Puvis de Chavannes were among her closest friends. Her sister Edma, who left Paris after her marriage, envied her their company:

> **To me, your life appears to be enchanting at the moment . . . chatting with Monsieur Degas while watching him draw, laughing with Manet, philosophizing with Puvis, seem to me to be so many things**

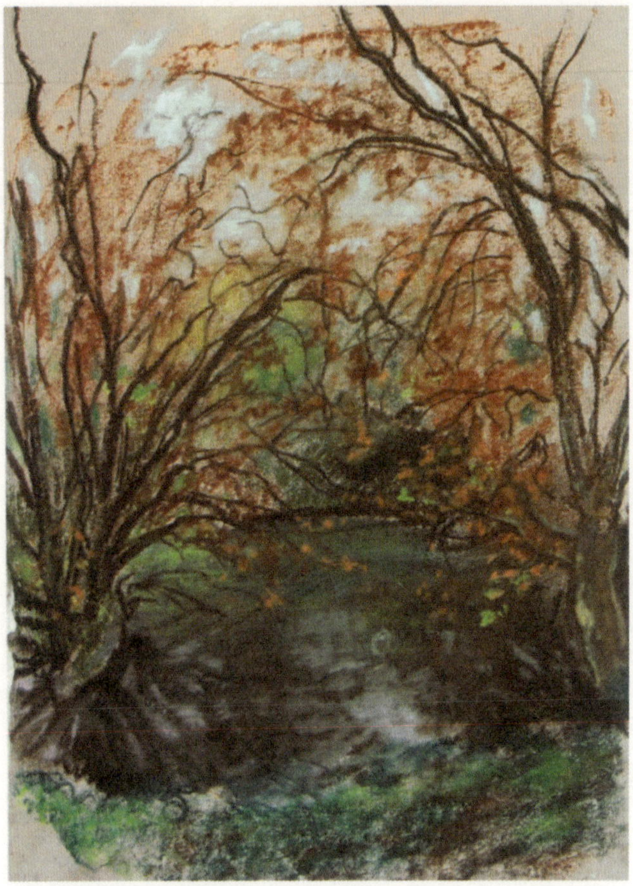

Léon Riesener (1808–1878)
Pond in the Woods, 1860–70
Pastel and charcoal on paper
Collection Musées de Lisieux (Château de Saint-Germain de Livet)

> **worthy of envy. You would see the effect it would have on you from afar.[32]**

These artists were the first to recognize Berthe's talent and they encouraged her in her vocation as a painter. Is it any wonder then that Berthe had a few mementoes of them from her early days? Degas was the first to offer her "Les nuits d'Espagne" after Alfred de Musset, elegantly painted on a delicate fan (p. 46 top). Framed without delay, presented as early as 1869, in a beautiful position in the living room of Madame Morisot *mère* (p. 46 bottom),[33] the work would always occupy a prominent place in the home of Eugène Manet and then in that of their daughter, Julie. Manet's first gifts arrived without delay, the aforementioned *The Bouquet of Violets*, in 1872, followed by *Berthe Morisot Reclining*, in 1873 (p. 239), the history of which is sufficiently well known not to be mentioned in this essay. Puvis de Chavannes was also represented. Berthe did not omit to add to her inventory a second number to include not one but two drawings: one in pen,[34] the other in red pencil.[35] This embryo of a collection held the work of another tutelary figure, that of Léon Riesener (1808–1878). This cousin of Delacroix became friends with the Morisots in 1864, when he rented the Beuzeval mill, where he had set up his easel on many occasions.[36] To a certain extent, Berthe followed in his footsteps and her senses were awakened on his land in the open air. The young woman was also interested in Riesener's writings, from which she copied passages. Last but not least, Mademoiselle Morisot formed lasting friendships with Léon's daughters, Rosalie and Louise. Was the *Autumn View*[37] in her collection a gift from the master to an aspiring artist, a memento offered by his daughters, or an acquisition made in 1878 at his estate sale? Was it one of the many sketches done at Beuzeval, a place dear to both of them?

The wedding gift offered by Degas to Berthe is well known: a *Portrait of Eugène Manet* (p. 223) sitting in the Normandy dunes—a background painted from memory as a souvenir of the region where the couple spent the summer prior to their marriage. We have no information about the gifts Berthe received. What became of *Portrait of Berthe Morisot Painting*[38] executed by her sister Edma in around 1865? Did the artist offer it to her sister when it had barely dried? How can we imagine that she took it to Lorient, where she moved with her husband in 1869? Although the precise date of this gift is not known, one thing is certain, the work did pass to Berthe and remained in the family. However, the painting does not appear on any list drawn up by the Impressionist or in her estate inventory. No one is a prophet in their own country. However, when Eugène and Berthe Manet moved to the avenue d'Eylau, works by their relatives were already keeping them company.

Is it any wonder that the first works to enrich this collection were portraits of Julie? In February 1880, Oncle Édouard could not resist the temptation to paint her at the age of fifteen months (p. 21)[39] on a decorative plaque of such delicacy that it has often been mistaken for a pastel.[40] Two years later, in the Rueil garden, he made a good-sized sketch of Julie Manet also called *Julie Manet on the Watering Can* (p. 188). Like Manet's other sketches, these pieces did not appear in the posthumous exhibition of 1884 and remained unknown to the public for a long time.

Berthe also indicated in her inventory drawn up around 1885 that she owned two other Degas paintings. The drawing *Singer at a Café-Concert*[41] cannot be identified with certainty. Of the works in the collection of Monsieur and Madame Ernest Rouart, the pastel on monotype dated around 1879 and entitled, as it happens, *Singer at a Café-Concert* (p. 231) is the only piece identified to date that comes close to this description. Finally, we are surprised to find in Berthe Morisot's list the pastel portrait of her sister Yves (p. 165) executed in rue Franklin in 1869.[42] Did Yves leave it with her sister in gratitude for her help? Obviously, Berthe did not consider herself the legitimate owner of this family portrait. The pastel does not appear in her estate inventory. From 1902, when the model's daughters and Paul Valéry moved to the third floor of the rue de Villejust, the work took pride of place in their living room.

Victor Vignon (1847–1909) also deserves to be mentioned.[43] A former pupil of Corot and a friend of Cals, he was also close to Pissarro and Cézanne, with whom he painted at Auvers-sur-Oise. We find him in Bougival, where he stayed in 1876 and 1877. He was familiar with the place. He set up his easel and visited the Eugène Manets, who rented a pied-à-terre there between 1880 and 1884. He remembered these joyful moments in a letter to Julie in 1905:

> I am deeply moved by the memories that you evoke and that, in my immense sorrow, remain the most precious consolation, because I loved your parents most sincerely and had for your mother an admiration as great as my friendship. In my misfortune,[44] I take refuge in the memories of the days of hope and I still see you as a little child with Madame your Mother, Monsieur your Father, Pazzi, or in Bougival, or in the townhouse in rue Villejust, where I was so kindly welcomed. And this past is dear to me and remains precious to me.[45]

Vignon exhibited several views of Bougival at the official Salon in 1878[46] as well as at the Impressionist exhibitions in which he participated from 1880 onwards.[47] In 1882, he was at Eugène's side as he arranged the works by his wife, who had remained in Nice with Bibi. In the report made to Berthe, Eugène indicated: "Nivard promised me your frames in two days. Vignon lent me a white frame in which your Nice beach looks very good. I have ordered similar frames for the others."[48]

In 1885, a view of Bougival[49] by Vignon belonged to the couple. Did Eugène exchange a work of art by his wife as a token of friendship and thanks for the assistance he had received? The approximate knowledge about this artist, rightly designated as the most little known of the Impressionists,[50] does not allow us to reconstruct the history of the work nor to identify any of his views of Bougival, at least to this day.

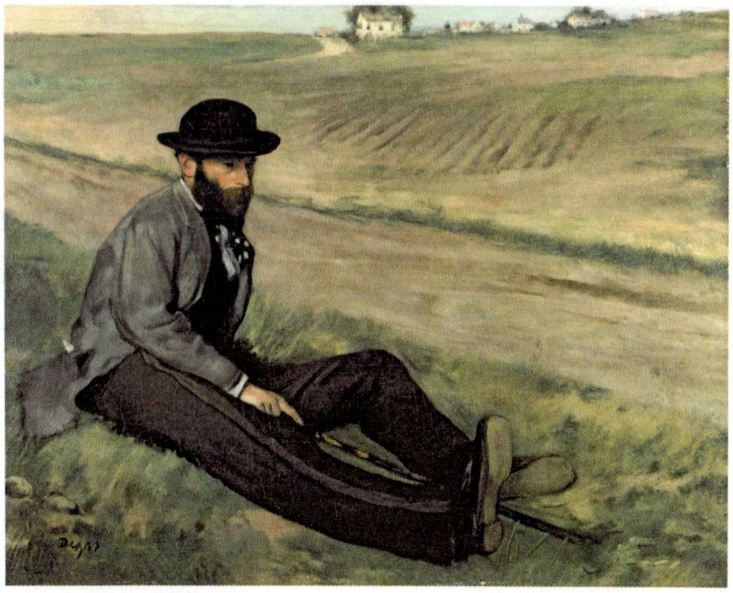

Edgar Degas (1834–1917)
Portrait of Eugène Manet, 1874
Oil on canvas, 52 × 65 cm
Private collection

AROUND THE ESTATE SALE OF ÉDOUARD MANET (1883–1884)

Édouard Manet's death was followed by artworks moving in various directions. Berthe got her portrait with a fan (p. 240), it is possible that Eugène received *Boy with Cherries* (p. 243) and Gustave the *Portrait of Mademoiselle Isabelle Lemonnier* (p. 224). The couple acquired many works at the estate sale. The use of different intermediaries—Jacob[51] and Duret being the best known—does not facilitate the analysis of official reports. As the lists drawn up by Berthe Morisot were not exhaustive, it is necessary to refer to sales invoices, mentions published in the press, and family correspondence in order to try to reconstruct this body of acquisitions. The most important pieces are well known: *Laundry* (p. 226), *The Lady with Fans* (p. 280–281), *Young Woman in a Garden* (p. 249), and *Singer at a Café-Concert*.[52] Also included: *Nude Arranging Her Hair* (p. 245), *Oysters and Champagne*,[53] *Departure of the Steamer*,[54] and *Under the Trees*.[55] Works on paper were not forgotten: two pastels (*Woman by the Sea*[56] and *Girl with a Summer Hat*[57]), a two-part drawing, now divided,[58] entitled *At the Concert*, with on one side *The Conductor* (p. 230), and on the other the public in the form of a series of top hats, also called *At the Concert*.[59] A lithograph of the *Execution of Maximilian* was mentioned by Tabarant. Finally, let us mention the enigmatic pastel *Young Man with a Blond Beard*,[60] acquired by La Narde. Although the sheet of paper could not be identified

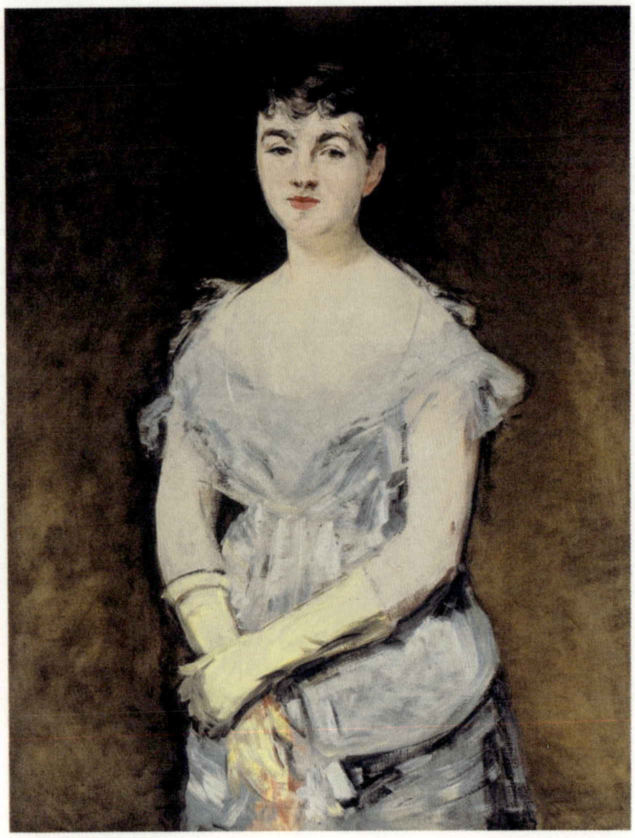

Édouard Manet (1832–1883)
Portrait of Mademoiselle Isabelle Lemonnier, 1879
Oil on canvas, 101 × 81 cm
Yoshino Gypsum Collection, on permanent loan at the Yamagata Art Museum

in the family inventories, Berthe Morisot's grandson, Denis Rouart—co-author of Édouard Manet's catalogue raisonné—gave it to his father Eugène Manet, and then to his mother Julie Manet-Rouart. Duret listed the work in 1902 without specifying its owner; therefore it doesn't rule out that it only entered the home of Julie Manet and her husband Ernest Rouart at the beginning of the twentieth century.

At the end of the sale, works went in various directions. In keeping with tradition, a memento of the late painter was reserved for family members and close friends. Berthe and Eugène immediately offered two Manets, which they had just bought, hence these works did not appear on any family inventory. *Woman by the Sea* was delivered to Monet on January 26, 1885, as confirmed by the recipient:

> **Dear Monsieur Manet, I received your brother's pastel in very good condition, and I am delighted to have it. Thank you so much for your kindness. My warmest regards to Madame Manet. Yours sincerely, Claude Monet.**[61]

Degas received equally rapidly *Departure of the Steamer*, which touched him deeply:

> **You wanted to give me great pleasure and you succeeded. There are even several intentions in your gift whose delicacy you will allow me to feel deeply.**[62]

We also note transactions. Berthe seemed to be in charge.

> **I am in talks to sell my child with cherries by Édouard. It's a relatively mediocre thing but was a huge hit at the Exposition. I'm asking for 5,000 and I would have them.**[63]

One may be surprised by the severity of the judgment, as *Boy with Cherries* (p. 243) is considered to be one of Manet's most accomplished early works. Does the tragedy associated with the painting explain Berthe's eagerness to get rid of it? The little model had indeed hanged himself in Manet's studio. The shock was such that Baudelaire wrote a short prose poem dedicated to the painter, whom he makes speak. Nine stanzas contain the whole story. The narrator "Manet-Baudelaire" recounts the meeting with the boy, his role in the studio—one day model, the other factotum— as well as the boy's mood swings. The narrator describes the discovery of the body, his efforts to untie it, the vain calls for help, then the announcement to the parents, and the preparation of the body for burial. The final point is given by the mother, who takes possession of the rope before leaving the studio forever, and perhaps longer. Since the publication of the poem in *Le Figaro* of February 7, 1864, Manet's painting had been irrevocably associated with the tragedy that Morisot mentioned in her notes.[64] The work left the rue de Villejust, sold on October 14, 1884 to Durand-Ruel for 3,600 francs.[65]

Berthe Morisot also made purchases by mutual agreement. She confided in her sister:

> **I bought for 1,700 francs a little corner of the garden which is a jewel. One of the prettiest he ever did [p. 248].**[66]

In the record of the paintings belonging to her, she specified:

> **sold to the Magasins du Louvre, or, rather, exchanged for a Turkish carpet, was then sold to my husband during the Exposition des Beaux-Arts for the sum of 1,200 francs.**[67]

Berthe also indicated that she possessed at this early date "a magnificent sketch of Madame Manet in a garden"[68] (p. 251) from her sister-in-law. As the work was exchanged for a portrait of Édouard and Suzanne, *Fishing* (p. 221), which was still hanging at that time in the apartment of Madame Manet *mère* in rue de Villejust,[69] it may be assumed that the Manet-Morisot-Leenhoff family had already agreed that the portraits for which they had posed would eventually revert to their sitter or their closest descendants, as a memento.

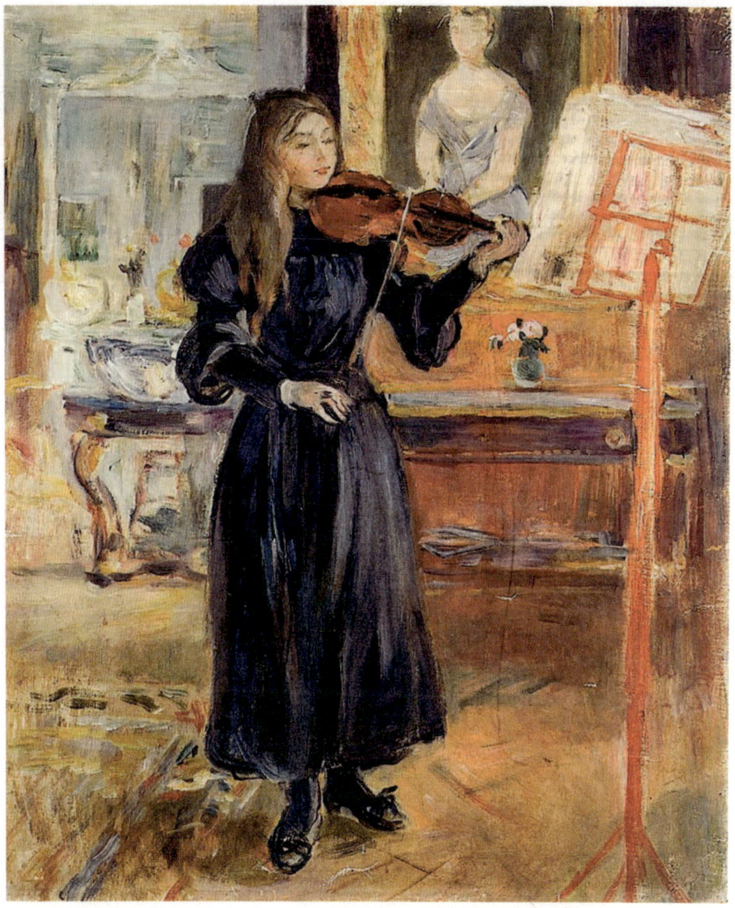

Berthe Morisot (1841–1895)
Learning the Violin, 1893
Oil on canvas, 41 × 33 cm
Private collection

ESTATES OF GUSTAVE MANET AND OF MADAME MANET *MÈRE* (1885)

Gustave Manet's death on December 18, 1884, was accompanied by works changing hands once again. This was the case with the *Portrait of Mademoiselle Isabelle Lemonnier* (p. 224), which passed on to the last surviving brother, Eugène. According to Rouart and Wildenstein, Eugène also recovered the copy of a self-portrait by Tintoretto[70] executed in the Louvre around 1854. If such were the case, the work quickly arrived at Eugène Spuller's home, and hence does not appear in any family inventory.

It was perhaps as part of Gustave's estate that three Monets were added to the couple's collection. Berthe Morisot wrote that it was only after Édouard Manet's death that she became involved with her fellow Impressionists, and in particular with Monet. Their budding friendship was sealed by a work of art: a decorative panel that Monet painted to decorate the living room in the rue de Villejust and which he delivered in person in November 1884.[71] In this case, how can we explain that, in 1885, Berthe possessed three Monets from the 1870s: *Boat, Rouen*,[72] 1872, *Boats in a Harbor* (p. 252),[73] 1873, *The Geldersekade in Amsterdam, Winter* (p. 252),[74] 1874? The explanation is undoubtedly to be found among the Manet family. The latter were indeed among the most loyal supporters of the leader of the Impressionists. To rescue the artist from a tight situation, in June 1875,[75] Gustave bought from him, a set of five paintings that Monet offered to sell to recover his stake.[76] It is very possible that the three paintings mentioned by Berthe Morisot came from what remained of this set. A purchase or rather assistance not declared as such.

The succession of Madame Manet *mère* marked the end of an era and brought the period of dividing up possessions to a close. None of the "paintings by various artists and objets d'art found in the home of Madame Manet *mère*" in the apartment she lived in on the third floor of the rue de Villejust passed to her two heirs, her son Eugène and little Julie. No fewer than six Monets, including the iconic painting *La Grenouillère*[77] in the Metropolitan Museum of Art in New York, a Pissarro, a Sisley, sketches by Fantin after Giorgione and Titian, works by Eva Gonzalès, de Nittis, Brandon, Balleroy, Monginot, Desboutin, and Ribot. Let us also mention two portraits of Édouard Manet: one by Fantin,[78] the other by Monet.[79] Berthe evoked this small painting in an unpublished letter she sent to its creator from Cowes in 1875:

> Dear Monsieur, Édouard Manet told me that you had been kind enough to bring the sketch you did of him. I didn't have time to thank you before leaving Paris. I am all the more sensitive to your memento because I greatly value what you do. In front of these very English seascapes which surround us, my husband and I often speak about your talent and your ability to depict this maritime motion. Please pass on my

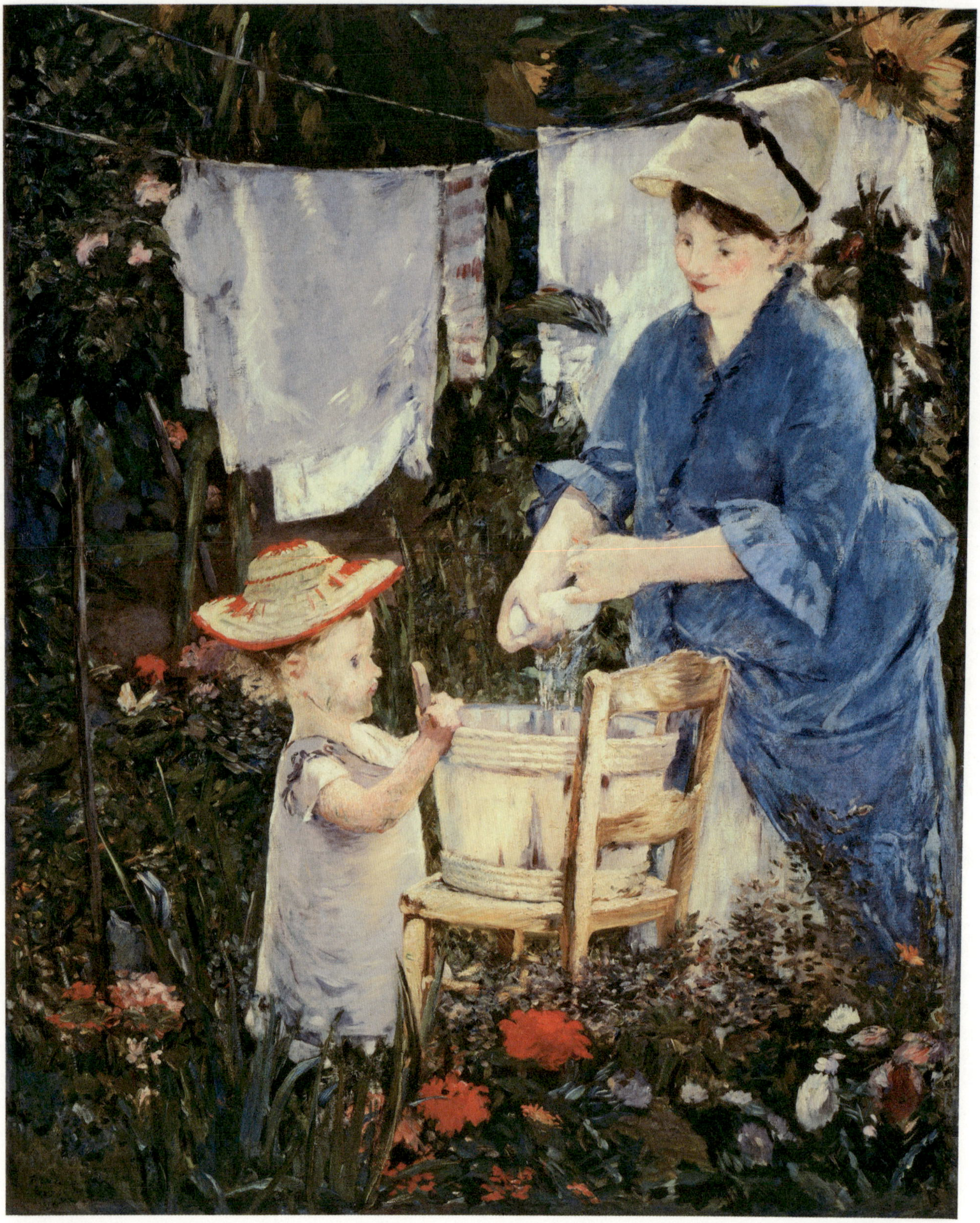

Édouard Manet (1832–1883)
Laundry, 1875
Oil on canvas, 145.4 × 114.9 cm
Philadelphia, Barnes Foundation

warmest regards to Madame Monet. Yours sincerely, Berthe Manet.[80]

Despite Berthe's obvious interest, the work, like all the others mentioned above, obviously belonged to Suzanne Leenhoff, Édouard Manet's wife. The above-mentioned exchange took place after the death of Madame Manet *mère* on January 8, 1885. Suzanne gave Berthe back one of her youthful works, *The Harbor at Lorient*,[81] which Berthe had offered to Manet in 1869. In gratitude and as a token of affection, perhaps Suzanne[82] offered her portrait in pastel[83] before definitively leaving the rue de Villejust for Gennevilliers.

The valuation of the furniture attached to the deed of succession of Madame Eugénie Manet née Fournier having disappeared,[84] we must rely on other sources to try to identify the paintings that she bequeathed to Eugène. The portrait of Monsieur and Madame Auguste Manet (p. 235)[85] and a drawing in red chalk after Monsieur Manet (p. 6)[86] were unquestionably from her. In the 1885 inventory, we note the presence of a copy of Titian,[87] a second entered the family collection after 1895.[88] *Jupiter and Antiope* (p. 242) was the largest, *Venus of Urbino*[89] was a small panel. Both belonged to Julie.

In 1885, Berthe also owned two Pissarros.[90] Although these two works are regularly found in all subsequent inventories, their brief designation and the lack of additional information do not allow them to be identified. It would be interesting to document the sincere friendship between the Manet-Morisot-Pissarro family. According to a family tradition, Pissarro saved the copy that Berthe did after *The Villa d'Este* by Corot[91] from destruction. The work probably entered his collection at an early date. Julie bought it in April 1907[92] from the painter's widow for a sum that varied, depending on the sources, between 2,000 and 3,000 francs.[93] Clearly, Pissarro encountered Berthe early on and visited her regularly, and he discovered some of her works when they were barely dry. On the subject of *Pasie Sewing in the Garden* (p. 284), which Ernest suggested presenting at the Impressionist exhibition of 1882, Berthe indicated:

> **Pissarro and Édouard saw it and neither of them seemed to be amazed. However, if it looks less bad than the others, put it in.**[94]

As a collector, Pissarro owned two other Morisot paintings[95] in addition to the Corot copy. As his financial situation did not allow him to purchase works, the master of Éragny favored exchanges. No doubt he did the same with Morisot. Last but not least, *Beneath the Wood* by Manet, acquired at Édouard's posthumous sale, and which appears on the inventory drawn up by Berthe in 1885, passed to Pissarro at a later date.[96] Could it be anything other than a gift in memory of Édouard?

FINAL ACQUISITIONS (1886–1895)

Should Eugène Manet and Berthe Morisot be considered collectors? The works that entered the rue de Villejust from 1886 onwards were above all family portraits or tokens of friendship. Around 1886, *Julie in the Garden*, a pastel by Guillaumin, now lost,[97] and in 1887 *Child with a Cat* by Renoir, of which the family kept at least two preparatory drawings, enriched their estate.

When Eugène died in 1892, perhaps because she needed ready cash, Berthe considered selling some works: Manet's *Laundry* (p. 226), which she liked less than *The Lady with Fans* (p. 280–281),[98] and a Monet. She initially turned to the Galerie Boussod et Valadon. Maurice Joyant wrote to her on April 26, 1892:

> **Dear Madam,**
> **I have received the two paintings by Monet and Manet: would you be so kind as to tell me what you are asking for each. Please excuse me also for insisting, but have you considered the possibility of holding an Exhibition of your paintings, pastels, and drawings (about 40) in my gallery around May 15? Yours faithfully.**[99]

On June 29, 1892, he wrote to her again:

> **Dear Madame,**
> **I've received your note informing me that you do not wish to let Manet's *Laundry* go for below 14,000 francs. It will be absolutely impossible for me to carry out the deal I told you about at that price. My client will not pay a penny more than the price he has set. Perhaps if you decided to let your Manet go for 12,000 francs net to you (cash of course) I could manage to close. I must tell you that if we miss out on this deal, I know of no one in Paris who is capable of buying your Manet at the moment. Indeed, some time ago, I tried to sell a Manet, *The Bullfighter*, and I couldn't even find a buyer at 10,000 francs. Please consider if you want to take advantage of this opportunity, perhaps unique, to sell your painting.**[100]

On July 5, 1892, a final letter from Joyant came to her:

> **Dear Madame, I am pleased to inform you that the deal involving your Manet has concluded and that**

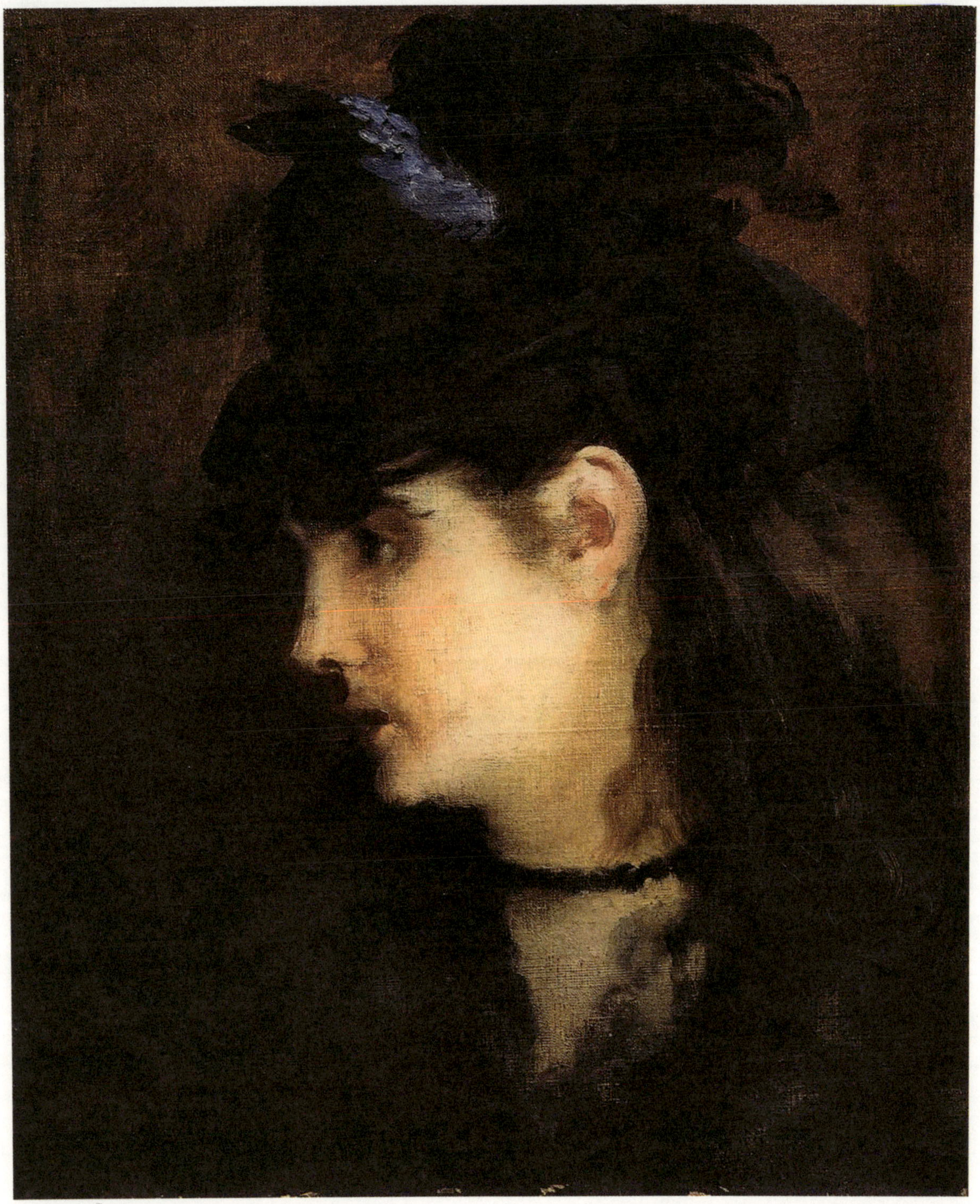

Édouard Manet (1832-1883)
Berthe Morisot in Profile, 1869
Oil on canvas, 41 × 32 cm
Private collection

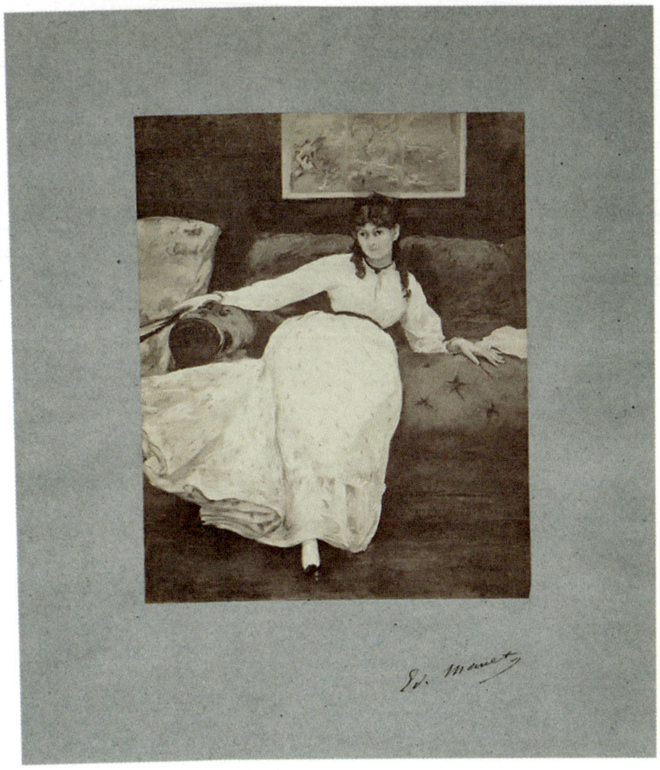

Photograph of The Rest *by Édouard Manet, signed by the artist,* n.d.
Julie Manet kept this work all her life
Private collection

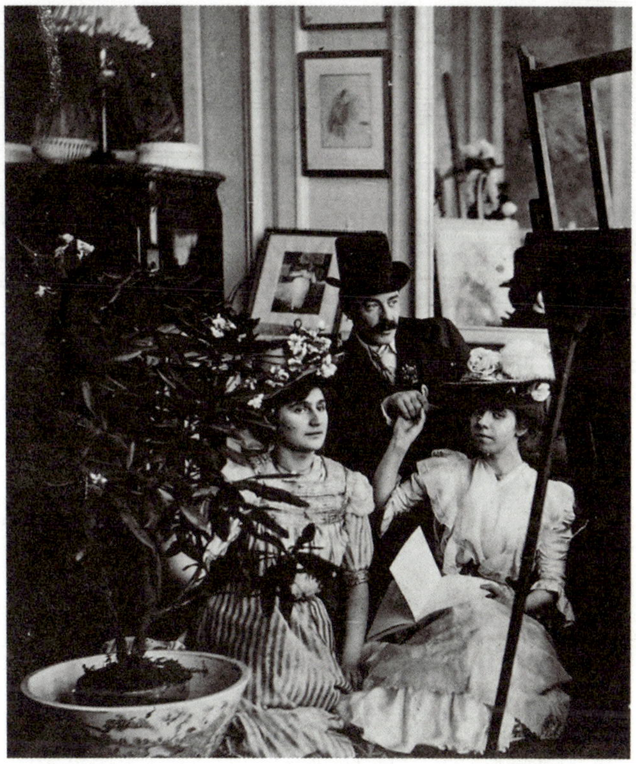

Julie Manet, Paul Valéry, and Jeannie Gobillard (left); in the background, a photograph of The Rest *signed by Édouard Manet,* March 23, 1900
Private collection

> **consequently I have credited to your account the sum of 12,000 francs (twelve thousand) for your painting *Laundry*.**[101]

Berthe Morisot accepted, and the work was sold the same day to Paul Gallimard (1850–1929) for the sum of 19,000 francs, which included the gallery's commission.[102] As the Galerie Boussod et Valadon did not add works to its stock until after sales had been concluded,[103] the stock book does not identify the Monet painting deposited by Berthe Morisot. In all likelihood, she recovered her property because she deposited her three "small" Monets[104] at Durand-Ruel on August 19, 1893. She asked for 5,000 francs for *Boat, Rouen* and 3,000 for each of the other two. A garden by Manet that can be identified, in view of the 6,000 francs expected, as the *The Garden at Bellevue* (p. 248)[105] was entrusted to the dealer on the same date. The Manet and two Monets were returned on December 16, 1893. The view of Rouen was not returned until November 8, 1895, which is why it does not appear in Berthe Morisot's estate inventory.

1894 saw an increase in the number of family portraits. Renoir painted a bust of Julie (p. 214) and a double portrait of Berthe Morisot and her daughter,[106] of which we know a preparatory pastel (p. 43 and 217). The Impressionist acquired her portrait with a bouquet of violets by Manet (p. 218) at the Duret sale. A misunderstanding would explain why she missed out on *The Rest* (p. 237).[107] The memory of the work remained very present. Julie would piously keep a photo of the painting signed by "E. Manet" in her living room (above).

The family portraits were soon one of the issues of Jules de Jouy's estate. In his will,[108] he bequeathed to Julie's family the portrait of Émilie Manet (sister of Eugénie Fournier, Manet's wife and Julie's great-aunt) by an unknown artist, as well as the portrait of Jules de Jouy by Manet (p. 17). Other works were reserved for his close circle, first of all: Monsieur Maugras, executor of his will. The portrait of Émilie would never be heard of again. The Manet, on the other hand, was claimed by Maugras and caused a lot of ink to flow. Suzanne Leenhoff took sides and confided to her sister-in-law on May 31, 1894:

> **My dear Berthe, What I think about the portrait is that it should go to Julie, it was first bequeathed by will to her father, and for Julie it will be a memento of her godfather uncle. Moreover, it was painted by**

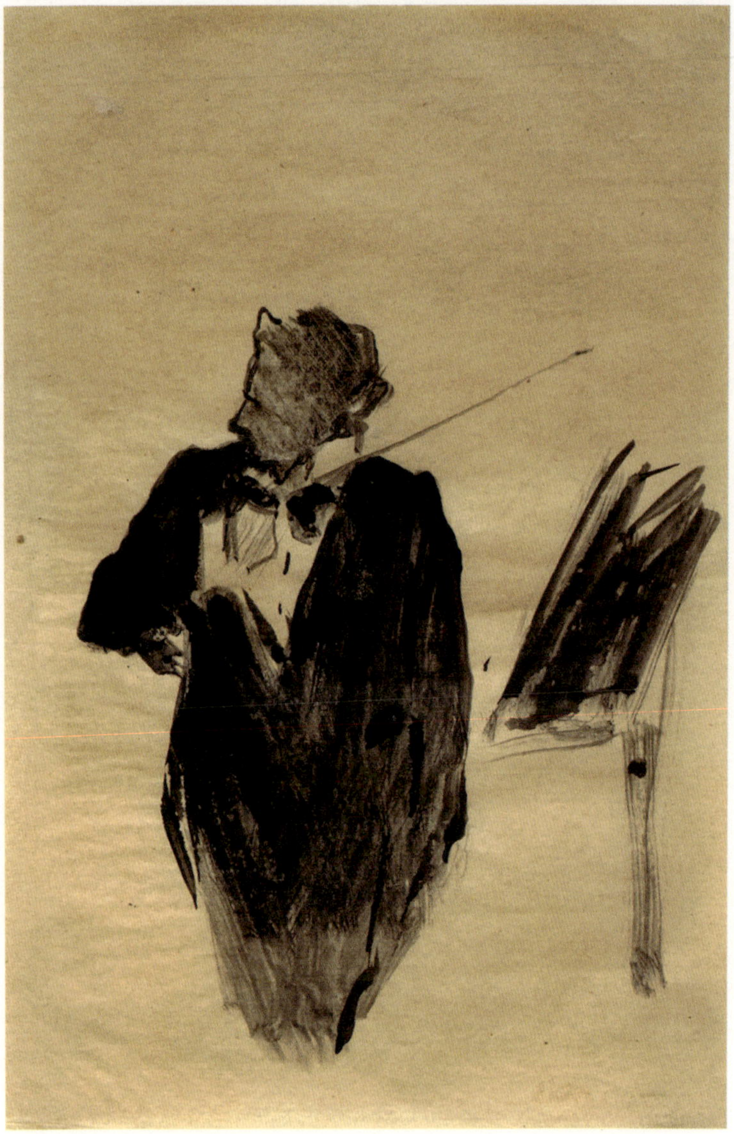

Édouard Manet (1832–1883)
The Conductor, c. 1878–80
Indian ink wash on paper, 18.3 × 12 cm
Private collection

> **her real paternal uncle (by friendship). This portrait is only valuable for yourself. If one wanted to sell it, it would get a low sum—portraits are not usually sold and do not offer any interest for a connoisseur, so I don't understand at all why Monsieur Maugras wants to have it—while there are very beautiful drawings by Fragonard in his cousin's living room which are much better. You had a good idea to offer it to the Louvre, at least everyone would see it—and that was indeed the opinion of the deceased for some time.[109]**

The work went to Maugras and was later sold to Emil Goeritz. Gone was the Louvre. Julie inherited—in addition to furniture and real estate—a portrait of her mother by Manet bought by her godfather uncle at the 1884 sale: *Berthe Morisot in Profile* (p. 228).

Tante Suzanne did not forget Julie's birthday. On the occasion of a visit to Gennevilliers on November 2, 1894, she gave her some mementos of Manet a few days before her sixteenth birthday. Julie evoked it in her diary:

> **We dropped in on Tante Suzanne, where we saw some sketchbooks of drawings which Oncle Édouard did on his travels—they're sketches in pen and ink of sculptures, paintings, etc. We brought back three of them—a red chalk drawing of a woman after Raphael,[110] I think, and two watercolour medallions, one of the Three Graces on a mauve ground [p. 246], that other, a woman with a violin at her side, probably Saint Celia [also known as *Allegorical Figure*].[111]**

In an unpublished letter of January 8, 1895, Suzanne mentioned other sketches:

> **My dear Berthe,**
> **I'm very upset that I cannot go out at the moment. The Gennevilliers' car is being used by a doctor, otherwise I would have already been at your house, in spite of the bad state of my health. Édouard was also supposed to bring you the promised sketches [p. 244] and the poor fellow is coughing a lot, which is serious for him.[112]**

Finally, let us mention two unidentified works that were only mentioned in Berthe Morisot's estate inventory: a painting by Blanche (Jacques-Émile, no doubt) and a poster by Chéret. There was no lack of Japanese prints, the detail of one of them can be seen in a photo taken at the home of Julie and Ernest Rouart at the beginning of the century.

Art was everywhere, including in Berthe's testamentary letter to Julie:

> **Give your Tante Edma a souvenir of me, and your cousins too; and give Monet's *Boats in a Harbor* [p. 252] to your cousin Gabriel. Tell Monsieur Degas that if he founds a museum he is to choose a Manet. A keepsake for Monet; one for Renoir; and one of my drawings for Bartholomé.[113]**

Such was Julie's artistic legacy. Such were the paintings of her life.

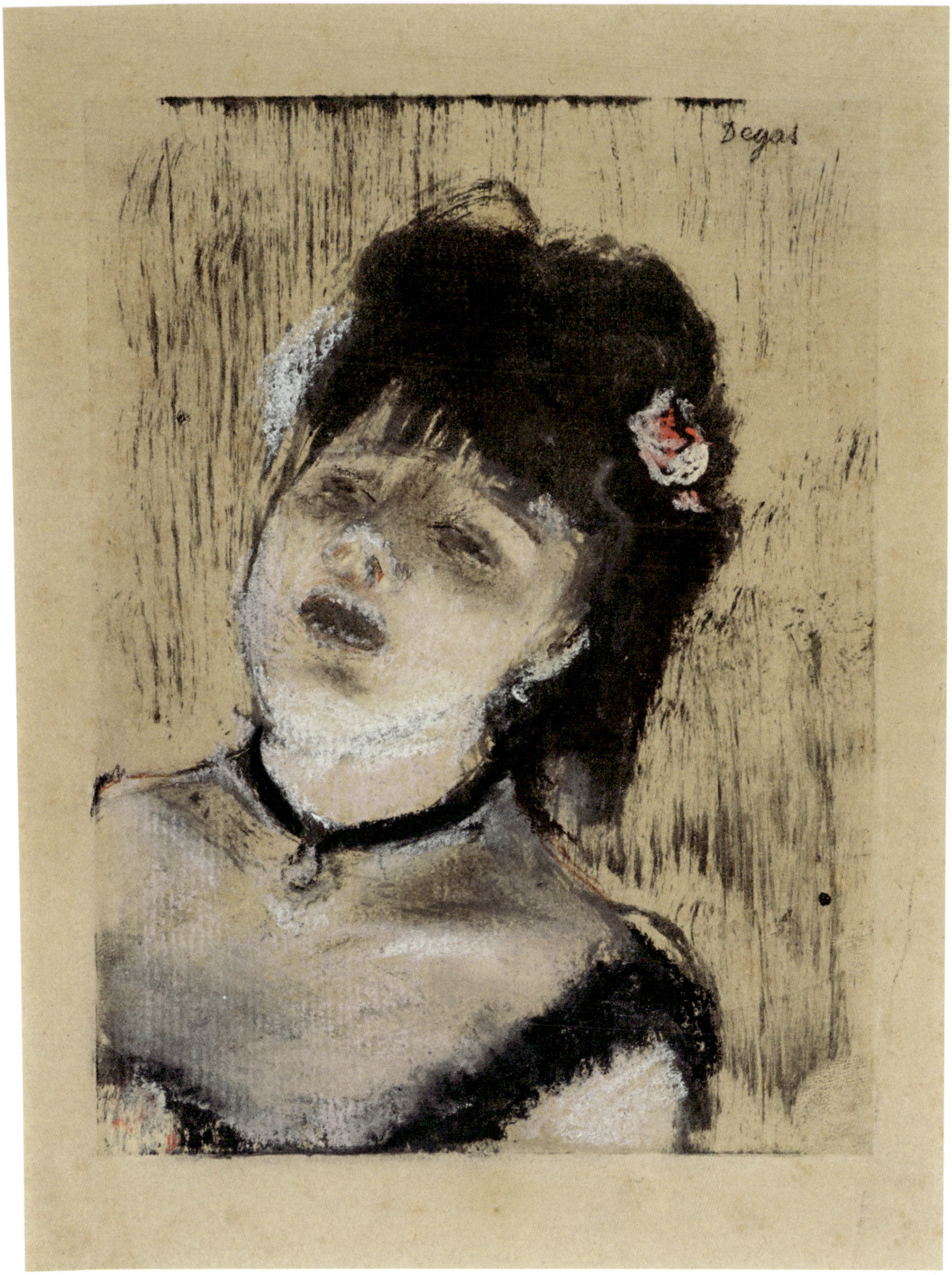

Edgar Degas (1834–1917)
Singer at a Café-Concert, c. 1879
Pastel and monotype on paper, 37 × 28 cm
Private collection

NOTES

1. Estate inventory of Madame Eugène Manet (widow), March 13, 1895, AN, MC/ET/XXX/1293.
2. Berthe Morisot, *Venus Asking Vulcan for Arms*, after Boucher, 1884 (CMR 145), private collection.
3. Estate inventory of Monsieur Eugène Manet, no work by Berthe Morisot was listed. We find the mention "A still life study by Manet, a landscape painting with a character and Love valued at one hundred francs" (AN, MC/ET/XXX/1263).
4. This amount also included a still life by Manet cited above.
5. Estate inventory of Camille Pissarro entitled "Liste des tableaux Paris," n.d., Oxford, Ashmoleum Museum. On Monet's role in Pissarro's succession, see exh. cat. Paris 2019, p. 196.
6. According to Sylvie Patry, eighty-five percent of the Morisots remain in the family. See exh. cat. Paris, Quebec, Philadelphia, and Dallas 2018–19, p. 24 (Quebec edition).
7. See the essay in the present volume "And so Ended the Existence of the Rue de Villejust," p. 124–133.
8. Berthe Morisot, "green notebook A", 1885–86, Paris, Musée Marmottan Monet, inv. D.5-1986.2014.2.
9. Henri Jennings was the owner of the land that Eugène and Berthe Manet bought on rue de Villejust to build their house.
10. Paris, Musée Marmottan Monet, inv. D.4-1986. 2013.727.
11. *Bulletin de la Société archéologique et historique du Limousin*, 1846, p. 7.
12. Housed in the bishop's palace, the establishment would then become the Musée des Beaux-Arts de Limoges.
13. Estate inventory of Edme Tiburce Morisot, February 25, 1874, AN, MC/ET/XL/478.
14. Rouart 1950, p. 119.
15. Évariste Fragonard, *Portrait known as "of Mme Morisot,"* c. 1805, private collection. Considering the style and fashion of dress, it is more likely to be the mother of Marie-Cornélie Morisot, Marie Caroline Mayniel (1793–1870).
16. Marriage contract between Berthe Morisot and Eugène Manet, December 21, 1874, AN, MC/ET/XL/487.
17. "Legros / n° 41 portrait d'Eugène Manet," in Berthe Morisot, *Tableaux* (handwritten manuscript c. 1885), Arch. BS, inv. 2021.2.198.
18. Alphonse Legros, *Portrait of Édouard Manet*, 1863, Paris, Petit Palais, Musée des Beaux-Arts de la Ville de Paris.
19. Édouard Manet, *The Luncheon on the Grass*, 1863, Paris, Musée d'Orsay.
20. He actually exhibited two paintings: *Scientific Discussion* (no. 1156 belonging to Doctor Bicord) and *The Lectern* (no. 1155).
21. Desnoyers 1863, p. 42.
22. Joos van Craesbeeck, *Painter Painting a Portrait*, formerly known as *Craesbeeck's Studio*, 1626, Paris, Musée du Louvre.
23. "Fantin La Tour / n° 39 *id.* [esquisse] Crasbeck," in Berthe Morisot, *Tableaux* (handwritten manuscript c. 1885), Arch. BS, inv. 2021.2.198.
24. "N° 365 Craesbeke (Copie d'après). *Craesbeke peignant un portrait*. Musée du Louvre. N° 2340. A Eugène Manet," in Fantin-Latour 1911, p. 50.
25. "Fantin La Tour / n° 37 esquisse d'après Rubens," in Berthe Morisot, *Tableaux* (handwritten manuscript c. 1885), Arch. BS, inv. 2021.2.198.
26. "N° 371 – D) Paysage. Musée du Louvre, n° 2119. Toile. H. 0m233. L 0m.482 A E. Manet," in Fantin-Latour 1911, p. 50.
27. The copies by Fantin-Latour appearing in the inventory after Édouard Manet's death were inspired by Titian and Giorgione. See Rouart and Wildenstein 1975, vol. I, p. 106. It is therefore likely that the landscape belonged to Eugène.
28. "Fantin La Tour / n° 38 *id* [esquisse] d'après Rembrandt," in Berthe Morisot, *Tableaux* (handwritten manuscript c. 1885), Arch. BS, inv. 2021.2.198.
29. "Fantin La Tour / n° 36 *id* nature morte," ibid., Arch. BS, inv. 2021.2.198.
30. "N° 366 Les deux Bellin (copie d'après). Musée du Louvre, n° 1156. A Eugène Manet (petite copie)," in Fantin-Latour 1911, p. 50.
31. Rouart 1950, p. 21.
32. Ibid., p. 31.
33. Degas's fan features in the background of *The Sisters* (p. 46) painted in Marie-Cornélie Morisot's living room, rue Franklin in Paris.
34. "Puvis de Chavanne [*sic*] (Pierre) / 34bis dessin à la plume," in Berthe Morisot, *Tableaux* (handwritten manuscript c. 1885), Arch. BS, inv. 2021.2.198.
35. "Puvis de Chavanne [*sic*] (Pierre) / 34 dessin au crayon rouge," ibid., Arch. BS, inv. 2021.2.198.
36. A section entitled "Studies done in the vicinity of Beuzeval (Calvados)" (nos. 89 to 109) featured in the *Catalogue de la vente qui aura lieu par suite de la mort de M. Riesener*, Paris, Hôtel Drouot, April 10–11, 1879.
37. "Riesener / 40 Vue d'automne," in Berthe Morisot, *Tableaux* (handwritten manuscript c. 1885), Arch. BS, inv. 2021.2.198.
38. Edma Morisot, *Portrait of Berthe Morisot Painting*, 1865, private collection.
39. "Manet Édouard / 12 Julie Manet bébé" in Berthe Morisot, *Tableaux* (handwritten manuscript c. 1885), Arch. BS, inv. 2021.2.198.
40. Berthe Morisot, March 13, 1895, AN, MC/ET/XXX/1293; Tabarant 1947, p. 366.
41. "de Gas (Edgard) / 30 chanteuse de café-concert (dessin)," in Berthe Morisot, *Tableaux* (handwritten manuscript c. 1885), Arch. BS, inv. 2021.2.198.
42. "de Gas (Edgard) / 28 portrait de Mme Gobillard (pastel)," in Berthe Morisot, *Tableaux* (handwritten manuscript c. 1885), Arch. BS, inv. 2021.2.198.
43. On the subject of Vignon, see exh. cat. Pontoise 2002.
44. He lost his eyesight.
45. Victor Vignon to Julie Manet-Rouart, January 26, 1905, in exh. cat. Lodève 2006, p. 116.
46. *The Seine at Bougival, Spring Day* (no. 2243), location unknown.
47. Impressionist exhibition of 1881: *Willow Plantation at Bougival* (no. 156) location unknown, *Green Path at Bougival* (no. 163) loc.inc.; exhibition of 1881: *The Seine at Bougival* (no. 195) location unknown.
48. Rouart 1950, p. 104.
49. "Victor Vignon / 35 Vue de Bougival," in Berthe Morisot, *Tableaux* (handwritten manuscript c. 1885), Arch. BS, inv. 2021.2 198.
50. Exh. cat. Pontoise 2002, p. 5. With thanks to Christophe Duvivier.
51. In *Almanach du commerce, de l'industrie, de la magistrature et de l'administration*. The art expert Fulgence Jacob established his premises at 9 rue Buffault in the 9th arrondissement under the name of Fulgence from 1880 to 1887, then under that of Jacob from 1887 to 1894. He moved in 1896 to rue Châteaudun.
52. Édouard Manet, *Singer at a Café-Concert*, c. 1879, oil on canvas, 73 × 92 cm, location unknown (RW 310)
53. Édouard Manet, *Still Life with Oysters*, c. 1877, location unknown.
54. Édouard Manet, *Departure of the Steamer*, 1869, Winterthur, Oskar Reinhart collection.
55. Édouard Manet, *Under the Trees*, also known as *The Outing in the Countryside*, 1878, location unknown.
56. Édouard Manet, *Woman by the Sea*, 1880–81, location unknown.
57. Édouard Manet, *Girl with a Summer Hat*, c. 1879, location unknown.
58. This was a family decision, as the work was already divided in 1932 when Eugène and Julie Rouart lent it to the Manet exhibition: it appeared under two separate numbers, 110 and 111.
59. Édouard Manet, *At the Concert* [c. 1878–80], location unknown.
60. Édouard Manet, *Young Man with a Blond Beard*, 1880, location unknown.

61. Letter from Claude Monet to Eugène Manet, January 26, 1885, Paris, Musée Marmottan Monet, inv. D.4-1986.2013.252.
62. Rouart 1950, p. 121.
63. Ibid., p. 119.
64. "*Boy with Cherries* which belonged to my husband was sold through Durand-Ruel. This child who in a fit of despair had hanged himself in Édouard's studio inspired one of Baudelaire's little prose tales," Berthe Morisot, "green notebook A", 1885–1886, Paris, Musée Marmottan Monet, inv. D.5-1986.2014.2.
65. With thanks to the Archives Durand-Ruel.
66. Rouart 1950, p. 119.
67. Berthe Morisot, "green notebook A", 1885–1886, Paris, Musée Marmottan Monet, inv. D.5-1986.2014.2.
68. Rouart 1950, p. 119.
69. "Paintings by various artists and objets d'art found in the home of Madame Manet *mère* . . . river landscape with small boat by Manet valued at 300," transcription of Édouard Manet's estate inventory in Rouart and Wildenstein 1975, I, p. 106.
70. Édouard Manet, *Self-Portrait by Tintoretto*, 1854, Dijon, Musée des Beaux-Arts.
71. On this point see exh. cat. Paris 2017–18.
72. "Monet (Claude) / 27 bateau effet du soir," in Berthe Morisot, *Tableaux* (handwritten manuscript c. 1885), Arch. BS, inv. 2021.2.198.
73. "Monet (Claude) / 25 bateau en réparation au Havre," ibid., Arch. BS, inv. 2021.2.198.
74. "Monet (Claude) / 26 vue de Hollande effet de neige," ibid., Arch. BS, inv. 2021.2.198.
75. Claude Monet's account book, 1872–77, Paris, Musée Marmottan Monet, inv. 5160.2013.1.
76. Letter from Claude Monet to Gustave Manet, Montgeron, December 4, 1876, Wildenstein, 1979, vol. II, p. 431, no. 97.
77. Claude Monet, *La Grenouillère*, 1869, New York, The Metropolitan Museum of Art.
78. Henri Fantin-Latour, *Portrait of Édouard Manet*, 1867, Chicago, The Art Institute of Chicago.
79. Claude Monet, *Manet Painting in Monet's Garden in Argenteuil*, 1874 (W. 342), location unknown.
80. Letter from Berthe Morisot to Claude Monet, Cowes, Isle of Wight, known from Julie Manet's transcription, in Julie Manet, *Recueil de transcriptions de lettres de Berthe Morisot*, fol. 23, Arch. BS, inv. 2021.2.579.
81. Berthe Morisot, *The Harbor at Lorient*, 1869, Washington, D.C., National Gallery of Art.
82. "Tableaux par M. Édouard Manet se trouvant dans l'appartement de Mme Manet rue de Villejust n° 40 . . . Portrait de Mme Manet au pastel," transcription of the estate inventory of Édouard Manet in Rouart and Wildenstein 1975, I, p. 106.
83. "Manet (Édouard) / 10 portrait de Mme Ed. Manet (pastel)," in Berthe Morisot, *Tableaux* (handwritten manuscript c. 1885), Arch. BS, inv. 2021.2.198; Édouard Manet, *Madame Édouard Manet*, 1873, Toledo, Toledo Museum of Fine Arts.
84. Declaration of the estate of Madame Eugène Manet née Fournier, Arch. Paris, DQ7 12 697.
85. "Manet (Édouard) / 7 portrait de Monsieur et Madame Manet," in Berthe Morisot, *Tableaux* (handwritten manuscript c. 1885), Arch. BS, inv. 2021.2.198.
86. "Manet (Édouard) / 21 dessin d'après M. Manet (crayon rouge)," ibid., Arch. BS, inv. 2021.2.198.
87. "Manet (Édouard) / 20 copie du Titien," ibid., Arch. BS, inv. 2021.2.198.
88. Unless the work was forgotten in Berthe Morisot's estate inventory.
89. Édouard Manet, *Venus of Urbino*, 1854–56 (RW 7), location unknown.
90. "Pissarro (Camille) / 32 effet d'automne / 33 un jardin," in Berthe Morisot, *Tableaux* (handwritten manuscript c. 1885), Arch. BS, inv. 2021.2. 198.
91. Rouart 1950, p. 14.
92. List of paintings sold or donated, Oxford, Ashmolean Museum, Pissarro Archive.
93. According to the list of paintings sold or donated, it was sold for 2,000 francs (Oxford, Ashmolean Museum, Pissarro Archive) and according to the list of friends' undivided paintings, it was sold for 3,000 francs (Musée de Pontoise).
94. Rouart 1950, p. 105.
95. A painting among twenty by Berthe Morisot appears in a list that serves as an inventory: "Collections of paintings, pastels, and watercolors by various painters," Musée de Pontoise. In exh. cat. Lodève 2006, Hugues Wilhem identifies this work—without however giving an explanation—as *In Bougival*, 1882, Cardiff, National Museum of Wales. He also mentions a *Toilet*: *Woman Putting on Makeup* (1877, Paris, Musée d'Orsay) or *Woman at her Toilet* (1877, location unknown, CMR 73), p. 108–110.
96. Estate inventory of Pissarro, entitled "List of paintings (Paris)," n.d., Oxford, Ashmolean Museum, Pissarro Archive.
97. Paris, Musée Marmottan Monet, inv. D. 4-1986. 2013.727.
98. Rouart 1950, p. 120.
99. Letter from Maurice Joyant to Berthe Morisot, April 26, 1892, Arch. BS, inv. 2021.2.482.
100. Letter from Maurice Joyant to Berthe Morisot, June 29, 1892, Arch. BS, inv. 2021.2.483.
101. Letter from Maurice Joyant to Berthe Morisot, July 5, 1892, Arch. BS, inv. 2021.2.481.
102. Boussod et Valadon stock book, vol. 13, stock no. 22428, p. 103.
103. Entries and sales frequently have the same date.
104. *The Geldersekade in Amsterdam, Winter* deposit DR 8296 (p. 252); *Boats in a Harbor*, deposit DR 8297 (p. 252); *Boat, Rouen*, deposit DR 8295.
105. Deposit DR 8294.
106. Pierre-Auguste Renoir, *Berthe Morisot and her Daughter, Julie Manet* [1894], private collection.
107. Rouart 1950, p. 179.
108. Will and codicil of Anatole Jules de Jouy, deposited on March 9, 1894 with Émile Pinguet, notary in Paris, 18, rue des Pyramides, AN, MC/ET/LXXIX/1017.
109. Letter from Suzanne Leenhoff to Berthe Morisot, May 31, 1894, Paris, Musée Marmottan Monet, inv. D.4-1986.2013.48.
110. Édouard Manet, *Lucrezia after Andrea del Sarto*, 1853–54, private collection.
111. Manet ed. 2017, Kindle edition, trans. Jane Roberts, p. 64.
112. Suzanne Leenhoff to Berthe Morisot, January 8, 1895, Arch. BS, inv. 2021.2.403.
113. Manet ed. 2017, Kindle edition, trans. Jane Roberts, p. 68–69.

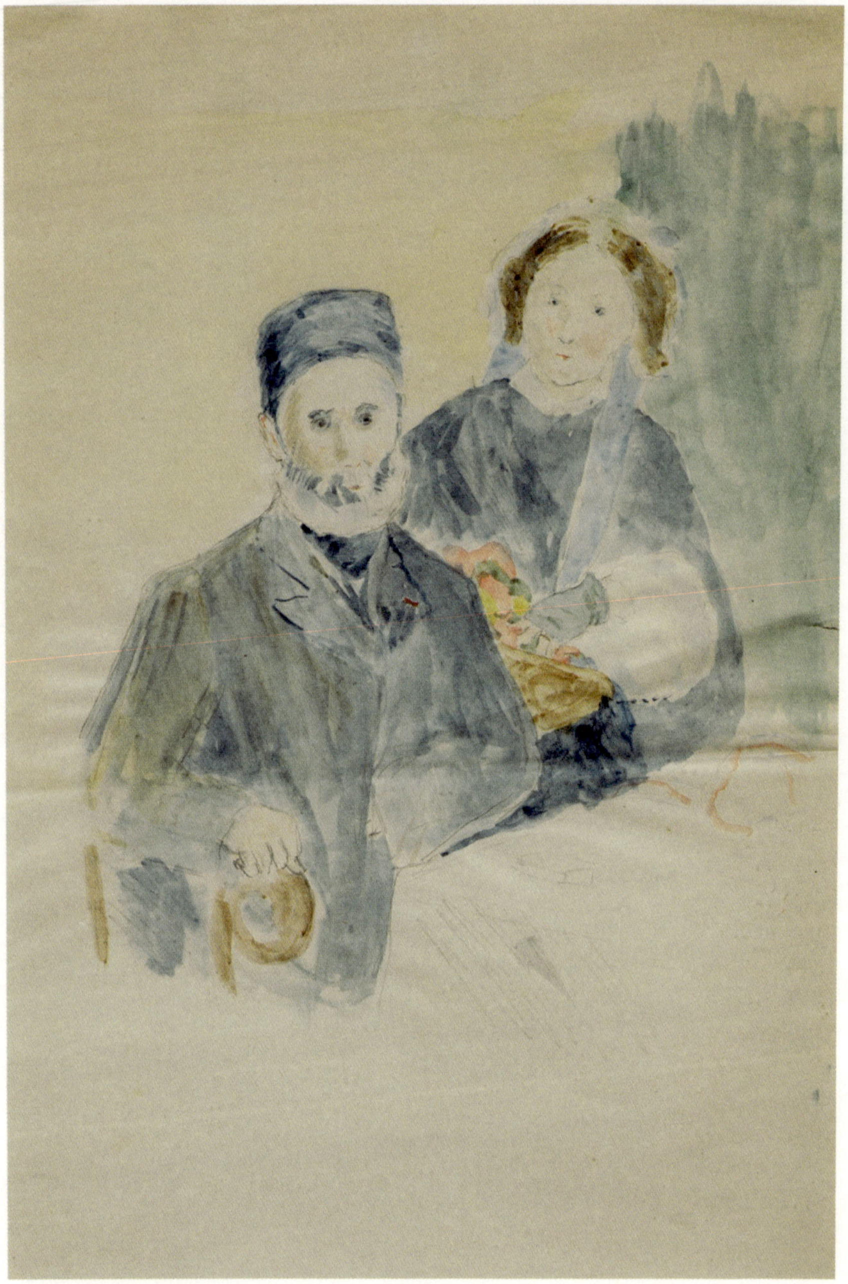

Julie Manet (1878–1966)
M. and Mme Auguste Manet or *Portrait of Manet's Parents* (after Édouard Manet), n.d.
Watercolor on paper, 29 × 19 cm
Paris, Musée Marmottan Monet

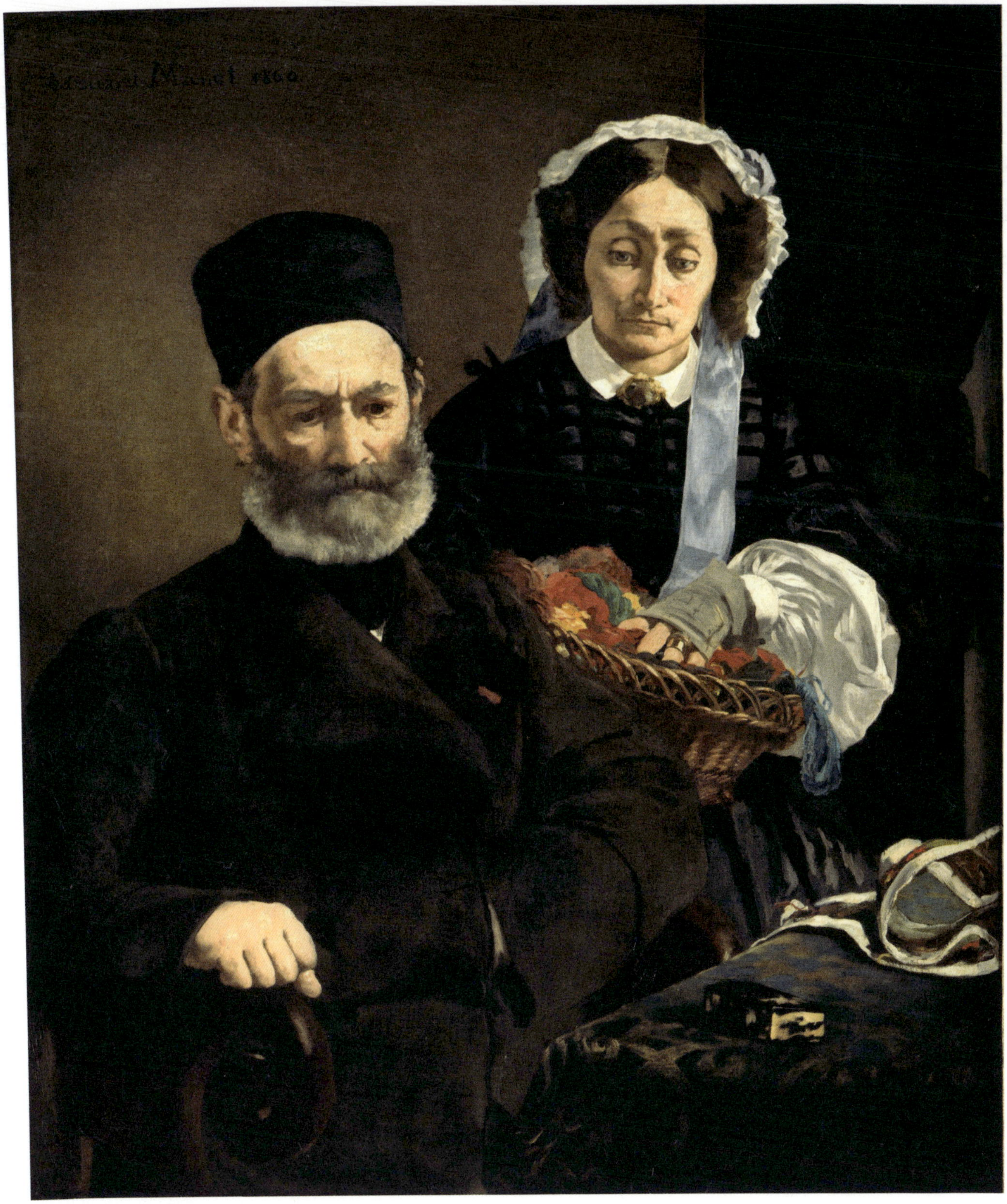

Édouard Manet (1832–1883)
M. and Mme Auguste Manet or *Portrait of Manet's Parents*, 1860
Oil on canvas, 110 × 90 cm
Paris, Musée d'Orsay, acquired thanks to the generosity of the Rouart-Manet family, of Mme Jeannette Veil-Picard and of a foreign benefactor, 1977

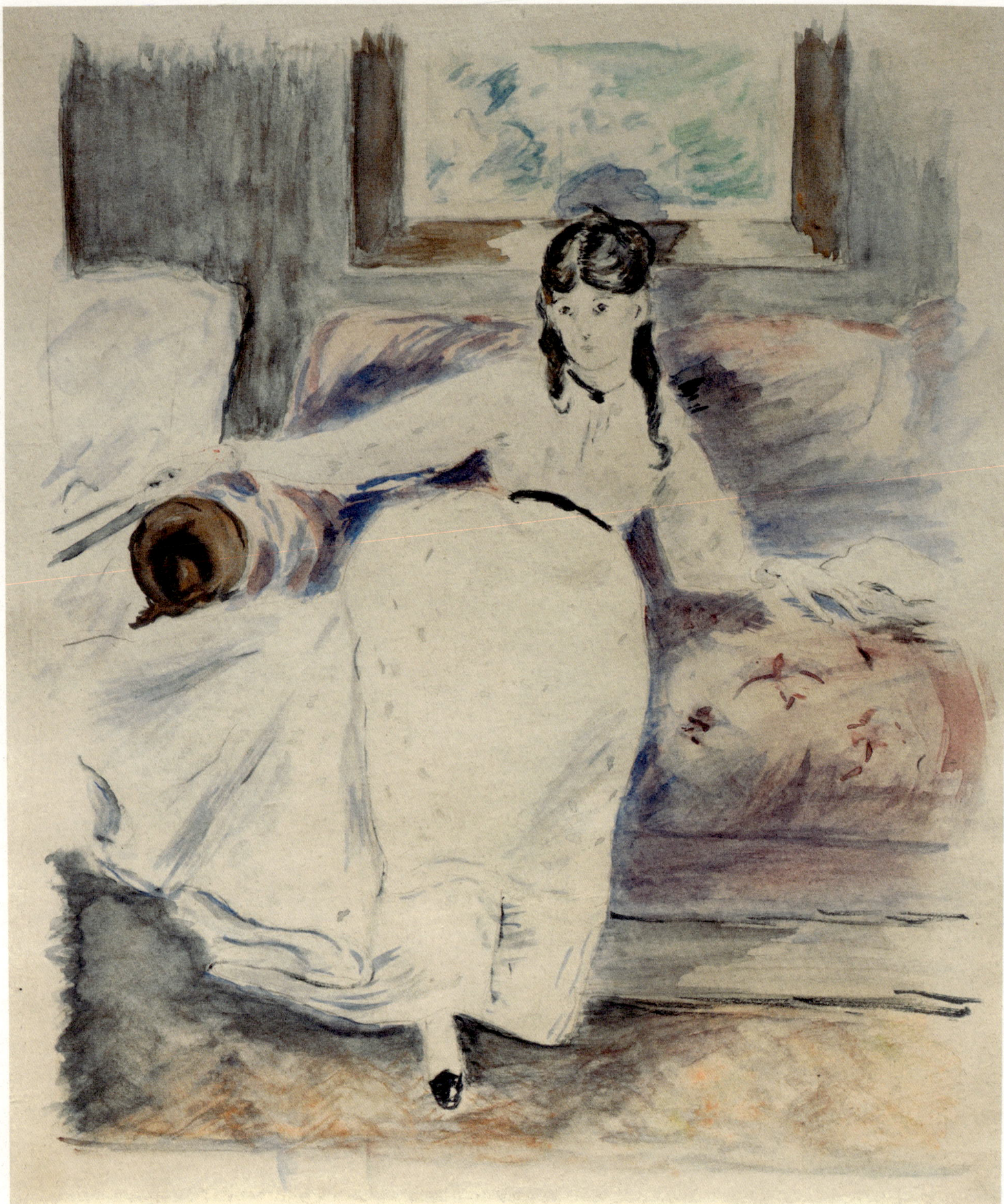

Julie Manet (1878–1966)
The Rest (after Édouard Manet), n.d.
Watercolor on paper, 26.5 × 22.5 cm
Private collection

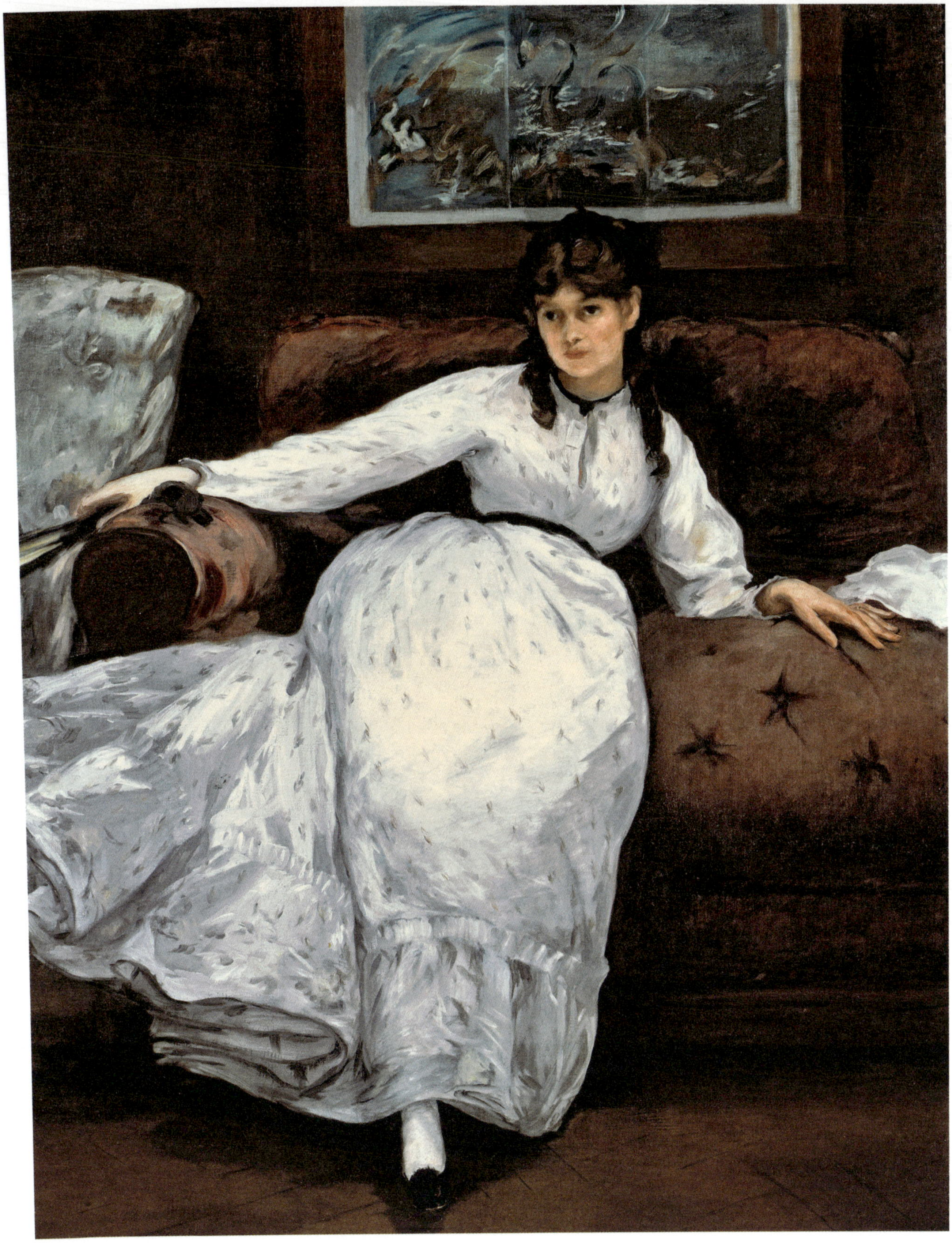

Édouard Manet (1832–1883)
The Rest (Berthe Morisot), c. 1871
Oil on canvas, 150.2 × 114 cm
Providence, RISD Museum, bequest of Mrs. Edith Stuyvesant Vanderbilt Gerry

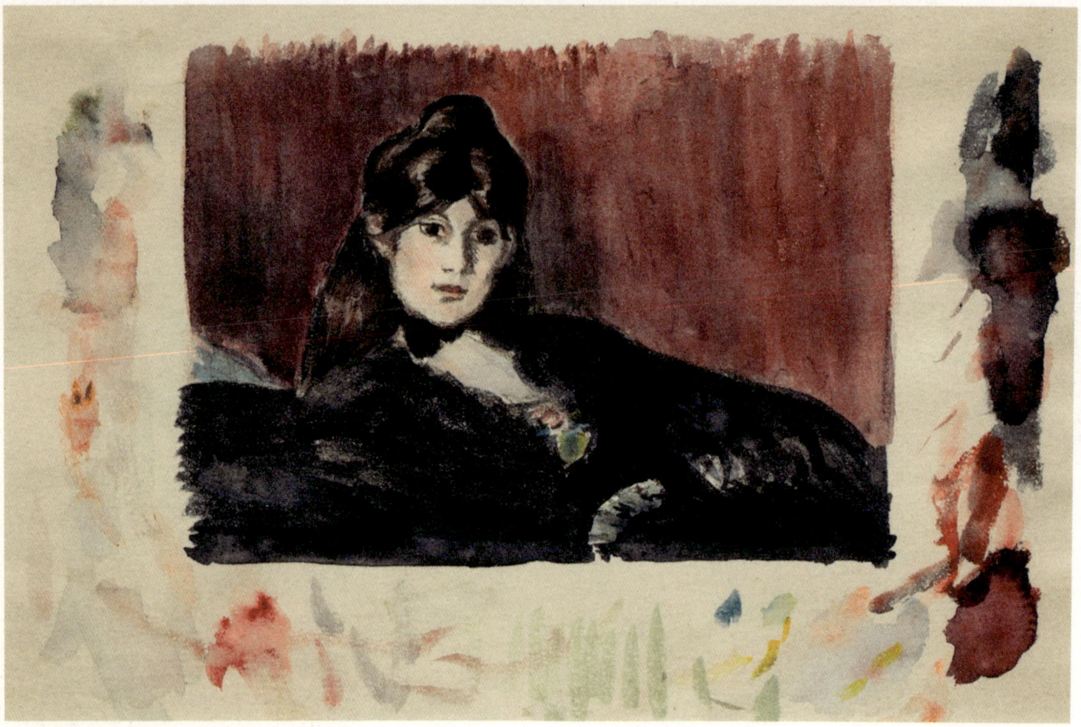

Julie Manet (1878–1966)
Berthe Morisot Reclining (after Édouard Manet), n.d.
Watercolor on paper, 15 × 22 cm
Paris, Musée Marmottan Monet

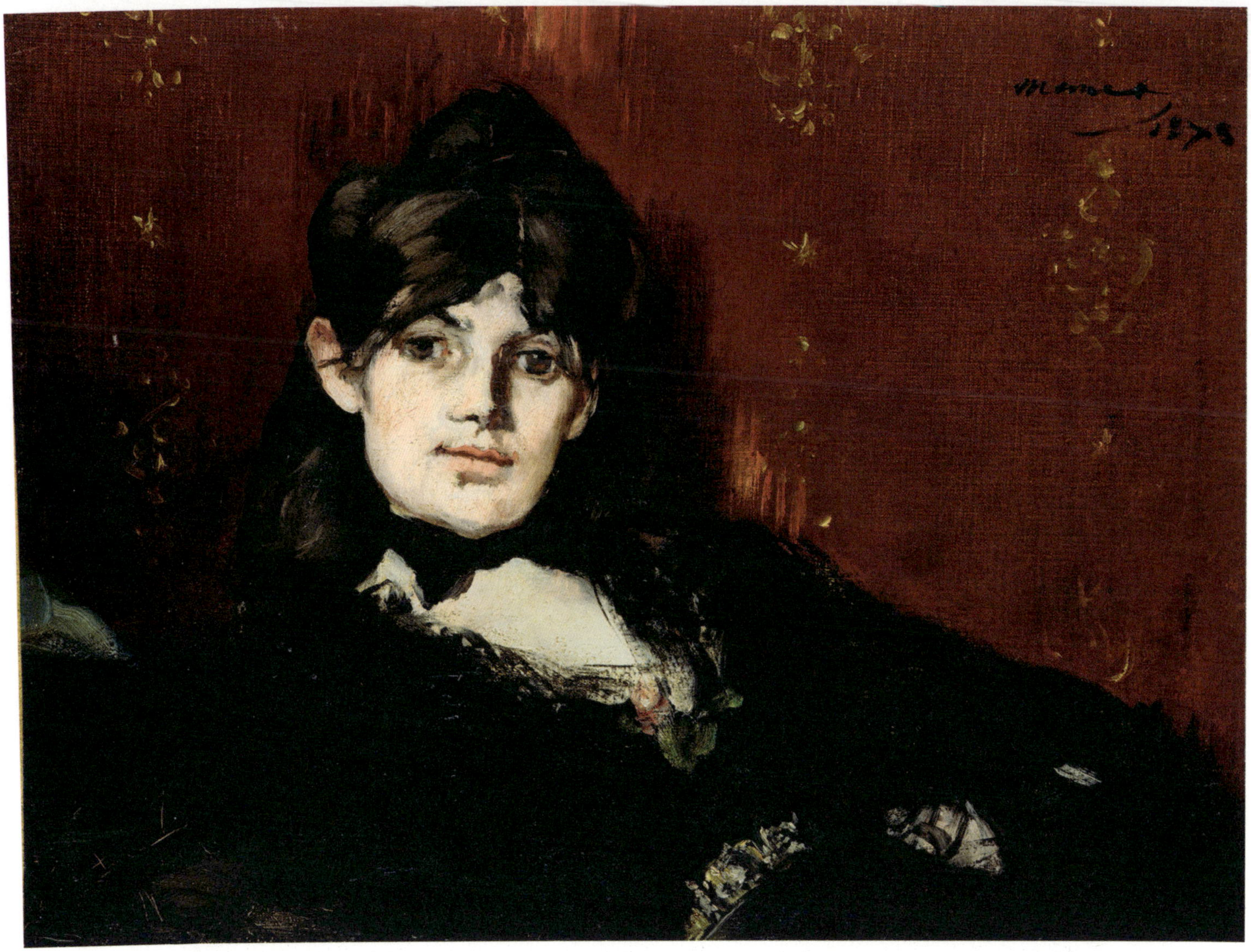

Édouard Manet (1832–1883)
Berthe Morisot Reclining, 1873
Oil on canvas, 26 × 34 cm
Paris, Musée Marmottan Monet

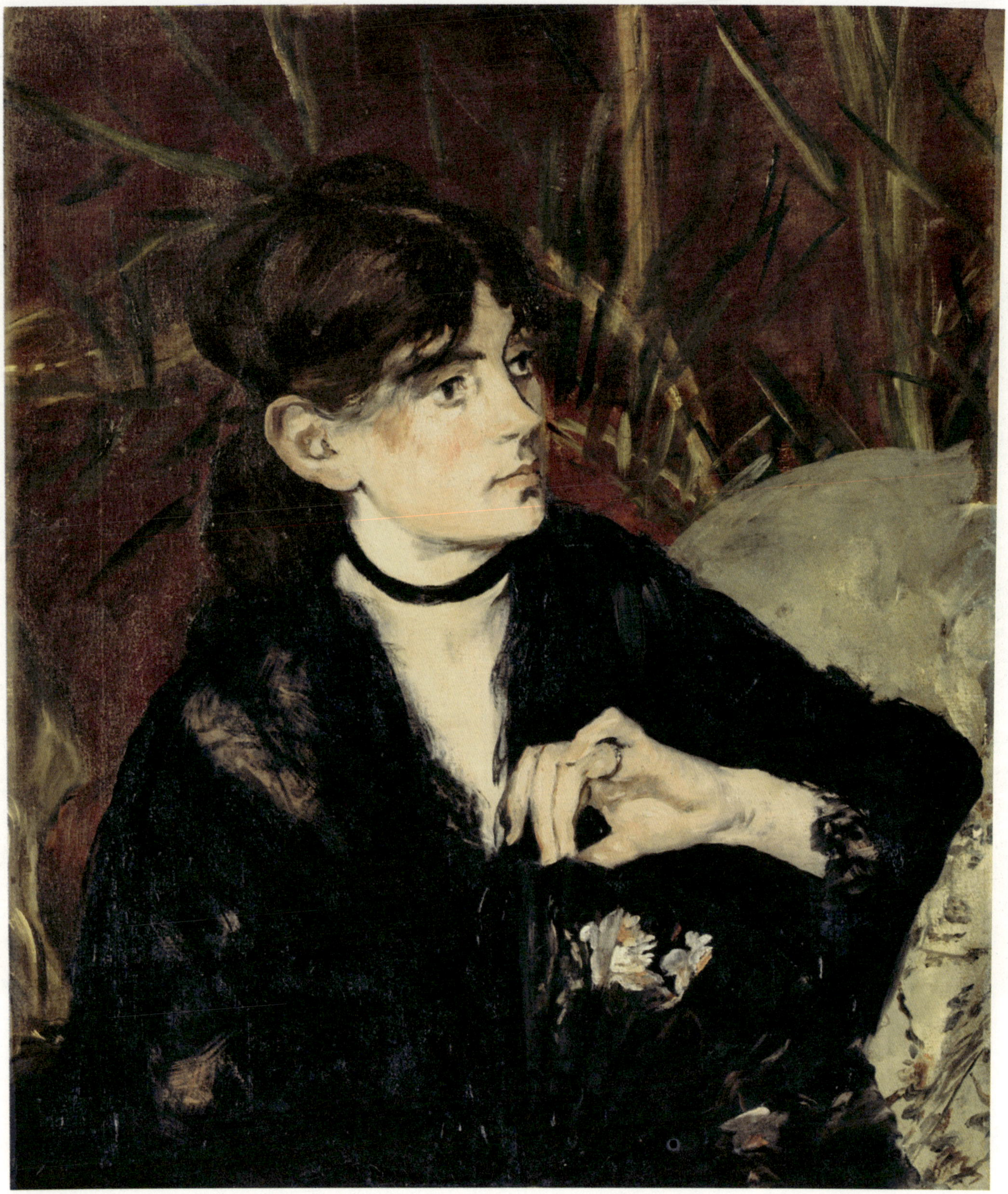

Édouard Manet (1832–1883)
Portrait of Berthe Morisot with a Fan, 1874
Oil on canvas, 61 × 50.5 cm
Paris, Musée d'Orsay, on permanent loan at the Palais des Beaux-Arts de Lille, accepted by the state in lieu of estate tax, 1999

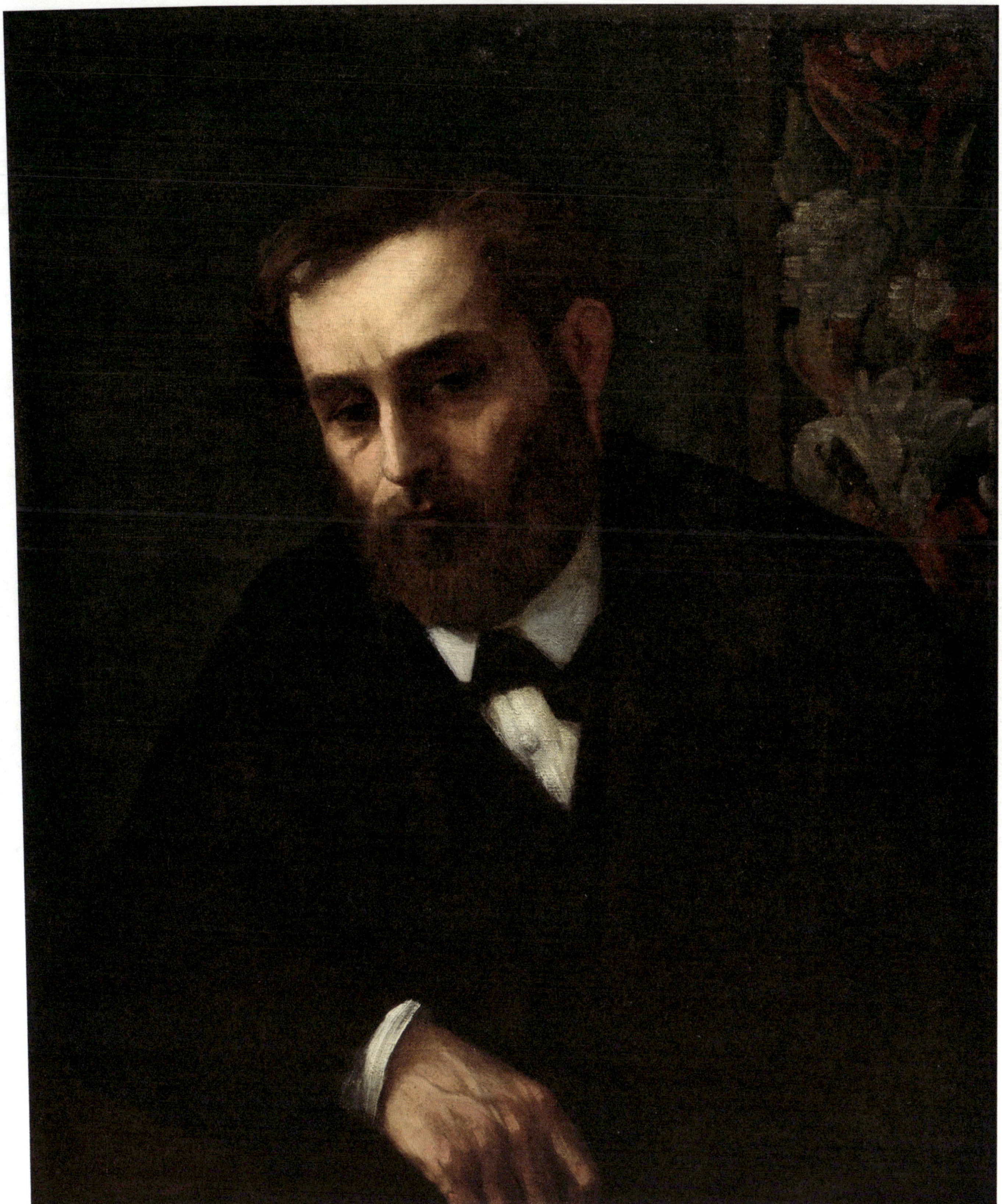

Alphonse Legros (1837–1911)
Portrait of Eugène Manet, 1862
Oil on canvas, 71 × 58 cm
Private collection

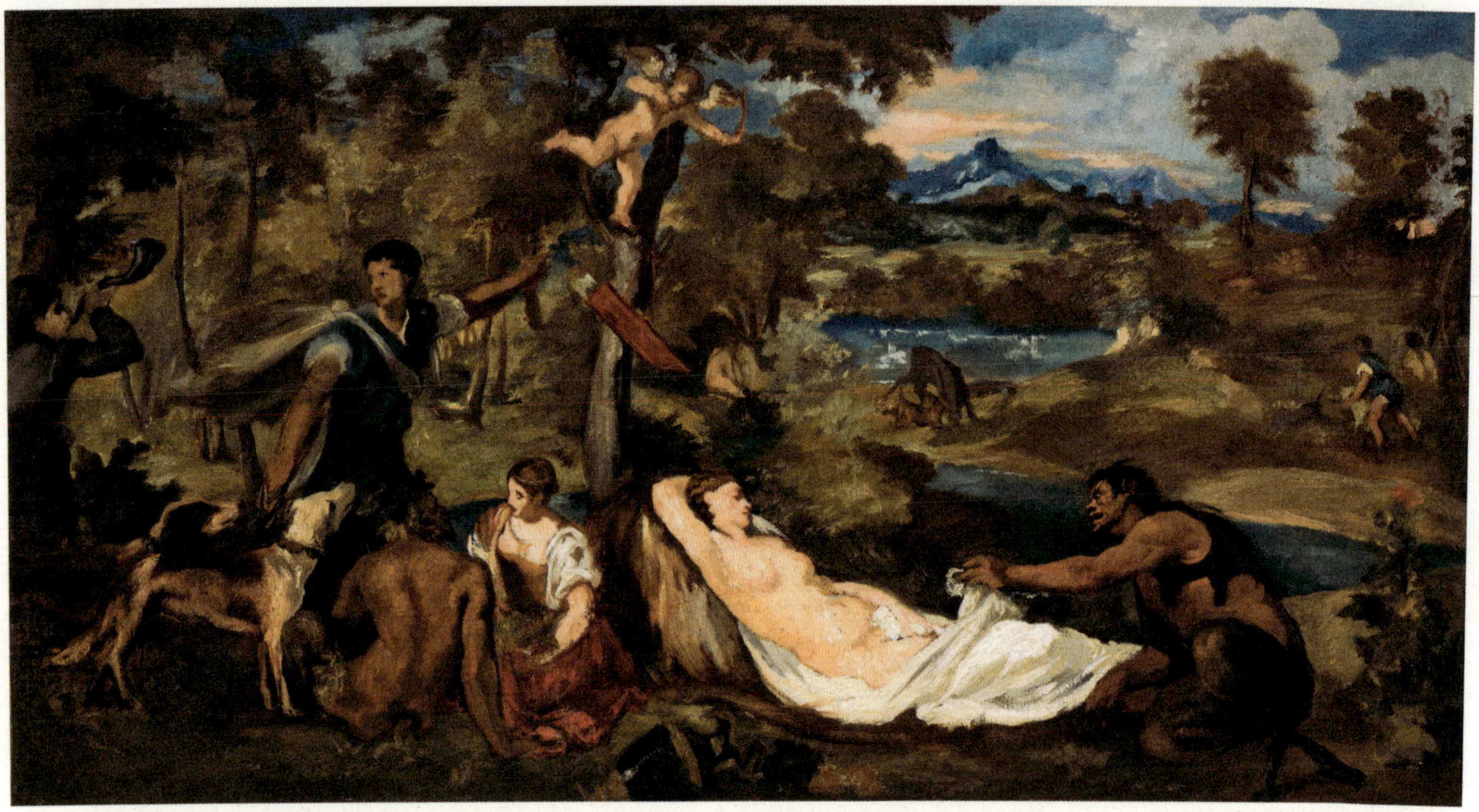

Édouard Manet (1832–1883)
Jupiter and Antiope (copy after Titian), 1856
Oil on canvas, 47 × 85 cm
Paris, Musée Marmottan Monet

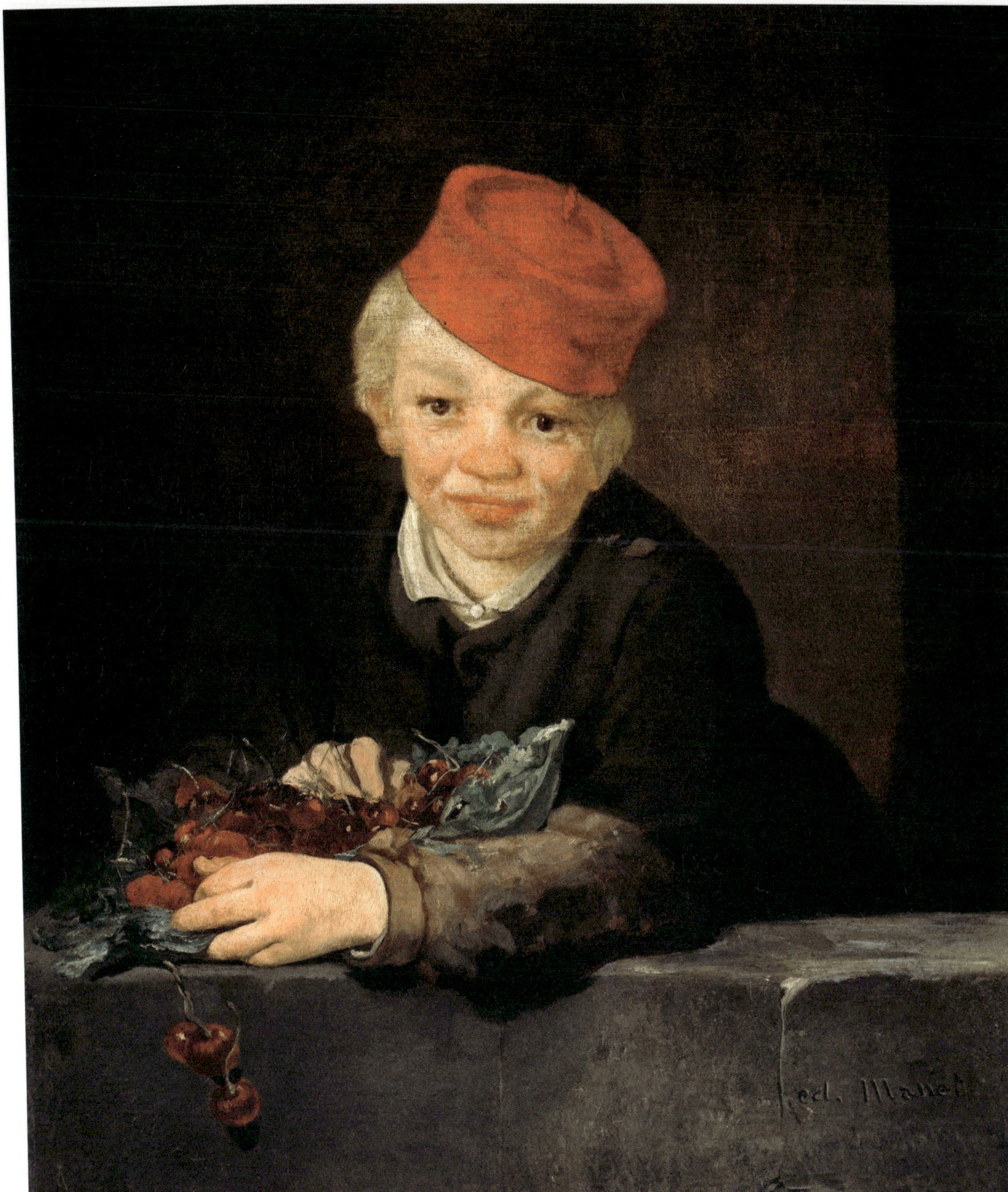

Édouard Manet (1832–1883)
Boy with Cherries, 1858
Oil on canvas, 65.5 × 54.5 cm
Lisbon, Calouste Gulbenkian Museum

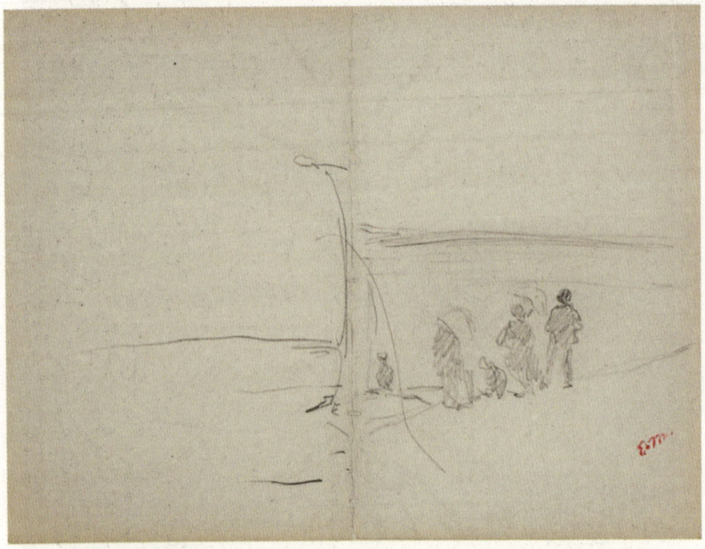

Édouard Manet (1832–1883)
Figures on a Beach, 1859–14
Graphite on squared paper, 11.5 × 18.5 cm
Private collection

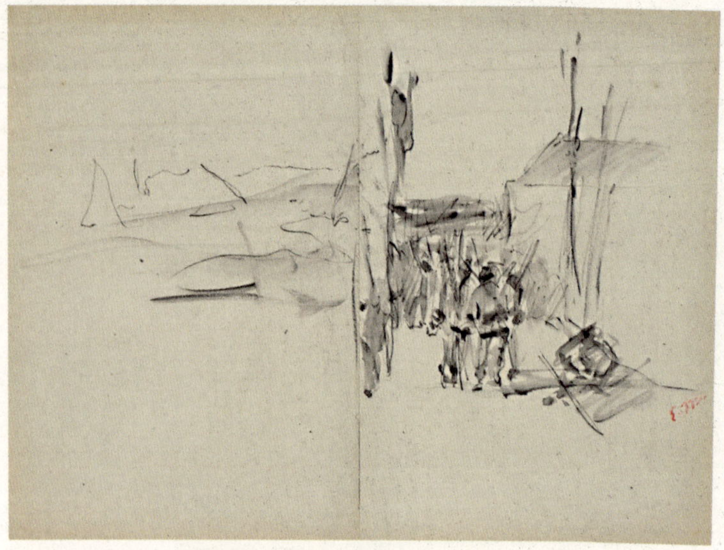

Édouard Manet (1832–1883)
Soldiers Making Their Way to the Outpost, 1870
Black pencil and wash on paper, 18.5 × 24 cm
Private collection

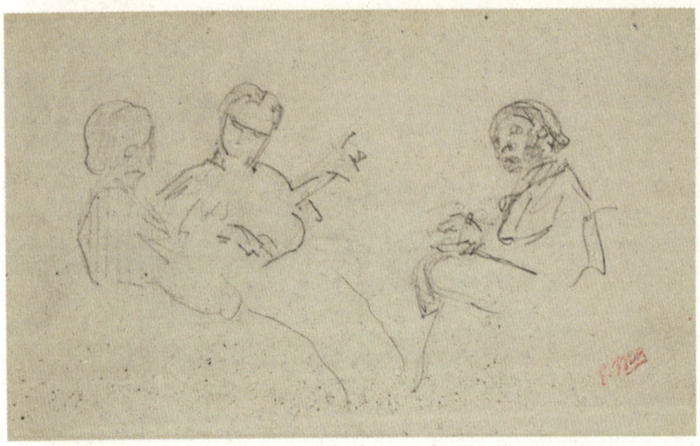

Édouard Manet (1832–1883)
The Musicians, c. 1862
Graphite on paper, 11.1 × 18.3 cm
Private collection

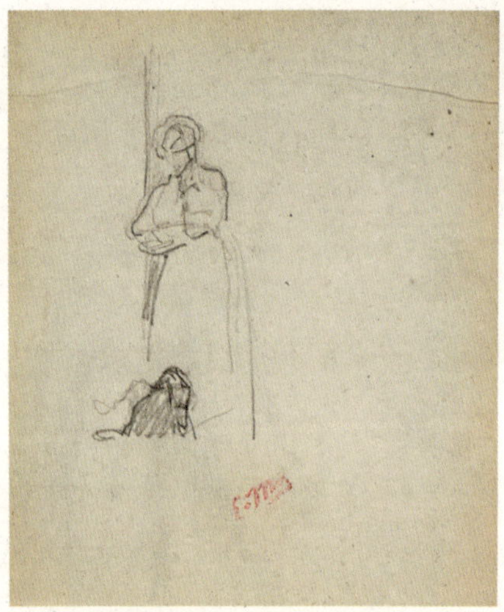

Édouard Manet (1832–1883)
Woman with Pug, 1881
Graphite on paper, 12.7 × 10.5 cm
Private collection

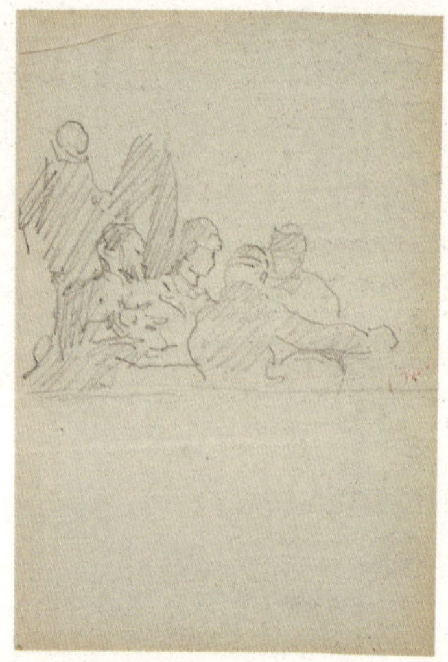

Édouard Manet (1832–1883)
In the Café, c. 1876
Graphite on squared paper, 18.5 × 11.9 cm
Private collection

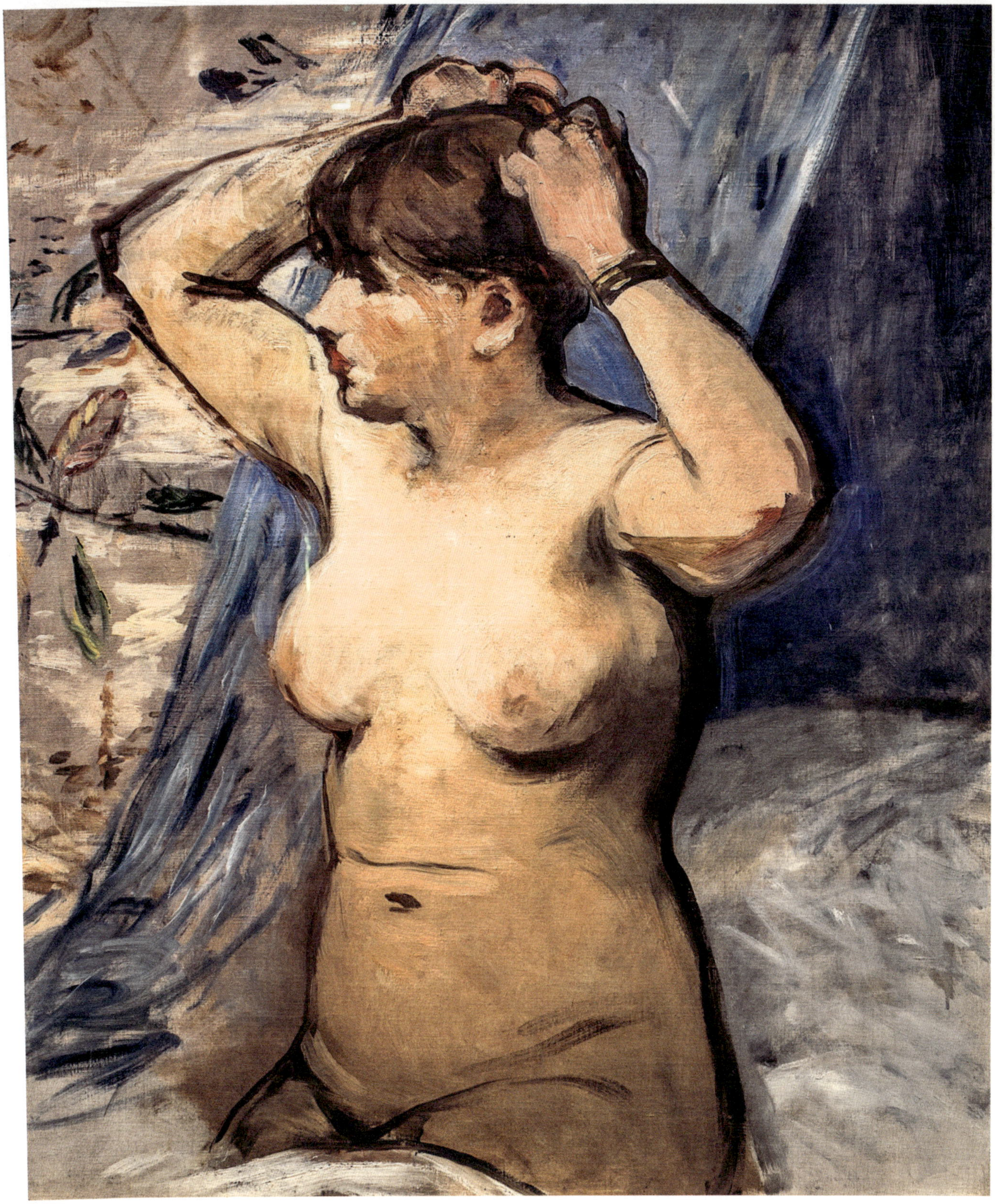

Édouard Manet (1832–1883)
Nude Arranging Her Hair, 1879
Oil on canvas, 80 × 65 cm
Koons Collection

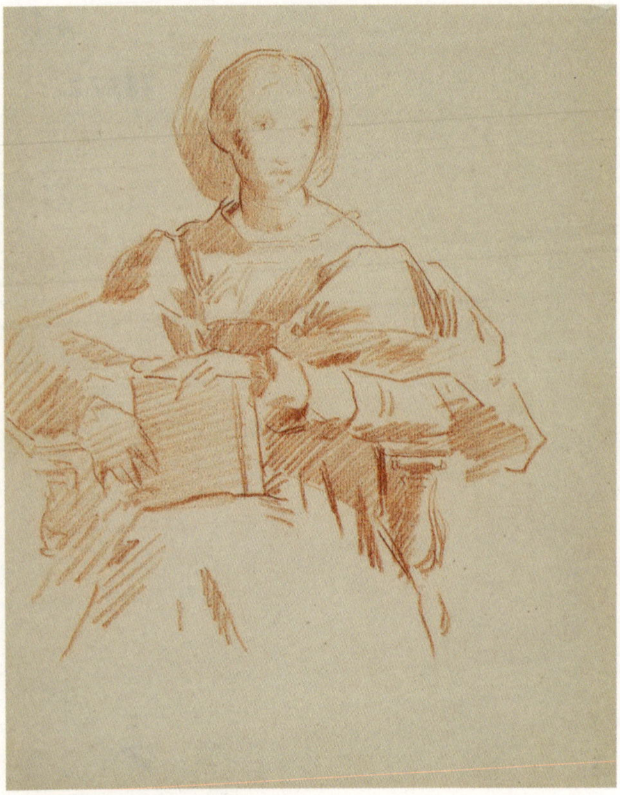

Édouard Manet (1832–1883)
Lucrezia, after *Portrait of Lucrezia del Fede*, Andrea del Sarto, Florence, Uffizi Musei, c. 1853–56
Red chalk on paper, 28.5 × 22 cm
Private collection

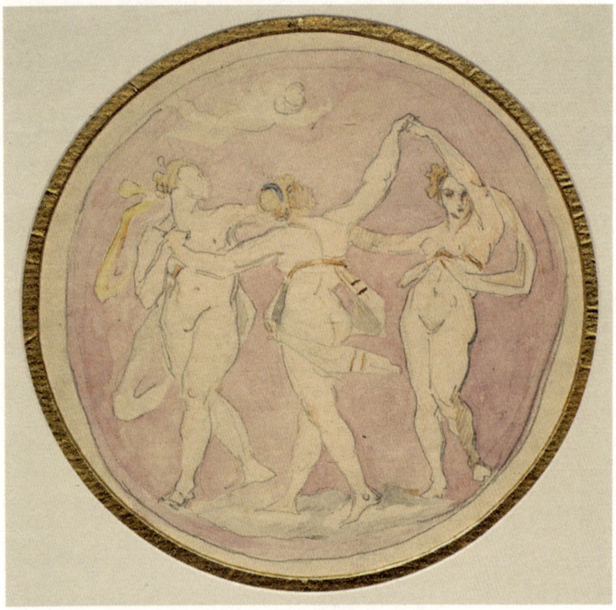

Édouard Manet (1832–1883)
Three Female Nudes, c. 1853–56
Watercolor and graphite on paper, 28.5 × 22 cm
Private collection

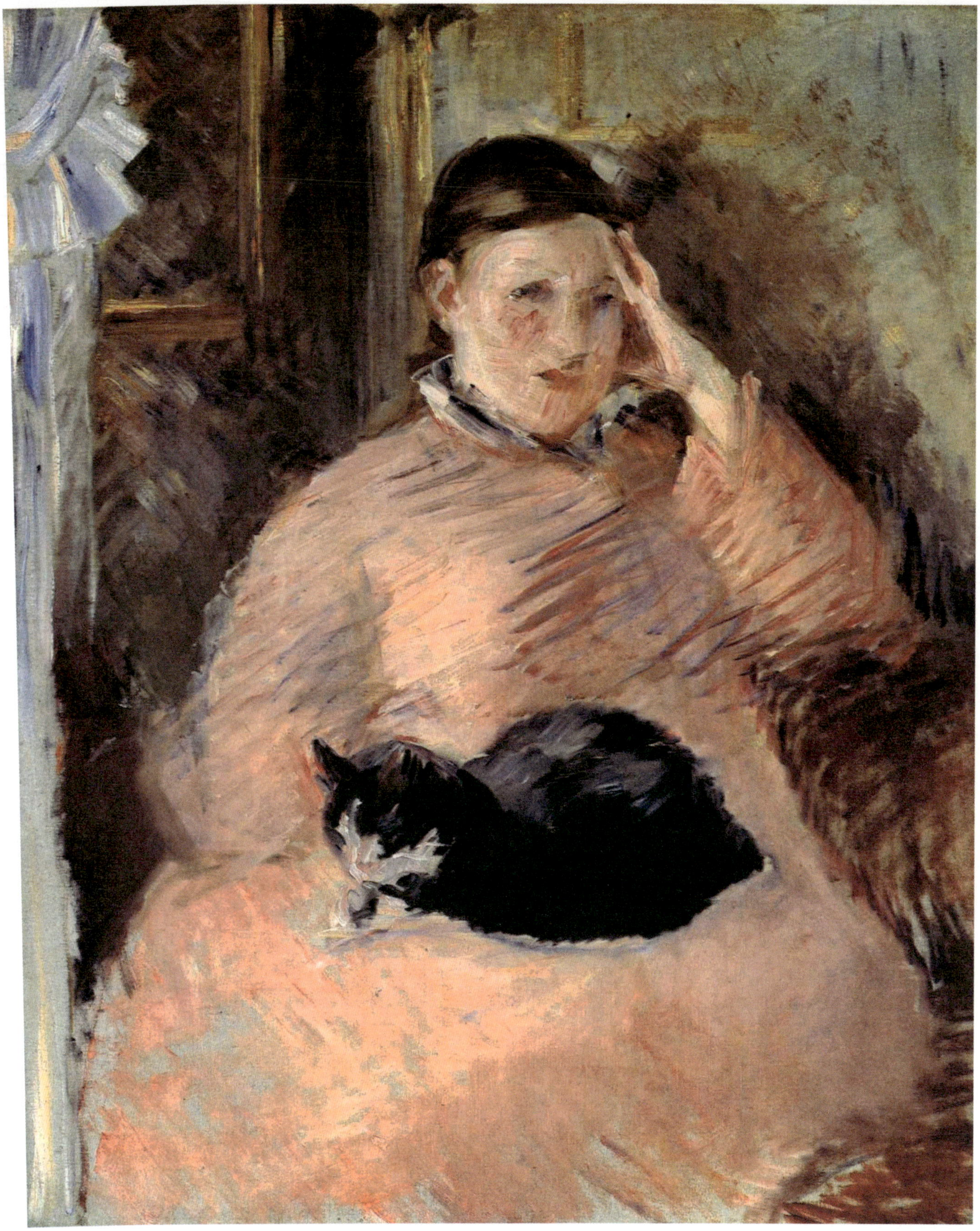

Édouard Manet (1832–1883)
Portrait of Madame Manet or *Woman with a Cat*, c. 1880
Oil on canvas, 92.1 × 73 cm
London, Tate, purchased 1918

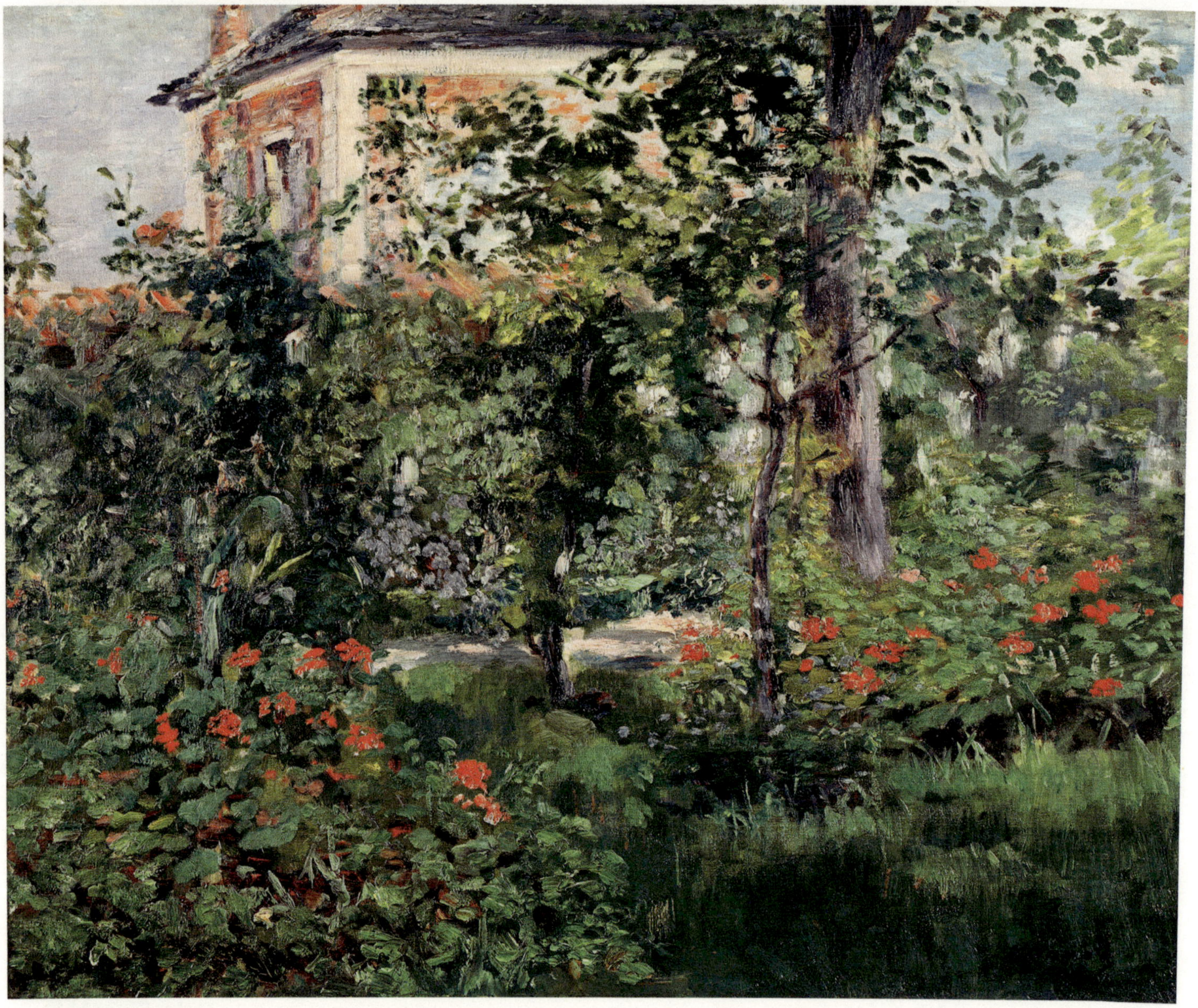

Édouard Manet (1832–1883)
The Garden at Bellevue, c. 1880
Oil on canvas, 54 × 65 cm
Location unknown

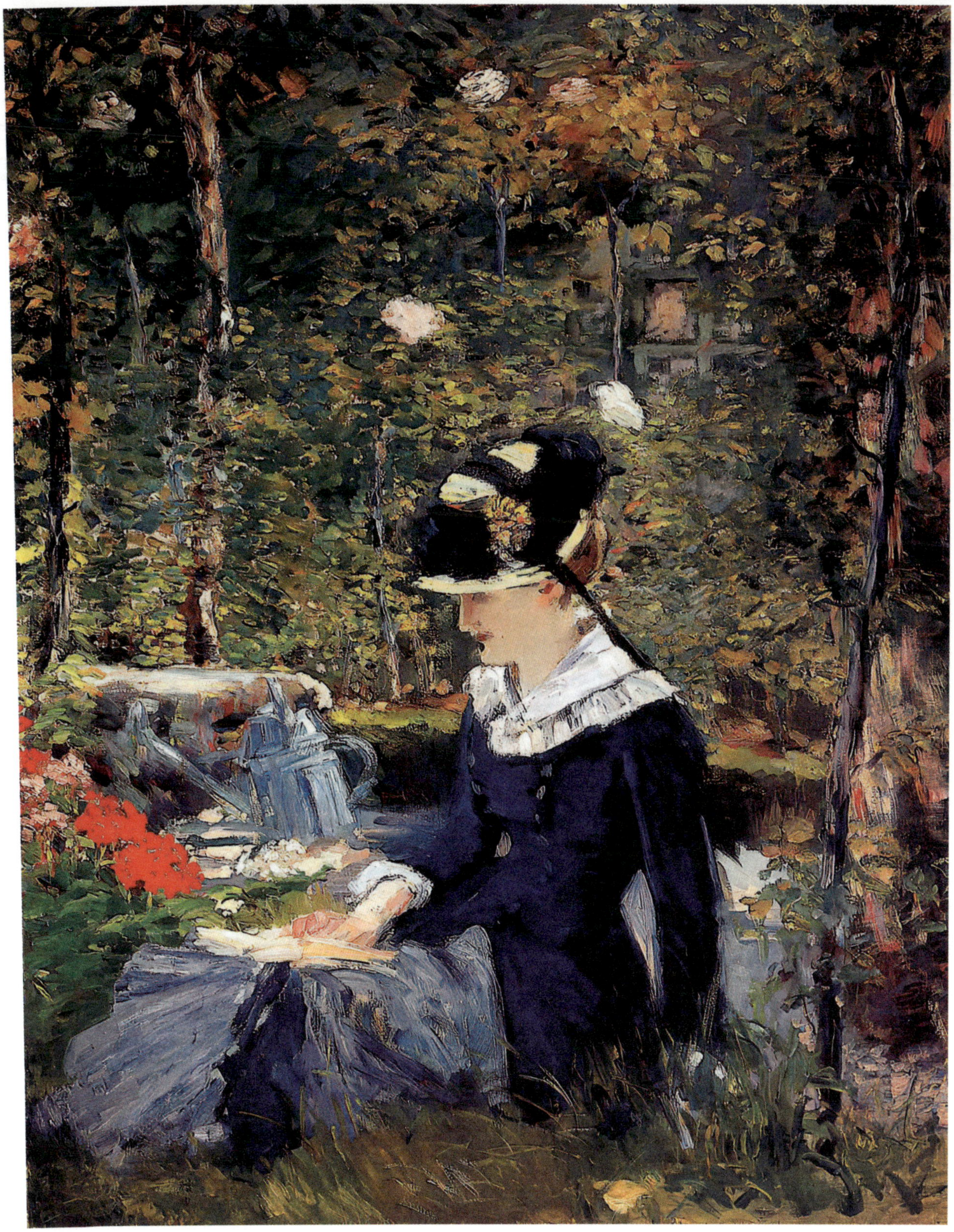

Édouard Manet (1832–1883)
Young Woman in a Garden, 1880
Oil on canvas, 151 × 115 cm
Location unknown

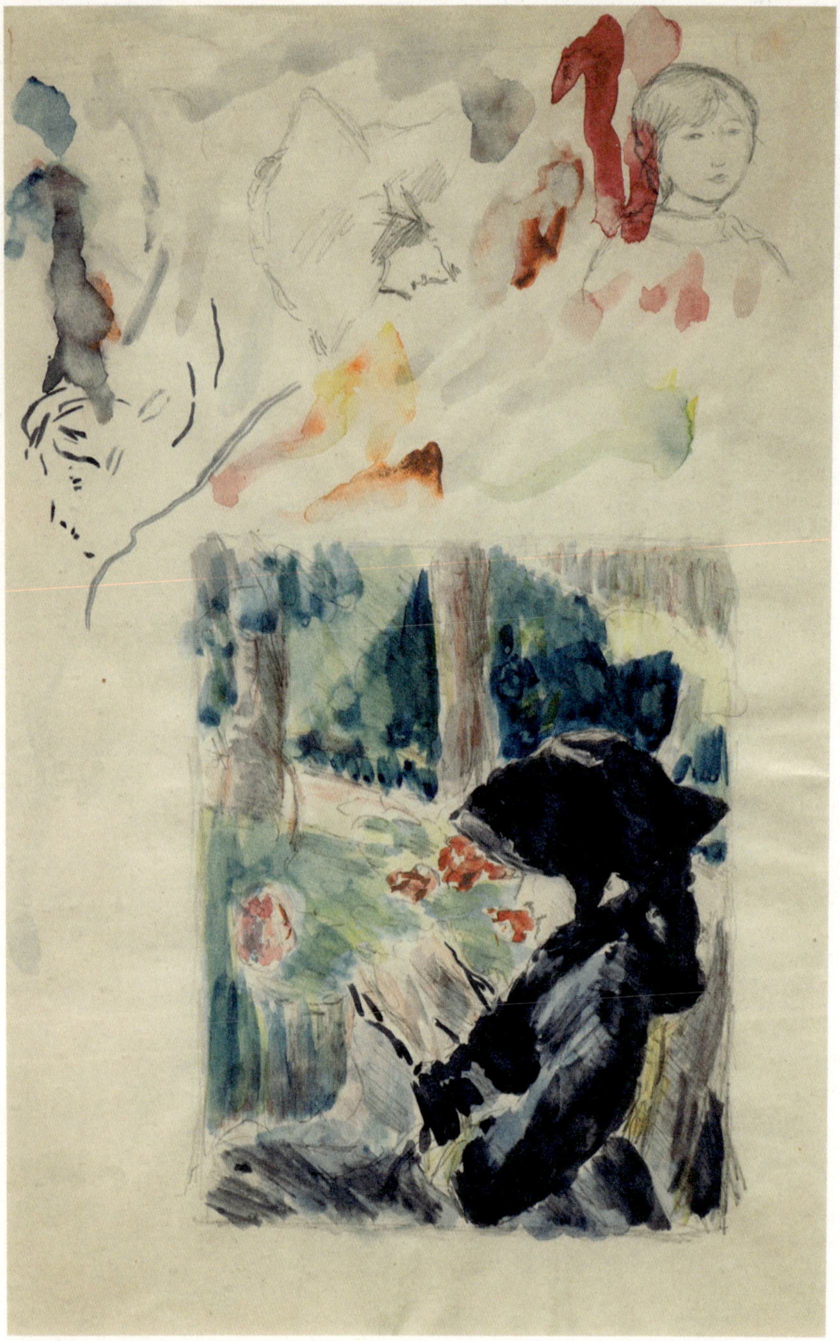

Julie Manet (1878–1966)
Mme Manet mère *in the Garden at Bellevue* (after Édouard Manet), n.d.
Watercolor on paper, 30 × 18.5 cm
Paris, Musée Marmottan Monet

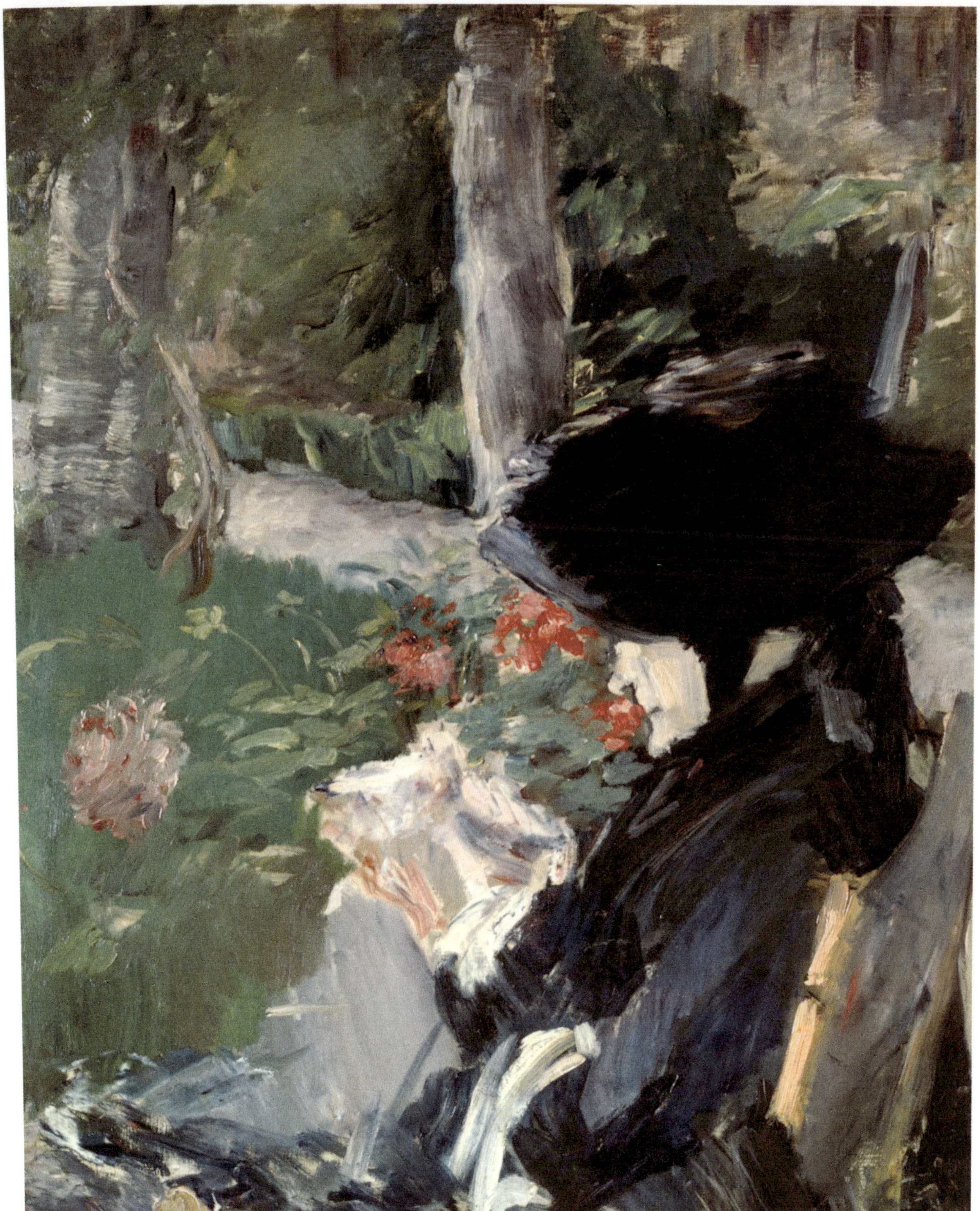

Édouard Manet (1832–1883)
Mme Manet mère *in the Garden at Bellevue*, 1880
Oil on canvas, 82 × 65 cm
Location unknown

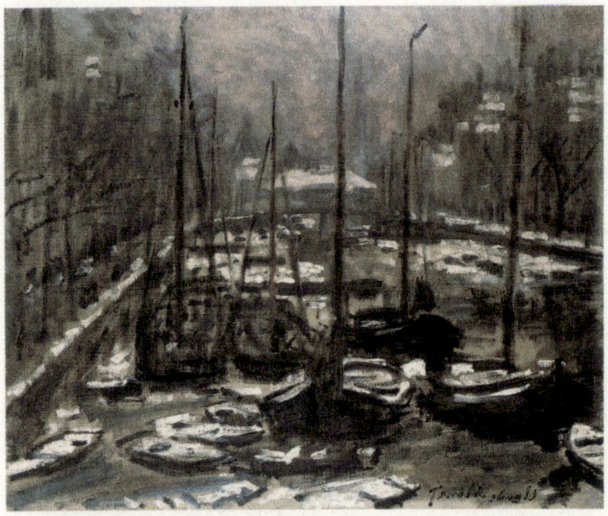

Claude Monet (1840–1926)
The Geldersekade in Amsterdam, Winter, 1871–74
Oil on canvas, 55 × 65 cm
Location unknown

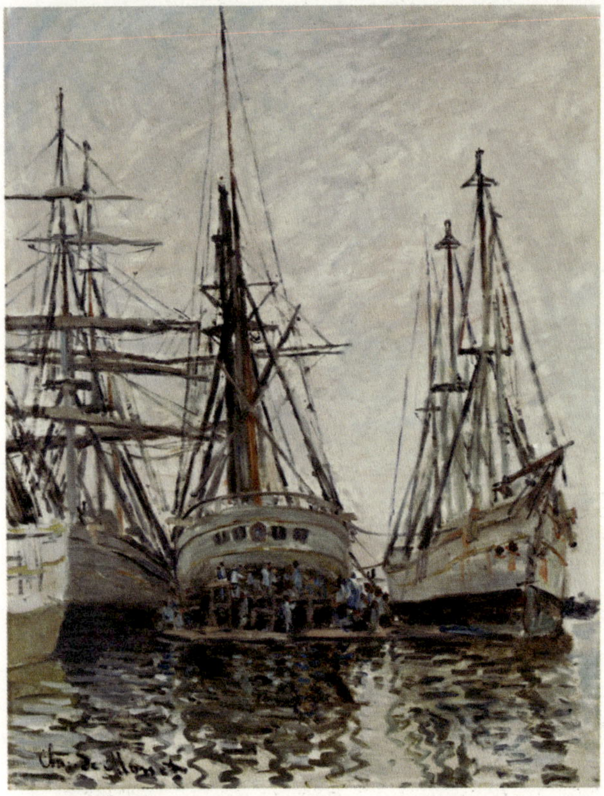

Claude Monet (1840–1926)
Boats in a Harbor, c. 1873
Oil on canvas, 71.2 × 54 cm
Edinburgh, National Galleries of Scotland

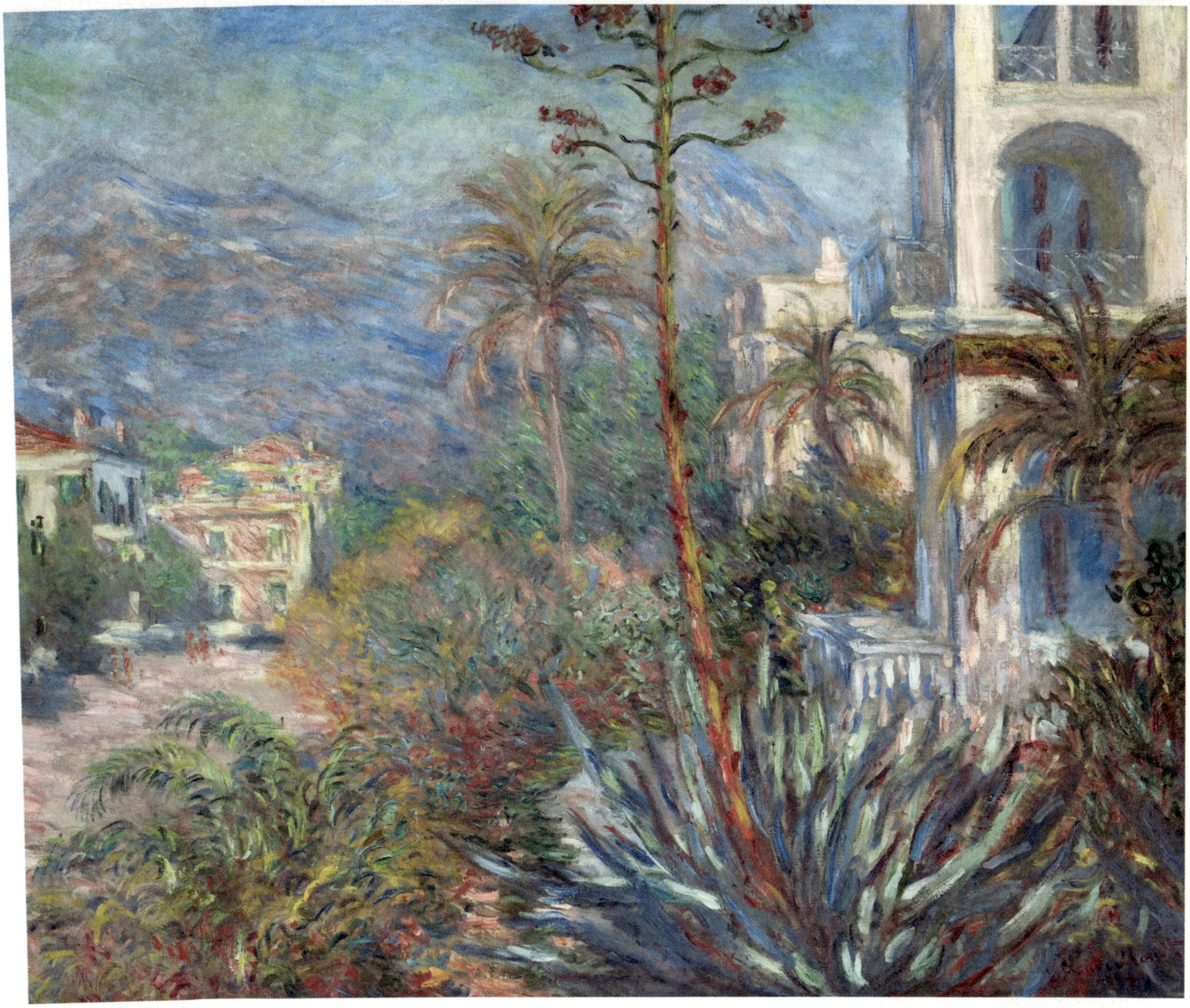

Claude Monet (1840–1926)
Villas at Bordighera, 1884
Oil on canvas, 116.5 × 136.5 cm
Paris, Musée d'Orsay, acquired in 2000

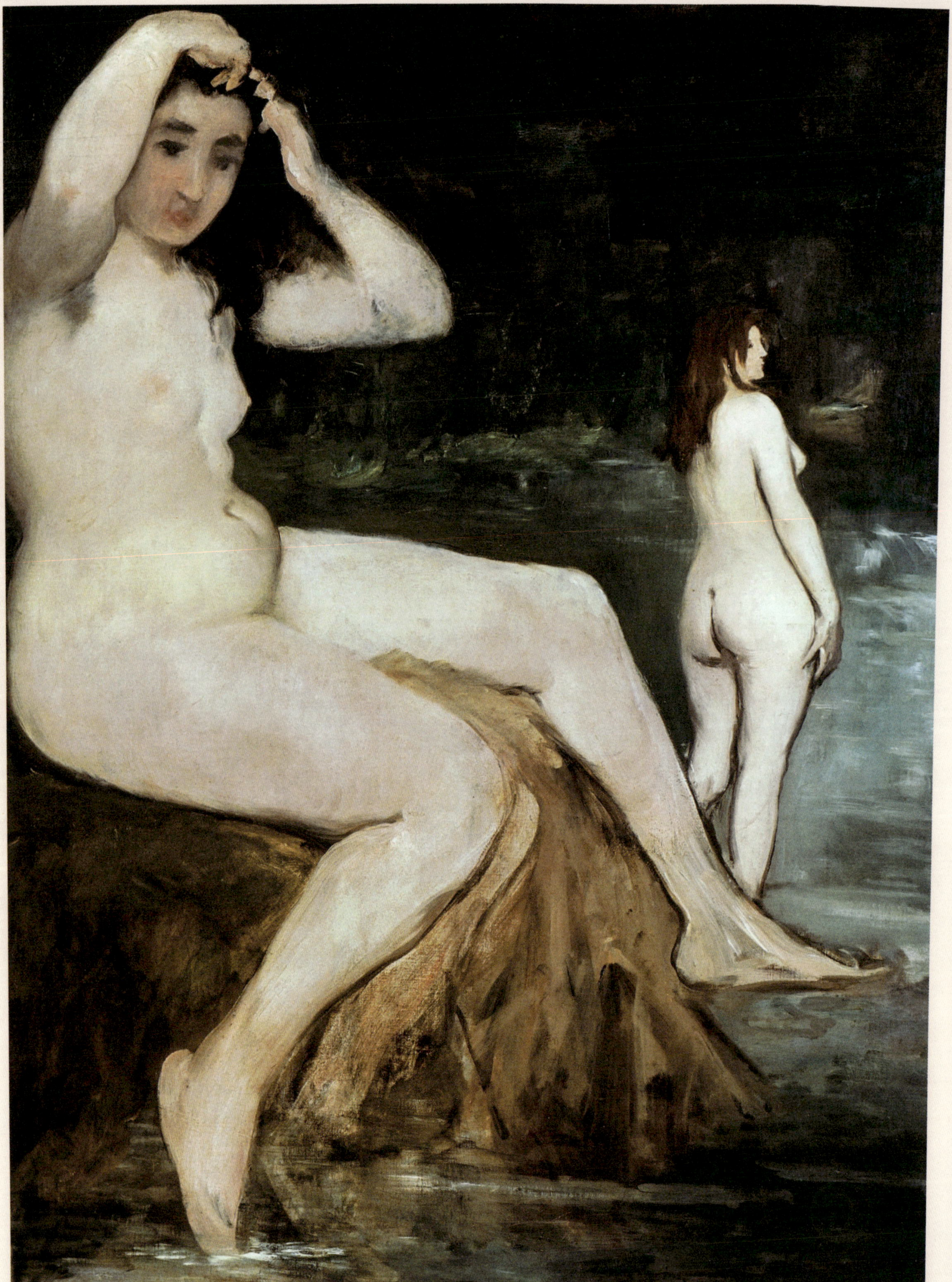

MONSIEUR AND MADAME ERNEST ROUART

COLLECTORS AND DONATORS

MARIANNE MATHIEU

JULIE'S EMANCIPATION

In 1895, Julie inherited a considerable artistic legacy: the collection of works in the studio of her mother, Berthe Morisot, and the collection of paintings, drawings, and prints assembled by her parents, a group largely dominated by the figure of her uncle, Édouard Manet. Julie was immediately moved by a duty of remembrance and of safeguarding memory. When it came to her mother's legacy, this led to studies, assistance with publications, and the organization of exhibitions. It also concerned the works themselves and their administration. Her mother's recognition inevitably relied on the diffusion of her oeuvre, in other words through sales and works entering museum collections. The issue was clearly identified in 1896, when Berthe Morisot's colleagues organized a posthumous exhibition at Durand-Ruel. Although Julie paid 4,339.45 francs for the "Exhibition expenses for the works of Madame Manet-Morisot, these expenses having been incurred with a view to the presentation and sale of these works,"[1] and although she was able to barter certain paintings on occasion and thus give "to Monsieurs Durand Ruel & fils in payment for the rental of the show room, a painting by Berthe Morisot (Le thé),"[2] estimated at 200 francs by the gallery, it soon became apparent that her status as a minor prevented Julie from selling the works she had inherited.

Facing page
Édouard Manet (1832–1883)
Bathers on the Seine, 1874–76
Oil on canvas, 132 × 98 cm
Collection Museu de Arte de São Paulo Assis Chateaubriand, gift of Arthur Lundgreen, 1952

This is what Joseph Durand-Ruel confirmed to her guardian, Gabriel Thomas, on February 28, 1896:

> **Monsieur, I've seen my solicitor about the matter you mentioned last night. He told me that it would indeed be almost impossible to obtain an amicable sale of Madame Manet's paintings and that we must give up this idea.[3]**

A solution was immediately sought to what was considered a major problem. The lawyer Maurice Bouts was approached; the solution envisaged was emancipation. On November 16, 1896, Bouts delivered his opinion and wrote to Gabriel Thomas:

> **I confirm what I told you about emancipation. You can take the initiative (I will take care of the formalities) by calling a meeting of the family council, which makes a sovereign decision; there is no question of ratification by the court. The emancipated minor can do all ordinary acts of administration, not exceeding nine years: works, alienation of property, etc. The [senator?] appointed will intervene only in real estate matters and for the acceptance of the guardianship account which you must render.[4]**

Shortly afterwards, Julie asked about the possibility of disposing of a small number of paintings. Her cousin answered her on June 16, 1897:

> **My dear Julie,**
> **On reflection, I don't believe that it's possible for you at this time, in your present situation as a minor, to bend the law which you demonstrated yesterday, by selling**

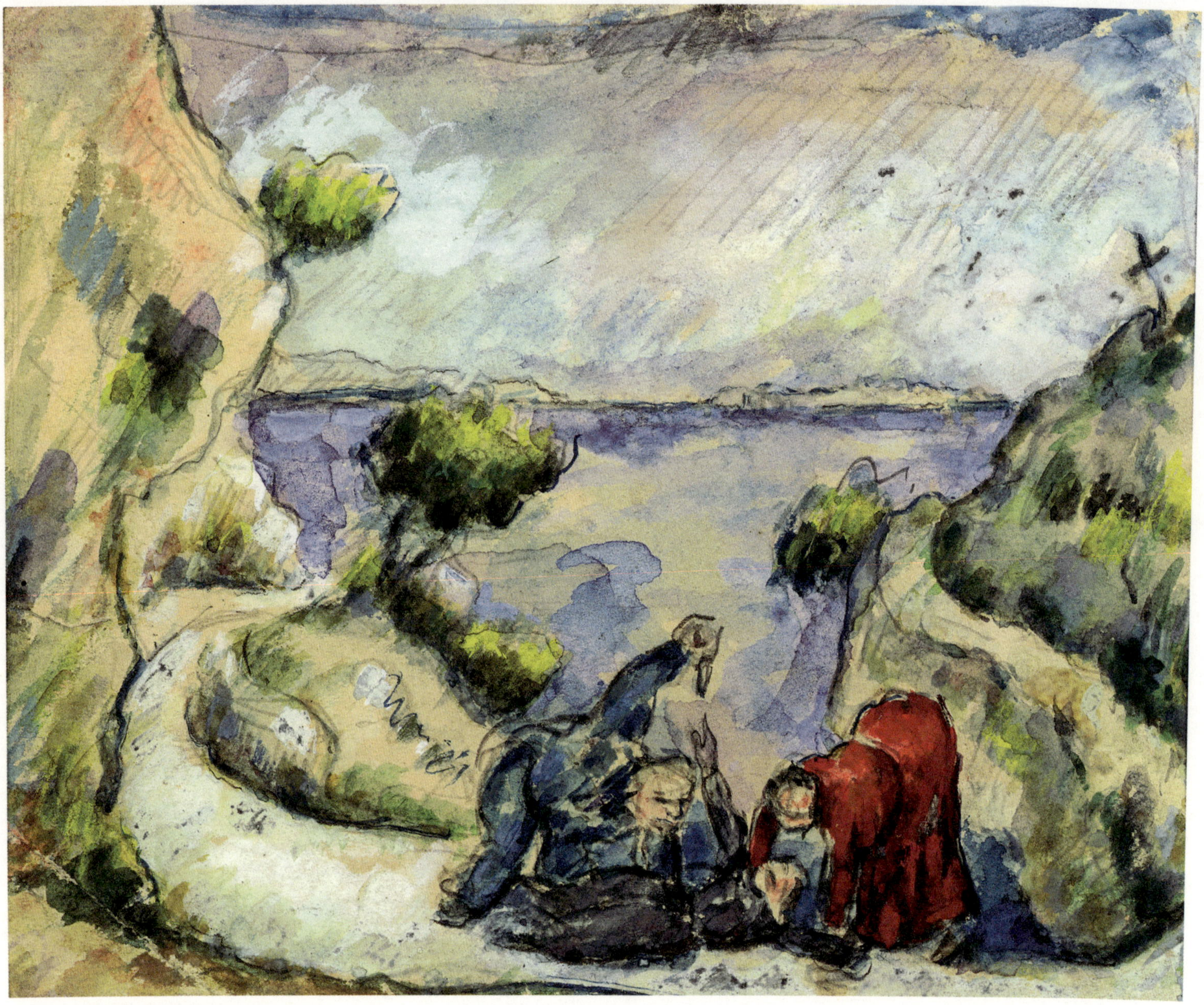

Paul Cézanne (1839–1906)
The Murder, c. 1874–75
Graphite, watercolor, and gouache on paper, 14.6 × 17.5 cm
Greenville, collection Keith D. Stoltz

paintings to which the catalogued and sensational exhibition of last year has well and truly given an official existence. This would be an action of perhaps greater significance than it seems, and I can see advantages in it only were it to happen regularly. If your desire concerning the execution of this affair is as formal as mine is not to cause you any aggravation, confirm it to me by asking for your emancipation (which will allow you to dispose of your personal property as well as of all your income as you see fit) and I will hasten to gather the family council to have it granted. I went to Durand-Ruel to ask him to postpone all negotiations until this situation is legally settled. And there is every advantage to this. Yours affectionately, my dear child.[5]

Julie did not hesitate, replying the next day:

> My dear cousin, it seems to me that it would be better for me to be emancipated. But won't that take a long time? Monsieur Renoir thinks it's important to sell some canvases now so that the painting overall becomes more valuable; besides, he will talk about this with you since he is writing to you to ask for an appointment.[6]

Julie was emancipated fifteen days later on June 29, 1897.[7] Henceforth, she would endeavor to ensure her mother's works circulated in selected places.

"TAKE A LOOK AT THIS LITTLE ART COLLECTOR"[8] (1895–1899)

Julie's entourage was not only made up of artists, some were also collectors. The most accomplished of them was undoubtedly Edgar Degas. The group of works he collected—two hundred and forty-seven numbers in the catalog of the first posthumous sale[9] and two hundred and sixty-four numbers in the catalog of the second sale[10]—was exceptional. Only a privileged few—including Julie—were invited to discover the treasures he kept in the first floor of his apartment, a room that Julie described as a "museum."[11] As well as being an artist and collector, Degas was also an expert. Julie was amused by this:

> Monsieur Degas . . . peering in a very comical way at each lot through his magnifying glass. He was sitting next to the Rouarts.[12]

These lifelong friends shared the same passion and the same exacting specialists' standards. The painter thus wrote to the engineer [Henri Rouart]:

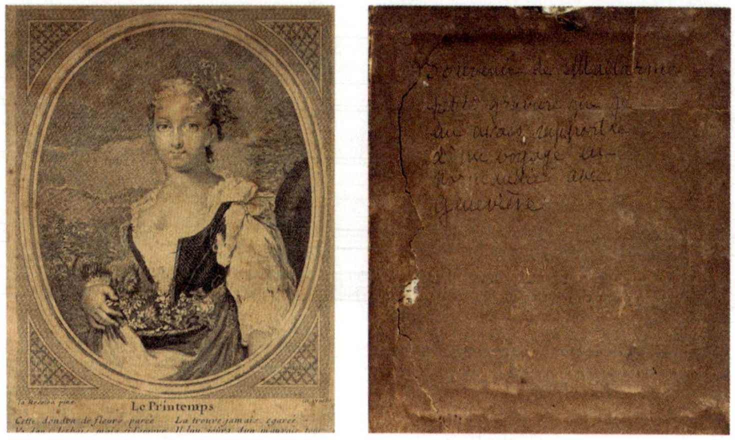

Rosalba Carriera (1675–1757)
The Four Seasons: The Spring, n.d.
On the back (right): a handwritten reference by Julie Manet, symbol of her attachment to the poet: "Souvenir of Mallarmé. A little print I brought him back from a trip to Normandy with Geneviève"
Etching, 15.5 × 13 cm
Private collection

> Try to find a moment, my dear friend, to go to Bernheim's to look at three sketches of flowers by Delacroix, so that we can talk about them tomorrow at your place. Best regards, Degas. There are also two old Corots to take a look at.[13]

It was not uncommon for the partners to acquire works in concert. This was the case with two Gauguins acquired on June 6, 1898 from George Daniel de Monfreid: Henri Rouart—whom de Monfried called Drouart!—chose *Nave Nave Mahana*[14] and Degas a *Bouquet of Flowers*.[15] His notebook indicated on June 8:

> Monsieur Drouart's servant came to take the Gauguins and gave me 450 francs. . . . Received for Gauguin from Monsieur Drouart *père* and from Monsieur Degas: 450 francs.

Like his models, Ernest Rouart also came the day before to choose a painting, *Fatata te Miti* (p. 304), we read on June 7:

> On the way home found Ern. Drouart coming to get his Gauguin painting. . . . Received from Ernest Drouart . . . 200 francs for a painting by Gauguin.[16]

The proximity of Degas and the Rouarts could only have encouraged Julie to take the plunge herself.

Berthe Morisot's daughter was also quick to collect and described in her diary on November 29, 1895 the circumstances of what seems to be her first acquisition:

> We went to Vollard's with Monsieur Degas and Monsieur Renoir to view the Cézanne exhibition.[17] . . .

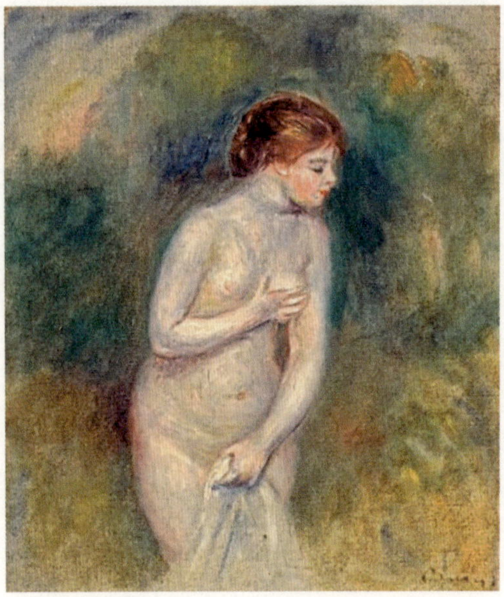

Pierre-Auguste Renoir (1841–1919)
Bather, c. 1885
Oil on canvas, 33 × 27 cm
Location unknown

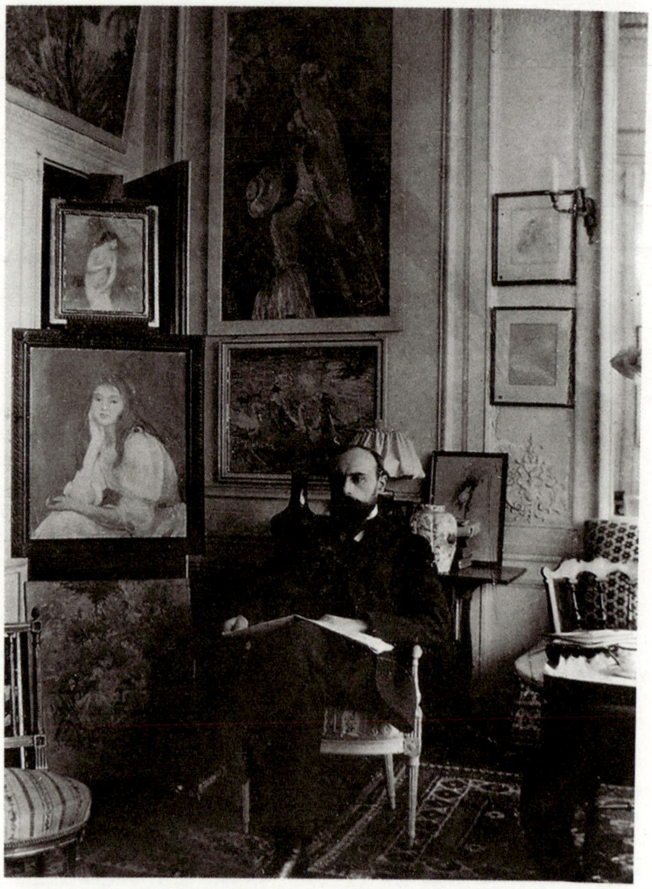

Ernest Rouart in the living room in the rue de Villejust, n.d.
Paris, Musée Marmottan Monet

> Monsieur Degas and Monsieur Renoir drew lots for a magnificent still-life watercolour of pears and a small one depicting an assassination in the Midi [p. 256], which isn't in the least bit horrifying – the figures stand out in exactly the right tones, red, blue, and violet in a landscape like those of Brittany or the Midi with round trees, areas of land against a blue sea, and, in the background, some islands. Monsieur Renoir liked this one very much too, so I bought it thinking it would be a sensible thing to do. "Well, take a look at this little art collector!" cried Monsieur Degas, patting me affectionately under the chin.[18]

Julie's collection was enriched in 1898 by a very small engraving after Rosalba Carriera (1675–1757), *The Spring* (p. 257), which Madame Mallarmé gave to the recently deceased poet's ward; two other seasons were reserved for the rest of the "Flying Squadron," Jeannie and Paule Gobillard. Julie confirmed the intention of the Mallarmé ladies:

> Madame Mallarmé and Geneviève gave them to us in memory of Monsieur Mallarmé, to whom we had brought them back from Rouen[19] and which he used as a paperweight.[20]

Which the poet had let her know on her eighteenth birthday:

> Goodbye, affectionately all three, whose portraits by the Rosalba, hold in place, during my work, the papers scattered on my small desk.[21]

Although modest, the memento was precious for Julie and her cousins: "It is sweet for us to have these objects that every working day he touched and that held in place these thousands of small pages on which he noted his thoughts."[22] Julie would keep this *Spring* throughout her life and, to avoid any equivocation, would annotate its reverse side: "Memento of Mallarmé, small engraving that I had brought back to him from a trip to Normandy with Geneviève."

Before the end of 1898, Renoir offered a painting to his protégée: "He gave me a small landscape painted in Essoyes which I wanted very much; I am delighted to have it."[23] Surrounded by these artist connoisseurs, Julie soon started reasoning as a collector, which is to say with regard to acquisitions. She dreamed of acquiring her portrait in a pink dress[24] painted by Renoir in 1899:

> My portrait is finished, it is delightful. The mastery of the figure, of the foliage's surface is marvelous [p. 191]. If Monsieur Renoir intends to give it to Durand-Ruel, I would like to arrange to buy it.[25]

The portrait was shown at Vollard's gallery and the project was short-lived. What became of *Young Woman in a Blue Hat in Profile*, a quickly sketched pastel,[26] and *Bather* (p. 258 left), a small canvas that we know from a late photograph of Julie's interior (p. 258 right)? Were they given or purchased? Both are possible. As modest as her acquisitions were, Julie did not hesitate. In this spirit, she played her cards at the sale of the Choquet collection, one of the events of 1899.

> I spent another day at the Choquet collection exhibition. I want to buy a small sketch by Delacroix after an engraving by Rubens if it doesn't go higher than 100 francs. I saw again with pleasure all these marvels. . . . I was very excited at the prospect of trying to buy a Delacroix. Paule and I went to the saleroom and asked Vollard to bid for me. . . . The Delacroix paintings went for practically nothing. *Ovid among the Scythians*,[27] which I thought was wonderful, only made 1,800 francs, whereas I had been expecting it to go for thousands. I'm almost sorry I didn't try bidding for it; it would have been worth having a fling. Still, I was pleased as in the end I got my little sketch after an engraving by Rubens for 460 francs.[28] After the sale, we went over to join Monsieur Degas and the Rouarts. Ernest immediately asked me if I had bought anything.[29]

At the following Monday's auction, he left with "a pretty drawing for 72 francs."[30]

MORAL DUTY

Julie had other dreams of acquisition in 1899, as she wrote in her diary:

> We went to see the Pellerin collection with Jeanne B.[audot]. . . . a sketch of Maman in profile in a violet hat and a fur coat, which is so lifelike. I would dearly love to have that one.[31]

However, it was above all the discovery of a painting by her Oncle Édouard, *Bathers on the Seine* (p. 254), that made her blood boil. She explained why a few days later:

> While we were talking about the P. collection, Madame Renoir told us that the Bernheims had repainted a picture by Oncle Édouard, which they had sold to Monsieur Pellerin for 100,00 francs. Paule and I realized it was the background to *Nude Women*, which looked so weird. . . . Paule stayed at home and received a visit from Jacques Blanche, who owned Oncle Édouard's *Bathers* with a rubbed green background and several legs. He sold it to the Bernheims this summer, who wanted it for Pellerin. So, no more doubt to be had about that repainted background. It's outrageous – I have a good mind to sue those horrible Bs.[32]

Julie therefore went to see the painter's widow to raise the issue, which didn't calm her, as these lines show:

> I went over to see Tante Suzanne to discuss Pellerin's retouched painting and to obtain her authorization to start proceedings. I find it quite unacceptable to allow Oncle Édouard's works to be damaged in this way. But when I left, I was beside myself with rage. There's nothing that can be done because Tante Suzanne had written on the back of the picture that she recognized it as authentic, although she hesitated at first, noticing several light alterations. "I couldn't say that the whole painting *wasn't* by my husband," she said to me with her Dutch nonchalance, "because the women were definitely by him." I told her outright that she shouldn't have signed. I got a little carried away. I think she feels I'm meddling in what doesn't concern me, and she remained very calm and said that it's always like that for the sketches; it's true that her own brother repainted several of Oncle Édouard's paintings. So, that's what happened. To keep themselves safe and sound, those cunning Bs arranged to have Tante Suzanne's signature before the painting was completely repainted. What can be done about such people! Tante Suzanne thinks that P. is in cahoots with them. I don't know, but if this is the case, he keeps it well hidden.[33]

Close friends and relatives were consulted:

> I told Monsieur Renoir that I had met Pellerin who had urged me to come and see his "new Manets," which have never been seen by anyone so far. "You should have told him that even Manet himself hasn't seen them yet!," laughed Monsieur Renoir.[34]
>
> . . . I returned with Aunt Edma to Pellerin's. I came back outraged and cried all day at the thought that I can

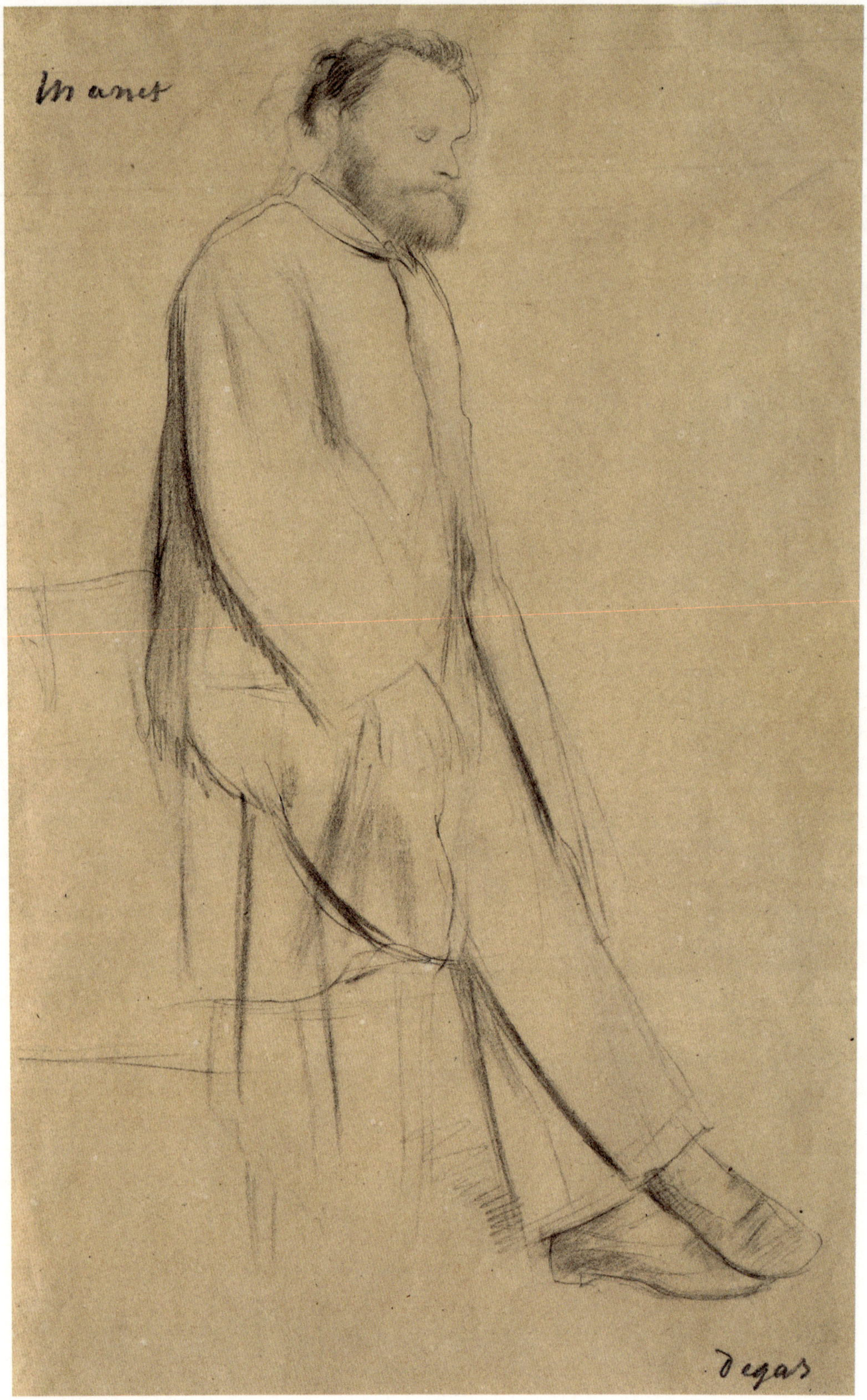

Edgar Degas (1834–1917)
Portrait of Édouard Manet, c. 1866
Pencil on paper, 40 × 26 cm
Paris, Musée Marmottan Monet

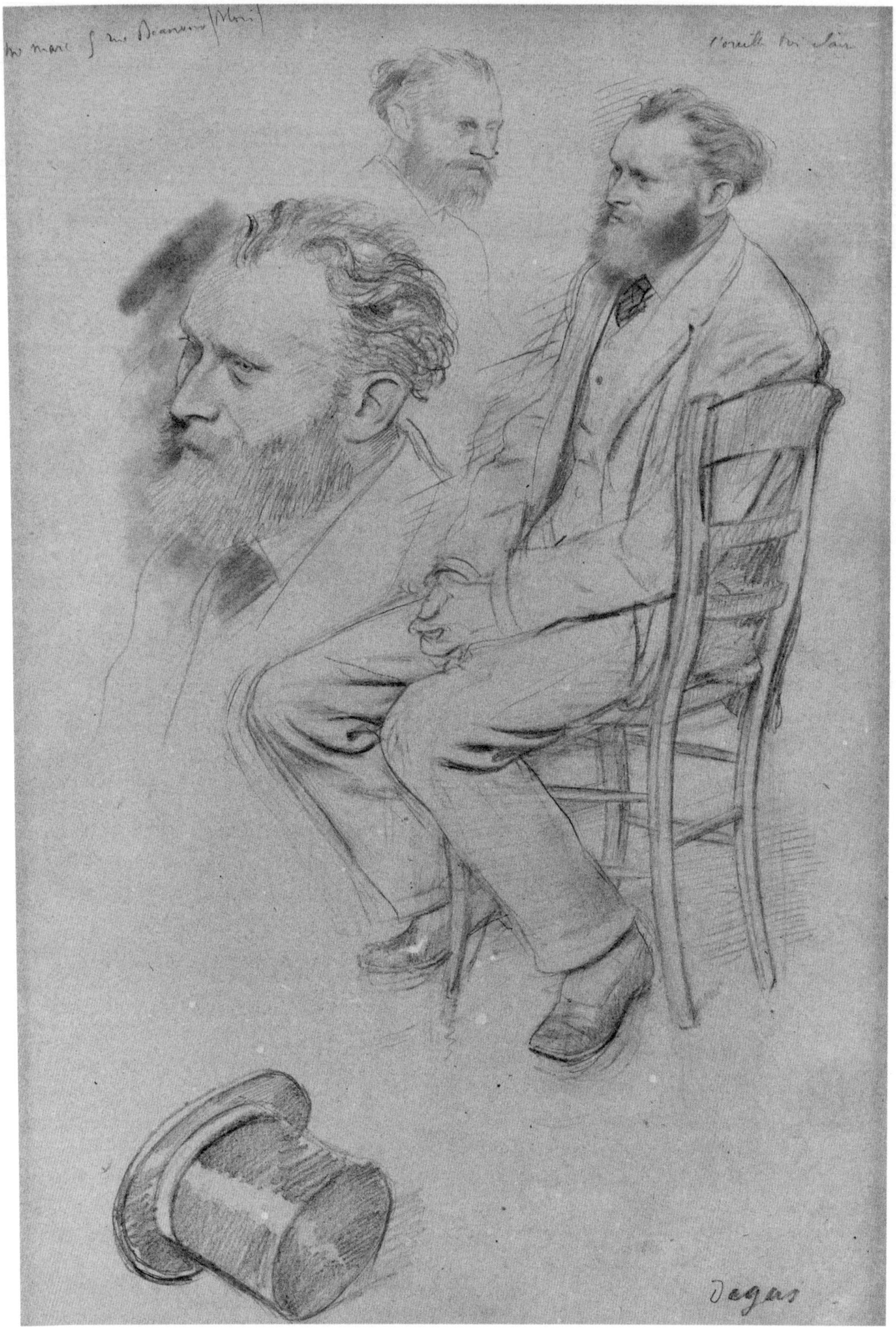

Edgar Degas (1834–1917)
Portrait of Édouard Manet, c. 1865–70
Graphite on paper, 40 × 25.5 cm
Paris, Musée d'Orsay, conserved at the Musée du Louvre

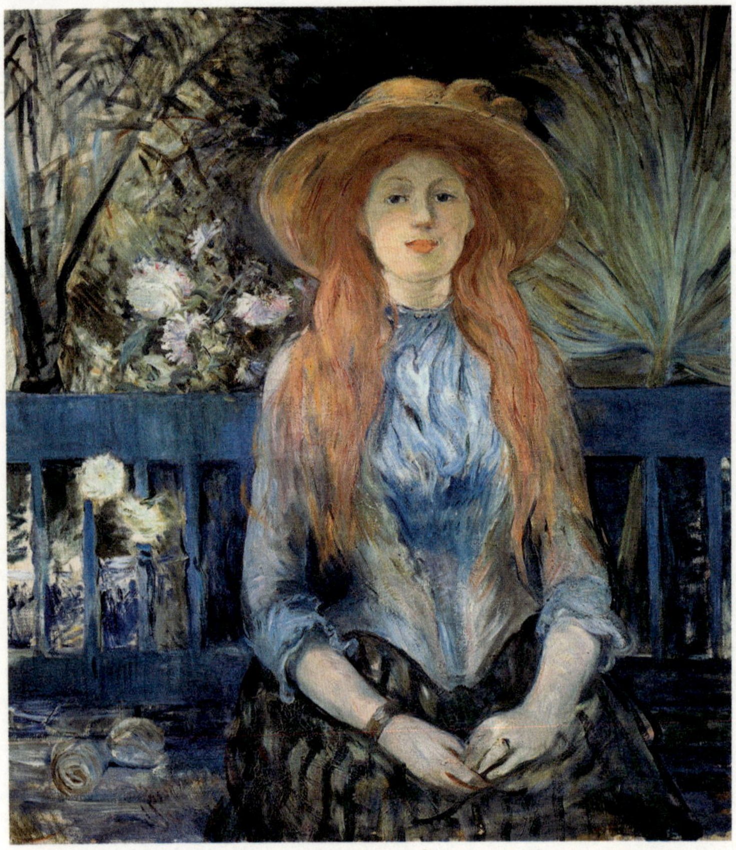

Berthe Morisot (1841–1895)
Young Girl in a Park or *On the Bench*, 1893
Oil on canvas, 90 × 81 cm
Toulouse, Musée des Augustins

> do nothing against this industry of Manet paintings. P. has quantities of fakes and he gets rid of the real ones. I'm starting to no longer hesitate in believing that he works in concert with those ignoble Bernheims that we met at his place. I bit my tongue so as not to respond with insults to the greetings and deep bows and to the over-attentiveness of these people with hats and shiny hair. . . . It was a pleasure to again see the beautiful things by Oncle Édouard and Maman that P owns, but it was most unpleasant seeing Oncle Édouard's sketches repainted and made horrible. I would have liked so much to be able to scream. I had to force myself to say nothing, and now I regret it. But I couldn't say a word since Tante Suzanne's signature is on the backs of these paintings. I cannot blame my aunt. Ah, these people have been careful to take cover. I'll have to go back to Tante Suzanne to talk to her about this and find out if she signed all these horrors, before they were completely retouched, which she probably did. This whole thing infuriates me, I wish I could do something about it. It makes me cry to see all the dirty business that goes on in the world. When seeing an affair like this, you think it's the terrible crisis that's shaking up our poor France at the moment.[35]

MARRIAGE AND SELF-SACRIFICE

Once married, Julie Manet and Ernest Rouart continued to share this mutual passion for art, acting as heirs, collectors, and donors. While Julie included in the marriage contract a brief inventory of the paintings belonging to her—for the first time in the family's history prominence was given to works by Berthe Morisot, of which there were seventy-four references, and by Édouard Manet, of which there were two paintings, several portraits and sketches, three Monets, one Degas, two portraits by Renoir and two landscapes by Pissarro—Ernest did not declare any works, even though it is known that he possessed some. As a wedding present, Degas reserved for them preparatory drawings for engraved portraits of Manet: one sheet shows him seated, in a three-quarter view, on a chair, with his hands crossed, *"Study of a Head Three Quarters to the Left"*;[36] a pencil drawing heightened with India ink wash shows him leaning against a table.[37] A final drawing depicting Manet in a similar attitude, annotated "Degas" in the lower right, "Manet" in the upper left, should be linked to this group (p. 260).[38] The question of the Manet paintings was evoked, to the point that Ernest's brother, the talented Louis, echoed it in one of his articles published in *L'Occident*, in 1902:

> Soon, for example, one will find in France only dubious Manets, entirely refurbished and finished by unscrupulous amateurs and dealers. Then undoubtedly the Louvre will decide to buy, at a very high price, a painting by this great master.[39]

However, the main concern of the young couple was to promote Berthe Morisot's work. To become part of the history of art, one must enter the museum. This was their objective. Social connections were the key and without the family nothing would have been possible. Hence close relations were appealed to.

In Haute-Garonne, Eugène Rouart was approached. Rouart, who was involved in politics—from 1906 to 1918 he was mayor of Castelnau-d'Estrétefonds, a town thirty-five kilometers from Toulouse, and a member of the Conseil Général in 1910, then a senator for Haute-Garonne from 1933 to 1936—had been working with the curator of Toulouse's museum since 1905. *On the Bench* (above), a bust figure from 1893, joined the institution's collections in May. A letter from Ernest confirms this:

> **Monsieur, As agreed with my brother, I have just had a painting by Madame Berthe Morisot, "Jeune fille sur un banc," sent to you by Monsieurs Durand-Ruel. My wife and I are offering this painting to the Musée de Toulouse, thinking that you will want to hang it in a good place.[40]**

The city of Pau also caught the couple's attention. On March 3, 1870, Julie's father had acquired an in-perpetuity concession in the centrally located Catholic cemetery for his relative Augustine Marie Manet.[41] Ernest also had ties to the city. From 1900 to 1918, Paul Lafond,[42] a close friend of Degas to whom Ernest had also become close, was the curator of the municipal museum. Lafond, who knew Henri Rouart and his immense modesty well, was undoubtedly sensitive to the initiative of his son, Ernest, who offered the museum *The Mandolin Player*,[43] thus acting in favor of the institutional recognition of Henri's work during the artist's lifetime. Lafond was undoubtedly associated with the project to donate a work by Berthe Morisot, *Pasie Sewing in the Garden at Bougival* (p. 284), which the mayor welcomed in a letter to Ernest on November 30, 1907:

> **The city council eagerly accepted, in its meeting of the 26th of this month, the gift that Madame Rouart and you kindly made to our museum of the remarkable painting by Madame Berthe Morisot "Jeune femme cousant" with the condition that it will be on permanent exhibition.[44]**

Although the acceptance of the donation was formalized on October 26, an agreement in principle was given much earlier, so that the work appeared in accordance with the Musée de Pau[45] in the catalog of the Berthe Morisot retrospective that Julie and Ernest organized from October 1 to 22, 1907 at the Salon d'Automne.

This savoir-faire also explains the acquisition of the *Peasant Woman from Nice* by the Musée de Lyon (p. 286). Since the beginning of the century, the museum had pursued a policy of openness to modern art and had set up an acquisition committee.[46] In order to follow new trends as closely as possible, its delegates were responsible for keeping abreast of sales and the Parisian Salons. As early as 1900, one of its most eminent members, the painter Jacques Martin, approached Renoir through Albert André, who was himself the companion of one of Martin's students, Marguerite Cornillac, whom the city did not neglect to commission. The intervention of Albert André, who had the full confidence of the Impressionist—he was to be his executor—facilitated the discussions and enabled the museum to acquire its first modern painting in 1901, *Woman Playing the Guitar*.[47] Given his links with Renoir, is it any wonder that André was a friend of Julie and Ernest and was one of the regulars at the Thursday gatherings in the rue de Villejust that Madame Rouart established, following in her mother's footsteps?[48]

It was in this context that the protagonists met again in 1907 at the Salon d'Automne. Martin went there as usual and bought a painting by his friend Albert André, *In Provence*, on behalf of the Musée de Lyon. No doubt Martin and André had the courtesy to visit the *Berthe Morisot* retrospective presented a few doors away and to admire *Woman from Nice*, a work, according to the exhibition catalog, from the collection of Madame Ernest Rouart. Albert André was certainly aware of Renoir's views on the need to circulate Morisot's oeuvre. And it goes without saying that he was aware of Julie's recent initiatives to this effect. Finally, there is no doubt that André advocated a purchase. Martin opted for *Peasant Woman from Nice*. The decision was made at the Salon. On November 7, 1907, the minutes of the committee's meeting confirmed that "the canvas was bought in Paris by the delegates of the committee." The purchase was effective on November 16, 1907, for the sum of 3,000 francs.

The promotion business being a family one, the Valéry family was asked to contribute. Paul's brother, Jules Valéry, a prominent Montpellier lawyer and professor of law at the university, was asked to contact the museum in his city and to act as Julie's intermediary with the head of the establishment:

> **Dear Sir,**
>
> **Confirming the conversation I had the honor of having with you, I am hereby putting in writing that Madame Ernest Rouart, née Manet, sole heiress of Berthe Morisot, her mother, and Édouard Manet, her uncle, would be willing to donate to the Musée de Montpellier some of the paintings, bearing one or other of these illustrious signatures, that she owns. The bonds of friendship and alliance that unite me to her give me the pleasure of passing on this proposal to you. If it is accepted, as I hope it will be, by the members of the museum's committee, they are invited to contact Madame Rouart who lives in Paris, 40 rue de Villejust.[49]**

The Musée de Montpellier committee ratified the gift of *Young Woman at the Window* (p. 285) on November 5, 1907 and did not fail to express its regrets to Julie, who finally did not wish to donate any work by her uncle.

The circumstances that led the Musée du Petit Palais in Paris to receive Morisot paintings were different. If works

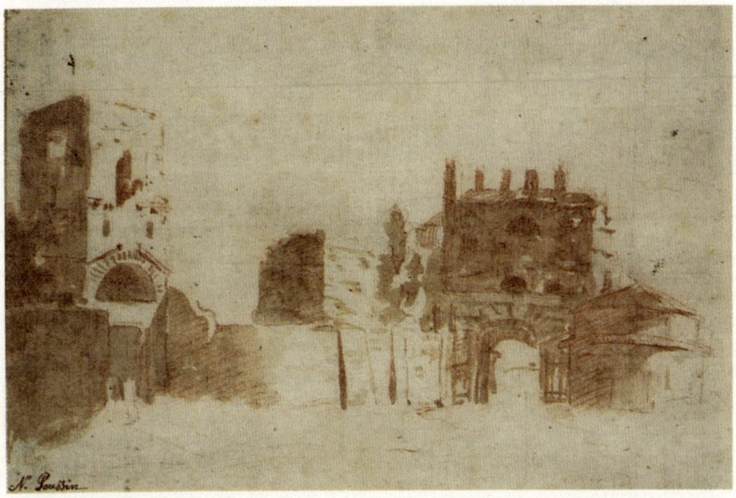

Nicolas Poussin (1594–1665)
View of Rome, n.d.
Sepia wash on paper, 16 × 23 cm
Paris, Musée Marmottan Monet

by the Impressionist were offered to it, it was not at the initiative of the artist's daughter, but at the request of its director, Henry Lapauze. This was not a customary occurrence. It must be said that the context was particular and the man remarkable for his initiatives. Founded in 1902 to "inhabit" a building built for the Exposition Universelle of 1900, the Petit Palais houses the collections of the City of Paris. Its first directors intended to enrich them. Henry Lapauze, who took over the reins of the institution in 1905, instigated numerous initiatives, one of the most notorious being the acquisition of several studio collections.[50] Another, launched in 1907, aimed at creating a "museum of modern drawing" for which many artists, descendants of artists, and collectors were called upon for contributions. Monsieur and Madame Ernest Rouart offered in this context a red chalk drawing by Berthe Morisot,[51] a preparatory study for the painting *Embroidery*.[52] Renoir, also contacted, chose the preparatory pastel (p. 43) for the *Portrait of Berthe Morisot and Her Daughter Julie Manet* (p. 217). Ernest's uncle, Alexis Rouart, donated fourteen drawings. Close to Lapauze, he became his intermediary with Ernest so that the museum could be offered a painting this time. On January 14, 1908, Ernest replied:

> **Monsieur,**
> **Taking into consideration the request made to us via our uncle, we have the honor to inform you that we are willing to offer a painting by Madame Berthe Morisot to the Musée du Petit Palais. We have set aside several from which we would ask you to choose. The only condition is that the painting must always be displayed for the public to see and placed on the picture rail.**[53]

Young Girl in a Low-Cut Dress with a Flower in Her Hair (p. 287), an oil painting from 1893, was added to the collections of the City of Paris. Julie and Berthe Morisot were associated for the last time with the Musée du Petit Palais. Charged with designing the decor of one of the building's cupolas on the theme of the history of French art, Maurice Denis decided to treat his subject by painting portraits of the artists he considered most important. For Berthe's portrait, he asked Julie to provide him with a model. The Impressionist's daughter sent him a full-length watercolor figure[54] from which the painter drew his inspiration to complete his decor, with Berthe finally reaching the firmament of art history.[55]

ROUART SALES 1911–1912. ACQUISITIONS AND DONATIONS

From the beginning of their marriage, Monsieur and Madame Ernest Rouart acted as collectors. Julie continued to frequent the Hôtel Drouot auction house and confided about the Fabre sale: "I might go with Jeannie today to see the Redon paintings for sale, which are really good."[56]

In circumstances that remain to be clarified, between 1902 and 1906 the couple acquired from Ambroise Vollard *Landscape with Horses* by Gauguin (p. 305), a painting that they lent to the Salon d'Automne in 1906[57] with *Fatata te Miti* (p. 304), of which they divested themselves at a still unknown date. At the Chéramy sale in 1908, Ernest was seduced by two drawings: a Corot sketched in Italy in September 1837[58] and a *Study of a Tiger's Head and Body* by Delacroix.[59] Throughout his life, he continued to acquire signed or anonymous pieces, thus giving free rein to what was undoubtedly one of his greatest passions: the sense of line, of the virtuoso line, drawing—a language in its own right. His wife was no stranger to these purchases: "Julie has certainly told you about his acquisition of engravings,"[60] his cousin Jeannie wrote to Ernest.

Was it during their peregrinations that they acquired a wash drawing by Poussin, *View of Rome* (above left), one or several drawings by Ingres, this *View of Algiers* (p. 265) by Delacroix and perhaps even *Summer* by Puvis de Chavannes (p. 265)? This was undoubtedly the case for the fifty-one engravings by Rembrandt and other engravings by Dürer, Van Ostade, Mantegna, Cranach, and Claude Lorrain that Julie mentioned in one of her inventories.[61]

The Rouart sales marked a turning point in their career. In 1911, Ernest acquired two works at the sale after his uncle Alexis' death.[62] For 200 francs, he purchased a work

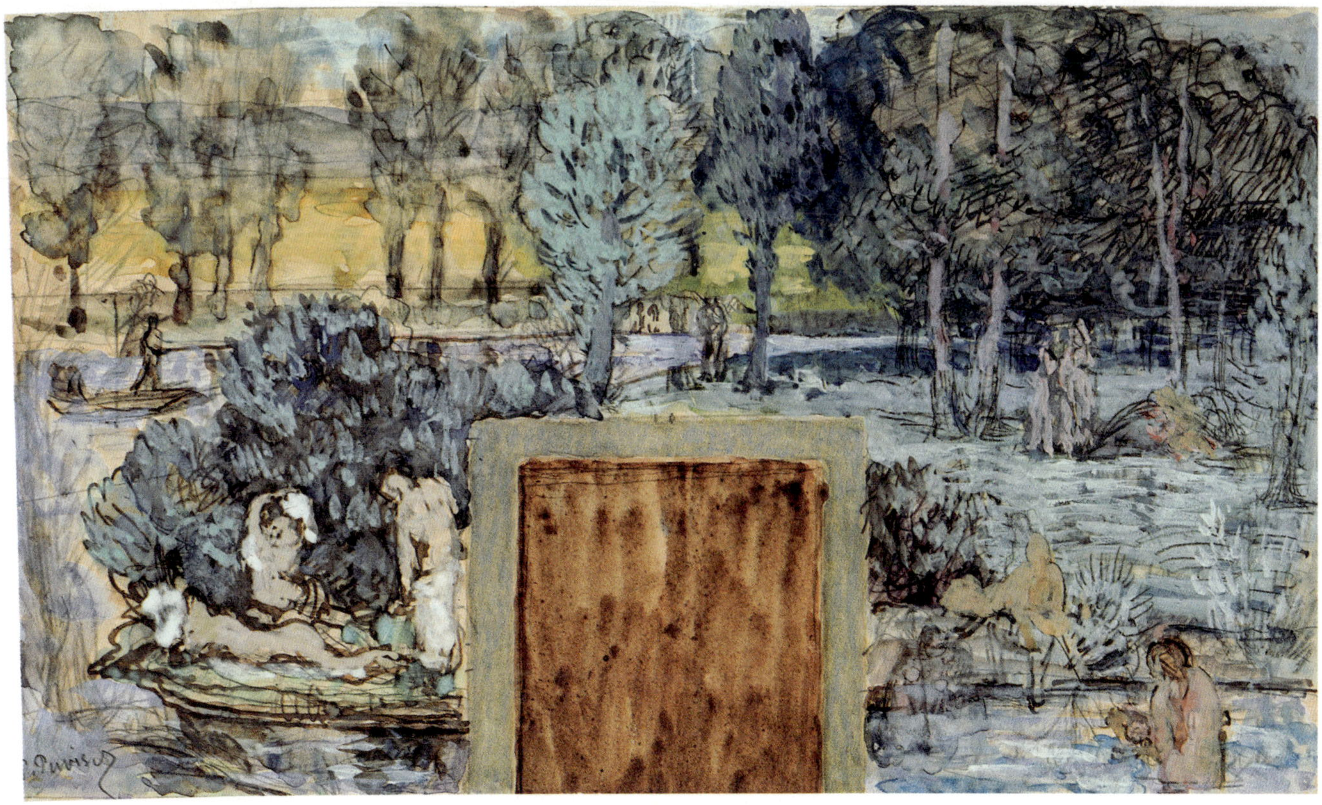

Pierre Puvis de Chavannes (1824–1898)
Summer, 1891
Watercolor and gouache on blue paper, 20 × 34 cm
Paris, Musée Marmottan Monet

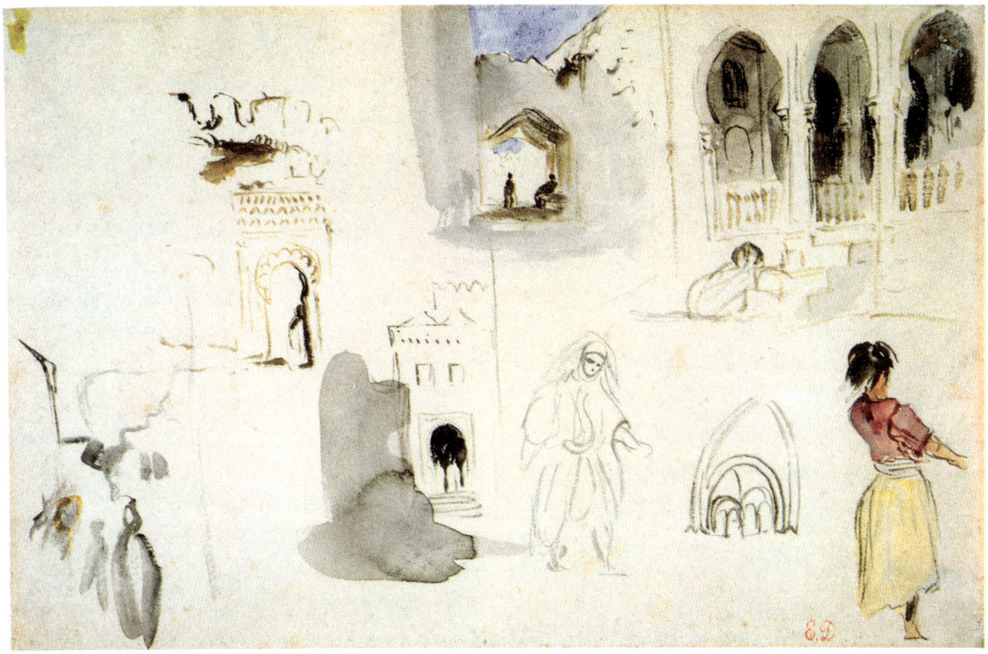

Eugène Delacroix (1798–1863)
View of Algiers, also known as *The Casbah, Tangier*, n.d.
Watercolor on paper, 21 × 32 cm
Paris, Musée Marmottan Monet

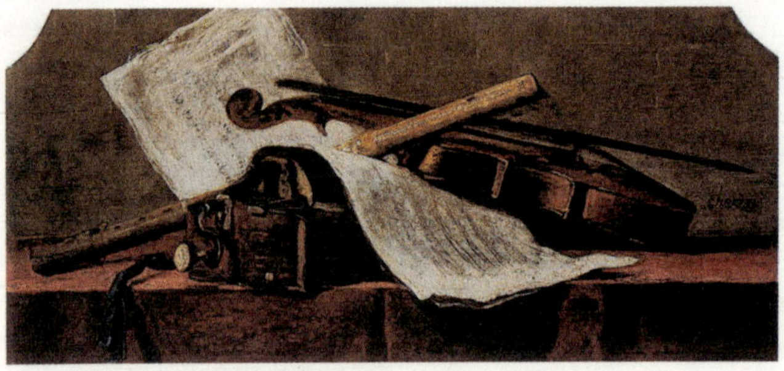

Jean Siméon Chardin (1699–1779)
Musical Instruments, c. 1735
Oil on canvas, 49 × 95 cm
Private collection

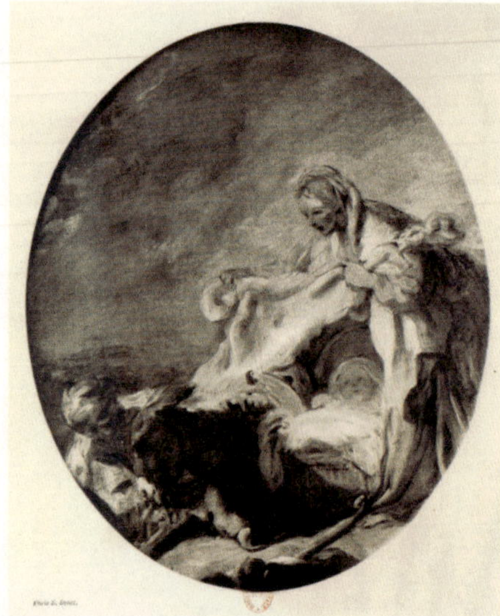

Jean Honoré Fragonard (1732–1806)
The Rest on the Flight into Egypt, n.d.
Oil on canvas, 53 × 43 cm
Location unknown

by one of his father's best friends, Gustave Colin,[63] and for 13,300 francs—which corresponded more or less to Paul Valéry's annual income[64]—a pastel on monotype by Degas, measuring a mere twenty-nine by twenty-six centimeters: *Dancers in Yellow* (p. 302).[65] This indicates how popular the artist's work had now become.

The fate of Henri Rouart's collection was the main event. At his death, works that did not appear on any inventory passed directly to his children. Many of these were mementoes. Eugène received the famous *Henri Rouart in Front of His Factory* (p. 299) painted by Degas around 1875. Alexis was reunited with the pastel by Degas for which he sat with his father in 1895.[66] Several paintings seem to have returned to Ernest. According to the archives of the Galerie Weill,[67] a portrait of Leconte de Lisle[68] by Jean-François Millet would have been attributed to him. The *Portrait of Léopold Levert* (p. 301) by Degas probably went to him, unless it had been acquired from Chéramy, to whom the historian Paul-André Lemoisne—author of the first catalog raisonné of Degas's oeuvre, published in four volumes between 1947 and 1949[69]—gave the painting. The acquisition would then be prior to 1908, as Levert's portrait was not included in the art connoisseur's posthumous sale. As this provenance is not mentioned in Paul Lafond's 1918 book, nor in the catalog for the *Degas portraitiste sculpteur* exhibition in 1931[70] (both well-researched), it is likely that Ernest received it in 1912. In any case, the portrait of Léopold Levert belonged to him, and it also belonged to his father and did not appear in the sale of his collection.

To be more precise, three sales, organized in December 1912 and April 1913,[71] were necessary to disperse the eight hundred and seventy-one lots offered at auction. Prices soared, the collection, estimated at 640,000 francs,[72] reached the historic sum of 5,736,231 francs.[73] Henri's five children purchased three hundred and twenty-nine lots for a total of 1,815,862 francs, or 31.66% of the proceeds of the sale. As these purchases were recorded in the minutes[74] under the joint ownership of Rouart, i.e. the five children together, we can only attempt to reconstruct the list of Ernest's acquisitions. Old photographs, family archives, exhibition catalogs, not forgetting the article devoted in 1932 to Ernest Rouart's collection in the magazine *Formes*,[75] are the main sources that allow us to draw up this list. Twenty-three lots were thus identified, representing 6.99% of the lots acquired jointly.

Let us evoke classic art first. Ernest took away *Musical Instruments* by Jean Siméon Chardin (above left),[76] *The Rest on the Flight into Egypt* by Jean Honoré Fragonard (above right),[77] now lost and similar to *Shepherds in a Landscape* (p. 288), also acquired jointly and now held by the Musée d'Annecy, and lastly *View of the Louvre. The Garden of the Infante* (p. 289)[78] by Hubert Robert.

The great nineteenth-century masters came next. Let us mention a pencil drawing by Pierre Paul Prud'hon, *Standing Nude Woman, Leaning on an Oar*,[79] a self-portrait by Delacroix (p. 291),[80] and a black pencil drawing by Jean-François Millet, *Woodcutters in the Forest*.[81] Five little drawings by Honoré Daumier: *At the Theatre* (p. 267),[82] *The Bedridden Patient* (p. 268),[83] *A Lawyer* (p. 268), *Two Defendants* (p. 268), and *Recollection of the Palais*.[84] With seven paintings, Jean-Baptiste Camille Corot, the artist who had most affected Julie during her first visit to rue de Lisbonne, is the best represented. Indeed, on

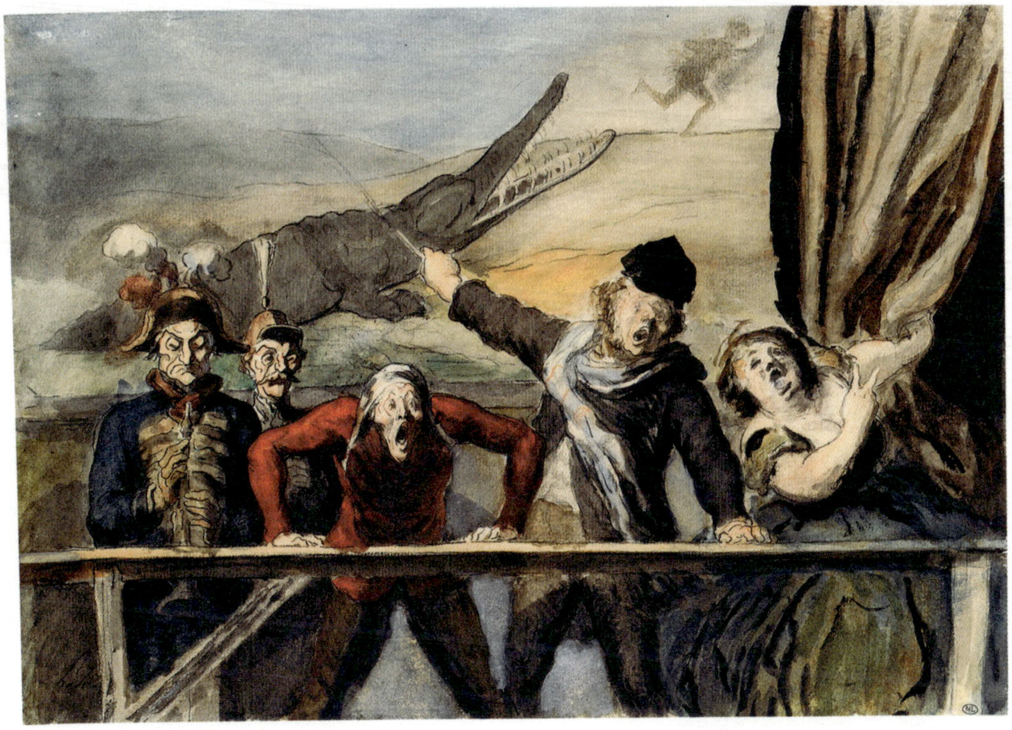

Honoré Daumier (1808–1879)
The Fairground Show, c. 1865
Pen, ink, watercolor, black chalk, red chalk, gray wash, Conté pencil and gouache on laid paper, 20 × 36.5 cm
Paris, Musée d'Orsay, conserved at the Musée du Louvre

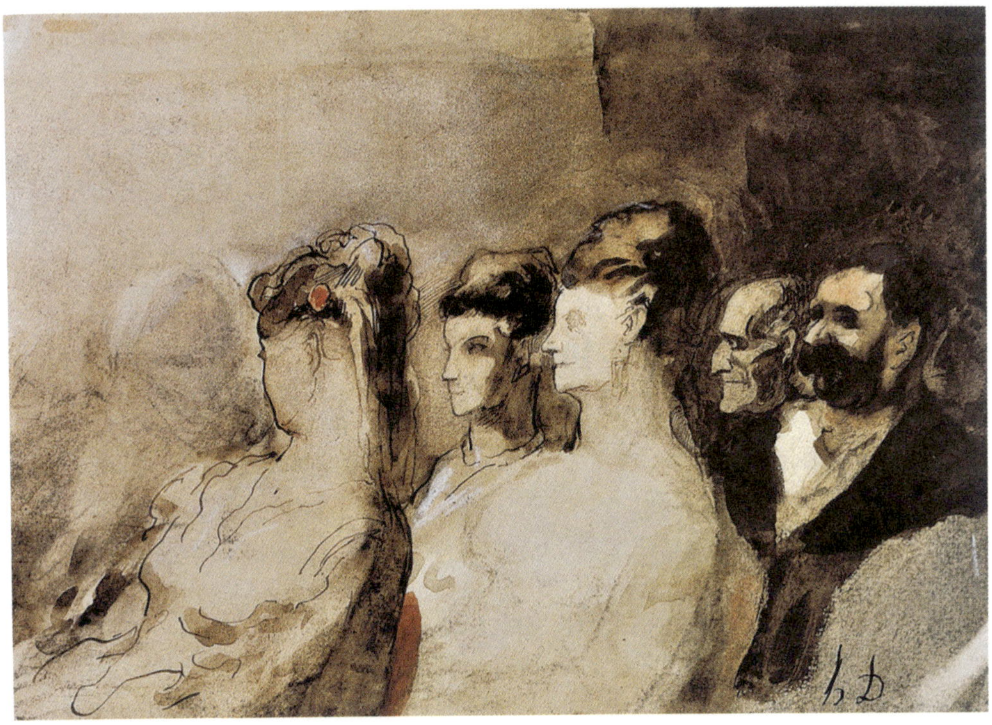

Honoré Daumier (1808–1879)
At the Theater, c. 1860–65
Pencil, ink and watercolor on paper, 19 × 27 cm
Location unknown

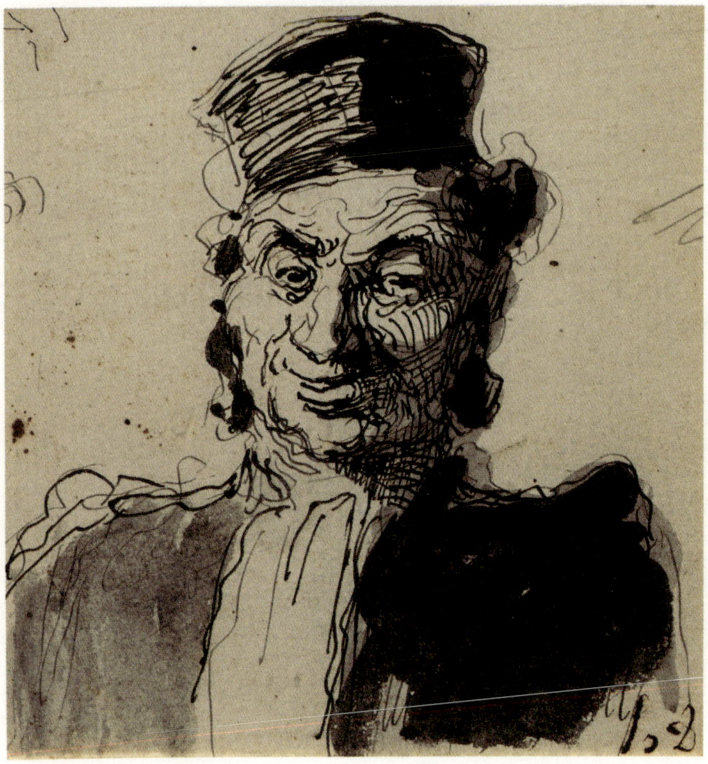

Honoré Daumier (1808–1879)
A Lawyer, n.d.
India ink and wash on paper, 11 × 10 cm
Paris, Musée Marmottan Monet

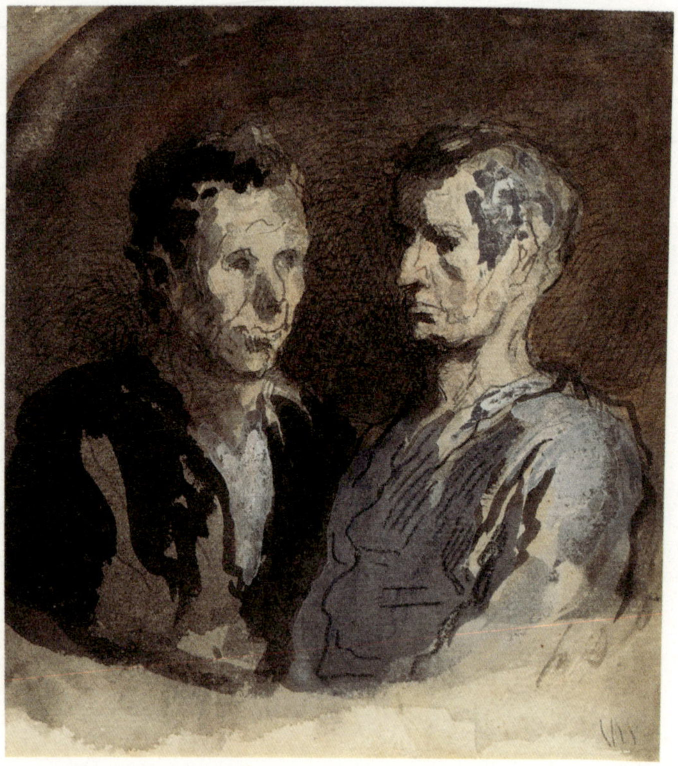

Honoré Daumier (1808–1879)
Two Defendants, n.d.
Watercolor on paper, 14 × 12 cm
Paris, Musée Marmottan Monet

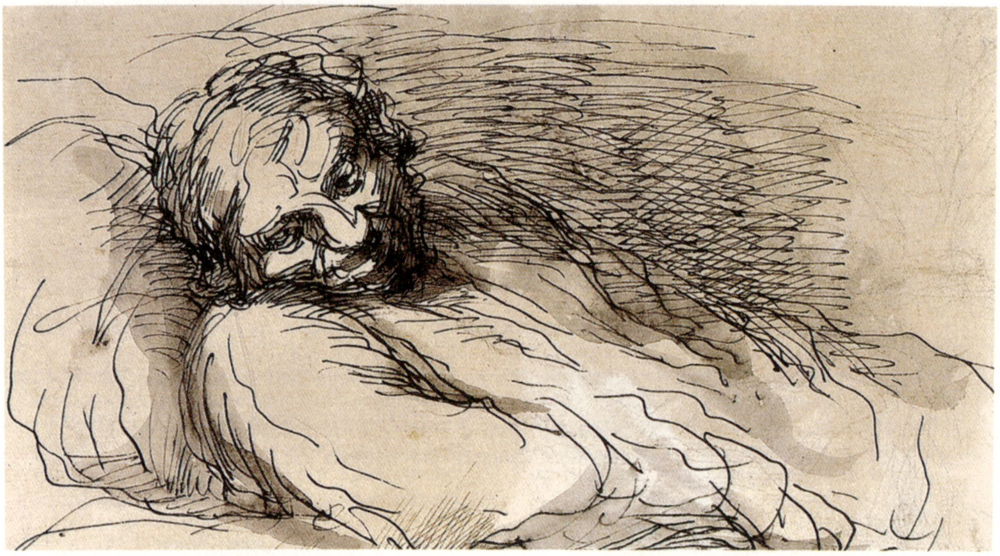

Honoré Daumier (1808–1879)
The Bedridden Patient, n.d.
Pen and wash on paper, 12 × 22 cm
Location unknown

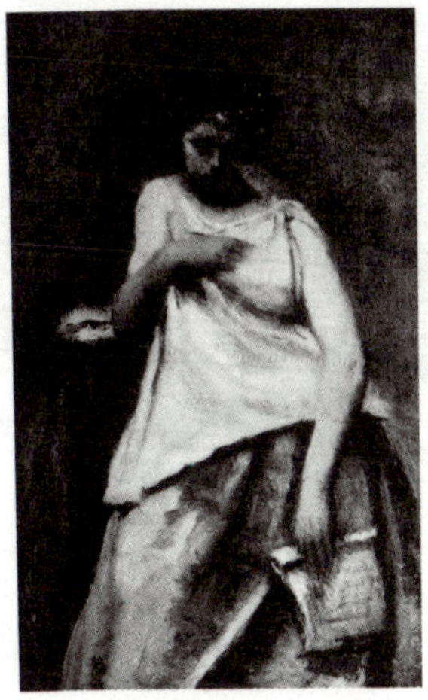

Jean-Baptiste Camille Corot (1796–1875)
Tragedy, c. 1860–65
Oil on canvas, 70 × 54 cm
Location unknown

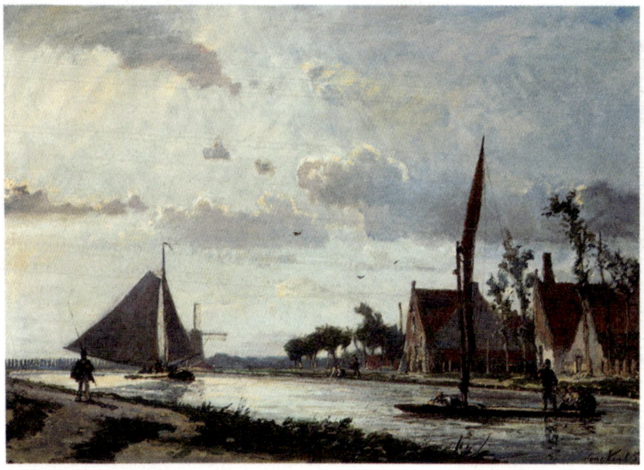

Johan Barthold Jongkind (1819–1891)
A Canal near Rotterdam, 1857
Oil on canvas, 41 × 56 cm
Private collection

January 27, 1898, Berthe Morisot's daughter noted on leaving Henri Rouart's house:

> For me, it was a revelation of Corot's talent; I thought I knew him through his delicious landscapes but I hadn't seen everything, of course. When Monsieur Renoir talked about his figures with such enthusiasm, I was unable to share his admiration as I had never seen any of them; but Corot's great genius was made apparent to me today. Until now, though I liked him, I didn't appreciate him at his proper value.[85]

It is therefore not surprising that the couple took away three figures: *Dreaming Bohemian Girl*,[86] *Peasant Woman with a White Blouse*,[87] and *The Source* (p. 293).[88] Then came the landscapes, three studies: *Recollection of Montpellier*,[89] *View of Genzano* (p. 292),[90] and *Volterra, Road Descending from the Town*,[91] and finally the masterpiece, *Tivoli. The Gardens of the Villa d'Este* (p. 295),[92] bought for 111,000 francs. They also acquired a painting by Jongkind, *A Canal near Rotterdam* (above).[93]

Then it was the turn of Manet and the Impressionists. By Oncle Édouard, only *On the Beach*[94] was purchased, which Julie had copied in watercolor and which shows her father from behind—the work attained the not inconsiderable sum of 92,000 francs. The couple preferred, for a slightly higher amount, *Brunette with Bare Breasts* (p. 273).[95] Monet appealed and so *Festival at Argenteuil*[96] was chosen. Degas concluded this inventory. For 145,000 francs, Ernest obtained three pastels by his master, who attended the sale with him: *At the Milliner's* (p. 270),[97] *In the Wings* (p. 303),[98] and *Dancer with a Fan* (p. 271).[99]

In total, Ernest paid 538,800 francs, a sum corresponding to 29.67% of the amount of the joint ownership purchases and 9.39% of the proceeds of the sale. The investment was considerable; it was equivalent to 40% of his inheritance. His son Julien, then ten years old, confirmed the importance of these acquisitions:

> My father bought back a very large part [of the collection], quite a lot. I think he must have repurchased almost everything that he could from his share of the inheritance.[100]

Marked by the extraordinary impact of the sale which, according to him, had made the headlines, he added:

> I remember that when I arrived in class the next day my classmates looked at me with astonishment. I had become another character for them, especially since I was quite shy and self-effacing, and I was a bit surprised by all this. It was beyond me.[101]

The story could make one giddy.

Henri Rouart's children did not forget the Louvre and reserved several lots for the museum, contributing to the enrichment of the public collections after their father's death. On January 14, 1913, a note from the Musées Nationaux stated:

> The Fairground Show [p. 267], watercolor by Daumier . . . is fully gifted by the children of Monsieur Henri Rouart, who bought it at the sale for 45,000 francs

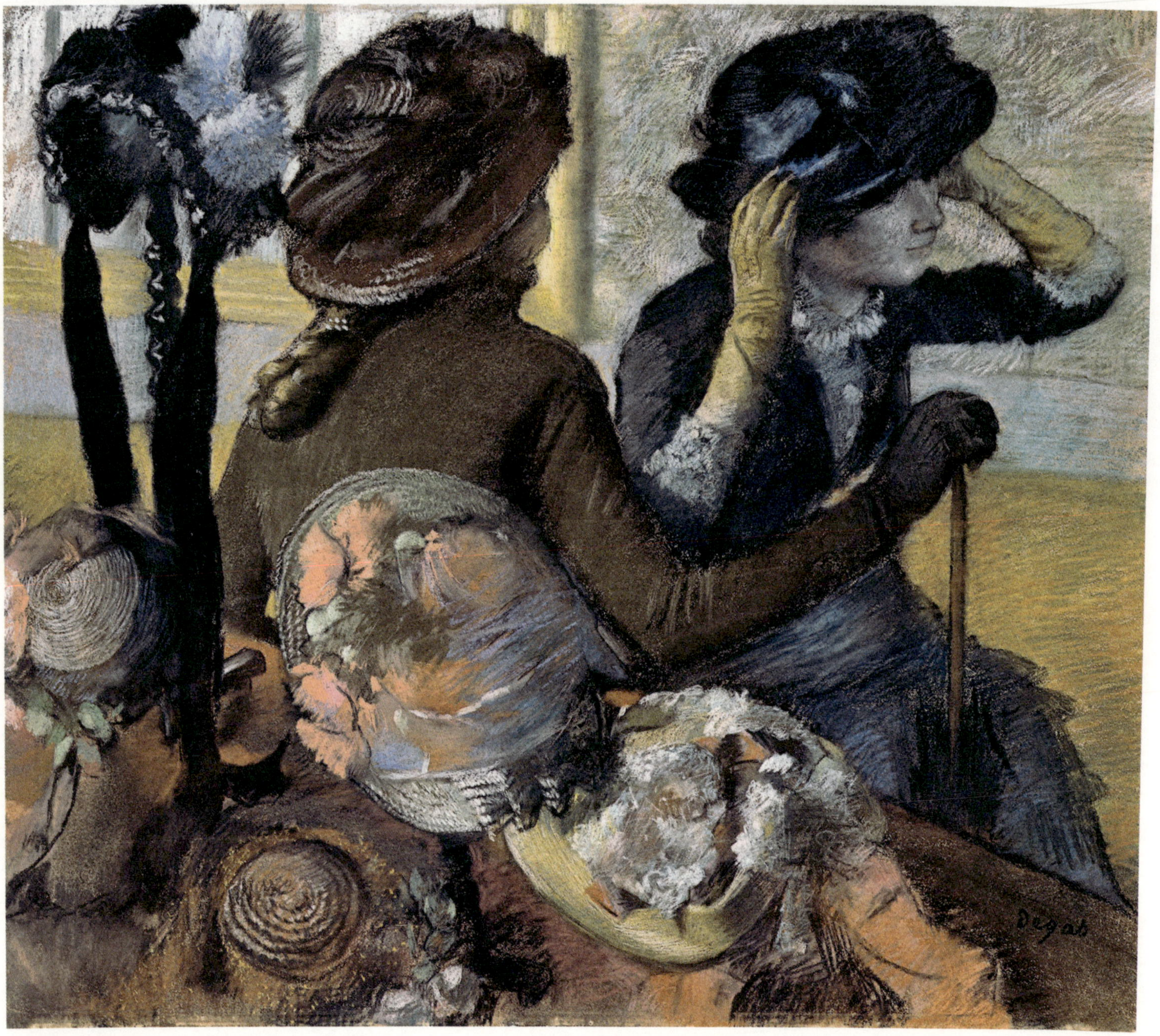

Edgar Degas (1834–1917)
At the Milliner's, 1882
Pastel on paper, 75.5 × 85.5 cm
Madrid, Museo Nacional Thyssen-Bornemisza

with the intention of offering it to us. Do not be mistaken. We must warmly thank Monsieur Alexis Rouart, 34, rue de Lisbonne (he is the eldest of the family) for this generosity and ask him to convey our gratitude to his brothers and sister. This donation is made jointly by Monsieur Alexis Rouart, his brothers, and his sister. Monsieur Henri Rouart's children have joined together under the same conditions to contribute to the donation of the Société des Amis du Louvre [*Crispin and Scapin* by Daumier, p. 296]. To a purchase made at the price of 60,000 francs, they participated for a sum of 35,000 francs, solely making it possible.[102]

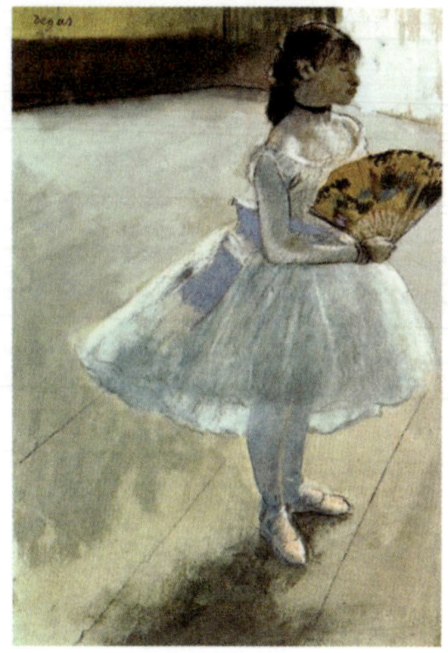

Edgar Degas (1834–1917)
Dancer with a Fan, c. 1879
Pastel on paper, 50.8 × 34.9 cm
Dallas Museum of Art, Eugene and Margaret McDermott Art Fund, bequest of Mrs. Eugene McDermott

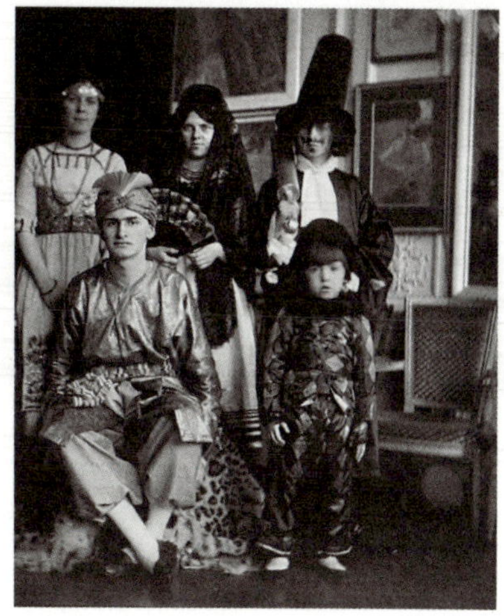

Julie Manet (1878-1966)
or Ernest Rouart (1874-1942)
Carnival rue de Villejust
Behind the Rouart and Valéry children: *Dancer with a Fan by Degas*, c. 1920
On permanent loan at the Musée Marmottan Monet

Henri Rouart's children also contributed in cash to the acquisition of Corot's *Lady in Blue* (p. 297), which was sold for 162,000 francs. The draft of a letter from the director of the Musées Nationaux to Alexis Rouart confirms this:

> The Conseil des Musées authorized me, last Tuesday, to collect the sum of 12,000 francs that you were kind enough to put at our disposal, in agreement with your brothers and sister, to pay for the acquisition of the painting by Corot "the lady in blue" sold to the Louvre at the sale of Monsieur Henri Rouart, your father.
>
> I would be most grateful if you would let me know the day and time that would be convenient for you so that . . . the Secrétaire of the Musées Nationaux could receive this sum from your hands, unless you would like to have it brought to the Louvre.[103]

Thus, Henri Rouart's heirs contributed 34% to the financing of three very important works: *The Fairground Show*, *Crispin and Scapin* by Daumier, and *Lady in Blue* by Corot. This explains the thanks addressed to them by the director of the Musées Nationaux:

> [Please accept] our deepest gratitude for the very effective assistance you gave us at the time of the dispersal of your father's famous collection, without which some eminently desirable acquisitions for France would have slipped by us.[104]

WAR AND SALES: AROUND THE DEGAS'S SALES (1918–1920)

The death of Degas and the sale of his studio were another heartbreak. Ernest lost his master, a man he looked up to as a father; Julie a protector and a friend. The dispersal of his "museum" and his studio collection echoed the drama of the dividing up of the rue de Lisbonne collection. So many major groups of works that they were unable to save. The pain was all the more acute since Degas died at the height of the First World War. Mobilized in Châlons (Marne), Ernest could attend neither the funeral nor the sales. Nor could Julie. On March 23, 1918, Paris was shelled by the Big Bertha. Julie was ordered by her husband to flee with the children. She took refuge with her cousins in Vassé, before spending the rest of 1918 in Rennes.

On March 22, the day before the first shelling and on the same day, a sale of *Modern and Antique Paintings, drawings, objets d'art and furniture, Chinese porcelain, eighteenth-century chairs and furniture and other items belonging to Monsieur X* was held at the Hôtel Drouot. The sale began with eighty-two lots of kitchen utensils, crockery, and other glassware, not included in the catalog, suggesting that it was a complete interior that was being dispersed. The seller? Eugène Rouart. His registered residence? Not his main residence—he lived in the Château de Saint-Caprais in Castelnau-d'Estrétefonds, in the Haute-Garonne—but 11 rue Boissière in Paris. Was it simply an address or a pied-à-terre? Was this the apartment he was leaving? Was it this apartment that he was emptying? We do not know.

Bad investments forced him to sell. Numerous works from his father's collection were included in the catalog. Ernest could not let this go. It is unlikely that he obtained permission to attend the sale. He was probably represented by his brother Louis, who put in several bids. His two most important acquisitions reflected his tastes. We find a figure by Corot, *Tragedy* (p. 269),[105] 13,000 francs,

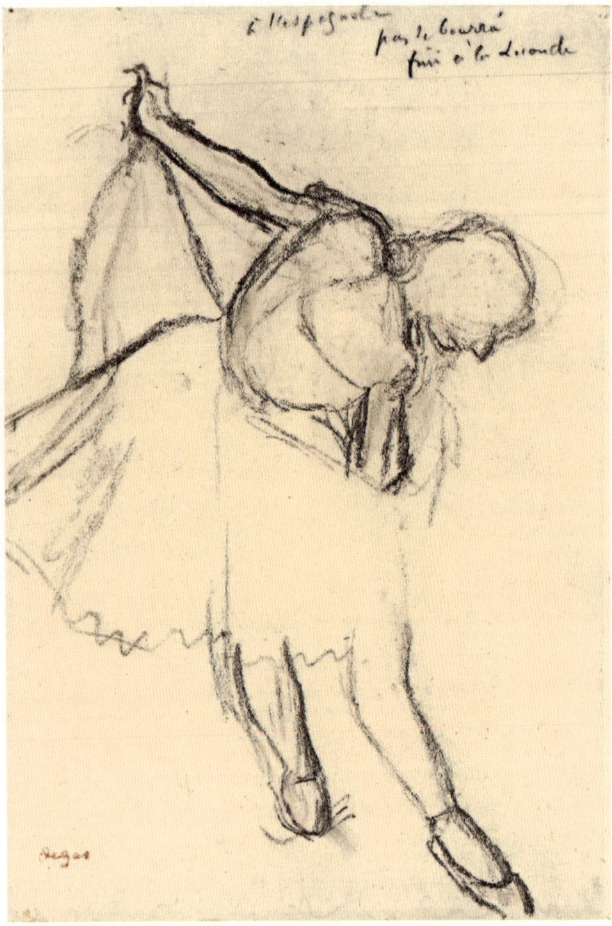

Edgar Degas (1834–1917)
Dancer (Pas de Bourrée), c. 1880–85
Brown Conté pencil and pink chalk on paper,
34.3 × 22.8 cm
Snite Museum of Art, University of Notre Dame

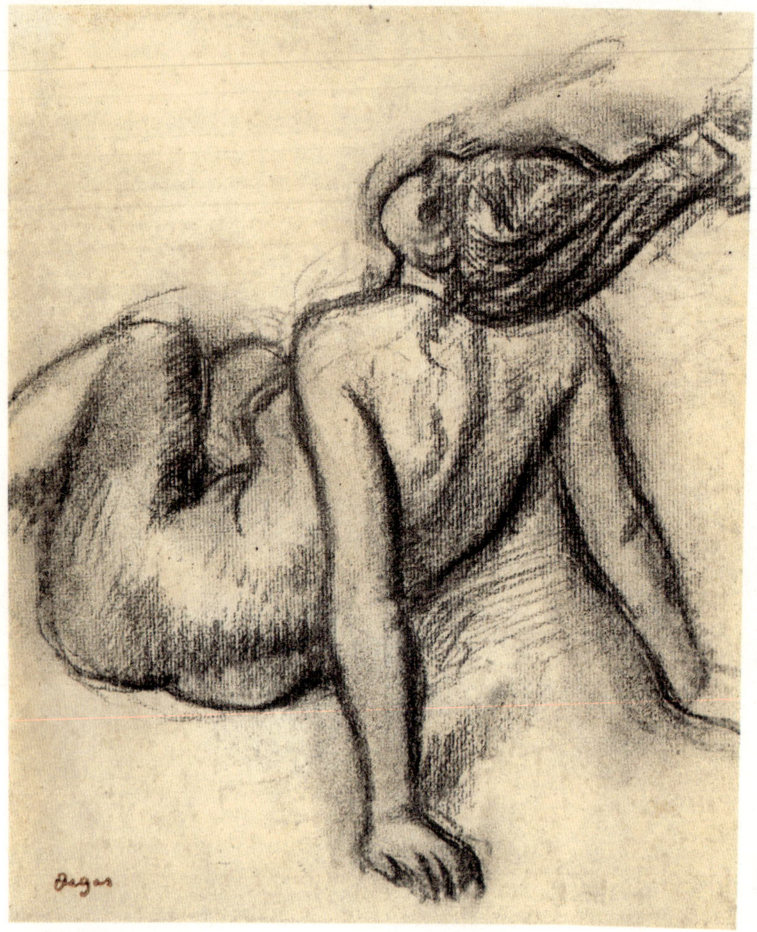

Edgar Degas (1834–1917)
The Coiffure, n.d.
Charcoal on laid paper, 34 × 26 cm
Paris, Musée Marmottan Monet

and for 1,820 francs a large watercolor by Delacroix, *An Arab* (p. 290).[106] It was precisely other drawings by Delacroix and Ingres patiently collected by his master that Ernest had to endure seeing vanish a few days later. Neither Eugène nor Julie could attend the sale of the Degas collection on March 26 and 27, 1918. Was Berthe Morisot's daughter, who so regretted having to leave Paris, leaving behind the portrait of her mother with a bouquet of violets, aware that another portrait of her by Manet, *Portrait of Berthe Morisot*,[107] was included in the sale? No more auctions on behalf of Ernest Rouart were recorded before his demobilization on January 9, 1919. After his discharge, he attended the third Degas sale, on April 7, 8, and 9, 1919, and for 8,750 francs bought ten or so sheets in three or four lots: two *Dancers*[108] in charcoal with white heightening, four *Dancers*[109] in charcoal with pastel heightening,[110] and four *Dancers* in charcoal with gouache heightening. A certain Monsieur Vigué took away three charcoal drawings. Was this for Ernest or did he acquire *The Coiffure* (above),[111] which was definitely part of his collection, later? This remains to be seen. Finally, at the fourth sale of old and modern prints, he bought a single engraving by his master for 730 francs: *After the Bath*.[112] Last but not least, Ernest recalled in *Degas, Danse, Dessin* the circumstances that led him to buy back the copy that his master had made of Mantegna's *Minerva Expelling the Vices from the Garden of Virtue* (p. 60), a symbolic, almost amorous act, since it was while he was copying the same painting in the Louvre that Degas introduced him to Julie:

> This painting was sold under the attribution "French School." I found it shortly after the war at a dealer's who had paid two hundred francs for it. (At that time, I was mobilized in Châlons, and had not been able to follow the sale.) The dealer had recognized it as a

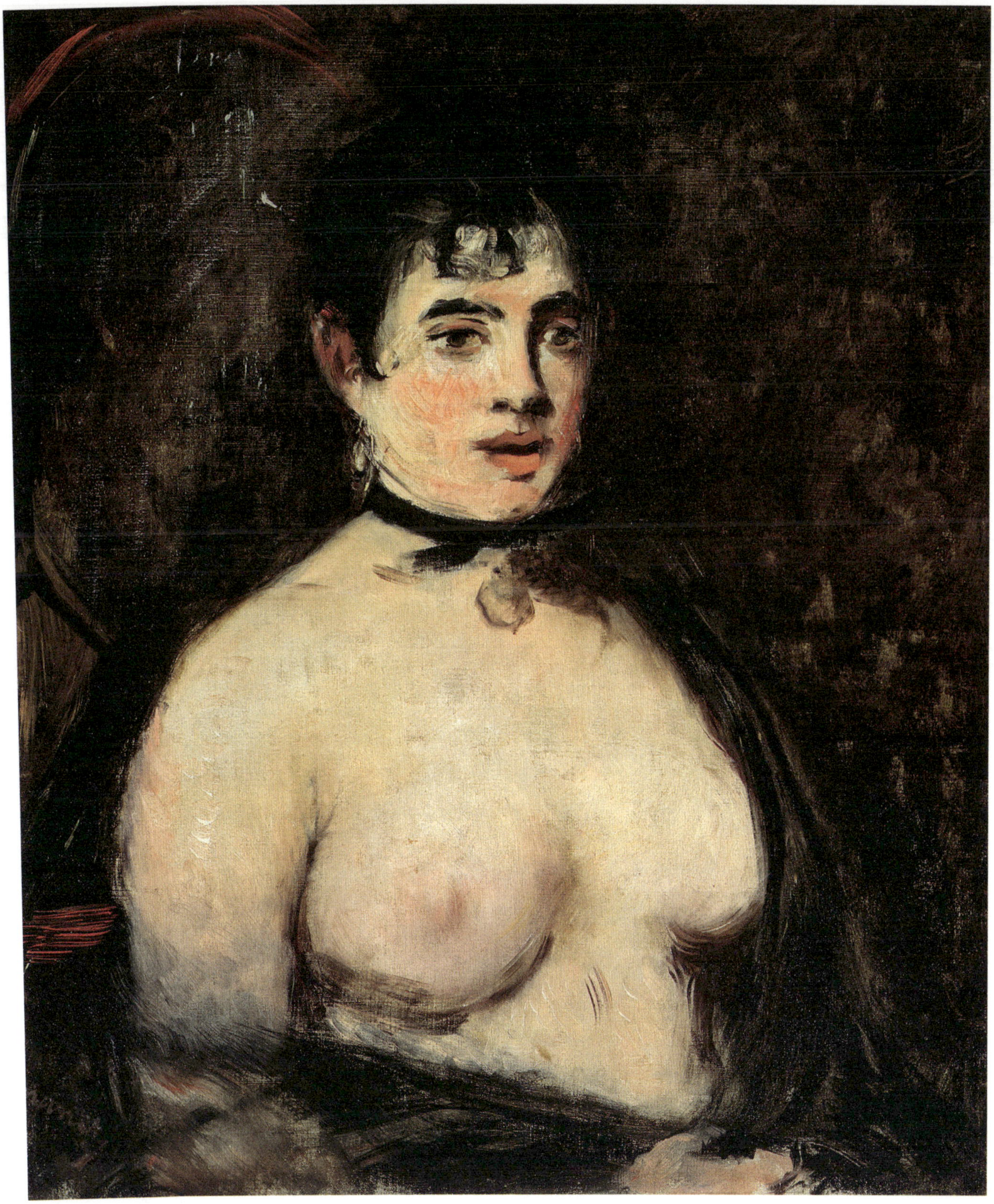

Édouard Manet (1832–1883)
Brunette with Bare Breasts, 1872
Oil on canvas, 60 × 49 cm
Location unknown

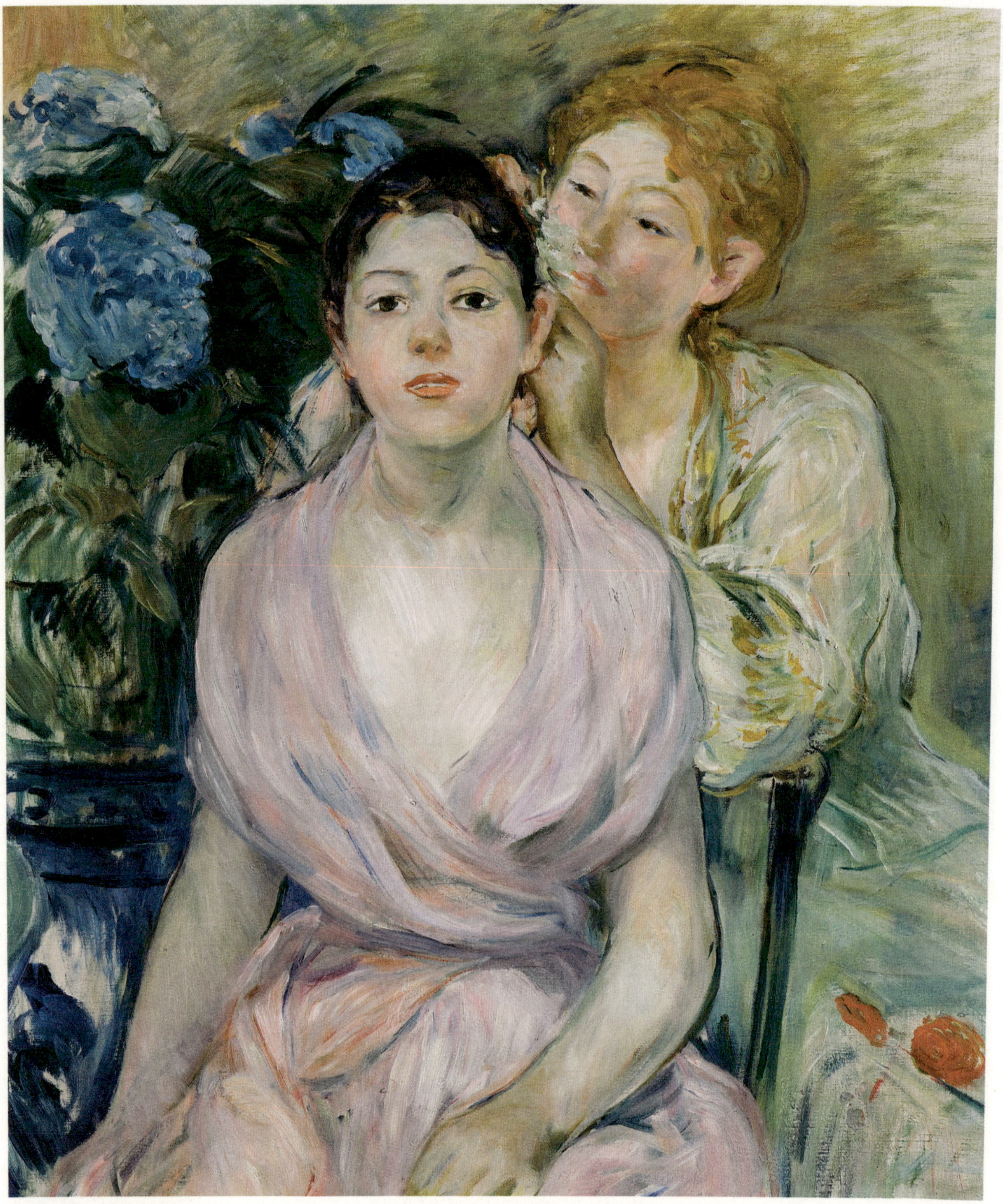

Berthe Morisot (1841–1895)
The Hortensia, 1894
Oil on canvas, 73.1 × 60.4 cm
Paris, Musée d'Orsay

work by Degas, and naturally, made me pay considerably more. (As it is, it is for me a precious memento.)[113]

With the war barely over, the enterprise of gaining recognition for Berthe Morisot's oeuvre resumed. Louis Rouart (p. 277)—who had already expressed his sincere admiration for the artist in his exhibition reports—was in charge. On June 25, 1920, he approached Paul Jamot, assistant curator of the Department of Paintings, Chalcography, and Drawings at the Louvre, with the aim of Morisot's work entering the museum's collections.

> Monsieur,
> I have forwarded your letter to my sister-in-law, Madame Ernest Rouart. If you are free next Monday either in the morning between eleven and noon or after lunch between two thirty and three thirty, my sister-in-law will be happy to show you . . . the painting she intends to offer to the Musée du Louvre.[114]

Julie selected a work presented at the 1896 and 1907 exhibitions, *The Hortensia* (p. 276), exhibited around 1919 in the living room in the rue de Villejust, as shown in a photo of Paul Valéry posing next to one of the children of the family (right).

A second letter from Louis, on the letterhead of the Librairie de l'Art Catholique, set the appointment for Monday at eleven. At the end of the visit, Paul Jamot annotated it and indicated:

> Monsieur and Madame Ernest Rouart offer to the Louvre a painting by Berthe Morisot (Madame Eugène Manet) mother of Madame Ernest Rouart: "The Hortensia." Two young girls (half-body) in a garden. One brunette, the other blonde. 1894. Excellent painting from the period of B.M. who, in the first part of her career had been influenced by Manet, turned to Renoir. Seen on June 28, 1920 P. J.[115]

The gift was accepted by decree on August 7, 1920.[116] In 1924, Paul Jamot joined the Fraternité du Tiers-Ordre and from then on established more direct ties with Ernest, which led them to work together to organize particularly ambitious heritage exhibitions.

Tante Edma also participated in this effort and donated a work by her sister to the Louvre. Upon her death, her son Edme acted on her instructions and contacted the museum administration:

> Monsieur,
> I have the honor to inform you that in accordance with the last wishes of my mother, Madame Pontillon née Morisot, we are holding at your disposal her portrait executed in pastel by Berthe Morisot, her sister. My cousin Monsieur Ernest Rouart will bring the painting to the museum next week.[117]

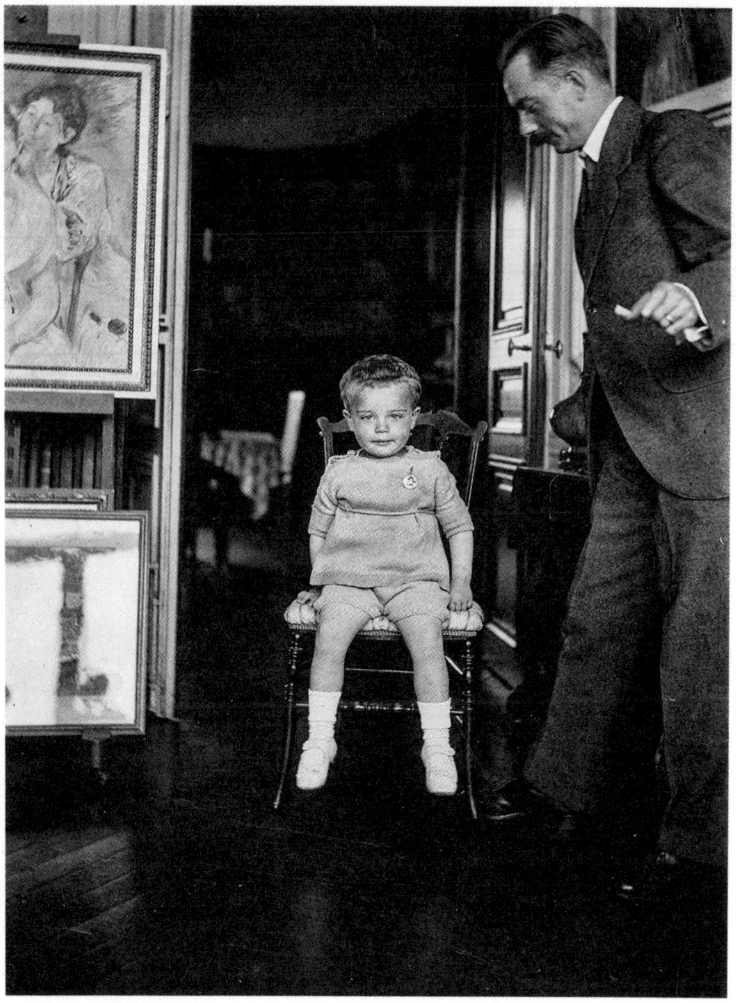

Paul Valéry and one of the children of the family in the living room in the rue de Villejust, c. 1919
The painting *The Hortensia* can be made out on the left
On permanent loan at the Musée Marmottan Monet

Edma thus destined to the Louvre what had always been considered by the family as one of her sister's youthful masterpieces. The sculptor Aimé Millet, who had particularly encouraged her in her early years, had copied for her in 1871 a review of the Salon where the work had been received:

> One must go and see the pastel by Mademoiselle Morisot, Portrait de Madame E. P., which is one of the Salon's most masterful works. It is a real surprise to see a portrait of such quality signed with an unknown name. Once you have seen it, you will never forget this expressive head, so gracefully treated, and its gaze remains in your eyes. The hands are magnificent, the whole is of

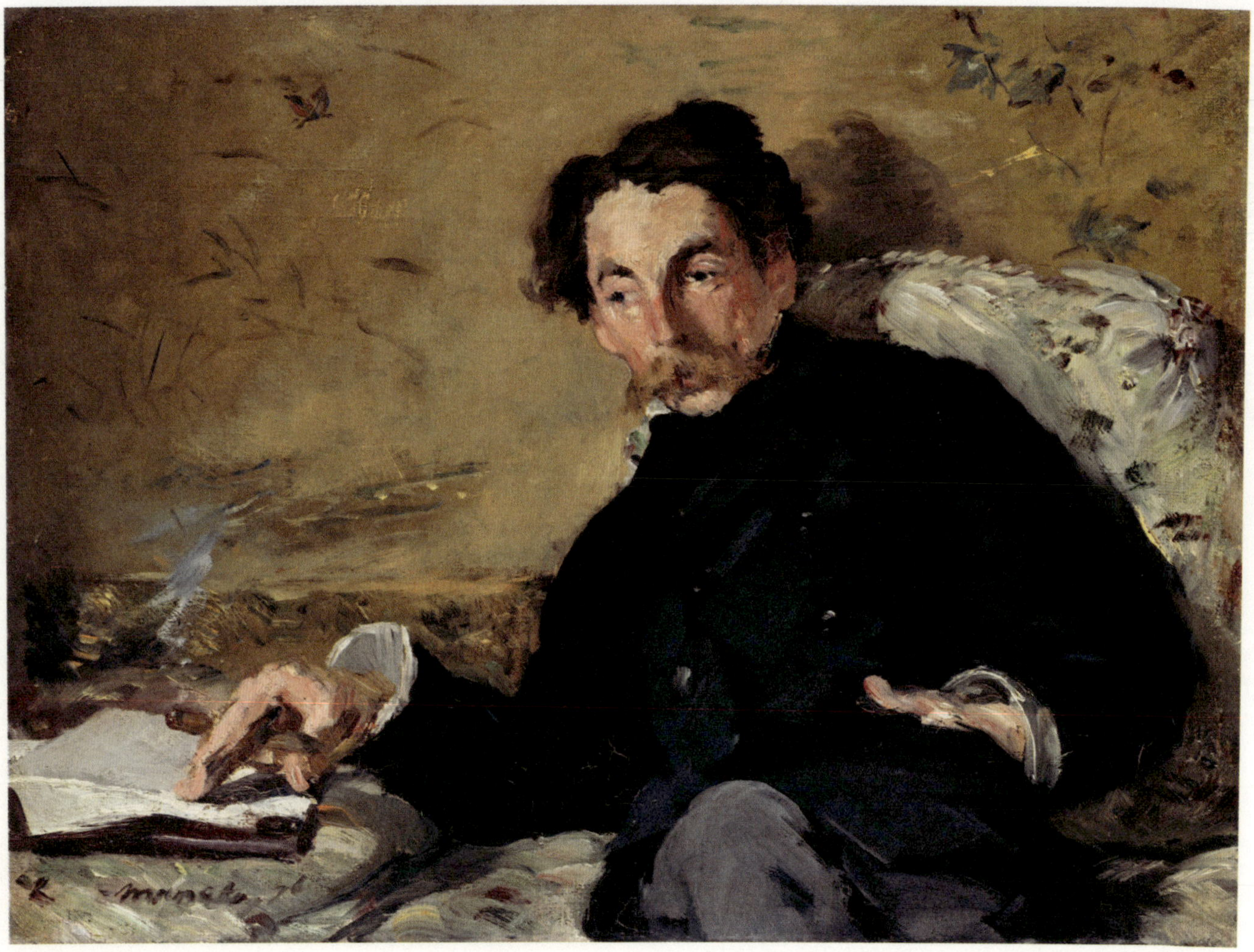

Édouard Manet (1832–1883)
Stéphane Mallarmé, 1876
Oil on canvas, 27.2 × 35.7 cm
Paris, Musée d'Orsay, acquired with the support of the Société des Amis du Louvre and of D. David Weill, 1928

> a marvelous breadth, character, and expression. Only the jury placed it so high [on the wall] that few people have seen this beautiful pastel which is among the most striking works of the Salon (C. Pelletan).[118]

The dossier was administered without delay and the decree published on July 12.[119]

FINAL DONATIONS, FINAL ACQUISITIONS

The enrichment of the national collections and the recognition of the works of Manet, Degas, and Berthe Morisot went hand in hand, and the undertaking never ceased to motivate the couple and their relatives.

At the end of the 1920s, the Musées Nationaux were worried that the masterpieces by Manet and the Impressionists would be lost en masse, as only the great foreign fortunes seemed able to acquire them. The Archives Nationales holds a note from Jacques-Émile Blanche summarizing the situation in 1926:

> I understand that the Louvre, or at least its Friends, are concerned about what is happening. But how do we avoid it? The 24 or 25 Renoirs that I have owned and almost as many Manets and Degas, little by little I have had to watch them go, over the last fifteen years. Life conditions no longer allow people like me to keep what they thought they could always possess. I am by no means free and often have to submit myself, with sorrow.[120]

The Société des Amis du Louvre, particularly dynamic, sought to recruit goodwill ambassadors and "naturally" turned to Ernest. Raymond Koechlin, president of the Conseil des Musées Nationaux, informed him on March 23, 1926 of their project:

> Several friends and I would be very happy if you would allow us to announce your name at the next elections to the council of the Société des Amis du Louvre and to propose you to our colleagues. Everything points to you to participate in it, including, among other things, the memory of your father who had sat among us. It is only a debt of gratitude that we would pay, for we cannot forget that it is thanks to you and your brothers that this Crispin and Scapin [p. 296] entered the Louvre.[121]

On May 5, the same man was pleased to inform Ernest that he had "been named a member of the board of directors of the Société des Amis du Louvre."[122]

It was in this context that the Louvre, with the support of the Amis and D. David Weill, acquired Manet's portrait of Stéphane Mallarmé for the sum of 200,000 francs.[123] The sellers, who were none other than Mallarmé's daughter and son-in-law, acted in concert with Ernest and Julie, their family at heart. Monsieur Rouart—who worked in the shadows but actively—informed the Louvre on January 28, 1928:

> Bonniot and I will bring you the portrait of Mallarmé next Wednesday, January 25 at three in the afternoon to your office in the Louvre. I hope that you won't mind and that in any case we will find someone to receive the painting.[124]

The context was finally favorable for fulfilling one of Berthe Morisot's dearest wishes, to have Manet's *Lady with Fans* (p. 280–281) enter the Louvre. Berthe had saved it at the sale after Manet's death. This Salon painting—judging by its size, and yet never exhibited during the artist's lifetime—was considered by Berthe to be a pure masterpiece. She did not hesitate to say so and to write about it, notably to her sister Edma shortly after Manet's estate sale:

> Did you see in the studio Madame de Callias, a woman in black, lying on a couch with Japanese screens on the background. It is a marvel that will go to the Louvre.

Or again:

> I am sure that you will be enthusiastic about *Madame de Callias*, I'm crazy about her . . . . In any case, I'll only let her go so she can enter the Museum and this will happen, if not in my lifetime, then in Bibi's.[125]

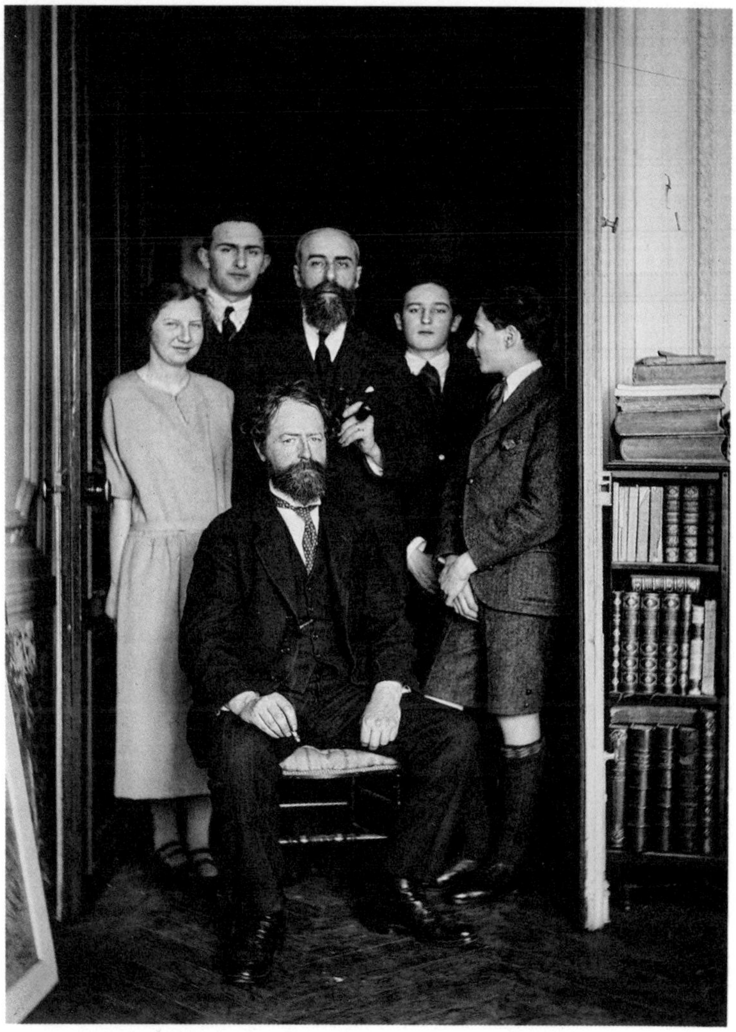

Attributed to Julie Manet (1878–1966)
Family photograph in the rue de Villejust around Louis Rouart, sat in the center. From left to right: Éléonore Rouart, Julien Rouart, Ernest Rouart, Clément Rouart, and Denis Rouart, c. 1925
Paris, Musée Marmottan Monet

Given the scandal provoked by *Olympia* and the almost insurmountable difficulties Manet's friends, led by Monet, faced in getting the nude into the Musée du Luxembourg, not the Louvre as they had hoped, it is not surprising that Berthe took no steps during her lifetime to donate the work. Manet was still misunderstood. In 1930, the situation was reversed. Manet was now an inaccessible master. This painting, which is almost twenty times larger than Mallarmé's portrait and which could be valued at approximately 3,500,000 to 4,000,000 francs, could easily have found a buyer on the other side of the Atlantic. Overriding her own interests, Julie offered the work to the Louvre, which accepted it in 1930. Their friend Albert André immediately sent a letter to Ernest:

My dear friend, I have just come from the Louvre and I cannot resist sending you my congratulations and my thanks as a painter for the gift you are giving us. Now, that is a class act! I received a shock when arriving in the room where this good lady is lounging, because I was not warned.[126]

From then on, the couple was one of the Louvre's major donors. In the same period, the Louvre acquired *The Cradle* (p. 125) by Berthe Morisot for 300,000 francs[127] from Blanche Pontillon-Forget, Julie's cousin and the child in the painting. Ernest wrote to the museum on July 11, 1930:

I thank you for your letter and am pleased that our offer has been so enthusiastically accepted by the Conseil des Musées. Our regret to see the painting go will be compensated by the pleasure of seeing it hanging in the Louvre among the modern French school. We will also be delighted to see Berthe Morisot represented by something as beautiful as *The Cradle*, which is perhaps her best work in this genre. We are grateful to the Conseil des Musées for having kindly inscribed our names next to those of the major patrons. It is our great pleasure to have been able to do something for this museum that we both love so much and to which we are linked by so many memories.[128]

In 1931, the Louvre accepted the gift of a work by Ernest, *Girl at Work*,[129] and in 1932, one by his father, *The Church of San Michele near Venice*.[130]

The 1930s were the years of the great exhibitions dedicated to Manet and Degas. As we saw earlier in this book, Ernest was the tireless craftsman. Although Manet was no longer contested, Degas's personality was still being singled out. His spiritual son would do everything possible to rehabilitate the man, who was often set against the artist. The organizer of these events, he was also one of the main lenders. Turning the pages of these catalogs, one discovers that Ernest owned some paintings that have not yet been mentioned. *Portrait of Madame Ducros* (p. 300), a little thirty-centimeter painting, as well as a portrait of Henri Rouart (p. 298), of the same dimensions, also belonged to him. The portrait of his father was described based on his indications in the catalog of 1931:

One of the numerous pictures of this talented painter and great connoisseur, a close friend of Degas, who was his comrade in arms during the 1870 war. Belonged to Monsieur Alphonse Cherfils, a mutual friend of Degas and Henri Rouart.[131]

Cherfils died in 1892, and it is not known under what circumstances the painting came to him. The same is true for the portrait of Madame Ducros. We have more information about two other portraits of his father by Degas. After Madame François Hepp lent the pastel depicting his father and grandfather, Alexis and Henri Rouart (p. 279), in 1931, Ernest acquired it and presented it as part of his collection in the 1937 exhibition. He also bought from his brother Eugène the portrait of *Henri Rouart in Front of His Factory* (p. 299). To help him after his reversal of fortune, it was acquired, but on what date and under what conditions? Since the work was not included in any of the exhibitions Ernest organized, one can imagine that he allowed Eugène to possess the painting during his lifetime and that it was only after his death in 1936 that his widow, Yvonne, gave it back to Ernest. Unless Eugène was afraid to leave it to him and another arrangement was made. Who knows?

After Ernest's death, his wife and children donated one of the paintings he had loved the most to the Louvre: Corot's *Tivoli. The Gardens of the Villa d'Este* (p. 295), acquired at a high price in 1912. The acquisitions ceased, until they were revived with a crowning piece worthy of an apotheosis. When the gallery owner Katia Granoff organized the first Monet exhibition ever dedicated to the *Waterlilies* in Paris, Julie, encouraged by her sons and grandchildren, leapt at the opportunity. Privileged witnesses of the genesis and evolution of this great work, Julie had for the first time the possibility of acquiring a painting from this period. She opted for a simple composition, a water lily, a single flower floating in the center of a light blue panel measuring one meter fifty (p. 306–307). She exchanged it for Manet's portrait of Suzanne in pastel. The painting would never leave the family until it entered the Musée Marmottan Monet, alongside the works of her mother and her collection bequeathed by her son and daughter-in-law, Denis and Annie Rouart, soon followed by Julien and Thérèse Rouart. This collection constitutes the world's foremost collection of the first female Impressionist's oeuvre. Her Degas, Manets, and so many other masterpieces that Berthe and Julie cherished enrich the museum's collections, making this property of the Académie des Beaux-Arts a major center of Impressionism. We thank them all. As for Monet's late panel, it is normally presented among the *Water Lilies* bequeathed by the painter's son, Michel Monet. In rue Louis Boilly, it bears the sobriquet "le Nymphéa de Julie" (Julie's Waterlily).

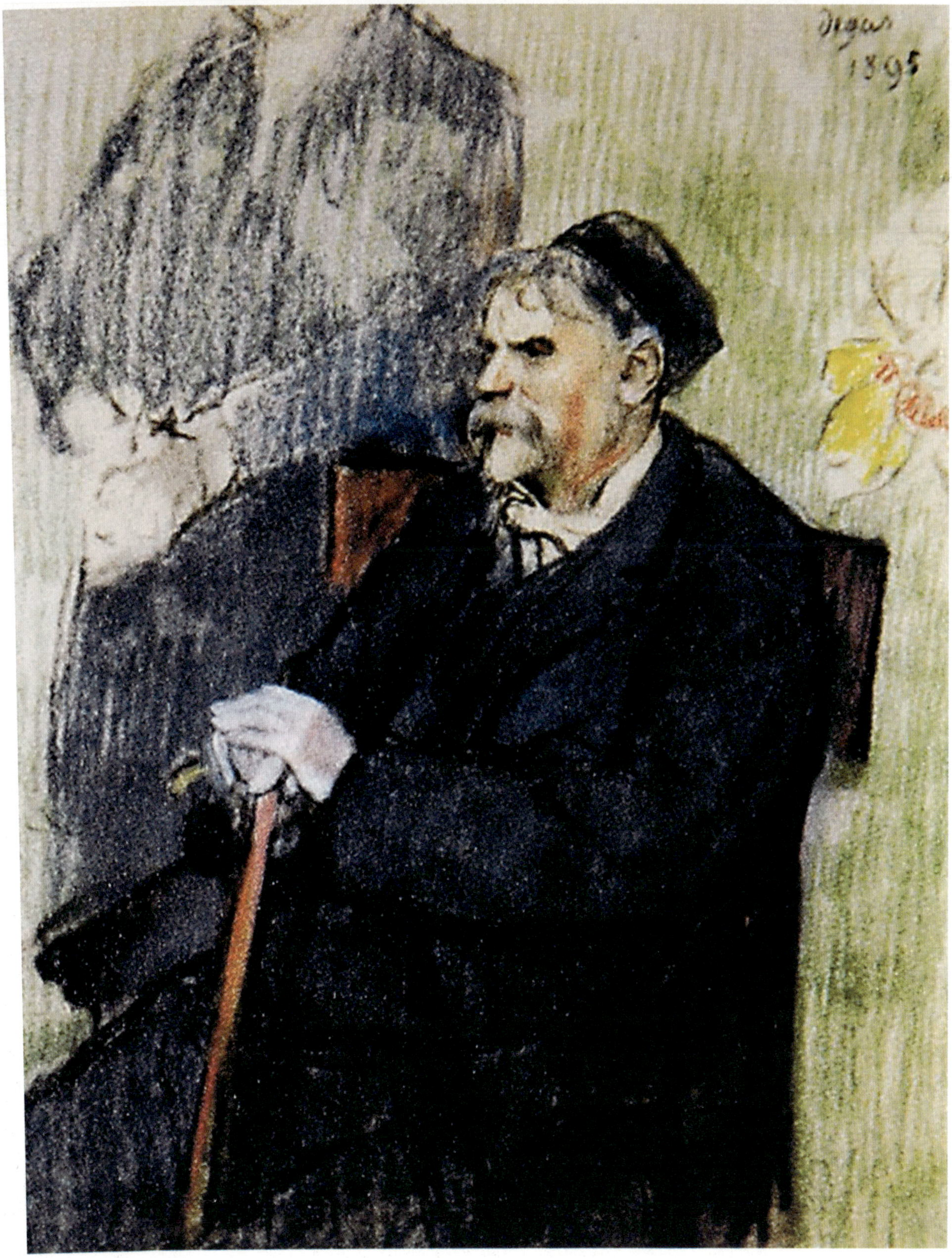

Edgar Degas (1834–1917)
Henri Rouart, 1895
Pastel and charcoal on paper, 60 × 45 cm
Private collection

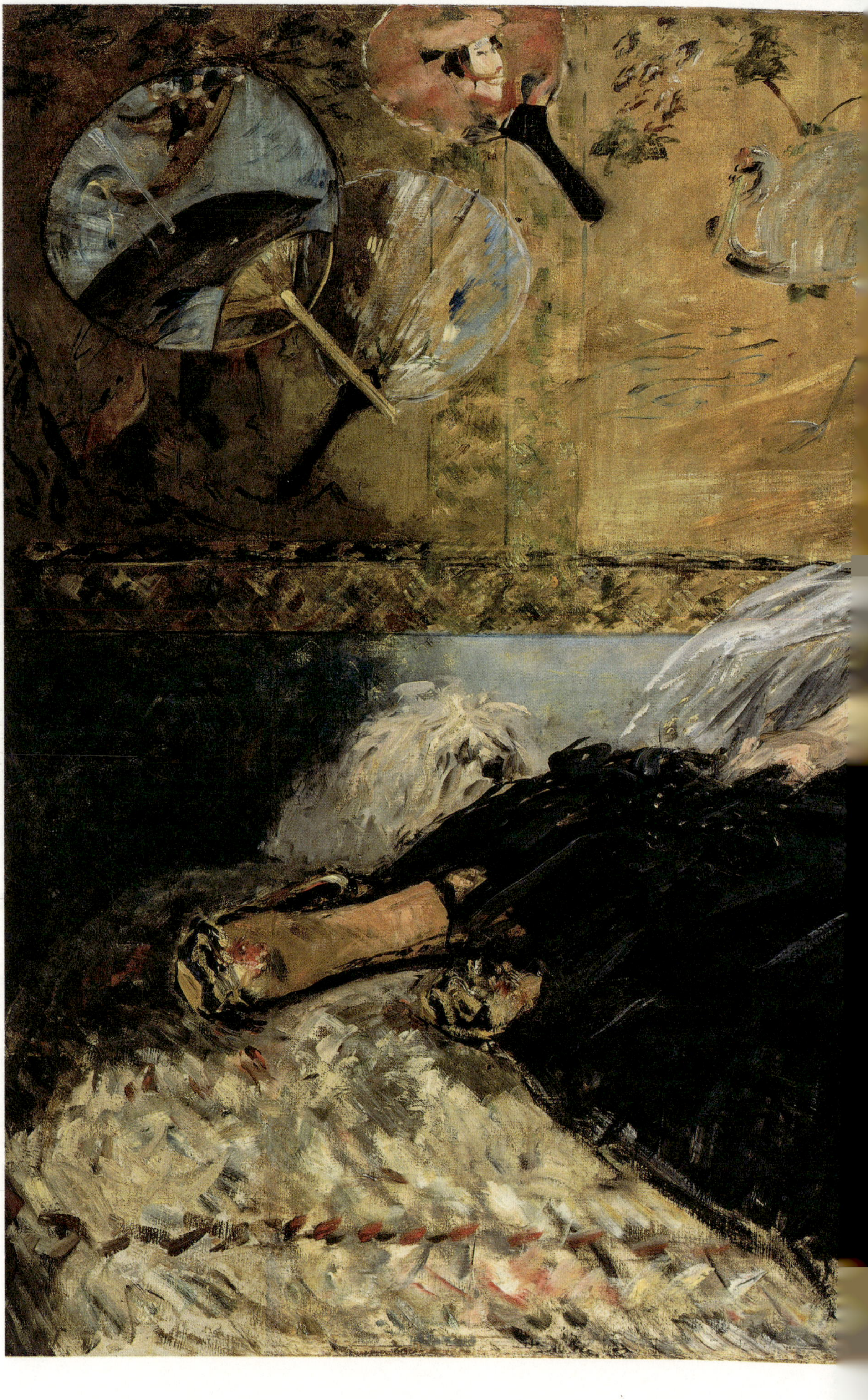

Édouard Manet (1832–1883)
Woman with Fans, 1873
Oil on canvas, 113 × 166 cm
Paris, Musée d'Orsay, gift of
M. and Mme Ernest Rouart, 1930

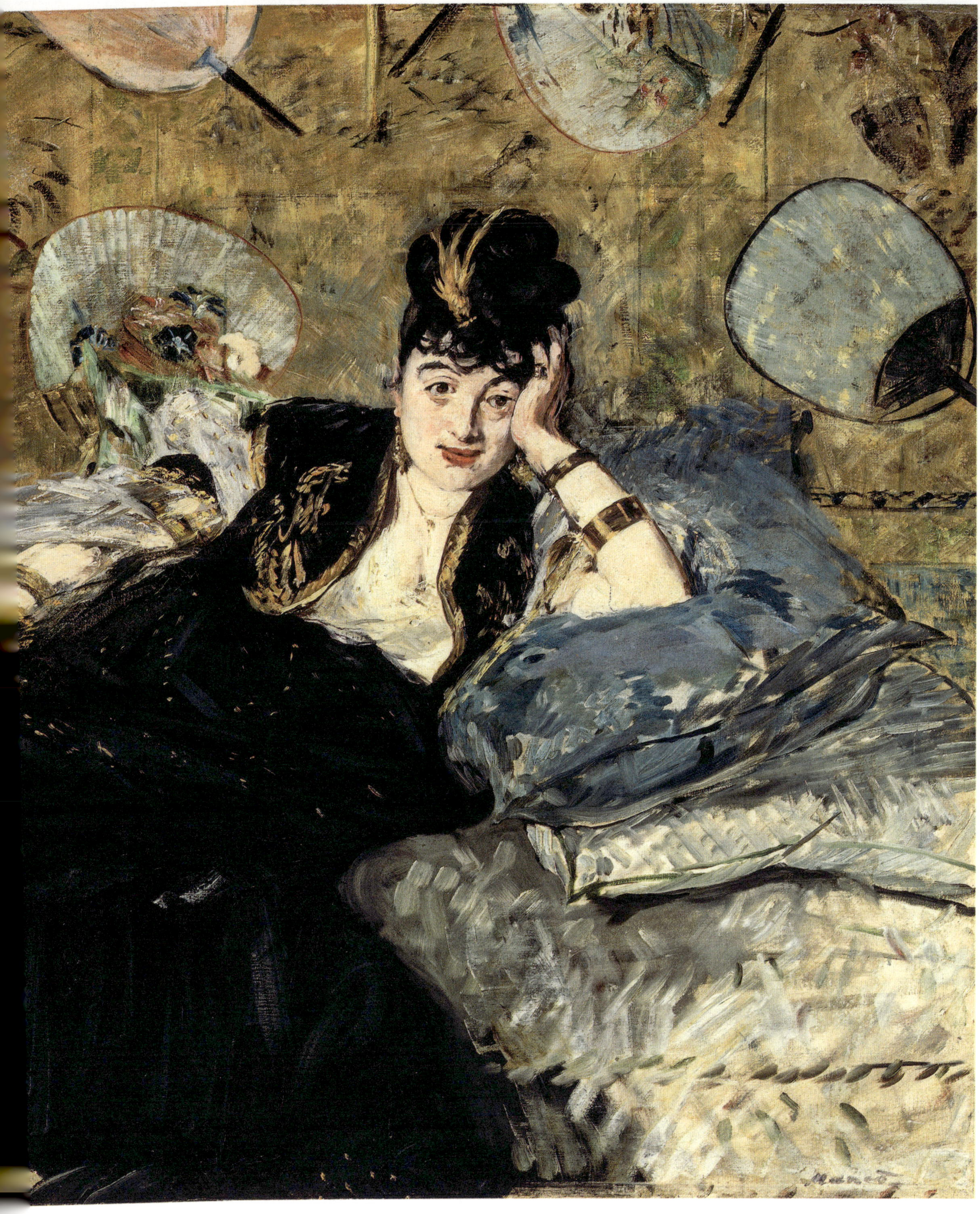
Manet

NOTES

1. Account given to Monsieur Gabriel Thomas, Mademoiselle Manet's tutor, by Monsieur Maurice Bouts, lawyer practicing at 13, rue Pasquier, Paris, following the one given on May 2, 1896, Arch. BS, inv. 2021.2.572.
2. Mention written in the daybook and dated March 25, 1896, Arch. Durand-Ruel.
3. Letter from Joseph Durand Ruel to Gabriel Thomas, February 28, 1896, Arch. BS, inv. 2021.2.584.
4. Letter from Maurice Bouts to Gabriel Thomas, November 16, 1896, Arch. BS, inv. 2021.2.586.
5. Letter from Gabriel Thomas to Julie Manet, June 16, 1897, Arch. BS, inv. 2021.2.585.
6. Letter from Julie Manet to Gabriel Thomas, Thursday, June 17 [1897], Arch. BS, inv. 2021.2.107.
7. See the essay in the present volume by Marianne Mathieu "The Flying Squadron," p. 44–57.
8. Manet 2017, Kindle edition, trans. Jane Roberts, p. 88.
9. *Catalogue des tableaux modernes et anciens, aquarelles, pastels, dessins... composant la collection Edgar Degas*, sale, Paris, Galerie Georges Petit, March 26 and 27, 1918.
10. *Catalogue des tableaux modernes, pastels, aquarelles, dessins anciens et modernes par Brandon, Braquaval, Mary Cassatt...* [et al.] *faisant partie de la collection Edgar Degas...*: 2nd sale, Paris, Hôtel Drouot, November 15 and 16, 1918.
11. Manet 1979, p. 232–233.
12. Manet 2017, Kindle edition, trans. Jane Roberts, p. 177.
13. Pneumatic card from Edgar Degas to Henri Rouart, June 30, 1898, Paris, Musée Marmottan Monet, inv. D.4-1986.2013.215.
14. Paul Gauguin, *Nave Nave Mahana*, 1896, Lyon, Musée des Beaux-Arts (W.548).
15. Paul Gauguin, *A Bouquet of Flowers*, 1896, London, The National Gallery.
16. Notebooks of George Daniel de Monfreid, 1898, Paris, Musée d'Orsay, George Daniel de Monfreid (1856–1929) collection.
17. *Paul Cézanne*, Paris, Galerie Vollard, November 11–December 15, 1895.
18. Manet 2017, Kindle edition, trans. Jane Roberts, p. 88.
19. See the essay in the present volume by Marianne Mathieu "The Flying Squadron," p. 44–57.
20. Manet 1979, p. 200.
21. Mallarmé 2019, letter no. 2761, p. 1510–1511.
22. Manet 1979, p. 200.
23. Ibid., p. 204. The work has unfortunately not been identified.
24. Pierre-Auguste Renoir, *Portrait of Julie Manet in a Pink Dress*, 1899, private collection.
25. Manet 1979, p. 247.
26. Ibid., p. 204.
27. Eugène Delacroix, *Ovid among the Scythians*, 1859, London, The National Gallery.
28. Eugène Delacroix, *Sketch after an Engraving by Rubens*, date unknown, oil on canvas, 23.5 × 25.25 cm, location unknown.
29. Manet 2017, Kindle edition, trans. Jane Roberts, p. 177.
30. Ibid., p. 239.
31. Manet 2017, Kindle edition, trans. Jane Roberts, p. 164.
32. Manet 2017, Kindle edition, trans. Jane Roberts, p. 165–166.
33. Manet 2017, Kindle edition, trans. Jane Roberts, p. 167.
34. Manet 2017, Kindle edition, trans. Jane Roberts, p. 170.
35. Manet 1979, p. 230.
36. According to the exhibition catalog *Degas: portraitiste, sculpteur* (Paris, 1931), not identified.
37. Edgar Degas, *Portrait of Édouard Manet Standing*, c. 1866–68, Paris, Musée du Louvre, Musée d'Orsay's collections, inv. RF 41651 recto.
38. Only three sheets were presented at the *Degas* exhibitions of 1931 and 1937 organized at the Orangerie des Tuileries, all accompanied by the mention "donated by Degas to Monsieur and Madame Ernest Rouart on the occasion of their wedding."
39. *L'Occident*, no. 2, January 1902, p. 69, cited in Haziot 2012, p. 257.
40. Letter from Ernest Rouart to, in all likelihood, the museum curator, May 27, 1905, Arch. du Musée de Toulouse, no. Ro 708 / Arch / 2R28 – April and June sessions 1905.
41. Extract from the register of decisions of the mayor of the city of Pau, March 3, 1870, Arch. BS, inv. 2021.2.480.
42. Paul Lafond (1847–1918), artist, art historian, director of the Musée de Pau. A friend of Degas, he sat for *Paul Lafond and Alphonse Cherfils Studying a Work* (1878–80, Cleveland Museum of Art). He published the first book dedicated to Degas. The two-volume work, *Degas*, was published by H. Floury in 1918.
43. Henri Rouart, *The Mandolin Player*, c. 1875, Pau, Musée des Beaux-Arts. In 1897, Ernest had already offered one of his father's works to the Musée de Pau, *A Lane in La Queue-en-Brie* (inv. 897.13.1).
44. Letter from the mayor of Pau to Ernest Rouart, November 30, 1907, Arch. du Mesnil, inv. 2021.1.1144.
45. Salon d'Automne catalog, 1907. *Berthe Morisot* retrospective, no. 127, *Woman Sewing* (belonging to the Musée de Pau).
46. On this subject, Bruyère 2015.
47. Pierre-Auguste Renoir, *Woman Playing the Guitar*, 1896–97, Musée des Beaux-Arts de Lyon.
48. See p. 25, 56 and 106.
49. Letter from Jules Valéry to the curator of the Musée de Montpellier, March 10, 1907, Arch. du Musée Fabre, Montpellier.
50. The first studio collections to join the Petit Palais were those of Jean-Joseph Carriès, Jules Dalou, Félix Ziem, and Jean-Jacques Henner.
51. Berthe Morisot, *Study for Embroidery*, also known as *Study of a Young Woman Sewing*, 1889, Paris, Petit Palais – Musée des Beaux-Arts de la Ville de Paris.
52. Berthe Morisot, *Embroidery*, 1889, private collection.
53. Letter from Ernest Rouart to Henry Lapauze, January 14, 1908, Arch. du Musée du Petit Palais.
54. Julie Manet, *Drawing of Julie Manet Rouart for Berthe Morisot of the cupola of the Petit Palais*, c. 1925, Saint-Germain-en-Laye, Musée Départemental Maurice-Denis.
55. Collet 2008.
56. In this letter, Julie evoked the Fabre sale. Letter from Julie Manet-Rouart to Ernest Rouart, Monday morning [1902], Arch. BS, inv. 2021.2.104.
57. Salon d'Automne, no. 202, *Landscape*, no. 203, *Fatata te Miti* (belonged to Monsieur Ernest Rouart).
58. Camille Corot, *Civita Castellana*, 1837, location unknown; Chéramy sale, 1908, no. 202; official sales report, Paris Arch, D42E[3] 107.
59. Eugène Delacroix, *Study of a Tiger's Head and Body*, location unknown; Chéramy sale, 1908, no. 354; official sales report, Paris Arch, D42E[3] 107.
60. Letter from Jeannie Gobillard-Valéry to Ernest Rouart, Monday, November 22 [1915], Arch. du Mesnil, inv. 2021.1.304.
61. Julie Manet, inventory of works deposited in different places during the Second World War entitled "paintings belonging to Monsieur and Madame Rouart," Arch. BS, inv. 2021.2.217.
62. As the minutes of the Alexis Rouart sales cannot be found, the results of the sale presented in this essay are taken from the annotated catalog from the collections of the Bibliothèque Nationale de France.
63. Gustave Colin, *Environs of Biarritz*, n.d., location unknown. Acquired by Ernest Rouart for 200 francs at the fourth Alexis Rouart sale, May 8–10, 1911, no. 37. On March 17, 1925, the artist's son, Charles Colin, asked Ernest Rouart for advice about his father's studio collection and added: "Is it too much to ask the son of my father's best friend?" Paris, Musée Marmottan Monet, inv. D.4-1986.2013.938.
64. See here p. 63.
65. Acquired by Ernest Rouart for 13,300 francs, fourth Alexis Rouart sale, May 8–10, 1911, no. 216.
66. Edgar Degas, *Portrait of Henri and Alexis Rouart*, 1895, private collection.
67. On this subject, see the National Gallery of Art archives, Washington, D.C.
68. Jean-François Millet, *Leconte de Lisle*, c. 1840–41, Washington, D.C, National Gallery of Art.
69. Lemoisne, *Degas et son œuvre*, 4 vols., Paris, Arts et Métiers graphiques, 1947–49.
70. *Degas portraitiste sculpteur*, Paris, Musée de l'Orangerie, July 19—October 1, 1931.
71. First sale, December 9, 10, and 11, 1912; second sale, December 16, 17, and 18, 1912; third sale, December 21 and December 22, 1913.
72. Declaration of transfer by death of Henri Rouart, May 29, 1913, Arch. Paris, DQ7 31831.
73. Minutes of the Henri Rouart sale, Arch. Paris, D42E3 124.
74. Minutes of the sale: *December 7 [1912], requisition in order to sell paintings, drawings, and pastels from the estate of Monsieur Henri Rouart, December 9 sale of said paintings etc. July 8, 1913 discharge of the product of the sale*, Arch. Paris, D42E3 124. The PV notation in the following notes refers to this document.
75. Dormoy 1932.
76. Henri Rouart sale, Paris, Galerie Manzi-Joyant, December 9, 10, 11, 1912, no. 10 in the catalog. PV no. 260: "1 other by Chardin, Musical instruments to Monsieurs Rouart requesting joint acquisition" for 41,000 francs.
77. Henri Rouart sale, Paris, Galerie Manzi-Joyant, December 9, 10, 11, 1912, no. 37 in the catalog (PV no. 255), acquired by the Rouart joint acquisition 75,000 francs.
78. Henri Rouart sale, Paris, Galerie Manzi-Joyant, December 9, 10, 11, 1912, no. 67 in the catalog (PV no. 261), acquired by the Rouart joint acquisition for 32,000 francs.
79. Pierre Paul Prudhon, *Standing Nude Woman, Leaning on an Oar*, n.d., location unknown. Henri Rouart sale, Paris, Galerie Manzi-Joyant, December 9,

10, 11, 1912, no. 449 in the catalog (PV no. 271), acquired by the Rouart joint acquisition for 15,100 francs.

80. Henri Rouart sale, Paris, Galerie Manzi-Joyant, December 9, 10, 11, 1912, no. 182 in the catalog (PV no. 78), acquired by the Rouart joint acquisition for 11,000 francs.

81. Jean-François Millet, *Woodcutters in the Forest*, n.d., location unknown. Henri Rouart sale, Paris, Galerie Manzi-Joyant, December 9, 10, 11, 1912, no. 228 in the catalog (PV no. 443), acquired by the Rouart joint acquisition for 14,600 francs.

82. Henri Rouart sale, Paris, Galerie Manzi-Joyant, December 9, 10, 11, 1912, no. 33 in the catalog (PV no. 342), acquired by the Rouart joint acquisition for 8,000 francs.

83. Henri Rouart sale, Paris, Galerie Manzi-Joyant, December 9, 10, 11, 1912, no. 47 in the catalog (PV no. 352), acquired by the Rouart joint acquisition for 1,500 francs.

84. Honoré Daumier, *A Lawyer* (p. 268); id., *Two Defendant*, (p. 268); id., *Recollection of the Palais*, n.d., Paris, Musée Marmottan Monet. Henri Rouart sale, Paris, Galerie Manzi-Joyant, December 9, 10, 11, 1912, no. 50 (II) in the catalog (PV no. 355), acquired by the Rouart joint acquisition for 2,500 francs (the lot).

85. Manet ed. 2017, p. 138.

86. Camille Corot, *Dreaming Bohemian Girl*, 1865–70, location unknown. Henri Rouart sale, Paris, Galerie Manzi-Joyant, December 9, 10, 11, 1912, no. 126 in the catalog (PV no. 50), acquired by the Rouart joint acquisition for 14,100 francs.

87. Camille Corot, *Peasant Woman with a White Blouse and Yellow Bonnet*, 1840–45, private collection. Henri Rouart sale, Paris, Galerie Manzi-Joyant, December 9, 10, 11, 1912, no. 139 in the catalog (PV no. 188), acquired by the Rouart joint acquisition for 11,000 francs.

88. Henri Rouart sale, Paris, Galerie Manzi-Joyant, December 9, 10, 11, 1912, no. 131 in the catalog (PV no. 182), acquired by the Rouart joint acquisition for 37,000 francs.

89. Camille Corot, *Recollection of the Environs of Montpellier*, 1840–45, private collection Henri Rouart sale, Paris, Galerie Manzi-Joyant, December 9, 10, 11, 1912, no. 115 in the catalog (PV no. 133), acquired by the Rouart joint acquisition for 15,000 francs.

90. Henri Rouart sale, Paris, Galerie Manzi-Joyant, December 9, 10, 11, 1912, no. 123 in the catalog (PV no. 136), acquired by the Rouart joint acquisition for 9,000 francs.

91. Camille Corot, *Volterra, Road Descending from the Town*, c. 1834, Paris, Musée Marmottan Monet. Henri Rouart sale, Paris, Galerie Manzi-Joyant, December 9, 10, 11, 1912, no. 110 in the catalog (PV no. 54), acquired by the Rouart joint acquisition for 13,500 francs.

92. Henri Rouart sale, Paris, Galerie Manzi-Joyant, December 9, 10, 11, 1912, no. 114 in the catalog (PV no. 67), acquired by the Rouart joint acquisition for 111,000 francs.

93. Henri Rouart sale, Paris, Galerie Manzi-Joyant, December 9, 10, 11, 1912, no. 218 in the catalog (PV no. 35), acquired by the Rouart joint acquisition for 5,000 francs.

94. Édouard Manet, *On the Beach*, 1873, Paris, Musée d'Orsay.

95. Henri Rouart sale, Paris, Galerie Manzi-Joyant, December 9, 10, 11, 1912, no. 236 in the catalog (PV no. 62), acquired by the Rouart joint acquisition for 97,000 francs.

96. Claude Monet, *Festival at Argenteuil*, 1873, private collection. Henri Rouart sale, Paris, Galerie Manzi-Joyant, December 9, 10, 11, 1912, no. 256 in the catalog (PV no. 58), acquired by the Rouart joint acquisition for 13,000 francs.

97. Henri Rouart sale, Paris, Galerie Manzi-Joyant, December 9, 10, 11, 1912, no. 70 in the catalog (PV no. 332), 82,000 francs.

98. Henri Rouart sale, Paris, Galerie Manzi-Joyant, December 9, 10, 11, 1912, no. 74 in the catalog (PV no. 335), 31,000 francs.

99. Henri Rouart sale, Paris, Galerie Manzi-Joyant, December 9, 10, 11, 1912, no. 75 in the catalog (PV no. 336), 32,000 francs.

100. Interview between Julien and Jean-Marie Rouart.

101. Ibid.

102. AN, 20144779-15 & 20144790-84.

103. AN, 201447779-15 & 20144790-66.

104. AN, 201447779-15 & 20144790-66.

105. Henri Rouart sale, Paris, Galerie Manzi-Joyant, December 9, 10, 11, 1912, no. 141 in the catalog (PV no. 180), acquired by the Rouart joint acquisition for 17,000 francs; anonymous sale (Eugène Rouart), Paris, Hôtel Drouot, March 22–23, 1918, no. 12 in the catalog (PV no. 52) acquired by Ernest Rouart for 13,000 francs.

106. Henri Rouart sale, Paris, Galerie Manzi-Joyant, December 9, 10, 11, 1912, no. 96 in the catalog (PV no. 288), acquired by the Rouart joint acquisition for 3,250 francs; Anonymous sale (Eugène Rouart), Paris, Hôtel Drouot, March 22–23, 1918, no. 49 in the catalog (PV no. 12), acquired by Ernest Rouart for 1,820 francs.

107. Édouard Manet, *Portrait of Berthe Morisot*, 1874, location unknown (RW 228).

108. Edgar Degas, *Dancer*, private collection, Cambridge (Massachusetts); Edgar Degas, *Two Studies*, c. 1874, private collection. Third Degas sale, Galerie Georges Petit, Paris, April 7–9, 1919, part of lot no. 359 (PV no. 1465), acquired by Ernest Rouart for 3,600 francs.

109. Edgar Degas, *Dancer Seen from Behind*, location unknown; Edgar Degas, *Dancer Tying Her Belt*, location unknown; Edgar Degas, *Dancer Adjusting Her Slipper*, c. 1879, Detroit, The Detroit Institute of Arts; Edgar Degas, *Dancer Seen in Profile*, location unknown. Third Degas sale, Galerie Georges Petit, Paris, April 7–9, 1919, part of lot no. 137 (PV no. 1183), acquired by Ernest Rouart for 2,150 francs.

110. Edgar Degas, *Dancer*, location unknown; Edgar Degas, *Dancer (pas de bourrée)* (p. 272); Edgar Degas, *Dancer (end of a variation)*, location unknown; Edgar Degas, *Dancer (preparation for inward turn)*, location unknown, third Degas sale, Galerie Georges Petit, Paris, April 7–9, 1919, part of lot no. 102 (PV no. 1147), acquired by Ernest Rouart for 1,450 francs.

111. Edgar Degas, *The Coiffure* (p. 272); id., *Woman Drying Herself*, n.d., location unknown; id., *Seated Woman*, n.d., location unknown, third Degas sale, Galerie Georges Petit, Paris, April 7–9, 1919, part of lot no. 116 (PV no. 1161), acquired by Monsieur Vigué for 1,550 francs.

112. Edgar Degas, *After the Bath*, c. 1898, print with colored heightening. Fourth Degas sale, Galerie Georges Petit, Paris, July 2–4, 1919, lot no. 314 (PV no. 1648), acquired by Ernest Rouart for 730 francs.

113. Valéry, 1936, p. 100, consulted on Gallica, Paul Valéry collection. A Œuvres. IX Pièces sur l'art. II. de 1936 à 1943, Paris, BnF, département des Manuscrits, NAF 19069.

114. Letter from Louis Rouart to Paul Jamot, June 25, 1920, AN, 20144790-85.

115. Letter from Louis Rouart to Paul Jamot, n.d., AN, 20144790-85.

116. AN, 20144790-85.

117. Letter from Edme Pontillon [unspecified recipient], June 9, 1921, AN, 20144779-33.

118. Note by Aimée Millet, Arch. BS, inv. 2021.2.581; retranscribed from Pelletan, 1872.

119. AN, 20144779-33.

120. Letter from Jacques-Émile Blanche [unspecified recipient], January 11, 1926, AN, 20144790-66.

121. Letter from Raymond Koechlin to Ernest Rouart, March 23, 1926, Paris, Musée Marmottan Monet, inv. D.4-1986.2013.960.

122. Letter from Raymond Koechlin to Ernest Rouart, May 5, 1926, Paris, Musée Marmottan Monet, inv. D.4-1986.2013.967.

123. Order of February 25, 1928, Arch. du Musée d'Orsay.

124. Letter from Ernest Rouart [unspecified recipient], January 28, 1928, AN, 20144790 66.

125. Rouart 1950, p. 120.

126. Letter from Albert André to Ernest Rouart, August 12, 1930, Arch. du Mesnil, inv. 2021.1.985.

127. Order of August 7, 1930, AN, 20144790-67.

128. Letter from Ernest Rouart [to Raymond Koechlin?], July 11, 1930, AN, 20144790-67.

129. Ernest Rouart, *Girl at Work*, n.d., Paris, Musée d'Orsay.

130. Henri Rouart, *The San Michele Church near Venice*, c. 1883, Paris, Musée d'Orsay.

131. Exh. cat. Paris 1931, no. 52, p. 53.

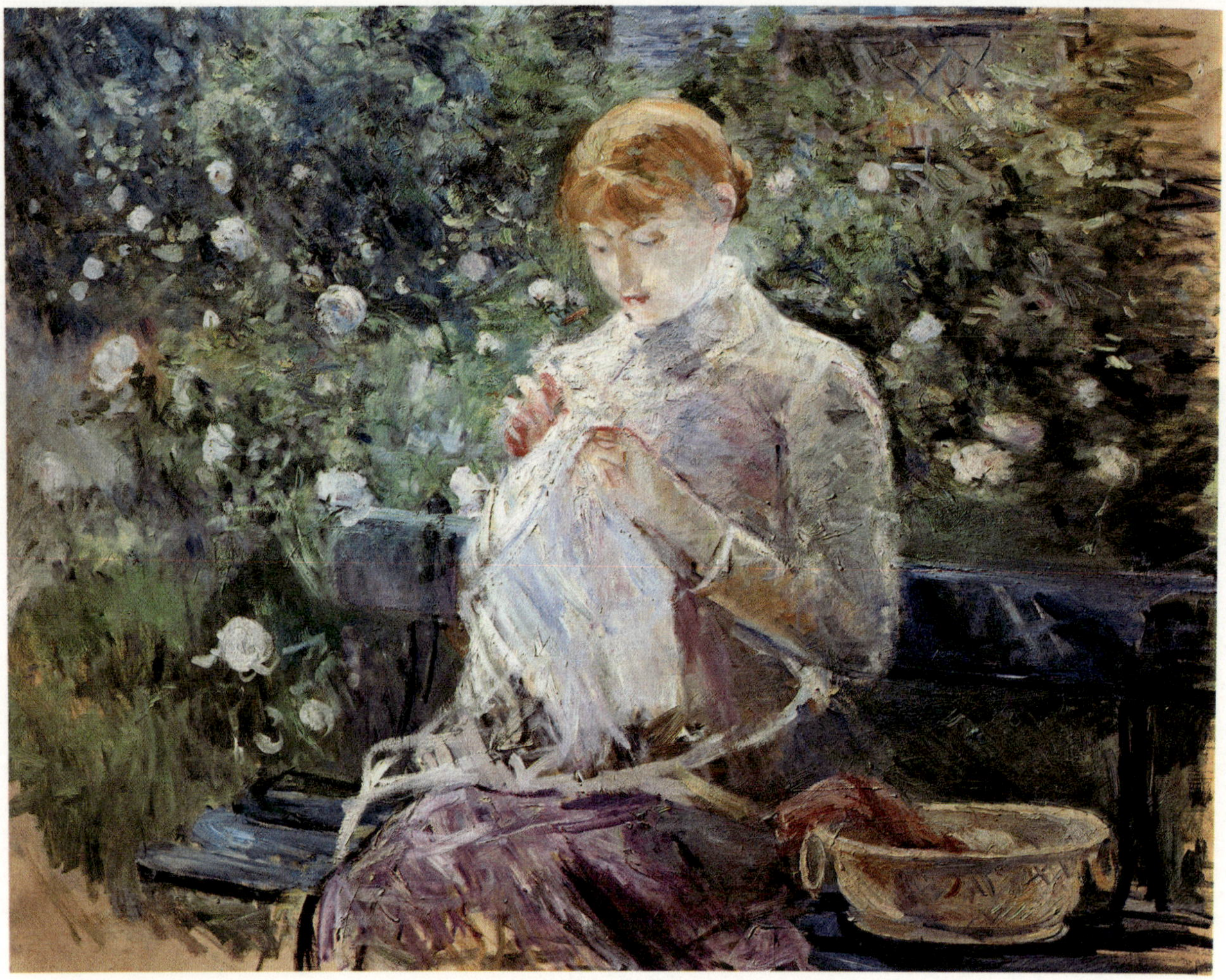

Berthe Morisot (1841–1895)
Pasie Sewing in the Garden at Bougival, 1881
Oil on canvas, 81 × 100 cm
Pau, Musée des Beaux-Arts

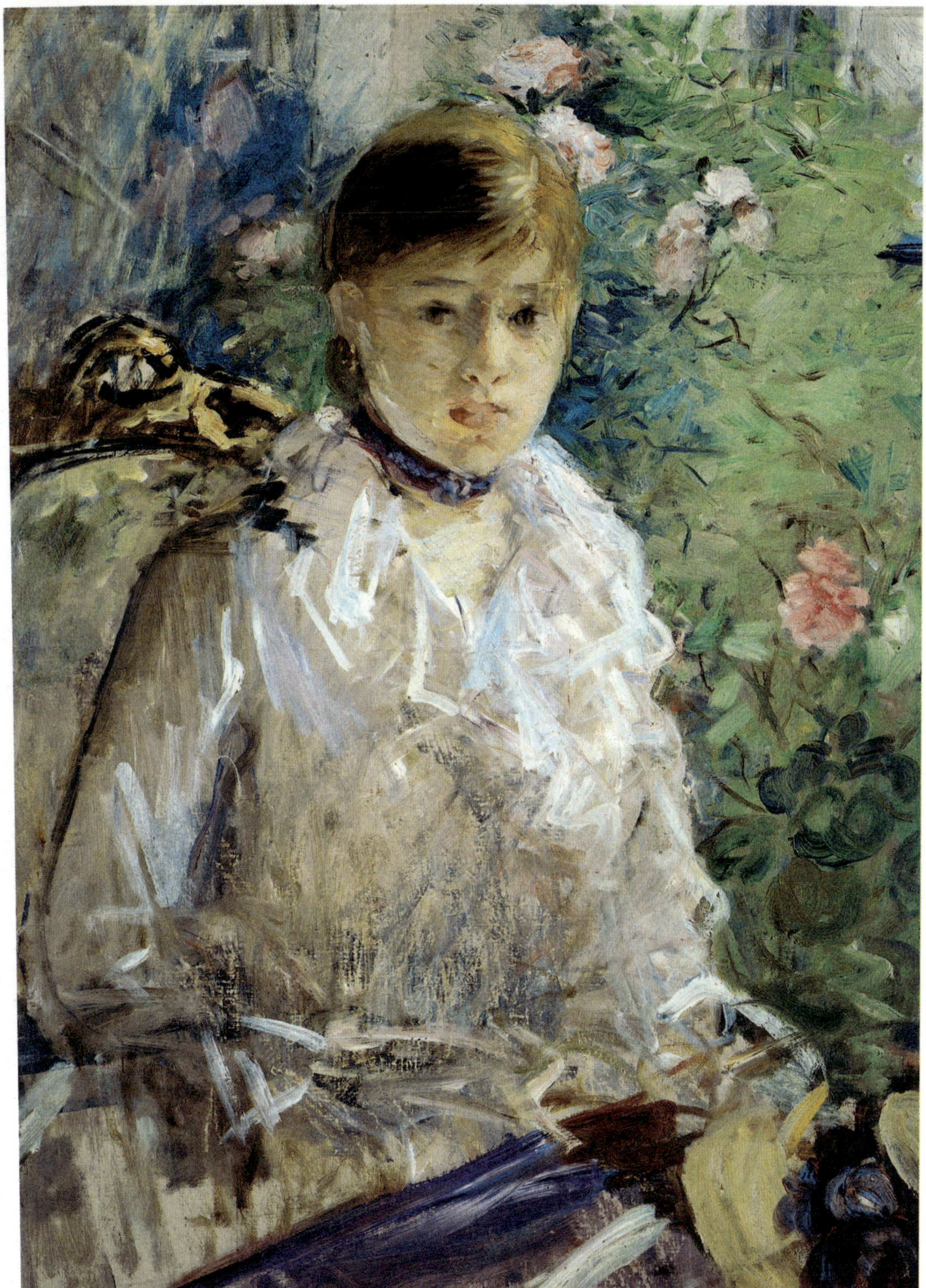

Berthe Morisot (1841–1895)
Young Woman at the Window, or *Summer*, 1879
Oil on canvas, 76 × 61 cm
Montpellier Méditerranée Métropole, Musée Fabre

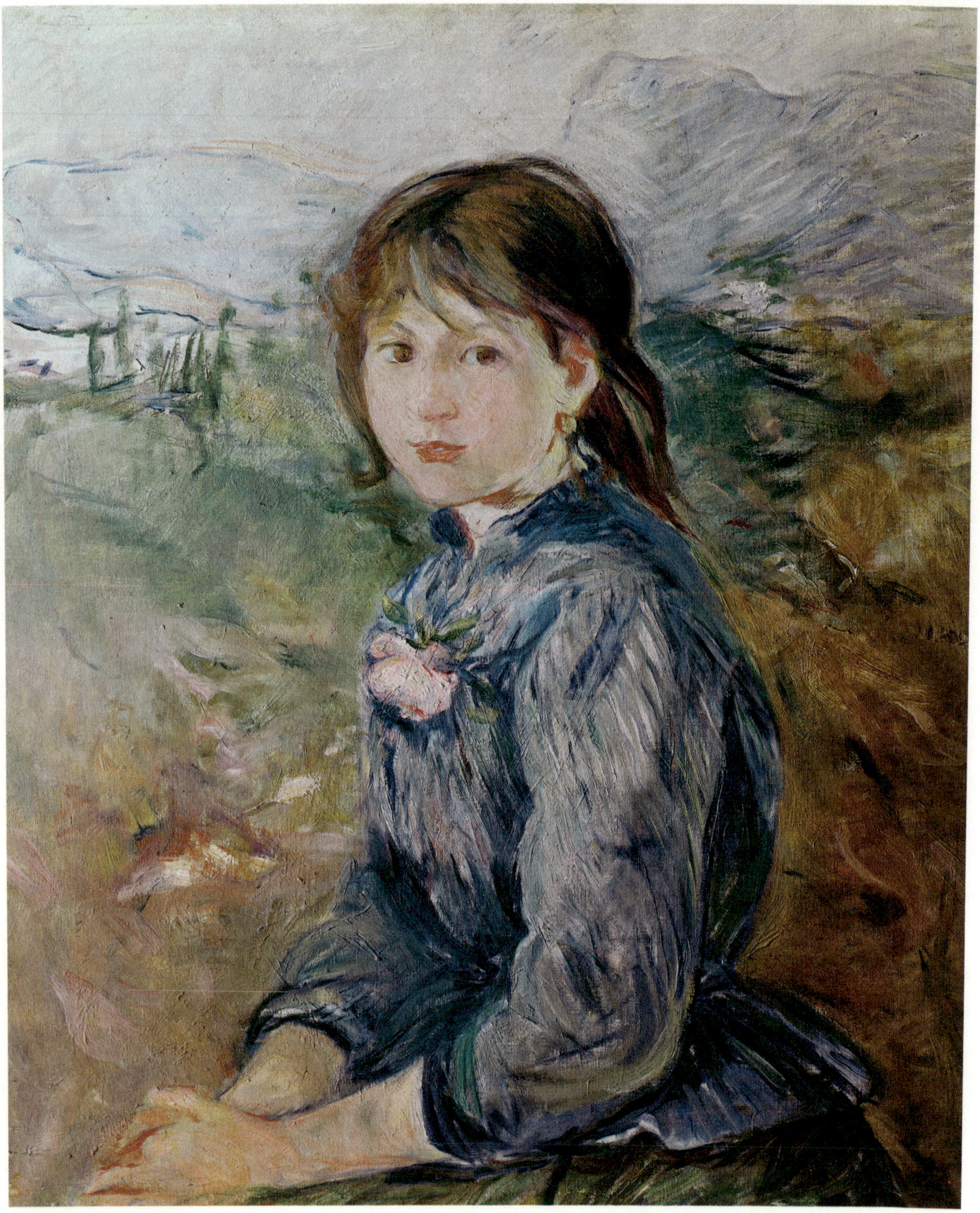

Berthe Morisot (1841–1895)
Peasant Woman from Nice, 1889
Oil on canvas, 64 × 52 cm
Lyon, Musée des Beaux-Arts

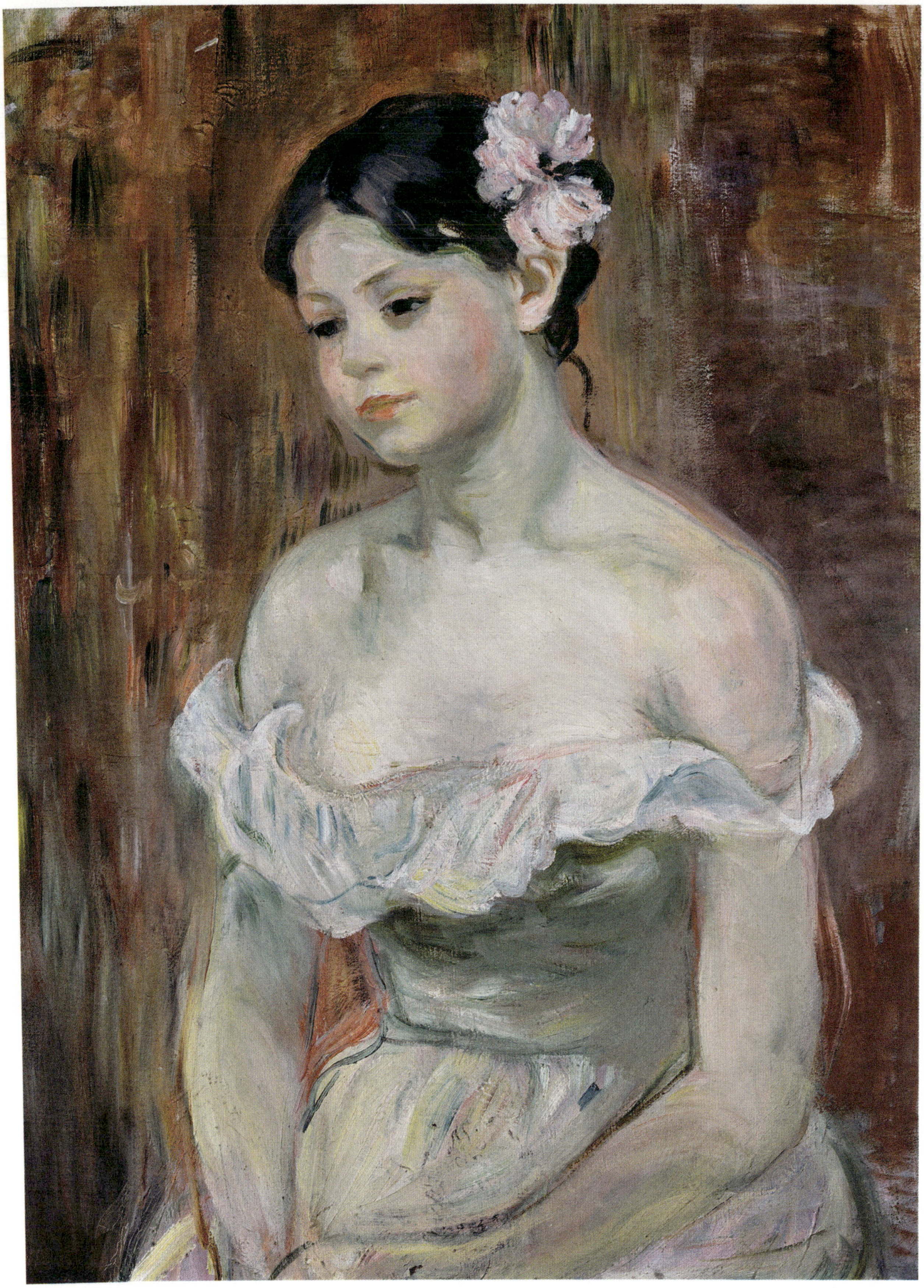

Berthe Morisot (1841–1895)
Young Girl in a Low-Cut Dress with a Flower in Her Hair, 1893
Oil on canvas, 70 × 51.5 cm
Paris, Petit Palais–Musée des Beaux-Arts de la Ville de Paris

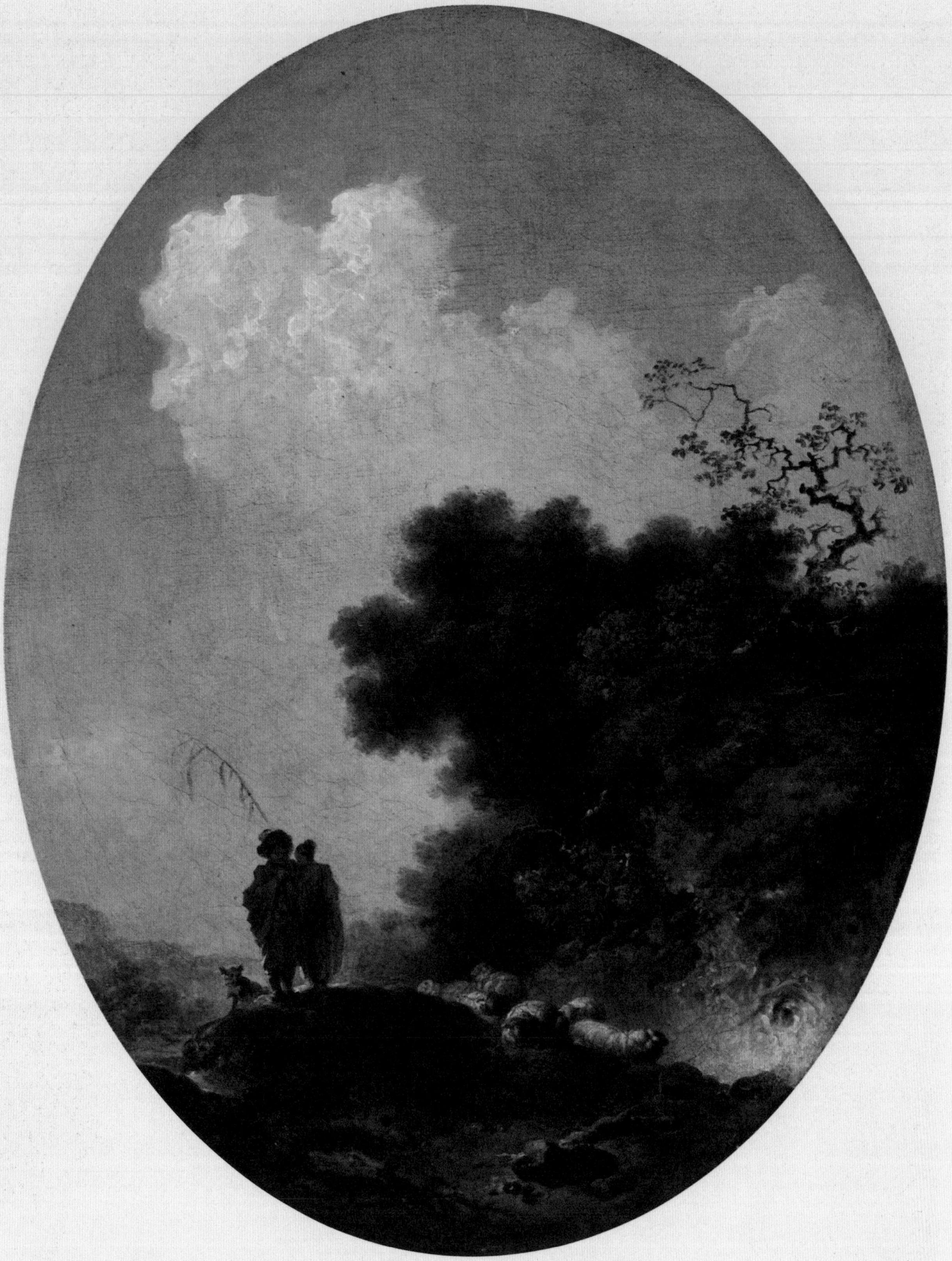

Jean Honoré Fragonard (1732–1806)
Shepherds in a Landscape, also known as *Shepherd Playing the Flute, Shepherdess Listening*, c. 1765
Oil on canvas, 40 × 30 cm
Annecy, Musée-Château, on permanent loan from the Musée du Louvre

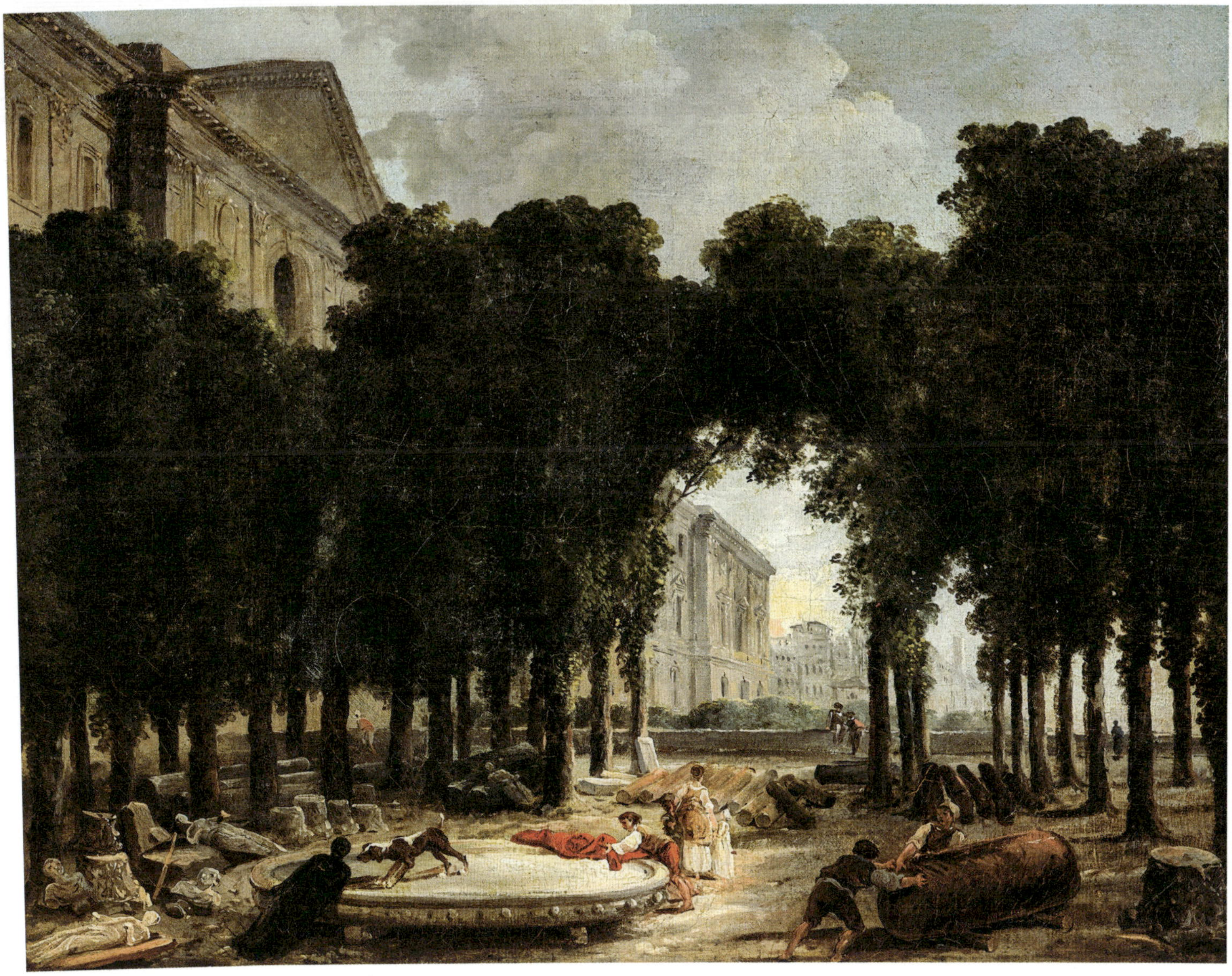

Hubert Robert (1733–1808)
View of the Louvre. The Garden of the Infante, 1798
Oil on canvas, 38 × 46 cm
Paris, Musée Marmottan Monet

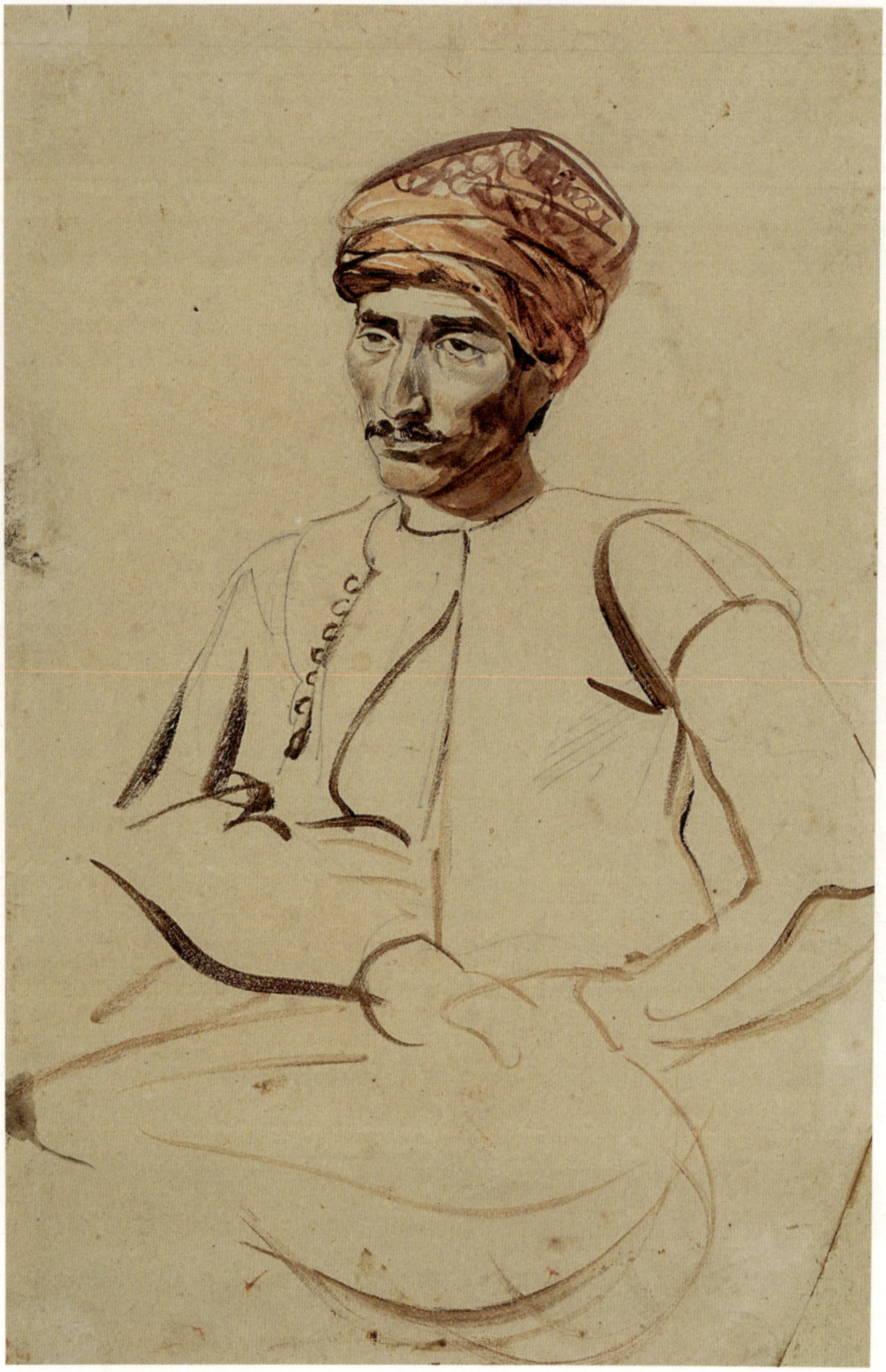

Eugène Delacroix (1798–1863)
An Arab, c. 1832
Graphite heightened with watercolor on paper, 30 × 19 cm
Private collection

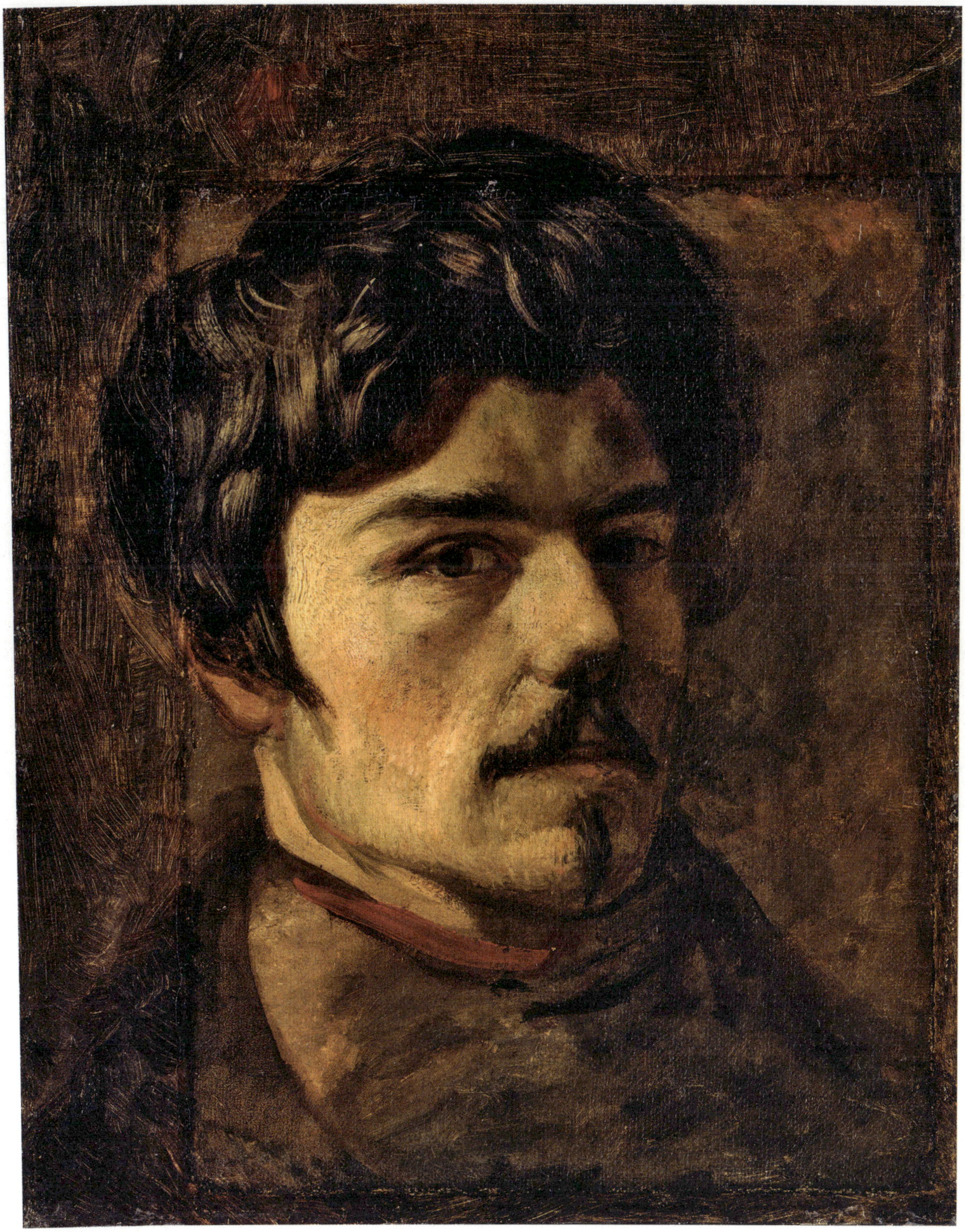

Eugène Delacroix (1798–1863)
Self-Portrait, c. 1830–35
Oil on canvas, 36 × 28 cm
Zurich, Emil Bührle collection

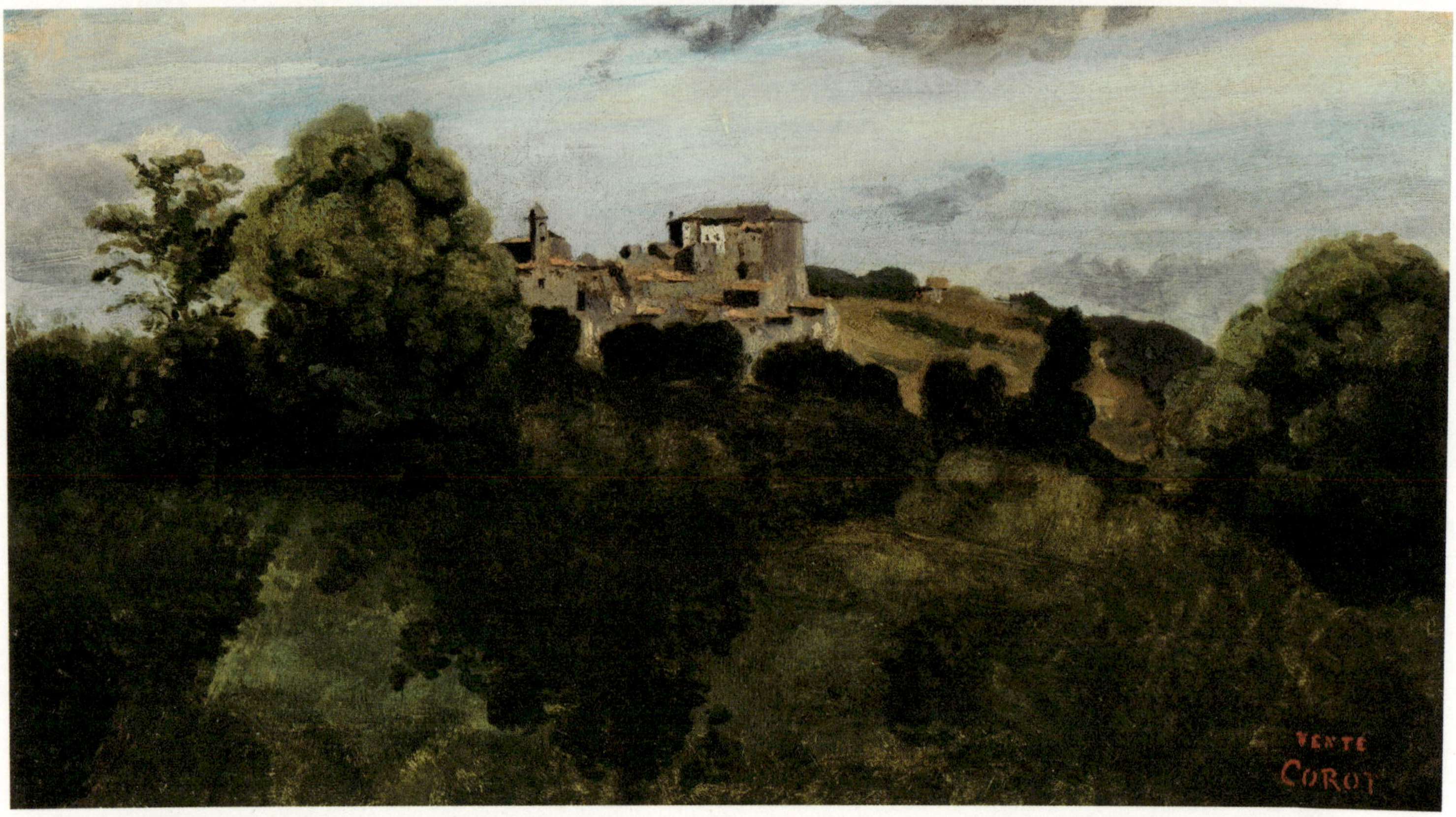

Jean-Baptiste Camille Corot (1796–1875)
View of Genzano, 1843
Oil on canvas, 15.9 × 28.9 cm
New York, The Metropolitan Museum of Art

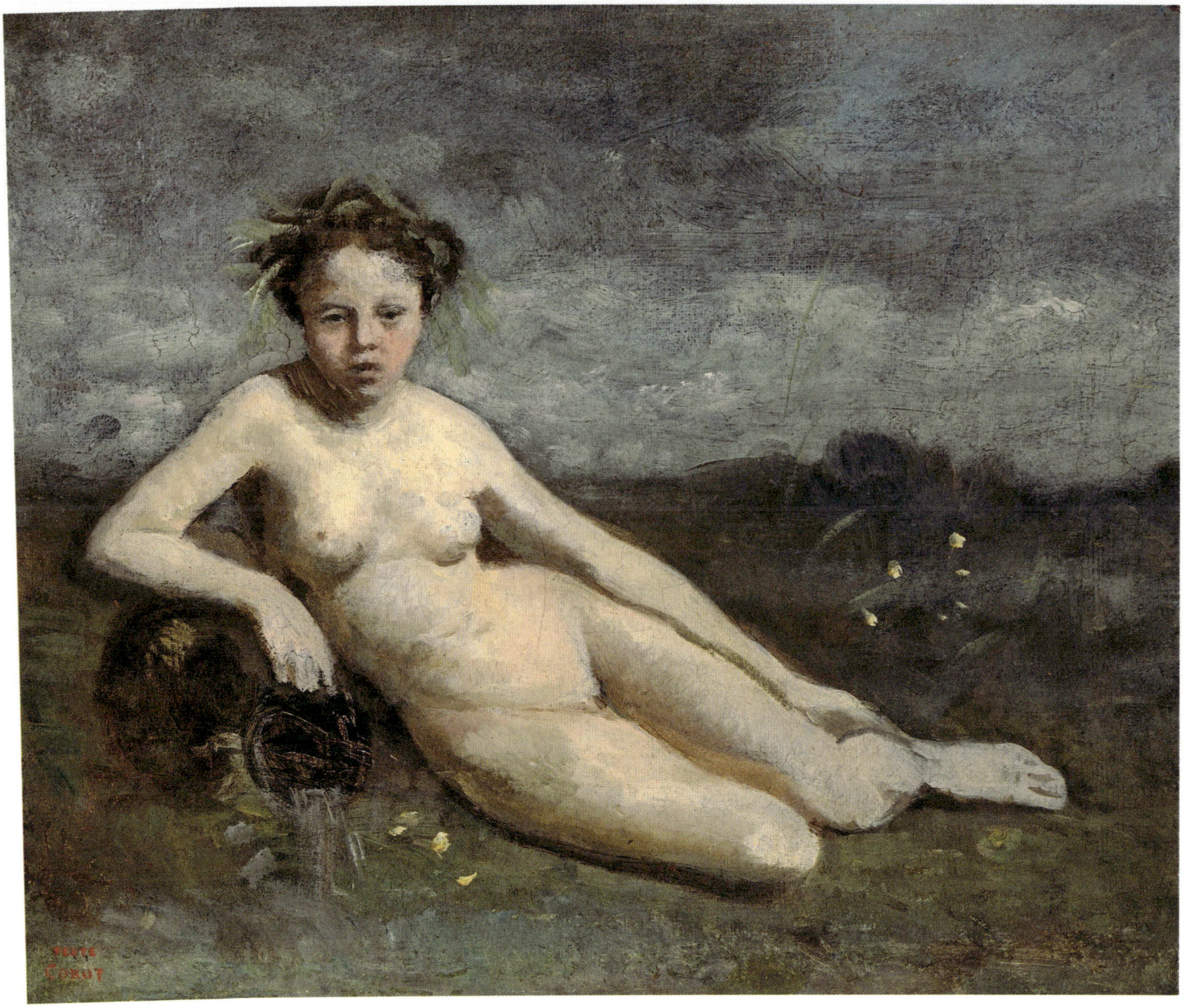

Jean-Baptiste Camille Corot (1796–1875)
The Source, c. 1850–55
Oil on canvas, 34 × 39.5 cm
David and Ezra Nahmad Collection

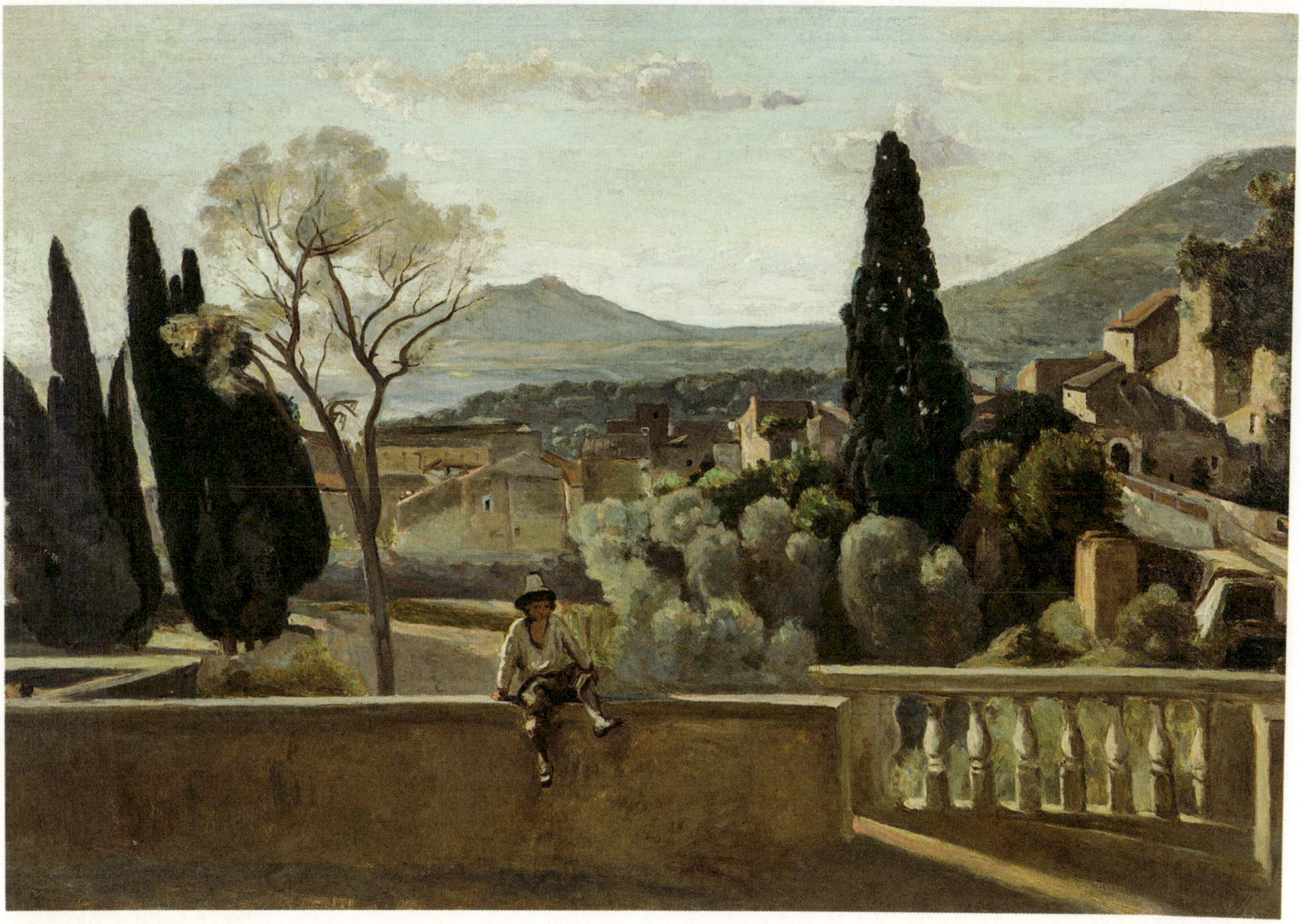

Berthe Morisot (1841–1895)
Tivoli. The Gardens of the Villa d'Este (after Jean-Baptiste Camille Corot), 1863
Oil on canvas, 42 × 59 cm
Private collection

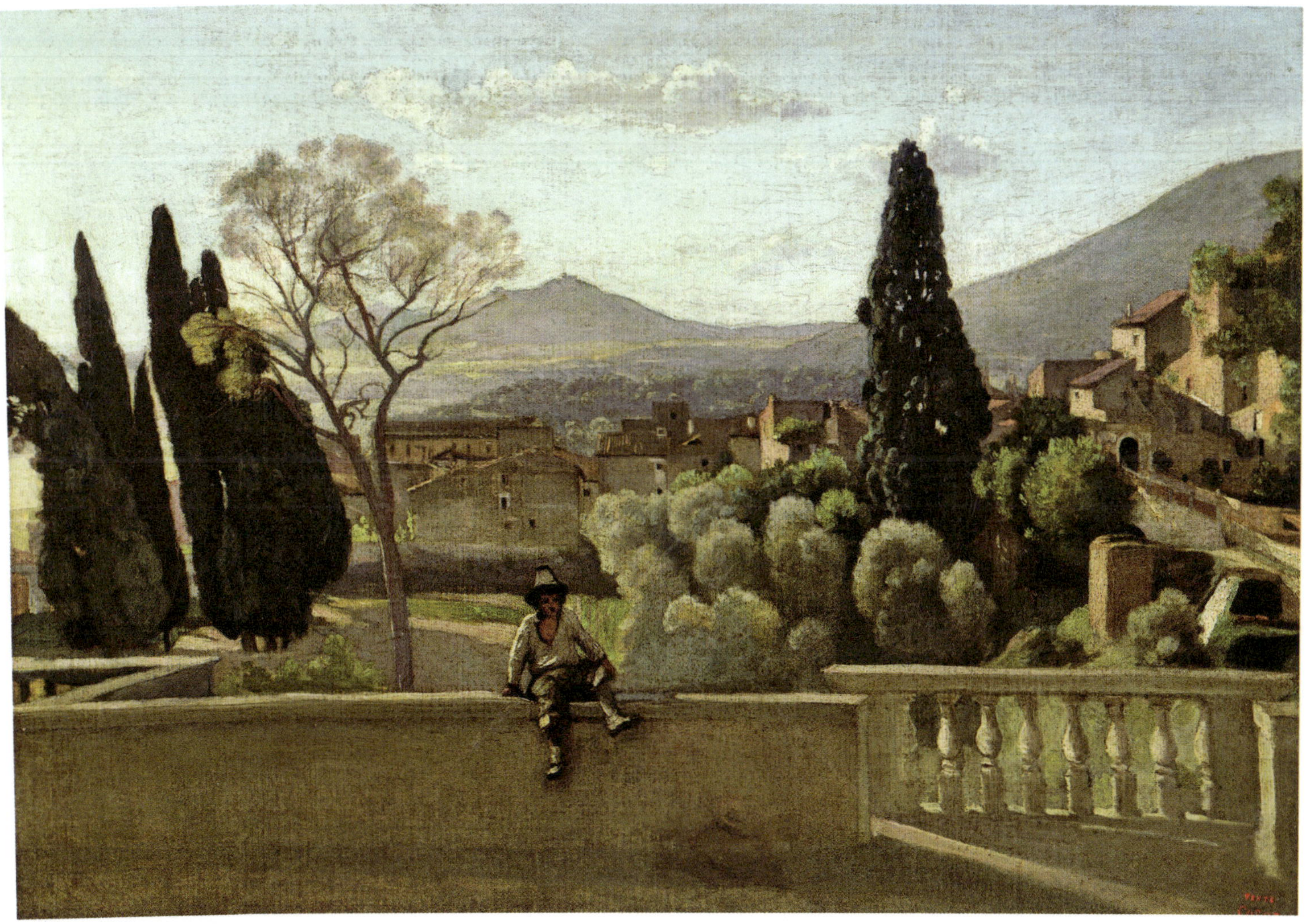

Jean-Baptiste Camille Corot (1796–1875)
Tivoli. The Gardens of the Villa d'Este, 1843
Oil on canvas, 43 × 60 cm
Paris, Musée du Louvre

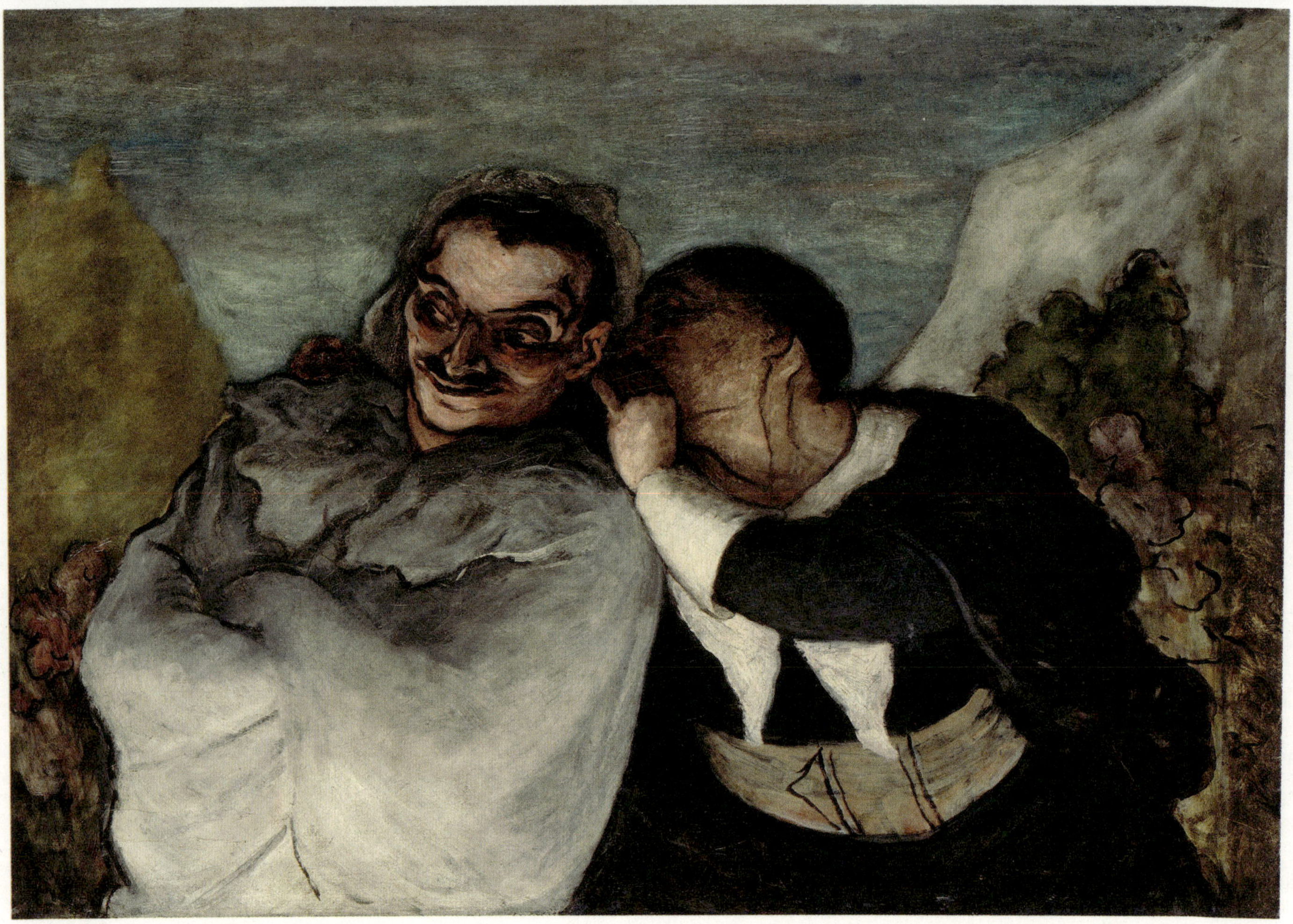

Honoré Daumier (1808–1879)
Crispin and Scapin, also known as *Scapin and Sylvestre*, c. 1864
Oil on canvas, 60.5 × 82 cm
Paris, Musée d'Orsay, gift of the Société des Amis du Louvre with the support of Henri Rouart's children, 1912

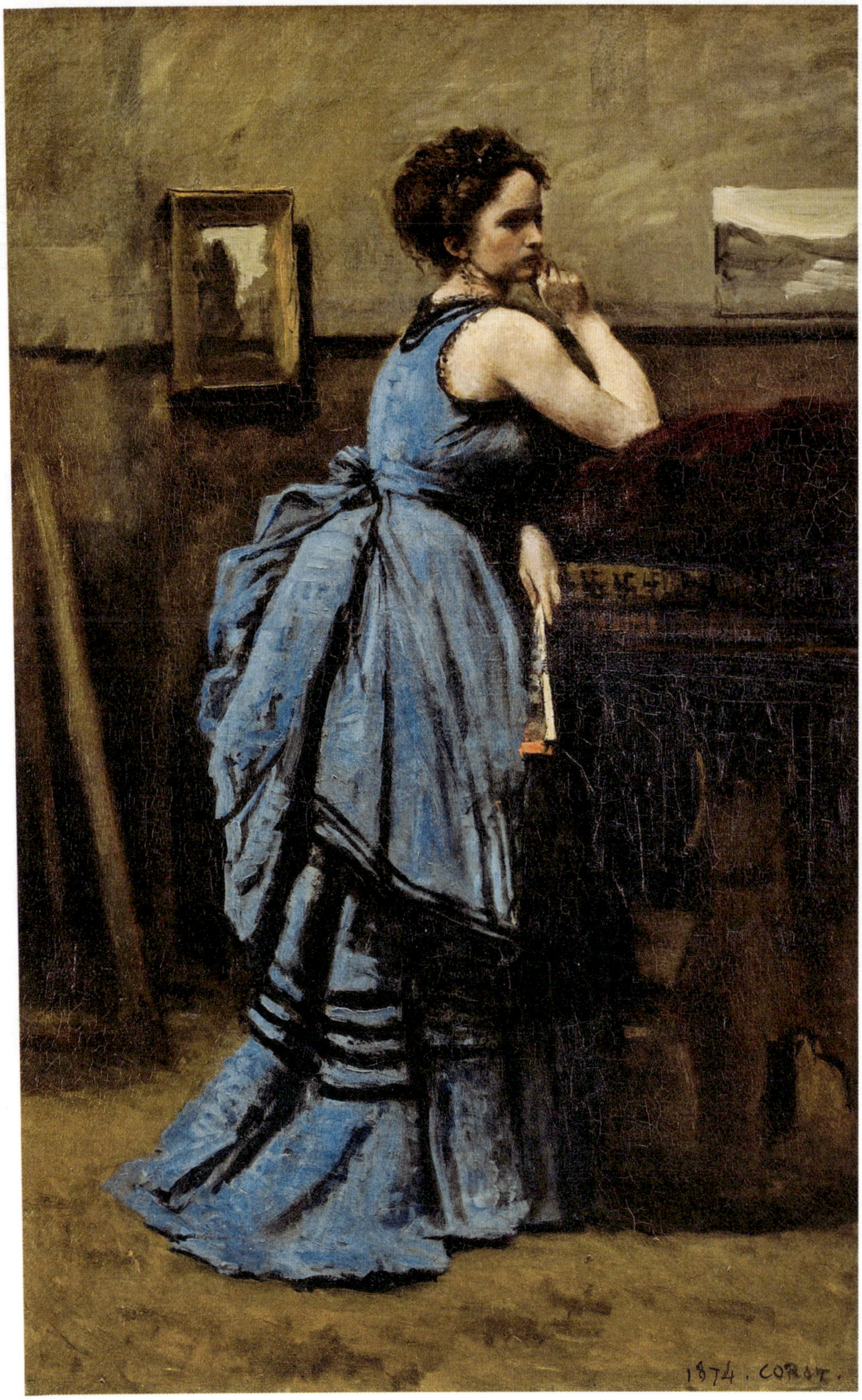

Jean-Baptiste Camille Corot (1796–1875)
Lady in Blue, 1874
Oil on canvas, 80 × 50.5 cm
Paris, Musée du Louvre

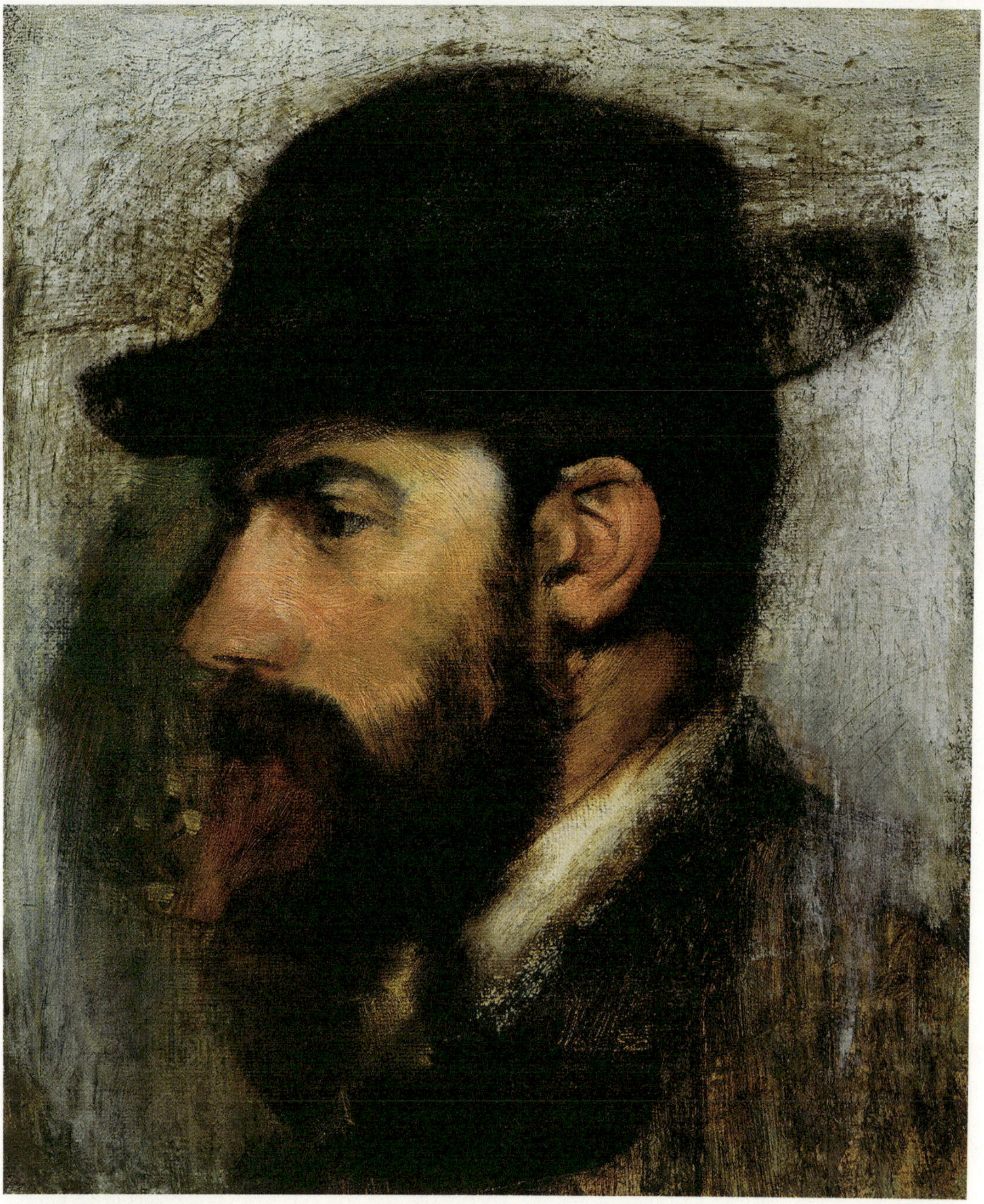

Edgar Degas (1834–1917)
Portrait of Henri Rouart, c. 1871–73
Oil on canvas, 27 × 22 cm
Paris, Musée Marmottan Monet

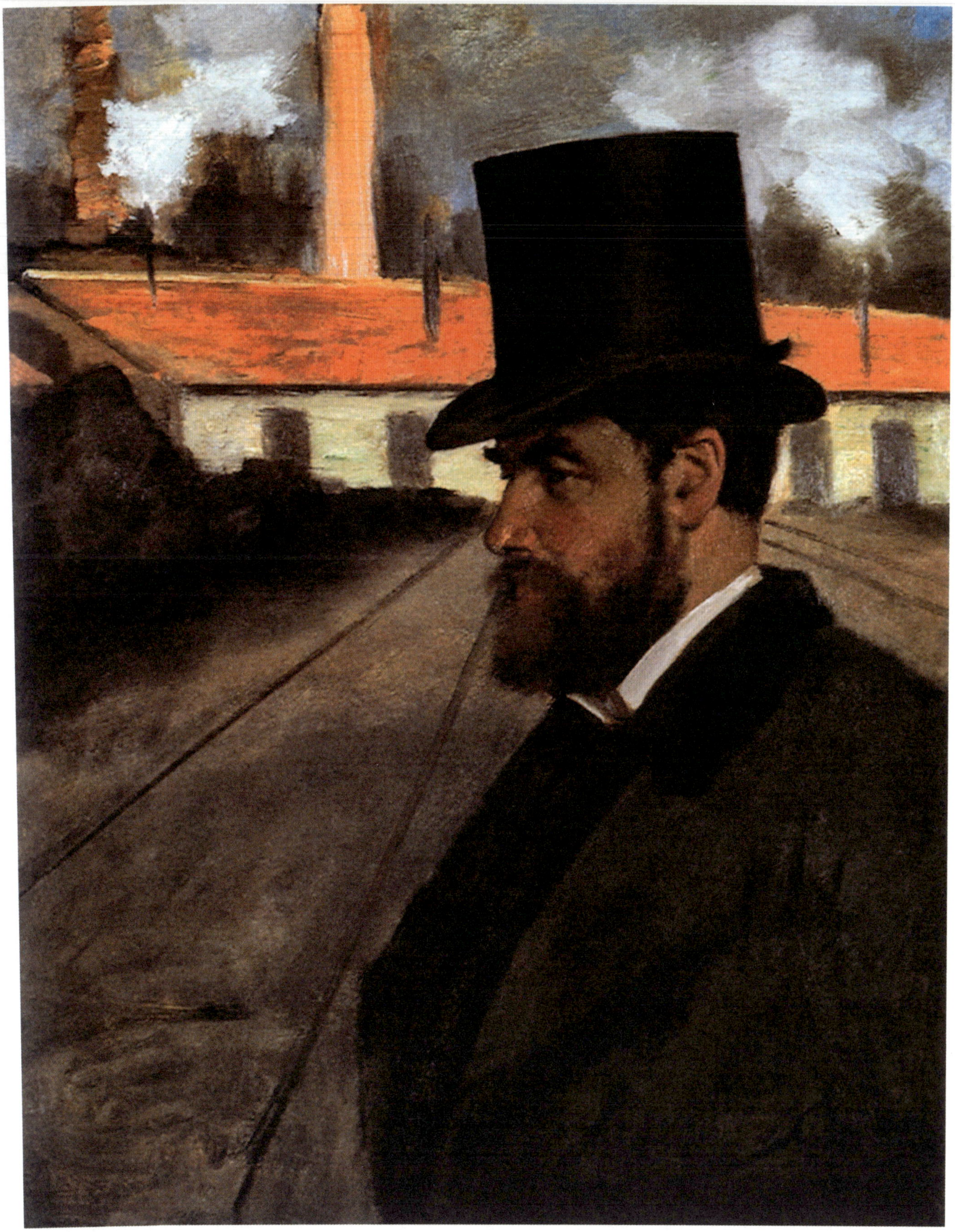

Edgar Degas (1834–1917)
Henri Rouart in Front of His Factory, c. 1875
Oil on canvas, 65.2 × 50.1 cm
Pittsburgh, Carnegie Museum of Art

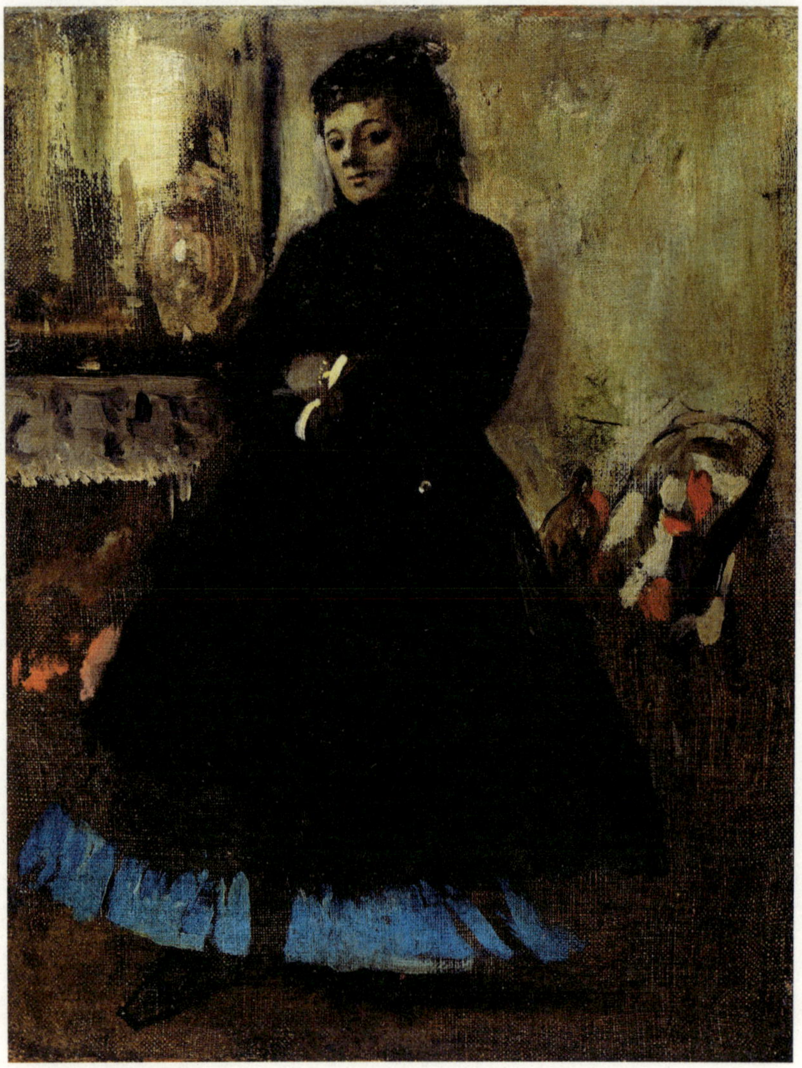

Edgar Degas (1834–1917)
Portrait of Madame Ducros, c. 1857–59
Oil on canvas, 33 × 25 cm
Paris, Musée Marmottan Monet

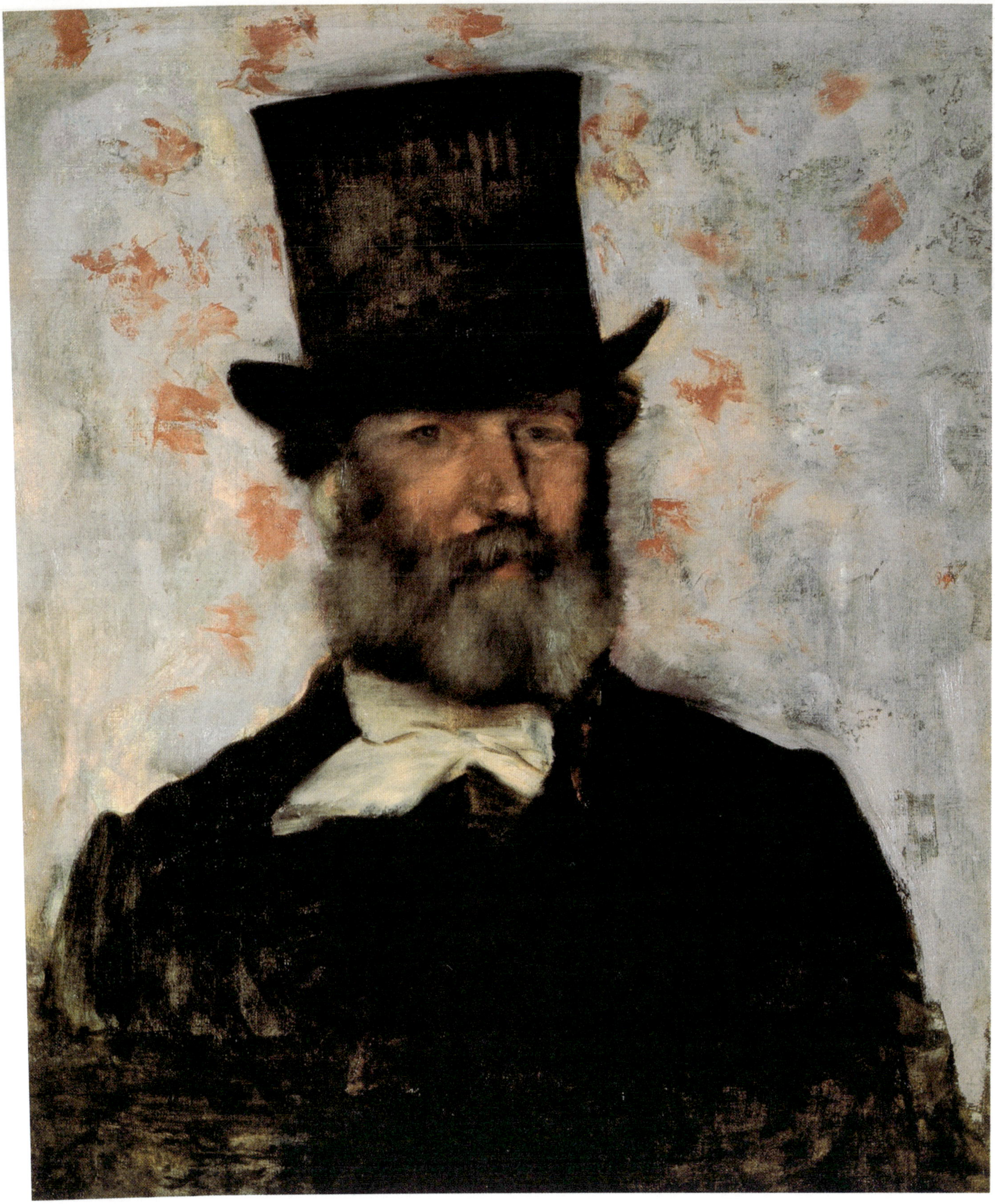

Edgar Degas (1834–1917)
Portrait of Léopold Levert, c. 1874
Oil on canvas, 65 × 54 cm
Tokyo, Artizon Museum, Ishibashi Foundation

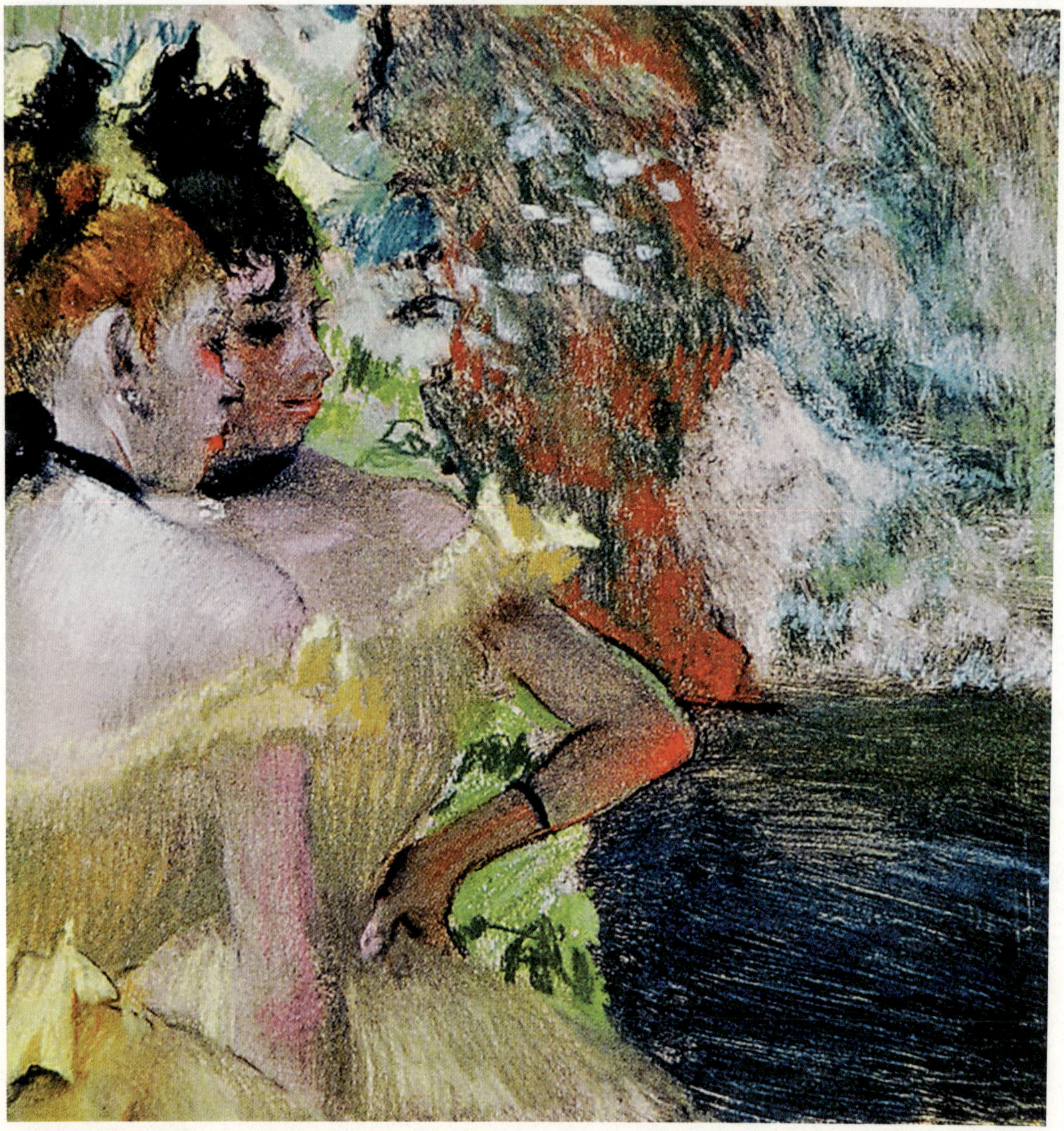

Edgar Degas (1834–1917)
Dancers in Yellow, c. 1878–80
Pastel and monotype on paper, 29 × 26 cm
Private collection

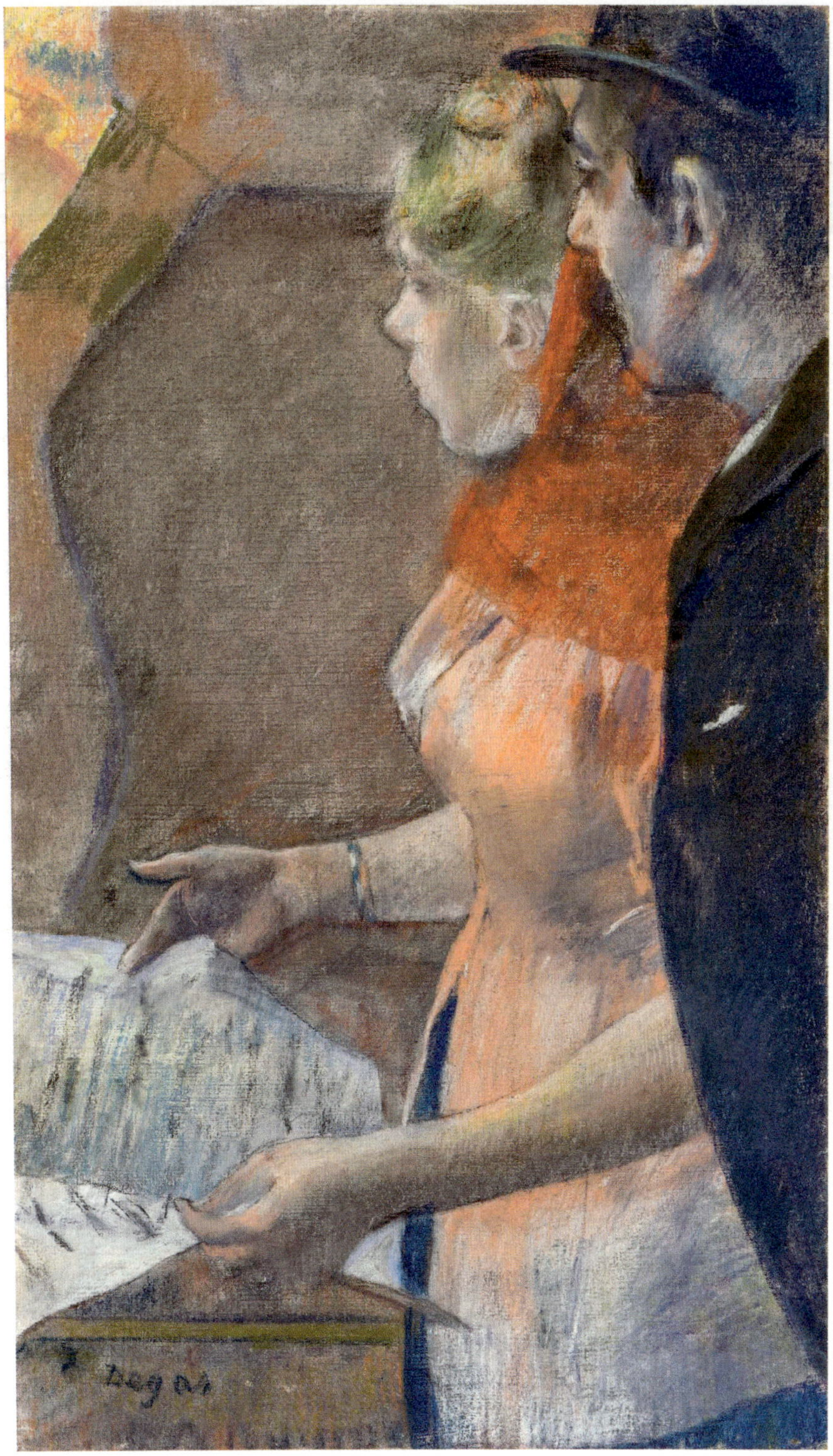

Edgar Degas (1834–1917)
In the Wings, c. 1878–80
Pastel on paper, 66 x 38 cm
Private collection

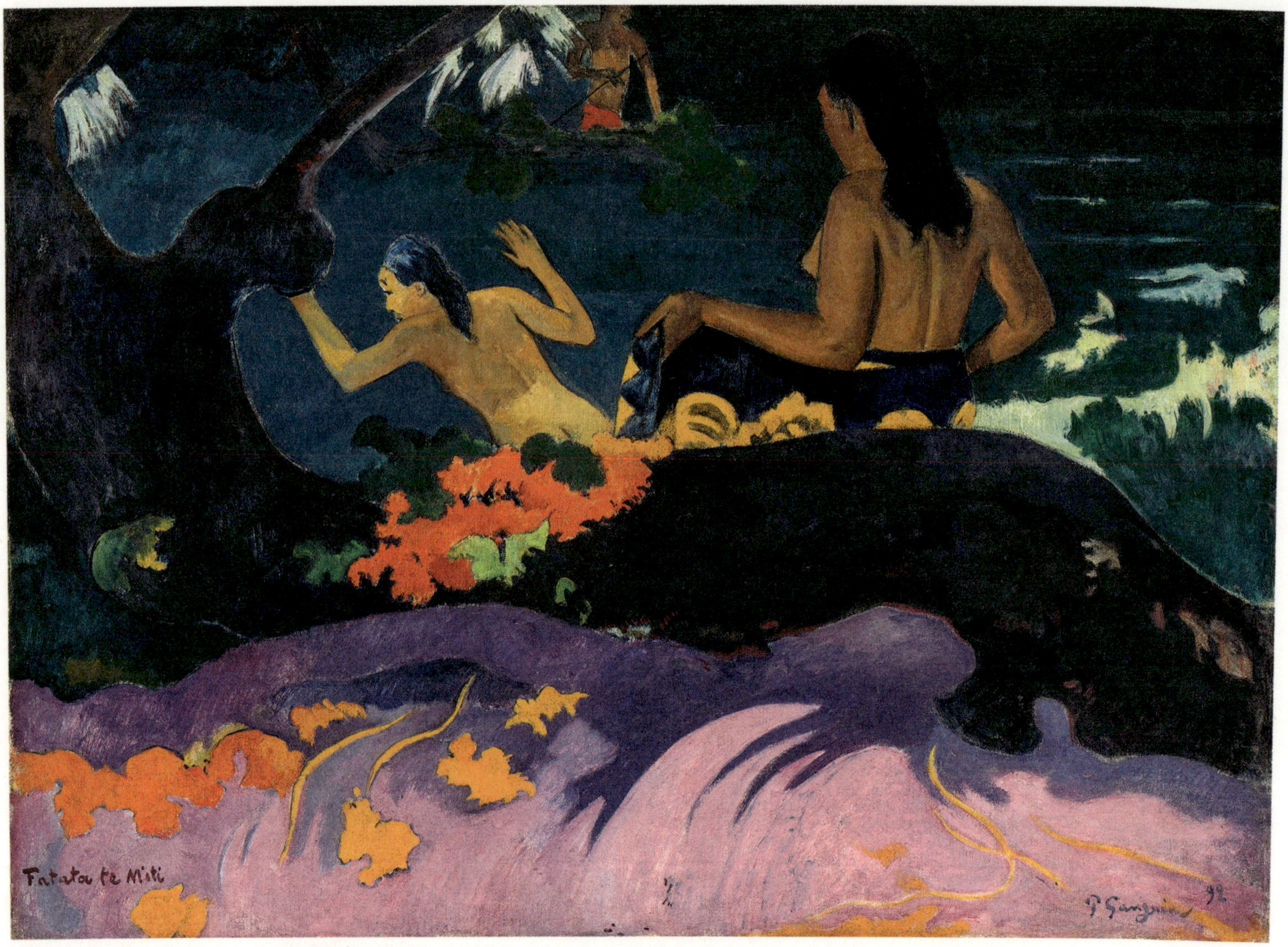

Paul Gauguin (1848–1903)
Fatata te Miti, 1892
Oil on canvas, 67.9 × 91.5 cm
Washington, D.C., National Gallery of Art

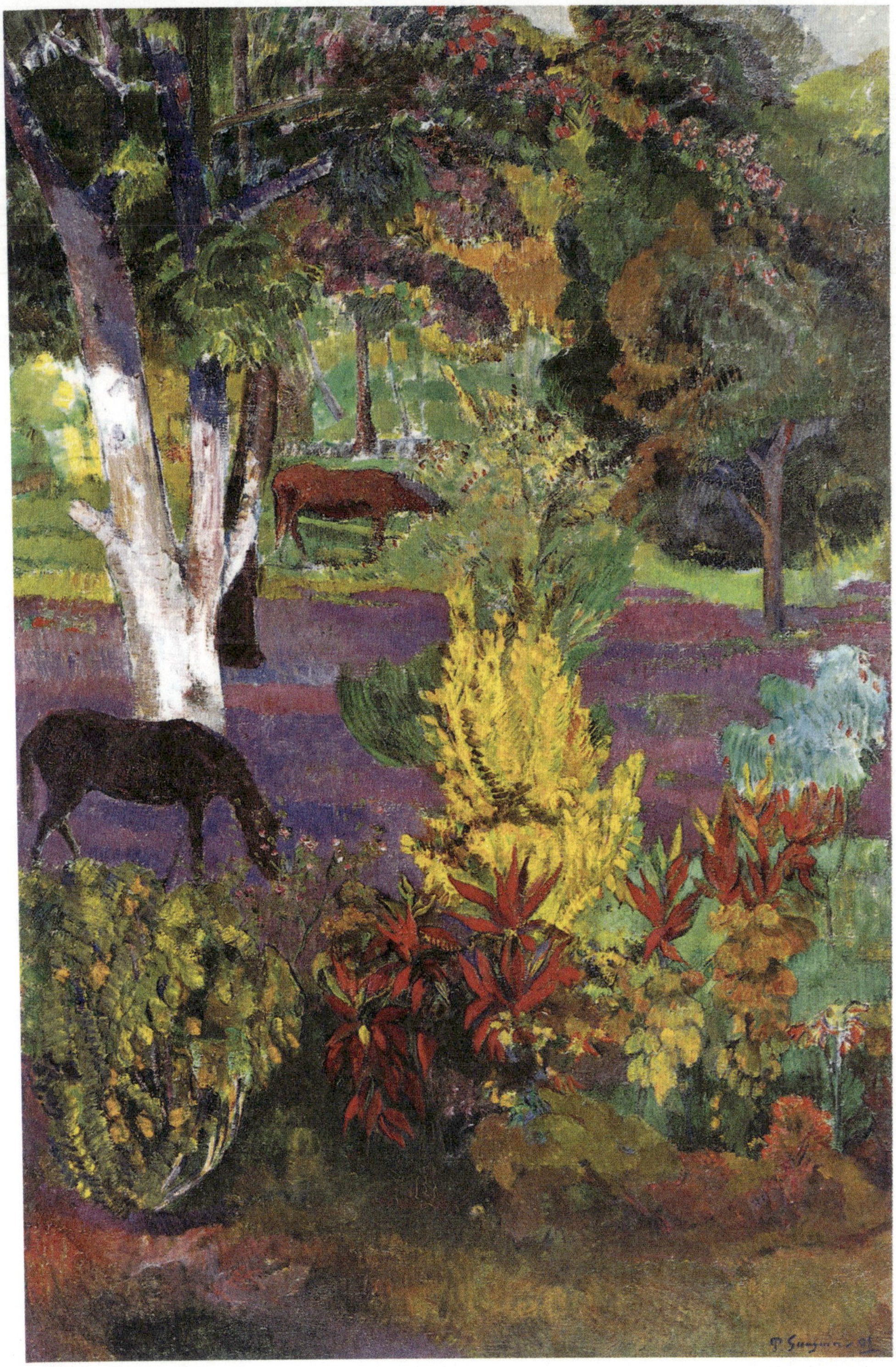

Paul Gauguin (1848–1903)
Landscape with Horses, 1901
Oil on canvas, 95 × 61 cm
Private collection

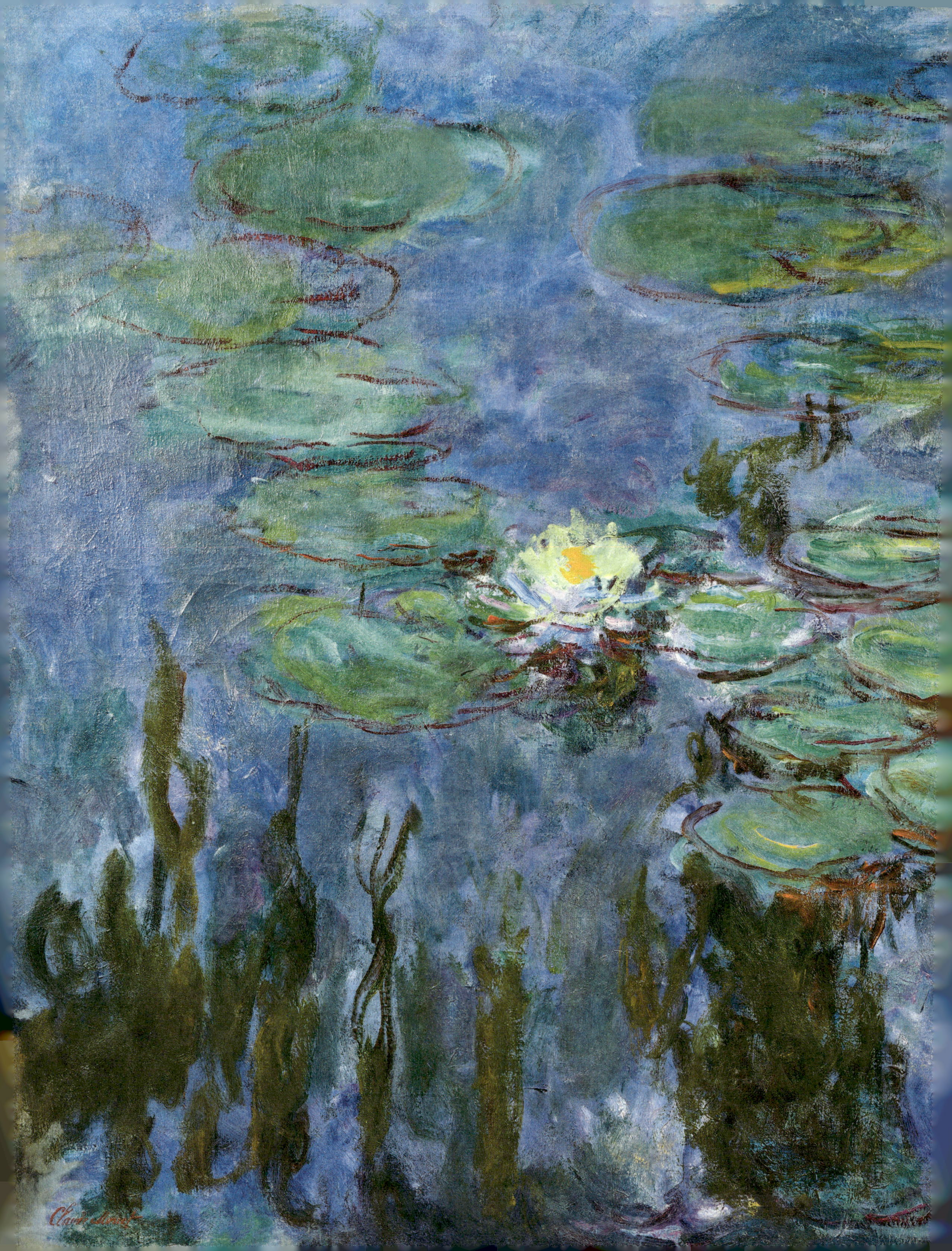

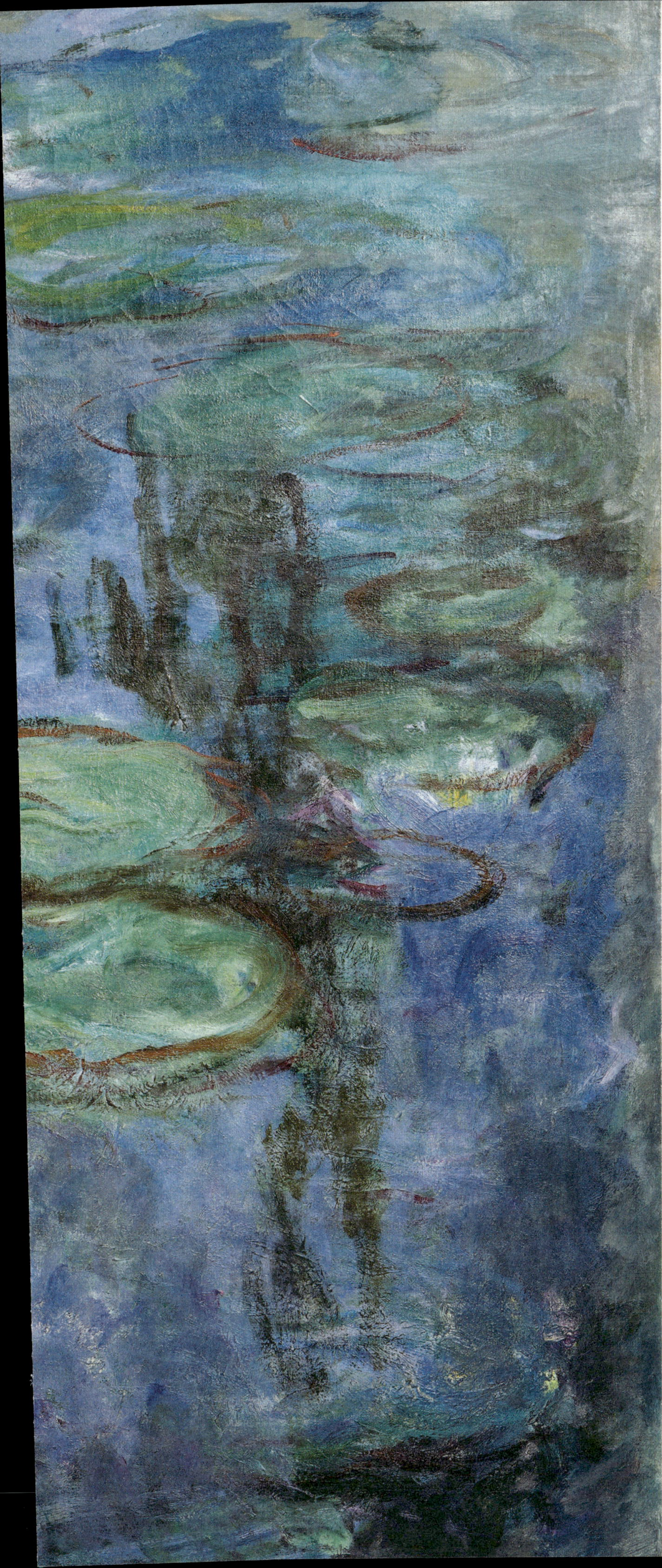

Claude Monet (1840–1926)
Water Lilies, 1914–17
Oil on canvas, 130 × 153 cm
Paris, Musée Marmottan Monet

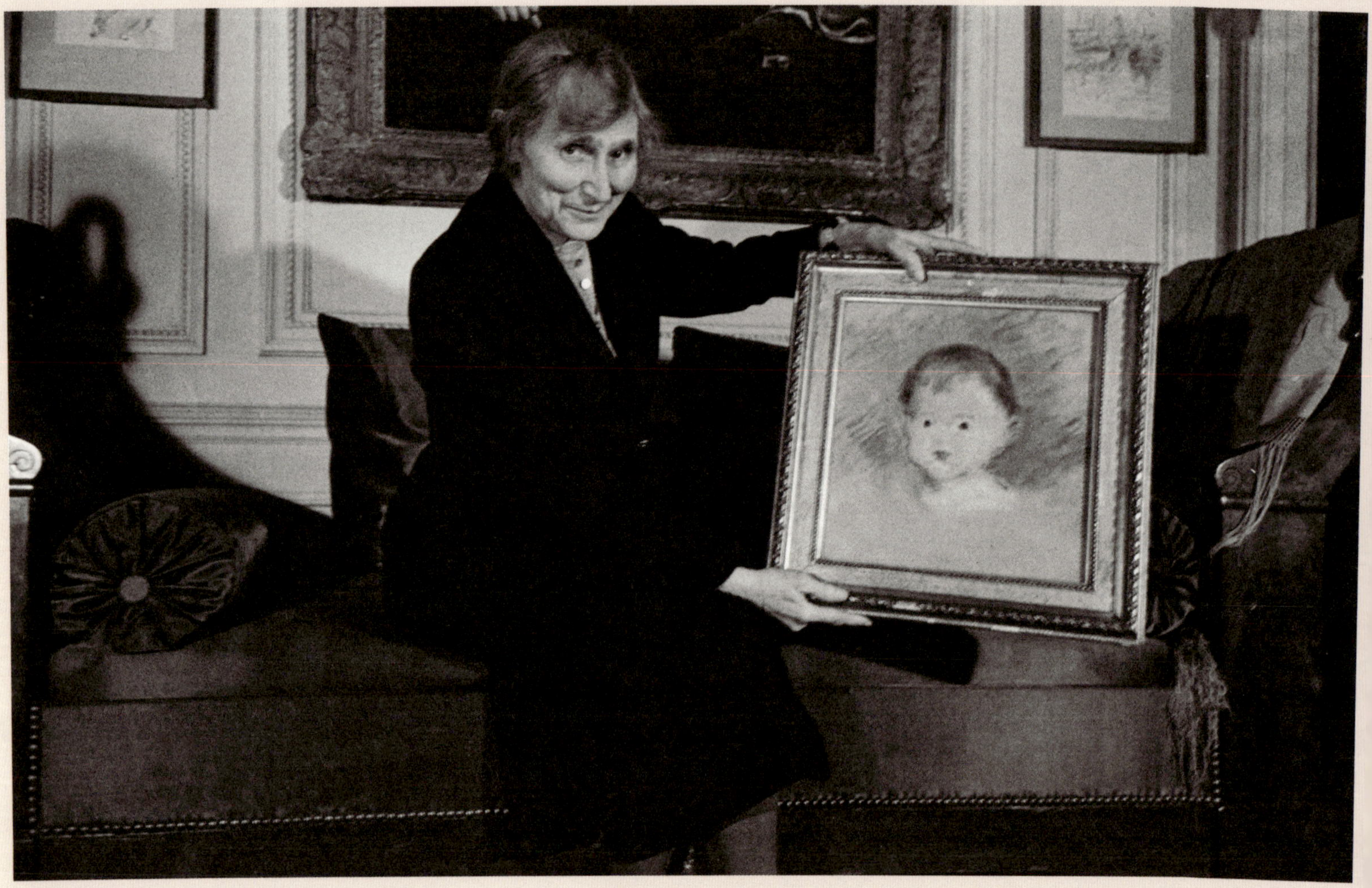

Julie Manet at home toward the end of her life, holding the portrait of her at fifteen months by Édouard Manet

LIST OF EXHIBITED WORKS

Jean-Baptiste Camille Corot (1796–1875)
Honfleur: Wood on the Côte de Grâce, c. 1830
Oil on paper mounted on canvas, 35 × 27 cm
Paris, Musée Marmottan Monet, inv. 2017.3.1

Jean-Baptiste Camille Corot (1796–1875)
Volterra. Road Descending from the Town, c. 1834
Oil on canvas, 29 × 39 cm
Paris, Musée Marmottan Monet, inv. 6505

Jean-Baptiste Camille Corot (1796–1875)
Tivoli. The Gardens of the Villa d'Este, 1843
Oil on canvas, 43 × 60 cm
Paris, Musée du Louvre, Department of Paintings, inv. RF 1943-5

Jean-Baptiste Camille Corot (1796–1875)
The Source, c. 1850–55
Oil on canvas, 34 × 39 cm
Collection David and Ezra Nahmad

Jean-Baptiste Camille Corot (1796–1875)
Lady in Blue, 1874
Oil on canvas, 80 × 50.5 cm
Paris, Musée du Louvre, Department of Paintings, inv. RF 2056

Honoré Daumier (1808–1879)
Crispin and Scapin, also known as *Scapin and Sylvestre*, c. 1864
Oil on canvas, 60.5 × 82 cm
Paris, Musée d'Orsay, gift of the Société des Amis du Louvre with the support of the children of Henri Rouart, 1912, inv. RF 2057

Honoré Daumier (1808–1879)
Two Defendants, n.d.
Watercolor on paper, 14 × 12 cm
Paris, Musée Marmottan Monet, inv. 6135.2

Honoré Daumier (1808–1879)
A Lawyer Pleading, n.d.
Graphite on paper, 15 × 12 cm
Paris, Musée Marmottan Monet, inv. 6135.3

Honoré Daumier (1808–1879)
A Lawyer, n.d.
India ink and wash on paper, 11 × 10 cm
Paris, Musée Marmottan Monet, inv. 6135.1

Edgar Degas (1834–1917)
Portrait of Madame Ducros, c. 1857–59
Oil on canvas, 33 × 25 cm
Paris, Musée Marmottan Monet, inv. 6090

Edgar Degas (1834–1917)
Portrait of Edouard Manet, c. 1866
Pencil on paper, 40 × 26 cm
Paris, Musée Marmottan Monet, inv. 6507

Edgar Degas (1834–1917)
Portrait of Henri Rouart, c. 1871–73
Oil on canvas, 27 × 22 cm
Paris, Musée Marmottan Monet, inv. 6089

Edgar Degas (1834–1917)
Portrait of Léopold Levert, c. 1874
Oil on canvas, 65 × 54 cm
Tokyo, Artizon Museum, Ishibashi Foundation, inv. Gaiyo 162

Edgar Degas (1834–1917)
Singer at a Café-Concert, c. 1879
Pastel and monotype on paper, 37 × 28 cm
Private collection

Edgar Degas (1834–1917)
Dancer (Pas de Bourrée), c. 1880–85
Brown Conté pencil and pink chalk on paper, 34 × 22 cm
Snite Museum of Art, University of Notre Dame. Gift of John D. Reilly ND '63, '64 B.S., inv. 2004.053.004

Edgar Degas (1834–1917)
Village Street, Saint-Valéry-sur-Somme, c. 1896–98
Oil on canvas, 67.5 × 81 cm
Copenhagen, Ny Carlsberg Glyptotek, inv. SMK 4324

Edgar Degas (1834–1917)
Minerva Expelling the Vices from the Garden of Virtue (copy from Mantegna), 1897
Pastel sur toile, 66 × 81 cm
Paris, Musée d'Orsay, acquired in 1954, inv. RF 30573

Edgar Degas (1834–1917)
The Coiffure, n.d.
Charcoal on laid paper, 34 × 26 cm
Paris, Musée Marmottan Monet, inv. 6091

Eugène Delacroix (1798–1863)
Self-Portrait, c. 1830–35
Oil on canvas, 36 × 28 cm
Zurich, Collection Emil Bührle, inv. 130

Eugène Delacroix (1798–1863)
An Arab, c. 1832
Graphite heightened with watercolor on paper, 30 × 19 cm
Private collection

Eugène Delacroix (1798–1863)
View of Algiers, also known as *The Casbah, Tangier*, n.d.
Watercolor on paper, 21 × 32 cm
Paris, Musée Marmottan Monet, inv. 6138

Maurice Denis (1870–1943)
Magnificat, 1909
Oil on canvas, 130 × 104 cm
Private collection

Maurice Denis (1870–1943)
Portrait of Gabriel Thomas, c. 1918
Charcoal and pastel on paper, 61.5 ×50 cm
Saint-Germain-en-Laye, Musée Départemental Maurice Denis, inv. PMD 016.1.1

Maurice Denis (1870–1943)
Baptism of Christ or *Baptism in the Jordan* (sketch for the mosaic in the church of Saint-Paul in Geneva), 1922
Oil on canvas, 86 × 57.5 cm
Private collection, France

Maurice Denis (1870–1943)
Funerary Portrait of Gabriel Thomas, 1932
Lithograph in brown ink on paper, 32.4 × 43.4 cm
Private collection

Georges d'Espagnat (1870–1950)
Portrait of Paul Valéry, c. 1910
Oil on canvas, 73 × 59.8 cm
Private collection

Alexandre Évariste Fragonard (1780–1850)
Portrait of Mme Morisot, c. 1805
Pen, wash, and pencil on paper, 32 × 38 cm
Private collection

Jean-Honoré Fragonard (1732–1806)
Shepherds in a Landscape, also known as *Shepherd Playing the Flute, Shepherdess Listening*, c. 1765
Oil on canvas, 40 × 30 cm
Annecy, Musée-Château, on permanent loan from the Musée du Louvre, inv. MNR 870

Paul Gauguin (1848–1903)
Portrait of Stéphane Mallarmé "with the Raven," 1891, print of 1919
Etching, 18.4 × 14.4 cm
Private collection

Paul Gauguin (1848–1903)
Study for Pape Moe (Mysterious Water) or *The Tahitian*, c. 1893–94
Monotype, 28 × 17 cm
Paris, Musée Marmottan Monet, inv. 6506

Paule Gobillard (1867–1947)
View of the Manet Exhibition at the Orangerie des Tuileries, 1932
Oil on canvas, 37.5 × 46 cm
Private collection

Paule Gobillard (1867–1947)
Portrait of Julie Manet, c. 1900
Oil on canvas, 37 × 45 cm
Private collection

Johan Barthold Jongkind (1819–1891)
A Canal near Rotterdam, 1857
Oil on canvas, , 41 × 56 cm
Private collection

Alphonse Legros (1837–1911)
Portrait of Eugène Manet, 1862
Oil on canvas, 71 × 58 cm
Private collection

Édouard Manet (1832–1883)
Three Nudes, c. 1853–56
Watercolor and graphite on paper, 28.5 × 22 cm
Private collection

Édouard Manet (1832–1883)
Lucrezia, after *Portrait of Lucrezia del Fede* by Andrea del Sarto (Uffizi, Florence), c. 1853–56
Red chalk on paper, 28.5 × 22 cm
Private collection

Édouard Manet (1832–183)
Madonna of the Rabbit (after Titian), 1854
Oil on canvas, 70 × 84 cm
Paris, Musée du Louvre, Department of Paintings, inv. RF 2017 7

Édouard Manet (1832–1883)
Jupiter and Antiope (after Titian), 1856
Oil on canvas, 47 × 85 cm
Paris, Musée Marmottan Monet, inv. 6087

Édouard Manet (1832–1883)
Boy with Cherries, 1858
Oil on canvas, 65.5 × 54.5 cm
Lisbon, Museu Calouste Gulbenkian, inv. 395

Édouard Manet (1832–1883)
M. and Mme Auguste Manet or *Portrait of Manet's Parents*, 1860
Oil on canvas, 110 × 90 cm
Paris, Musée d'Orsay, acquired thanks to the generosity of the Rouart-Manet family, of Mme Jeannette Veil-Picard and of a foreign benefactor, 1977, inv. RF 1977 12

Édouard Manet (1832–1883)
Portrait of Auguste Manet, the Artist's Father, c. 1860
Red chalk on paper, 17 × 13.7 cm
Private collection

Édouard Manet (1832–1883)
The Musicians, c. 1862
Graphite on paper, 11.1 × 18.3 cm
Private collection

Édouard Manet (1832–1883)
The Mexican, c. 1862
Watercolor on paper, 19 × 12.5 cm
Paris, Musée Marmottan Monet, inv. 6088

Édouard Manet (1832–1883),
Soldiers Making Their Way to the Outpost, 1870
Pencil and wash on double notebook page, squared paper, 18.5 × 24 cm
Private collection

Édouard Manet (1832–1883)
Figures on a Beach, 1873
Graphite on double notebook page, squared paper, 19 × 24.5 cm
Private collection

Édouard Manet (1832–1883)
Berthe Morisot Reclining, 1873
Oil on canvas, 26 × 34 cm
Paris, Musée Marmottan Monet, inv. 6086

Édouard Manet (1832–1883)
Woman with Fans, 1873
Oil on canvas, 113 × 166 cm
Paris, Musée d'Orsay, gift of M. and Mme Ernest Rouart, 1930, inv. RF 2850

Édouard Manet (1832–1883)
Portrait of Berthe Morisot with a Fan, 1874
Oil on canvas, 61 × 50.5 cm
Paris, Musée d'Orsay, on permanent loan at the Palais des Beaux-Arts de Lille, accepted by the State in lieu of estate tax, 1999, inv. RF 1999 12/D. 2000-1-1

Édouard Manet (1832–1883)
Bathers on the Seine, c. 1874–76
Oil on canvas, 132 × 98 cm
Collection Museu de Arte de Sao Paulo Assis Chateaubriand, gift of Arthur Lundgreen, 1952, inv. MASP.00078

Édouard Manet (1832–1883)
Stéphane Mallarmé, 1876
Oil on canvas, 27.2 × 35.7 cm
Paris, Musée d'Orsay, acquired with the support of the Société des Amis du Louvre and of D. David Weill, 1928, inv. RF 2661

Édouard Manet (1832–1883)
In the Café, c. 1876–78
Graphite on squared paper, 18.5 × 12 cm
Private collection

Édouard Manet (1832–1883)
The Conductor, c. 1878–80
India ink wash on paper, 18.3 × 12 cm
Private collection

Édouard Manet (1832–1883)
Portrait of Mme Manet or *Woman with a Cat*, c. 1880
Oil on canvas, 92.1 × 73 cm
London, Tate, purchased 1918, inv. N03295

Édouard Manet (1832–1883)
Woman with a Pug, c. 1881
Graphite on paper, 12.7 × 10.5 cm
Private collection

Eugène Manet (1833–1892)
Sketchbook, c. 1882–83
Pencil on paper, 18 × 9 cm
Paris, Musée Marmottan Monet, inv. D.5-1986.2014.5

Julie Manet (1878–1966)
Nice, 1889
Watercolor on paper, 10.5 × 16.7 cm
Private collection

Julie Manet (1878–1966)
Woman and Girl beside a Lake, 1893
Oil on canvas, 53 × 35 cm
Private collection

Julie Manet (1878–1966)
Portrait of Paule Gobillard, c. 1894
Oil on canvas, 59.5 × 49.5 cm
Private collection

Julie Manet (1878–1966)
Martha in a Green Velvet Dress, 1898
Oil on canvas, 41 × 33 cm
Private collection

Julie Manet (1878–1966)
Young Girl with Dog, 1898
Oil on canvas, 61 × 50 cm
Private collection

Julie Manet (1878–1966)
The Piano Duo, c. 1898
Oil on canvas, 55 × 46 cm
Private collection

Julie Manet (1878–1966)
Portraits of Jeannie at the Piano and Paule Listening to Her, 1899
Oil on canvas, 90 × 90 cm
Private collection

Julie Manet (1878–1966)
Before the Ball, January 1899
Oil on canvas, 100 × 81 cm
Private collection

Julie Manet (1878–1966)
Portrait of Jeanne Baudot, January–February 1899
Oil on canvas, 55 × 46.5 cm
Private collection

Julie Manet (1878–1966)
Nude on the Couch, c. 1899
Oil on canvas, 61.5 × 50.5 cm
Private collection

Julie Manet (1878–1966)
Julien Rouart Painting in the Dining Room in the Rue de Villejust, c. 1904
Oil on canvas, 65.5 × 54.5 cm
Private collection

Julie Manet (1878–1966)
Carentec, View of Saint-Pol-de-Léon, August 29, 1911
Watercolor on paper, 22.5 × 28.3 cm
Private collection

Julie Manet (1878–1966)
Jean-Michel in a Pierrot Collar, c. 1935
Oil on canvas, 41 × 33 cm
Private collection

Julie Manet (1878–1966)
Françoise as a Baby, c. 1941
Oil on canvas, 25 × 36 cm
Private collection

Julie Manet (1878–1966)
Yves Holding a Book, c. 1941
Oil on canvas, 46 × 36 cm
Private collection

Julie Manet (1878–1966)
Jean-Michel's Catechism Book, c. 1941
Ink and watercolor on paper, 24.5 × 19 cm
Private collection

Julie Manet (1878–1966)
M. and Mme Auguste Manet or *Portrait of Manet's Parents* (after Édouard Manet), n.d.
Watercolor on paper, 29 × 19 cm
Paris, Musée Marmottan Monet, inv. 6168

Julie Manet (1878–1966)
Berthe Morisot Reclining (after Édouard Manet), n.d.
Watercolor on paper, 15 × 22 cm
Paris, Musée Marmottan Monet, inv. 6173

Julie Manet (1878–1966)
Mme Manet Senior in the Garden at Bellevue (after Édouard Manet), n.d.
Watercolor on paper, 30 × 18.5 cm
Paris, Musée Marmottan Monet, inv. 6172

Julie Manet (1878–1966)
Singer at a Café-Concert (after Édouard Manet), n.d.
Watercolor on paper, 22 × 25 cm
Paris, Musée Marmottan Monet, inv. 6167

Julie Manet (1878–1966)
Still Life with Pheasant, n.d.
Oil on canvas, 32.6 × 46 cm
Private collection

Julie Manet (1878–1966)
In the Wood, n.d.
Oil on canvas, 41 × 33 cm
Private collection

Julie Manet (1878–1966)
Woman Sitting at Her Fireplace, n.d.
Oil on canvas, 64 × 54 cm
Private collection

Julie Manet (1878–1966),
Selection of Painted Plates, n.d.
Porcelain
Private collection

Julie Manet (1878–1966)
Still Life with Quinces, n.d.
Oil on canvas, 26 × 42 cm
Private collection

Julie Manet (1878–1966)
Le Mesnil, n.d.
Oil on canvas, 67.5 × 50 cm
Private collection

Julie Manet (1878–1966)
In the Wood, n.d.
Oil on canvas, 55 × 38 cm
Private collection

Julie Manet (1878–1966)
Picking Peaches, n.d.
Oil on canvas, 92 × 60 cm
Private collection

Julie Manet (1878–1966)
Swans, n.d.
Oil on canvas, 19 × 33.3 cm
Private collection

Julie Manet (1878–1966)
Julie Manet or *Child with a Cat* (after Pierre-Auguste Renoir), n.d.
Black pencil on tracing paper, 17 × 18 cm
Paris, Musée Marmottan Monet, inv. 6169

Julie Manet (1878–1966)
After the Self-Portrait by Berthe Morisot, n.d.
Black pencil on paper, 30 × 22 cm
Paris, Musée Marmottan Monet, inv. 6162

Julie Manet (1878–1966)
After the Self-Portrait by Berthe Morisot, n.d.
Watercolor on laid paper, 29 × 20 cm
Paris, Musée Marmottan Monet, inv. 6161

Julie Manet (1878–1966)
The Rest (after Édouard Manet), n.d.
Watercolor on paper, 26.5 × 22.5 cm
Private collection

Julie Manet (1878–1966)
Woman with Fans (after Édouard Manet), n.d.
Oil on canvas, 40.3 × 60.2 cm
Private collection

Julie Manet (1878-1966)
Portrait of Berthe Morisot, n.d.
Watercolor on paper, 25.5 × 19.7 cm
Saint-Germain-en Laye, Musée Départemental Maurice-Denis, PMD 976.3.99

Claude Monet (1840–1926)
Villas at Bordighera, 1884
Oil on canvas, 116.5 × 136.5 cm
Paris, Musée d'Orsay, acquired in 2000, inv. RF 2000 94 / DO 1992 1

Claude Monet (1840–1926)
Water Lilies, 1914–17
Oil on canvas, 130 × 153 cm
Paris, Musée Marmottan Monet, inv. 6085

Berthe Morisot (1841–1895)
The Meal at the House of Simon (after Veronese), 1860
Oil on canvas, 53 × 112 cm
Paris, Musée Marmottan Monet, inv. 6023

Berthe Morisot (1841–1895)
Tivoli. The Gardens of the Villa d'Este (after Corot), 1863
Oil on canvas, 42 × 59 cm
Private collection

Berthe Morisot (1841–1895)
Young Woman at the Window, or *Summer*, 1879
Oil on canvas, 76 × 61 cm
Musée Fabre, Montpellier Méditerranée Métropole, inv. 07.5.1

Berthe Morisot (1841–1895)
Eugène Manet and Her Daughter in the Garden at Bougival, 1881
Oil on canvas, 73 × 92 cm
Paris, Musée Marmottan Monet, inv. 6018

Berthe Morisot (1841–1895)
Pasie Sewing in the Garden at Bougival, 1881
Oil on canvas, 81 × 100 cm
Pau, Musée des Beaux-Arts, inv. 07.10.1 / 867

Berthe Morisot (1841–1895)
Young Girl Siting in the Grass, 1882
Watercolor on paper, 26 × 32 cm
Paris, Musée Marmottan Monet, inv. 6030

Berthe Morisot (1841–1895)
Studies for Little Girl with a Doll, 1884
Graphite on paper, 22 × 35 cm
Paris, Musée Marmottan Monet, inv. 6069

Berthe Morisot (1841–1895)
Portrait of Berthe Morisot and Her Daughter, 1885
Oil on canvas, 72 × 91 cm
Private collection

Berthe Morisot (1841–1895)
"Green notebook A," c. 1885–86
Black pencil on paper, 17.3 × 11.6 cm
Paris, Musée Marmottan Monet, inv. D.5–1986.2014.2

Berthe Morisot (1841–1895)
"Beige notebook," c. 1885–88
Black pencil on paper, 15 × 10.3 cm
Paris, Musée Marmottan Monet, inv. D.5–1986.2014.1

Berthe Morisot (1841–1895)
Portrait of the Artist and Her Daughter, also known as *The Drawing Lesson*, 1889
Drypoint, 20.5 × 15.5 cm
Private collection

Berthe Morisot (1841–1895)
Little Girl in a Blue Dress, 1886
Pastel on canvas, 100 × 81 cm
Paris, Musée Marmottan Monet, inv. 6502

Berthe Morisot (1841–1895)
Bust of Julie Manet, 1886
Patinated bronze and marble, H. 36 cm (with base)
Private collection

Berthe Morisot (1841–1895)
Paule Gobillard Painting, 1887
Oil on canvas, 86 × 94 cm
Paris, Musée Marmottan Monet, inv. 6500

Berthe Morisot (1841–1895)
"Green notebook B," 1888–1889
Black pencil on paper, 17.3 × 11.6 cm
Paris, Musée Marmottan Monet,
inv. D.5–1986.2014.3

Berthe Morisot (1841–1895)
Little Girl with Cat, 1889
Drypoint, 13.5 × 10.7 cm
Paris, Musée Marmottan Monet, 6081

Berthe Morisot (1841–1895)
The Mandolin, 1889
Oil on canvas, 55 × 57 cm
Private collection

Berthe Morisot (1841–1895)
Peasant Woman from Nice, 1889
Oil on canvas, 64 × 52 cm
Lyon, Musée des Beaux-Arts, inv. B 814

Berthe Morisot (1841–1895)
Mézy or "Black notebook," 1891
Black pencil on paper, 15 × 8.5 cm
Paris, Musée Marmottan Monet,
inv. D.5–1986.2014.4

Berthe Morisot (1841–1895)
Julie Manet and Her Greyhound Laërtes, 1893
Oil on canvas, 73 × 80 cm
Paris, Musée Marmottan Monet, inv. 5027

Berthe Morisot (1841–1895)
The Seine at Valvins, 1893
Oil on canvas, 35 × 28 cm
Private collection

Berthe Morisot (1841–1895)
Young Girl in a Park or *On the Bench*, 1893
Oil on canvas, 90 × 81 cm
Toulouse, Musée des Augustins, inv. RO 708

Berthe Morisot (1841–1895)
Young Girl in a Low-Cut Dress with a Flower in Her Hair, 1893
Oil on canvas, 70 × 51.5 cm
Petit Palais, Musée des Beaux-Arts de la Ville de Paris, inv. PPP488

Berthe Morisot (1841–1895)
The Children of Gabriel Thomas, c. 1893–94
Watercolor on paper, 24 × 20 cm
Private collection

Berthe Morisot, (1841–1895)
Julie Dreaming, 1894
Oil on canvas, 65 × 54 cm
Private collection

Berthe Morisot (1841–1895)
Julie Manet in the Liberty Hat, 1895
Oil on canvas, 73 × 55 cm
Private collection

Edgar Allan Poe (1809–1849)
French translation by Stéphane Mallarmé (1842-1898), illustrations by Édouard Manet (1832-1883)
Le Corbeau, 1875
Printed monograph in 240 copies (print no. 105), 55 × 35 cm
Private collection

Nicolas Poussin (1798–1863)
View of Rome, n.d.
Sepia wash on paper, 16 × 23 cm
Paris, Musée Marmottan Monet, inv. 6128

Pierre Puvis de Chavannes (1824–1898)
Summer, 1891
Watercolor and gouache on blue paper, 20 × 34 cm
Paris, Musée Marmottan Monet, inv. 6121

Odilon Redon (1840–1916)
Face, n.d.
Etching on paper, 15.5 × 19.5 cm
Paris, Musée Marmottan Monet, inv. 6132

Pierre-Auguste Renoir (1841–1919)
Portrait of Paule Gobillard, c. 1885
Red chalk on paper, 41.6 × 34.3 cm
Private collection

Pierre-Auguste Renoir (1841–1919)
Young Woman with Blue Hat in Profile, 1885
Pastel on paper, 31 × 26 cm
Paris, Musée Marmottan Monet, inv. 6093

Pierre-Auguste Renoir (1841–1919)
Julie Manet or *Child with Cat*, 1887
Oil on canvas, 65 × 54 cm
Paris, Musée d'Orsay, accepted by the State in lieu of estate tax, 1999, RF 1999 13

Pierre-Auguste Renoir (1841–1919)
Julie Manet or *Child with Cat* (preparatory drawing), c. 1887
Pencil on paper, 62 × 47 cm
Private collection

Pierre-Auguste Renoir (1841–1919)
Julie Manet or *Child with Cat* (preparatory drawing), c. 1887
Pencil on paper, 61 × 47.5 cm
Private collection

Pierre-Auguste Renoir (1841–1919)
Portrait of Julie Manet, 1894
Oil on canvas, 55 × 46 cm
Paris, Musée Marmottan Monet, inv. 6092

Pierre-Auguste Renoir (1841–1919)
Berthe Morisot and Her Daughter Julie, 1894
Pastel and charcoal on paper glued on cardboard, 58.5 × 46 cm
Paris, Petit Palais, Musée des Beaux-Arts de la Ville de Paris, inv. PPD895

Pierre-Auguste Renoir (1841–1919)
Pinning the Hat, 1898
Lithograph in seven colors on laid paper, 60 × 49 cm
Private collection

Hubert Robert (1733–1808)
View of the Louvre. The Garden of the Infante, 1798
Oil on canvas, 38 × 46 cm
Paris, Musée Marmottan Monet, inv. 6094

Ernest Rouart (1874–1942)
Minerva Expelling the Vices from the Garden of Virtue (copy from Mantegna), 1897
Oil on canvas, 160.5 × 192.6 cm
Paris, Musée d'Orsay, gift of Clément Rouart and his brothers, the artist's sons, 1975, inv. RF 1975 8

Ernest Rouart (1874–1942)
Julie Manet Painting, 1905
Oil on canvas, 70 × 82.7 cm
Private collection

Ernest Rouart (1874–1942)
Portraits of Mme Ernest Rouart and Her Three Sons, c. 1917
Oil on canvas, 162 × 130 cm
Private collection

Ernest Rouart (1874–1942)
Self-Portrait, 1908
Oil on panel, 17.2 × 14.4 cm
Private collection

Ernest Rouart (1874–1942)
Portrait of Julie Manet, n.d.
Oil on canvas, 116.7 × 89.2 cm
Private collection

Ernest Rouart (1874–1942)
Portrait of Julie Manet, n.d.
Oil on canvas, 92 × 73 cm
Private collection

Nicolas François Octave Tassaert (1800–1874)
The Temptation of Saint Anthony, c. 1850
Oil on canvas, 61.6 × 50.8 cm
Bremen, Kunsthalle Bremen, inv. 992–1968/4

BIBLIOGRAPHY

Angoulvent 1933
Monique Angoulvent, *Berthe Morisot*, Paris, Éditions Albert Morancé, 1933.

Arnoult 2014
Dominique d'Arnoult, *Jean-Baptiste Perronneau, 1715–1783, un portraitiste dans l'Europe des Lumières*, foreword by Daniel Roche, preface by Xavier Salmon, Paris, Arthena, 2014.

Arnoult 2017
Dominique d'Arnoult, "Le portrait d'après nature : l'approche des pastellistes depuis Robert Nanteuil," in "Le pastel : regards croisés sur une technique singulière," symposium (Paris, INHA and Petit Palais, October 16–17, 2017), on the occasion of the exhibition *L'Art du pastel de Degas à Redon : catalogue des collections de pastels du Petit Palais* (Paris, Petit Palais, September 15, 2017 – April 8, 2018), [unpublished].

Bailly-Hertzberg 1979
Janine Bailly-Hertzberg, "Les estampes de Berthe Morisot," *Gazette des Beaux-Arts*, May–June 1979, p. 215–227.

Bailly-Hertzberg 1989
Janine Bailly-Hertzberg, *Correspondance de Camille Pissarro*, Paris, Éd. du Valhermeil, IV, 1989.

Bashkirtseff 1890
Marie Bashkirtseff, *Journal de Marie Bashkirtseff*, Paris, Charpentier, 1890.

Bassanville 1847
Anaïs de Bassanville, *Du perfectionnement de l'éducation des filles*, Paris, A. Desesserts, 1847.

Bataille and Wildenstein 1961
Marie-Louise Bataille and Georges Wildenstein, *Berthe Morisot, catalogue des peintures, pastels et aquarelles*, Paris, Les Beaux-Arts, 1961.

Baudot 1949
Jeanne Baudot, *Renoir, ses amis, ses modèles*, Paris, Éditions littéraires de France, 1949.

Bèhne 1885
Edgar Bèhne, *Le Nouveau Petit Poucet, conte raisonnable*, Paris, Hinrichsen et Cie, 1885.

Bertinot [n.d.]
Michel Bertinot, *Gabriel Thomas, le moine des capucins*, n.d. [unpublished].

Bertrand 2008
Pierre-Michel Bertrand, "Les gauchers ne sont pas faits pour l'écriture occidentale," *Le Figaro*, August 13, 2008, interview conducted by Claire Conruyt.

Blanche 1921
Jacques-Émile Blanche, "Les dames de la Grand Rue," in *Propos de peintre*, 2nd series, Paris, Émile-Paul frères éditeurs, 1921, p. 16–24.

Bona 2012
Dominique Bona, *Deux sœurs, Yvonne et Christine Rouart, les muses de l'impressionnisme*, Paris, Grasset, 2012.

Bougeard and Cariou, 2015
Christian Bougeard and Nathalie Cariou, "Les prisonniers de guerre de 1940–1945 en Bretagne : approches générales et exemple finistérien," in *La Captivité des prisonniers de guerre : Histoire, art et mémoire, 1939–1945. Pour une approche européenne*, Rennes, Presses universitaires de Rennes, 2015, p. 117–130.

Breuille 1992
Jean-Philippe Breuille (ed.), *L'Impressionnisme et la peinture de plein air, 1860–1914. Dictionnaire : histoire et sources, épanouissement, prolongements*, Paris, Larousse, 1992.

Bruyère 2015
Gérard Bruyère, "Postimpressionnistes en contexte : les beaux-arts à l'exposition internationale urbaine de Lyon de 1914," in *Le Postimpressionnisme et Rhône-Alpes (1886-1914) : la couleur dans la lumière*, exh. cat. (Villefranche-sur-Saône, musée Paul-Dini, October,11 2015 – February 7, 2016), edited by Sylvie Carlier and Dominique Lobstein, Villefranche-sur-Saône, Musée Paul Dini, 2015, p. 28–35.

C. E. 1881
C. E. [Charles Ephrussi], "Exposition des peintres indépendants," *Chronique des arts et de la curiosité, supplément à la Gazette des Beaux-Arts*, April 23, 1881, p. 134–135.

Cabanne 1989
Pierre Cabanne, *Monsieur Degas*, Paris, Jean-Claude Lattès, 1989.

Cabanne 2003
Pierre Cabanne, *Les Grands Collectionneurs*, I, Paris, Éditions de l'Amateur, 2003.

Cahn 2006
Isabelle Cahn, "Vollard et ses archives, entre mythe et réalité," in exh. cat. New York, Chicago, and Paris 2006–2007, p. 281–289.

Cariou 2003
André Cariou, "1889–1890, de Pont-Aven au Pouldu," in *L'Aventure de Pont-Aven et Gauguin*, exh. cat. (Paris, Musée du Luxembourg, April 2 – June 22, 2003; Quimper, Musée des Beaux-Arts, July 12 – September 30, 2003), Milan, Skira, 2003, p. 141–194.

Cennini 1858
Cennino Cennini, *Il Libro dell'arte*, in *Traité de la peinture de Cennino Cennini mis en lumière pour la première fois avec des notes par le Chevalier G. Tambroni, traduit par Victor Mottez*, Paris, Vve Jules Renouard, 1858.

Cézan 1963
Claude Cézan, *Gabriel Thomas. Souvenirs et témoignages*, 1963, unpaginated.

Chavence 1920
René Chavence, "Atelier d'art sacré," *Art et décoration*, November 1920, p. 3.

CMR 1997
Alain Clairet, Delphine Montalant, and Yves Rouart, *Berthe Morisot, 1841–1895* : catalogue *raisonné de l'œuvre peint*, Montolivet, CÉRA-nrs éd., 1997.

Collet 2008
Isabelle Collet, "L'histoire de l'art français, iconographie du décor de Maurice Denis au Petit Palais," *Les Cahiers d'histoire de l'art*, no. 6, 2008, p. 16–25.

Coppens 2014
Thera Coppens, *Suzanne en Edouard Manet: De liefde van een Hollandse pianiste en een Parijse schilder*, Amsterdam, Meulenhoff, 2014.

Cosnier 2001
Colette Cosnier, *Le Silence des filles. De l'aiguille à la plume*, Paris, Fayard, 2001.

Coutin 2012
Cécile Coutin, *Tromper l'ennemi. L'invention du camouflage moderne en 1914–1918*, Paris, Éditions Pierre de Taillac, 2012.

D'Acq 1881
Louise d'Acq, *Le nouveau savoir-vivre universel dans toutes les circonstances de la vie*, Paris, Bureaux des Conseils familiers, 1881.

Dauberville 2010
Guy-Patrice Dauberville, *Renoir. Catalogue raisonné des tableaux, pastels, dessins et aquarelles. III. 1895–1902*, Paris, Éditions Bernheim-Jeune, 2010.

Delacroix 1893–95
Journal de Eugène Delacroix, précédé d'une étude sur le maître par M. Paul Flat, 3 vols., Paris, Plon-Nourrit, 1893–95.

Denis 1922
Maurice Denis, *Nouvelles théories sur l'art moderne, sur l'art sacré. 1914–1921*, Paris, L. Rouart et J. Watelin éditeurs, 1922.

Desmoulins 1995
Lucile Desmoulins. Journal : 1788–1793, Paris, Éditions des Cendres, 1995.

Desnoyers 1863
Fernand Desnoyers, *La Peinture en 1863 : Salon des Refusés*, Paris, A. Dutil, 1863.

Distel 1990
Anne Distel, "Il y a cent ans, ils ont donné l'*Olympia*," *Quarante-huit / Quatorze*, 1990–4, p. 44–50.

Dormoy 1932
Marie Dormoy, "La collection d'Ernest Rouart," *Formes, revue internationale des arts plastiques*, no. 24, April 1932, p. 257–259.

Du Camp 1867
Maxime Du Camp, *Les Forces perdues*, Paris, Michel Lévy frères, libraires éditeurs, 1867.

Fantin-Latour 1911
Catalogue de l'œuvre complet de Fantin Latour (1849–1904), Paris, Henri Floury éditeur, 1911.

Fargue 1942
Léon-Paul Fargue, "Grand bourgeois, grand artiste," *Aujourd'hui*, Tuesday July 7, 1942, p. 1–2.

Fargue 1946
Léon-Paul Fargue, *Rue de Villejust*, Paris, chez Jacques Haumont, 1946.

Fargue, 1946a
Léon-Paul Fargue, "Ernest Rouart," in Fargue, 1946, p. 55-59.

Fargue 2014
Léon-Paul Fargue, "Ernest Rouart sous la férule de Degas," in exh. cat. Nancy and Yerres 2014–15, p. 69–71.

Fourreau 1925
Armand Fourreau, *Berthe Morisot*, Paris, F. Rieder et Cie, 1925.

Geffroy 1896
Gustave Geffroy, "Berthe Morisot", *Le Journal*, no. 1256, March 6, 1896, p. 1.

Gobillard 2021
Jeannie Gobillard, *Journal*, Paris, Éditions des Cendres and Musée Marmottan Monet, 2021.

Halévy 1960
Daniel Halévy, *Degas parle...*, Paris and Geneva, La Palatine, 1960.

Haziot 2012
David Haziot, *Le Roman des Rouart 1850–2000*, Paris, Fayard, 2012.

Jamot 1924
Paul Jamot, "Degas, peintre d'assiettes," *Gazette des Beaux-Arts*, 1st semester 1924, p. 295–300.

Janvier 1936
R. P. Janvier OP, *La Fraternité du S. Sacrement de Paris 1910–1935*, Paris, Labergerie, 1936.

Kang, 2018
Cindy Kang, "Morisot sur le seuil," in cat. exh. Quebec, Philadelphia, Dallas, and Paris 2018–2019, p. 201–212.

Lacordaire 1919
Henri-Dominique Lacordaire, *Vie de saint Dominique*, introduction by Marie-Albert Janvier, 2 vols., Paris, Jacques Beltrand, 1919.

Lacoue-Labarthe 2011
Isabelle Lacoue-Labarthe, "Lettres et journaux de femmes. Entre écriture contrainte et affirmation de soi," *Tumultes*, no. 36, 2011, p. 113–132.

Lafenestre [1885]
Georges Lafenestre, *La Peinture italienne. I. Depuis les origines jusqu'à la fin du xve siècle*, Paris, A. Quantin [1885].

Laroche-Gisserot 1988
Florence Laroche-Gisserot, "Pratiques de la dot en France au xixe siècle," *Annales. Économies, sociétés, civilisations*, 43rd year, no. 6, 1988, p. 1433–1452.

Lejeune 1984
Philippe Lejeune, "'La cote Ln 27.' Pour un répertoire des autobiographies écrites en France au xixe siècle," *Études littéraires*, vol. 17, no. 2, autumn 1984, p. 213–237.

Lejeune 1993
Philippe Lejeune, *Le moi des demoiselles: enquête sur le journal de jeune fille*, Paris, Seuil, 1993.

Lemoisne 1947–49
Paul-André Lemoisne, *Degas et son œuvre*, 4 vols., Paris, Arts et Métiers graphiques, 1947–49.

Lesko 1994
Diane Lesko (ed.), *Catalogue of the Collection. Museum of Fine Arts, St. Petersburg, Florida*, St. Petersburg, Museum of Fine Arts, 1994.

Lévy 1984
Marie-Françoise Lévy, *De mères en filles. L'éducation des Françaises 1850–1880*, Paris, Calmann-Lévy, 1984.

Lobstein 2003
Dominique Lobstein, *Dictionnaire des Indépendants 1884–1914*, Dijon, L'Échelle de Jacob, II, 2003.

Louis 1917
Le Tiers-Ordre de saint Dominique par le R.P. Raymond Louis, Paris, L'Art catholique, 6 place Saint-Sulpice, 1917.

Loyrette 1991
Henri Loyrette, *Degas*, Paris, Fayard, 1991.

Mallarmé 1876
Stéphane Mallarmé, *L'après-midi d'un Faune, églogue*, Paris, Alphonse Derenne, 1876.

Mallarmé 1886
Stéphane Mallarmé, "Notes sur le théâtre : Hamlet ; Pierrot assassin de sa femme," *La Revue indépendante : politique, littéraire et artistique*, November 1886, p. 37ff.

Mallarmé 2019
Stéphane Mallarmé, correspondance 1854–1898, annotated by Bertrand Marchal, edited by Jean-Yves Tadié, Paris, Gallimard, 2019.

Manet 1979
Julie Manet, *Journal (1893–1899). Sa jeunesse parmi les peintres impressionnistes et les hommes de lettres*, Paris, C. Klincksieck, 1979.

Manet 1987
Julie Manet, *Journal (1893–1899)*, introduction by Rosalind de Boland Roberts and Jane Roberts, Paris, Scala, 1987.

Manet 2013
Julie Manet, *Journal 1893–1899. Dans l'intimité des peintres impressionnistes et des hommes de lettres de la Belle Époque*, preface by Pascale Filoche, Paris, A. Baudry and Cie, 2013.

Manet 2017
Julie Manet, *Journal (1893–1899)*, Paris, Mercure de France, 2017.

Manet 2017a
Julie Manet, *Growing up with the Impressionists: the Diary of Julie Manet*, trans. by Jane Roberts, London, I. B. Tauris & Co. Ltd, 2017.

Mathieu 2017
Marianne Mathieu, "Berthe Morisot dans la collection Monet," in exh. cat. Paris 2017–18, p. 132–149.

Mathieu 2019
Marianne Mathieu, "Une artiste en devenir," in *Berthe Morisot*, Paris, Musée d'Orsay and Flammarion, 2019, p. 163–176.

Montalant 1986
Delphine Montalant, in *L'Œil*, September 1986, p. 52–57.

Nivet and Michel 1990
Jean-François Nivet and Pierre Michel, *Octave Mirbeau, l'imprécateur au cœur fidèle*, Paris, Librairie Séguier, 1990.

Nonnis Vigilante 2005
Serenella Nonnis Vigilante, "Le corps en deuil : la mise en scène de la mémoire dans les traités de savoir-vivre. France-Italie, xixe et xxe siècles," in *Les Narrations de la mort*, Aix-en-Provence, Presses universitaires de Provence, 2005, p. 231–240.

Oudry 1749
Jean-Baptiste Oudry, in Jacqueline Lichtenstein and Christian Michel (eds.), *Conférences de l'Académie royale de Peinture et de Sculpture. V. 1747–1751*, Paris, École Nationale Supérieure des Beaux-Arts, 2012, p. 319–340.

Papon 2002
Claire Papon, "Arrêt sur image : Paule Gobillard," *La Gazette de l'hôtel Drouot*, December 13, 2002.

Peeters 2016
Benoît Peeters, *Paul Valéry, une vie*, Paris, Flammarion (Champs Biographie), 2016.

Pelletan 1872
Camille Pelletan, "Le Salon," *Le Rappel*, July 2, 1872, p. 2.

Pouly 2012
Marie-Pierre Pouly, "La différenciation sociale de l'apprentissage de la langue anglaise en France au xixe siècle," *Histoire de l'éducation*, no. 133, 2012, p. 5–41.

Proust 1954
Marcel Proust, *À la recherche du temps perdu. Le côté de Guermantes II* (1906–1920), Paris, Gallimard (Bibliothèque de la Pléiade), II, 1954.

Reff 1964
Theodore Reff, "Copyists in the Louvre, 1850–1870," *The Art Bulletin*, vol. 46, no. 4, December 1964, p. 552–559.

Roger-Marx 1933
Claude Roger-Marx, *Renoir*, Paris, Librairie Floury, 1933.

Rouart 1908
Louis Rouart, "Berthe Morisot (Mme Eugène Manet) 1841–1895," *Art et Décoration*, 1908, p. 166–182.

Rouart 1937
Ernest Rouart, "Le marchand de couleurs," *Le Soir*, March 4, 1937.

Rouart 1941
Louis Rouart, *Berthe Morisot*, Paris, Plon, 1941.

Rouart 1950
Denis Rouart, *Correspondance de Berthe Morisot avec sa famille et ses amis, Manet, Puvis de Chavannes, Degas, Monet, Renoir et Mallarmé*, Paris, Quatre Chemins-Éditart, 1950.

Rouart 1956
Louis Rouart, *Ernest Rouart 1874–1942*, Paris, Rouart Éditeur, 1956.

Rouart 2000
Jean-Marie Rouart, *Une jeunesse à l'ombre de la lumière*, Paris, Gallimard, 2000.

Rouart 2012
Martine Rouart, *La Cuisinière de Mallarmé*, Paris, Michel de Maule, 2012.

Rouart and Wildenstein, 1975
Denis Rouart and Daniel Wildenstein, *Édouard Manet : catalogue raisonné*, 2 vols., Paris and Lausanne, Bibliothèque des Arts, 1975.

Salon d'automne 1946
Salon d'automne. Catalogue : peinture, sculpture, dessin..., October 4–November 10, 1946, Musée des Beaux-Arts de la Ville de Paris, Paris, Société du Salon d'Automne, 1946.

Serry 2004
Hervé Serry, *Naissance de l'intellectuel catholique*, Paris, La Découverte, 2004.

Signorile 2015
Patricia Signorile, *Paul Valéry, regards sur la guerre. La Grande Guerre des écrivains*, edited by Romain Vignest and Jean-Nicolas Corvisier, Paris, Classiques Garnier, 2015.

Simonet-Tenant 2018
Françoise Simonet-Tenant (ed.), *Dictionnaire de l'autobiographie. Écritures de soi de langue française*, Paris, Honoré Champion, 2018.

Société Nationale des Beaux-Arts [1896–1900] 2001
Gaïté Dugnat, *Catalogues des salons de la Société nationale des Beaux-Arts : 1896-1900*, preface de Dominique Lobstein, Dijon, L'Échelle de Jacob, 2001.

Société Nationale des Beaux-Arts 1897
Catalogue des ouvrages de Peinture, Sculpture Dessins, Gravure Architecture et Objets d'Art exposés au Champ-de-Mars Le 24 Avril 1897, Évreux, Ch. Hérissey éditeur, 1897.

Tabarant 1947
Adolphe Tabarant, *Manet et ses œuvres*, Paris, Gallimard, 1947.

Valéry 1936
Paul Valéry, "Souvenirs de M. Ernest Rouart," in *Id., Degas, Danse, Dessin*, Paris, A. Vollard, 1936, p. 219–239.

Valéry [1936] 1965
Paul Valéry, "Souvenirs de Monsieur Ernest Rouart," in *Id., Degas, Danse, Dessin* (1936), Paris, Gallimard, 1965, p. 219–239.

Valéry 1938
Paul Valéry, *Degas, Danse, Dessin*, Paris, Gallimard, 1938.

Valéry 1942
Paul Valéry, "In memoriam Ernest Rouart," *Le Figaro*, July 7, 1942, p. 4.

Viallefond 1955
Geneviève Viallefond, *Le Peintre Léon Riesener, 1808–1878. Sa vie, son œuvre avec des extraits d'un manuscrit inédit de l'artiste, de David à Berthe Morisot*, Paris, éd. Albert Morancé, 1955.

White 1985
Barbara Ehrlich White, *Renoir*, Paris, Flammarion, 1985.

Wildenstein 1979
Daniel Wildenstein, with the collaboration of Rodolphe Walter, France Daguet, Madeleine Manigler, and Michèle Paret, *Claude Monet. 2. 1882–1886 : peintures*, Lausanne and Paris, Bibliothèque des Arts, 1979.

Wojciechowski 2019
Amalia Wojciechowski, "Chronologie," in *Berthe Morisot*, Paris, Musée d'Orsay and Flammarion, 2019, p. 234–248.

EXHIBITIONS

Lille and Martigny 2002
Berthe Morisot 1841–1895 (Lille, Palais des Beaux-Arts, March 10 – June 9, 2002; Martigny, Fondation Pierre Gianadda, June 20 – November 19, 2002). Exh. cat. edited by Sylvie Patry, Hugues Wilhelm, and Sylvie Patin, Paris, Réunion des Musées Nationaux, 2002.

Lodève 2006
Berthe Morisot : regards pluriels (Lodève, Musée de Lodève, June 17 – October 29, 2006). Exh. cat., Milan, Mazzotta, 2006.

Nancy and Yerres 2014–15
Les Rouart. De l'impressionnisme au réalisme magique (Nancy, Musée des Beaux-Arts, November 7, 2014 – February 23, 2015; Yerres, propriété Caillebotte, Centre d'Art et d'Exposition de la Ferme Ornée, March 28 – July 5, 2015). Exh. cat. edited by Dominique Bona, Paris, Gallimard, 2014.

New York 1989
The Julian Academy Paris, 1868–1939, spring exhibition (New York, Shepherd Gallery, 1989). Exh. cat. by Catherine Fehrer, New York, Shepherd Gallery, 1989.

New York, 1997–98
The Private Collection of Edgar Degas (New York, Metropolitan Museum of Art, octobre 1, 1997 – January 11, 1998). New York, The Metropolitan Museum of Art, 1997.

New York, Chicago, and Paris 2006–07
Cézanne to Picasso, Ambroise Vollard Patron of the Avant-Garde (New York, The Metropolitan Museum of Art, September 13, 2006 – January 7, 2007; Chicago, The Art Institute of Chicago, February 17 – May 12, 2007; Paris, Musée d'Orsay, June 19 – September 16, 2007). Exh. cat. by Maryline Assante di Panzillo et al., New York, The Metropolitan Museum of Art and New Haven, Yale University Press, 2006.

Paris 1882
Septième exposition des Artistes indépendants (Paris, Salle des Panoramas, 251 rue Saint-Honoré, March 1 – 31, 1882). 1882.

Paris 1931
Degas : portraitiste, sculpteur (Paris, Musée de l'Orangerie, 1931). Exh. cat., Paris, Musées Nationaux, 1931.

Paris 1941
Berthe Morisot (1841–1895) (Paris, Musée de l'Orangerie, summer 1941). Exh. cat., preface by Paul Valéry, Paris, impr. d'Aulard, 1941.

Paris 1942
Exposition rétrospective des œuvres d'Ernest Rouart (Paris, galerie Berri-Raspail, June 20 – July 9, 1942). Cat. with a foreword by Paul Valéry, "In memoriam Ernest Rouart," Paris, [s. n.], 1942.

Paris 1951
Henri Rouart (1833–1912) Ernest Rouart (1874–1942) (Paris, Galerie Durand-Ruel, April 17 – May 5, 1951). Exh. cat., Paris, Galerie Durand-Ruel, 1951.

Paris 1956
Paul Valéry (Paris, Bibliothèque Nationale, January 31 – March 31, 1956). Exh. cat. by Marcel Thomas, Paris, Bibliothèque Nationale, 1956.

Paris 1999
Edgar Degas photographe (Paris, Bibliothèque Nationale de France, Galerie Mansart, May 27 – August 22, 1999). Exh. cat. by Malcolm Daniel, Eugenia Parry, and Theodore Reff, with the collaboration of Sylvie Aubenas, Paris, Bibliothèque Nationale de France, 1999.

Paris 2004
Au cœur de l'impressionnisme, la famille Rouart (Paris, Musée de la Vie Romantique, February 3 – June 13, 2004). Exh. cat., Paris, Paris Musées, 2004.

Paris 2017–18
Monet collectionneur (Paris, Musée Marmottan Monet, September 14, 2017 – January 14, 2018). Exh. cat. by Marianne Mathieu and Dominique Lobstein, Vanves, Hazan, and Paris, Musée Marmottan Monet, 2017.

Pontoise 2002
Victor Vignon, 1847–1909 (Pontoise, Musée Tavet-Delacour, May 25 – September 15, 2002). Exh. cat., Pontoise, Ville de Pontoise, 2002.

Quebec, Philadelphia, Dallas, and Paris 2018–19
Berthe Morisot, Woman Impressionist/Berthe Morisot, femme impressionniste (Québec, Musée National des Beaux-Arts du Québec, June 21 – September 16, 2018; Philadelphia, Barnes Foundation, October 20, 2018 – January 14, 2019; Dallas, Dallas Museum of Art, February 24 – May 26, 2019; Paris, Musée d'Orsay, June 17 – September 22, 2019). Exh. cat. edited by Sylvie Patry, New York, Rizzoli Electa and Philadelphia, Barnes Foundation, 2018.

Washington, D.C., and San Francisco 1986
The New Painting, Impressionism, 1874–1886 (Washington, D.C., National Gallery of Art, January 17 – April 6, 1986; San Francisco, The Fine Arts Museums of San Francisco, M. H. de Young Memorial Museum, April 19 – July 6, 1986). Exh. cat. by Charles S. Moffett, Ruth Berson, and Barbara Lee Williams, San Francisco, Fine Arts Museum, 1986.

WEBSITES

Guide Labreuche
Le Guide des fournisseurs de matériel pour artistes, France, XVIIIe–XXe siècles
[http://www.guide-labreuche.com]

Musée d'Orsay, catalogues of the Salons
[http://salons.musee-orsay.fr/]

Schulman
Michel Schulman, *Edgar Degas, 1834–1917. Le catalgue raisonné numérique*
[http://www.degas-catalogue.com/fr/]

PRINCIPAL ARCHIVES CONSULTED

BULLOT MARIE JOSÉPHINE
(Montrouge, September 28, 1849 — Nice, March 5, 1904)

Marriage certificate, married name Hippolyte Henri Gamby, April 25, 1865, Clichy-sur-Seine (Archives Départementales des Hauts-de-Seine, ref. E_NUM_CLI193)
Marriage certificate, Paris 6th, October 4, 1887, married name Charles Marie Tiburce Morisot (Archives de Paris, ref. V4E 5914)
Death certificate (Archives Départementales des Alpes-Maritimes, Nice, register of deaths, 1904, deed no. 572)

DE JOUY JULES
(Gennevilliers, March 7, 1815 — Paris 1st, March 9, 1894)

Birth certificate (Archives Départementales des Hauts-de-Seine, ref. E_NUM_GEN49)
Marriage certificate, April 27, 1847 (Archives Nationales (Soubise), Central Minute Book of Parisian Notaries, ref. MC/ET/LXXIX/1017)
Death certificate (Archives de Paris, ref. V4E 8032)
Will and codicil, registered March 9, 1894 with Me Émile Pinguet, notary in Paris, 18, rue des Pyramides (Archives Nationales (Soubise), Central Minute Book of Parisian Notaries, ref. MC/ET/LXXIX/1017)
Post-mortem inventory, March 24, April 10, 11, and 12, 1894 (Archives Nationales (Soubise), Central Minute Book of Parisian Notaries, ref. MC/ET/LXXIX/1017)
Declarations of succession (1st office, July 5, 1894, Archives de Paris, ref. DQ7 10956 / 1st office, September 10, 1894, Archives de Paris, ref. DQ7 10957)

FANFILLON MARIE EUGÉNIE MATHILDE
(Maintenon, March 8, 1852 — Sarcelles, August 11, 1917)

Birth certificate (Archives Départementales de l'Eure-et-Loir, ref. 3 E 227/019)
Marriage certificate
(Archives de Paris, ref. V4E 8627)
Table of deaths (Archives Départementales du Val-d'Oise, ref. 4 E 1262)
Death certificate
(town of Sarcelles, no. 000067/1917)

FOURNIER MARRIED NAME MANET EUGÉNIE
(formerly Paris 10th (today 7th), February 11, 1811 — Paris 16th, January 8, 1885)

Table of births (Archives de Paris, Reconstituted civil records, ref. V3E/N 918)
Death certificate (Archives de Paris, ref. V4E 7322)
Declaration of succession
(Archives de Paris, ref. DQ7 12 697)
Handwritten will, dated February 12, 1871 and registered January 8, 1885 (Archives Nationales (Soubise), ref. MC/ET/XCIV/1635)

GAMBY ALICE MARGUERITE
(Brussels, April 4, 1874 — date and place of death unknown)

Birth certificate (Archives of the city of Brussels)
Registered deed of transfer (*hypothèques*), September 4, 1909, foreclosure sale of the Villa l'Hermitage (Archives Départementales de Nice)

GAMBY HIPPOLYTE HENRI
(Paris 12th, December 15, 1841 —)

Marriage certificate, married name Marie Joséphine Bullot, April 25, 1865, Clichy-sur-Seine (Archives Départementales des Hauts-de-Seine, ref. E_NUM_CLI193)

GOBILLARD MARRIED NAME VALÉRY JEANNIE
(Paris 16th, January 16, 1877 — Paris 16th, July 7, 1970)

Birth certificate (Archives de Paris, ref. V4E 4676)
Marriage contract (Archives Nationales (Soubise), Central Minute Book of Parisian Notaries, ref. MC/ET/XL/812)
Marriage certificate (civil), May 29, 1900 (Archives de Paris, ref. V4E 10066)
Marriage certificate (religious)
(Archives de Paris, ref. D6J 9521)
Death certificate (Archives de Paris, ref. 16D 234)

GOBILLARD MARCEL
(Mirande, March 17, 1872 — Mexico, October 25, 1920)

Birth certificate
(Archives Départementales du Gers, ref. 5 E 18096)
Military recruitment of Seine, Recruitment register (1887–1921), No. 3341, class 1892 (Archives de Paris, ref. D4R1 697)

GOBILLARD PAULE
(Quimperlé, December 3, 1867 — Paris 16th, February 27, 1946)

Birth certificate
(Archives of Finistère, ref. 1 MI EC 289/7)
Death certificate (Archives de Paris, ref. 16D 176)
Annual list of burials, Père-Lachaise cemetery. Division 31, line 1/32, no. 22/36. Plot 826, year 1827 (Archives de Paris, ref. CPL_RA19461950_01)
Daily register of burials, Père-Lachaise cemetery (Archives de Paris, ref. CPL_RJ19441946_01)

GOBILLARD THÉODORE
(Quimper, June 4, 1833 — Saint-Maurice, January 6, 1883)

Ten-year tables, births (Archives Départementales du Finistère, ref. 5 E 240/2/4)
Medical records of Théodore Gobillard
Public hospital of Ville-Évrard (24/06/1876–24/10/1876) ref. 205R143
Maison de Charenton, Hôpital Esquirol, Saint-Maurice.
Register of male patients by date of admission, 1874–85 (Archives Départementales du Val-de-Marne, ref. 4X 524)
Death certificate (Archives Départementales du Val-de-Marne, ref. 1MI 2484)

KOËLLA LÉON ÉDOUARD
(Paris 6th, January 29, 1852 — Bizy (Eure), September 3, 1927)

Table of births (Archives de Paris, Reconstituted civil records, ref. V3E/N 1248)
Birth certificate (Archives de Paris, Reconstituted civil records, ref. 5Mi1 734)
Death certificate (Archives Départementales de l'Eure, ref. D (1927) (2 E 8791))

LEENHOFF MARRIED NAME MANET SUZANNE
(Delft, October 30, 1829 — Paris 7th, March 8, 1906)

Birth certificate
(Dutch, Stadsarchief DELFT, no. 478/1829)
Marriage certificate transcribed in Paris 9th on 12/08/1863
(Archives de Paris, ref. V4E 996) / Wedding in Zaltbommel (Netherlands), October 28, 1863
Death certificate (Archives de Paris, ref. 7D 127)
Declaration of succession
(Archives de Paris, ref. DQ7 30792)
Will, registered March 9, 1906 with Me Cotelle, notary in Paris (Archives Nationales (Soubise), Central Minute Book of Parisian Notaries, ref. MC/ET/LXXXIX/2142)

MALLARMÉ GENEVIÈVE
(Tournon-sur-Rhône, November 19, 1864 — Paris 17th, May 26, 1919)

Birth certificate (Archives Départementales de l'Ardèche, ref. NC-17064)
Marriage certificate June 19, 1901, with Paul Charles BONNIOT
(Archives de Paris, ref. V4E 10242)
Death certificate (Archives de Paris, ref. 17D 209)

MALLARMÉ STÉPHANE
(formerly Paris 2nd, now 8th), March 18, 1842 — Valvins, September 9, 1898)
Table of births (Archives de Paris, Reconstituted civil records, ref. V3E/N 1514)
Death certificate (Archives Départementales du Seine-et-Marne, ref. 6E561/6)
Declaration of succession
(Archives de Paris, ref. DQ7 12014)

MANET AUGUSTE
(Paris 3rd, August 30, 1796 — Paris 9th, September 25, 1862)

Death certificate (Archives de Paris, ref. V4E 986)

MANET ÉDOUARD
(Paris 8th, January 23, 1832 — Paris 8th, April 30, 1883)

Birth certificate (Fonds Andriveau)
Death certificate (Archives de Paris, ref. V4E 6133)
Declaration of succession, April 30, 1883 (Archives de Paris, ref. DQ7 12150)
Post-mortem inventory (Archives Nationales, ref. MC/RS//885)
Minutes of the posthumous sale (Archives de Paris, ref. D48E3C72)

MANET EUGÈNE
(Paris 6th or 11th former, November 21, 1833 — Paris 16th, April 13, 1892)

Birth certificate (Andriveau archives)
Marriage contract, December 21, 1874 (Archives Nationales (Soubise), ref. MC/ET/XL/487)
Marriage certificate, December 22, 1874 (Archives de Paris, ref. V4E 4661)
Death certificate (Archives de Paris, ref. V4E 7336)
Declaration of succession, October 12, 1892 (Archives de Paris, ref. DQ7 12762)
Post-mortem inventory (Archives Nationales (Soubise), Central Minute Book of Parisian Notaries, ref. MC/ET/XXX/1263)

MANET GUSTAVE
(Paris 10th, March 16, 1835 — Menton, December 18, 1884)

Birth certificate (Andriveau archives)
Death certificate (Civil records of the town of Menton, 1884)
Declaration of succession, December 18, 1884 (Archives de Paris, ref. DQ7 12455)

MANET MARRIED NAME ROUART JULIE
(Paris 16th, November 14, 1878–Paris 16th, November 21, 1966)

Birth certificate (Archives de Paris, ref. V4E 4682)
Baptism certificate, February 8, 1879, parish of Sainte-Madeleine (Archives de Paris, Registers of Catholicity of the Archbishopric of Paris, ref. D6J 4284)
Marriage contract, May 25, 1900, with Me Albert Morel d'Arleux (Archives Nationales (Soubise), ref. MC/ET/CI1741)
Marriage certificate, May 29, 1900 (Archives de Paris, ref. V4E 10066)
Religious marriage, May 31, 1900, parish of Saint-Honoré (Archives de Paris, ref. D6J 9521)
Death certificate (Archives de Paris, ref. 16D 223)
Deed of succession, December 20 and 21, 1966 (Archives of the SCP Le Gonidec de Kerhalic, Koenig, Gaudry, Cheval et Bonnet, 20, rue de la Paix, 75002 Paris)

MORISOT MARRIED NAME MANET BERTHE
(Bourges, January 14 , 1841 — Paris 16th, March 2, 1895)

Birth certificate (Archives Départementales du Cher, ref. 3E2538)
Marriage contract, December 21, 1874 (Archives Nationales (Soubise), ref. MC/ET/XL/487)
Marriage certificate, December 22, 1874 (Archives de Paris, ref. V4E 4661)
Death certificate (Archives de Paris, ref. V4E 10016)
Declaration of succession (Archives de Paris, ref. DQ7 12 791)
Will registered March 15, 1895 with Me Fermé, notary in Suresnes (Archives Départementales des Hauts-de-Seine, ref. 3E/SUR_661)
Post-mortem inventory, March 13, 1895 (Archives Nationales (Soubise), Central Minute Book of Parisian Notaries, ref. MC/ET/XXX/1293)

MORISOT CHARLES MARIE TIBURCE
(Limoges, December 11, 1845 – Aspremont, June 13, 1927)

Birth certificate (Archives Départementales de la Haute-Vienne, ref. 3 E 85 / 180)
Marriage certificate, Paris 6th, October 4, 1887, married name Marie Joséphine Bullot (Montrouge, 09/28/1849–Nice, 03/05/1904) (Archives de Paris ref. V4E 5914)
Death certificate (Archives Départementales des Alpes-Maritimes, ref. 02 E 0461)

MORISOT MARRIED NAME PONTILLON EDMA
(Valenciennes, December 13, 1839 — Paris 16th, May 2, 1921)

Birth certificate (Archives Départementales du Nord ref. D [1838], NMD [1839] (1838–1839))
Marriage certificate, March 8, 1869 (Archives de Paris, ref. V4E 1966)
Death certificate (Archives de Paris, ref. 16D 121)

MORISOT EDME TIBURCE
(Paris 3rd, March 11, 1806 — Paris 16th, January 24, 1874)

Table of births (Archives de Paris, Reconstituted civil records, births, ref. V3E/N 1664)
Birth certificate (Archives de Paris, reconstituted civil records, ref. 5Mi1 134)
Marriage certificate, April 6, 1836 in Paris 1st (Archives de Paris, Reconstituted civil records, ref. 5Mi1 2088)
Death certificate (Archives de Paris, ref. V4E 4662)
Daily register of burials, Père-Lachaise cemetery. "Vault 17, alongside Chemin Labédoyère, 60th right of Hernos, beside Bassano" (Archives de Paris, ref. CPL_RJ18741874_01)
Annual list of burials, Père-Lachaise cemetery (Archives de Paris, ref. CPL_RA18701874_04)
Will, registered February 2, 1874 with Me Amy, notary in Paris (Archives Nationales (Soubise), Central Minute Book of Parisian Notaries, ref. MC/ET/XL/478)
Post-mortem inventory, February 25, 1874 (Archives Nationales (Soubise), Central Minute Book of Parisian Notaries, ref. MC/ET/XL/478)
Declaration of succession (Archives Nationales, refs DQ7 12618 and DQ7 12619)

MORISOT MARRIED NAME GOBILLARD YVES
(Valenciennes, October 4, 1838 — Marly-le-Roi, June 8, 1893)

Birth certificate (Archives Départementales du Nord, ref. NMD 1126/1341)
Marriage certificate, December 1, 1866 (Archives de Paris, ref. V4E 1948)
Death certificate (Archives Départementales des Yvelines, ref. 2MIEC245)
Annual list of burials, Père-Lachaise cemetery. Plot no. 30636 (Archives de Paris, ref. CPL_RA18901894_01)
Daily register of burials, Père-Lachaise cemetery (Archives de Paris, ref. CPL_RJ18921893_01)
Declaration of succession (no declaration was registered: table of successions and absences, Archives Départementales des Yvelines, ref. Q 2062)

PONTILLON ADOLPHE
(Paris 2nd, April 28, 1832 — Cherbourg, September 9, 1894)

Annual list of burials, Père-Lachaise cemetery. Plot no 30636 (Archives de Paris, ref. CPL_RA18901894_01)
Daily register of burials, Père-Lachaise cemetery (Archives de Paris, ref. CPL_RJ18931894_01)

PONTILLON MARRIED NAME FORGET BLANCHE
(Paris 16th, December 23, 1871 — Paris 16th, July 8, 1941)

Birth certificate, December 23, 1871, 16, rue Franklin (Archives de Paris, ref. V4E 4644)
Marriage certificate, October 17, 1908, Paris 16th (Archives de Paris, ref. 16M 161)
Death certificate, July 8, 1941, Paris 16th, 40, rue de Villejust (Archives de Paris, ref. 16D 163)

PONTILLON MARRIED NAME MARTIN JEANNE
(Paris 16th, January 17, 1870 — 1921)

Birth certificate, January 17, 1870, 16, rue Franklin (Archives de Paris, ref. V4E 1970)
Marriage certificate civil, December 3, 1896, Paris 16th, married name Adrien Paul Alexandre MARTIN (Archives de Paris, ref. V4E 10025)

ROUART ALEXIS STANISLAS
(Montcornet, September 2, 1800 — Paris 8th, February 16, 1875)

Birth certificate (Archives Départementales de l'Aisne, ref. 5Mi0460)
Death certificate (Archives de Paris, ref. V4E 3407)

ROUART ALEXIS HUBERT
(Paris 2nd, March 21, 1839 — Paris 8th, January 2, 1911)

Marriage certificate, September 4, 1865, Paris 3rd (Archives de Paris, ref. V4E 261)
Death certificate (Archives de Paris, ref. 8D 138)
Declaration of succession (Archives de Paris, ref. DQ731795)
Will (and annexes), January 2, 1911 (Office of Mes Roux and Lavigne, 3, avenue du Président Wilson, 75116 Paris)
Post-mortem inventory (and annexes), January 9, 1911 (Office of Mes Roux and Lavigne, 3, avenue du Président Wilson, 75116 Paris)
Sale of the estate, May 15, 1911 (Office Mes Roux and Lavigne, 3, avenue du Président Wilson, 75116 Paris)

Division of the estate, June 21, 1911 (Office of Ms Roux and Lavigne, 3, avenue du Président Wilson, 75116 Paris)
Declarations of succession, June 26, and July 1, 1911 (Archives de Paris, ref. DQ7 31795)
Division between Jean and Henri Rouart, son of Alexis Hubert Rouart, May 21 1912 (Office of Mes Roux and Lavigne, 3, avenue du Président Wilson, 75116 Paris)

Rouart Alexis Marie Stanislas

(Le Mée-sur-Seine, October 7, 1869 – Paris 8th, November 1, 1821)

Birth certificate (Archives Départementales de Seine-et-Marne, ref. 5MI2148)
Death certificate (Archives de Paris, ref. 8D 180)
Declaration of succession, July 21, 1923 (Archives de Paris, ref. DQ7 32000)
Post-mortem inventory
(Office of Mes Roux and Lavigne, 3, avenue du Président Wilson, 75116 Paris)
Donation between married names (Office of Mes Roux and Lavigne, 3, avenue du Président Wilson, 75116 Paris)

Rouart Ernest

(Paris 8th, August 24, 1874 – Paris 16th, February 27, 1942)

Birth certificate (Archives de Paris, ref. V4E 3392)
Baptism certificate, December 14, 1874, Paris, parish of Saint-Augustin (Archives du Mesnil, inv. 2021.1.1146)
Marriage contract, May 25, 1900, at Me Albert Morel d'Arleux
(Archives Nationales (Soubise), ref. MC/ET/CI1741)
Marriage certificate, May 29, 1900 (Archives de Paris, ref. V4E 10066)
Religious wedding, May 31, 1900, parish of Saint-Honoré (Archives de Paris, ref. D6J 9521)
Lease from Ernest Rouart to Mme Chaniot, rue de Villejust, February 19, 1906
(Office of Mes Roux and Lavigne, 3, avenue du Président Wilson, 75116 Paris)
Sale by M. and Mme Ernest Rouart to M. Ythier of a plot of land in Gennevilliers, February 19, 1906 (Office of Mes Roux and Lavigne, 3, avenue du Président Wilson, 75116 Paris)
Sale by M. and Mme Ernest Rouart to M. Veron of a plot of land in Gennevilliers, May 28, 1907 (Office of Mes Roux and Lavigne, 3, avenue du Président Wilson, 75116 Paris)
Promissory note from Mlle Vos to M. Ernest Rouart, June 2, 1910
(Office of Mes Roux and Lavigne, 3, avenue du Président Wilson, 75116 Paris)
Donation of grave of Ernest Rouart to Alexis Hubert Rouart, January 8, 1930
(Office of Mes Roux and Lavigne, 3, avenue du Président Wilson, 75116 Paris)
Death certificate (Archives de Paris, ref. 16D 165)
Burial, register of burials at Père Lachaise 1940–45
(Archives de Paris, ref. CPL_RA19401945_01)
Daily register of burials, Père-Lachaise cemetery. Tayssedre provisional vault, 4th div. Case 16 (Archives de Paris, ref. CPL_RJ19411943_01)
Will, dated December 25, 1914, registered March 12, 1942 (Office of Mes Roux and Lavigne, 3, avenue du Président Wilson, 75116 Paris)
Post-mortem inventory, March 9, 1943
(Office of Mes Roux and Lavigne, 3, avenue du Président Wilson, 75116 Paris)
Approval of Ernest Rouart's will, December 1, 1943 (Office of Mes Roux and Lavigne, 3, avenue du Président Wilson, 75116 Paris)
Liquidation-division Rouart/Manet, December 17, 1943 (Office of Mes Roux and Lavigne, 3, avenue du Président Wilson, 75116 Paris)
Declaration of succession, April 28, 1944 (Archives de Paris, ref. DQ7 34150)

Rouart Eugène

(Le Mée-sur-Seine, August 22, 1872 – Granada, July 6, 1936)

Birth certificate (Archives Départementales de Seine-et-Marne, ref. 5MI2148)
Marriage certificate, December 24, 1898 (Archives de Paris, ref. V4E 8652)

Rouart married name Marin Hélène

(Paris 9th, July 25, 1863 – Montpellier, February 27, 1929)

Birth certificate (Archives de Paris, ref. V4E 989)
Marriage certificate, May 9, 1885, Paris 8th (Archives de Paris, ref. V4E 6100)
Death certificate
(Municipal Archives of Montpellier, ref. 3E142)

Rouart Henri

(Paris 4th, October 2, 1833 – Paris 8th, January 2, 1912)

Table of births (Archives de Paris, Reconstituted civil records, ref. V3E/N 1979)
Death certificate (Archives de Paris, ref. 8D 141)
Post-mortem inventory, January 15, 1912 (Office of Mes Roux and Lavigne, 3, avenue du Président Wilson, 75116 Paris)
Division of the estate of the widow Mme Henri Rouart, April 10, 1912
(Office of Mes Roux and Lavigne, 3, avenue du Président Wilson, 75116 Paris)
Declarations of succession, April 11, 20, and 27, 1912, June 12, 1912, January 8, 1913, May 24, 1913 (Archives de Paris, refs DQ7 31810 (for the DS of April 11, 1912) / DQ7 31811 (for the DSes of April 20 and 27, 1912) / DQ7 31814 (for the DS of June 12, 1912) / DQ7 31824 (for the DS of January 8, 1913) / DQ7 31831 (for the DS of May 29, 1913))
Record of sale December 7 [1912] Requisition for the sale of paintings, drawings, and pastels from the estate of M. Henri Rouart, December 9, sale of said paintings etc.., July 8, 1913 discharge of proceeds from sale (Archives de Paris, ref. D42E3 124)

Rouart Louis

(Le Mée-sur-Seine, October 5, 1875 – Paris 7th, June 28, 1964)

Birth certificate (Archives Départementales de Seine-et-Marne, ref. 5MI2149)
Marriage certificate, February 12, 1901 (Archives de Paris, ref. V4E 8674)
Death certificate (Archives de Paris, ref. 7D 261)
Declaration of succession
(Archives de Paris, ref. DQ750151)

Thomas Gabriel

(Paris 16th, January 15, 1854 – Meudon, February 14, 1932)

Marriage certificate, July 27, 1882 at Saint-Germain-en-Laye, married name Jenny Guastalla (Archives Départementales des Yvelines, ref. 2MIEC298)
Death certificate (Archives Départementales des Hauts-de-Seine, ref. 1E_NUM_MEU_D1932)
Post-mortem inventory, begun May 3, 1932, closed July 12, 1932
(Archives de Paris, ref. MC/ET/XL1332)
Declarations of succession and referrals (Archives Départementales des Hauts-de-Seine, refs 3Q-SEV-735, 3Q-SEV-737, 3Q-SEV-740 and 3Q-SEV-765)

Thomas married name Morisot Marie-Cornélie

(Paris former 12th, October 5, 1819 – Paris 16th, December 15, 1876)

Table of births (Archives de Paris, reconstituted civil records, births, ref. V3E/N 2122)
Birth certificate (Archives de Paris, reconstituted civil records, ref. 5Mi1 209)
Marriage certificate April 6, 1836, Paris 1st (Archives de Paris, register on reconstituted civil records, ref. 5Mi1 2088)
Death certificate (Archives de Paris, ref. V4E 4675)
Annual list of burials, Père-Lachaise cemetery. Plot no 33007
(Archives de Paris, ref. CPL_RA18751879_02)
Daily register of burials, Père-Lachaise cemetery. "Vault 31st division, alongside ch. Labédoyère, right of Néruas, beside Bassano"
(Archives de Paris, ref. CPL_RJ18761877_02)
Declaration of succession, February 24, 1877 (Archives de Paris, ref. DQ712633)
Post-mortem inventory, February 19, 1877 (Archives Nationales (Soubise), Central Minute Book of Parisian Notaries, ref. MC/ET/XL/512)

Valéry Paul

(Sète, October 30, 1871 – Paris 16th, July 20, 1945)

Birth certificate (Archives Départementales de l'Hérault, ref. 5 MI 12/11)
Marriage contract(Archives Nationales (Soubise), Central Minute Book of Parisian Notaries, ref. MC/ET/XL/812)
Marriage certificate (civil), May 29, 1900 (Archives de Paris, ref. V4E 10066)
Marriage certificate (religious) (Archives de Paris, ref. D6J 9521)
Death certificate (Archives de Paris, ref. 16D 174)
Declaration of succession
(Archives de Paris, ref, DQ734214 (for the DS of January 31, 1947) and DQ734321 (for the DS of December 16, 1949)

LIST OF ABBREVIATIONS

The BS and Le Mesnil archives are private. Their content has been inventoried and is accessible to researchers at the Musée Marmottan Monet.

AMN	Archives des Musées Nationaux
AN	Archives Nationales
APDF	Archives de la Province Dominicaine de France
Arch.	Archives
Arch. dép.	Archives Départementales
b.	bottom
BnF	Bibliothèque Nationale de France
BS	private archive
BW	See Bataille and Wildenstein 1961
cm	centimeters
CMR	See CMR 1997
d.	dated
r.	right
ed.	edition
l.	left
t.	top
Ibid.	ibidem
inv.	inventory no.
L	see Lemoisne 1947–49
MC	Minutier Central des Notaires de Paris
MS	see Schulman [on line]
no	number
n.d.	not dated
n.p.	not paginated
op. cit.	in the work already cited
p.	page
repr.	reproduced
RW	see Rouart and Wildenstein 1975
s.	signed
W	see Wildenstein 1979

GUIDE TO THE FAMILLY TREES

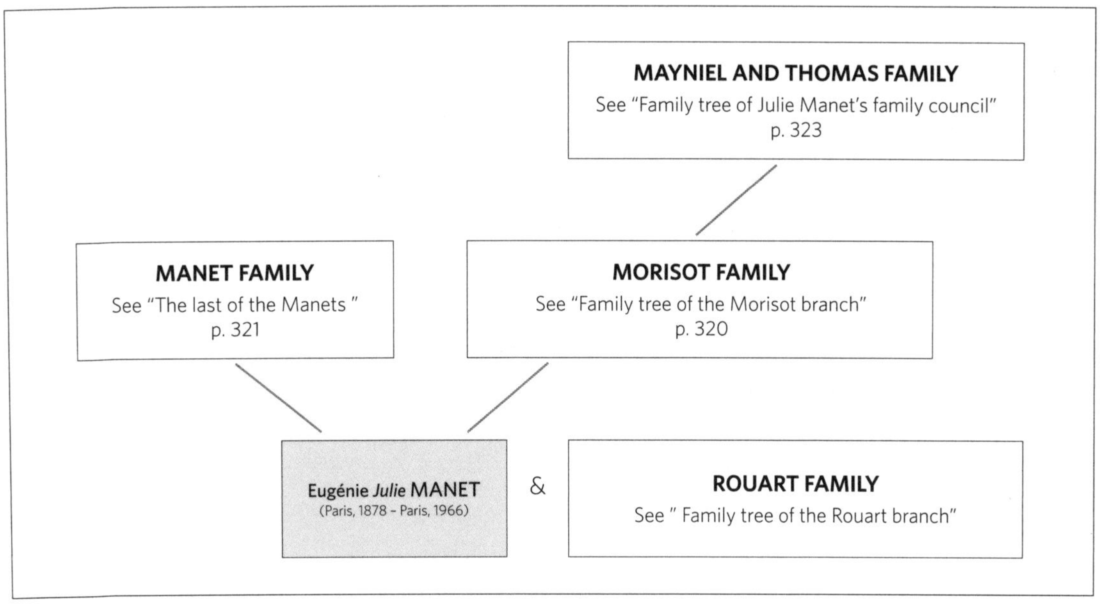

Key

&	married to
(dark grey bar)	member of Julie Manet's family council
(line)	direct relation
(wavy line)	relation via another union
DWI	died without issue
in italics	Usual first name (except when there is only one)

These family trees are based on research by Marianne Mathieu and Claire Gooden, with the invaluable help of Antoine Left and Bernard Thomas. We thank them.

FAMILY TREE OF THE MORISOT BRANCH

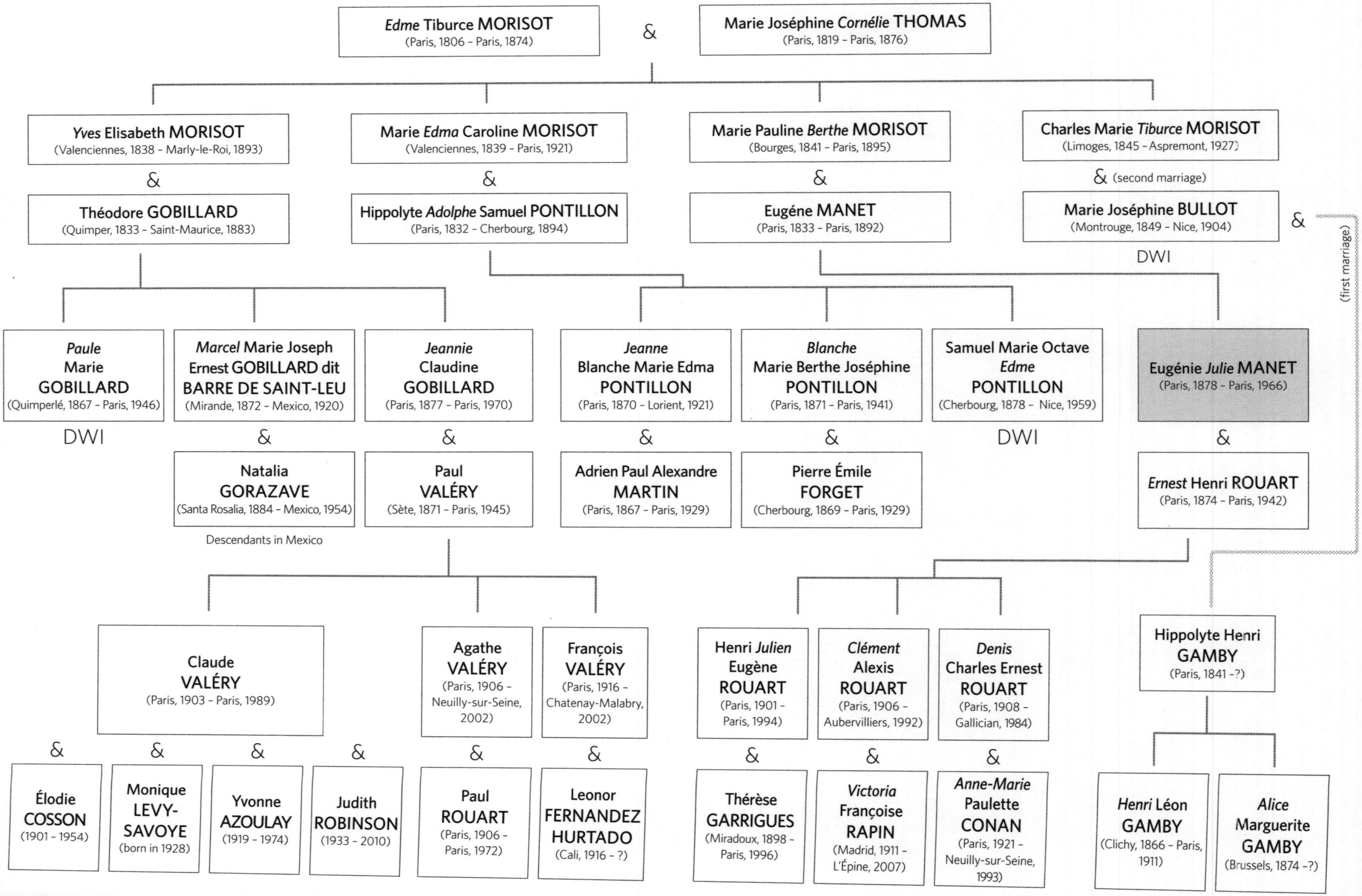

THE LAST OF THE MANETS

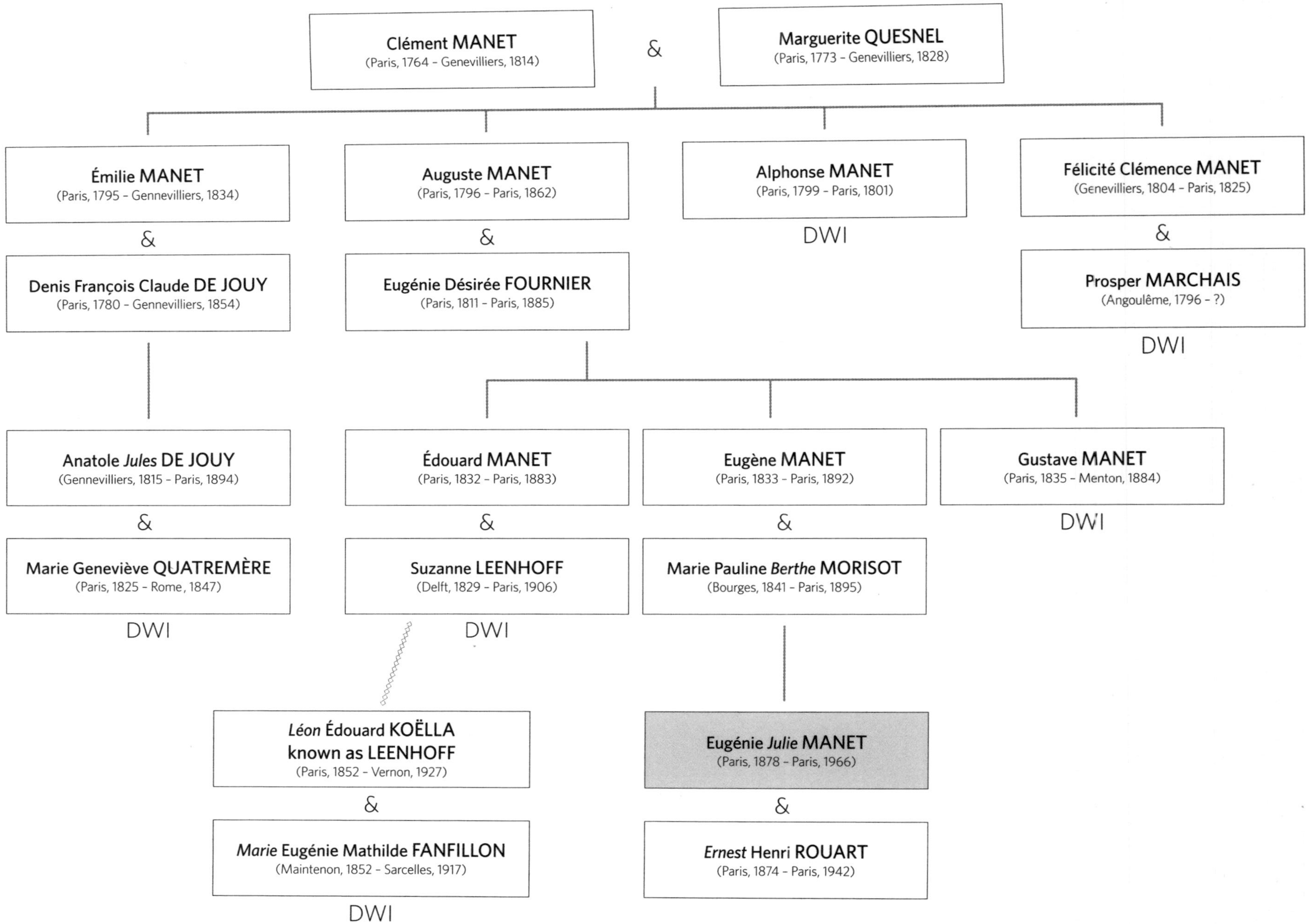

FAMILY TREE OF THE ROUART BRANCH

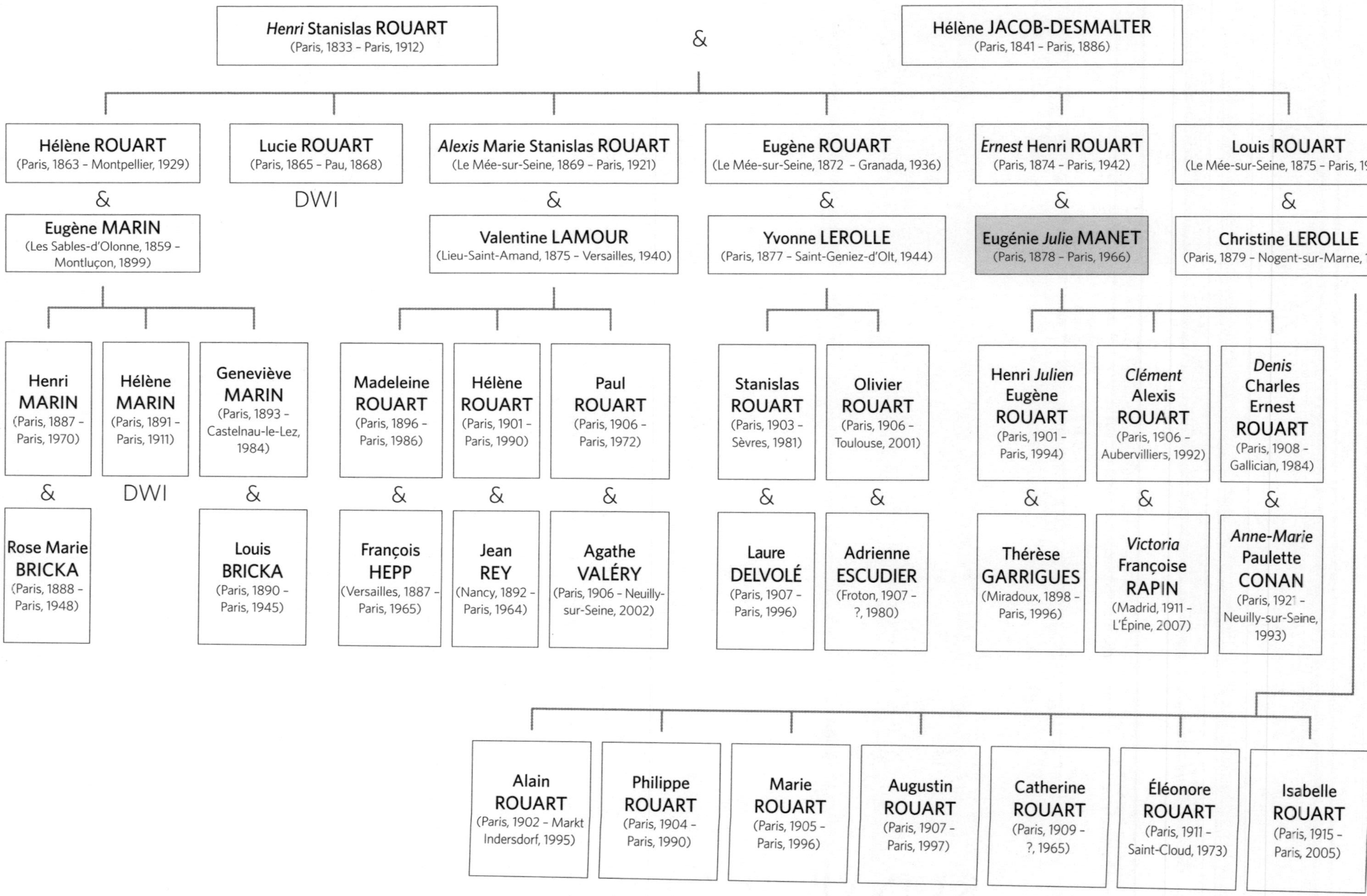

FAMILY TREE OF JULIE MANET'S FAMILY COUNCIL

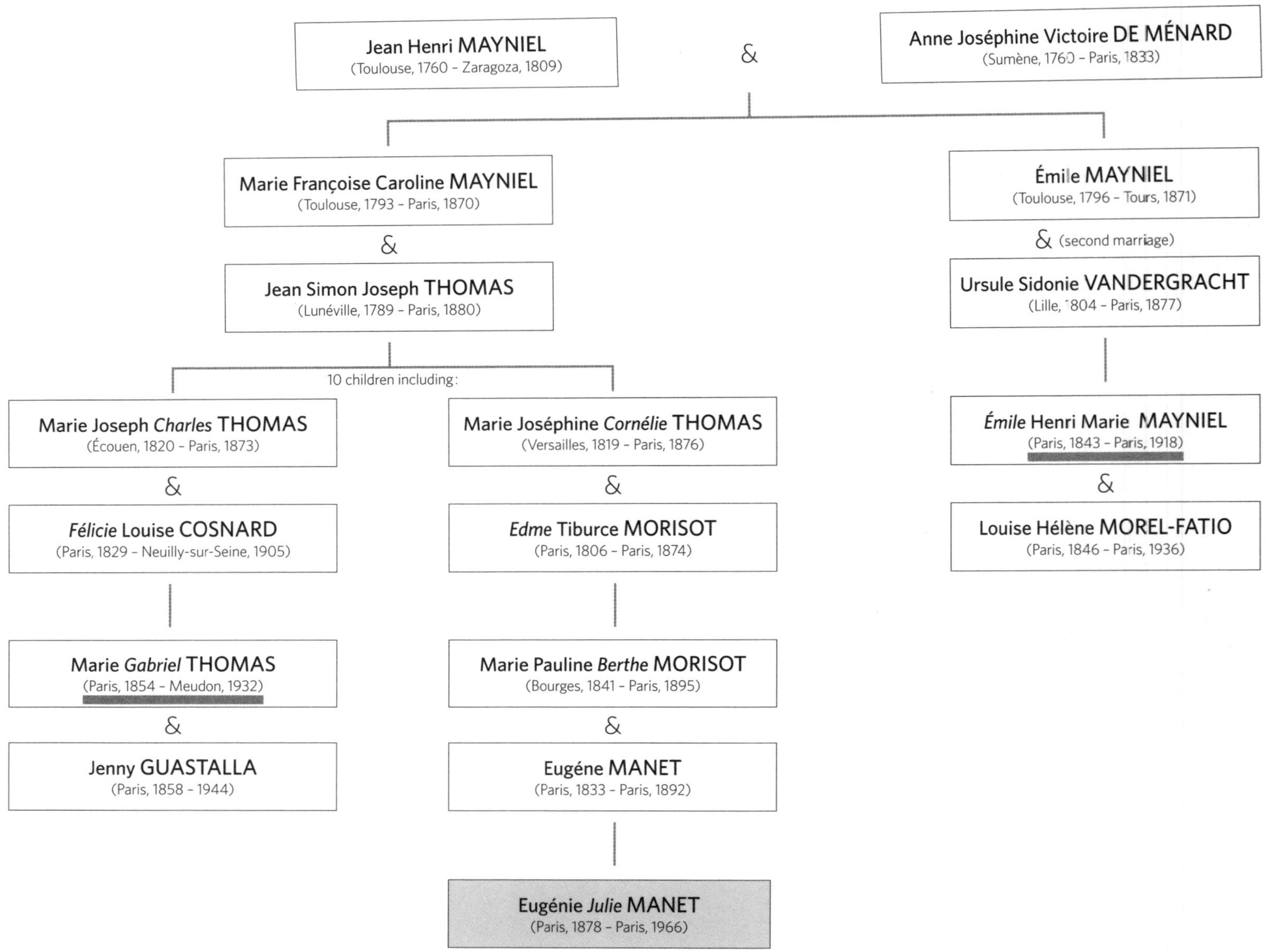

PHOTO CREDITS

akg-images: p. 243, 251

akg-images / André Held: p. 216

akg-images / De Agostini Picture Lib. / G. Dagli Orti: p. 254

akg-images / Erich Lessing: p. 192 (l), 219

akg-images / Laurent Lecat: p. 125,

Alamy Stock Photo: p. 17 (tr, br), 228, 247, 279, 301

Annecy, Musée-Château, on loan at the Musée du Louvre, inv. MNR 870: p. 288

Archives Charmet / Bridgeman Images: p. 55 (l)

Art Heritage / Alamy Stock Photo: p. 271 (l)

Artefact / Alamy Stock Photo: p. 249

Bibliothèque Nationale de France: p. 15 (tr), 16, 17 (tl, bl), 18, 23 (l), 102, 103, 104, 105, 266 (r)

Bridgeman Images: p. 19, 35 (c), 43, 190 (r), 223, 226, 237, 248, 256, 286, 295, 297, 303, 304

CCI / Bridgeman Images: p. 109

Catalogue raisonné Maurice Denis: p. 118, 119

Christie's Images / Bridgeman Images: p. 167 (l), 217, 224, 293

Private collection: p. 162, 166, 167 (r), 302

Private collection / © Christian Baraja SLB: back cover, p. 6, 12, 15 (tl), 21, 31, 41, 52, 58, 63, 68, 70, 78, 107, 120, 121, 122, 123, 126 (l), 155, 158, 159, 160, 163 (2nd image), 164, 170, 172, 177, 180, 181, 182, 183, 184, 185, 188 (r), 191 (l), 193, 194 (l), 196, 197, 198, 199, 204, 206, 208, 211, 216, 229, 230, 231, 236, 241, 242, 244, 245, 246, 257, 269 (r), 290, 294

Private collection / rights reserved: p. 14, 26, 34 (t), 35 (tl and tr), 50 (c and r), 55 (r), 57, 69, 77 (b), 88, 91, 94 (t), 99, 110 (tl, tr, bl and br), 112 (l), 161 (l and r), 163 (1st and 4th images), 194 (r), 205, 222, 225, 252 (t), 258 (l), 266 (r), 267 (b), 268 (b), 269 (l), 305

Private collection on loan at the musée Marmottan Monet / © Franck Boucourt: p. 47, 50 (l), 51, 53, 54, 62 (r), 71, 77 (t), 79 (c and r), 86, 89 (r), 95, 96, 97, 108, 110 (c), 111, 113, 115, 116, 126 (r), 133, 153, 271 (r), 275

Edinburgh, National Galleries of Scotland: p. 252 (b)

Editions Scala/ rights reserved: p. 158

Emil Bührle Collection, Zurich Photo: SIK-ISEA, Zurich (J.-P. Kuhn): p. 291

Fine Art Images / Bridgeman Images: p. 270

Los Angeles, J. Paul Getty Museum: p. 94 (b)

Monaco, Collection Nahmad / © Nahmad Collection Monaco: p. 293

Musée d'Orsay, Dist. RMN-Grand Palais / Patrice Schmidt: p. 64, 253, 276

Musée du Louvre, Dist. RMN-Grand Palais / Angèle Dequier: p. 60 (l)

Nationaal Archief/Collectie Spaarnestad/ Fotograaf onbekend / Bridgeman Images: p. 34 (b)

New York, The Metropolitan Museum of Art /Gift of Paul F. Walter, 2000: p. 48 (l)

New York, The Metropolitan Museum of Art / gift of Paul F. Walter 2000: p. 48 (b)

New York, The Metropolitan Museum of Art, Dist. RMN-Grand Palais / image of the MMA: p. 221 (r)

Paris, Musée d'Orsay / © Christian Baraja SLB: p. 61

Paris, Musée Marmottan Monet / © Christian Baraja SLB: p. 147, 234, 238, 250, 268 (tl and tr)

Paris, Musée Marmottan Monet / © Franck Boucourt: endpapers, p. 10, 20, 23 (r), 24, 27, 28, 29, 35 (c), 40, 44, 45, 49, 67, 72, 73, 74, 75, 80, 81 (b), 82, 83, 84 (l), 149, 166 (r), 188 (l), 220 (l and c), 277

Paris, Musée Marmottan Monet / © Musée Marmottan Monet, Paris: front cover, p. 8, 15 (tl, bl, bc and br), 30, 32, 35 (b), 37, 39, 57, 59, 62 (l), 76, 79 (l), 81 (tl and tr), 84 (r), 85, 89 (l and c), 90, 92, 93, 98, 99, 112 (r), 142, 152, 186, 187, 190 (l and c), 192 (r), 202, 203, 207, 212, 214, 215, 239, 258 (r), 260, 264, 265, 272 (r), 289, 298, 300, 306–307

Peter Willi / Bridgeman Images: p. 273

Photo Josse / Bridgeman Images: p. 262, 284, 285

Pictures Now / Alamy Stock Photo: p. 127, 299

RMN-Grand Palais (Musée d'Orsay) / Hervé Lewandowski: p. 218, 220 (r), 235, 274, 280-281, 296

RMN-Grand Palais (Musée d'Orsay) / Adrien Didierjean: p. 261,

RMN-Grand Palais (Musée d'Orsay) / Franck Raux: p. 60 (r), 267 (t)

RMN-Grand Palais (Musée du Louvre) / Franck Raux: p. 221,

RMN-Grand Palais / Agence Bulloz: p. 287

RMN-Grand Palais (musée d'Orsay) / Stéphane Maréchalle: p. 209

Saeml Parisienne de photographie: p. 130

Saint-Denis de La Réunion, Musée Léon Dierx: p. 161 (c)

Snite Museum of Art, University of Notre Dame, gift of John D. Reilly: p. 272 (l)

Sotheby's/akg-images: p. 163 (3th image)

Tajan: p. 191 (r)

Thaw Collection, jointly owned by The Metropolitan Museum of Art and The Morgan Library & © Museum, Gift of Eugene V. Thaw, 2009: p. 292

Tully Potter / Bridgeman Images: p. 25

Walter Carone/ParisMatch/Scoop: p. 124, 308

Washington, D.C., National Gallery of Art / Gift of Mrs. Charles S. Carstairs: p. 46 (b)

Washington, D.C., National Gallery of Art / Woodner Collection: p. 46 (t)

Yvan Bourhis: p. 48 (r)

Translation from French into English
Charles Penwarden and Sandra Reid

Graphic design (except for the cover)
Julien Boitias

Cover design
Jean-Marc Barrier

Director of Éditions Hazan
Jérôme Gille

Editorial manager
Soline Massot

Copy-editor
Bernard Wooding

Picture researchers
Anne Tailleux and Claire Gooden

Production manager
Francis Verdelet

Photoengraving
Reproscan, Orio al Serion, Italy

Printed in September 2021 by
Printer Trento, Trento, Italy

Endpapers
Attributed to Ernest Rouart (1874–1942)
Julie Manet-Rouart and her son Julien in the garden at Le Mesnil, c. 1904
Archives BS, Paris, Musée Marmottan Monet

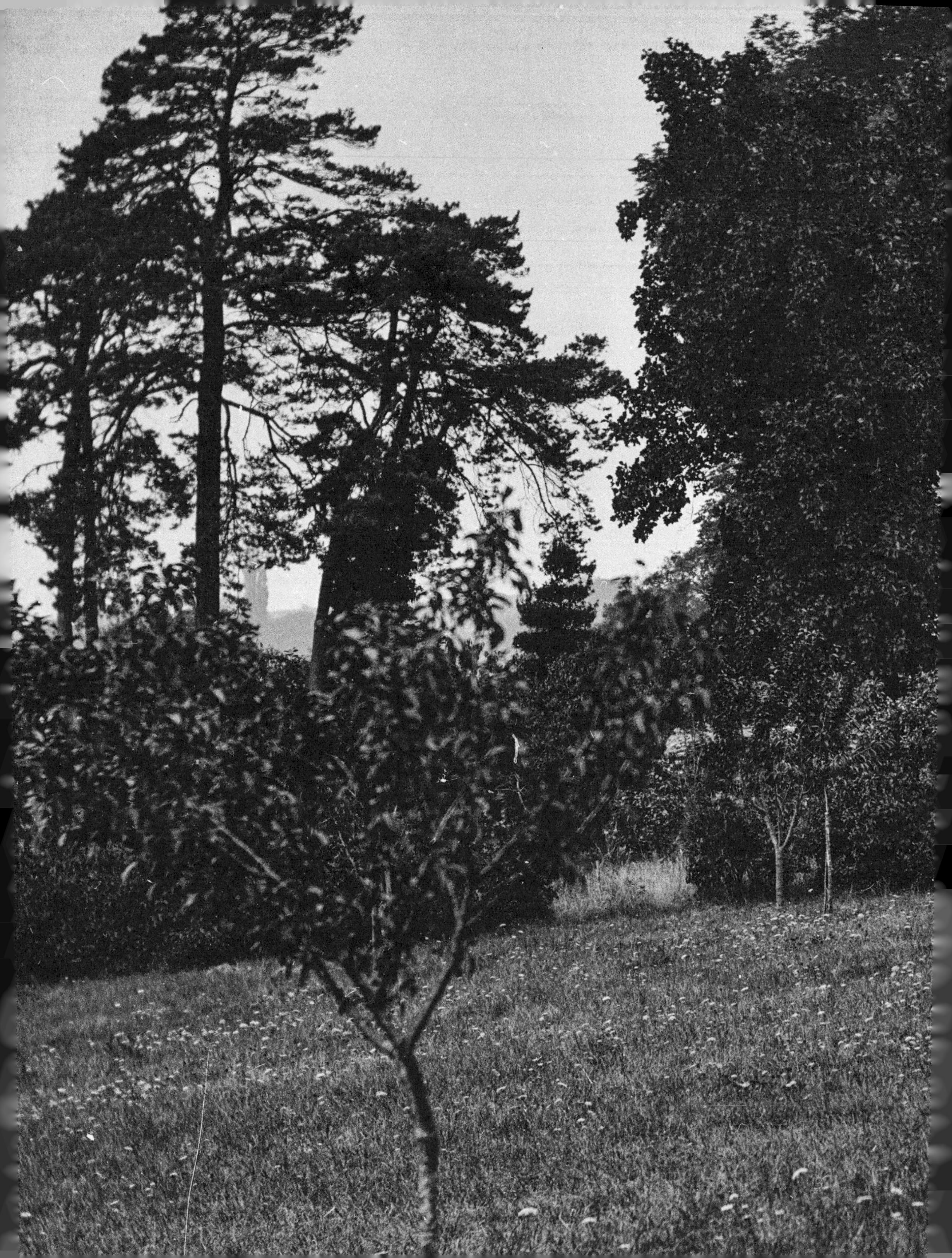